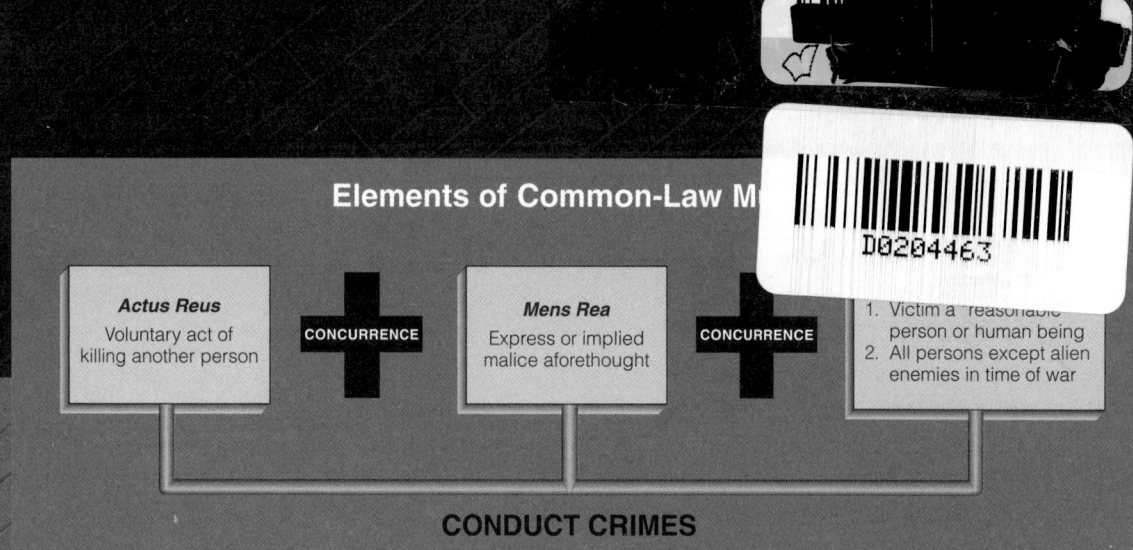

Elements of Common-Law M[urder]

| **Actus Reus** Voluntary act of killing another person | CONCURRENCE | **Mens Rea** Express or implied malice aforethought | CONCURRENCE | 1. Victim a "reasonable person or human being 2. All persons except alien enemies in time of war |

CONDUCT CRIMES

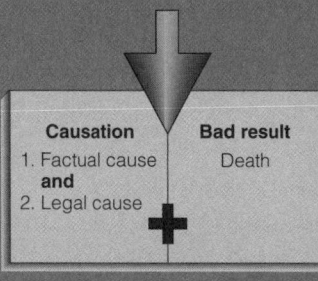

| **Causation** 1. Factual cause **and** 2. Legal cause | **Bad result** Death |

RESULT CRIMES

Elements of Material Support to Terrorists

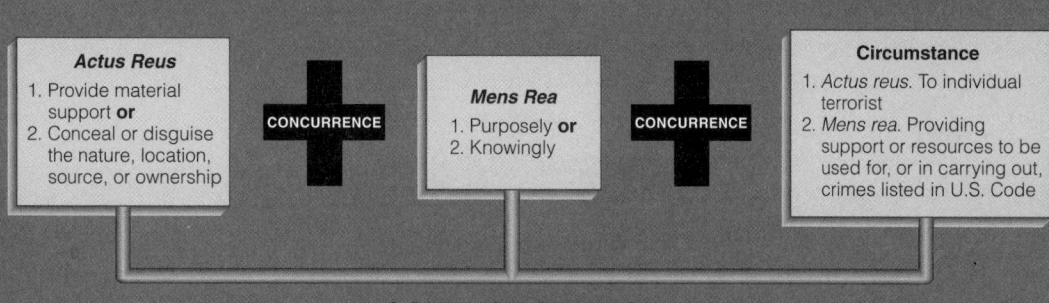

| **Actus Reus** 1. Provide material support **or** 2. Conceal or disguise the nature, location, source, or ownership | CONCURRENCE | **Mens Rea** 1. Purposely **or** 2. Knowingly | CONCURRENCE | **Circumstance** 1. *Actus reus.* To individual terrorist 2. *Mens rea.* Providing support or resources to be used for, or in carrying out, crimes listed in U.S. Code |

CONDUCT CRIMES

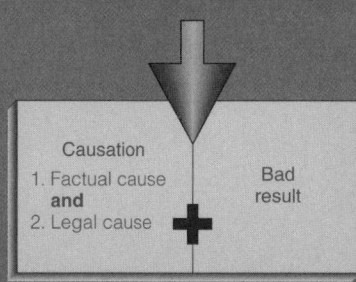

| Causation 1. Factual cause **and** 2. Legal cause | Bad result |

RESULT CRIMES

CRIMINAL LAW

Ninth Edition

JOEL SAMAHA
*Morse Alumni Distinguished Teaching
Professor of Sociology
University of Minnesota*

THOMSON
WADSWORTH

Australia • Brazil • Canada • Mexico • Singapore • Spain
United Kingdom • United States

THOMSON

WADSWORTH

Criminal Law, Ninth Edition
Joel Samaha

Senior Acquisitions Editor, Criminal Justice: Carolyn Henderson Meier
Assistant Editor: Rebecca Johnson
Editorial Assistant: Beth McMurray
Technology Project Manager: Amanda Kaufmann
Marketing Manager: Terra Schultz
Marketing Assistant: Emily Elrod
Marketing Communications Manager: Tami Strang
Project Manager, Editorial Production: Jennie Redwitz
Creative Director: Rob Hugel
Art Director: Vernon Boes

Print Buyer: Becky Cross
Permissions Editor: Bob Kauser
Production Service: Ruth Cottrell
Text Designer: Adriane Bosworth
Photo Researcher: Billie Porter
Copy Editor: Lura Harrison
Illustrator: Judith Ogus
Cover Designer: Yvo Riezebos Design
Cover Image: © Hisham Ibrahim/Photov.com/Alamy
Compositor: International Typesetting and Composition
Text and Cover Printer: R. R. Donnelley/Willard

Library of Congress Control Number: 2007920752
ISBN-13: 978-0-495-09539-2
ISBN-10: 0-495-09539-7

Thomson Higher Education
10 Davis Drive
Belmont, CA 94002-3098
USA

For more information about our products, contact us at:
Thomson Learning Academic Resource Center
1-800-423-0563
For permission to use material from this text or product, submit a request online at
http://www.thomsonrights.com.
Any additional questions about permissions can be submitted by e-mail to
thomsonrights@thomson.com.

For my students, and Doug and Steve

About the Author

Professor Joel Samaha teaches Criminal Law, Criminal Procedure, Introduction to Criminal Justice, and The Constitution in Crisis Times at the University of Minnesota. He is both a lawyer and an historian whose primary interest is crime control in a constitutional democracy. He received his B.A., J.D., and Ph.D. from Northwestern University. Professor Samaha also studied under the late Sir Geoffrey Elton at Cambridge University, England. He was named the College of Liberal Arts Distinguished Teacher in 1974. In 2007 he was awarded the title of University of Minnesota Morse Alumni Distinguished Teaching Professor and inducted into the Academy of Distinguished Teachers.

Professor Samaha was admitted to the Illinois Bar in 1962 and practiced law briefly in Chicago. He taught at UCLA before going to the University of Minnesota in 1971. At the University of Minnesota, he served as Chair of the Department of the Department of Criminal Justice Studies from 1974 to 1978. He now teaches and writes full time. He has taught both television and radio courses in criminal justice and has co-taught a National Endowment for the Humanities seminar in legal and constitutional history. He was named Distinguished Teacher at the University of Minnesota in 1974.

In addition to *Law and Order in Historical Perspective* (1974), an analysis of law enforcement in pre-industrial English society, Professor Samaha has transcribed and written a scholarly introduction to a set of local criminal justice records from the reign of Elizabeth I. He has also written several articles on the history of criminal justice, published in the *Historical Journal, The American Journal of Legal History, Minnesota Law Review, William Mitchell Law Review,* and *Journal of Social History.* In addition to *Criminal Law,* he has written two other textbooks, *Criminal Procedure* in its sixth edition, and *Criminal Justice* in its seventh edition.

Brief Contents

Contents

Preface

Criminal Law was my favorite course as a first-year law student at Northwestern University Law School in 1958. I've loved teaching it since I came to the University of Minnesota in 1971. I've also loved writing *Criminal Law*, now for the ninth time. And, it's a source of great satisfaction that my modest innovation to the study of criminal law, the combined text/case book—which brings together the description, analysis, and critique of general principles with excerpts of cases edited for nonlawyers—has been successful.

Like its predecessors, *Criminal Law*, Ninth Edition stresses both the general principles that apply to all of criminal law and the specific elements of particular crimes that prosecutors have to prove beyond a reasonable doubt. Learning the principles of criminal law isn't just a good mental exercise, although it does stimulate students to use their minds. Understanding the general principles is an indispensable prerequisite for understanding the elements of specific crimes. The general principles have lasted for centuries. The definitions of the elements of specific crimes, on the other hand, differ from state to state and over time because they have to meet the varied and changing needs of new times and different places.

That the principles have stood the test of time testifies to their strength as a framework for explaining the elements of crimes as they're defined in the fifty states and the U.S. criminal codes. But there's more to their importance than durability; knowledge of the principles is also practical. The general principles are the bases both of the elements that prosecutors have to prove beyond a reasonable doubt to convict defendants and of the defenses that justify or excuse the guilt of defendants.

So, *Criminal Law*, Ninth Edition rests on a solid foundation. But it can't stand still any more than the subject of criminal law can remain frozen in time. The more I teach and write about criminal law, the more I learn and rethink what I've already learned; the more "good" cases I find that I didn't know were there; and the more I'm able to include cases that weren't decided and reported when the previous edition went to press.

Of course, it's my obligation to incorporate into the Ninth Edition these now-decided and reported cases and this new learning, rethinking, and discovery. But obligation doesn't describe the pleasure that preparing now nine editions of *Criminal Law* brings me. Finding cases that illustrate a principle in terms students can understand while at the same time stimulating them to think critically about subjects worth thinking about is the most exciting part of teaching and writing and why I take such care in revising this book, edition after edition.

 AN OVERVIEW OF THE TEXT/CASE APPROACH

Criminal Law, Ninth Edition continues the interactive approach to learning that lies at the heart of the text/case method. The text explains general principles. Then, the main case excerpts that follow the explanation apply the principles explained in the text to specific facts of a real case. The text/case approach invites students to participate actively in learning. They can agree or disagree with the application made by the court in its opinion, but they have to understand the principles and definitions to apply them. The text/case approach has repeatedly demonstrated that students not only understand what they've learned, that they not only actually enjoy what they've learned, but also that they remember what they've learned. Perhaps the most gratifying part of teaching criminal law by the text/case method is having students tell me many years after they've taken the course that they remember the cases and the principles the cases stood for.

The **Case Excerpts** portray the criminal law in action because they apply the general principles to real-life events. Students have to think about, formulate their own interpretations of, and apply the principles of criminal law to these real-life events. Students in my classes have to act as legislators, prosecutors, defense attorneys, judges, and juries so they can see the principles and rules of criminal law from all perspectives. They have to show that they understand the principles and rules first by stating them as the text presents them, and then by applying them to the facts and reasoning of the case excerpts.

This close relationship between the principles and rules that appear in the text and the case excerpts remains central to *Criminal Law,* Ninth Edition. Case excerpts remain tailored to teach students the principles, doctrines, and rules of criminal law but with an eye toward policy rather than the technical knowledge needed by lawyers. Also, the case excerpts remain distinct from the text, as they have in previous editions. The text covers all of the main points, so it can stand alone as an analysis of the criminal law. Instructors can choose to omit the cases altogether from assignments; use them as illustrations and elaborations of the points made in the text; use them to test students' grasp of the text; or integrate them fully into the course.

An **Opening Question** introduces each case excerpt, focusing students' attention on the principle or issue that the case excerpt addresses. The **Case History** summarizes the procedural steps from the lowest court, verdict, sentence where available, and judgment to the judgment in the final appeals court.

The excerpts present the **Facts** and the **Opinion** of the case in the actual words of the court. **Case Questions** follow the excerpts. The case questions test students' mastery of the facts and their understanding of the principle illustrated by the case excerpt. The questions also provoke students to think critically by inviting them to evaluate and propose alternatives to the arguments and the decisions of the court as presented in the case excerpt. Questions frequently ask students to play the role of prosecutor, defense counsel, judge, jury, or legislator.

The **Exploring Further** feature follows some of the case excerpts. This feature provides brief synopses of cases that illustrate how courts vary in interpreting and applying the principles of criminal law and the definitions of crimes involved in the primary case excerpt. Instructors and students have convinced me that the Exploring Further cases are a valuable tool both in understanding and applying the topics covered in the text.

CHAPTER ORGANIZATION

The chapters in the text organize the criminal law into a traditional scheme that is widely accepted and can embrace, with minor adjustments, the criminal law of any state and/or the federal government. The logic of the arrangement is first to cover the **general part of the criminal law,** namely principles and doctrines common to all or most crimes, and then the **special part of criminal law,** namely the application of the general principles to the elements of specific crimes.

Chapters 1–8 cover the general part of criminal law: the nature, origins, structure, sources, and purposes of criminal law and criminal punishment; the constitutional limits on the criminal law; the general principles of criminal liability; the defenses of justification and excuse; parties to crime and vicarious liability; and incomplete crimes (attempt, conspiracy, and solicitation).

Chapters 9–13 cover the special part of the criminal law: the major crimes against persons; crimes against homes and property; crimes against public order and morals; and crimes against the state.

CHANGES TO THE NINTH EDITON

Criminal Law has always followed the three-step analysis of criminal liability (criminal conduct, justification, and excuse), and the Ninth Edition brings this analysis into even sharper focus in two ways. First, it changes the chapter sequence. Chapters 3 and 4 cover the principles of criminal conduct as they always have. But Chapter 5 now covers the defenses of justification, the second step in the analysis of criminal liability, and Chapter 6 covers the defenses of excuse, the third step, so the chapter sequence in the Ninth Edition precisely mirrors the three-step analysis of criminal liability.

The second way the Ninth Edition sharpens the focus on the three-step analysis is through the newly designed **Elements of Crime** art. The new design is consistent throughout the chapters involving the special part of criminal law.

All three of these steps are included in each "Elements of Crime" graphic, but elements that are not required in certain crimes—like crimes that don't require a "bad" result—are grayed out. The new figures go right to the core of the three-step analysis of criminal liability, making it easier for students to master the essence of criminal law: applying general principles to specific individual crimes.

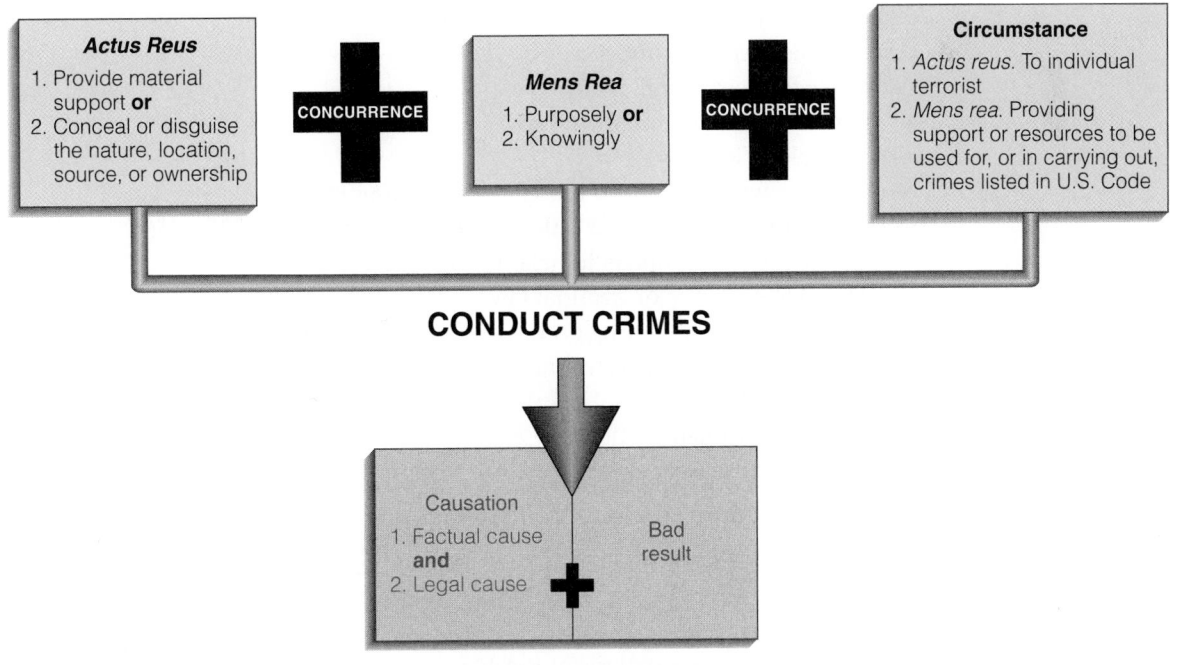

Elements of Material Support to Terrorists

The text part of *Criminal Law* has undergone substantial rewriting and revision (see below) to improve readability; readers will find more description, explanation, and analysis; more examples and more tables; and more background information such as crime statistics and other materials that put the rules of criminal law into a contemporary social context. Finally, included in the text itself are more synopses of facts and opinions in cases that illustrate the principles and elements of crimes than in previous editions. The Ninth Edition contains 25 new case excerpts. Why so many? The new cases are needed to keep the text current and relevant to students. Second, the discovery of older cases that explain the general principles better and apply the facts in clearer and more interesting ways than cases in previous editions requires the addition of new cases.

Most case excerpts retained from previous editions have been re-edited to streamline them by removing all but what's necessary in their opinion sections. Other excerpts have been moved to the "Exploring Further" feature, incorporated into the main text, or moved to the accompanying website.

In every case excerpt, whether new or re-edited, I've left the facts section of the excerpts as full and rich as the court provides. It's the opinion section of the case excerpts where I used the electronic editing scissors, leaving only enough to provide students with an understanding of the principle of the case. But, I also take pains to leave enough of the opinion to stimulate critical thinking and class discussion of the issues in the case. Most of the re-editing grows out of my experience teaching the cases in my classes at the University of Minnesota.

CHAPTER-BY-CHAPTER CHANGES

Chapter 1, The Nature and Limits of Criminal Law in U.S. Society

- A new opening vignette based on actual case excerpts from the book (not hypothetical cases as was true in previous editions)
- New or expanded sections:
  - Who's responsible for what?
  - Crimes and noncriminal wrongs
  - Principle of legality
  - No crime without law; no punishment without law
  - lawmaking," especially on difference between judicial and legislative lawmaking and limits on judicial lawmaking
  - "Expressive" nature of criminal law
  - Rule of lenity: Elaborating on the rules of statutory interpretation
  - Common law (state and federal)
  - Model Penal Code (MPC)
  - Municipal ordinance offenses
  - Administrative agency crimes

Chapter 2, Constitutional Limits on Criminal Law

- New or expanded sections:
  - *Ex post facto* laws
  - Void for vagueness
  - Free speech; added analysis of *R.A.V. v. St. Paul*
  - Right to privacy
  - "Proportional punishments" and imprisonment
  - Death penalty and the mentally retarded

- — Death penalty and juveniles
- — Three-strikes law

- New case excerpts:
  - — Right to privacy: *Griswold v. Connecticut* (crime of married couples using contraceptives)
  - — Three-strikes law: *Ewing v. California* (25 years to life for stealing golf clubs worth $399)

Chapter 3, The General Principles of Criminal Liability: *Actus Reus*

- New or expanded sections:
  - — Elements of criminal liability: Clarifying and expanding three-step analysis of criminal liability
  - — Voluntary act
  - — *Actus reus* and the Constitution

- New "Elements of Crime" art first appears in this chapter, and in subsequent chapters

- New case excerpts:
  - — Voluntary act: *Brown v. State*
  - — Omission: *Commonwealth v. Pestinakas*
  - — Possession: *Miller v. State*

Chapter 4, The General Principles of Criminal Liability: *Mens Rea*, Concurrence, and Causation

- **New or expanded sections:**
  - — General intent and specific intent
  - — Ignorance and mistake of law and/or fact

- **New case excerpts:**
  - — General/specific intent: *People v. Disimone*
  - — Knowingly: *State v. Jantzi*
  - — Causation: *Commonwealth v. McCloskey*

Chapter 5, Defenses to Criminal Liability: Justifications

- New case regarding necessity (choice of evils): *U.S. v. Aguiler* (harboring illegal immigrants)

Chapter 6, Defenses to Criminal Liability: Excuse

- New or expanded sections:
  - — Myths and reality about the way the insanity defense works in practice, including results of empirical research
  - — Diminished capacity and diminished responsibility, especially the confusion and differences between them

- New case excerpts:
  - — Insanity: right-wrong test: *State v. Odell* (mentally ill man kills his father because he thinks God ordered him to do it)
  - — Insanity: substantial capacity test: *People v. Drew* (schizophrenic attacks police officer in a bar)

Chapter 7, Parties to Crime and Vicarious Liability

- New section: enterprise vicarious liability

- New case excerpts:

— Enterprise vicarious liability: *State v. Zeta Chi Fraternity* (fraternity liable for underage drinking and prostitution)
— Individual vicarious liability: *State v. Tomaino* (owner of video store liable for clerk renting pornography to a minor)

Chapter 8, Inchoate Crimes: Attempt, Conspiracy, and Solicitation

- New or expanded sections:
  — Attempt criminal act: Extensive text revision elaborates on the major tests for determining how close to completion defendants' actions have proceeded, set clearly within the theories of dangerous acts (how much remains to be done) and dangerous people (how much defendants have already done)
  — Impossibility: Expanded discussion of definition and distinction between factual and legal impossibility

- New case excerpts:
  — Attempt mental element: *People v. Kimball* (joke or intent to rob?)
  — Attempt *actus reus: Young v. State* (MPC substantial steps test adopted and thoroughly analyzed in attempted bank robbery)
  — Conspiracy: *U.S. v. Garcia* (conspiracy of a Blood to kill a Crip in gang rivalry)
  — Solicitation: *State v. Cotton* (did husband solicit his wife to intimidate a witness?)

Chapter 9, Crimes Against Persons I: Criminal Homicide

- New or expanded sections:
  — Criminal homicide in context. Statistical data comparing homicide to other crimes—rarity of homicides; model for three-step analysis used in this text
  — When does life begin? Full discussion of leading case *People v. Chavez* and the meaning of "person," in the context of "baby in process of being born"
  — History of murder: Clarify the difference between MPC and non-MPC terms. Much fuller and clearer discussion of "malice aforethought"; "depraved heart" murder; and "intent-to-cause-serious-injury" murder.
  — First-degree murder: Difference between "premeditated" and "deliberate"
  — Death penalty: Significance of aggravating and mitigating circumstances to determine whether to impose death penalty; full treatment of two-phase (bifurcated) proceedings: guilt phase and penalty phase
  — Proving premeditated deliberate intent: A new table (Table 9.1) includes leading cases and application of standards and categories of facts to prove premeditation and deliberation
  — Felony murder: Discussion of specific felony murder statutes; fuller discussion of debate over and trend toward abolition of felony murder category; discussion and application of "inherently dangerous to life" felonies and the "case-by-case" approach
  — Manslaughter: Fuller treatment of the meaning of "adequate/reasonable provocation"
  — Criminal negligence/vehicular/firearms manslaughter: Discussion of "criminal negligence" manslaughter applying almost exclusively to deaths involving vehicles and firearms

- New case excerpts:
  — Premeditation/deliberation: *Byford v. State* (application of aggravating circumstance facts in death penalty case)

— Second-degree murder: *People v. Protopappas* ("depraved heart" murder: care-takers paid to take care of an elderly man instead took his money and let him slowly starve to death)

Chapter 10, Crimes Against Persons II: Criminal Sexual Conduct, Bodily Injury, and Personal Restraint

- New or expanded sections:
  - Rape *actus reus*: Force and resistance rule
  - Resistance and danger to victim: Discussion of statistical evidence regarding whether victim resistance to rape increases or decreases chances of injury to victim
  - Rape *mens rea:* "Reasonable mistake" regarding consent of victim as a defense to rape charge; extended discussion of famous English case (*Rex v. Morgan*) that caused great stir in U.S.
  - Stalking: Extended discussion of stalking as a social problem, stalking statistics, high-profile cases, and types of anti-stalking laws
  - Stalking *mens rea*

- New case excerpt: Stalking: *State v. Hoying* (stalking co-worker by e-mail)

Chapter 11, Crimes Against Property

- New and expanded sections:
  - Taking other people's property: Reduced coverage of history of the old laws of larceny, embezzlement, and false pretenses, and expanded coverage of modern theft law
  - Cyber crime: Extensive new coverage of the social problem of cyber crime, the enormous extent of damage caused by it, and detailed subsections on identity theft and intellectual property crimes

- New case excerpts:
  - Receiving stolen property: *Sonnier v. State* (15-year sentence for receiving stolen speakers)
  - Burglary: *Jewell v. State* (can you burglarize your own home?)
  - Cyber crime: identity theft: *Remsburg v. Docusearch* (defendant paid $150 to Docusearch, an investigation and information service company, to find his ex-girlfriend, whom he then murdered; her parents sued Docusearch and its owners)
  - Cyber crime: intellectual property: *U.S. v. Ancheta* (21-year-old Ancheta received the harshest sentence ever imposed [57-month sentence and forfeiture of his BMW and other property], for profiting from selling "botnets" [armies of compromised computers])

Chapter 12, Crimes Against Public Order and Morals

- Case excerpts streamlined to reduce length

Chapter 13, Crimes Against the State

- Case excerpts streamlined to reduce length

- Expanded section: Patriot Act discussion updated to reflect revisions in the law enacted in 2004 and 2006

- New case excerpt: Providing "material support or resources" to terrorists or terrorist organizations: *Humanitarian Law Project v. Gonzalez* (providing support for lawful non-terrorist activities of organizations designated as terrorist organizations)

SUPPLEMENTS

An extensive package of supplemental aids accompanies this edition of *Criminal Law.* They are available to qualified adopters. Please consult your local sales representative for details.

For the Instructor

Instructor's Resource Manual   The fully updated and revised *Instructor's Resource Manual* for this edition includes learning objectives, key terms with definitions, chapter outlines, chapter summary, discussion topics, lecture suggestions, recommended readings, and holdings of leading cases, as well as a complete test bank. Also included is a Resource Integration Guide, which will help you make maximum use of the rich supplement package available for this text by integrating media, Internet, video, and other resources into each chapter. Each chapter's test bank contains approximately 80 multiple-choice, true-false, fill-in-the-blank, and essay questions coded according to difficulty level. Also included is a full answer key. Each question in the Test Bank has been carefully reviewed by experienced criminal justice instructors for quality, accuracy, and content coverage. Our Instructor Approved seal, which appears on the front cover, is our assurance that you are working with an assessment and grading resource of the highest caliber.

ExamView® Computerized Testing   The comprehensive *Instructor's Resource Manual* is backed up by ExamView, a computerized test bank available for PC and Macintosh computers. With ExamView you can create, deliver, and customize tests and study guides (both print and online) in minutes. You can easily edit and import your own questions and graphics, change test layouts, and reorganize questions. And using ExamView's complete word processing capabilities, you can enter an unlimited number of new questions or edit existing questions.

JoinIn™ on Turning Point®   Spark discussion and assess your students' comprehension of chapter concepts with interactive classroom quizzes and background polls developed specifically for use with this edition of *Criminal Law.* Also available are polling/quiz questions that enable you to maximize the educational benefits of the ABC® News video clips we custom-selected to accompany this textbook. Thomson Wadsworth's agreement with TurningPoint software enables you to run our tailor-made Microsoft® PowerPoint® slides in conjunction with the "clicker" hardware of your choice. Enhance how your students interact with you, your lecture, and each other. For college and university adopters only. Please consult your Wadsworth representative for details or visit www.thomsonedu.com.

WebTutor™ ToolBox on Blackboard® and WebCT®   A powerful combination: easy-to-use course management tools for whichever program you use—WebCT or Blackboard—and content from this text's rich companion website, all in one place. You can use ToolBox as is, from the moment you log on—or, if you prefer, customize the program with web links, images, and other resources.

The Wadsworth Criminal Justice Video Library So many exciting new videos—so many great ways to enrich your lectures and spark discussion of the material in this text! A list of our unique and expansive video program follows. Or, visit www.thomsonedu.com/criminaljustice/media_center for a complete, up-to-the-minute list of all of Wadsworth's video offerings (many of which are also available in DVD format) as well as clip lists and running times. The library includes these selections and many others:

- *ABC Videos:* Featuring short, high-interest clips from current news events specially developed for courses including Introduction to Criminal Justice, Criminology, Corrections, Terrorism, and White-Collar Crime, these videos are perfect for use as discussion starters or lecture launchers. The brief video clips provide students with a new lens through which to view the past and present, one that will greatly enhance their knowledge and understanding of significant events and open up to them new dimensions in learning. Clips are drawn from such programs as *World News Tonight, Good Morning America, This Week, PrimeTime Live, 20/20, and Nightline,* as well as numerous ABC News specials and material from the Associated Press Television News and British Movietone News collections.

- *The Wadsworth Custom Videos for Criminal Justice:* Produced by Wadsworth and Films for the Humanities, these videos include short (5- to 10-minute) segments that encourage classroom discussion. Topics include white-collar crime, domestic violence, forensics, suicide and the police officer, the court process, the history of corrections, prison society, and juvenile justice.

- *Court TV Videos:* One-hour videos presenting seminal and high-profile cases such as the interrogations of Michael Crowe and serial killer Ted Bundy, as well as crucial and current issues such as cyber crime, double jeopardy, and the management of the prison on Riker's Island.

- *A&E American Justice:* Forty videos to choose from, on topics such as deadly force, women on death row, juvenile justice, strange defenses, and Alcatraz.

- *Films for the Humanities:* Nearly 200 videos to choose from on a variety of topics such as elder abuse, supermax prisons, suicide and the police officer, the making of an FBI agent, domestic violence, and more.

- *Oral History Project:* Developed in association with the American Society of Criminology, the Academy of Criminal Justice Society, and the National Institute of Justice, these videos will help you introduce your students to the scholars who have developed the criminal justice discipline. Compiled over the last several years, each video features a set of Guest Lecturers—scholars whose thinking has helped to build the foundation of present ideas in the discipline.

The Wadsworth Criminal Justice Resource Center

www.thomsonedu.com/criminaljustice

Designed with the instructor in mind, this website features information about Wadsworth's technology and teaching solutions, as well as several features created specifically for today's criminal justice student. Supreme Court updates, timelines, and hot-topic polling can all be used to supplement in-class assignments and discussions. You'll also find a wealth of links to careers and news in criminal justice, book-specific sites, and much more.

For the Student

Study Guide The already extensive student study guide that accompanies *Criminal Law* has been thoroughly revised and updated for the latest edition. Because students learn in different ways, the guide includes a variety of pedagogical aids. Each chapter is outlined and summarized, major terms and figures are defined, and worksheets and self-tests are provided.

Companion Website

www.thomsonedu.com/criminaljustice/samaha

Correlated with every chapter in Samaha's *Criminal Law* (an icon appears throughout the text's narrative and cases directing students to related content on the website), this information-rich site includes the U.S. Constitution, state constitutions, state statutes, complete unedited versions of the cases in the textbook, links to relevant websites, Internet research exercises, electronic versions of all the "Elements of Crime" art, and interactive cases that enable students to develop their skills in identifying the various types of crime.

Handbook of Selected Supreme Court Cases, Third Edition This supplementary handbook covers nearly 40 landmark cases, each of which includes a full case citation, an introduction, a summary from WestLaw, excerpts from the case, and the decision. The updated edition includes *Hamdi v. Rumsfeld, Roper v. Simmons, Ring v. Arizona, Atkins v. Virginia, Illinois v. Caballes,* and much more.

ACKNOWLEDGMENTS

Criminal Law, Ninth Edition didn't get here by my efforts alone; I had a lot of help. I am grateful for all those who have provided feedback over the years and as always, I'm particularly indebted to the reviewers for this edition (see p. xxi).

Criminal Justice Editor Carolyn Henderson Meier has helped me at every stage of the book. Jennie Redwitz helped with the photos, and as always, in other matters ironed out all kinds of rough spots along the way. The book also benefited once more from Lura Harrison's painstaking copy editing. Ruth Cottrell's calm efficiency, warm kindnesses, careful editing, and extraordinary patience were as welcome and necessary as they have been in earlier editions.

What would I do without Doug and Steve? Doug takes me there and gets me here and everywhere, day in and day out, days that now have stretched into years. And my old and dear friend Steve, who from the days when he watched over my kids to now decades later keeps the Irish Wolfhounds, the Siamese cat, the Standard Poodle, me, and a lot more around here in order. And they do it all while putting up with what my beloved mentor at Cambridge, Sir Geoffrey Elton, called "Joel's mercurial temperament." Only those who really know me can understand how I can try the patience of Job! Friends and associates like these have made *Criminal Law,* Ninth Edition whatever success it enjoys. As for its faults, I claim total ownership.

JOEL SAMAHA
Minneapolis

Reviewers of *Criminal Law*

Jim Beckman, University of Tampa
Kathleen Block
Bonnie Bondavalli, Lewis University
William Calathes, Jersey City State College
Frances Coles, California State University, San Bernardino
Dianne Daan
George Dery, California State University, Fullerton
Jerry Dowling
Donald Downs
Daniel Doyle, University of Montana
Aaron Fichtelberg, University of Delaware
Richard Frey
Phyllis Gerstenfeld, California State University, Stanislaus
Richard Given, Eastern Kentucky University
Jona Goldschmidt, Loyola University of Chicago
Richard Gwen
Robert Harvie, Montana State University
Craig Hemmens, Boise State University
Daniel Hillyard, Southern Illinois University Carbondale
Louis Holscher
Tom Hughes, University of Louisville
William E. Kelly, Auburn University
Julius Koefoed
Thomas Lateano, Kean University
James Maddox

Leon Manning, Northeastern Oklahoma A&M College
Leroy Maxwell, Missouri Western State College
Mickey McDermott, Alabama State University
William Michalek, Broome Community College
Rick Michelson, Grossmont-Cuyamaca Community College
Anne Miller, Vincennes University
James Newman
Kathleen Nicolaides, University of North Carolina, Charlotte
Laura Otten
Robert Partel
William Pelkey
Gregory Russel
Steve Russell, Indiana University
Richard Stempien, SUNY Mohawk Valley Community College
Rebecca Stevens
Gene Straughan, Lewis-Clark State College
Susette Talarico, University of Georgia
Carol Tebben
R. Bankole Thompson
Victoria Time, Old Dominion University
James Todd
Jonah Triebwasser
Donald Wallace, Central Missouri State University
James Wallace
Lee S. Weinberg, University of Pittsburgh
Wayne Wolff, Thornton Community College

CRIMINAL LAW

The Nature and Limits of Criminal Law in U.S. Society

MAIN POINTS

- Criminal law is about blaming and punishing people for crimes.
- Criminal law is only *one* kind of social control.
- The *most* important difference between torts and crimes is the conviction, which expresses the community's hatred of, fear of, or contempt for the convict.
- Classifying crimes reflects the urge to make sense of criminal law.
- Criminal law consists of a general part, which includes principles that apply to more than one crime, and a special part, which defines the elements of specific crimes.
- The purposes of punishment include retribution, which looks back to punish past criminal conduct, and prevention, which looks ahead to prevent future criminal conduct.
- Law, not individuals, controls government power.
- Judges are restrained in their lawmaking power by the rule of lenity, precedent, and stare decisis.
- The sources of criminal law in our federal system can be found mostly in state criminal codes and municipal codes.
- There's a substantial and growing body of criminal law in the U.S. Criminal Code and in administrative agencies.
- The common denominator in U.S. criminal law is the Model Penal Code.

Photograph ©Jean Coughlin

Jail Time for an Overdue Library Book?

A Burlington, WA, man has been ordered to pay a library $150 and do community service after he was arrested for overdue library books. The arrest was for failure to appear before a judge to answer charges of "Detaining Property." The property was library books the man had checked out eight months earlier.

Jeremy Jones called Burlington police to his apartment recently to report an incidence of mail theft. Police ran a background check and told Jones and his girlfriend there was a warrant for Jones' arrest. They explained about the library books. Jones insists he tried to give his overdue library books to police. "They wouldn't even take them. That kind of irked me," he said. "I told them they are right on the table, take them. They said 'No, we have a warrant, we have to arrest you.'"

"They handcuffed him," said Jones' friend, Misty Colburn. "He didn't put up a fight or anything, but they handcuffed him and went away." Arrested for,

(continued)

among other things, having the book Mysteries of the Unexplained: How Ordinary Men and Women Have Experienced the Strange, the Uncanny, and the Incredible, *Jones was released after spending an hour at the county jail.*

At the Burlington Library, they insist this isn't strange. They tried over and over again to get their books back—letters and seven phone calls, they said. "After months of dealing with this, we sent a letter from the police chief giving them one last chance," said Librarian Christine Perkins, "and warning if they do not respond they will be invited to talk to a judge about it." Perkins says Jones didn't show up for a court hearing and a warrant was issued. She said the library didn't send out the police; they just did a normal check for outstanding warrants.

"I'm sorry; they are books for crying out loud. If it was a computer part or a CD or something, I could understand," Colburn said. "You know, they are books; they are replaceable. I could see them revoking my library privileges, but having me arrested is a little bit extreme," Jones added.

The library insists no one wanted to arrest anyone, but the librarian suspects the arrest could have an upside. "Well, I'm interested to see if we get a lot of books turned in in the next week or so." 🌀

(JOHNSON 2005, MARCH 3)

1. A young man beat a stranger on the street with a baseball bat for "kicks." The victim died.

2. A husband begged his wife, who had cheated on him for months, not to leave him. She replied, "No, I'm going to court, and you're going to have to give me all the furniture. You're going to have to get the hell out of here; you won't have nothing." Then, pointing to her crotch, she added, "You'll never touch this again, because I've got something bigger and better for it."

   Breaking into tears, he begged some more, "Why don't you try to save the marriage? I have nothing more to live for."

   "Never. I'm never coming back to you."

   He cracked, ran into the next room, got a gun, and shot her to death.

3. Another wife wanted to leave her husband, but he wanted her to stay. Coaxing her into his car, he drove off with her, hoping he could convince her, with the help of a gun, to keep their marriage together. When they stopped at a coffee shop, she jumped out of the car, and tried to run away. When he ran after her with the gun, she fell, and he put the gun to her head. He pulled the trigger; nothing happened.

Repeatedly pulling the trigger, he shouted, "It won't fire! It won't fire!" The gun was unloaded.

4. Two robbers met a drunk man in a bar displaying a wad of money. When the man asked them for a ride, they agreed, drove him out into the country, robbed him, forced him out of the car without his glasses, and drove off. A college student, driving at a reasonable speed, didn't see the man standing in the middle of the road waving him down, couldn't stop, and struck and killed him.

5. A young woman on a 3-day "crack" cocaine binge propped up a bottle so her 3-month-old baby could feed himself. The baby died of dehydration.

6. During the Korean War, a mother dreamed an enemy soldier was on top of her daughter. In her sleep, she got up, walked to a shed, got an ax, went to her daughter's room, and plunged the ax into her, believing she was killing the enemy soldier. The daughter died instantly; the mother was beside herself with grief.

7. A neighbor told an 8-year-old boy and his friend not to play behind a building, because it was dangerous. The boy answered belligerently, "In a minute."

   Losing patience, the neighbor said, "No, not in a minute; get out of there now!"

   A few days later, he broke into her house, pulled a goldfish out of its bowl, chopped it into little pieces with a steak knife, and smeared it all over the counter. Then, he went into the bathroom, plugged in a curling iron, and clamped it onto a towel.

8. A young man lived in a ground-level apartment with a large window opening onto the building parking lot. At 8 o'clock one morning, he stood naked in front of the window eating his cereal in full view of those getting in and out of their cars.

9. A college student was sentenced to jail for failing to return two library books.

10. A husband watched his wife suffer from the agony of dying from an especially painful terminal cancer. He shot her with one of his hunting guns; she died instantly.

11. A man knew he was HIV positive. Despite doctors' instructions about safe sex and the need to tell his partners before having sex with them, he had sex numerous times with three different women without telling them. Most of the time, he used no protection, but, on a few occasions, he withdrew before ejaculating. He gave one of the women an anti-AIDS drug, "to slow down the AIDS." None of the women contracted the HIV virus.

12. A woman met a very drunk man in a bar. He got into her car, and she drove him to her house. He asked her for a spoon, which she knew he wanted to use to take drugs. She got it for him and waited in the living room while he went into the bathroom to "shoot up." He came back into the living room and collapsed; she went back to the bar. The next morning she found him "purple, with flies flying

around him." Thinking he was dead, she told her daughter to call the police and left for work. He was dead.

13. A young man played the online video game "Border Patrol" on his home computer. The game showed immigrants running across the border where a sign reads, "Welcome to the U.S. Welfare office this way." There are three kinds of targets: Mexican nationalists, drug smugglers, and "breeders" (pregnant women with children). The game says, "Kill them at any cost." When you hit a "target," it explodes into bits with appropriate visual and audio effects. When the game ends, it gives a score using a derogatory term (Branson 2006).

14. A 22-year-old plumber's apprentice, while working on a sewer pipe in a trench 10-feet deep, was buried alive under a rush of collapsing muck and mud. He didn't die easily. Clawing for the surface, sludge filled his throat. Thousands of pounds of dirt pressed on his chest, squeezing until he couldn't draw another breath.

    He worked for a plumbing company with a long record of safety violations. Only 2 weeks before, a federal safety investigator had caught men from the same company working unprotected in a 15-foot-deep trench, a clear violation of federal safety laws. On that day, the dead apprentice, when questioned by the investigator, described many unsafe work practices. The investigator knew the company well. Some years earlier, he'd investigated another death at the company. The circumstances were nearly identical: a deep trench, no box, and a man buried alive (Barstow 2003).

15. A young waiter in an upscale restaurant is addicted to crystal meth, which "everyone" knows.

16. A criminal justice major smokes marijuana on weekends.

17. A man in his mid-twenties dances nude in a local bar. A sign outside the bar reads: "Gay male strippers inside. Adults welcome."

The summaries you just read are of real cases; you'll read more about them in later chapters. Here, we'll use them to introduce you to the government practice of "blaming and punishing" (Kadish 1987) people for crimes. The approach in this book is to explore and think critically about the answers to the question criminal law always boils down to, "Who's responsible for what?" (Dubber 2002, 5). Or, as the lawyers ask, "Who's liable for what?" We'll explore other questions in this book, but they all flow from this one. One other point about the issues of criminal law raised in the summaries: The questions are easy to ask but hard to answer for reasons that we'll explore throughout the book.

CONDUCT THAT UNJUSTIFIABLY INFLICTS HARM

Now you can start learning about criminal law as we'll approach the subject in this book. First, assign each of the previous 17 case summaries to one of the five following categories. Don't worry about whether you know enough about criminal law. In fact, try to ignore what you already know; just choose the category you believe the summary should be in. Then, without reading further, try to explain why you assigned them to the categories you chose.

1. *Crime* If you put the case summary into this category, also grade it as very serious, serious, or minor, thereby stamping it with both the amount of disgrace (stigma) that a convicted "criminal" should suffer and roughly the severity of the punishment you think he or she deserves.

2. *Noncriminal wrong* This is a wrong that justifies suing someone and getting money. In other words, name a price that the wrongdoer has to pay to another individual, but don't put the stamp of "criminal" on it (Coffee 1992, 1876–77).

3. *Regulation* Let government action—for example, a heavy cigarette tax to discourage smoking—discourage the behavior (Harcourt 2005, 11–12). In other words, make the price high, but don't stamp it with the stigma of "crime."

4. *License* Charge a price for it—for example, a driver's license fee for the privilege to drive—but don't try to encourage or discourage it. Make the price affordable, and attach no stigma to it.

5. *Lawful* Let individual conscience and/or group (social) disapproval condemn it, but create no *legal* consequences.

Now that you've categorized them, consider this definition of criminal liability: "conduct that unjustifiably and inexcusably inflicts or threatens substantial harm to individual or public interests" (American Law Institute—hereafter ALI—Model Penal Code—hereafter MPC—1985, § 1.02(1)(a)). Here's a breakdown of the words and phrases in the definition; each represents a fundamental requirement of criminal law:

- Conduct that
- Unjustifiably *and* inexcusably
- Inflicts or threatens *substantial* harm
- To individual or public interests

Compare the case summaries against each word and phrase in the definition. Did you change your mind about any of your categorizations? Which ones do you think meet the test of criminal liability?

Learning what's needed to answer these kinds of questions is what most of the rest of this book is about. But, first, we'll explore throughout the rest of this chapter and Chapter 2, which discusses the constitutional limits placed on the criminal law, some broad propositions about criminal law. These will help prepare you to follow and understand the later chapters, which look at "Who's liable for what?" in more detail.

CRIMES AND NONCRIMINAL WRONGS

The five categories you put the summaries into demonstrate a very important point about criminal law—namely, that it's only *one* kind of social control, *one* form of responsibility for deviance from social norms. So in criminal law, the basic question, to be exact, boils down to "Who's *criminally* responsible for what *crime?*" We won't often discuss the noncriminal kinds of responsibility in this book. But you should keep them in mind anyway, because in the real world criminal liability is the exceptional form of social control. The norm is the other four categories. And they should be, because the criminal liability response is the harshest and most expensive response; it's frequently not effective; and it has the most serious side effects.

In this section, we'll concentrate on the noncriminal wrongs called **torts,** private wrongs for which you can sue the party who wronged you and recover money. Crimes and torts represent two different ways our legal system responds to social and individual harm. Before we look at their differences, let's look at how they're similar. First, both are sets of rules telling us what we can't do (steal money or sell diseased food) and what we must do (pay taxes or provide safe transportation). Second, the rules apply to everybody in the community, and they speak on behalf of everybody, with the power and prestige of the whole community behind them. Third, the power of the law backs up the enforcement of the rules (Hart 1958, 403).

How are they different? Some believe crimes injure the whole community, whereas torts harm only individuals. But that's not really true. Almost every crime is also a tort. Many crimes and torts even have the same name (there's both a crime and a tort called "assault"). Other crimes are torts even though they don't have the same names; for example, the crime of murder is also the tort of wrongful death. In fact, the same killing sometimes is tried as murder and later as a civil wrongful death suit. One famous example is in the legal actions against the great football player O. J. Simpson. He was acquitted in the murder of his ex-wife and her friend in a criminal case but then lost in a tort case for their wrongful deaths. Also, torts don't just harm other individuals; they can also harm the whole community. For example, breaches of contract don't just hurt the parties to the contract. Much of what keeps daily life running depends on people keeping their word when they agree to buy, sell, perform services, and so on.

So, are crimes and torts the same things with different names? No. One difference is that criminal prosecutions are brought by the government against individuals; that's why criminal cases always have titles like *"U.S. v. Rasul," "People v. Menendez," "State v. Erickson,"* or *"Commonwealth v. Wong."* (The first name in the case title is what that government entity calls itself, and the second name, the defendant's, is the individual being prosecuted.) Nongovernment parties bring tort actions against other parties who may or may not be governments. A second difference is that injured **plaintiffs** (those who sue for wrongs in tort cases) get money (called **damages**) for the injuries they suffer.

These differences are important, but the *most* important difference between torts and crimes is the conviction itself. The conviction "is the expression of the community's hatred, fear, or contempt for the convict . . ." (Hart 1958, 405). Professor Henry M. Hart sums up the difference this way:

> [Crime] . . . is not simply anything which a legislature chooses to call a "crime." It is not simply antisocial conduct which public officers are given a responsibility to suppress. It is not simply any conduct to which the legislature chooses to attach a criminal penalty. It is

conduct which . . . will incur a formal and solemn pronouncement of the moral condemnation of the community. (405)

Does this mean that words of condemnation by themselves make crimes different from torts. Not at all. When the legislature defines a crime, it's issuing a threat—"Don't do this, or else . . . "; "Do that, or else. . . ." The "or else" is the threat of punishment, a threat that will be carried out against anyone who commits a crime. In fact, so intimately connected are condemnation and criminal punishment that some of the most distinguished criminal law scholars say that punishment has two indispensable components, condemnation *and* "hard treatment." According to Andrew von Hirsch, honorary professor of Penal Theory and Penal Law at the University of Cambridge, England, and prolific writer on the subject, and his distinguished colleague, Andrew Ashworth, the Vinerian Professor of Law at Oxford University:

> Punishment conveys censure, but it does not consist solely of it. The censure in punishment is expressed through the imposition of a deprivation ("hard treatment") on the offender. (von Hirsch and Ashworth 2004, 21)

If the threat isn't carried out when a crime is committed, condemnation is meaningless, or worse it sends a message that the victim's suffering is worthless. Punishment has to back up the condemnation. According to another respected authority on this point, Professor Dan Kahan (1996):

> When society deliberately forgoes answering the wrongdoer through punishment, it risks being perceived as endorsing his valuations; hence the complaint that unduly lenient punishment reveals that the victim is worthless in the eyes of the law. (598)

The case of *Chaney v. State* (1970) makes clear the need for punishment to make condemnation meaningful. Two young soldiers in the U.S. Army picked up a young woman in Anchorage, Alaska, brutally beat and raped her four times, and took her money. After a trial jury found one of them guilty of rape and robbery, the judge sentenced the defendant to two one-year prison sentences, to be served concurrently, and he suspended sentence for robbing her.

When he sentenced Chaney, the judge recommended that the defendant be confined in a minimum-security prison. He further remarked that he was "sorry that military regulations would not permit keeping Chaney in the service if he wanted to stay because it seems to me that is a better setup for everybody concerned than putting him in the penitentiary." At a later point in his remarks, the trial judge seemed to invite the parole board to, or even recommend that it, release him:

> I have sentenced you to a minimum on all 3 counts here but there will be no problem as far as I'm concerned for you to be paroled at the first day the Parole Board says that you're eligible for parole. . . . If the Parole Board should decide 10 days from now that you're eligible for parole and parole you, it's entirely satisfactory with the court. (445)

In a review of the sentence authorized under Alaska law, the Alaska supreme court ruled that the trial judge's "sentence was too lenient considering the circumstances surrounding the commission of these crimes."

> Forcible rape and robbery rank among the most serious crimes. . . . Considering . . . the violent circumstances surrounding the commission of these dangerous crimes, we have difficulty in understanding why one-year concurrent sentences were thought appropriate. Review of the sentencing proceedings leads to the impression that the trial judge was apologetic in regard to his decision to impose a sanction of incarceration. Much was made of Chaney's fine military record and his potential eligibility for early parole. Seemingly all but forgotten is the victim of appellee's rapes and robbery. [A military spokesman at the time of sentencing noted that] what happened "is very common and happens many times

each night in Anchorage. Needless to say, Donald Chaney was the unlucky 'G.I.' that picked a young lady who told." . . . (445–46)

> We . . . think that the sentence imposed falls short of effectuating the goal of community condemnation, or the reaffirmation of societal norms for the purpose of maintaining respect for the norms themselves. In short, knowledge of the calculated circumstances involved in the commission of these felonies and the sentence imposed could lead to the conclusion that forcible rape and robbery are not reflective of serious antisocial conduct. Thus, respect for society's condemnation of forcible rape and robbery is eroded and reaffirmation of these societal norms negated. . . . A sentence of imprisonment for a substantially longer period of imprisonment . . . would reaffirm society's condemnation of forcible rape and robbery. (447)

We'll come back to the subject of punishment later in this chapter, where we'll discuss the purposes of punishment more fully, and again in Chapter 2, where we'll discuss the constitutional ban on "cruel and unusual punishment." But here it's important to emphasize the often overlooked intimate connection between punishment and the meaning of crime itself.

Nevertheless, even on this important point of expression of condemnation backed up by punishment, the line between torts and crime can get blurred. In tort cases involving violence and other especially "wicked" circumstances, plaintiffs can recover not only damages for their actual injuries but also substantial **punitive damages** to make an example of defendants and to "punish" them for their "evil behavior" (Black 1983, 204).

CLASSIFYING CRIMES

The urge to make sense of criminal law is ancient. That urge has produced several schemes to classify the content of criminal law. Although it might not be the most exciting part of your study of criminal law, knowing something about these schemes will help you follow the remaining chapters in the book and understand and think critically about criminal law. Let's look at the most common classification schemes:

1. Felony and misdemeanor (classification by penalty)
2. Inherently evil and legally wrong (classification by the moral character of the crime)
3. General and special parts of criminal law (classification by general principles of criminal law and by subject matter of kinds of crimes)

Felony and Misdemeanor

The most widely used scheme for classifying crimes is according to punishment. **Felonies** are punishable by death or confinement in the state's prison for one year to life without parole; **misdemeanors** are punishable by fine and/or confinement in the local jail for up to one year. Notice the word "punishable"; the classification depends on the *possible* punishment, not the *actual* punishment. For example, Viki Rhodes pled guilty to "Driving under the Influence of Intoxicants, fourth offense," a felony. The trial court sentenced her to 120 days of home confinement. When she later argued she was a misdemeanant because of the home confinement sentence, the appeals court ruled that "a person whose . . . felony sentence is reduced . . . does not become a misdemeanant by virtue of the reduction but remains a felon" (*Commonwealth v. Rhodes* 1996, 532).

Why should the label "felony" or "misdemeanor" matter? First, the designation might be an element in another crime. For example, an element of burglary is breaking and entering with the intent to commit a felony once inside; intent to commit a misdemeanor won't do (Chapter 11). Second, procedure for felonies differs from that for misdemeanors. For example, felony defendants have to be in court for their trials; misdemeanor defendants don't. Third, prior felony convictions make offenders eligible for longer sentences. Fourth, the legal consequences of felony convictions last after punishment. In many states, former felons can't vote, can't serve in public office, and can't be attorneys. Further, a felony conviction can be a ground for divorce.

Malum in Se and *Malum Prohibitum*

The second classification is based on whether a crime is inherently evil (***malum in se***)—that is, "immoral in its nature, and injurious in its consequences" (Black 1983, 494)—or wrong that isn't evil but wrong only because a statute says it's a crime (***malum prohibitum***).

The *malum in se/malum prohibitum* distinction, one with strong moral overtones, is ancient, going back as far as 1497. It's not always easy to decide which category specific crimes belong in. Some courts have said only crimes requiring criminal intent (Chapter 4) are *mala in se*. In fact, in the beginning, these included only the ancient common-law felonies—murder, manslaughter, rape, burglary, and theft (discussed later in this chapter in the section, "Common-Law Crimes"). Other courts say that any crimes dangerous to life or limb qualify as *mala in se*. For example, in one case, a man dozed off while he was driving; he continued to drive, dozed off again, ran head-on into an oncoming car, and killed a 14-year-old passenger in the car he hit. According to the court, he was guilty of manslaughter because his act was *malum in se*. What he did, the court said, was the same as "firing a gun into a crowded street, or dropping a heavy object into such a street from a tall building (*Grindstaff v. State* 1964, 927).

Mala prohibita is a catchall category that includes all crimes that aren't *mala in se*. Table 1.1 includes a list of *mala in se* and *mala prohibita* crimes based on a variety of court decisions applying one or the other of these criteria. As you can see, the line between the two isn't always easy to figure out.

TABLE 1.1	Crimes *Mala in Se* and *Mala Prohibita*
Mala in Se	***Mala Prohibitum***
Battery	Speeding
Robbery	Driving on a suspended or a revoked license
Larceny	Failure to yield right of way
Malicious property damage	Leaving the scene of an accident
Drunk driving	Drunk driving
Public drunkenness	Hunting without a license
Possession of drugs	Illegal sale of alcohol
Abortion	Carrying a concealed weapon
Attempted suicide	Shooting in a public place
	Tax evasion
	Passing through a tollgate without paying

Source: Based on LaFave 2003a, 37–38.

Why does it matter which category a crime falls into? In criminal law cases, the difference is most important in two crimes, nonintentional manslaughter and battery, where liability may depend on whether the act that caused the injury in battery or the death in manslaughter was *malum in se* or *malum prohibitum* (Chapters 9 and 10). But it's also important in several civil proceedings, for example, excluding or deporting aliens, disbarring lawyers, and revoking doctors' licenses (LaFave 2003a, 39–40).

THE GENERAL AND SPECIAL PARTS OF CRIMINAL LAW

Criminal law consists of two parts: a general part and a special part. The **general part of criminal law** consists of principles that apply to more than one crime. Most state criminal codes today include a general part. The **special part of criminal law** defines specific crimes and arranges them into groups according to subject matter. All states include the definitions of at least some specific crimes, and most group them according to subject matter.

The special part of the criminal law is a classification scheme, but it's also part of the larger organizational structure of the whole criminal law, and the one followed in this book. So we'll discuss the classification scheme in the context of the general and special parts of the criminal law.

The General Part

The general principles are broad propositions that apply to more than one crime. Some general principles (covered in Chapters 3–8) apply to all crimes (for example, all crimes have to include a voluntary act); other principles (for example, criminal intent) apply to all felonies; still others apply only to some crimes (for example, the use of force is justified to prevent murder, manslaughter, assault, and battery).

In addition to the general principles of criminal law in the general part of criminal law, there are also two kinds of what we call "offenses of general applicability" (Dubber 2002, 142). The first is **complicity,** crimes that make one person criminally liable for someone else's conduct. There's no general crime of complicity; instead, there are the specific crimes of accomplice to murder; accomplice to robbery; or accomplice to any other crime for that matter (Chapter 7). Similarly, other crimes of general applicability are the crimes of attempt, conspiracy, and solicitation. Like complicity, there are no general crimes of attempt, conspiracy, and solicitation, but there are the specific crimes of attempting, conspiring, and soliciting to commit specific crimes—for example, attempted murder, conspiring to murder, and soliciting to murder (Chapter 8).

Finally, the general part of criminal law includes the principles of justification (Chapter 5) and excuse (Chapter 6), the principles that govern most defenses to criminal liability. In the defenses of justification, defendants accept responsibility for their actions but claim what they did was right. Their defense goes like this: "I'm responsible for committing the crime, but under the circumstances it was right to commit it." The classic justification is self-defense ("Kill or be killed"). According to the principle of justification, under some circumstances, it's right to commit crimes. If so, committing the crime is justified and doesn't deserve punishment.

Excused conduct doesn't deserve punishment either—but for a different reason. According to the principle of excuse, it's wrong to punish someone who's not responsible for his or her conduct. The argument for excuse goes like this: "Committing the crime was wrong, but I wasn't responsible for my actions." So even if it was wrong to commit the crime, the defendant can't be blamed. The classic excuse is insanity ("I was too insane to know what I was doing; so, even though what I did was wrong, you can't blame me for it").

The Special Part

The special part of criminal law (covered in depth in Chapters 9–13) defines specific crimes, according to the principles set out in the general part. The definitions of crimes are divided into four groups: crimes against persons (such as murder and rape, discussed in Chapters 9 and 10); crimes against property (stealing and trespass, discussed in Chapter 11); crimes against public order and morals (aggressive panhandling and prostitution, discussed in Chapter 12); and crimes against the state (domestic and foreign terror, discussed in Chapter 13).

The definitions of specific crimes are the elements prosecutors have to prove beyond a reasonable doubt to convict defendants. From the standpoint of understanding how the general principles relate to specific crimes, every definition of a specific crime is an application of one or more general principles. To show you how this works, let's look at an example from the Alabama criminal code. One section of the general part of the code reads, "A person is criminally liable for an offense [only] if it is committed by his own behavior" (Alabama Criminal Code 1975, ß 13A-2-20). This general principle of criminal liability (**liability** is the technical legal term for responsibility) is required in the definition of *all* crimes in Alabama.

According to Chapter 7 in the special part of the Alabama Criminal Code, "Offenses Involving Damage to and Intrusion upon Property," the crime of first-degree criminal trespass is defined as "A person is guilty of criminal trespass in the first degree if he . . . enters or remains unlawfully in a dwelling" (ß 13A-7-4). So the general principle of requiring behavior is satisfied by the acts of either entering or remaining.

CRIMINAL PUNISHMENT

The aims of criminal law don't end with defining and classifying crimes or even with understanding the grand organizational structure of the general and special parts of the criminal law. In fact, as you've already learned (page 9), criminal condemnation means nothing without criminal punishment to back it up. And, as you'll learn later in the "The Principle of Legality" section, every criminal law has to define the crime *and* prescribe a punishment. Some go so far as to say that the very purpose of defining, condemning, and classifying crimes—organizing the content into general principles and their application to specific crimes—is so we can decide the kind and amount of punishment.

Punishment, in general, takes many forms. A parent grounds a teenager; a club expels a member; a church excommunicates a parishioner; a friend rejects a companion; a school expels a student for cheating—all these are punishments in the sense that they intentionally inflict pain or other unpleasant consequences ("hard treatment") on the recipient. However, none of these is *criminal* punishment. To qualify as **criminal punishment,** penalties have to meet four criteria:

1. They have to inflict pain or other unpleasant consequences.
2. They have to prescribe a punishment in the same law that defines the crime.
3. They have to be administered intentionally.
4. The state has to administer them.

The last three criteria don't need explanation; the first does. "Pain or other unpleasant consequences" is broad and vague. It doesn't tell us what kind of, or how much, pain. A violent mental patient confined indefinitely to a padded cell in a state security hospital suffers more pain than a person incarcerated for five days in the county jail for disorderly conduct. Nevertheless, only the jail sentence is criminal punishment. The difference lies in the purpose. Hospitalization aims to treat and cure the mental patient; the pain is a necessary but an unwanted side effect, not the reason for the confinement. On the other hand, the pain of confinement in the jail is inflicted intentionally to punish the inmate's disorderly conduct.

This distinction between criminal punishment and treatment is rarely clear-cut. For example, the government may sentence certain convicted criminals to confinement to maximum-security hospitals while sentencing others to prison for "treatment" and "cure." Furthermore, pain and pleasure don't always distinguish punishment from treatment. Shock treatment and padded cells inflict more pain than confinement in some minimum-security federal prisons with their "country club" atmospheres. When measured by pain, punishment may often be preferable to treatment. Some critics maintain that the major shortcoming of treatment is that "helping" a patient sometimes justifies extreme measures: massive surgery, castration, and lobotomy (Hart 1958, 403–5).

We'll divide the purposes of punishment into two broad categories: retribution, which looks back for the purpose of punishing individual criminals for crimes they've already committed, and prevention, which looks forward to prevent future crimes committed by criminals and those who might be thinking about committing crimes.

Retribution

Striking out to hurt what hurts us is a basic human impulse. It's what makes us kick the table leg we stub our toe on. This impulse captures the idea of retribution, which appears in the Old Testament:

> Now a man, when he strikes down any human life, he is put to death, yes death! And a man, when he renders a defect in his fellow, as he has done, thus is to be done to him—break in place of break, eye in place of eye, tooth in place of tooth. (Fox 1995, translating Leviticus 24: 17, 19–20)

Of course, we don't practice this extreme form of payback in the United States, except for murder—and, even for murder, the death penalty is rarely imposed (Chapter 2). In other cases, the Old Testament version of retribution is unacceptable to most retributionists and highly unrealistic: raping a rapist? robbing a robber? burning down an arsonist's house? I think you get the point.

Retribution looks back to past crimes and punishes individuals for committing them, because it's right to hurt them. According to the great Victorian English judge and historian of the criminal law Sir James F. Stephen (1883b), the wicked deserve to suffer for their evil deeds:

> The infliction of punishment by law gives definite expression and a solemn ratification and justification to the hatred which is excited by the commission of the offense. The criminal law thus proceeds upon the principle that it is morally right to hate criminals, and it confirms and justifies that sentiment by inflicting on criminals punishments which express it.
>
> I think it highly desirable that criminals should be hated, that the punishments inflicted upon them should be so contrived as to give expression to that hatred, and to justify it so far as the public provision of means for expressing and gratifying a healthy natural sentiment can justify and encourage it. The forms in which deliberate anger and

righteous disapprobation are expressed, and the execution of criminal justice is the most emphatic of such forms, stand to the one set of passions in the same relation in which marriage stands to sexual passion. (81–82)

Retributionists contend that punishment benefits not only society, as Stephen emphasized, but also criminals. Just as society feels satisfied by "paying back" criminals, giving criminals their "just deserts," offenders benefit through putting right their evil. Society pays back criminals by retaliation; criminals pay back society by accepting responsibility through punishment. Both paybacks are at the heart of retribution.

Retribution is only right if offenders *choose* between committing and not committing crimes. In other words, we can only blame criminals if they had these choices and made the wrong choice. So in the popular "You do the crime, you do the time," what we really mean is, "You *chose* to do the crime, so you *have to* do the time." Their wrong choice makes them blameworthy. *And* their blameworthiness (the criminal law calls it their **culpability**) makes them responsible (the criminal law calls it "liable"). So as culpable, responsible individuals, they have to suffer the consequences of their irresponsible behavior.

Retribution has several appealing qualities. First, it assumes free will, or individual autonomy. This assumption upholds a basic value—that individuals have the power to determine their own destinies and aren't at the mercy of forces they can't control. Retribution also seems to accord with human nature. Hating and hurting wrongdoers— especially murderers, rapists, robbers, and other violent criminals—appear to be natural impulses (Gaylin 1982; Wilson and Herrnstein 1985, chap. 19).

From the Old Testament's philosophy of taking an eye for an eye, to the 19th-century Englishman's claim that it's right to hate and hurt criminals, to today's "three strikes and you're out" and "do the crime, do the time" sentences, the desire for retribution has run strong and deep in both religion and criminal justice. Its sheer tenacity seems to validate retribution.

Retributionists, however, claim that retribution rests not only on long use but also on a firm philosophical foundation. Two reasons support this claim: the first centers on culpability, the second on justice. According to its proponents, retribution requires culpability; it requires that criminals choose and intend to harm their victims. Accidents don't qualify for retribution. So people who load, aim, and fire guns into their enemies' chests deserve punishment; hunters who fire at what they think is a deer and hit their companions who they should know are in the line of fire, don't. Civil law can deal with careless people; the criminal law ought to punish only people who harm their victims "on purpose."

Retributionists also claim that justice is the only proper measure of punishment. Justice is a philosophical concept whose application depends on culpability. Only those who deserve punishment can justly receive it; if they don't deserve it, it's unjust. Similarly, justice is the only criterion by which to determine the quality and quantity of punishment (Chapter 2, "Proportional Punishments").

There are several problems with retribution. First, it's difficult to translate abstract justice into concrete penalties. What are a rapist's just deserts? Is castration for a convicted rapist justice? How many years in prison is robbery worth? How much offender suffering will repay the pain of a maimed aggravated assault victim? Of course, it's impossible to match exactly the pain of punishment and the suffering caused by the crime.

Another criticism is that the urge to retaliate isn't part of human nature in a civilized society; it's the last remnant of barbarism. Retributionists can only assume that human nature cries out for vengeance; they can't prove it. So it's time for the law to reject retribution as a purpose for punishment.

Determinists, among whom are many criminologists, reject the free-will assumption underlying retribution (Mayer and Wheeler 1982; Wilson and Herrnstein 1985). They maintain that forces beyond human control determine individual behavior. Social scientists have shown the relationship between social conditions and crime. Psychiatrists point to subconscious forces beyond the conscious will's control that determine criminal conduct. A few biologists have linked violent crime to biological and biochemical abnormalities. Determinism undermines the theory of retribution because it rejects blame, and punishment without blame is unjust.

Probably the strongest argument against retribution is that the vast numbers of crimes don't require culpability to qualify for criminal punishment (Diamond 1996, 34). This includes almost all the crimes against public order and morals (discussed in Chapter 12). It includes some serious crimes, too—for example, statutory rape—where neither the consent of the victim nor an honest and reasonable mistake about the victim's age relieves statutory rapists from criminal liability (discussed in Chapter 10)— and several kinds of unintentional homicides (discussed in Chapters 4 and 9).

Prevention

Prevention looks forward and inflicts pain, not for its own sake, but to prevent future crimes. There are four kinds of prevention. **General deterrence** aims, by the threat of punishment, to prevent the general population who haven't committed crimes from doing so. **Special deterrence** aims, by punishing already convicted offenders, to prevent them from committing any more crimes in the future. **Incapacitation** prevents convicted criminals from committing future crimes by locking them up, or more rarely, by altering them surgically or executing them. **Rehabilitation** aims to prevent future crimes by changing individual offenders so they'll want to play by the rules and won't commit any more crimes in the future. As you can see, all four forms of prevention inflict pain, not for its own sake, but to prevent future crimes.

General and special deterrence: Jeremy Bentham, an 18th-century English law reformer, promoted deterrence. Bentham was part of the intellectual movement called "the Enlightenment." At the core of the movement was the notion that natural laws govern the physical universe and, by analogy, human society. One of these laws, hedonism, is that human beings seek pleasure and avoid pain. A related law, rationalism, states that individuals can, and ordinarily do, act to maximize pleasure and minimize pain. Rationalism also permits human beings to apply natural laws mechanistically (according to rules) instead of discretion (according to the judgment of individual decision makers).

These ideas, oversimplified here, led Bentham to formulate the classical deterrence theory. It states that rational human beings won't commit crimes if they know that the pain of punishment outweighs the pleasure gained from committing crimes. Prospective criminals weigh the pleasure they hope to get from committing a crime now against the threat of pain they believe they'll get from future punishment. According to the natural law of hedonism, if prospective criminals fear future punishment more than they derive pleasure from present crime, they won't commit crimes. In other words, they're deterred.

Supporters of deterrence argue that the **principle of utility**—permitting only the minimum amount of pain necessary to prevent the crime—limits criminal punishment more than retribution does. English playwright George Bernard Shaw, a strong deterrence supporter, put it this way: "Vengeance is mine saith the Lord; which means it is not the Lord Chief Justice's" (Morris 1974). According to this argument, divinity enables only God, the angels, or some other divine being to measure just deserts, while social scientists can determine how much pain, or threat of pain, deters crime. With this knowledge, the state can scientifically inflict the minimum pain needed to produce the maximum crime reduction.

Its supporters concede that that there are impediments to putting deterrence into operation. The emotionalism surrounding punishment impairs objectivity, and often, prescribed penalties rest more on faith than evidence. For example, the economist Isaac Ehrlich's (1975) sophisticated econometric study showed that every execution under capital punishment laws may have saved seven or eight lives by deterring potential murderers. His finding sparked a controversy having little to do with the study's empirical validity. Instead, the arguments turned to ethics—whether killing anyone is right, no matter what social benefits it produces. During the controversy over the study, one thoughtful state legislator told me that he didn't "believe" the findings, but if they were true, then "we'll have to deep-six the study."

Critics find several faults with the deterrence theory and its application to criminal punishment. According to the critics, the rational, free-will individual that deterrence supporters assumes exists is as far from reality as the 18th-century world that spawned the idea. Complex forces within the human organism and in the external environment, both of which are beyond individual control, strongly influence behavior (Wilson and Herrnstein 1985).

Furthermore, critics maintain that individuals and their behavior are too unpredictable to reduce to a mechanistic formula. For some people, the existence of criminal law is enough to deter them from committing crimes; others require more. Who these others are and what the "more" consists of hasn't been sufficiently determined to base punishment on deterrence. Besides, severity isn't the only influence on the effectiveness of punishment. Certainty and speed may have greater deterrent effects than severity (Andenæs 1983, 2:593).

Also, threats don't affect all crimes or potential criminals equally. Crimes of passion, such as murder and rape, are probably affected little by threats; speeding, drunk driving, and corporate crime are probably affected greatly by threats. The leading deterrence theorist, Johannes Andenæs (1983), sums up the state of our knowledge about deterrence this way:

> There is a long way to go before research can give quantitative forecasts. The long-term moral effects of the criminal law and law enforcement are especially hard to isolate and quantify. Some categories of crime are so intimately related to specific social situations that generalizations of a quantitative kind are impossible. An inescapable fact is that research will always lag behind actual developments. When new forms of crime come into existence, such as hijacking of aircraft or terrorist acts against officers of the law, there cannot possibly be a body of research ready as a basis for the decisions that have to be taken. Common sense and trial by error have to give the answers. (596)

Finally, critics maintain that even if we could obtain empirical support for criminal punishment, deterrence is unjust because it punishes for example's sake. Supreme Court Justice Oliver Wendell Holmes (Howe 1953) offered this analogy:

> If I were having a philosophical talk with a man I was going to have hanged (or electrocuted) I should say, "I don't doubt that your act was inevitable for you but to make it more avoidable by others we propose to sacrifice you to the common good. You may regard yourself as a soldier dying for your country if you like. But the law must keep its promises." (806)

Punishment shouldn't be a sacrifice to the common good; it's only just if it's administered for the redemption of particular individuals, say the retributionists. Punishment is personal and individual, not general and societal. Deterrence proponents respond that as long as offenders are in fact guilty, punishing them *is* personal; hence, it *is* just to use individual punishment for society's benefit.

Incapacitation: Incapacitation restrains convicted offenders from committing further crimes. At the extreme, incapacitation includes mutilation—castration, amputation, and lobotomy—or even death in capital punishment. Incapacitation in most cases means imprisonment. Incapacitation works: Dead people can't commit crimes, and prisoners don't commit them—at least not outside prison walls. Incapacitation, then, has a lot to offer to a society determined to repress crime. According to criminologist James Q. Wilson (1975):

> The chances of a persistent robber or burglar living out his life, or even going a year with no arrest are quite small. Yet a large proportion of repeat offenders suffer little or no loss of freedom. Whether or not one believes that such penalties, if inflicted, would act as a deterrent, it is obvious that they could serve to incapacitate these offenders and, thus, for the period of the incapacitation, prevent them from committing additional crimes. (209)

Like deterrence and retribution, incapacitation has its share of critics. They argue that incapacitation merely shifts criminality from outside prisons to inside prisons. Sex offenders and other violent criminals can and do still find victims among other prisoners; property offenders trade contraband and other smuggled items. As you might imagine, this criticism finds little sympathy (at least among many of my students, who often answer this criticism with an emphatic, "Better them than me").

Rehabilitation: In his widely acclaimed book *The Limits of the Criminal Sanction*, Herbert Packer (1968) succinctly summarized the aims of rehabilitation: "The most immediately appealing justification for punishment is the claim that it may be used to prevent crimes by so changing the personality of the offender that he will conform to the dictates of law; in a word, by reforming him" (50).

Rehabilitation borrows from the "medical model" of criminal law. In this model, crime is a "disease," and criminals are "sick." The major purpose of punishment is to "cure" criminal patients by "treatment." The length of imprisonment depends upon how long it takes to cure the patient. Supporters contend that treating offenders is more humane than punishing them.

Two assumptions underlie rehabilitation theory. The first is determinism; that is, forces beyond offenders' control cause them to commit crimes. Because offenders don't freely choose to commit crimes, they can't be blamed. Second, experts can, through the right therapy, reform (rehabilitate) criminals and change their behavior to prevent them from committing any more crimes in the future. After rehabilitation, former criminals will control their own destinies, at least enough so that they won't commit crimes. To this extent, rehabilitationists subscribe to free will: Criminals can choose to change their life habits and often do; so, in the future, society can hold them responsible for their actions.

The view that criminals are sick has profoundly affected criminal law—and generated acrimonious debate. The reason isn't because reform and rehabilitation are new ideas; quite the contrary is true. Victorian Sir Francis Palgrave summed up a 700-year-old attitude when he stated the medieval church's position on punishment: It was not to be "thundered in vengeance for the satisfaction of the state, but imposed for the good of the offender; in order to afford the means of amendment and to lead the transgressor to repentance, and to mercy." Sixteenth-century Elizabethan pardon statutes were laced with the language of repentance and reform; the queen hoped to achieve a reduction in crime by mercy rather than by vengeance. Even Jeremy Bentham, most closely associated with deterrence, claimed that punishment would "contribute to the reformation of the offender, not only through fear of being punished again, but by a change in his character and habits" (Samaha 1978, 763).

Despite this long history, rehabilitation has suffered serious attacks. First, and most fundamental, critics maintain that rehabilitation is based on false, or at least unproven, assumptions. The causes of crime are so complex, and the wellsprings of human behavior as yet so undetermined, that sound policy can't depend on treatment. Second, it makes no sense to brand everyone who violates the criminal law as sick and needing treatment (Schwartz 1983, 1364–73).

Third, some critics call rehabilitation inhumane because the cure justifies administering large doses of pain. British literary critic C. S. Lewis (1953) argued:

> My contention is that good men (not bad men) consistently acting upon that position would act as cruelly and unjustly as the greatest tyrants. They might in some respects act even worse. Of all tyrannies a tyranny sincerely exercised for the good of its victims may be the most oppressive. It may be better to live under robber barons than under omnipotent moral busybodies. The robber baron's cruelty may sometimes sleep, his cupidity may at some point be satiated; but those who torment us for our own good will torment us without end for they do so with the approval of their own conscience. They may be more likely to go to Heaven yet at the same time likelier to make a Hell of earth. Their very kindness stings with intolerable insult. To be "cured" against one's will and cured of states which we may not regard as disease is to be put on a level with those who have not yet reached the age of reason or those who never will; to be classed with infants, imbeciles, and domestic animals. But to be punished, however severely, because we have deserved it, because we "ought to have known better," is to be treated as a human person made in God's image. (224)

Trends in Punishment

Historically, societies have justified punishment on the grounds of retribution, deterrence, incapacitation, and rehabilitation. But the weight given to each has shifted over the centuries. Retribution and rehabilitation, for example, run deep in English criminal law from at least the year 1200. The church's emphasis on atoning for sins and rehabilitating sinners affected criminal law variously. Sometimes the aims of punishment and reformation conflict in practice.

In Elizabethan England, for example, the letter of the law was retributive: the penalty for all major crimes was death. Estimates show that in practice, however, most accused persons never suffered this extreme penalty. Although some escaped death because they were innocent, many were set free on the basis of their chances for rehabilitation. The law's technicalities, for example, made death a virtually impossible penalty for first-time property offenders. In addition, the queen's general pardon, issued almost annually, gave blanket clemency in the hope that criminals, by this act of mercy, would reform their erring ways (Samaha 1974, 1978).

Gradually, retribution came to dominate penal policy, until the 18th century, when deterrence and incapacitation were introduced to replace what contemporary humanitarian reformers considered ineffective, brutal, and barbaric punishment in the name of retribution. By the turn of the 20th century, humanitarian reformers had concluded that deterrence was neither effective nor humane. Rehabilitation replaced deterrence as the aim of criminal sanctions and remained the dominant form of criminal punishment until the 1960s. Most states enacted indeterminate sentencing laws that made prison release dependent on rehabilitation. Most prisons created treatment programs intended to reform criminals so they could become law-abiding citizens. Nevertheless, considerable evidence indicates that rehabilitation never really won the hearts of most criminal justice professionals, despite their strong public rhetoric to the contrary (Rothman 1980).

In the early 1970s, little evidence existed to show that rehabilitation programs reformed offenders. The "nothing works" theme dominated reform discussions, prompted by a highly touted, widely publicized, and largely negative study evaluating the effectiveness of treatment programs (Martinson 1974). At the same time that academics and policy makers were becoming disillusioned with rehabilitation, public opinion was hardening into demands for severe penalties in the face of steeply rising crime rates. The time was clearly ripe for retribution to return to the fore as a dominant aim of punishment.

California, a rehabilitation pioneer in the early 20th century, reflected this shift in attitude in 1976. In its Uniform Determinate Sentencing Law, the state legislature abolished the indeterminate sentence, stating boldly that "the purpose of imprisonment is punishment," not treatment or rehabilitation. Called "just deserts" or even simply "deserts," retribution was touted as "right" by conservatives who believed in punishment's morality and as "humane" by liberals convinced that rehabilitation was cruel and excessive. Public opinion supported it, largely on the ground that criminals deserve to be punished (Feeley 1983, 139).

Since the mid-1980s, reformers have heralded retribution and incapacitation as the primary criminal punishments. There are, to be sure, some powerful holdouts. One is the Model Penal Code (described later in the "Model Penal Code" section), first written in 1961, when rehabilitation dominated penal policy. After thoroughly reviewing current research and debate, its reporters decided to retain rehabilitation as the primary form of punishment (American Law Institute 1985, 3:11–30).

THE PRINCIPLE OF LEGALITY

Now, let's turn to a principle that applies to all criminal laws and their punishment—the principle of legality. Speaking broadly, the **principle of legality** (also called the "rule of law"), the general proposition that law controls the power of government, is ancient. In 350 B.C., Aristotle wrote:

> He who bids the law rule may be deemed to bid God and Reason alone rule, but he who bids man rule adds an element of the beast; for desire is a wild beast, and passion perverts the minds of rulers, even when they are the best of men. The law is reason unaffected by desire. (quoted in Allen 1993, 3)

Almost nine hundred years later, in 1215, in the Magna Carta, King John promised his barons that he wouldn't proceed with force against any free man, "except by the lawful judgment of his equals or by the law of the land." In 1240, the great English jurist Bracton (1968) wrote that even the king ruled "under God and the law," and "it is a saying worthy of the majesty of a ruler that the prince acknowledges himself bound by the laws (2:305–6).

The principle of legality consists of a mixture of four values (Moore 1999, 208):

1. *Fairness* It's unfair to surprise individuals by charging them with criminal liability when they reasonably believed their actions weren't criminal when they acted.

2. *Liberty* Criminal law interferes with liberty if individuals can't know its content well enough to take into account the possibility of criminal liability when they plan their actions.

3. *Democracy* Democratic decision making demands that elected legislatures, not unelected courts, create crimes.

4. *Equality* Legislatures and courts should treat alike individuals who are "in all morally relevant respects" equal.

"NO CRIME WITHOUT LAW; NO PUNISHMENT WITHOUT LAW"

More narrowly, as it applies to criminal law, the principle of legality refers to a ban on **retroactive criminal lawmaking.** The ban is expressed in another ancient proposition, "No crime without law; no punishment without law." For our purposes, the proposition means a person can't be convicted of, or punished for, a crime unless the law defined the crime and prescribed the punishment *before* she acted. It's called "*the* first principle of criminal law" (Packer 1968, 79); all other principles you'll learn about in this book are subordinate to it. And it applies even when following it allows morally blameworthy, dangerous people to go free without punishment (Dressler 2001, 39).

The case of Treva Hughes (*Hughes v. State* 1994) is an excellent example. Hughes, while driving drunk, ran into Reesa Poole's car and killed Poole's fetus; Poole was due to deliver in 4 days. The appeals court reversed her conviction because the law didn't give Hughes fair warning that it included the unborn in its homicide statute (731). The court had this to say about its decision:

> That Hughes will go largely unpunished for having taken the life of another is frustrating. There are, however, basic principles upon which this country is founded which compel the result we reach. . . . The retroactive application of criminal law . . . is so abhorrent that we must occasionally endure some frustration in order to preserve and protect the foundation of our system of law. (736)

Let's look more closely at two types of retroactive criminal lawmaking, legislative and judicial, and discover why some think the latter form is sometimes a good idea.

Legislative Retroactive Criminal Lawmaking

Why is a retroactive criminal law so "abhorrent" that we don't punish people like Treva Hughes for killing Reesa Poole's ready-to-be-born baby? Because retroactive criminal laws undermine the "central values" of free societies (Allen 1993, 15)—namely, fairness, liberty, democracy, and equality. Limiting punishment to conviction for violating *existing* criminal laws promotes the value of "fair notice" as to what the law commands. Knowing what the law commands provides individuals with the opportunity to obey the law and avoid punishment. Providing individuals with this opportunity promotes the value of human autonomy and dignity. The ban on retroactive criminal lawmaking also prevents officials from punishing conduct they think is wrong but which no existing criminal law prohibits. To allow this would threaten the rule of law itself; it would become a rule of officials instead (Kahan 1997, 96).

Legislatures can't pass retroactive criminal statutes. The Constitution bans them from doing so (as you'll learn in Chapter 2). Why? Jeremy Bentham argued that crime legislation leans toward too much severity, "What is too little is more clearly observed than what is too much" (quoted in Kahan 1997, 112).

Legislators react quickly when it comes to passing severe criminal laws and punishments. "Antipathy, or a want of compassion for individuals who are represented as dangerous and vile, pushes them onward to an undue severity" (Kahan 1997, 112). They can also lean toward severity when it comes to overriding court opinions interpreting statutes favorable to criminals. In one empirical study covering the years 1969 to 1990, Congress passed legislation overriding U.S. Supreme Court interpretations of criminal statutes in 18 cases; they overrode 15 interpretations favorable to criminals and only 3 favorable to the state (Eskridge 1991, 363).

Judicial Retroactive Criminal Lawmaking

You've just learned some of the reasons for banning *legislative* retroactive criminal lawmaking, but what about *judicial* retroactive criminal lawmaking? Should the ban apply to judges' rulings, too? Some say no, because judges are different; so they should get some leeway and be allowed to interpret statutes to include cases of people who clearly deserve punishment, such as drunk driver Treva Hughes and high school principal George Ray Thompson.

George Ray Thompson, a Montana high school principal and boys' high school coach, forced a student to have oral sexual intercourse with him by threatening her that she wouldn't graduate from high school if she didn't. In *State v. Thompson* (1990), he was charged with "sexual assault without consent," a felony in Montana. According to the statute, "without consent" means "the victim is compelled to submit by force against the victim or another."

The trial court dismissed the charges because Thompson didn't use *physical* force to coerce the victim. On appeal, the Montana supreme court affirmed. The court conceded that the case showed "disgusting acts of taking advantage of a young person by an adult who occupied a position of authority over the young person." The court based its decision on the principle of legality:

> If we could rewrite the statutes to define the alleged acts here as sexual intercourse without consent, we would willingly do so. The business of courts, however, is to interpret statutes, not to rewrite them, or insert words not put there by the legislature. With a good deal of reluctance, and with a strong condemnation of the alleged acts, we affirm the District Court. (1107)

To the advocates of wise use of judicial retroactive criminal lawmaking, this case seemed like a good time to use it. Critics, such as Professor Dan Kahan, don't agree with the sweeping condemnation of retroactive criminal lawmaking. They claim that if used wisely, retroactive lawmaking doesn't threaten the values of fair notice, individual autonomy, and abuse of government power; in fact, it *promotes* them (Kahan 1997, 97).

The court could've created a new crime to cover this case (Professor Kahan calls it "sextortion" (97)). Why? First, because the principal *deserves* to be punished. Just because he didn't commit an existing crime doesn't make what he did "any less culpable and deserving—morally speaking—of punishment" than others legally guilty of having sexual intercourse without consent (98). Second, if Thompson had known that courts could fill in "unintended and embarrassing gaps" in existing statutes, this might have *prevented* his disgusting behavior from ever occurring in the first place (99).

Proponents don't recommend retroactive criminal lawmaking "across the board, but rather to exercise it judicially." It only applies in cases where conduct "violates clear moral norms," such as Thompson's (Kahan 1997, 101); we don't need notice to tell us it's "wrong" (*malum in se*; see the *"Malum in Se"* section earlier). Judicial retroactive criminal lawmaking shouldn't apply to *malum prohibita* offenses, many of which most of us don't recognize as wrong and really need notice to tell us are against the law.

Why judges?: Why are judges different? According to supporters of judicial retroactive criminal lawmaking, it's not because judges have better values than legislators or the people legislators represent. After all, judges are socialized pretty much to the same moral norms as ordinary members of the public. It's because they play a moderator's role in criminal law. Read this passage from Professor Kahan (1997), one of judicial retroactive criminal lawmaking's most articulate advocates:

> [Judges] not only see the gruesome cases that dominate the headlines, but also the humdrum, everyday ones that do not even make it onto the back page. They also see the destructive effects of severe policies that do not work as intended. . . . (114)
>
> . . . Judges . . . have a more refined perception of what the law should be made to look like in order to realize those shared values. In particular, they understand how excessive severity in punishment can waste the resources needed for deterrence, and do violence to the expressive norms that inform the public's sense of desert. A criminal law that is made at least in part by judges is thus more likely to secure the ends that the public itself values than is one made entirely by the legislature. The very pervasiveness and stability of delegated common-lawmaking confirm that this is so. (116)
>
> It is precisely in the aftermath of a high profile crime that "antipathy, or a want of compassion for individuals who are represented as dangerous and vile" is most likely to "push [legislators and members of the public] onward to an undue severity"; it is exactly then that legislators are most likely to perceive that the only gesture they can make to reaffirm the values that the wrongdoer's conduct denies is to enact a new, retroactively applicable law, condemning that behavior all the more. Judges are much less likely to succumb to these pressures and frustrations. Their assessment of the case at hand is tempered by their exposure to a vast catalogue of past misdeeds; their temptation to lash out against any one wrongdoer is disciplined by their (sad) awareness that future opportunities to vindicate good values through punishment are likely to be inexhaustible. They take—and are generally expected to take—a longer view of the task of criminal lawmaking. (116)

Professor Kahan concedes that retroactive judicial lawmaking has its problems. Trusting judges to decide what conduct is immoral enough to be treated as criminal when a statute hasn't defined it as criminal "is hardly beyond criticism" (111). Let's look next at some of the limits on judicial criminal lawmaking, including the rule of lenity, precedent, and stare decisis.

The limits on judicial criminal lawmaking: Judges' criminal lawmaking power leaves them lots of leeway for making decisions based on their professional training and experience. Legislators, law enforcement officers, and all other public officials also engage in this **discretionary decision making.** But they don't have total discretion; they have to act within the admittedly very broad boundaries of the principle of legality.

Some of these boundaries are drawn by the U.S. and state constitutions, which you'll learn about in Chapter 2. Others are set by statutes. Some boundaries are made clear by the words in the constitutional provisions and statutes; however, often they're not. They suffer from "that malady which so often afflicts legislation of all types—ambiguity" (LaFave 2003a, 85). *Ambiguity* means statutory definitions of crimes and punishments can have more than one meaning. Let's look at the nonconstitutional rules that help judges resolve the ambiguity problem; they're called the "rules of judicial interpretation of statutes."

The rule of lenity: Ambiguity arises for several reasons. The two most commonly given are (1) words aren't like numbers; they're imperfect symbols for expressing ideas, and (2) situations come up after statutes are enacted that legislators couldn't have thought of when they wrote them. "Who can anticipate every set of facts which the ever changing waves of life can wash ashore?" (Hart and Sacks 1994, 1372).

There are a number of rules of statutory interpretation that are supposed to help courts resolve the ambiguity problem. They're all related, and they all can apply to interpreting criminal statutes. But we'll focus on the one that's directed only at criminal statutes—the **rule of lenity**; the rule is also called "strict construction of criminal statutes." (Throughout the book, we'll use the "rule of lenity," or just "lenity," strict construction of criminal statutes, or just "strict construction" interchangeably.) The rule means that when judges apply a criminal statute to the defendant in the case before them, they have to stick "clearly within the letter of the statute," resolving all ambiguities in favor of defendants and against the application of the statute (Black 1983, 741).

The reason for the rule of lenity is:

> Because of the seriousness of criminal penalties, and because criminal punishment usually represents the moral condemnation of the community, legislatures and not courts should define criminal activity. This policy embodies the instinctive distastes against men languishing in prison unless the lawmaker has clearly said they should. Thus, where there is ambiguity in a criminal statute, doubts are resolved in favor of the defendant. (*U.S. v. Bass* 1971, 348)

Just where do we find ambiguity in the law? An excellent example is the case of *People v. Shabtay* (2006). A jury convicted Yerev Shabtay of two separate offenses growing out of a sophisticated identity theft scheme. Shabtay owned and operated "Simply Discount." He used his customers' credit card number to order electronics equipment. When detectives armed with a warrant searched his home, where he operated his business, they seized 270 items, including computers, digital cameras, and camcorders. Between February 6 and May 8, 2001, Shabtay used 11 victims' credit card numbers without their permission to buy all the items found in his house. California's grand theft statute makes it a felony to use without their permission credit card numbers of four or more persons to obtain "goods or any other thing of value," *"within any consecutive 12-month period."*

On appeal, the California Court of Appeal had to decide whether Shabtay committed one or two grand thefts during 2001. According to the court:

> If a statute is amenable to two alternative interpretations, the one that leads to the more reasonable result will be followed. If there is no ambiguity, then we presume the lawmakers meant what they said, and the plain meaning of the language governs. Ambiguous means "susceptible to more than one reasonable interpretation."
>
> In our view, the language of [the grand theft statute] is clear and unambiguous, and leads to the inescapable conclusion that there can be only one violation of the statute within any consecutive 12-month period. . . . By defining grand theft as acquiring access cards of "four *or more*" persons, makes explicitly clear that no matter how many cards are accessed in excess of four, there is only one offense within any consecutive 12-month period. (227)

One judge disagreed:

> Unlike my colleagues, I believe the application of the "who within any consecutive 12-month period, acquires access cards issued in the names of four or more persons" is guilty of grand theft language . . . is cloaked in ambiguity. On one hand, it can be argued . . . that since the 11 credit card numbers were all possessed in a 3-month, 2-day period . . . only one act of grand theft occurred. On the other hand . . . the first set of 4 victims can be segregated into one count which concludes a consecutive 12-month period. There is evidence that defendant between February 19 and March 29, 2001, used the credit card numbers of four victims to order merchandise. There is also evidence that between April 3

and May 8, 2001, defendant used the credit card numbers of 4 other victims to purchase electronic equipment. . . . A jury could reasonably conclude that any *new* "consecutive 12-month period" . . . began to run with the commission of the fifth possession of the stolen credit card number on April 3, 2001. Each theory finds a basis in logic because the Legislature never defines when the controlling "any 12-month" period begins or terminates.

Defendant is entitled, in matters of statutory interpretation, to the benefit of the "rule of 'lenity'" which is as follows: We have repeatedly stated that when a statute defining a crime or punishment is susceptible of two reasonable interpretations, the appellate court should ordinarily adopt that interpretation more favorable to the defendant.

However, the Supreme Court has explained the limited nature of the lenity rule thusly: ". . . The rule [of lenity] applies only if the court can do no more than guess what the legislative body intended; there must be an egregious ambiguity and uncertainty to justify invoking the rule."

. . . The rule of statutory interpretation that ambiguous penal statutes are construed in favor of defendants is inapplicable unless two reasonable interpretations of the same provision stand in relative equipoise, i.e., that resolution of the statute's ambiguities in a convincing manner is impracticable. Thus, although true ambiguities are resolved in a defendant's favor, an appellate court should not strain to interpret a penal statute in defendant's favor if it can fairly discern a contrary legislative intent." (227)

There's evidence that courts rarely apply the rule of lenity to the cases before them. U.S. Circuit Court Judge Harry Edwards reported that the rule was an issue in about one hundred federal cases during one ten-year period. Although the courts paid lip service to the rule, they used it to overturn the convictions of only three defendants (*U.S. v. Nofziger* 1989, 456).

Several reasons might explain why courts apply the rule so rarely. One is that judges fear they'll be seen as using it to further their own personal, political, and political agendas:

We often cling to the belief that the judge has a secret gift for fashioning, without adding his own creative labors, a clear and consistent decision in every case. . . . [But in reality] the jurist has at his command a full rack of torture, called the rules of interpretation, enabling him to force the silent law into speech, [including] . . . the rules of liberal and of strict construction . . . , yet unfortunately, nowhere is there a rule telling him when the one and not the other must be applied. (Hart and Sacks 1994, 1372–73)

The quote may be true, but it doesn't necessarily mean that the judges' personal views drive their interpretations. There may be, as Professor Kahan argues, an unstated rule at work—the rule that legislatures want and need to share their criminal lawmaking power with courts (Kahan 1995, 389–98). So they delegate it to legislatures.

Professor Francis Allen (1993) gives us this revealing anecdote about legislative delegation of its criminal lawmaking power to courts:

A member of a state legislature who had just succeeded in getting a criminal statute enacted was asked the meaning of a particular provision. His answer was, "We don't know. The courts haven't spoken yet." (82)

Professor Allen wasn't amused. The willingness of the courts to "come to the rescue of ailing legislation . . . permits legislatures to evade their obligation to determine substantive policy" (82).

Professor Kahan concedes that retroactive judicial lawmaking has its problems. Trusting judges to decide what conduct is immoral enough to be treated as criminal when a statute hasn't defined it as criminal "is hardly beyond criticism" (111).

Precedent and stare decisis: Two more restraints on judges' criminal lawmaking power are courts' past decisions (called **precedent**) and **stare decisis** (standing by the precedents set in past cases). According to U.S. Supreme Court Justice and respected judicial philosopher Benjamin Cardozo (1921), in his essay on legal reasoning:

> [I]t is easier to follow the beaten track than it is to clear another. In doing this, I shall be treading in the footsteps of my predecessors, and illustrating the process that I am seeking to describe, since the power of precedent, when analyzed, is the power of the beaten path. (62)

The idea of "following the beaten track" isn't special to criminal law, nor is it the basis only of legal reasoning. We're accustomed to following precedent in ordinary life, even if we don't call it by the fancy name *stare decisis*. We like to do things the way we've done them in the past. Suppose your criminal law professor tells you on the first day of class that you'll be able to use your notes on the four exams scheduled for the semester. True to what she told you on the first day, she lets you use your notes on the first, second, and third exams. Then, on the fourth exam, before she passes it out, she says, "Oh, by the way—no notes today."

I'm sure if your professor broke with the beaten path of the first three exams' precedent of "notes allowed" by her "no notes today" rule in the fourth exam, you wouldn't (to put it mildly) like it. Your reaction gives you a sense of stare decisis. Now, let's look more closely at stare decisis, so you can understand its nature and operation in deciding criminal cases.

Stare decisis isn't a constitutional command; it's a judicial policy guiding decision making (Costello 2005, 2). According to Associate Supreme Court Justice Louis Brandeis:

> *Stare decisis* is usually the wise policy because in most matters it is more important that the applicable rule of law be settled than that it be settled right. (*Burnet v. Coronado Oil and Gas Co.* 1932, 406)

Why is it better to settle a case than settle it right? How can this be "the wise policy"? According to U.S. Supreme Court Chief Justice John Roberts, it's because "adherence to precedent promotes evenhandedness, promotes fairness, promotes stability and predictability" (quoted in Franck 2006). Kentucky Supreme Court Justice William Cooper gave this down-to-earth answer in his blistering dissent from his court's majority opinion, breaking the beaten path to reverse a methamphetamine possession conviction:

> I am reminded of a conversation many years ago with a prominent practicing attorney, who later served with distinction as a Kentucky Circuit Court Judge. I asked him why he always appealed every case as far as the appellate process would allow. He replied, "I know what the law is today, but who knows what it will be tomorrow?" In fact, the most significant moment in the legal profession is not when the Supreme Court renders a seminal decision. It is when a client inquires of an attorney: "These are my facts; what is your advice?" Without stability and predictability in the law, an attorney may become a skilled litigator but will never become an informed counselor. If for no other reason, therein lies the importance of stare decisis. (*Matheney v. Commonwealth* 2006, 12)

A Pennsylvania court put the case for stare decisis more bluntly:

> There should be some certainty to the law so that the bar has definite guidelines. The theory of "stare decisis" has received a modern buffeting in many legal quarters and of course bad law should not remain in force because of errors in the past, but to change the concept of the law every other month makes a mockery of its majesty and a yo-yo of its practice. (*Commonwealth v. Rozanski* 1965, 159)

Critics concede that the values Chief Justice Roberts cited and those stated in the *Matheney v. Commonwealth* dissent are important, but they ask "why a court of law should perpetuate a wrong merely because it has continued until people get used to it and counted on its continuation" (Franck 2006). And they quote Lincoln's answer,

"No one has a right to do wrong" (Franck 2006). The Kentucky Supreme Court majority in *Matheney* agreed:

> Stare decisis is an important guiding principle in American jurisprudence. . . . However, . . . stare decisis does not commit us to the sanctification of ancient or relatively recent fallacy. While we recognize this Court should decide cases with a respect for precedent, this respect does not require blind imitation of the past or unquestioned acceptance ad infinitum. Rather, in many ways, respect for precedent *demands* proper reconsideration when we find sound legal reasons to question the correctness of our prior analysis. (3)

In practice, there's a need for a "safety valve" in the application of stare decisis. Justice Brandeis recognized this when he wrote that stare decisis is "*usually* the wise policy." Curiously, his further comments referencing the safety valve hardly ever appear when his dissent in the *Burnet* case (on page 26), which overruled a precedent, is quoted. But courts have recognized the safety valve throughout the history of stare decisis as it operates in the United States.

American courts in the 1800s routinely overruled precedents, "and the leading judges of the day fully encouraged this practice" (Healy 2001, 90). In 1826, the very distinguished Judge Kent, in his widely read *Kent's Commentaries*, wrote that "hasty and crude decisions" should "be examined without fear, and revised without reluctance," rather than have the "beauty and harmony of the system destroyed by the perpetuity of error" (90).

Author Thomas Healy (2001) said this of Kent's writings:

> He also acknowledged that the "revision of a decision very often resolves itself into a mere question of expediency." These are not the statements of a judge who considered courts bound by decisions with which they disagreed. And taken together with similar statements by other judges and the Supreme Court's lack of attention to precedent, they make it difficult to conclude that the founding generation had adopted the principle of stare decisis. (90)

Apparently, the courts are still taking advantage of the safety valve. The U.S. Supreme Court, as of 2005, had overruled its own decisions 228 times (Costello 2005, 1)!

Matheney v. Commonwealth *and the Safety Valve:* Let's close this section with an extended look at the facts and opinion of *Matheney v. Commonwealth* (2006). Think about the principle of legality, the rule of lenity, and the principle of stare decisis. Then reread the portion of the dissent in *Matheney* quoted on page 26. In your opinion, is this an appropriate case for the safety valve? Or, should the legislature change the law?

Here's what happened. On March 4, 2001, Jeff Matheney and his wife and children traveled to Madisonville, Kentucky. In Madisonville, Mrs. Matheney bought two boxes of cold medicine at the Dollar Store. Matheney then bought two boxes of cold medicine at the More for Less Store. Then, the family traveled to an auto parts store and bought three cans of Pyro (starting fluid) and to a hardware store and bought a gallon of Liquid Fire. They traveled to another shopping center and bought two boxes of Sudafed. After this purchase, the family traveled to yet another shopping center, where Matheney purchased two more boxes of Sudafed from a Rite Aid drug store. The store manager of this Rite Aid recognized Matheney as the same individual who had bought two boxes of Sudafed 3 weeks earlier and called the police to report the purchases.

The evidence at trial established that the following chemicals are necessary to manufacture methamphetamine:

- Ephedrine or pseudoephedrine
- Potassium, lithium, or some other reactive metal
- Anhydrous ammonia
- Ether

- Acid

- Salt or potassium

Matheney possessed only ephedrine (in the Sudafed and cold pills), acid (Liquid Fire can serve as the requisite acid), and ether (starting fluid contains ether).

Here are excerpts from the Kentucky Supreme Court's opinion:

From July 15, 1998, when manufacturing methamphetamine was first made a crime by the Kentucky legislature, until June 20, 2005, the relevant part of the statute provided: "A person is guilty of manufacturing methamphetamine when he . . . possesses the chemicals or equipment for the manufacture of methamphetamine. . . .

In *Kotila v. Commonwealth* (2003), this Court held that the statute required possession of *all* the chemicals or equipment necessary to manufacture methamphetamine. Essentially, this Court found that the statute's use of the word "the" meant that a person could be convicted . . . only for possession of *all the* chemicals or equipment (as opposed to "any" or "some" of the chemicals or equipment) for the manufacture of methamphetamine. . . . Since *Kotila* was rendered, over two years ago, it has become increasingly clear that . . . requiring possession of *all* the chemicals or equipment to uphold a conviction . . . defies common sense. . . . Therefore, we . . . hold that *Kotila's* construction . . . was incorrect. (2)

. . . While we recognize this Court should decide cases with a respect for precedent, this respect does not require blind imitation of the past or unquestioned acceptance ad infinitum. Rather, in many ways, respect for precedent *demands* proper reconsideration when we find sound legal reasons to question the correctness of our prior analysis. (3)

We construe the language . . . "the chemicals or equipment for the manufacture of methamphetamine" to mean that one must possess two or more chemicals or items of equipment with the intent to manufacture methamphetamine to fall within the statute. This construction is based on a common sense approach that gives proper import to the use of the plural "chemicals."(3)

Is this case an appropriate one for applying the safety valve, or should the legislature change the law? What do you think?

THE SOURCES OF CRIMINAL LAW

Legislative and judicial criminal lawmaking are closely related to the sources of criminal law. Most criminal law is found in state criminal codes created by state legislatures and municipal codes created by city and town councils elected by the people. There's also a substantial body of criminal law in the U.S. Criminal Code created by Congress.

Sometimes, these elected bodies invite administrative agencies, whose members aren't elected by the people, to participate in creating criminal law. (Coincidentally, as I'm writing this, the U.S. House of Representatives has passed a bill making gas price-gouging a federal crime. Echoing Professor Allen's anecdote about the legislator waiting for the courts to say what the law he and his co-workers had just passed meant, when asked what "price-gouging" means, one representative answered, "We'll let the Interstate Commerce Commission decide.")

Legislatures weren't always the main source of criminal law. Judges' court opinions were the original source of criminal law, and it remained that way for several centuries. By the 1600s, judges had created and defined the only crimes known to our law. Called **common-law crimes,** they included everything from disturbing the peace to murder.

Let's look first at the common-law crimes created by judges' opinions and then at the legislated criminal codes, including state and municipal codes, the Model Penal Code. Then, we'll look briefly at the participation in legislating criminal law by administrative agencies.

Common-Law Crimes

Criminal codes didn't spring full-grown from legislatures. They evolved from a long history of ancient offenses called "common-law crimes." These crimes were created before legislatures existed and when social order depended on obedience to unwritten rules (the *lex non scripta*) based on community customs and traditions. These traditions were passed on from generation to generation and modified from time to time to meet changed conditions. Eventually, they were incorporated into court decisions.

The common-law felonies still have familiar names and have maintained similar meanings (murder, manslaughter, burglary, arson, robbery, stealing, rape, and sodomy). The common-law misdemeanors do, too (assault, battery, false imprisonment, libel, perjury, corrupting morals, and disturbing the peace [LaFave 2003a, 75]).

Exactly how the common law began is a mystery, but like the traditions it incorporated, it grew and changed to meet new conditions. At first, its growth depended mainly on judicial decisions (Chapter 2). As legislatures became more established, they added crimes to the common law. They did so for a number of reasons: to clarify existing common law; to fill in blanks left by the common law; and to adjust the common law to new conditions. Judicial decisions interpreting the statutes became part of the growing body of precedent making up the common law. Let's look further at common-law crimes at both the state and federal levels.

State common-law crimes: The English colonists brought this common law with them to the New World and incorporated the common-law crimes into their legal systems. Following the American Revolution, the 13 original states adopted the common law. Almost every state created after that enacted "reception statutes" that adopted the English common law. For example, the Florida reception statute reads: "The Common Law of England in relation to crimes . . . shall be of full force in this state where there is no existing provision by statute on the subject" (*West's Florida Statutes* 2005, Title XLVI, 775.01).

Most states have abolished the common-law crimes. But the common law is far from dead. Several states, including Florida, still recognize the common law of crimes. Even in **code states** (states that have abolished the common law), the codes frequently use the names of the common-law crimes without defining them. So to decide cases, the courts have to go to the common-law definitions and interpretations of the crimes against persons, property, and public order and morals (you'll learn about these in Chapters 9–12); the common law of parties to crime (in Chapter 7) and attempt, conspiracy, and solicitation (in Chapter 8); and the common-law defenses, such as self-defense and insanity (in Chapters 5–6).

California, a code jurisdiction, includes all of the common-law felonies in its criminal code (*West's California Penal Code* 1988, § 187(a)). The California Supreme Court relied on the common law to determine the meaning of its murder statute in *Keeler v. Superior Court* (1970). Robert Keeler's wife Teresa was pregnant with another man's child. Robert kicked the pregnant Teresa in the stomach, causing her to abort the fetus. The California court had to decide whether fetuses were included in the murder statute. The court decision, in the following passage, reveals the importance of the common law in interpreting present statutes:

> Penal code § 187 provides: "Murder is the unlawful killing of a human being, with malice aforethought." The dispositive question is whether the fetus which petitioner is accused of killing was, on February 23, 1969, a "human being" within the meaning of this statute. . . .
>
> We therefore undertake a brief review of the origins and development of the common law of abortional homicide. . . . From that inquiry it appears that by the year 1850—the

date with which we are concerned—an infant could not be the subject of homicide at common law unless it had been born alive. . . . Perhaps the most influential statement of the "born alive" rule is that of Coke, in mid-seventeenth century: "If a woman be quick with childe and by a potion or otherwise killeth it in her wombe, or if a man beat her, whereby the childe dyeth in her body, and she is delivered of a dead childe, this is a great misprision (i.e., misdemeanor), and no murder; but if the childe be born alive and dyeth of the potion, battery, or other cause, this is murder; for in law it is accounted a reasonable creature . . . when it is born alive." (3 Coke, Institutes 58 [1648]) . . .

We hold that in adopting the definition of murder in Penal Code § 187 the Legislature intended to exclude from its reach the act of killing an unborn fetus. (*Keeler v. Superior Court* 1970)

As a result of the court's decision, the California legislature changed the criminal homicide statute to include fetuses (Chapter 9).

Federal common-law crimes: In *U.S. v. Hudson and Goodwin* (1812), the U.S. Supreme Court stated clearly that there are no federal common-law crimes. During the War of 1812, Hudson and Goodwin published the lie that President Madison and Congress had secretly voted to give $2 million to Napoleon. They were indicted for criminal libel. But there was a catch; there was no federal criminal libel statute. The Court ruled that without a statute, libel can't be a federal crime. Why? According to the Court:

The courts of [the U.S.] are [not] vested with jurisdiction over any particular act done by an individual in supposed violation of the peace and dignity of the sovereign power. The legislative authority of the Union must first make an act a crime, affix a punishment to it, and declare the Court that shall have jurisdiction of the offence. Certain implied powers must necessarily result to our courts of justice from the nature of their institution. But jurisdiction of crimes against the state is not among those powers. (34)

The rule of *U.S. v. Hudson and Goodwin* seems perfectly clear: There's no federal criminal common law. But like so many other rules you'll learn in your study of criminal, the reality is more complicated. It's more like:

There is no federal criminal common law. But there is. . . . The shibboleth that there is no federal criminal common law—that Congress, not the courts, creates crimes—is simply wrong. There are federal common law crimes. (Rosenberg 2002, 202)

Here's what Associate U.S. Supreme Court Justice Stevens had to say about federal criminal common lawmaking:

Statutes like the Sherman Act, the civil rights legislation, and the mail fraud statute were written in broad general language on the understanding that the courts would have wide latitude in construing them to achieve the remedial purposes that Congress had identified. The wide open spaces in statutes such as these are most appropriately interpreted as implicit delegations of authority to the courts to fill in the gaps in the common law tradition of case-by-case adjudication. (*McNally v. U.S.* 1987)

According to Professor Dan Kahan (1994), Congress has accepted the prominent role Justice Stevens ascribes to the federal courts in developing a "federal common law" in noncriminal subjects. Moreover, Kahan contends that Congress actually *prefers* "lawmaking collaboration" to a "lawmaking monopoly" (369). Judicial common criminal lawmaking *can* be a good thing when it punishes conduct "located not on the border but deep within the interior of what is socially undesirable" (400). The U.S. Supreme Court engaged in judicial lawmaking when to reach the "interior" evil of assaulting a federal officer, in *U.S. v. Feola* (1975), the Court upheld the conviction of several narcotics dealers for assaulting federal officers they didn't know were undercover officers. (See the "Judicial Retroactive Criminal Lawmaking" section for more on this subject.)

 Go to the Criminal Law 9e website to find Exercise 1.1, Common-Law Crimes: www.thomsonedu.com/ criminaljustice/samaha.

State Criminal Codes

From time to time in U.S. history, reformers have called for the abolition of the common-law crimes and their replacement with **criminal codes** created and defined by elected legislatures. The first criminal codes appeared in 1648, the work of the New England Puritans. The Laws and Liberties of Massachusetts *codified* (put into writing) the colonies' criminal law, defining crimes and spelling out punishments.

The authors stated their case for a code this way: "So soon as God had set up political government among his people Israel he gave them a body of laws for judgment in civil and criminal causes. . . . For a commonwealth without laws is like a ship without rigging and steerage" (Farrand 1929, A2).

Some of the codified offenses sound odd today (witchcraft, cursing parents, blasphemy, and idolatry), but others—for example, rape—don't:

> If any man shall ravish any maid or single woman, committing carnal copulation with her by force, against her own will, that is above ten years of age he shall be punished either with death or some other grievous punishment. (5)

Another familiar codified offense was murder:

> If any man shall commit any wilful murder, which is manslaughter, committed upon premeditate malice, hatred, or cruelty not in a man's necessary and just defense, nor by mere casualty against his will, he shall be put to death. (6)

Hostility to English institutions after the American Revolution spawned another call by reformers for written legislative codes to replace the English common law. The 18th-century Enlightenment, with its emphasis on reason and natural law, inspired reformers to put aside the piecemeal "irrational" common law scattered throughout judicial decisions and to replace it with criminal codes based on a natural law of crimes. Despite anti-British feelings, reformers still embraced Blackstone's *Commentaries* (1769) and hoped to transform his complete and orderly outline of criminal law into criminal codes.

Reformers contended that law created by judges was not just disorderly and incomplete; it was antidemocratic. They believed legislatures representing the popular will should make laws, not aloof judges out of touch with public opinion. Thomas Jefferson proposed such a penal code for Virginia (Bond 1950). The proposed code never passed the Virginia legislature, not because it codified the law but because it recommended too many drastic reductions in criminal punishments (Preyer 1983, 53–85).

There was also a strong codification movement during the 19th century, but two codes stand out. The first, the most ambitious and least successful, was Edward Livingston's draft code for Louisiana, completed in 1826. Livingston's goal was to rationalize into one system the laws of criminal law, criminal procedure, criminal evidence, and punishment. Livingston's draft never became law.

The second, David Dudley Field's code, was less ambitious but more successful. Field was a successful New York lawyer who wanted to make criminal law more accessible, particularly to lawyers. According to Professors Paul Robinson and Markus Dubber (2004):

> Field's codes were designed to simplify legal practice by sparing attorneys the tedium of having to sift through an ever rising mountain of common law. As a result, Field was more concerned with streamlining than he was with systematizing or even reforming New York penal law. (3)

Field's New York Penal Code was adopted in 1881 and remained in effect until 1967, when New York adopted most of the Model Penal Code (described later in the "Model Penal Code" section).

The codification movement gathered renewed strength after the American Law Institute (ALI) decided to "tackle criminal law and procedure" (Dubber 2002, 8). ALI was founded by a group of distinguished jurists "to promote the clarification and simplification of the law and its better adaptation to social needs, to secure the better administration of justice, and to encourage and carry on scholarly and scientific legal work" (8). After its first look at criminal law and procedure in the United States, "it was so appalled by what it saw that it decided that . . . what was needed was a fresh start in the form of *model* codes (8).

Go to the Criminal Law 9e website to find Exercise 1.2, 19th-Century Codification Movement: www .thomsonedu.com/ criminaljustice/samaha.

The Model Penal Code (MPC)

The Great Depression and World War II stalled the development of a model penal code. But after World War II, led by reform-minded judges, lawyers, and professors, ALI was committed to replacing the common law with codification. From the earliest of 13 drafts written during the 1950s to the final version in 1962, in the **Model Penal Code (MPC),** ALI (1985) made good on its commitment to draft a code that abolished common-law crimes. Section 1.05, which is right at the beginning of its core provisions, reads: "No conduct constitutes an offense unless it is a crime or violation under this Code or another statute of this State." ([1], § 1.01 to 2.13).

One measure of the MPC's success is its influence on criminal law today. After its adoption in 1962, more than forty states changed their criminal codes. None of these states adopted the MPC completely, but it influenced all of them to some extent (Dubber 2002, 6). The MPC has also influenced the criminal law in all states, not just those with rewritten codes. Over two thousand opinions from every U.S. state, the District of Columbia, and the federal courts have cited the MPC (7).

Many of the opinions excerpted in this book are drawn from among those opinions. Also, this book follows the general structure and analysis of the MPC, because understanding the MPC's structure and analysis will help you to understand criminal law. You'll encounter many variations of the MPC throughout the book, but "if there is such a thing as a common denominator in American criminal law, it's the Model Penal Code" (Dubber 2002, 5). So let's look at the structure and analysis of the MPC.

The structure of the MPC follows closely the description of the "General and Special Parts of Criminal Law" section, so we won't repeat it here. Instead, we'll focus on the analysis of criminal liability—that is, how to analyze statutes and cases to answer the question posed at the beginning of the chapter, "Who's responsible for what?"

We begin by repeating the MPC's definition of criminal liability: "conduct that unjustifiably and inexcusably inflicts or threatens substantial harm to individual or public interests" (ALI 1985, MPC § 1.02(1)(a)). Now let's break down this definition into its three elements, which we can state as three main and two subsidiary questions:

1. Is the conduct a crime? (Chapters 3–4, 5–6, 9–13)
   a. Does the conduct inflict or threaten?
   b. Does the conduct inflict or threaten substantial harm to individual or public interests?

2. If the conduct is a crime, is it wrong? Or, under special circumstances, was the conduct justified, as in self-defense? In other words, the actor admits responsibility for the conduct but proves that under the special circumstances the conduct was right. (Chapter 7)

3. If the conduct was unjustified, should we blame the actor for it? Or, under special circumstances, such as insanity, was the actor not responsible? In other words, the

actors admit their conduct was wrong, but they maintain that under the special circumstances, they weren't responsible for their conduct. (Chapter 8)

There you have, in a nutshell, the elements of criminal liability, not just in the MPC, but in American criminal law in all code states, common-law states, and the federal government. Most of the rest of this book elaborates on these elements of criminal liability and their application to specific crimes.

Municipal Ordinances

City and town governments enjoy broad powers to create criminal laws, a power local governments are enthusiastically using in today's atmosphere of "zero tolerance" for drugs, violence, public disorder, and other "quality of life" offenses that violate community standards of good manners in public. Municipalities have a "chorus of advocates" among criminal law reformers who've helped cities write a "new generation" of their old vagrancy and loitering ordinances that "cleanse" them of prior objections that they're unconstitutional and discriminatory (Logan 2001, 1418). (These matters are discussed in Chapters 2 and 12.) Throughout the book, you'll read cases involving a number of municipal offenses.

Municipal criminal lawmaking isn't new; neither is the enthusiasm for it. In his book *The People's Welfare* (1996), the historian William Novak convincingly documents the "powerful government tradition devoted in theory and practice to the vision of a well-regulated society" from 1787 to 1877:

> At the heart of the well-regulated society was a plethora of bylaws, ordinances, statutes, and common law restrictions regulating nearly every aspect of early American economy and society. . . . These laws—the work of mayors, common councils, state legislators, town and county officers, and powerful state and local judges . . . taken together . . . demonstrate the pervasiveness of regulation in early American versions of the good society: regulations for *public safety* and security; . . . the policing of *public space* . . .; all-important restraints on *public morals* (establishing the social and cultural conditions of public order). (1–2)

> Here's a sample of current ordinances collected by Professor Wayne Logan (2001):

> pick-pocketing; disturbing the peace; shoplifting; urinating in public; disorderly conduct; disorderly assembly; unlawful restraint; obstruction of public space; harassment over the telephone; resisting arrest; obscenity; nude dancing; lewdness, public indecency, and indecent exposure; prostitution, pimping, or the operation of "bawdy" houses; gambling; graffiti and the materials associated with its inscription; littering; aggressive begging and panhandling; vandalism; trespass; automobile "cruising"; animal control nuisances; excessive noise; sale or possession of drug paraphernalia; simple drug possession; possession of weapons other than firearms; possession of basic firearms and assault-style firearms; discharge of firearms; sleeping, lying, or camping in public places; driving under the influence of drugs or alcohol; carrying an open container of alcohol; underage drinking; and public drinking and intoxication; vagrancy and loitering; curfews for minors; criminal assault and battery. (1426–28)

Municipal ordinances often duplicate and overlap state criminal code provisions. When they conflict, state criminal code provisions are supposed to trump municipal ordinances. A number of technical rules control whether they're in conflict, and we don't to need get into the details of these rules, but their gist is that unless state criminal codes make it very clear they're preempting local ordinances, local ordinances remain in effect.

A good example is the case of *Chicago v. Roman* (1998). Edwin Roman attacked 60-year-old Anthony Pupius. He was convicted of the Chicago municipal offense of assault against the elderly and was sentenced to 10 days of community service and one year of probation. However, the ordinance contained a mandatory minimum sentence of at least 90 days of incarceration. The city appealed, claiming the sentence violated the mandatory minimum required by the ordinance. The trial court's decision was reversed.

According to the Illinois Supreme Court, the Illinois legislature can restrict Chicago's power to create crimes, but it has to pass a law *specifically* spelling out the limit. Because the legislature hadn't passed a law preempting the penalty for assaulting the elderly, Chicago's mandatory minimum had to stand.

The long list of ordinances Professor Logan found illustrates the broad power of municipalities to *create* local crimes. But, as the example of *Chicago v. Roman* indicates, the power of municipalities goes further than creating crimes; it includes the power to determine the punishment, too. They also have the power to enact forfeiture laws. Under New York City's alcohol and other drug-impaired driver's law, thousands of impaired drivers have forfeited their vehicles (Fries 2001, B2). Another example: an Oakland, California, ordinance authorizes forfeiture of vehicles involved in "solicitation of prostitution or acquisition of controlled substances." The ordinance was passed after residents complained about individuals driving through their neighborhoods looking to buy drugs or hire prostitutes (*Horton v. City of Oakland* 2000, 372).

Don't get the idea from what you've just read that municipalities have *unlimited* powers to create crimes and prescribe punishments. They don't. We've already noted two limits—constitutional limits (which we'll discuss further in Chapters 2 and 12) and the power of states to preempt municipal criminal lawmaking and punishment. Municipalities also can't create felonies, and they can't prescribe punishments greater than one year in jail.

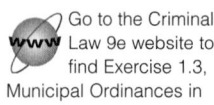 Go to the Criminal Law 9e website to find Exercise 1.3, Municipal Ordinances in the United States: www.thomsonedu.com/criminaljustice/samaha.

Administrative Agency Crimes

Both federal and state legislatures frequently grant administrative agencies the authority to make rules. For example, the fat manual of U.S. Internal Revenue Service income tax regulations is based on the rule-making authority granted by Congress to the IRS. On the state level, state legislatures commonly authorize the state highway patrol agencies to make rules regarding vehicle safety inspections. We call violations of these federal and state agency rules **administrative crimes;** they're a rapidly growing source of criminal law. Administrative crimes might conflict with the Constitution if they delegate Congress's exclusive power to make laws to administrative agencies.

Let's look at three situations where administrative laws have raised constitutional questions (LaFave 2003a, 124):

1. Can legislatures authorize administrative agencies to create regulations when there's a criminal penalty for violating these regulations?

2. Can legislatures go further and authorize agencies to prescribe penalties for violating regulations created by the agency?

3. Can legislatures go even further and allow agencies to set up their own courts to decide cases involving violations of the regulations they've created?

The U.S. Supreme Court answered the first question, almost a century ago. In *U.S. v. Grimaud* (1911), Pierre Grimaud and J. P. Carajou drove and grazed their sheep on the Sierra Forest Reserve without a permit, in violation of a Department of Agriculture rule. The defendants argued that it was unconstitutional for Congress to delegate its lawmaking power to the Secretary of the Agriculture. The Court held that the delegation was constitutional because "it was impractical for Congress to provide general regulations for . . . various and varying details of management" of the forest preserves. "Authorizing the Secretary of Agriculture to meet these local conditions, Congress was merely conferring administrative functions on an agent, and not delegating to him legislative power" (516).

The Court admitted that it's "difficult to define the line which separates legislative power to make laws, from administrative authority to make regulations." But, according to the Court, once Congress makes its will known in a statute, it can grant to the agency the "power to fill up the details" by establishing rules and regulations, "the violation of which could be punished by fine or imprisonment fixed by Congress, or by penalties fixed by Congress" (517).

In a long line of cases since *Grimaud*, the Court has continued to uphold delegations in cases where Congress sets the punishment. State courts have followed the pattern of the federal courts (LaFave 2003a, 125).

"Can legislatures delegate the power to set penalties for administrative crimes?" Some courts say yes, others say no (LaFave 2003a, 127–28). The answer to the third question is clearly no; administrative agencies can't decide guilt in individual cases of administrative crimes. But there's a catch. Some administrative agency cases aren't considered criminal, even when the penalty is severe. Administrative agencies often revoke or suspend individuals' licenses, deny their benefits, and seize their property; there are even cases where courts have called fining individuals noncriminal (cases cited in LaFave 2003a, 128).

CRIMINAL LAW IN A FEDERAL SYSTEM

Until now, we've referred to criminal law, *inaccurately*, in the singular, and throughout the rest of the book, you'll see this inaccuracy repeated, mainly because it's convenient. But let's clear up the inaccuracy. In our federal system, there are 52 criminal codes, one for each of the 50 states, one for the District of Columbia, and the U.S. Criminal Code, which overlays the other 51 codes. The U.S. government power to ban, interpret, and punish crimes is limited to crimes specifically related to national interests, such as crimes committed on military bases and other national property; crimes against federal officers; and crimes that are difficult for one state to prosecute—for example, drug, weapons, organized and corporate crime, and crimes involving domestic and international terrorism (Chapter 13). The rest of criminal law, which is most of it, is left to the state codes. These are the crimes against persons, property, and public order and morals in the special part of the criminal law. You'll learn about these in Chapters 9–12.

So we have 52 criminal codes, each defining specific crimes and establishing general principles for the territory and people within it. And they don't, in practice, define specific crimes the same. For example, in some states, to commit burglary, you have to actually break into and then enter a building. In other states, it's enough that you enter a building unlawfully, as in opening an unlocked door to a house the owners forgot to lock, looking to steal their HDTV inside. In still other states, all you have to do is stay inside a building you've entered lawfully—for example, hiding until after closing time in a store restroom during business hours, so you can steal stuff after the store closes (Chapter 11).

The defenses to crime also vary across state lines. In some states, insanity requires proof *both* that defendants didn't know what they were doing and that they didn't know it was wrong to do it. In other states, it's enough to prove *either* that defendants didn't know what they were doing or that they didn't know that it was wrong (Chapter 6). Some states permit individuals to use deadly force to protect their homes from intruders; others require proof that the occupants in the home were in danger of serious bodily harm or death before they can shoot intruders (Chapter 5).

Punishments also differ widely among the states. Several states prescribe death for some convicted murderers; others prescribe life imprisonment. Capital punishment states differ in how they execute murderers: by electrocution, lethal injection, the gas chamber, hanging, or even the firing squad. The death penalty is only the most dramatic example of different punishments. Other, less dramatic examples affect far more people. Some states lock up individuals who possess small quantities of marijuana for private use; in other states, it's not a crime at all.

This diversity among the criminal codes makes it clear there's no single U.S. criminal code. But this diversity shouldn't obscure the broad outline that's common to all criminal law in the United States. They're all based on the general principles of liability and crimes of general applicability that we touched on earlier in this chapter (which you'll learn about more in depth in Chapters 3–6), and they all include defenses of justification and excuse (which you'll learn about in Chapters 5–6). The definitions of the crimes you'll learn about in Chapters 9–12 do differ, and we'll take account of the major differences. But when it comes to the serious crimes, even these definitions resemble one another more than they differ.

 Go to the Criminal Law 9e website to find Exercise 1.4, Individual State Criminal Codes: www.thomsonedu .com/criminaljustice/samaha

For example, *murder* means killing someone on purpose; criminal sexual assault includes sexual penetration by force; *robbery* means taking someone's property by force or threat of force; *theft* means taking, and intending to keep permanently, someone else's property. And, of course, the crimes against the state (in Chapter 13) and other crimes in the U.S. Criminal Code don't recognize state lines; they apply everywhere in the country.

THE TEXT-CASE METHOD

Now that you've got the big picture of criminal liability and punishment, the overarching principles that apply to all of criminal law, and the sources of criminal law in a federal system, it's time to take a closer look at the method this book uses to help you learn, understand, and think critically about criminal law. I call it the "text-case method," and *Criminal Law 9* is what I call a "text-case book"; it's part text and part excerpts from criminal law cases edited for nonlawyers. The text part of the book explains the general principles of criminal law and the definitions of specific crimes. The case excerpts involve real-life crimes that apply the general information in the text to real-life situations.

The application of principles and definitions of crimes to the facts of specific cases serves two important purposes. First, it helps you understand the principles and the elements of specific crimes. Second, it stimulates you to think critically about the principles and their application. I believe the combination of text and case excerpts is the best way to test whether you *understand* and can *think about* general concepts rather than just memorizing and writing them by rote. So although you can learn a lot from the text without reading the case excerpts, you won't get the full benefit of what you've learned without applying and thinking about it by reading the case excerpts.

For most of my students (and many of you who send me e-mails), reading and discussing the case excerpts are their favorite part of the book. That's good. Cases bring criminal law to life by applying the abstract general principles, doctrines, and rules described in the text to real events in the lives of real people. But keep in mind that judges write the reports of the cases the excerpts are taken from. So don't be surprised to learn that they don't all write with college students or other nonlawyers in mind. Reading the excerpts may take some getting used to. This section is designed to help you get the most out of the cases.

The cases in this book are all excerpts; that is, they're edited versions of the complete reports of the cases. In almost all the case excerpts, you'll be reading reports of the appeals of guilty verdicts, not transcripts of the criminal trial. In other words, the defendant has been convicted already by a trial court and has asked an appeals court to review the conviction.

You'll never read a review of a case in which a defendant was acquitted. Why not? In the criminal law of the United States, a "not guilty" verdict is final and not subject to review. (There's an exception, sort of, to this rule, but we'll take it up in the first of the few case excerpts where the exception applies.)

Let's look at a few technical, but essential, points about the verdicts "not guilty" and "guilty." Not guilty doesn't mean innocent; it means the government didn't prove its case beyond a reasonable doubt. Think of "not guilty" as "not *legally* guilty." Guilty doesn't mean not innocent; it means the government proved its case beyond a reasonable doubt. Think of "guilty" as "*legally* guilty." These technical differences are not just technicalities. As you read the cases, remember that some of the *legally* guilty defendants you're reading about are *factually* innocent. The flip side is also true; some acquitted defendants are *factually* guilty. The number of factually guilty people who "got off" is probably less than many people believe ("Symposium: Wrongful Convictions and Systemic Reform" 2005).

Criminal cases start in trial courts. It's in the trial courts that the cases for the state and the defense are presented; where their witnesses and the physical evidence are introduced; and where the *fact finders* (juries in jury trials or judges in nonjury bench trials) decide what the "true" story is and whether the evidence all adds up to proof of guilt beyond a reasonable doubt). If there's reasonable doubt, the jury renders its "not guilty" verdict; the judge enters a judgment of Acquittal; and, the case is over—for good. There's no appeal to an acquittal; the fact finders' verdict is final.

If there's proof beyond a reasonable doubt, the fact finders render their "guilty" verdict; the judge enters a judgment of Guilty—and the case *might* be over. Sometimes, defendants appeal judgments of guilt. These appeals go to appellate courts. (The case excerpts are drawn from the official reports of these courts' decisions.) Most states and the federal government have two levels of appeals courts (see Figure 1.1): an intermediate court of appeals and a supreme court. The usual procedure is to appeal first to the intermediate court of appeals and then to the state supreme court. In a very few cases involving issues about the U.S. Constitution, the case may go to the U.S. Supreme Court. That's where the case excerpts in this book enter the picture. Let's look at the parts of the appellate cases you'll be reading excerpts from.

The Parts of Case Excerpts

Don't worry if reading cases intimidates you at first. Like students before you, you'll get the hang of it before long. To help you get the most out of the case excerpts, I've outlined the main parts of each case: the (1) title, (2) citation, (3) procedural history, (4) judge, (5) facts, (6) decision, and (7) opinion. Now we'll take a closer look at all the

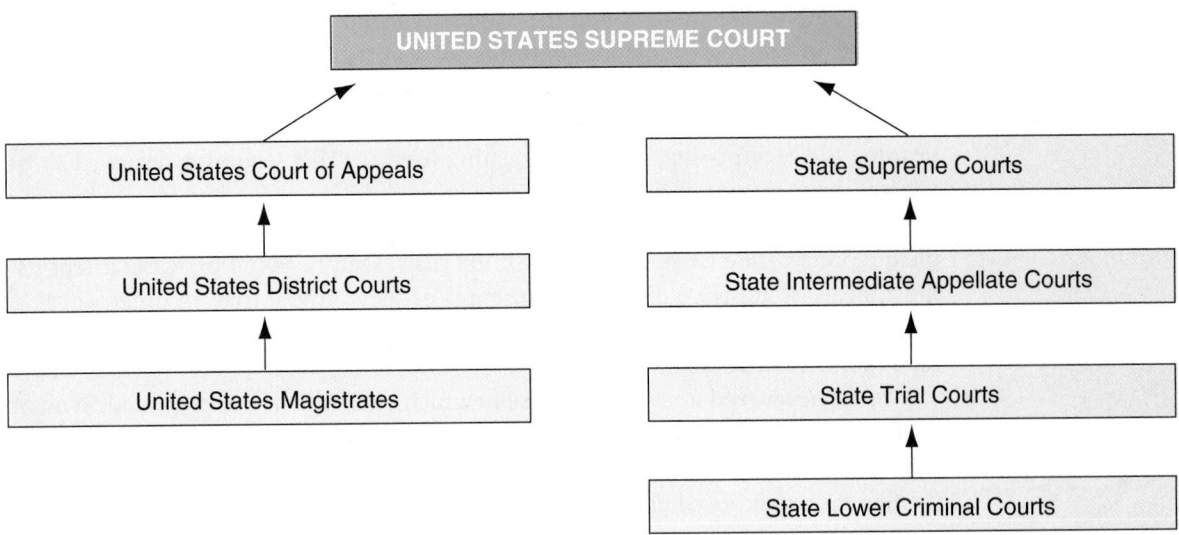

FIGURE 1.1 Criminal Court Structure

parts of the case excerpts to guide you through reading and understanding what each contains and what each means.

Title: The case title consists of the names of the parties, either *appellants* (the party appealing the case) and *appellees* (party appealed against) or *petitioners* (parties bringing a case in habeas corpus or certiorari) and *respondents* (parties petitioned against in habeas corpus and certiorari).

Citation: The citation is like the footnote or endnote in any text; it tells you where to find the case. (See "Finding Cases" later.)

Procedural history: The case history is a brief description of the procedural steps and judgments (decisions) made by each court that has heard the case.

Judge: The name of the judge who wrote the opinion and issued the court's judgment in the case.

Facts: The facts of the case are the critical starting point in reading and analyzing cases. If you don't know the facts, you can't understand the principle the case is teaching. One of my favorite law professors, Professor Hill, frequently reminded us: "Cases are stories with a point. You can't get the point if you don't know the story." He also gave us some helpful advice: "Forget you're lawyers. Tell me the story as if you were telling it to your grandmother who doesn't know anything about the law."

Judgment (Decision): The court's judgment (sometimes called the court's "decision") is how the court disposes of the case. In the trial court, the judgments are almost always guilty or not guilty. In appeals courts, the judgments are affirmed, reversed, or reversed and remanded. This is the most important legal action of the court, because it's what decides what happens to the defendant and the government.

Opinion: For students wanting to learn criminal law, the court's opinion is more important than the judgment: it's "the point of the story." In the opinion, the court backs up its judgment by explaining how and why the court applied the law (general principles and the elements of crimes) to the facts of the case. The law in the case excerpts includes the constitutional principles in Chapter 2; the principles of criminal liability in Chapters 3 and 4; the defenses in Chapters 5 and 6; the law of parties to crime and incomplete offenses in Chapters 7 and 8; and the law of crimes against persons, property, public order, and the state in Chapters 9–13.

The opinion contains two essential ingredients:

1. The court's holding—the legal rule the court has decided to apply to the facts of the cases.

2. The court's reasoning—the reasons the court gives to support its holding. In some cases, the justices write majority and dissenting opinions.

A *majority opinion,* as its name indicates, is the opinion of the majority of the justices on the court who participated in the case. The majority opinion lays out the law of the case. Although the majority opinion represents the established law of the case, *dissenting opinions* present a plausible alternative to the majority opinion. Dissents of former times sometimes become the law of later times. For example, dissents in U.S. Supreme Court opinions of the 1930s became the law in the 1960s, and many of the dissents of the 1960s became law by the 1990s.

Occasionally, you'll see a concurring opinion. In concurring opinions, justices agree with the conclusions of either the majority or the dissenting opinion, but they have different reasons for reaching the conclusion. Sometimes (mostly in U.S. Supreme Court cases), enough justices agree with the *result* in the case to make up a majority decision, but not enough agree on the *reasoning* to make up a majority opinion. In these cases, there's a *plurality opinion,* an opinion that represents the reasoning of the greatest number (but less than a majority) of justices.

All of the differing perspectives in the opinions get you to think about the principles of criminal law. They also clearly demonstrate that there's almost always more than one reasonable way to look at important questions.

Briefing the Case Excerpts

To get the most from your reading of the case excerpts, you should write out the answers to the following questions about each. This is what we call "briefing" a case.

1. *What are the facts?* State the facts in simple narrative form in chronological order. As Professor Hill said, "Tell me the story as if you were telling it to your grandmother." Then, select, sort, and arrange the facts into the following categories:
   a. *Actions of the defendant* List what the defendant did in chronological order. (Remember, there's no criminal case without criminal acts by the defendant.)
   b. *Intent of the defendant required, if any* If none is required, say "none."
   c. *Circumstances required by the statute defining the crime (such as age in statutory rape), if any* If none is required, say "none."
   d. *Causing a harmful result, if one is required* If none is required, say "none."
   e. *Justification and excuse (defense), if any* If none, say "none."

2. *What's the legal issue in the case?* State the principle and/or element of a specific crime raised by the facts of the case.

3. *What are the arguments in the court's opinion?* List the reasons the court gives for its decision. The court's opinion consists of how and why the court applies the principle, doctrine, and/or rule to the facts of the case.

4. *State the court's judgment (decision).* The most common judgments are
   a. *Affirmed* Upheld the judgment (decision) of the lower court
   b. *Reversed* Overturned the judgment (decision) of the lower court
   c. *Reversed and remanded* Overturned the judgment (decision) of the lower court and sent the case back for further proceedings in accord with the appellate court's decision

Summary of briefing cases: You can't answer all these questions in every case. First, the answers depend on the knowledge you'll accumulate as the text and your instructor introduce more principles, doctrines, and rules. Second, courts don't necessarily follow the same procedure in reviewing an appeal as the one outlined here. Third, not all of the questions come up in every case—except for one: What did the defendant do? That's because there's no criminal case without some action by the defendant.

Developing the skills needed to sort out the elements of the case excerpts requires practice, but it's worth the effort. Answering the questions can challenge you to think not only about the basic principles, doctrines, and rules of criminal law but also about your own fundamental values regarding life, property, privacy, and morals.

Finding Cases

Knowing how to read and brief cases is important. So is knowing how to find cases. You may want to look up cases on your own, either in the library or in the rapidly expanding cases published on the Internet. These might include cases your instructor talks about in class, those discussed in the text, or the full versions of the case excerpts and the note cases following the excerpts. You may even want to look up a case you read or hear about outside of class.

The case citation consists of the numbers, letters, and punctuation that follow the title of a case in the excerpts or in the bibliography at the end of the book. These letters and numbers tell you where to locate the full case report. For example, in *State v. Metzger*, just after the title of the case, "State v. Metzger," you read "319 N.W. 2d 459 (Neb. 1982)." Here's how to interpret this citation:

319 = Volume 319

N.W.2d = Northwestern Reporter, Second Series

459 = page 459

(Neb. 1982) = Nebraska Supreme Court in the year 1982

So if you're looking for the full version of *State v. Metzger*, you'll find it in Volume 319 of the *Northwestern Reporter*, second series, page 459. The Northwestern Reporter, Second Series, is the second series of a multivolume set of law books that publishes reports of cases decided by the supreme courts and intermediate appellate courts in Nebraska and several other states in the region. There are comparable reporters for other regions, including the Northeast (N.E.), Southern (So.), Southwest (S.W.), and Pacific (P.).

Case citations always follow the same order. The volume number always comes before the title of a reporter and the page always comes immediately after the title. The abbreviation of the name of the court and the year the case was decided follow the page number in parentheses. You can tell if the court was the highest or an intermediate appellate court by the abbreviation. For example, in *Metzger*, the court is the Nebraska Supreme Court. (If the Nebraska intermediate appeals court had decided the case, you'd see "Neb. App.")

SUMMARY

I. **Criminal law always boils down to "Who's responsible for what?" Or, as the lawyers ask, "Who's liable for what?"**

II. **Criminal liability is:**
   A. Conduct that
   B. Unjustifiably *and* inexcusably
   C. Inflicts *or* threatens *substantial* harm
   D. To individual or public interests

III. **The law classifies behaviors into one of five categories:**
   A. *Crime* The degree of severity should reflect the amount of stigma that a criminal should suffer and the severity of "hard punishment."
   B. *Noncriminal wrong (tort)* This reflects the price that the wrongdoer has to pay to another individual without labeling the behavior "criminal."
   C. *Regulation* Government places this burden on behaviors to discourage them; for example, an alcohol tax makes the user pay a high price, but drinking it isn't a criminal act.
   D. *License* This is a small user fee, which neither encourages nor discourages the behavior.
   E. *Lawful* There are no legal consequences for the act but it can still be deemed as a deviant behavior by peers and the community.

IV. **Crimes vs. noncriminal (civil) wrongs**
   A. Noncriminal (civil) wrongs, called "torts," allow one party to sue another to recover monetary damages for the injuries they've suffered.
   B. Crimes are actions brought by the government against individuals.
   C. Conviction is the most important difference between torts and crimes. Conviction for a crime leads to punishment, which has two indispensable components: (1) condemnation and (2) "harsh treatment."

V. **Crime classification**
   A. *Felony and misdemeanor* Crimes are also classified by the penalty assessed. Felonies are punishable by death or confinement in a state prison for one year to life without parole; misdemeanors are punishable by a fine and/or confinement in the local jail for up to one year.
   B. *Inherently evil and legally wrong* Crimes can be classified by the moral character of the crime. Inherently evil (*malum in se*) crimes are immoral in nature and injurious in their consequences. Legally wrong (*malum prohibitum*) crimes aren't evil in nature but are crimes because there are statutes that say they're crimes.
   C. The general and specific parts of criminal law divide criminal law between the general principles and doctrines of criminal law and the applications of the general information to the definitions of specific crimes.
   D. The definitions of crimes are divided into four groups:
      1. Crimes against persons: murder and rape
      2. Crimes against property: stealing and trespass
      3. Crimes against public order and morals: aggressive panhandling and prostitution
      4. Crimes against the state: domestic and foreign terror

VI. Criminal punishment

A. Every criminal law has to define the crime *and* prescribe a punishment.

B. To qualify as *criminal* punishment, penalties have to meet four criteria:

  1. Inflict pain or other unpleasant consequences

  2. Be prescribed within the law defining the crime

  3. Be administered intentionally

  4. Be administered by the state as punishment

C. Punishment has two goals: retribution and prevention.

  1. Retribution looks back to past crimes and punishes individuals for committing them because it's right to hurt them.

  2. Prevention looks forward and inflicts pain not for its own sake but to prevent future crimes. There are four kinds of prevention:

    a. General deterrence aims to prevent the general population from committing crimes through the threat of punishment.

    b. Special deterrence aims to prevent convicted offenders from committing more crimes in the future.

    c. Incapacitation prevents convicted criminals from committing future crimes by locking them up.

    d. Rehabilitation aims to prevent future crimes from happening by changing individual offenders.

D. Trends in punishment

  1. Historically, societies have justified punishment on the grounds of retribution, deterrence, incapacitation, and rehabilitation.

  2. Retribution and rehabilitation have been in English criminal law for at least eight hundred years.

  3. Gradually, retribution came to dominate penal policy, until the 18th century, when deterrence and incapacitation were introduced to replace the "barbaric and ineffective" punishment form of retribution.

  4. Rehabilitation replaced deterrence in the late 20th century and remained the dominant form of punishment until 1960.

  5. In the 1960s a wave of public opinion that "nothing worked" to rehabilitate the offenders swept the nation.

  6. By the mid-1980s, reformers were heralding retribution and incapacitation as the primary criminal punishments.

VII. The principle of legality is also called the "rule of law." The belief is that law controls the power of government. From Aristotle in 350 B.C. to the Magna Carta in 1215, the principle of legality has been a mixture of four values:

A. Fairness

B. Liberty

C. Democracy

D. Equality

VIII. Retroactive criminal lawmaking

A. It's illegal to charge a culprit with a crime that's not on the books.

B. Judicial retroactive criminal lawmaking allows judges to exercise their judgment (discretionary decision making) in cases, but there are limits:

  1. Judges are bound by the U.S. and state constitutions.

  2. When applying a criminal statute to a defendant in a current case, judges have to follow the rule of lenity and stick "clearly within the letter of the statute."

3. *Precedent*, courts' past decisions, restrains judicial discretion.
4. *Stare decisis*, which is standing by the precedents set in past cases, is a judicial policy, not a constitutional command.

IX. Sources of criminal law
  A. The original source of criminal law, common-law crimes, was created by judges. These crimes ranged from murder to disturbing the peace.
  B. Although most states have abolished state common-law crimes, which were carried over from the English colonists into the New World, they still use the codes in common-law crimes.
  C. Today, most criminal law is found in state criminal codes created by state legislatures and municipal codes created by city and town councils. The U.S. Congress also details laws in the U.S. Criminal Code.
  D. The Model Penal Code focuses on the analysis of criminal liability, meaning, "Who's responsible for what?"
  E. By beginning with the definition of criminal liability—which is, "conduct that unjustifiably and inexcusably inflicts or threatens substantial harm to individual or public interest"—we can break down the Model Penal Code into three main and two subsidiary questions:
    1. Is the conduct a crime?
      a. Does the conduct inflict or threaten?
      b. Does the conduct inflict or threaten substantial harm to the individual or public interests?
    2. If the conduct is a crime, is it wrong?
    3. If the conduct was unjustifiable, should we blame the actor for it?
  F. Municipal ordinances often duplicate and overlap state criminal code provisions. However, when they're in conflict with state criminal codes, the state criminal codes trump municipal ordinances.
    1. Municipalities have the power to both create crimes and prescribe punishment for them.
    2. Municipalities can also enact forfeiture laws.
    3. Municipality ordinances aren't unlimited in their powers:
      a. They cannot create felonies.
      b. They cannot prescribe punishment for more than one year in jail.
  G. Administrative agency crimes are written by administrative agencies who've been granted the authority from both the federal and state legislatures to create laws. They're a rapidly growing source of criminal law, but they often raise constitutional questions:
    1. Can legislatures authorize administrative agencies to create regulations when there's a criminal penalty for violating these regulations?
    2. Can legislatures go further and authorize agencies to prescribe penalties for violating regulations created by the agency?
    3. Can legislatures go even further and allow agencies to set up their own courts to decide cases involving violations of the regulations they've created?

X. Criminal law in a federal system
  A. There are 52 criminal codes, one for each of the 50 states, one for the District of Columbia, and the U.S. Criminal Code, which overlays the other 51 codes.
  B. Definitions, defenses, and punishment of crimes vary across state lines.

XI. The text-case method

A. It's important to understand that you'll never read a case in which a defendant was acquitted, because an acquittal is final and can never be reviewed.

B. The application of principle definitions and facts to specific cases is important, because it stimulates you to think critically and furthers your understanding of these definitions.

C. Think of "not guilty" as "not legally guilty."

D. Think of "guilty" as "legally guilty."

E. All criminal cases start in trial courts with two levels of appeals courts:
1. An intermediate court of appeals
2. A supreme court (state or federal when a constitutional issue is involved)

REVIEW QUESTIONS

1. List and describe each part of the definition of *criminal liability*.

2. List and give an example of each typology used to classify the case summaries at the beginning of the chapter.

3. What are two differences between criminal and civil wrongs?

4. What's the most important difference between criminal and civil wrongs?

5. Name and describe the two indispensable components of punishment.

6. List and describe the three most common schemes for classifying crimes.

7. List four reasons why the label "felony" or "misdemeanor" matters.

8. Identify, describe, and give an example of the two parts of criminal law.

9. To qualify as *criminal* punishment, what four criteria have to be met?

10. Identify, explain, and give an example of the two general purposes of criminal punishment.

11. List four kinds of prevention.

12. Describe the historical trends in punishment.

13. Define the principle of legality and the four values it incorporates.

14. Describe retroactive criminal lawmaking. Is it legal?

15. Identify and describe how judges are bound in their discretionary decision making.

16. Why are precedent and stare decisis important?

17. Define the rule of lenity.

18. Identify the sources of criminal law.

19. Identify the two ways municipalities are limited in their criminal lawmaking powers.

20. Administrative crimes raise what three constitutional questions?

21. In what three ways do criminal codes differ from state to state? Provide an example of each one.

22. List the main steps in the development of U.S. criminal law from its common-law origins to the 21st century.

23. Identify and describe two levels of appeals from trial court decisions.

KEY TERMS

Constitutional Limits on Criminal Law

MAIN POINTS

- In a constitutional democracy, there are limits placed on the power of the government to create crimes.
- Retroactive statutes, called "ex post facto laws," are unconstitutional. These laws criminalize innocent acts, increase punishments for a crime, and take away a defense that was available to a defendant when the crime was committed.
- The ban on ex post facto laws protects private individuals by giving them a fair warning about what criminal behavior is and banning legislators from passing arbitrary and vindictive legislation.
- According to the U.S. Supreme Court, vague laws deny individuals their right to "due process" in both federal and state criminal justice.
- The variety of human behavior and the limits of human imagination make it impossible for lawmakers to predict all the variations that might arise under the provisions of statutes.
- Equal protection under the law doesn't require the government to treat everybody exactly alike.
- Criminals can be classified based on their prior criminal record, but the classification of criminals based on race falls under strict scrutiny and is never justified.
- The First Amendment rights to freedom of speech, religion, and associations can't be banned as crimes.
- Obscenity, profanity, libel and slander, fighting words, and expressions that pose a clear and present danger aren't protected by the First Amendment.
- The constitutional right to privacy bans "all governmental invasions of the sanctity of a man's home and the privacies of life."
- The cruel and unusual punishments clause bans "barbaric" punishments and punishments that are disproportionate to the crime.
- It's cruel and unusual punishment to execute the mentally retarded and criminals who committed their crimes as juveniles.

2

The nine members of the U.S. Supreme Court make decisions that are the final word regarding constitutional limits on the power to create crimes and prescribe punishments.

The Death Penalty for Child Rape?

She could have been anyone's 8-year-old daughter. The image of the Harvey, IL, youngster sorting Girl Scout cookies in the family garage when two men grabbed her and dragged her to a vacant lot where she was raped was recounted repeatedly by the girl and her stepfather. Then the story fell apart. The stepfather was charged with the crime and then convicted by a Jefferson Parish jury that also decided he should pay the ultimate price for the crime: his life.

The 2½-week trial reached a historic climax when the 38-year-old Harvey man became the first person in the nation in more than 25 years to be sentenced to death for rape. But whether the sentence will stand is in doubt. Some legal experts said the U.S. Supreme Court will never allow an execution for a crime other than murder after the nation's high court outlawed the death penalty for rape of adults in 1977.

(DARBY 2003, 1)

The authors of the U.S. Constitution were suspicious of power, especially power in the hands of government officials. They were also devoted to the right of individuals to control their own destinies without government interference. But they were realists who knew that freedom depends on order, and order depends on social control. So they created a Constitution that balanced the power of government and the liberty of individuals. No one has expressed the kind of government the Constitution created better than James Madison (1961), one of its primary authors:

> If men were angels, no government would be necessary. If angels were to govern men, neither external nor internal controls on government would be necessary. In framing a government which is to be administered by men over men, the great difficulty is this: You must first enable the government to control the governed; and in the next place, oblige it to control itself. (349)

James Madison was describing the kind of democracy we live in—a *constitutional* democracy—not a *pure* democracy. In a pure democracy, the majority can have whatever it wants. In a constitutional democracy, the majority can't make a crime out of what the Constitution protects as a fundamental right. Even if all the people want to make it a crime to say, "The president is a war criminal," they can't. Why? Because the First Amendment to the U.S. Constitution guarantees the fundamental right of free speech.

A central feature of criminal law in a constitutional democracy is that limits are placed on the power of government to create crimes (see "The Principle of Legality," in Chapter 1). In this chapter, we focus on the limits imposed by the U.S. and state constitutions. These limits include:

- The ban on ex post facto laws
- The right to due process of law
- The right to equal protection of the law
- The right to free speech, association, press, and religion
- The right to privacy
- The ban on "cruel and unusual punishment"

EX POST FACTO LAWS

In Chapter 1, you learned how essential the ban on retroactive lawmaking is to the principle of legality, generally, and that it lies at the heart of criminal lawmaking. It's expressed in the ancient principle of "no crime without law; no punishment without law." So fundamental did the authors of the Constitution consider a ban on *legislative* retroactive criminal lawmaking that they raised it to constitutional status in Article I of the U.S. Constitution, the article that defines legislative power. Further, they put it in two places (*Kring v. Missouri* 1883, 227). Article I, Section 9 bans the U.S. Congress, and Section 10 state legislatures, from passing *ex post facto laws*. Most state constitutions include their own ban on retroactive statutes (LaFave 2003b, 1:153).

The Kinds of Ex Post Facto Laws

An **ex post facto law** is a statute that does one of three things:

1. It criminalizes an act that was innocent when it was committed.

2. It increases the punishment for a crime after the crime was committed.

3. It takes away a defense that was available to a defendant when the crime was committed. (*Beazell v. Ohio* 1925, 169)

Statutes that criminalize innocent acts after they're committed are the clearest example of ex post facto laws; they're also the rarest, because legislatures practically never try it. Equally clear, and equally rare, are statutes that change an element of a crime after it's committed—for example, raising the age of the victim in statutory rape from 16 to 21. Statutes that modify punishment are common. They're also more problematic because, as you've learned in Chapter 1, it's not easy to define what criminal punishment is, let alone what's more, and what's less, punishment (LaFave 2003b, 1:154).

Courts have struggled especially with whether a new punishment is more severe than the old. An excellent example is *Garner v. Jones* (2000). Robert Jones began serving a life sentence for murder under a Georgia statute that required parole boards initially to consider prisoners with life sentences for parole after 7 years. The parole board adopted a rule that required a rehearing every 3 years for prisoners denied parole on their first hearing. Jones escaped from prison and committed a second murder, but he was caught, convicted, and began serving a second life sentence.

After he committed the second murder, the parole board increased the interval for a rehearing from 3 to 8 years. Jones sued the parole board, claiming the rule increasing the interval for a rehearing violated the ban on ex post facto laws. The U.S. Eleventh Circuit Court ruled that the increased interval "seems certain to insure that some number of inmates will find the length of their incarceration extended in violation of the *Ex Post Facto* clause of the Constitution" (248).

A five-member majority of the U.S. Supreme Court disagreed, holding that the increased interval "created only the most speculative . . . possibility of . . . increasing the measure of punishment" (251) because, "given Jones's criminal history, including his escape from prison and the commission of a second murder, it is difficult to see how the Board increased the risk of his serving a longer time when it decided that its parole review should be exercised after an 8-year, not a 3-year, interval" (255).

Justice Scalia went further:

> I know of no precedent for the proposition that a defendant is entitled to the same degree of mercy or clemency that he could have expected at the time he committed his offense. Under the traditional system of minimum-maximum sentences (20 years to life, for example), it would be absurd to argue that a defendant would have an *ex post facto* claim if the compassionate judge who presided over the district where he committed his crime were replaced, prior to the defendant's trial, by a so-called "hanging judge." Discretion to be compassionate or harsh is inherent in the sentencing scheme, and being denied compassion is one of the risks that the offender knowingly assumes. (258)

The three dissenting justices saw it differently. They concluded that "common sense can lead to an inference of a substantial risk of increased punishment, and it does so here" (261). And they backed up their commonsense conclusion with the parole board's and its chairman's own words. The board's website reported that "Since 1991 the Board has steadily and consistently amended and refined its guidelines and policies to provide for lengthier prison service for violent criminals" (quoted at 261–62).

The Purposes of the Ban on Ex Post Facto Laws

The ex post facto ban has two major purposes. One is to protect private individuals by ensuring that legislatures give them fair warning about what's criminal and that they can rely on that requirement. The second purpose is directed at legislators, preventing them from passing arbitrary and vindictive legislation. (*Arbitrary* means legislation is based on random choice or personal whim, not on reason and standards.)

DUE PROCESS

Vague laws violate the principle of legality (see Chapter 1). According to the **void-for-vagueness doctrine,** the U.S. Supreme Court has decided that vague laws also deny individuals their right to "due process." This right is protected by the Fifth Amendment in federal criminal justice and the Fourteenth Amendment in state criminal justice. The reasoning behind the void-for-vagueness doctrine goes like this:

1. Criminal punishment deprives individuals of life (capital punishment), liberty (imprisonment), or property (fines).

2. The Fifth and Fourteenth Amendments to the U.S. Constitution ban both federal and state governments from taking any person's "life, liberty, or property without due process of law."

3. Failure to warn adequately private persons of what the law forbids and/or allowing officials the chance to define arbitrarily what the law forbids denies individuals life, liberty, and/or property without due process of law.

The Aims of the Void-for-Vagueness Doctrine

The void-for-vagueness doctrine takes aim at two evils (which in various forms should be becoming familiar to you). First, void laws fail to give fair warning to individuals as to what the law prohibits. Second, they allow arbitrary and discriminatory criminal justice administration. A famous case from the 1930s gangster days, *Lanzetta v. New Jersey* (1939), still widely cited and relied on today is an excellent example of both the application of the doctrine and its purposes. The story begins with a challenge to this New Jersey statute:

> Any person not engaged in any lawful occupation, known to be a member of any gang consisting of two or more persons, who has been convicted at least three times of being a disorderly person, or who has been convicted of any crime, in this or in any other State, is declared to be a gangster. . . . Every violation is punishable by fine not exceeding $10,000 or imprisonment not exceeding 20 years, or both. (452)

The challengers attacking the statute for vagueness were Ignatius Lanzetta, Michael Falcone, and Louie Del Rossi. On June 12, 16, 19, and 24, 1936, the four challengers, "not being engaged in any lawful occupation"; "known to be members of a gang, consisting of two or more persons"; and "having been convicted of a crime in the State of Pennsylvania" were "declared to be gangsters."

The trial court threw out their challenge that the law was void-for-vagueness; they were tried, convicted, and sentenced to prison for "not more than ten years and not less than five years, at hard labor." The New Jersey intermediate appellate court and the New Jersey supreme court also threw out their challenges. But they finally prevailed when a unanimous U.S. Supreme Court ruled that the New Jersey statute was void-for-vagueness. Why? The reasons are so clearly stated, and so often still quoted in opinions today, that you should read them in the original:

No one may be required at peril of life, liberty or property to speculate as to the meaning of penal statutes. All are entitled to be informed as to what the State commands or forbids. (453)

That the terms of a penal statute creating a new offense must be sufficiently explicit to inform those who are subject to it what conduct on their part will render them liable to its penalties is a well-recognized requirement, consonant alike with ordinary notions of fair play and the settled rules of law; and a statute which either forbids or requires the doing of an act in terms so vague that men of common intelligence must necessarily guess at its meaning and differ as to its application violates the first essential of due process of law. (453)

The phrase "consisting of two or more persons" is all that purports to define "gang." The meanings of that word indicated in dictionaries and in historical and sociological writings are numerous and varied. Nor is the meaning derivable from the common law, for neither in that field nor anywhere in the language of the law is there definition of the word. Our attention has not been called to, and we are unable to find, any other statute attempting to make it criminal to be a member of a "gang." (454–55)

Notice this important point: The answer to the question, "What's fair notice?" isn't subjective; that is, it's not what a particular defendant actually knows about the law. For example, the Court didn't ask what Lanzetta and his cohorts knew about the gangster ordinance: Were they aware it existed? Did they get advice about what it meant? Did their life experiences inform them that their behavior was criminal (Batey 1997, 4)?

According to the courts, what's fair notice is an objective question; that is, "Would an ordinary, reasonable person know that what he was doing was criminal?" Perhaps the best definition of objective fair warning is U.S. Supreme Court Justice Oliver Wendell Holmes's "language that the common world will understand, of what the law intends to do if a certain line is passed" (*U.S. v. Lanier* 1997, 265). Justice Byron White put it more bluntly: "If any fool would know that a particular category of conduct would be within the reach of the statute, if there is an unmistakable core that a reasonable person would know is forbidden by the law, the enactment is not unconstitutional. . . . (*Kolender v. Lawson* 1983, 370–71).

Despite the importance of giving fair warning to individuals, in 1983, the Supreme Court decided that providing "minimal guidelines to govern law enforcement" trumps notice to private individuals as the primary aim of the void-for-vagueness doctrine (*Kolender v. Lawson* 1983, 357). According to the Court:

Where the legislature fails to provide such minimal guidelines, a criminal statute may permit a standardless sweep [that] allows policemen, prosecutors, and juries to pursue their personal predilections. (358)

And, quoting from an old case (*U.S. v. Reese* 1875), the Court in *Lawson* elaborated further on the choice to give priority to controlling arbitrary and discriminatory enforcement:

It would certainly be dangerous if the legislature could set a net large enough to catch all possible offenders, and leave it to the courts to step inside and say who could be rightfully detained, and who should be set at large. This would, to some extent, substitute the judicial for the legislative department of government. (221)

Go to the Criminal Law 9e website and find Exercise 2.1 to learn more about *Kolender v. Lawson:* www.thomsonedu .com/criminaljustice/samaha.

Giving priority to controlling law enforcement is more realistic than giving fair notice to hypothetical reasonable, ordinary people. Police officers and prosecutors are more likely to read what's in the criminal statutes and know about the cases that interpret them. So it makes sense for courts to ask whether statutes clearly indicate to ordinary police officers and prosecutors what the law prohibits. Inquiries that seem "wrongheaded" when they're directed at guaranteeing fair notice to ordinary noncriminal justice experts become reasonable when they're examined to decide whether they're clear enough to limit arbitrary and discriminatory enforcement (Batey 1997, 6–7).

Defining Vagueness

Whether the emphasis is on notice to individuals or control of officials, the void-for-vagueness doctrine can never cure the uncertainty in all laws. After all, laws are written in words, not numbers. U.S. Supreme Court Justice Thurgood Marshall expressed this opinion when he wrote, "Condemned to the use of words, we can never expect mathematical certainty from our language" (*Grayned v. City of Rockford* 1972, 110). It's not just the natural uncertainty of words that creates problems. It's also because the variety of human behavior and the limits of human imagination make it impossible for lawmakers to predict all the variations that might arise under the provisions of statutes. So courts allow considerable leeway in the degree of certainty required to pass the two prongs of fair warning and avoidance of arbitrary law enforcement.

Still, the strong presumption of constitutionality (referred to earlier) requires challengers to prove the law is vague. The Ohio Supreme Court summarized the heavy burden of proof challengers have to carry:

> The challenger must show that upon examining the statute, an individual of ordinary intelligence would not understand what he is required to do under the law. Thus, to escape responsibility . . . [the challenger] must prove that he could not reasonably understand that . . . [the statute] prohibited the acts in which he engaged. . . . The party alleging that a statute is unconstitutional must prove this assertion beyond a reasonable doubt. (*State v. Anderson* 1991, 1226–27)

State v. Metzger (1982) is a good example of how one court applied the void-for-vagueness doctrine. The Nebraska supreme court held that a Lincoln, Nebraska, city ordinance that made it a crime to "commit any indecent, immodest, or filthy act" was void-for-vagueness. (Please make sure you review the "The Text-Case Method" section in Chapter 1 before you read this first excerpt.)

CASE | *Was His Act "Indecent, Immodest, or Filthy"?*

State v. Metzger

319 N.W.2d 459 (Neb. 1982)

HISTORY

Douglas E. Metzger was convicted in the municipal court of the city of Lincoln, Nebraska, of violating ß 9.52.100 of the Lincoln Municipal Code. The District Court, Lancaster County, affirmed the District Court judgment. Metzger appealed to the Nebraska supreme court. The supreme court reversed and dismissed the District Court's judgment.

KRIVOSHA, CJ.

FACTS

Metzger lived in a garden-level apartment located in Lincoln, Nebraska. A large window in the apartment faces a parking lot which is situated on the north side of the apartment building. At about 7:45 A.M. on April 30, 1981, another resident of the apartment, while parking his automobile in a space directly in front of Metzger's apartment window, observed Metzger standing naked with his arms at his sides in his apartment window for a period of 5 seconds. The resident testified that he saw Metzger's body from his thighs on up.

The resident called the police department and two officers arrived at the apartment at about 8 A.M. The officers testified that they observed Metzger standing in front of the window eating a bowl of cereal. They testified that Metzger was standing within a foot of the window and his nude body, from the mid-thigh on up, was visible.

The pertinent portion of ß 9.52.100 of the Lincoln Municipal Code, under which Metzger was charged, provides as follows: "It shall be unlawful for any person within the City of Lincoln . . . to commit any indecent, immodest or filthy act in the presence of any person, or in such a situation that persons passing might ordinarily see the same."

OPINION

The . . . issue presented to us by this appeal is whether the ordinance, as drafted, is so vague as to be unconstitutional. We believe that it is. There is no argument that a violation of the municipal ordinance in question is a criminal act. Since the ordinance in question is criminal in nature, it is a fundamental requirement of due process of law that such criminal ordinance be reasonably clear and definite. Moreover, a crime must be defined with sufficient definiteness and there must be ascertainable standards of guilt to inform those subject thereto as to what conduct will render them liable to punishment thereunder.

The dividing line between what is lawful and unlawful cannot be left to conjecture. A citizen cannot be held to answer charges based upon penal statutes whose mandates are so uncertain that they will reasonably admit of different constructions. A criminal statute cannot rest upon an uncertain foundation. The crime and the elements constituting it must be so clearly expressed that the ordinary person can intelligently choose in advance what course it is lawful for him to pursue.

Penal statutes prohibiting the doing of certain things and providing a punishment for their violation should not admit of such a double meaning that the citizen may act upon one conception of its requirements and the courts upon another. A statute which forbids the doing of an act in terms so vague that men of common intelligence must necessarily guess as to its meaning and differ as to its application violates the first essential elements of due process of law.

It is not permissible to enact a law which in effect spreads an all-inclusive net for the feet of everybody upon the chance that, while the innocent will surely be entangled in its meshes, some wrongdoers may also be caught.

. . . The test to determine whether a statute defining an offense is void for uncertainty (1) is whether the language may apply not only to a particular act about which there can be little or no difference of opinion, but equally to other acts about which there may be radical differences, thereby devolving on the court the exercise of arbitrary power of discriminating between the several classes of acts. (2) The dividing line between what is lawful and what is unlawful cannot be left to conjecture.

In the case of *Papachristou v. City of Jacksonville*, 405 U.S. 156 (1972), the U.S. Supreme Court said: "Living under a rule of law entails various suppositions, one of which is that '[all persons] are entitled to be informed as to what the State commands or forbids.'" In *Papachristou*, the U. S. Supreme Court declared a vagrancy statute of the city of Jacksonville, Florida, invalid for vagueness, saying "It would certainly be dangerous if the legislature could set a net large enough to catch all possible offenders, and leave it to the courts to step inside and say who could be rightfully detained, and who should be set at large."

The ordinance in question makes it unlawful for anyone to commit any "indecent, immodest or filthy act." We know of no way in which the standards required of a criminal act can be met in those broad, general terms. There may be those few who believe persons of opposite sex holding hands in public are immodest, and certainly more who might believe that kissing in public is immodest. Such acts cannot constitute a crime. Certainly one could find many who would conclude that today's swimming attire found on many beaches or beside many pools is immodest. Yet, the fact that it is immodest does not thereby make it illegal, absent some requirement related to the health, safety, or welfare of the community. The dividing line between what is lawful and what is unlawful in terms of "indecent," "immodest," or "filthy" is simply too broad to satisfy the constitutional requirements of due process. Both lawful and unlawful acts can be embraced within such broad definitions. That cannot be permitted. One is not able to determine in advance what is lawful and what is unlawful.

We do not attempt, in this opinion, to determine whether Metzger's actions in a particular case might not be made unlawful, nor do we intend to encourage such behavior. Indeed, it may be possible that a governmental subdivision using sufficiently definite language could make such an act as committed by Metzger unlawful. We simply do not decide that question at this time because of our determination that the ordinance in question is so vague as to be unconstitutional.

We therefore believe that ß 9.52.100 of the Lincoln Municipal Code must be declared invalid. Because the ordinance is therefore declared invalid, the conviction cannot stand.

REVERSED AND DISMISSED.

DISSENT

BOSLAUGH, J.

The ordinance in question prohibits indecent acts, immodest acts, *or* filthy acts in the presence of any person. Although the ordinance may be too broad in some respects . . . the exhibition of his genitals under the circumstances of this case was, clearly, an indecent act. Statutes and ordinances prohibiting indecent exposure generally have been held valid. I do not subscribe to the view that it is only "possible" that such conduct may be prohibited by statute or ordinance.

CLINTON and HASTINGS, JJ., join in this dissent.

Questions

1. State the exact wording of the offense Douglas Metzger was convicted of.

2. List all of Metzger's acts and any other facts relevant to deciding whether he violated the ordinance.

3. State the test the court used to decide whether the ordinance was void-for-vagueness.

4. According to the majority, why was the ordinance vague?

5. According to the dissent, why was the ordinance clear enough to pass the void-for-vagueness test?

6. In your opinion, was the statute clear to a reasonable person? Back up your answer with the facts and arguments in the excerpt and information from the void-for-vagueness discussion in the text.

EQUAL PROTECTION OF THE LAWS

In addition to the due process guarantee, the Fourteenth Amendment to the U.S. Constitution commands that "no state shall deny to any person within its jurisdiction the equal protection of the laws." Equal protection is far more frequently an issue in criminal procedure than it is in criminal law; we'll note briefly here the limits it puts on criminal lawmaking and punishment.

First, equal protection doesn't require the government to treat everybody exactly alike. Statutes can, and often do, classify particular groups of people and types of conduct for special treatment. For example, almost every state ranks premeditated killings as more serious than negligent homicides. Several states punish habitual criminals more harshly than first-time offenders. Neither of these classifications violates the equal protection clause. Why? Because they make sense. Or, as the courts say, they have a "rational basis" (*Buck v. Bell* 1927, 208).

Classifications in criminal codes based on race are another matter. The U.S. Supreme Court subjects all racial classifications to "strict scrutiny." In practice, strict scrutiny means race-based classifications are never justified. According to the U.S. Supreme Court, any statute that "invidiously classifies similarly situated people on the basis of the immutable characteristics with which they were born . . . always [emphasis added] violates the Constitution, for the simple reason that, so far as the Constitution is concerned, people of different races are always similarly situated."

Gender classifications stand somewhere between the strict scrutiny applied to race and the rational basis applied to most other classifications. The Supreme Court has had difficulty deciding exactly how carefully to scrutinize gender classifications in criminal statutes. The plurality, but not a majority, of the justices in *Michael M. v. Superior Court of Sonoma County* (1981, 477) agreed that gender classifications deserve *heightened scrutiny,* meaning there has to be a "fair and substantial relationship" between classifications based on gender and "legitimate state ends."

Go to the Criminal Law 9e website and find Exercise 2.2 to learn more about *Michael M. v. Superior Court of Sonoma County:* www .thomsonedu.com/ criminaljustice/samaha.

Michael M., a 17-year-old male challenged on gender-based equal protection grounds California's statutory rape law, which defines unlawful sexual intercourse as "an act of sexual intercourse accomplished with a female not the wife of the perpetrator, where the female is under the age of 18 years." The U.S. Supreme Court denied the equal protection challenge. "The question . . . boils down to whether a State may attack the problem of sexual intercourse and teenage pregnancy directly by prohibiting a male from having sexual intercourse with a minor female. We hold that such a statute is sufficiently related to the State's objectives to pass constitutional muster" (473).

THE BILL OF RIGHTS AND CRIMINAL LAW

The ban on ex post facto laws, denial of due process, and equal protection of the laws are broad constitutional limits that cover all of criminal law. The Bill of Rights bans defining certain kinds of behavior as criminal. One is the ban on making a crime out of the First Amendment rights to speech, religion, and associations; the other is criminalizing behavior protected by the right to privacy created by the U.S. Supreme Court. Let's look at criminal law and the right to free speech, and then at the right to privacy.

Free Speech

"Congress shall make no law . . . abridging the freedom of speech," the First Amendment commands. The U.S. Supreme Court has expanded the ban beyond this already sweeping scope. First, the Court has expanded the meaning of "speech" by holding that the protection of the amendment "does not end with the spoken or written word" (*Texas v. Johnson* 1989, 404). It also includes *expressive conduct*, meaning actions that communicate ideas and feelings. So free speech includes wearing black armbands to protest war; "sitting in" to protest racial segregation; and picketing to support all kinds of causes from abortion to animal rights. It even includes giving money to political candidates.

Second, although the amendment itself directs its prohibition only at the U.S. Congress, the Court has applied the prohibition to the states since 1925 (*Gitlow v. New York*). Third, the Court has ruled that free speech is a fundamental right, one that enjoys preferred status. This means that the government has to provide more than a *rational basis* for restricting speech and other forms of expression. It has the much higher burden of proving that a *compelling government interest* justifies the restrictions.

Despite these broad prohibitions and the heavy burden the government faces in justifying them, the First Amendment doesn't mean you can express yourself anywhere, anytime, on any subject, in any manner. According to the Supreme Court, there are five categories of expression not protected by the First Amendment:

1. _Obscenity_ Material whose predominant appeal is to nudity, sexual activity, or excretion. *something deemed to be obscene is NOT free speech*
2. *Profanity* Irreverence toward sacred things, particularly the name of God. *Burning crosses, not just language but actions*
3. *Libel and slander* Libels are damages to reputation expressed in print, writing, pictures, or signs; slander damages reputation by spoken words. *Hurt more of the public features than private*
4. *Fighting words* Words that are likely to provoke the average person to retaliation and cause a "breach of the peace."

5. *Clear and present danger* Expression that creates a clear and present danger of an evil, which legislatures have the power to prohibit. (*Chaplinsky v. New Hampshire* 1942, 574)

Why doesn't the First Amendment protect these forms of expression? Because they're not an "essential element of any exposition of ideas, and are of such slight value as a step to truth that any benefit that may be derived from them is clearly outweighed by the social interest in order and morality" (*Gitlow v. New York* 1925, 572).

These exceptions create the opportunity for the government to make these kinds of expression a crime, depending on the manner, time, and place of expression. For example, under the clear and present danger doctrine, the government can punish words "that produce clear and present danger of a serious substantive evil that rises far above public inconvenience, annoyance, or unrest." So the First Amendment didn't save Walter Chaplinsky from conviction under a New Hampshire statute that made it a crime to call anyone an "offensive or derisive name" in public. Chaplinsky had called the marshal of the City of Rochester, New Hampshire, "a God damned racketeer." In perhaps the most famous reference to the doctrine, U.S. Supreme Court Justice Oliver Wendell Holmes wrote, "The most stringent protection of free speech would not protect a man in falsely shouting fire in a theatre and causing a panic" (*Schenck v. U.S.* 1919, 52).

The most difficult problem in making a crime out of speech and expressive conduct is when laws reach so far they include not just expression the Constitution bans but also expression it protects. According to the **void-for-overbreadth doctrine,** laws that include not only prohibited but also protected expression are void because they deny people freedom of expression without due process of law. Why? Because people will hesitate to express themselves if they fear criminal prosecution. This **"chilling effect"** on the exercise of the fundamental right to freedom of expression violates the right to liberty guaranteed by the Fifth and Fourteenth amendments to the U.S. Constitution.

The U.S. Supreme Court dealt with the chilling effect of a St. Paul, Minnesota hate, crime ordinance in *R.A.V. v. City of St. Paul* (1992). In this case, R.A.V., a juvenile, was alleged to have burned a crudely constructed wooden cross on a Black family's lawn. He was charged with violating St. Paul's Bias-Motivated Crime Ordinance. The ordinance provided that anyone who places a burning cross, Nazi swastika, or other symbol on private or public property knowing that the symbol would arouse "anger, alarm or resentment in others on the basis of race, color, creed, religion, or gender commits disorderly conduct and shall be guilty of a misdemeanor."

The Minnesota Supreme Court found that the ordinance was constitutional because it could be construed to ban only "fighting words," which aren't protected by the First Amendment (380). The U.S. Supreme Court, on the other hand, ruled that, even when a statute addresses speech that's not protected (in this case "fighting words"), states still can't discriminate on the basis of the content. The Court concluded that the St. Paul ordinance violated the First Amendment because it would allow the proponents of racial tolerance and equality to use fighting words to argue in favor of tolerance and equality but would prohibit similar use by those opposed to racial tolerance and equality:

> Although the phrase in the ordinance, "arouses anger, alarm or resentment in others," has been limited by the Minnesota Supreme Court's construction to reach only those symbols or displays that amount to "fighting words," the remaining, unmodified terms make clear that the ordinance applies only to "fighting words" that insult, or provoke violence, "on the basis of race, color, creed, religion or gender." Displays containing abusive invective, no matter how vicious or severe, are permissible unless they are addressed to one of the specified disfavored topics. Those who wish to use "fighting words" in connection with other ideas—to express hostility, for example, on the basis of political affiliation, union membership, or homosexuality—are not covered. The First Amendment does not permit St. Paul to impose special prohibitions on those speakers who express views on disfavored subjects.
>
> In its practical operation, moreover, the ordinance goes even beyond mere content discrimination, to actual viewpoint discrimination. Displays containing some words—odious racial epithets, for example—would be prohibited to proponents of all views. But "fighting words" that do not themselves invoke race, color, creed, religion, or gender—aspersions upon a person's mother, for example—would seemingly be usable in the placards of those arguing *in favor* of racial, color, etc., tolerance and equality, but could not be used by those speakers' opponents. One could hold up a sign saying, for example, that all "anti-Catholic bigots" are misbegotten; but not that all "papists" are, for that would insult and provoke violence "on the

Go to the Criminal Law 9e website and find Exercise 2.3 to learn more about *R.A.V. v. City of St. Paul:* www.thomsonedu.com/criminaljustice/samaha.

basis of religion." St. Paul has no such authority to license one side of a debate to fight freestyle, while requiring the other to follow Marquis of Queensberry rules. (391–92)

The Illinois Appellate Court ruled that Illinois's hate crime statute, at least when a prosecution is based on "disorderly conduct," doesn't run afoul of the First Amendment. The case was *People v. Rokicki*.

Does the Hate Crime Statute Violate Free Speech?

People v. Rokicki
718 N.E.2d 333 (Ill.App. 1999)

HISTORY

Kenneth Rokicki was charged with a hate crime based on the predicate (underlying) offense of disorderly conduct. Before trial, Rokicki moved to dismiss the charges alleging, among other things, that the hate crime statute was unconstitutional. The trial court denied his motion. Rokicki waived his right to a jury, and the matter proceeded to a *bench trial* (trial without a jury). Rokicki was convicted, sentenced to two years' probation, and ordered to perform 100 hours of community service and to attend anger management counseling. He appealed, contending that the hate crime statute is unconstitutionally overly broad and chills expression protected by the First Amendment to the United States Constitution. Conviction and sentence affirmed.

HUTCHINSON, J.

FACTS

Donald Delaney testified that he is the store manager of a Pizza Hut in South Elgin. On October 20, 1995, at approximately 1:30 P.M., Rokicki entered the restaurant. The victim was a server there and took Rokicki's order. The victim requested payment, and Rokicki refused to tender payment to him. Delaney, who was nearby, stepped in and completed the sale. Rokicki told Delaney not to let "that faggot" touch his food. When Rokicki's pizza came out of the oven, Delaney was on the telephone, and the victim began to slice the pizza. Delaney saw Rokicki approaching the counter with an irritated expression and hung up the telephone. Before Delaney could intervene, Rokicki leaned over the counter and began yelling at the victim and pounding his fist on the counter. Rokicki directed a series of epithets at the victim including "Mary," "faggot," and "Molly Homemaker." Rokicki continued yelling for 10 minutes and, when not pounding his fist, shook his finger at the victim. Delaney asked Rokicki to leave several times and threatened to call the police. However, Delaney did not call the police because he was standing between the victim and Rokicki and feared that Rokicki would physically attack the victim if Delaney moved. Eventually, Delaney returned Rokicki's money and Rokicki left the establishment.

The victim testified that he was working at the South Elgin Pizza Hut on October 20, 1995. Rokicki entered the restaurant and ordered a pizza. When Rokicki's pizza came out of the oven, the victim began to slice it. Rokicki then began yelling at the victim and pounding his fist on the counter. Rokicki appeared very angry and seemed very serious. The victim, who is much smaller than Rokicki, testified that he was terrified by Rokicki's outburst and remained frightened for several days thereafter. Eventually, the manager gave Rokicki a refund and Rokicki left the restaurant. The victim followed Rokicki into the parking lot, recorded the license number of his car, and called the police.

Christopher Merritt, a sergeant with the South Elgin police department, testified that, at 2:20 P.M. on October 20, 1995, Rokicki entered the police station and said he wished to report an incident at the Pizza Hut. Rokicki told Merritt that he was upset because a homosexual was working at the restaurant and he wanted someone "normal" to touch his food. Rokicki stated that he became angry when the victim touched his food. He called the victim a "Mary," pounded on the counter, and was subsequently kicked out of the restaurant. Merritt asked Rokicki what he meant by a "Mary," and Rokicki responded that a "Mary" was a homosexual. Merritt conducted only a brief interview of Rokicki because shortly after Rokicki arrived at the police station Merritt was dispatched to the Pizza Hut.

Deborah Hagedorn, an employee at the Pizza Hut in St. Charles, testified that in 1995 Rokicki came into the restaurant and asked for the address of the district manager for Pizza Hut. When asked why he wanted the address, Rokicki complained that he had been arrested at the South Elgin restaurant because he did not want a "f___g faggot" touching his food.

Rokicki testified that he was upset because the victim had placed his fingers in his mouth and had not washed his hands before cutting the pizza. Rokicki admitted calling the victim "Mary" but denied that he intended to suggest the victim was a homosexual. Rokicki stated that he used the term "Mary" because the victim would not stop talking and "it was like arguing with a woman." Rokicki denied yelling and denied directing other derogatory terms toward the victim. Rokicki admitted giving a statement to Merritt but denied telling him that he pounded his fist on the counter or used homosexual slurs. Rokicki testified that he went to the St. Charles Pizza Hut but that Hagedorn was not present during his conversation with the manager. Rokicki testified that he complained about the victim's hygiene but did not use any homosexual slurs.

The trial court found Rokicki guilty of a hate crime. In a posttrial motion, Rokicki again argued that the hate crime statute was unconstitutional. The trial court denied Rokicki's motion and sentenced him to two years' probation. As part of the probation, the trial court ordered Rokicki not to enter Pizza Hut restaurants, not to contact the victim, to perform 100 hours' community service, and attend anger management counseling. Rokicki timely appeals.

OPINION

On appeal, Rokicki does not challenge the sufficiency of the evidence against him. Rokicki contends only that the hate crime statute is unconstitutional when the predicate offense is disturbing the peace. Rokicki argues that the statute is overly broad and impermissibly chills free speech.

The Illinois hate crime statute reads in part as follows:

A person commits a hate crime when, by reason of the actual or perceived race, color, creed, religion, ancestry, gender, sexual orientation, physical or mental disability, or national origin of another individual or group of individuals, [she or] he commits assault, battery, aggravated assault, misdemeanor theft, criminal trespass to residence, misdemeanor criminal damage to property, criminal trespass to vehicle, criminal trespass to real property, mob action or disorderly conduct. . . .

1. Infringement on Free Speech Rights

Rokicki's conviction was based on the predicate offense of disorderly conduct. A person commits disorderly conduct when she or he knowingly "[d]oes any act in such an unreasonable manner as to alarm or disturb another and to provoke a breach of the peace." Disorderly conduct is punishable as a Class C misdemeanor. However, hate crime is punishable as a Class 4 felony for a first offense and a Class 2 felony for a second or subsequent offense. . . .

The overbreadth doctrine protects the freedom of speech guaranteed by the first amendment by invalidating laws so broadly written that the fear of prosecution would discourage people from exercising that freedom. A law regulating conduct is facially overly broad if it (1) criminalizes a substantial amount of protected behavior, relative to the law's plainly legitimate sweep, and (2) is not susceptible to a limiting construction that avoids constitutional problems. A statute should not be invalidated for being overly broad unless its overbreadth is both real and substantial.

. . . [There is a] long-standing principle that speech alone cannot form the basis for a disorderly conduct charge. . . . It is no crime to express an unpopular view even if the person expressing those views draws attention to herself or himself or annoys others nearby . . . : Vulgar language, however distasteful or offensive to one's sensibilities, does not evolve into a crime because people standing nearby stop, look, and listen. The State's concern becomes dominant only when a breach of the peace is provoked by the language. . . . The hate crime statute does not reach those who, in Rokicki's words, simply "express themselves loudly and in a highly-animated, passionate manner" but applies only when their conduct is unreasonable and provokes a breach of the peace.

Rokicki is not being punished merely because he holds an unpopular view on homosexuality or because he expressed those views loudly or in a passionate manner. Defendant was charged with a hate crime because he allowed those beliefs to motivate unreasonable conduct. Rokicki remains free to believe what he will regarding people who are homosexual, but he may not force his opinions on others by shouting, pounding on a counter, and disrupting a lawful business. Rokicki's conduct exceeded the bounds of spirited debate, and the first amendment does not give him the right to harass or terrorize anyone. Therefore, because the hate crime statute requires conduct beyond mere expression . . . , the Illinois hate crime statute constitutionally regulates conduct without infringing upon free speech.

2. Content Discrimination

Rokicki cites *R.A.V. v. City of St. Paul* and argues that the hate crime statute is constitutionally impermissible because it discriminates based on the content of an offender's beliefs. Rokicki argues that the statute enhances disorderly conduct to hate crime when the conduct is motivated by, *e.g.*, an offender's views on race or sexual orientation but that it treats identical conduct differently if motivated, *e.g.*, by an offender's beliefs regarding abortion or animal rights. . . .

However, the portions of *R.A.V.* upon which defendant relies do not affect our analysis. In *R.A.V.*, the Court recognized several limitations to its content discrimination analysis, including statutes directed at conduct rather than speech, which sweep up a particular subset of proscribable speech. The Court noted, for example, that certain sexually derogatory words may violate general prohibitions against sexual discrimination. One year later, in *Wisconsin v. Mitchell*, the Court further examined this exception. . . . The *Mitchell* Court held that the State could act to redress the harm it perceived as associated with bias-motivated crimes by punishing bias-motivated offenses more severely. . . . We too decide that the legislature was free to determine as a matter of sound public policy that bias-motivated crimes create greater harm than identical conduct not motivated by bias and should be punished more harshly. Consequently, we reject defendant's content discrimination argument.

3. Chilling Effect

Rokicki also argues that the hate crime statute chills free expression because individuals will be deterred from expressing unpopular views out of fear that such expression will later be used to justify a hate crime charge. We disagree. The overbreadth doctrine should be used sparingly and only when the constitutional infirmity is both real and substantial. The *Mitchell* Court rejected identical arguments and held that any possible chilling effects were too speculative to support an overbreadth claim. The first amendment does not prohibit the evidentiary use of speech to establish motive or intent. Similarly, we find Rokicki's argument speculative, and we cannot conclude that individuals will refrain from expressing controversial beliefs simply because they fear that their statements might be used as evidence of motive if they later commit an offense identified in the hate crime statute.

Conclusion

We hold that the hate crime statute is not facially unconstitutional when the predicate offense is disorderly conduct because (1) the statute reaches only conduct and does not punish speech itself; (2) the statute does not impermissibly discriminate based on content; and (3) the statute does not chill the exercise of first amendment rights. Defendant contends only that the statute is unconstitutional and does not challenge the sufficiency of the evidence against him or assert any other basis for reversal. Accordingly, we affirm defendant's conviction.

The judgment of the circuit court of Kane County is affirmed.

Questions

1. State the elements of the Illinois hate crime statute.

2. List all of the facts relevant to deciding whether Kenneth Rokicki violated the hate crime statute.

3. According to the court, why doesn't the Illinois "hate crime" statute violate Rokicki's right to free speech?

4. In your opinion, does the statute punish speech or nonexpressive conduct?

5. Do you think the purpose of this statute is to prevent disorderly conduct or expression?

6. Does Rokicki have a point when he argues that the statute prohibits only some kinds of hatred—race, ethnic, and sexual orientation—but not other kinds, for example, hatred for animal rights and abortion? Defend your answer.

EXPLORING FURTHER

Free Speech

1. Is "Nude Dancing" Expressive Speech?

Barnes v. Glen Theatre, Inc. et al., 501 U.S. 560 (1991)

FACTS An Indiana statute prohibits nude dancing in public. Glen Theatre, a bar that featured nude dancing, sought an injunction against enforcing the law, arguing it violated the First Amendment. The law permitted erotic dancing, as long as the dancers wore "G-strings" and "pasties." It prohibited only totally nude dancing. The law

argued that dancers can express themselves erotically without total nudity. Did the ordinance unduly restrict expressive conduct protected by the right to free speech?

DECISION No, said the U.S. Supreme Court. Chief Justice Rehnquist, writing for a plurality, admitted that nude dancing is expressive conduct, but he concluded that the public indecency statute is justified because it "furthers a substantial government interest in protecting order and morality." So the ban on public nudity was not related to the erotic message the dancers wanted to send.

2. Is Flag Burning Expressive Conduct?

Texas v. Johnson, 491 U.S. 397 (1989)

FACTS During the 1984 Republican National Convention in Dallas, Gregory Lee Johnson participated in a political demonstration called the "Republican War Chest Tour." The purpose of this event was to protest the policies of the Reagan administration and of certain Dallas-based corporations. The demonstrators marched through the Dallas streets, chanting political slogans and stopping at several corporate locations to stage "die-ins" intended to dramatize the consequences of nuclear war. On several occasions, they spray-painted the walls of buildings and overturned potted plants, but Johnson himself took no part in such activities. He did, however, accept an American flag handed to him by a fellow protestor who had taken it from a flagpole outside one of the targeted buildings.

The demonstration ended in front of Dallas City Hall, where Johnson unfurled the American flag, doused it with kerosene, and set it on fire. While the flag burned, the protestors chanted, "America, the red, white, and blue, we spit on you." After the demonstrators dispersed, a witness to the flag-burning collected the flag's remains and buried them in his backyard. No one was physically injured or threatened with injury, though several witnesses testified that they had been seriously offended by the flag-burning.

Johnson was charged and convicted under Texas's "desecration of a venerated object" statute, sentenced to one year in prison, and fined $2,000. Did the flag-burning statute violate Johnson's right to free speech?

DECISION Yes, said a divided U.S. Supreme Court:

> The First Amendment literally forbids the abridgment only of "speech," but we have long recognized that its protection does not end at the spoken or written word.
>
> While we have rejected "the view that an apparently limitless variety of conduct can be labeled 'speech' whenever the person engaging in the conduct intends thereby to express an idea, we have acknowledged that conduct may be sufficiently imbued with elements of communication to fall within the scope of the First and Fourteenth Amendments." . . .
>
> Texas claims that its interest in preventing breaches of the peace justifies Johnson's conviction for flag desecration. However, no disturbance of the peace actually occurred or threatened to occur because of Johnson's burning of the flag. Although the State

stresses the disruptive behavior of the protestors during their march toward City Hall, it admits that "no actual breach of the peace occurred at the time of the flag burning or in response to the flag burning." . . .

Nor does Johnson's expressive conduct fall within that small class of "fighting words" that are "likely to provoke the average person to retaliation, and thereby cause a breach of the peace." No reasonable onlooker would have regarded Johnson's generalized expression of dissatisfaction with the policies of the Federal Government as a direct personal insult or an invitation to exchange fisticuffs.

We thus conclude that the State's interest in maintaining order is not implicated on these facts. The State need not worry that our holding will disable it from preserving the peace. We do not suggest that the First Amendment forbids a State to prevent "imminent lawless action." . . .

If there is a bedrock principle underlying the First Amendment, it is that the Government may not prohibit the expression of an idea simply because society finds the idea itself offensive or disagreeable. We have not recognized an exception to this principle even where our flag has been involved. Justice Jackson described one of our society's defining principles in words deserving of their frequent repetition: "If there is any fixed star in our constitutional constellation, it is that no official, high or petty, can prescribe what shall be orthodox in politics, nationalism, religion, or other matters of opinion or force citizens to confess by word or act their faith therein." . . .

Although Justice Kennedy concurred, the flag burning obviously disturbed him. He wrote:

The hard fact is that sometimes we must make decisions we do not like. We make them because they are right, right in the sense that the law and the

Constitution, as we see them, compel the result. And so great is our commitment to the process that, except in the rare case, we do not pause to express distaste for the result, perhaps for fear of undermining a valued principle that dictates the decision. This is one of those rare cases. Our colleagues in dissent advance powerful arguments why respondent may be convicted for his expression, reminding us that among those who will be dismayed by our holding will be some who have had the singular honor of carrying the flag in battle. And I agree that the flag holds a lonely place of honor in an age when absolutes are distrusted and simple truths are burdened by unneeded apologetics. . . . The case here today forces recognition of the costs to which [our] . . . beliefs commit us. It is poignant but fundamental that the flag protects those who hold it in contempt. . . . So I agree with the court that he must go free.

Four justices dissented. Perhaps none of the justices felt more strongly than the World War II naval officer Justice Stevens, who wrote:

The ideas of liberty and equality have been an irresistible force in motivating leaders like Patrick Henry, Susan B. Anthony, and Abraham Lincoln, schoolteachers like Nathan Hale and Booker T. Washington, the Philippine Scouts who fought at Bataan, and the soldiers who scaled the bluff at Omaha Beach. If those ideas are worth fighting for—and our history demonstrates that they are—it cannot be true that the flag that uniquely symbolizes their power is not itself worthy of protection from unnecessary desecration. I respectfully dissent.

 Go to the Criminal Law 9e website for the full versions of the Exploring Further excerpts: www.thomsonedu.com/criminaljustice/samaha.

The Right to Privacy

Unlike the right to free speech, which is clearly spelled out in the First Amendment, you won't find the word privacy anywhere in the U.S. Constitution. Nevertheless, the U.S. Supreme Court has decided there is a constitutional **right to privacy**, a right that bans "all governmental invasions of the sanctity of a man's home and the privacies of life" (*Griswold v. Connecticut* 1965, 484). Not only is privacy a constitutional right, it's a *fundamental* right that requires the government to prove a compelling interest justifies invading it.

According to the Court (*Griswold v. Connecticut* 1965), the fundamental right to privacy originates in six amendments to the U.S. Constitution:

- The First Amendment rights of free speech, religion, and association
- The Third Amendment ban on the quartering of soldiers in private homes

- The Fourth Amendment right to be secure in one's "person, house, papers, and effects" from "unreasonable searches"

- The Ninth Amendment provision that "the enumeration in the Constitution, of certain rights, shall not be construed to deny or disparage others retained by the people"

- The Fifth and Fourteenth amendments' due process right to liberty

This cluster of amendments sends the implied but strong message that we have the right to be let alone by the government. In the First Amendment, it's our beliefs and expression of them and our associations with other people that are protected from the government. In the Third and Fourth Amendments, our homes are the object of protection. And, in the Fourth Amendment, it's not only our homes but our bodies, our private papers, and even our "stuff" that fall under its protection. The Ninth, or catchall, Amendment acknowledges we have rights not named in the Constitution. In other words, "specific guarantees in the Bill of Rights have penumbras, formed by emanations from those guarantees that help give them life and substance" (484).

According to the Court, privacy is one of these rights. *Griswold* was the first case that specifically recognized the fundamental constitutional right to privacy when it struck down a Connecticut statute that made it a crime for married couples to use contraceptives.

<table>
<tr><td>CASE</td><td>Can a State Make It a Crime for Married Couples to Use Contraceptives?</td></tr>
</table>

Griswold v. Connecticut
381 U.S. 479 (1965)

HISTORY

Estelle Griswold and others were convicted in a Connecticut trial court. They appealed, and the intermediate appellate court affirmed their conviction. They appealed to the Connecticut Supreme Court of Errors, which affirmed the intermediate appellate court's judgment. They appealed to the U.S. Supreme Court. The Supreme Court reversed, holding that the Connecticut law forbidding use of contraceptives unconstitutionally intrudes upon the right of marital privacy.

DOUGLAS, J.

FACTS

[The facts are taken, in part, from the Connecticut Supreme Court of Errors, 400 A2d 479, 480.] In November, 1961, The Planned Parenthood League of Connecticut occupied offices at 79 Trumbull Street in New Haven. For ten days during that month the league operated a planned parenthood center in the same building. The defendant Estelle T. Griswold is the salaried executive director of the league and served as acting director of the center. The other defendant, C. Lee Buxton, a physician, who has specialized in the fields of gynecology and obstetrics, was the medical director of the center. The purpose of the center was to provide information, instruction and medical advice to married persons concerning various means of preventing conception. In addition, patients were furnished with various contraceptive devices, drugs or materials. A fee, measured by ability to pay, was collected from the patient. At the trial, three married women from New Haven testified that they had visited the center, had received advice, instruction and certain contraceptive devices and materials from either or both of the defendants and had used these devices and materials in subsequent marital relations with their husbands. Upon these facts, there is no doubt that, within the meaning of [the statute] . . . , the defendants did aid, abet and counsel married women. . . .

The statutes whose constitutionality is involved in this appeal are ßß 53-32 and 54-196 of the General Statutes of Connecticut. The former provides:

Any person who uses any drug, medicinal article or instrument for the purpose of preventing conception shall be fined not less than fifty dollars or imprisoned not less than sixty days nor more than one year or be both fined and imprisoned.

Section 54-196 provides:

Any person who assists, abets, counsels, causes, hires or commands another to commit any offense may be prosecuted and punished as if he were the principal offender.

The appellants were found guilty as accessories and fined $100 each, against the claim that the accessory statute as so applied violated the Fourteenth Amendment. The Appellate Division of the Circuit Court affirmed. The Supreme Court of Errors affirmed that judgment.

OPINION

. . . We are met with a wide range of questions that implicate the Due Process Clause of the Fourteenth Amendment. . . . We do not sit as a super-legislature to determine the wisdom, need, and propriety of laws that touch economic problems, business affairs, or social conditions. This law, however, operates directly on an intimate relation of husband and wife and their physician's role in one aspect of that relation.

The association of people is not mentioned in the Constitution or in the Bill of Rights. The right to educate a child in a school of the parents' choice—whether public or private or parochial—is also not mentioned. Nor is the right to study any particular subject or any foreign language. Yet the First Amendment has been construed to include certain of those rights. . . . We protected the "freedom to associate and privacy in one's associations," noting that freedom of association was a peripheral First Amendment right. . . . In like context, we have protected forms of "association" that are not political in the customary sense but pertain to the social, legal, and economic benefit of the members. . . .

Those cases involved more than the "right of assembly"— a right that extends to all irrespective of their race or ideology. The right of "association," like the right of belief, is more than the right to attend a meeting; it includes the right to express one's attitudes or philosophies by membership in a group or by affiliation with it or by other lawful means. Association in that context is a form of expression of opinion; and while it is not expressly included in the First Amendment its existence is necessary in making the express guarantees fully meaningful.

The foregoing cases suggest that specific guarantees in the Bill of Rights have penumbras, formed by emanations from those guarantees that help give them life and substance. Various guarantees create zones of privacy. The right of association contained in the penumbra of the First Amendment is one, as we have seen. The Third Amendment in its prohibition against the quartering of soldiers "in any house" in time of peace without the consent of the owner is another facet of that privacy. The Fourth Amendment explicitly affirms the "right of the people to be secure in their persons, houses, papers, and effects, against unreasonable searches and seizures." The Fifth Amendment in its Self-Incrimination Clause enables the citizen to create a zone of privacy which government may not force him to surrender to his detriment. The Ninth Amendment provides: "The enumeration in the Constitution, of certain rights, shall not be construed to deny or disparage others retained by the people." . . .

The present case, then, concerns a relationship lying within the zone of privacy created by several fundamental constitutional guarantees. And it concerns a law which, in forbidding the use of contraceptives rather than regulating their manufacture or sale, seeks to achieve its goals by means having a maximum destructive impact upon that relationship. Such a law cannot stand in light of the familiar principle, so often applied by this Court, that a governmental purpose to control or prevent activities constitutionally subject to state regulation may not be achieved by means which sweep unnecessarily broadly and thereby invade the area of protected freedoms. Would we allow the police to search the sacred precincts of marital bedrooms for telltale signs of the use of contraceptives? The very idea is repulsive to the notions of privacy surrounding the marriage relationship.

We deal with a right of privacy older than the Bill of Rights—older than our political parties, older than our school system. Marriage is a coming together for better or for worse, hopefully enduring, and intimate to the degree of being sacred. It is an association that promotes a way of life, not causes; a harmony in living, not political faiths; a bilateral loyalty, not commercial or social projects. Yet it is an association for as noble a purpose as any involved in our prior decisions.

REVERSED.

DISSENT

STEWART, J.

Since 1879 Connecticut has had on its books a law which forbids the use of contraceptives by anyone. I think this is an uncommonly silly law. As a practical matter, the law is obviously unenforceable, except in the oblique context of the present case. As a philosophical matter, I believe the use of contraceptives in the relationship of marriage should be left to personal and private choice, based upon each individual's moral, ethical, and religious beliefs. As a matter of social policy, I think professional counsel about methods of birth control should be available to all, so that each individual's choice can be meaningfully made. But we are not asked in this case to say whether we think this law is unwise, or even asinine. We are asked to hold that it violates the United States Constitution. And that I cannot do. . . .

What provision of the Constitution . . . makes this state law invalid? The Court says it is the right of privacy "created by several fundamental constitutional guarantees." With all deference, I can find no such general right of privacy in the Bill of Rights, in any other part of the Constitution, or in any case ever before decided by this Court.

At the oral argument in this case we were told that the Connecticut law does not "conform to current community standards." But it is not the function of this Court to decide cases on the basis of community standards. We are here to decide cases "agreeably to the Constitution and laws of the United States." It is the essence of judicial duty to subordinate our own personal views, our own ideas of what legislation is wise and what is not. If, as I should surely hope, the law before us does not reflect the standards of the people of Connecticut, the people of Connecticut can freely exercise their . . . rights to persuade their elected representatives to repeal it. That is the constitutional way to take this law off the books.

Questions

1. Summarize how Justice Douglas arrived at the conclusion that there is a "fundamental constitutional right to privacy" when the word *privacy* never appears in the Constitution or any of its amendments.

2. Summarize Justice Stewart's reasons for concluding there is no right to privacy in the U.S. Constitution.

3. Do you think the Connecticut law violates a fundamental right? Back up your answer with arguments from the case and the discussion of the right to privacy in the text preceding the case.

4. Do you think the Connecticut law is "uncommonly silly"? If you think it is, explain why. If not, how would you characterize it?

EXPLORING FURTHER

The Right to Privacy

1. Does the Right to Privacy Protect Pornography?

Stanley v. Georgia, 394 U.S. 557 (1969)

FACTS Federal and state law enforcement agents, armed with a search warrant, searched Eli Stanley's home for evidence of his alleged bookmaking activities. They didn't find evidence of bookmaking, but while they were searching his bedroom, they found three pornography films. Stanley was charged, indicted, and convicted under a Georgia statute that made it a crime to "knowingly have(ing) possession of . . . obscene matter. . . . The Georgia Supreme Court affirmed the conviction. The U.S. Supreme Court reversed.

DECISION According to the Court:

Georgia contends that since obscenity is not within the area of constitutionally protected speech or press, the States are free, subject to the limits of other provisions of the Constitution, to deal with it any way deemed necessary, just as they may deal with posses-

sion of other things thought to be detrimental to the welfare of their citizens. If the State can protect the body of a citizen, may it not, argues Georgia, protect his mind?

. . . In the context of this case—a prosecution for mere possession of printed or filmed matter in the privacy of a person's own home—is the . . . fundamental . . . right to be free . . . from unwanted governmental intrusions into one's privacy.

The makers of our Constitution undertook to secure conditions favorable to the pursuit of happiness. They recognized the significance of man's spiritual nature, of his feelings and of his intellect. They knew that only a part of the pain, pleasure and satisfactions of life are to be found in material things. They sought to protect Americans in their beliefs, their thoughts, their emotions and their sensations. They conferred, as against the government, the right to be let alone—the most comprehensive of rights and the right most valued by civilized man [quoting *Olmstead v. U.S.* and citing *Griswold v. Connecticut*].

2. Is There a Constitutional Right to Engage in Sodomy?

Lawrence v. Texas, 123 S.Ct. 2472 (2003)

FACTS Houston police answered an anonymous tip of a disturbance in an apartment. The police went to the apartment, entered it, and saw John Lawrence and Tyron Garner having anal sex. They arrested the two men. Lawrence and Garner were later convicted and fined $200 under a Texas statute making "deviate sexual intercourse" a crime. The Texas Court of Criminal Appeals affirmed their convictions and rejected their privacy and equal protection challenges to the Texas law. The U.S Supreme Court by a vote of 6 to 3 declared the law unconstitutional.

DECISION Justice Kennedy, writing for five members of the Court, concluded that consenting adults have a fundamental right to engage in private sexual activity. He wrote that the right is part of the right to "liberty" protected by the Fourteenth Amendment due process clause. In so doing, the Court overruled *Bowers v. Hardwick* (1986), which held that the U.S. Constitution "confers [no] fundamental right upon homosexuals to engage in sodomy. . . ." So *Lawrence v. Texas* "invalidates the laws of the many States that still make such conduct illegal."

According to Justice Kennedy, the *Bowers* holding:

discloses the Court's own failure to appreciate the extent of the liberty at stake. To say that the issue in *Bowers* was simply the right to engage in certain sexual conduct demeans the claim the individual put forward, just as it would demean a married couple were it to be said marriage is simply about the right to have sexual intercourse. . . . When sexuality finds overt expression in intimate conduct with another person, the conduct can be but one element in a personal bond that is more enduring. The liberty protected by the Constitution allows homosexual persons the right to make this choice."

Justice O'Connor, concurred in the judgment, but not with Justice Kennedy's opinion. She wouldn't have overruled *Bowers*. Instead, she said the Texas law denied homosexual couples the right to equal protection of the laws because the law applied only to same-sex couples, whereas the Georgia law in *Bowers* applied both to opposite-sex and same-sex couples.

Justice Scalia, Chief Justice Rehnquist, and Justice Thomas, dissented. They argued that states should be able to make the moral judgment that homosexual conduct is wrong and embody that judgment in criminal statutes.

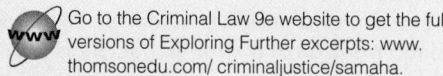 Go to the Criminal Law 9e website to get the full versions of Exploring Further excerpts: www. thomsonedu.com/ criminaljustice/samaha.

Unlike the U.S. Constitution, several state constitutions contain specific provisions guaranteeing the right to privacy. For example, the Florida Declaration of Rights provides: "Every natural person has the right to be let alone and free from governmental intrusion into his private life" (Florida Constitution 1998). Other states have followed the example of the U.S. Supreme Court and implied a state constitutional right to privacy.

CRUEL AND UNUSUAL PUNISHMENTS

The Eighth Amendment commands that "cruel and unusual punishments" shall not be "inflicted." According to the U.S. Supreme Court, there are two kinds of cruel and unusual punishments: "barbaric" punishments and punishments that are disproportionate to the crime committed (*Solem v. Helm* 1983, 284). Let's look at each.

Barbaric Punishments

Barbaric punishments are punishments that are considered no longer acceptable to civilized society. At the time the amendment was adopted, these included burning at the stake, crucifixion, breaking on the wheel, torturing or lingering death (*In re Kemmler* 1890, 446); drawing and quartering, the rack and screw (*Chambers v. Florida* 1940, 227); and extreme forms of solitary confinement (*In re Medley* 1890, 160).

For more than a hundred years after the adoption of the Bill of Rights, no "cruel and unusual" punishment cases reached the U.S. Supreme Court because these medieval forms of execution weren't used in the United States. But, in 1885, the governor of the state of New York, in his annual message to the legislature, questioned the use of hanging as a method of execution:

> The present mode of executing criminals by hanging has come down to us from the dark ages, and it may well be questioned whether the science of the present day cannot provide a means for taking . . . life . . . in a less barbarous manner. (*In re Kemmler* 1890, 444)

The legislature appointed a commission to study the matter. The commission reported that electrocution was "the most humane and practical method [of execution] known to modern science (*In re Kemmler* 1890, 444)." In 1888, the legislature replaced the hangman's noose with the electric chair.

Shortly thereafter, William Kemmler, convicted of murdering his wife, and sentenced to die in the electric chair, argued that electrocution was "cruel and unusual punishment." The U.S. Supreme Court disagreed. The Court said that electrocution was certainly unusual but not cruel. For the first time, the Court defined what "cruel" means in the Eighth Amendment. According to the Court, punishment by death isn't cruel as long as it isn't "something more than the mere extinguishment of life." The Court spelled out what it meant by this phrase: First, death has to be both instantaneous and painless. Second, it can't involve unnecessary mutilation of the body. So, according to the Court, beheading is cruel because it mutilates the body. Crucifixion is doubly cruel because it inflicts a "lingering" death *and* mutilates the body (*In re Kemmler* 1890, 446–47).

Proportional Punishments

The **principle of proportionality**—namely, that punishment should fit the crime—has an ancient history. The Magna Carta, adopted in 1215 before imprisonment was a form of punishment, prohibited "excessive" fines. The English Bill of Rights, in 1689, repeated the principle of proportionality in language that later appeared in the Eighth Amendment.

The U.S. Supreme Court first applied proportionality as a principle required by the Eighth Amendment in 1910, in *Weems v. U.S.* Weems was convicted of falsifying a public document. The trial court first sentenced him to 15 years in prison at hard labor in chains and then took away all of his civil rights for the rest of his life. The Court ruled that the punishment was "cruel and unusual," because it was disproportionate to his crime. *Weems* banned disproportionate punishments in *federal* criminal justice.

In extending the cruel and unusual punishment ban to *state* criminal justice in the 1960s, the Court in *Robinson v. California* (1962) reaffirmed its commitment to the proportionality principle. The Court majority ruled that a 90-day sentence for drug addiction was disproportionate because addiction is an illness, and it's cruel and unusual to punish persons for being sick. "Even one day in prison would be a cruel and unusual punishment for the 'crime' of having a common cold," wrote Justice Marshall for the Court majority.

Let's look at the issues surrounding whether many modern forms of punishment are proportional punishments.

The Death Penalty: "Death Is Different"   A majority of the U.S. Supreme Court has consistently agreed that the proportionality principle applies to death penalty cases; as the Court puts it, "death is different." There are numerous capital crimes where no one is killed; they include treason, espionage, kidnapping, aircraft hijacking, large-scale drug trafficking, train wrecking, and perjury that leads to someone's execution (Liptak 2003).

But, in practice, no one's actually sentenced to death for them, so it's difficult to tell whether the Court would rule that death is disproportionate to a crime where no one gets killed. With one exception—rape. In 1977, the Court heard *Coker v. Georgia;* it decided that death was disproportionate punishment for raping an adult woman. In fact, it looked as if a majority of the Court was committed to the idea that death is always disproportionate except in some aggravated murders. But the state of Louisiana has challenged this notion by making child rape a capital offense. In *State v. Wilson* (1996), the subject of the case excerpt that follows, the Louisiana supreme court decided that the death penalty *was* proportionate to the crime of child rape.

Is the Death Penalty for Child Rape Cruel and Unusual?

State v. Wilson

685 So.2d 1063 (1996 La)

HISTORY

Anthony Wilson, Defendant, was charged by a grand jury indictment with the aggravated rape of a five-year-old girl. Defendant moved to quash the indictment. The Criminal District Court, Parish of Orleans, quashed the defendant's indictment on the ground that the death penalty was constitutionally excessive for the crime of rape. The Supreme Court, Bleich, J., held that the death penalty is not excessive punishment nor is it susceptible of being applied arbitrarily and capriciously for a crime of rape of a child under age 12. Reversed and indictment vacated; remanded.

BLEICH, J.

FACTS

On December 21, 1995, Anthony Wilson was charged by grand jury indictment with the aggravated rape of a five-year-old girl. He moved to quash the indictment, alleging that the crime of rape could never be punished with the death penalty. The trial court granted Wilson's motion to quash, resulting in this appeal by the state.

OPINION

Excessive Punishment Argument

The defendant's primary argument is that death is a disproportionate penalty for the crime of rape. The contention is based on *Coker v. Georgia* (1977) decided by the Supreme Court in a plurality [4 justices] opinion. The Coker court rejected capital punishment as a penalty for the rape of an adult woman. . . . The plurality took great pains in referring only to the rape of *adult women* [emphasis added] throughout their opinion, leaving open the question of the rape of a child. The defendants argue that the *Coker* findings cannot be limited to the rape of an adult. They contend the following words used by the Court would apply with equal force to the crime of statutory rape when no life is taken:

> Rape is without doubt deserving of serious punishment; but in terms of moral depravity and of the injury to the person and to the public, it does not compare with murder, which does involve the unjustified taking of human life. Although it may be accompanied by another crime, rape by definition does not include the death or even the serious injury to another

person. The murderer kills; the rapist, if no more than that, does not. Life is over for the victim of the murderer; for the rape victim, life may not be nearly so happy as it was, but it is not over and normally is not beyond repair. We have the abiding conviction that the death penalty, which is unique in its severity and irrevocability, . . . is an excessive penalty for the rapist who, as such, does not take human life.

Rape of a child less than twelve years of age is like no other crime. Since children cannot protect themselves, the State is given the responsibility to protect them. Children are a class of people that need special protection; they are particularly vulnerable since they are not mature enough or capable of defending themselves. A "maturing society," through its legislature has recognized the degradation and devastation of child rape, and the permeation of harm resulting to victims of rape in this age category. The damage a child suffers as a result of rape is devastating to the child as well as to the community.

. . . In determining whether a penalty is excessive, the Supreme Court has declared that we should take into account the "evolving standards of decency," and in making this determination, the courts should not look to their own subjective conceptions, but should look instead to the conceptions of modern American society as reflected by objective evidence. As evidence of society's attitudes, we look to the judgment of the state legislators, who are representatives of society.

Louisiana's legislature determined a "standard of decency" by amending La. R.S. 14:42(C) to permit the death penalty in cases of aggravated rape when the victim is less than twelve, and deference must be given to that decision. The legislature alone determines what are punishable as crimes and the proscribed penalties. The legislature is not required to select the least severe penalty for the crime as long as the selected penalty is not cruelly inhumane or disproportionate to the offense. . . . "In a democratic society legislatures, not courts, are constituted to respond to the will and consequently the moral values of the people."

One of the most conservative and acceptable methods of determining the excessiveness of a penalty is to examine the statutes of the other states. . . . Louisiana is the only state that presently has a law in effect that provides for the death penalty for the rape of a child less than twelve. This fact, however, cannot be deemed determinative. . . . The fact that Louisiana is presently the sole state allowing the death penalty for the rape of a child is not conclusive.

There is no constitutional infirmity in a state's statute simply because that jurisdiction chose to be first. Statutes applied in one state can be carefully watched by other states so that the experience of the first state becomes available to all other states. That one State is "presently a minority does not, in my view, make [its] judgment less worthy of deference. Our concern for human life must not be confined to the guilty; a state legislature is not to be thought insensitive to human values because it acts firmly to protect the lives and related values of the innocent."

The needs and standards of society change, and these changes are a result of experience and knowledge. If no state could pass a law without other states passing the same or similar law, new laws could never be passed. To make this the controlling factor leads only to absurd results. Some suggest that it has been over a year since Louisiana has amended its law to permit the death penalty for the rape of a child, and that no other state has followed suit. Since its enactment, the statute has been under constant scrutiny. It is quite possible that other states are awaiting the outcome of the challenges to the constitutionality of the subject statute before enacting their own.

Crime without Death

It has been argued that the death penalty should not be an option when the crime committed produces no death. The Supreme Court has held that the death penalty is an excessive penalty for a robber who does not take a human life (*Enmund v. Florida* 1982). However . . . [the Louisiana statute] contemplates a defendant who rapes a child. The legislature has determined that this crime is deserving of the death penalty because of its deplorable nature, being a "grievous affront to humanity."

. . . Contemporary standards as defined by the legislature indicate that the harm inflicted upon a child when raped is tremendous. That child suffers physically as well as emotionally and mentally, especially since the overwhelming majority of offenders are family members. Louisiana courts have held that sex offenses against children cause untold psychological harm not only to the victim but also to generations to come. "Common experience tells us that there is a vast difference in mental and physical maturity of an adolescent teenager . . . and a pre-adolescent child . . . It is well known that child abuse leaves lasting scars from generation to the next . . . such injury is inherent in the offense." . . .

While the Eighth Amendment bars the death penalty for minor crimes under the concept of disproportionality, the crime of rape when the victim is under the age of twelve is certainly not a minor crime. The *Coker* Court recognized the possibility that the degree of harm caused by an offense could be measured not only by the injury to a particular victim but also by the resulting public injury. This implies that some offenses, in particular the rape of a child, might be so injurious to the public that death would not be disproportionate in relation to the crime for which it is imposed. "In part, capital punishment is an expression of society's moral outrage at particularly offensive conduct. This function may be unappealing to many, but it is essential in an ordered society that asks its citizens to rely on legal processes rather than self-help to vindicate their wrongs."

Thus, we conclude that given the appalling nature of the crime, the severity of the harm inflicted upon the victim, and the harm imposed on society, the death penalty is not an excessive penalty for the crime of rape when the victim is a child under the age of twelve years old. . . .

Goals of Punishment

Two legitimate goals of punishment are retribution and deterrence. The defendant argues that the death sentence in the case of child rape fails to meet either of these goals. They say the imposition of the death penalty will have a chilling effect on the already inadequate reporting of this crime. Since arguably, most child abusers are family members, the victims and other family members are concerned about the legal, financial and emotional consequences of coming forward. According to defendant, permitting the death penalty for the crime will further decrease the reporting since no child wants to be responsible for the death of a family member. But what defendant fails to understand is that the child is not the one responsible. The child is the innocent victim. The offender is responsible for his own actions. The subject punishment is for the legislature to determine, not this Court. . . .

Our holding today permits the death penalty without a death actually occurring. In reaching this conclusion, we give great deference to our legislature's determination of the appropriateness of the penalty. This is not to say, however, that the legislature has free reign in proscribing penalties. They must still conform to the mandates of the Eighth Amendment and Article I, ß 20 of the Louisiana Constitution, and they are still subject to judicial review by the courts. We hold only that in the case of the rape of a child under the age of twelve, the death penalty is not an excessive punishment nor is it susceptible of being applied arbitrarily and capriciously.

For the reasons stated above, we find La. R.S. 14:42(C) to be constitutional. The motion to quash is reversed and vacated. The case is remanded to the trial courts.

DISSENT

CALOGERO, CJ.

No other State in the union imposes the death penalty for the aggravated rape of a child under twelve years of age. The reason for this, in my view, is that the statute fails constitutional scrutiny under the decisions of the United States Supreme Court in *Coker v. Georgia* (1977), *Furman v. Georgia* (1972), and *Gregg v. Georgia* (1976). I therefore dissent and would hold R.S. 14:42(C) facially unconstitutional under the Eighth Amendment to the United States Constitution.

Note: This case was never reviewed by the U.S. Supreme Court because Wilson never got to death row; the case ended in a plea bargain for a life sentence. In declining to hear the appeal, three U.S. Supreme Court justices wrote that the decision not to hear the case "does not in any way constitute a ruling on the merits," suggesting they had reservations about the constitutionality of the law (Liptak 2003). But, in 2003, a Louisiana jury convicted and sentenced Patrick O. Kennedy to death for raping his 8-year-old stepdaughter; he became the first person in more than 28 years to be sentenced to death for rape (Darby 2003, 1). At the time I write this (June 1, 2006), the convicted rapist is on death row.

Questions

1. According to the court, why is death a proportionate penalty for child rape? Do you agree? Explain your reasons.

2. Who should make the decision as to what is the appropriate penalty for crimes? Courts? Legislatures? Juries? Defend your answer.

3. In deciding whether the death penalty for child rape is cruel and unusual, is it relevant that Louisiana is the only state that punishes child rape with death?

4. According to the court, some crimes are worse than death. Do you agree? Is child rape one of them? Why? Why not?

The Death Penalty for the Mentally Retarded Thirty-five mentally retarded persons were executed between 1976 when the death penalty was reinstated and 2001 (Human Rights Watch 2002). The American Association on Mental Retardation (AAMR) includes three elements in its definition of mental retardation:

1. The person has substantial intellectual impairment.

2. That impairment impacts the everyday life of the mentally retarded individual.

3. Retardation is present at birth or during childhood. (quoted in *Atkins v. Virginia* 2002, 308)

In *Atkins v. Virginia* (2002), the U.S. Supreme Court ruled that executing anyone who proved the three elements in the AAMR definition applied to them violated the ban on cruel and unusual punishment. The decision grew out of a grisly case. On August 16, 1996, Daryl Atkins and William Jones were drinking alcohol and smoking "pot." At about midnight, they drove to a convenience store to rob a customer. They picked Eric Nesbitt, an airman from Langley Air Force Base, abducted him, took him in their pickup truck to an ATM machine, and forced him to withdraw $200. Then, they drove him to a deserted area. Ignoring his pleas not to hurt him, they ordered Nesbitt to get out of the car. Nesbitt took only a few steps when (according to Jones, who made a deal with prosecutors to testify against Atkins in exchange for a life instead of a death sentence), Atkins fired eight shots into Nesbitt's thorax, chest, abdomen, arms, and legs (338).

The jury convicted Atkins of capital murder. At the penalty phase of Atkins's trial, the jury heard evidence about his 16 prior felony convictions, including robbery, attempted robbery, abduction, use of a firearm, and maiming. He hit one victim over the head with a beer bottle; "slapped a gun across another victim's face, clubbed her in the head with it, knocked her to the ground, and then helped her up, only to shoot her in the stomach" (339).

The jury also heard evidence about Atkins's mental retardation. After interviewing people who knew Atkins, reviewing school and court records, and administering a standard intelligence test, which revealed Atkins had an IQ of 59, Dr. Evan Nelson, a forensic psychologist concluded that Atkins was "mildly mentally retarded." According to Nelson, mental retardation is rare (about 1 percent of the population); it would automatically qualify Atkins for Social Security disability income; and that "of the over 40 capital defendants that he had evaluated, Atkins was only the second" who "met the criteria for mental retardation." Nelson also testified that, "in his opinion, Atkins' limited intellect had been a consistent feature throughout his life, and that his IQ score of 59 is not an 'aberration, malingered result, or invalid test score'" (309).

In reversing the death sentence, the U.S. Supreme Court based its decision on a change in public opinion since its 1989 decision that it's not cruel and unusual punishment to execute retarded offenders (*Penry v. Lynaugh* 1989). How did the Court measure this change in public opinion? First, since 1989, 19 states and the federal government had passed statutes banning the execution of mentally retarded offenders (*Atkins v. Virginia* 2002, 314). Second, it's not just the number of bans that's significant, it's "the consistency of the direction of the change":

> Given the well-known fact that anticrime legislation is far more popular than legislation providing protections for persons guilty of violent crime, the large number of States prohibiting the execution of mentally retarded persons (and the complete absence of States passing legislation reinstating the power to conduct such executions) provides powerful evidence that today our society views mentally retarded offenders as categorically less culpable than the average criminal.
>
> The evidence carries even greater force when it is noted that the legislatures that have addressed the issue have voted overwhelmingly in favor of the prohibition.
>
> Moreover, even in those States that allow the execution of mentally retarded offenders, the practice is uncommon. Some states, for example New Hampshire and New Jersey, continue to authorize executions, but none have been carried out in decades. Thus there is little need to pursue legislation barring the execution of the mentally retarded in those States.
>
> And it appears that even among those States that regularly execute offenders and that have no prohibition with regard to the mentally retarded, only five have executed offenders possessing a known IQ less than 70 since we decided Penry. The practice, therefore, has become truly unusual, and it is fair to say that a national consensus has developed against it. (315–16)

Third, executing retarded offenders doesn't serve the main purposes for having death sentences: retribution and deterrence. Mentally retarded offenders aren't as blameworthy or as subject to deterrence as people with normal intelligence because of their "diminished capacity to understand and process information, to learn from experience, to engage in logical reasoning, or to control their impulses" (319–20).

 Go to the Criminal Law 9e website and find Exercise 2.4 to learn more about *Atkins v. Virginia:* www.thomsonedu.com/criminaljustice/samaha.

The Death Penalty for Juveniles   The execution of juveniles began in 1642, when Plymouth Colony hanged 16-year-old Thomas Graunger for bestiality with a cow and a horse (Rimer and Bonner 2000). It continued at a rate of about one a year until Oklahoma executed Scott Hain on April 3, 2003, after the U.S. Supreme Court refused to hear his appeal. Hain and a 21-year-old acquaintance killed two people in the course of a carjacking and robbery. He was a "deeply troubled" 17-year-old kid who dropped out of the seventh grade after repeating the sixth grade three times. As a teenager, Scott's father got him a job in a warehouse so he could steal stuff and give it to his father, who sold it. At the time of the carjacking murders, Scott was living on the street in Tulsa, drinking, and using other drugs daily, but he'd never committed a violent crime (Greenhouse 2003, A18).

Just a few months before the U.S. Supreme Court refused to hear Scott Hain's case, four Supreme Court justices (John Paul Stevens, David Souter, Ruth Bader Ginsburg, and Stephen Breyer) had called the death penalty for juveniles a "shameful practice," adding that "the practice of executing such offenders is a relic of the past and is inconsistent with the evolving standards of decency in a civilized society" (Greenhouse 2003, A18).

In *Trop v. Dulles* (1958), the Court first adopted the "evolving standards" test to decide whether sentences run afoul of the Eighth Amendment ban on "cruel and unusual punishments." In 1944, U.S. Army private Albert Trop escaped from a military stockade at Casablanca, Morocco, following his confinement for a disciplinary violation. The next day, Trop willingly surrendered. A general court martial convicted Trop of desertion and sentenced him to 3 years at hard labor, loss of all pay and allowances, and a dishonorable discharge. In 1952, Trop applied for a passport. His application was rejected on the ground that he had lost his citizenship due to his conviction and dishonorable discharge for wartime desertion. The Court decided the punishment was "cruel and unusual." Why? Because "the words of the Amendment are not precise, and their scope is not static. The Amendment must draw its meaning from the evolving standards of decency that mark the progress of a maturing society" (100–101).

The Court applied the "evolving standards of decency" approach in *Thompson v. Oklahoma* (1988) to ban the execution of juveniles under 16. But the next year, in *Stanford v. Kentucky* (1989), the Court ruled that executing juveniles between 16 and 18 didn't offend "evolving standards of decency." (After serving 14 years on death row, Stanford was granted clemency in 2003 and is now serving a life sentence.)

In 2005, the Court decided whether standards of decency had evolved enough since 1989 to be offended by executing Christopher Simmons for a carjacking murder he committed when he was 17 (*Roper v. Simmons* 2005). By a vote of 5–4, the U.S. Supreme Court held that the Eighth and Fourteenth Amendments forbid the execution of offenders who were under the age of 18 when they committed their crimes. According to Justice Kennedy:

> When a juvenile offender commits a heinous crime, the State can exact forfeiture of some of the most basic liberties, but the State cannot extinguish his life and his potential to attain a mature understanding of his own humanity. (554)

The Court relied on "the evolving standards of decency that mark the progress of a maturing society" (561) to determine which punishments are so disproportionate as to be cruel and unusual. The Court argued that the majority of states' rejection of the death penalty for juveniles; its infrequent use in the states that retain the penalty; and the trend toward its abolition, show that there's a national consensus against it. The Court determined that today our society views juveniles as categorically less culpable than the average criminal.

Justice Stevens, joined by Justice Ginsburg, wrote in a concurring opinion, that "if the meaning of . . . [the Eighth] Amendment had been frozen when it was originally drafted, it would impose no impediment to the execution of 7-year-old children today" (587).

 Go to the Criminal Law 9e website and find Exercise 2.5 to learn more about *Roper v. Simmons*: www.thomsonedu .com/criminaljustice/samaha.

Justice Scalia, joined by Justice Thomas and Chief Justice Rehnquist, dissented. Justice Scalia maintained that the Court improperly substituted its own judgment for the state legislatures.' He criticized the majority for counting non–death penalty states toward a national consensus against juvenile executions. Scalia also objected to the Court's use of international law to support its opinion, claiming that, "Acknowledgement of foreign approval has no place in the legal opinion of this Court . . ." (628).

Imprisonment   The consensus that the ban on cruel and unusual punishment includes a proportionality requirement in capital punishment does not extend to prison sentences. The important case of *Solem v. Helm* (1983) revealed that the U.S. Supreme Court was deeply divided over whether the principle of proportionality applied to sentences of imprisonment. The case involved Jerry Helm, who by 1975 the state of South Dakota had convicted of six nonviolent felonies. The crimes consisted of three third-degree burglaries, one in 1964, one in 1966, and one in 1969; obtaining money under false pretenses in 1972; committing grand larceny, in 1973; and "third-offense driving while intoxicated" in 1975. A bare majority of five in the U.S. Supreme Court held that "a criminal sentence must be proportionate to the crime for which the defendant has been convicted" (290).

The split over the constitutional status of proportionality in prison sentences was revealed again when the constitutionality of three-strikes-and-you're-out laws reached the Court in 2003. Before we look at the Court's division, let's put three-strikes laws in some perspective. Three-strikes laws are supposed to make sure offenders who are convicted of a third felony get locked up for a very long time (sometimes for life). The laws are controversial, and they generate passions on both sides. Supporters claim that the laws "help restore the credibility of the criminal justice system and will deter crime." Opponents believe the harsh penalties won't have much effect on crime, and they'll cost states more than they can afford to pay (Turner et al. 1995, 75).

Despite controversy, three-strikes laws are popular and widespread. Twenty-four states have passed three-strikes laws (Shepherd 2002). California's law, the toughest in the nation, includes a 25-year-to-life sentence if you're "out" on a third strike. The law passed in 1994, after the kidnapping, brutal sexual assault, and murder of 12-year-old Polly Klaas in 1993 (Ainsworth 2004, 1; Shepherd 2002, 161). A bearded stranger broke into Polly Klaas's home in Petaluma, California, and kidnapped her. He left behind two other girls bound and gagged. Polly's mother was asleep in the next room. Nine weeks later, after a fruitless search by hundreds of police officers and volunteers, a repeat offender, Richard Allen Davis, was arrested, and, in 1996, convicted and sentenced to death.

Liberals and conservatives, Democrats and Republicans, and the public all jumped on the three-strikes bandwagon, taking it for granted these laws were a good idea. Why were they popular? Here are three reasons:

1. They addressed the public's dissatisfaction with the criminal justice system.

2. They promised a simple solution to a complex problem—the "panacea phenomenon."

3. The use of the catchy phrase "three strikes and you're out" was appealing; it put old habitual offender statute ideas into the language of modern baseball. (Benekos and Merlo 1995, 3; Turner et al. 1995)

What effects have three-strikes laws had? Everybody agrees that they *incapacitate* second- and third-strikers while they're locked up. But incapacitate them from doing what? Some critics argue that most strikers are already past the age of high offending. Most of the debate centers on deterrence: Do the laws prevent criminals from committing further crimes? The conclusions, based on empirical research, are decidedly mixed: Three-strikes laws deter crime; three-strikes laws have no effect on crime; three-strikes laws *increase* crime.

Whatever the effectiveness of three-strikes laws may be, the U.S. Supreme Court has ruled they're constitutional, even if the justices can't agree on the reasons. This is clear from the Court's 5–4 decision in *Ewing v. California*, upholding the constitutionality of California's three-strikes law.

Ewing v. California
538 U.S. 11 (2003)

HISTORY

Gary Ewing was convicted in a California trial court of felony grand theft and sentenced to 25 years to life under that state's three-strikes law. The California Court of Appeal, Second Appellate District, affirmed the sentence, and the State Supreme Court denied review. Certiorari was granted. The Supreme Court held that the sentence did not violate the Eighth Amendment's prohibition against cruel and unusual punishment.

O'CONNOR, J.

FACTS

On parole from a 9-year prison term, petitioner Gary Ewing walked into the pro shop of the El Segundo Golf Course, in Los Angeles County, on March 12, 2000. He walked out with three golf clubs, priced at $399 apiece, concealed in his pants leg. A shop employee, whose suspicions were aroused when he observed Ewing limp out of the pro shop, telephoned the police. The police apprehended Ewing in the parking lot.

Ewing is no stranger to the criminal justice system. In 1984, at the age of 22, he pleaded guilty to theft. The court sentenced him to six months in jail (suspended), three years' probation, and a $300 fine. In 1988, he was convicted of felony grand theft auto and sentenced to one year in jail and three years' probation. After Ewing completed probation, however, the sentencing court reduced the crime to a misdemeanor, permitted Ewing to withdraw his guilty plea, and dismissed the case. In 1990, he was convicted of petty theft with a prior and sentenced to 60 days in the county jail and three years' probation. In 1992, Ewing was convicted of battery and sentenced to 30 days in the county jail and two years' summary probation. One month later, he was convicted of theft and sentenced to 10 days in the county jail and 12 months' probation. In January 1993, Ewing was convicted of burglary and sentenced to 60 days in the county jail and one year's summary probation. In February 1993, he was convicted of possessing drug paraphernalia and sentenced to six months in the county jail and three years' probation. In July 1993, he was convicted of appropriating lost property and sentenced to 10 days in the county jail and two years' summary probation. In September 1993, he was convicted of unlawfully possessing a firearm and trespassing and sentenced to 30 days in the county jail and one year's probation.

In October and November 1993, Ewing committed three burglaries and one robbery at a Long Beach, California, apartment complex over a 5-week period. He awakened one of his victims, asleep on her living room sofa, as he tried to disconnect her video cassette recorder from the television in that room. When she screamed, Ewing ran out the front door. On another occasion, Ewing accosted a victim in the mailroom of the apartment complex. Ewing claimed to have a gun and ordered the victim to hand over his wallet. When the victim resisted, Ewing produced a knife and forced the victim back to the apartment itself. While Ewing rifled through the bedroom, the victim fled the apartment screaming for help. Ewing absconded with the victim's money and credit cards.

On December 9, 1993, Ewing was arrested on the premises of the apartment complex for trespassing and lying to a police officer. The knife used in the robbery and a glass cocaine pipe were later found in the back seat of the patrol car used to transport Ewing to the police station. A jury convicted Ewing of first-degree robbery and three counts of residential burglary. Sentenced to nine years and eight months in prison, Ewing was paroled in 1999.

Only 10 months later, Ewing stole the golf clubs at issue in this case. He was charged with, and ultimately convicted of, one count of felony grand theft of personal property in excess of $400. As required by the three-strikes law, the prosecutor formally alleged, and the trial court later found, that Ewing had been convicted previously of four serious or violent felonies for the three burglaries and the robbery in the Long Beach apartment complex.

As a newly convicted felon with two or more "serious" or "violent" felony convictions in his past, Ewing was sentenced under the three-strikes law to 25 years to life.

OPINION

The Eighth Amendment, which forbids cruel and unusual punishments, contains a "narrow proportionality principle" that "applies to noncapital sentences." . . . This Court "has on occasion stated that the Eighth Amendment prohibits imposition of a sentence that is grossly disproportionate to the severity of the crime." Although we stated that the proportionality principle "would . . . come into play in the extreme example, (if a legislature made overtime parking a felony punishable by life imprisonment,") we held that a mandatory life sentence [of a repeat offender didn't] constitute cruel and unusual punishment under the Eighth and Fourteenth Amendments" [*Solem v. Helm* (1983)]; . . . [neither did] the sentence of a repeat offender] to two consecutive terms of 20 years in prison for possession with intent to distribute nine ounces of marijuana and distribution of marijuana [*Hutto v. Davis* (1982)]; [or a life sentence without possibility of parole for a first time offender who possessed more than 650 grams of cocaine (*Harmelin v. Michigan* (1991)]. . . . [These cases] stand for the proposition that federal courts should be reluctant to review legislatively mandated terms of imprisonment, and that successful challenges to the proportionality of particular sentences should be exceedingly rare." . . .

For many years, most States have had laws providing for enhanced sentencing of repeat offenders. Yet between 1993 and 1995, three strikes laws effected a sea change in criminal sentencing throughout the Nation. These laws responded to widespread public concerns about crime by targeting the class of offenders who pose the greatest threat to public safety: career criminals. . . . Throughout the States, legislatures enacting three strikes laws made a deliberate policy choice that individuals who have repeatedly engaged in serious or violent criminal behavior, and whose conduct has not been deterred by more conventional approaches to punishment, must be isolated from society in order to protect the public safety.

Though three strikes laws may be relatively new, our tradition of deferring to state legislatures in making and implementing such important policy decisions is long-standing. Our traditional deference to legislative policy choices finds a corollary in the principle that the Constitution "does not mandate adoption of any one penological theory." A sentence can have a variety of justifications, such as incapacitation, deterrence, retribution, or rehabilitation. Some or all of these justifications may play a role in a State's sentencing scheme. Selecting the sentencing rationales is generally a policy choice to be made by state legislatures, not federal courts.

When the California Legislature enacted the three strikes law, it made a judgment that protecting the public safety requires incapacitating criminals who have already been convicted of at least one serious or violent crime. Nothing in the Eighth Amendment prohibits California from making that choice. . . . The State's interest in deterring crime also lends some support to the three strikes law. We have long viewed both incapacitation and deterrence as rationales for recidivism. . . . To be sure, California's three strikes law has sparked controversy. Critics have doubted the law's wisdom, cost-efficiency, and effectiveness in reaching its goals. This criticism is appropriately directed at the legislature, which has primary responsibility for making the difficult policy choices that underlie any criminal sentencing scheme. We do not sit as a "super-legislature" to second-guess these policy choices. It is enough that the State of California has a reasonable basis for believing that dramatically enhanced sentences for habitual felons "advance[s] the goals of [its] criminal justice system in any substantial way." . . .

Against this backdrop, we consider Ewing's claim that his three strikes sentence of 25 years to life is unconstitutionally disproportionate to his offense of "shoplifting three golf clubs." . . . Ewing's sentence is justified by the State's public-safety interest in incapacitating and deterring recidivist felons, and amply supported by his own long, serious criminal record. . . . To be sure, Ewing's sentence is a long one. But it reflects a rational legislative judgment, entitled to deference, that offenders who have committed serious or violent felonies and who continue to commit felonies must be incapacitated. The State of California "was entitled to place upon [Ewing] the onus of one who is simply unable to bring his conduct within the social norms prescribed by the criminal law of the State." Ewing's is not "the rare case in which a threshold comparison of the crime committed and the sentence imposed leads to an inference of gross disproportionality."

We hold that Ewing's sentence of 25 years to life in prison, imposed for the offense of felony grand theft under the three strikes law, is not grossly disproportionate and therefore does not violate the Eighth Amendment's prohibition on cruel and unusual punishments. The judgment of the California Court of Appeal is affirmed.

It is so ordered.

CONCURRING OPINION

SCALIA, J. concurring in the judgment.

In my opinion in *Harmelin v. Michigan*, (1991), I concluded that the Eighth Amendment's prohibition of "cruel and unusual punishments" was aimed at excluding only certain *modes* of punishment, and was not a "guarantee against disproportionate sentences." Out of respect for the principle of *stare decisis*, I might nonetheless accept the contrary holding of *Solem v. Helm*, (1983)—that the Eighth Amendment contains a narrow proportionality principle—if I felt I could intelligently apply it. This case demonstrates why I cannot.

Proportionality—the notion that the punishment should fit the crime—is inherently a concept tied to the penological goal of retribution. "[I]t becomes difficult even to speak intelligently of 'proportionality,' once deterrence and rehabilitation are given significant weight,"—not to mention giving weight to the purpose of California's three strikes law: incapacitation. In the present case, the game is up once the plurality has acknowledged that "the Constitution does not mandate adoption of any one penological theory," and that a "sentence can have a variety of justifications, such as incapacitation, deterrence, retribution, or rehabilitation." That acknowledgment having been made, it no longer suffices merely to assess "the gravity of the offense compared to the harshness of the penalty" . . . Perhaps the plurality should revise its terminology, so that what it reads into the Eighth Amendment is not the unstated proposition that all punishment should be reasonably proportionate to the gravity of the offense, but rather the unstated proposition that all punishment should reasonably pursue the multiple purposes of the criminal law. That formulation would make it clearer than ever, of course, that the plurality is not applying law but evaluating policy.

Because I agree that petitioner's sentence does not violate the Eighth Amendment's prohibition against cruel and unusual punishments, I concur in the judgment.

CONCURRING OPINION

THOMAS, J. concurring in the judgment.

In my view, the Cruel and Unusual Punishments Clause of the Eighth Amendment contains no proportionality principle. Because the plurality concludes that petitioner's sentence does not violate the Eighth Amendment's prohibition on cruel and unusual punishments, I concur in the judgment.

DISSENT

STEVENS, J., joined by SOUTER, GINSBURG, and BREYER, JJ.

. . . Proportionality review is not only capable of judicial application but also required by the Eighth Amendment. "The Eighth Amendment succinctly prohibits 'excessive' sanctions." Faithful to the Amendment's text, this Court has held that the Constitution directs judges to apply their best judgment in determining the proportionality of fines, bail, and other forms of punishment, including the imposition of a death sentence (*Coker v. Georgia* (1977)). It "would be anomalous indeed" to suggest that the Eighth Amendment makes proportionality review applicable in the context of bail and fines but not in the context of other forms of punishment, such as imprisonment. Rather, by broadly prohibiting excessive sanctions, the Eighth Amendment directs judges to exercise their wise judgment in assessing the proportionality of all forms of punishment.

The absence of a black-letter rule does not disable judges from exercising their discretion in construing the outer limits on sentencing authority that the Eighth Amendment imposes. After all, judges are "constantly called upon to draw . . . lines in a variety of contexts," and to exercise their judgment to give meaning to the Constitution's broadly phrased protections. For example, the Due Process Clause directs judges to employ proportionality review in assessing the constitutionality of punitive damages awards on a case-by-case basis. Also, although the Sixth Amendment guarantees criminal defendants the right to a speedy trial, the courts often are asked to determine on a case-by-case basis whether a particular delay is constitutionally permissible or not.

Throughout most of the Nation's history—before guideline sentencing became so prevalent—federal and state trial judges imposed specific sentences pursuant to grants of authority that gave them uncabined discretion within broad ranges. It was not unheard of for a statute to authorize a sentence ranging from one year to life, for example. In exercising their discretion, sentencing judges wisely employed a proportionality principle that took into account all of the justifications for punishment—namely, deterrence, incapacitation, retribution, and rehabilitation. Likewise, I think it clear that the Eighth Amendment's prohibition of "cruel and unusual punishments" expresses a broad and basic proportionality principle that takes into account all of the justifications for penal sanctions. It is this broad proportionality principle that would preclude reliance on any of the justifications for punishment to support, for example, a life sentence for overtime parking.

Accordingly, I respectfully dissent.

Questions

1. List Gary Ewing's crimes, and match them to the three-strikes law.

2. Define proportionality, as the plurality opinion defines it. Summarize how the majority applies proportionality to Ewing's sentence. How does Justice Scalia define proportionality, and how does his application of it to the facts differ from the majority's? Summarize how the dissent applies the principle of proportionality to the facts of the case.

3. In your opinion, was Ewing's punishment proportional to the crime? Back up your answer with the facts of the case and the arguments in the opinions.

4. If Justice Thomas is right that the Eighth Amendment contains no proportionality principle, what is cruel and unusual punishment?

SUMMARY

I. A central feature of criminal law in a constitutional democracy is that limits, written in U.S. and state constitutions, are placed on the power of the government to create crimes.

II. These limits include:
   A. The ban on ex post facto laws
   B. The right to due process of law
   C. The right to equal protection of the law

D. The right to free speech, association, the press, and religion
E. The right to privacy
F. The ban on "cruel and unusual punishment"

III. Ex post facto laws

A. Article 1, sections 9 and 10 of the U.S. Constitution ban both the U.S. Congress and state legislatures from passing ex post facto laws.
B. An ex post facto law is a statute that does one of three things:
1. It criminalizes an act that was innocent when it was committed.
2. It increases the punishment for a crime after the crime was committed.
3. It takes away a defense that was available to a defendant when the crime was committed.
C. Statutes that criminalize innocent acts after they're committed are the clearest example of ex post facto laws; they're also the rarest because legislatures practically never try it.
D. The ex post facto ban serves two major purposes:
1. One is to protect private individuals by ensuring that legislatures give them fair warning about what's criminal and that they can rely on that requirement.
2. The ban is directed at legislatures, preventing them from passing arbitrary (random choice or personal view) and vindictive legislation.

IV. Due process

A. According to the void-for-vagueness doctrine, the U.S. Supreme Court has decided that vague laws deny individuals their right to "due process." This right is protected by the Fifth Amendment in federal criminal justice and the Fourteenth Amendment in state criminal justice.
B. There are three clear arguments that uphold the void-for-vagueness doctrine:
1. Criminal punishment deprives individuals of life (capital punishment), liberty (imprisonment), or property (fines).
2. The Fifth and Fourteenth Amendments to the U.S. Constitution ban both federal and state governments from taking any person's "life, liberty, or property without due process of law."
3. Failure to warn private persons adequately of what the law forbids and/or allowing officials the chance to define arbitrarily what the law forbids denies individuals life, liberty, and/or property without due process of law.
C. The void-for-vagueness doctrine takes aim at two evils:
1. Void laws fail to give fair warning to individuals as to what the law prohibits.
2. They allow arbitrary and discriminatory criminal justice administration.
D. But what's fair notice?
1. The answer is not subjective; that is, it doesn't mean having to notify the defendant personally of what is a crime.
2. The answer is objective; that is, it's the kind of notice in which an ordinary person would know what they did was a crime.
E. Defining vagueness: The presumption of constitutionality requires challengers to prove the law is vague.

V. Equal protection of the laws

A. The Fourteenth Amendment to the U.S. Constitution commands that "no state shall deny to any person within its jurisdiction the equal protection of the laws."

B. Equal protection does not require the government to treat everybody exactly the same. A good example of this is ranking criminals as habitual offenders vs. first-time offenders.

C. Classifications based on race or any other immutable characteristics are held to "strict scrutiny."

D. Gender classifications stand somewhere between the strict scrutiny applied to race and the rational basis applied to most other classifications.

VI. The Bill of Rights bans defining certain kinds of behavior as criminal.

A. *Free speech* The First Amendment commands "Congress shall make no law . . . abridging the freedom of speech." The court has expanded the First Amendment in three ways:

1. The meaning of speech doesn't end with the spoken or written word; it also includes expressive conduct.

2. The court has expanded the amendment, applying it to the states since 1925.

3. The court has ruled that free speech is a fundamental right, one that enjoys preferred status.

4. Five categories of expression aren't protected by the First Amendment:

   a. Obscenity

   b. Profanity

   c. Libel and slander

   d. Fighting words

   e. Clear and present danger

B. *The right to privacy* Although you won't find the word privacy anywhere in the U.S. Constitution, the U.S. Supreme Court has decided there is a constitutional and fundamental right to privacy.

VII. Cruel and unusual punishment

A. The Eighth Amendment commands that "cruel and unusual punishments" shall not be "inflicted."

B. According to the Court, there are two kinds of cruel and unusual punishments:

1. *Barbaric punishments* are punishments that are considered no longer acceptable to civilized society.

2. Disproportionate punishments are punishments that do not fit the crime. The *principle of proportionality* is the idea that punishment should fit the crime. This was first applied in 1910.

   a. *Proportionality and the death penalty* A majority of the Court has consistently agreed that the proportionality principle applies to death penalty cases because "death is different."

   b. *Proportionality and the death penalty for the mentally retarded* According to the Supreme Court, executing anyone who proved the three elements in the American Association of Mental Retardation definition applied to them violated the ban on cruel and unusual punishment.

   c. *Proportionality and the death penalty for juveniles* By a 5–4 vote in 2005, the U.S. Supreme Court held that the Eighth and Fourteenth Amendments forbid the execution of offenders who were under the age of 18 when they committed their crimes.

   d. *Proportionality and imprisonment* Although there is a proportionality requirement in capital punishments, this does not extend to prison sentences. The U.S. Supreme Court has found the highly controversial three-strikes laws constitutional, even though the justices cannot agree on the reasons.

REVIEW QUESTIONS

1. Describe the difference between a pure democracy and a constitutional democracy.

2. List six limits on criminal law imposed by the U.S. and state constitutions.

3. List and describe three elements of an ex post facto law.

4. What are the two main purposes of ex post facto law bans?

5. Describe the void-for-vagueness doctrine and the two evils it aims to combat.

6. How do the courts answer the question, "What's fair notice?"

7. List and describe the two legal and one illegal way to classify particular groups of people.

8. Identify and describe five categories of expression that aren't protected by the First Amendment.

9. Define the "chilling effect."

10. What six amendments to the U.S. Constitution send a strong message that people have the right to be let alone by the government?

11. Identify and describe two forms of cruel and unusual punishment recognized by the Supreme Court.

12. What two elements need to exist to make a death penalty valid?

13. Describe the history of the principle of proportionality.

14. In practice, what crime is punishable by death even though no one gets killed?

15. Describe the three elements the American Association on Mental Retardation includes in its definition of mental retardation.

16. Identify and describe three reasons why the Supreme Court reversed its decision to execute retarded offenders.

17. What is the Supreme Court's holding on proportionality and the death penalty for juveniles?

18. Define the essence of three-strikes laws.

19. What views do supporters and opponents hold about three-strikes laws?

20. List and describe the three reasons why three-strikes laws became popular.

KEY TERMS

ex post facto laws, p. 49
void-for-vagueness doctrine,
   p. 50

void-for-overbreadth doctrine,
   p. 56
chilling effect, p. 56

right to privacy, p. 60
barbaric punishments, p. 64
principle of proportionality, p. 65

The General Principles of Criminal Liability: *Actus Reus*

MAIN POINTS

- The criminal act (*actus reus*) is one element that the prosecution has to prove beyond a reasonable doubt to convict individual defendants.
- Offenses that don't require *mens rea* almost always include an attendant circumstance element.
- Criminal acts are physical bodily movements; criminal conduct is the combination of *actus reus* triggered by *mens rea*.
- Criminal law demands that intention turns into action.
- Every crime has to include at least one voluntary act.
- Status (race, age, sex, sexual orientation, ethnicity) can never qualify as *actus reus*.
- Failures to act can be *actus reus* when there's a legal duty to act.
- Possession is *not* action; it's a passive condition that can qualify as a criminal act.

3

In 1964 Catherine ("Kitty") Genovese (inset) was stalked, raped, and killed during three attacks by Winston Moseley near her home in Kew Gardens, Queens, New York City (shown here). During the attacks, which spanned 30 minutes, 37 people either heard or witnessed part of the attacks, but did not assist Genovese and did no[t] call the police until well afte[r] Genovese had died. Did the bystanders have a legal duty to respond to Genovese's cries for help?

Did Mrs. Cogdon Voluntarily Kill Pat?

Mrs. Cogdon went to sleep. She dreamed that "the war was all around the house," that soldiers were in her daughter Pat's room, and that one soldier was on the bed attacking Pat. Mrs. Cogdon, still asleep, got up, left her bed, got an ax from a woodpile outside the house, entered Pat's room, and struck her two accurate forceful blows on the head with the blade of the axe, thus killing her.

(MORRIS 1951, 29)

Criminal law is primarily concerned with general rules for defining whether a crime has been committed. Recall, here, the Model Penal Code (MPC) (ALI 1985) definition of criminal liability from Chapter 1:

> *Conduct that unjustifiably and inexcusably inflicts or threatens substantial harm to individual or public interests. (§ 1.02(1)(a))*

This definition breaks down criminal liability into three general components that apply to all crimes:

1. Conduct that is
2. Without justification *and*
3. Without excuse

These components provide the basis for a three-step scheme for determining criminal liability. Let's put these steps in the form of questions. First and foremost, "Is there a criminal act of some kind?" If not, then there's no criminal liability. If there is, we proceed to the second question, "Is the act justified?" If it is, then there's no criminal liability. If not, then we advance to the third question, "Is the unjustified act nonetheless excused?" If yes, then there's no criminal liability. If not, then the defendant is guilty. This scheme applies whether it's the federal government or the government of the state, city, or town you live in; or whether it's the common law, a criminal code, or the MPC being analyzed.

This three-step analytical scheme requires that we look further into the general principles of criminal liability—*actus reus* (the criminal act), in this chapter, and *mens rea* (criminal intent) and causation, in Chapter 4. We examine the principle (defenses) of justification in Chapter 5 and the principle (defenses) of excuse in Chapter 6.

THE ELEMENTS OF CRIMINAL LIABILITY

The drafters of criminal codes have four building blocks at their disposal when they write the definitions of the thousands of crimes that make up the special part of their criminal law. These are the **elements of a crime** that the prosecution has to prove beyond a reasonable doubt to convict individual defendants of the crimes they're charged with committing:

1. Criminal act (*actus reus*)
2. Criminal intent (*mens rea*)
3. Concurrence
4. Attendant circumstances
5. Bad result (causing a criminal harm)

All crimes have to include, at a minimum, a criminal act (*actus reus* or "evil act"). The vast majority of minor crimes against public order and morals (the subject of Chapter 12) don't include either criminal intent (*mens rea*) or causing a bad result. But it's a rare crime that includes only *actus reus*. This is partly because without something more than an act, a criminal statute would almost certainly fail to pass the test of constitutionality (Chapter 2). For example, a criminal statute that made the simple act of "driving" a car a crime surely would be void for vagueness or for overbreadth; a ban on "driving while intoxicated" just as surely would not (Dubber 2002, 44). That's why most offenses that don't require a *mens rea* include what we call an **attendant circumstance** element. This element isn't an act, an intention, or a result; rather, it's a "circumstance" connected to an act, an intent, and/or a result. In our driving example, "while intoxicated" is the circumstantial element.

Serious crimes, such as murder (Chapter 9), sexual assault (Chapter 10), robbery (Chapter 11), and burglary (Chapter 11), include both *actus reus* and a second element, the mental attitudes included in what's called a *mens rea* ("evil mind"). You'll learn about *mens rea* in Chapter 4. Crimes consisting of a criminal act and a *mens rea* have a third element called **concurrence,** meaning some kind of mental state has to trigger the criminal act. Although concurrence is a critical element that you have to know exists, you won't read much about it as an element in crimes because it's practically never a problem proving it in real cases.

We call crimes requiring a criminal act triggered by criminal intent **conduct crimes.** Let's look at burglary as an example of a criminal conduct crime. It consists of the *actus reus* of breaking and entering a house, triggered by the *mens rea* of, say, stealing an iPod once inside the house. The crime of burglary is complete whether or not the burglar actually steals the iPod. So the crime of burglary is criminal conduct

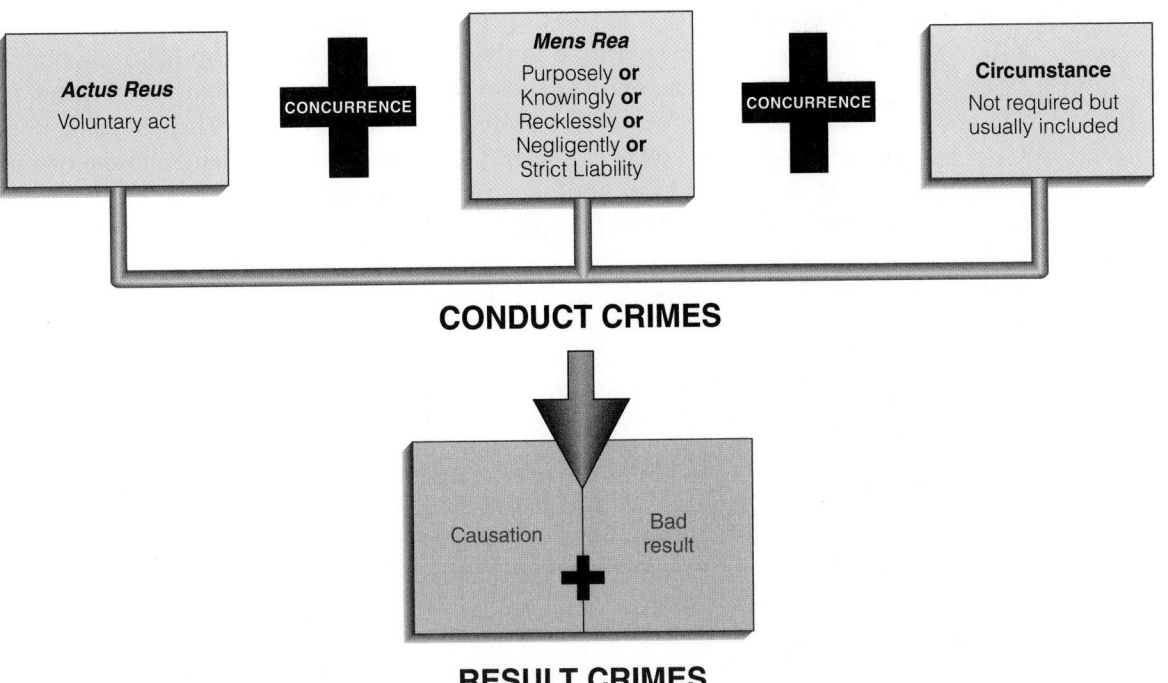

Elements of Criminal Conduct Crimes

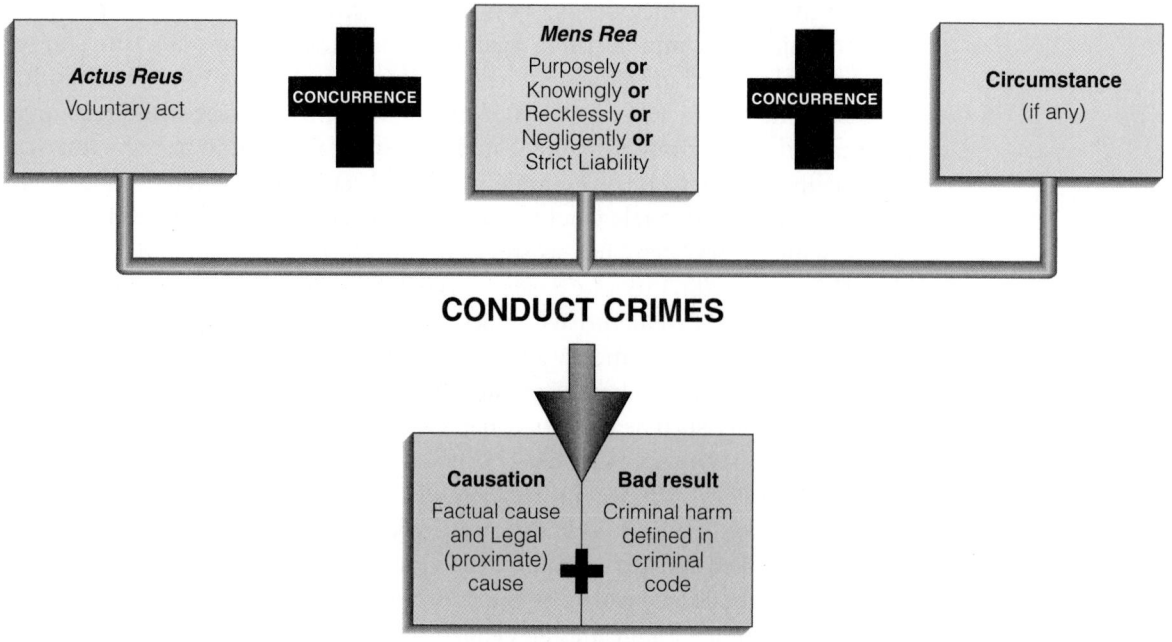

Elements of Bad Result Crimes

whether or not it causes any harm beyond the conduct itself. It's very important that you don't confuse criminal act with criminal conduct as we use these terms in the book. Criminal acts are voluntary physical bodily movements (Holmes 1963, 45–47); criminal conduct is the *actus reus* triggered by a *mens rea*.

Some serious crimes include all five elements; in addition to (1) a voluntary act, (2) the mental element, and (3) circumstantial elements, they include (4) causation (5) of criminal harm. We call these crimes **bad result crimes.** There are a number of these crimes (LaFave 2003b, 1:464–65), but the most prominent, and the one most discussed in this and most books, is *criminal homicide*—defined as criminal conduct that causes someone's death (Chapter 9). For example, murder consists of (1) a criminal act (it can be any act—shooting, stabbing, running down with a car, beating with a baseball bat), (2) triggered by the (3) intent to kill, (4) that causes (5) someone's death.

ACTUS REUS: THE FIRST PRINCIPLE OF LIABILITY

> No one should be punished except for something she does. She shouldn't be punished for what wasn't done at all; she shouldn't be punished for what someone else does; she shouldn't be punished for being the sort of person she is, unless it is up to her whether or not she is a person of that sort. She shouldn't be punished for being blond or short, for example, because it isn't up to her whether she is blond or short. Our conduct is what justifies punishing us. (Corrado 1994, 1529)

These are common expressions that capture the idea of the first principle of criminal liability. So it's not a crime to wish your cheating boyfriend would die; to fantasize about nonconsensual sex with the person sitting next to you in your criminal law class;

or to think about taking your roommate's wallet when he's not looking. "Thoughts are free," said a medieval judge.

Imagine a statute that makes it a crime merely to intend to kill another person. Why does such a statute strike us as absurd? Here are three reasons. First, it's impossible to prove a mental attitude by itself. In the words of a medieval judge, "The thought of man is not triable, for the devil himself knoweth not the thought of man." Second, a mental attitude by itself doesn't hurt anybody. Although the moral law may condemn you if you think about committing crimes, and religion may call thoughts sins ("I have sinned exceedingly in thought, word, and deed"), the criminal law demands conduct—a mental attitude that turns into action. So punishing the mere intent to kill (even if we could prove it) misses the harm the statute targets—another's death (Morris 1976, chap. 1).

A third problem with punishing a state of mind is that it's terribly hard to separate daydreaming and fantasy from intent. The angry thought, "I'll kill you for that!" rarely turns into actual killing (or for that matter even an attempt to kill; discussed in Chapter 8), because it's almost always just a spur of the moment way of saying, "I'm really angry." Punishment has to wait for enough action to prove the speaker really intends to commit a crime (Chapter 8).

Punishing thoughts stretches the reach of the criminal law too far when it puts within its grasp a "mental state that the accused might be too irresolute even to begin to translate into action." The bottom line: We don't punish thoughts because it's impractical, inequitable, and unjust (Williams 1961, 1–2). Now you know why the first principle of criminal liability is the requirement of an act. This requirement is as old as our law. Long before there was a principle of *mens rea*, there was the requirement of a criminal act.

The requirement that attitudes have to turn into deeds is called **manifest criminality.** Manifest criminality leaves no doubt about the criminal nature of the act. The modern phrase "caught red-handed" comes from the ancient idea of manifest criminality. Then it meant catching murderers with the blood still on their hands; now, it means catching someone in the act of wrongdoing. For example, if bank customers see several people enter the bank, draw guns, threaten to shoot if the tellers don't hand over money, take the money the tellers give them, and leave the bank with the money, their criminality—the *actus reus* and the *mens rea* of robbery—is manifest (Fletcher 1978, 115–16).

The *actus reus* requirement serves several purposes. First, it helps to prove the *mens rea*. We can't observe states of mind; we can only infer them from actions. Second, it reserves the harsh sanction of the criminal law for cases of actual danger. Third, it protects the privacy of individuals. The law doesn't have to pry into the thoughts of individuals unless the thinker crosses "the threshold of manifest criminality." Many axioms illustrate the *actus reus* principle: "Thoughts are free." "We're punished for what we do, not for who we are." "Criminal punishment depends on conduct, not status." "We're punished for what we've done, not for what we might do." Although simple to state as a general rule, much in the principle of *actus reus* complicates its apparent simplicity (Fletcher 1978, 117). We'll examine four of these: the requirement that the act be *voluntary*; status or condition and the Constitution; criminal omissions; and criminal possession.

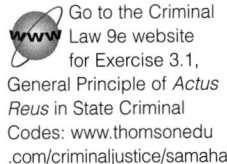 Go to the Criminal Law 9e website for Exercise 3.1, General Principle of *Actus Reus* in State Criminal Codes: www.thomsonedu .com/criminaljustice/samaha.

Voluntary Acts

Only *voluntary* acts qualify as *actus reus*. In the words of the great justice and legal philosopher Oliver Wendell Holmes, "An act . . . is a muscular contraction, and something more. . . . The contraction of muscles must be willed" (Holmes 1963, 46–47). The prestigious American Law Institute's Model Penal Code's (MPC) widely adopted definition of *actus reus* provides: "A person is not guilty of an offense unless his liability is based on conduct that includes a *voluntary* act . . ." (emphasis added) (ALI 1985, ß 2.01).

So *actus reus* consists of two requirements: bodily movements, but only *voluntary* bodily movements. Why the voluntary requirement? The rationale goes like this:

1. Criminal law punishes people.

2. We can only punish people we can blame.

3. We can only blame people who are responsible for their acts.

4. People are only responsible for their voluntary acts.

The MPC, and many state criminal codes, define voluntary only indirectly—that is, they list what are *in*voluntary acts. Most commonly, the list includes reflexes or convulsions; movements during sleep (sleepwalking) or unconsciousness (automatism); and actions under hypnosis. The MPC adds a fourth catchall category that (sort of) defines voluntary acts: "a bodily movement that otherwise is not a product of the effort or determination of the actor, either conscious or habitual" (ALI 1985 ß 2.01(2)).

Notice that according to the MPC, not *all* "bodily movements" have to be voluntary; conduct only has to "*include* a voluntary act." So as long as there's *one* voluntary act, other acts surrounding the crime may be *involuntary*. For example, a person who's subject to frequent fainting spells voluntarily drives a car; he faints while he's driving, loses control of the car, and hits a pedestrian. The driver's voluntary act is the one that counts; the fainting spell doesn't relieve the driver of criminal liability (*Brown v. State* 1997, 284). Most statutes follow the MPC's one-voluntary-act-is-enough definition.

But what if after a defendant's voluntary act someone else's act triggers an involuntary act of that defendant? There was some evidence of that in *Brown v. State* (the case excerpt included here). Aaron Brown pulled a gun, which he admitted was a voluntary act. Then, his friend, Ryan Coleman, bumped into Brown; the gun fired and killed Joseph Caraballo. The majority of the court found there was enough evidence to require the trial judge to give a voluntary act instruction. The dissent disagreed.

C A S E | *Was the Shooting Accidental?*

Brown v. State
955 S.W.2d 276 (Tex. 1997)

HISTORY

Alfred Brown, Defendant, was convicted in the 268th Judicial District Court, Fort Bend County, of murder. Defendant appealed. The Houston Court of Appeals reversed and remanded. State petitioned for discretionary review. The Court of Criminal Appeals, Overstreet, J., held that defendant was entitled to jury charge on voluntariness of his acts. Decision of Court of Appeals affirmed.

OVERSTREET, J.

FACTS

On the evening of July 17, 1992, Alfred Brown, appellant, was drinking beer and talking with friends in the parking lot of an apartment complex. Brown was involved in an altercation with James McLean, an individual with whom he had an encounter one week prior, in which McLean and some other individuals had beaten Brown. Brown testified that following the altercation on the day in question, he obtained a .25 caliber handgun in order to protect himself and his friends from McLean and his associates, who were known to possess and discharge firearms in the vicinity of the apartment complex.

Brown, who is right-handed, testified that he held the handgun in his left hand because of a debilitating injury to his right hand. Brown testified that during the course of the events in question, the handgun accidentally fired when he was bumped from behind by another person, Coleman, while raising the handgun.

Coleman testified that he bumped Brown and the handgun fired. Brown testified that the shot that fatally wounded the victim, Joseph Caraballo, an acquaintance and associate of Brown, was fired accidentally. The victim was not one of the persons Brown was at odds with, but a person aligned with Brown.

OPINION

Jury Instruction

Appellant requested that the jury charge include a required finding of voluntariness with regard to the commission of the offense. The trial court denied appellant's request. . . .

APPELLANT'S REQUESTED CHARGE Appellant's requested jury charge, denied by the trial court, included a required finding of voluntariness. Specifically, appellant stated:

> . . . You are instructed that a person commits an offense only if he voluntarily engages in conduct, including an act, omission, or possession; conduct is not rendered involuntary merely because a person did not intend the results of his conduct. Therefore, if you believe from the evidence beyond a reasonable doubt that on the occasion in question the Defendant, Alfred Brown, did cause the death of Joseph Caraballo by shooting him with a gun as alleged in the indictment, but you further believe from the evidence or have a reasonable doubt thereof that the shooting was the result of an accidental discharge of the gun and was not the voluntary act or conduct of the Defendant, you will acquit the Defendant and say by your verdict not guilty.

Evidentiary Sufficiency

Appellant testified at trial that the handgun in his possession accidentally discharged after he was bumped from behind by Ryan Coleman. Coleman also testified at trial that his bumping appellant precipitated the discharge of the gun and that idiosyncrasies of the handgun may have also allowed its discharge. . . .

. . . When a defensive theory is raised by evidence from any source and a charge is properly requested, it must be submitted to the jury. This rule is designed to insure that the jury, not the judge, will decide the relative credibility of the evidence. When a judge refuses to give an instruction on a defensive issue because the evidence supporting it is weak or unbelievable, he effectively substitutes his judgment on the weight of the evidence for that of the jury. The weight of the evidence in support of an instruction is immaterial.

. . . In the instant case, Coleman's corroborating testimony simply added to the threshold evidentiary requirements consistent with this Court's holdings in *George* and the cases cited therein. Thus, "if the issue is raised by the evidence, a jury may be charged that a defendant should be acquitted if there is reasonable doubt as to whether he voluntarily engaged in the conduct of which he is accused."

. . . When such conduct also includes a bodily movement of the accused sufficient for the gun to discharge a bullet [and something more] . . .—such as precipitation by another individual . . .—a jury . . . [must] be charged on the matter of whether the accused voluntarily engaged in the conduct with which he is charged." The evidence admitted at appellant's trial satisfies this requirement for an affirmative jury charge on voluntariness.

. . . Section 6.01(a) of the Texas Penal Code states that a person commits an offense only if he engages in voluntary conduct, including an act, an omission, or possession. Only if the evidence raises reasonable doubt that the defendant voluntarily engaged in the conduct charged should the jury be instructed to acquit. "Voluntariness," within the meaning of section 6.01(a), refers only to one's physical bodily movements. While the defense of accident is no longer present in the penal code, this Court has long held that homicide that is not the result of voluntary conduct is not to be criminally punished. . . .

We hold that if the admitted evidence raises the issue of the conduct of the actor not being voluntary, then the jury shall be charged, when requested, on the issue of voluntariness. The trial court did not grant appellant's request and the court of appeals correctly reversed the trial court. We hereby affirm the decision of the court of appeals.

DISSENT

PRICE, J.

The inquiry begins with the literal text of the statute. We start here because the literal text of the statute is the law—it is the version approved and adopted by the legislators. It is the only definitive evidence of the legislators' intent. Furthermore, we are constitutionally required to follow the text adopted by the Legislature. Thus, if the meaning of the literal text, when read applying the canons of construction, is plain and unambiguous, we give effect to that plain meaning. There is, necessarily, an exception to this rule: when literal application of a statute leads to absurd consequences or results in ambiguity, then and only then, may a court interpret a statute by using extra textual sources. . . .

. . . With the foregoing in mind, I turn to Section 6.01(a). Section 6.01(a) provides in part: "A person commits an offense only if he voluntarily engages in conduct, including an act, an omission or possession." Definitions for "act" and "conduct" are set out in Section 1.07 of the Penal Code. "Conduct" means an act or an omission plus its accompanying mental state, and "act" means a bodily movement, whether voluntary or involuntary. The enacted Penal Code does not contain a definition of "voluntary act." However, the 1970 proposed Code did. It defined a "voluntary act" as "a bodily movement performed consciously as a result of effort or determination."

. . . For conduct to support criminal responsibility, the conduct must "include a voluntary act . . . so that, for example, a drunk driver charged with involuntary manslaughter may not successfully defend with the argument he fell asleep before the collision since his conduct included the voluntary act of starting up and driving the car." Interestingly, these comments suggest that one voluntary act—regardless of subsequent acts—may form a basis for criminal responsibility. . . .

. . . Although a voluntary act is an absolute requirement for criminal liability, it does not follow that every act up to the moment that the harm is caused must be voluntary. This concept is best demonstrated by an example: A who is subject to frequent fainting spells voluntarily drives a car; while driving he faints, loses control of the vehicle and injures a pedestrian; A would be criminally responsible. Here, A's voluntary act consists of driving the car, and if the necessary mental state can be established as of the time he entered the car, it is enough to find A guilty of a crime.

Section 6.01(a) functions as a statutory failsafe. Due process guarantees that criminal liability be predicated on at least one voluntary act. In all criminal prosecutions the State must prove that the defendant committed at least one voluntary act—voluntary conduct is an implied element of every crime. Because it is an implied element, the State is not required to allege it in the charging instrument. For most offenses, proof of a voluntary act, although a separate component, is achieved by proving the other elements of the offense. . . .

. . . I believe the trial court properly denied appellant's request for an affirmative submission on voluntary conduct. I would reverse the court of appeals and affirm the trial court. Because the majority does not, I must dissent.

Questions

1. State the facts relevant to deciding whether Aaron Brown "voluntarily" shot Joseph Caraballo.

2. State the majority's definition of "voluntary act."

3. Summarize the majority's reasons for holding that the trial judge was required to instruct the jury on voluntary act.

4. Summarize the dissent's reasons for dissenting.

5. Which decision do you agree with? Back up your answer.

EXPLORING FURTHER

Voluntary Acts

1. Was Killing Her Daughter a Voluntary Act?

King v. Cogdon (Morris 1951, 29)

FACTS Mrs. Cogdon worried unduly about her daughter Pat. She told how, on the night before her daughter's death, she had dreamed that their house was full of spiders and that these spiders were crawling all over Pat. In her sleep, Mrs. Cogdon left the bed she shared with her husband, went into Pat's room, and awakened to find herself violently brushing at Pat's face, presumably to remove the spiders. This woke Pat. Mrs. Cogdon told her she was just tucking her in. At the trial, she testified that she still believed, as she had been told, that the occupants of a nearby house bred spiders as a hobby, preparing nests for them behind the pictures on their walls. It was these spiders which in her dreams had invaded their home and attacked Pat.

There had also been a previous dream in which ghosts had sat at the end of Mrs. Cogdon's bed and she had said to them, "Well, you have come to take Pattie." It does not seem fanciful to accept the psychological explanation of these spiders and ghosts as the projections of Mrs. Cogdon's subconscious hostility toward her daughter; a hostility which was itself rooted in Mrs. Cogdon's own early life and marital relationship.

The morning after the spider dream, she told her doctor of it. He gave her a sedative and, because of the dream and certain previous difficulties she had reported, discussed the possibility of psychiatric treatment.

That evening, while Pat was having a bath before going to bed, Mrs. Cogdon went into her room, put a hot water bottle in the bed, turned back the bedclothes, and placed a glass of hot milk beside the bed ready for Pat. She then went to bed herself. There was some desultory conversation between them about the war in Korea, and just before she put out her light, Pat called out to her mother, "Mum, don't be so silly worrying there about the war, it's not on our front doorstep yet."

Mrs. Cogdon went to sleep. She dreamed that "the war was all around the house," that soldiers were in Pat's room, and that one soldier was on the bed attacking Pat. This was all of the dream she could later recapture. Her first "waking" memory was of running from Pat's room, out of the house to the home of her sister who lived next door. When her sister opened the front door, Mrs. Cogdon fell into her arms, crying "I think I've hurt Pattie." In fact, Mrs. Cogdon had, in her somnambulistic state, left her bed, fetched an axe from the woodheap, entered Pat's room, and struck her two accurate forceful blows on the head with the blade of the axe, thus killing her.

At Mrs. Cogdon's trial for murder, Mr. Cogdon testified that, "I don't think a mother could have thought any more of her daughter. I think she absolutely adored her." On the conscious level, at least, there was no reason to doubt Mrs. Cogdon's deep attachment to her daughter. Mrs. Cogdon pleaded not guilty. Was she guilty?

DECISION Mrs. Cogdon's story was supported by the evidence of her physician, a psychiatrist, and a psychologist. The jury believed Mrs. Cogdon. The jury concluded that Mrs. Cogdon's account of her mental state at the time of the killing, and the unanimous support given to it by the medical and psychological evidence, completely rebutted the presumption that Mrs. Cogdon intended the natural consequences of her acts. [She didn't plead the insanity defense "because the experts agreed that Mrs. Cogdon was not psychotic." [See "Insanity" in Chapter 6.] The jury acquitted her because "the act of killing itself was not, in law, regarded as her act at all."

2. Were His Acts Committed During an Epileptic Seizure Voluntary?

People v. Decina, 138 N.E.2d 799 (N.Y.1956)

FACTS Emil Decina suffered an epileptic seizure while driving his car. During the seizure, his car ran up over the curb and killed four children walking on the sidewalk. Was the killing an "involuntary act" because it occurred during the seizure?

DECISION The court said no:

> This defendant knew he was subject to epileptic attacks at any time. He also knew that a moving vehicle uncontrolled on a public highway is a highly dangerous instrumentality capable of unrestrained destruction. With this knowledge, and without anyone accompanying him, he deliberately took a chance by making a conscious choice of a course of action, in disregard of the consequences which he knew might follow from his conscious act, which in this case did ensue.

3. Were His Acts Following Exposure to Agent Orange Voluntary?

State v. Jerrett, 307 S.E.2d 339 (1983)

FACTS Bruce Jerrett terrorized Dallas and Edith Parsons—he robbed them, killed Dallas, and kidnapped Edith. At trial, Jerrett testified that he could remember nothing of what happened until he was arrested, and that he had suffered previous blackouts following exposure to Agent Orange during military service in Vietnam. The trial judge refused to instruct the jury on the defense of automatism. Did he act voluntarily?

DECISION The North Carolina Supreme Court reversed and ordered a new trial.

> Where a person commits an act without being conscious thereof, the act is not a criminal act even though it would be a crime if it had been committed by a person who was conscious. . . .
>
> [In this case,] there was corroborating evidence tending to support the defense of unconsciousness. . . . Defendant's very peculiar actions in permitting the kidnapped victim to repeatedly ignore his commands and finally lead him docilely into the presence and custody of a police officer lends credence to his defense of unconsciousness.
>
> We therefore hold that the trial judge should have instructed the jury on the defense of unconsciousness.

4. Are Any of the Following Voluntary Acts?

a. Drowsy drivers who fall asleep while they're driving and hit and kill someone while they're asleep.

b. Drunk drivers who are so intoxicated they're not in control when they hit and kill someone.

c. Drivers with dangerously high blood pressure who suffer strokes while they're driving and kill someone while the stroke has incapacitated them.

Examples 4a–c are examples of what we might call voluntarily induced involuntary acts. In all three examples, the drivers voluntarily drove their cars, creating a risk they could injure or kill someone. In all three examples, involuntary acts followed that killed someone. Should we stretch the meaning of voluntary to include them within the grasp of the voluntary act requirement using the MPC's "conduct including a voluntary act" definition? Why should we punish them? Because they deserve it? Because it might deter people with these risky conditions from driving? Because it will incapacitate them?

 Go to the Criminal Law 9e website to find the full text of the Exploring Further excerpts: www.thomsonedu.com/criminaljustice/samaha.

Status

Action refers to what we *do*; **status** (or condition) denotes who we *are*. Most statuses or conditions don't qualify as *actus reus*. Status can arise in two ways. Sometimes, it results from prior voluntary acts—methamphetamine addicts voluntarily used methamphetamine the first time and alcoholics voluntarily took their first drink. Other conditions result from no act at all. The most obvious examples are the characteristics we're born with: sex, age, sexual orientation, race, and ethnicity.

ACTUS REUS AND THE U.S. CONSTITUTION

It's clear that, according to the general principle of *actus reus*, every crime has to include at least one voluntary act, but is *actus reus* a constitutional command? Twice during the 1960s, the U.S. Supreme Court considered this question. In *Robinson v. California* (1962), Lawrence Robinson was convicted and sentenced to a mandatory 90 days in jail for violating a California statute making it a misdemeanor "to be addicted to" narcotics. Five justices agreed that punishing Robinson *solely* for his addiction to heroin was cruel and unusual punishment (Chapter 2). The constitutional ban on status crimes was expressed in various ways: The California statute created a crime of *personal condition*, punishing Robinson for who he was (heroin addict) not for what he did. The statute punished the *sickness* of heroin addiction—"even one day in prison would be a cruel and unusual punishment for the 'crime' of having a common cold" (*Robinson v. California* 1962, 667); the statute punished a *condition* that may be "contracted innocently and involuntarily" (667).

The decision that legislatures can't make status or personal condition by itself a crime brought into question the constitutionality of many old status crimes, such as being a prostitute, a drunkard, or a disorderly person, if the statutes didn't include the requirement of some act in addition to the condition. That's where *Powell v. Texas* (1968) comes in.

On December 19, 1966, Leroy Powell was arrested and charged with being found in a state of intoxication in a public place. He was tried, found guilty, and fined $50. Powell's story, as told in the brief he filed in the U.S. Supreme Court, is

> typical of the stories of many indigent Americans who are afflicted with the disease of chronic alcoholism. At the time of his trial he was 66 years old with a history of drinking dating back to 1925. He estimated he has been arrested for being drunk approximately 100 times. In Travis County alone, the records reflect 73 arrests since 1949.
>
> Powell drinks every day and gets drunk about once each week. He earns an average of $12.00 a week working in a tavern shining shoes. Instead of using his meager earnings to purchase groceries or support his family, he uses his $12.00 of weekly earnings to purchase more liquor. Indeed, the total fines imposed on Powell for being drunk in 1966 exceed 20% of his total earnings.
>
> He remembers at least two jobs he has lost because of his drinking problem and readily admits that he has no control of his drinking. In fact, he was again arrested for being drunk pending the appeal of this case . . . from the Corporation Court to the County Court at Law.
>
> In short, Powell is an alcoholic who would like to be medically treated but is without sufficient financial resources to obtain such help. And given the ability to choose, he would not voluntarily appear in public in a state of intoxication. (*Powell v. Texas* 1967, Brief for Appellant, 3–4)

Powell's argument to the U.S. Supreme Court was that "the disease of chronic alcoholism" destroyed "his will power to resist drinking and appearing drunk in public." In other words, there was no *actus reus*, defined as a voluntary act. So the statute, which "criminally punishes an ill person for conduct" he can't control, violates the ban on cruel and unusual punishment (6).

In its brief, Texas relied on Powell's own witness, a nationally recognized psychiatrist, author, and lecturer on alcoholism, to make its own case that Powell's being drunk in public was a voluntary act.

Q: " . . . At the time that he takes the first drink from a sober condition, would you say that is a voluntary exercise of his will?

A: Yes. . . . These individuals have a compulsion, and this compulsion, while not completely overpowering, is a very strong influence, an exceedingly strong influence, and this compulsion coupled with the firm belief in their mind that they are going to be able to handle it from now on causes their judgment to be somewhat clouded. (*Powell v. Texas* 1968, Brief for Appellee, 8)

From this and other expert testimony, Texas argued that although it's very tough, chronic alcoholics can become "chronic abstainers, although perhaps not moderate drinkers" (8). In other words, with a lot of effort, they can stop themselves from taking the first, but not the second, drink of a "drinking bout." You might want to think about it this way: "barely" voluntary is good enough.

The U.S. Supreme Court's opinions reflected contrasting views on the critical question of how far the U.S. Constitution goes into the principle of *actus reus*. A plurality of four justices answered firmly, not one bit further than *Robinson v. California*. The plurality first distinguished Leroy Powell from Lawrence Robinson:

Powell was convicted, not for being a chronic alcoholic, but for being in public while drunk on a particular occasion. The State of Texas thus has not sought to punish a mere status, as California did in *Robinson*; nor has it attempted to regulate Powell's behavior in the privacy of his own home. Rather, it has imposed upon Powell a criminal sanction for public behavior which may create substantial health and safety hazards, both for Powell and for members of the general public, and which offends the moral and esthetic sensibilities of a large segment of the community. This seems a far cry from convicting one for being an addict, being a chronic alcoholic, being mentally ill, or a leper. (532)

After making clear that the Constitution bans only pure status as a basis for criminal liability, the plurality concluded:

Robinson so viewed brings this Court but a very small way into the substantive criminal law. And unless *Robinson* is so viewed it is difficult to see any limiting principle that would serve to prevent this Court from becoming, under the aegis of the Cruel and Unusual Punishment Clause, the ultimate arbiter of the standards of criminal responsibility, in diverse areas of the criminal law, throughout the country. (533)

Finally, the plurality invoked federalism to support its hands-off position regarding the principles of criminal liability:

We cannot cast aside the centuries-long evolution of the collection of interlocking and overlapping concepts which the common law has utilized to assess the moral accountability of an individual for his antisocial deeds. The doctrines of actus reus, mens rea, insanity, mistake, justification, and duress have historically provided the tools for a constantly shifting adjustment of the tension between the evolving aims of the criminal law and changing religious, moral, philosophical, and medical views of the nature of man. This process of adjustment has always been thought to be the province of the States. (535–36)

Justice White wrote a separate opinion concurring in the plurality's judgment, because "Powell showed nothing more than that he was to some degree compelled to drink and that he was drunk at the time of his arrest. He made no showing that he was unable to stay off the streets on the night in question" (553–54).

Justice White argued that *Robinson* would apply, however, if Powell had shown he couldn't stay off the streets:

If it cannot be a crime to have an irresistible compulsion to use narcotics (*Robinson*), I do not see how it can constitutionally be a crime to yield to such a compulsion. Punishing an addict for using drugs convicts for addiction under a different name. Distinguishing between the two crimes is like forbidding criminal conviction for being sick with flu or epilepsy but permitting punishment for running a fever or having a convulsion. Unless

Robinson is to be abandoned, the use of narcotics by an addict must be beyond the reach of the criminal law. Similarly, the chronic alcoholic with an irresistible urge to consume alcohol should not be punishable for drinking or for being drunk. (548–49)

Four dissenting justices were eager to bring the Court, by means of the U.S. Constitution, fully into the business of supervising the general principles of criminal liability. Writing for the dissent, Justice Fortas wrote:

> Powell is charged with a crime composed of two elements—being intoxicated and being found in a public place while in that condition. The crime, so defined, differs from that in *Robinson*. The statute covers more than a mere status. But the essential constitutional defect here is the same as in *Robinson*, for in both cases the particular defendant was accused of being in a condition which he had no capacity to change or avoid. . . . Powell was powerless to avoid drinking; that having taken his first drink, he had "an uncontrollable compulsion to drink" to the point of intoxication; and that, once intoxicated, he could not prevent himself from appearing in public places. (567–68)

Most criminal law books, and I'm sure most criminal law classes, spend lots of time and space on the Constitution and the general principles of criminal liability. At the time the cases were decided, there was great hope, and great fear (depending on your point of view), that an "activist" Supreme Court would use the "cruel and unusual punishment" ban and other provisions in the U.S. Constitution to write a constitutional doctrine of criminal liability and responsibility. It never happened. Real cases in real courts since *Powell* haven't tried to bring the Constitution further into the principles of criminal liability than *Robinson* brought it in 1962. It's left in the hands of legislatures to adopt general principles of liability and elements of specific crimes in criminal codes; and, it's left in the hands of courts to interpret and apply the code's provisions in decisions involving individual defendants.

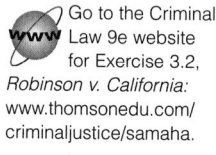 Go to the Criminal Law 9e website for Exercise 3.2, *Robinson v. California:* www.thomsonedu.com/ criminaljustice/samaha.

 OMISSIONS

We support punishment for people who rape, murder, and rob because their actions caused harm. But what about people who stand by and do nothing while bad things are happening around them? As Professor George Fletcher describes these people, "They get caught in a situation in which they falter. Someone needs help and they cannot bring themselves to render it." Can these failures to act (omissions) satisfy the *actus reus* requirement? Yes, but only when it's outrageous to fail to do something to help someone in danger.

There are two kinds of criminal failure to act (**criminal omission**). One is the simple failure to act, usually the **failure to report** something required by law, such as reporting an accident or child abuse, filing an income tax return, registering a firearm, or notifying sexual partners of positive HIV status. The other type of omission is the **failure to intervene** to prevent injuries and death to persons or the damage and destruction of property.

Failures to report or intervene are criminal omissions only if defendants had a **legal duty** (a duty enforced by law), not just a moral duty, to act. Legal duty is an attendant circumstance element that the prosecution has to prove beyond a reasonable doubt.

Legal duties are created in three ways:

1. Statutes

2. Contracts

3. Special relationships

Statutes are the basis for most legal duties to report—for example, the duty to file income tax returns, report accidents and child abuse, and register firearms. Individuals can also contract to perform duties; for example, law enforcement officers agree to "protect and serve." Failure to perform those duties can create criminal liability. The main special relationships are the parent-child relationship, the doctor-patient relationship, the employer-employee relationship, the carrier-passenger relationship, and, in some states, the husband-wife relationship.

Failure to perform moral duties (enforced by conscience, religion, and social norms) doesn't qualify as a criminal omission. According to Professors Wayne LaFave and Austin Scott (1986):

> Generally one has no legal duty to aid another person in peril, even when that aid can be rendered without danger or inconvenience to himself. He need not shout a warning to a blind man headed for a precipice or to an absent-minded one walking into a gunpowder room with a lighted candle in hand. He need not pull a neighbor's baby out of a pool of water or rescue an unconscious person stretched across the railroad tracks, though the baby is drowning or the whistle of the approaching train is heard in the distance. A doctor is not legally bound to answer a desperate call from the frantic parents of a sick child, at least if it is not one of his regular patients. A moral duty to take affirmative action is not enough to impose a legal duty to do so. But there are situations which do give rise to legal duties. (203)

There are two approaches to defining a legal duty to rescue strangers or call for help. One is the **"Good Samaritan" doctrine**, which "imposes a legal duty to render or summon aid for imperiled strangers." Only a few jurisdictions follow the Good Samaritan approach. Nearly all follow the approach of the **American bystander rule** (*State v. Kuntz* 2000, 951). According to the bystander rule, there's no legal duty to rescue or summon help for someone who's in danger, even if the bystander risks nothing by helping. So it might be a revolting breach of the *moral law* for an Olympic swimmer to stand by and watch a kid drown, without so much as even placing a 911 call on her cell phone, but the *criminal law* demands nothing from her.

Limiting criminal omissions to the failure to perform legal duties is based on three assumptions: First, individual conscience, peer pressure, and other informal mechanisms condemn and prevent behavior more effectively than criminal prosecution. Second, prosecuting omissions puts too much of a burden on an already overburdened criminal justice system. Third, criminal law can't force "Good Samaritans" to help people in need. The Pennsylvania Superior Court upheld a conviction for failure to act in *Commonwealth v. Pestinakas*.

C A S E   *Did They Owe Mr. Kly a Legal Duty?*

Commonwealth v. Pestinakas
617 A.2d 1339 (1992, Pa.Sup.)

HISTORY

Walter Pestinakas and Helen Pestinakas were convicted of third-degree murder in the Court of Common Pleas, Criminal Division, Lackawanna County. Each was sentenced to serve a term of imprisonment for not less than five (5) years or more than ten (10) years. Defendants

appealed. The Superior Court, Nos. 375 and 395 Philadelphia 1989, affirmed.

WIEAND, J.

FACTS

Joseph Kly met Walter and Helen Pestinakas in the latter part of 1981 when Kly consulted them about pre-arranging his funeral. In March, 1982, Kly, who had been living with a stepson, was hospitalized and diagnosed as suffering from Zenker's diverticulum, a weakness in the walls of the esophagus, which caused him to have trouble swallowing food. In the hospital, Kly was given food which he was able to swallow and, as a result, regained some of the weight which he had lost. When he was about to be discharged, he expressed a desire not to return to his stepson's home and sent word to The Pestinakases that he wanted to speak with them. As a consequence, arrangements were made for The Pestinakases to care for Kly in their home on Main Street in Scranton, Lackawanna County.

Kly was discharged from the hospital on April 12, 1982. When The Pestinakases came for him on that day they were instructed by medical personnel regarding the care which was required for Kly and were given a prescription to have filled for him. Arrangements were also made for a visiting nurse to come to The Pestinakases' home to administer vitamin B-12 supplements to Kly. The Pestinakases agreed orally to follow the medical instructions and to supply Kly with food, shelter, care and the medicine which he required.

According to the evidence, the prescription was never filled, and the visiting nurse was told by The Pestinakases that Kly did not want the vitamin supplement shots and that her services, therefore, were not required. Instead of giving Kly a room in their home, The Pestinakases removed him to a rural part of Lackawanna County, where they placed him in the enclosed porch of a building, which they owned, known as the Stage Coach Inn. This porch was approximately nine feet by thirty feet, with no insulation, no refrigeration, no bathroom, no sink and no telephone. The walls contained cracks which exposed the room to outside weather conditions.

Kly's predicament was compounded by The Pestinakases' affirmative efforts to conceal his whereabouts. Thus, they gave misleading information in response to inquiries, telling members of Kly's family that they did not know where he had gone and others that he was living in their home.

After Kly was discharged from the hospital, The Pestinakases took Kly to the bank and had their names added to his savings account. Later, Kly's money was transferred into an account in the names of Kly or Helen Pestinakas, pursuant to which moneys could be withdrawn without Kly's signature. Bank records reveal that from May, 1982, to July, 1983, The Pestinakases withdrew amounts roughly consistent with the three hundred ($300) dollars per month which Kly had agreed to pay for his care.

Beginning in August 1983, and continuing until Kly's death in November 1984, however, The Pestinakases withdrew much larger sums so that when Kly died, a balance of only fifty-five ($55) dollars remained. In the interim, The Pestinakases had withdrawn in excess of thirty thousand ($30,000) dollars.

On the afternoon of November 15, 1984, when police and an ambulance crew arrived in response to a call by The Pestinakases, Kly's dead body appeared emaciated, with his ribs and sternum greatly pronounced. Mrs.

Pestinakas told police that she and her husband had taken care of Kly for three hundred ($300) dollars per month and that she had given him cookies and orange juice at 11:30 A.M. on the morning of his death. A subsequent autopsy, however, revealed that Kly had been dead at that time and may have been dead for as many as thirty-nine (39) hours before his body was found. The cause of death was determined to be starvation and dehydration. Expert testimony opined that Kly would have experienced pain and suffering over a long period of time before he died.

At trial, the Commonwealth contended that after contracting orally to provide food, shelter, care and necessary medicine for Kly, The Pestinakases engaged in a course of conduct calculated to deprive Kly of those things necessary to maintain life and thereby cause his death. The trial court instructed the jury that The Pestinakases could not be found guilty of a malicious killing for failing to provide food, shelter and necessary medicines to Kly unless a duty to do so had been imposed upon them by contract. The court instructed the jury, inter alia, as follows:

> In order for you to convict the defendants on any of the homicide charges or the criminal conspiracy or recklessly endangering charges, you must first find beyond a reasonable doubt that the defendants had a legal duty of care to Joseph Kly.
>
> There are but two situations in which Pennsylvania law imposes criminal liability for the failure to perform an act. One of these is where the express language of the law defining the offense provides for criminal [liability] based upon such a failure. The other is where the law otherwise imposes a duty to act.
>
> Unless you find beyond a reasonable doubt that an oral contract imposed a duty to act upon Walter and Helen Pestinakas, you must acquit the defendants.

OPINION

The Pestinakases contend that this was error. The applicable law appears at 18 Pa.C.S. ß 301(a) and (b) as follows:

(a) General rule. A person is not guilty of an offense unless his liability is based on conduct which includes a voluntary act or the omission to perform an act of which he is physically capable.

(b) Omission as basis of liability. Liability for the commission of an offense may not be based on an omission unaccompanied by action unless:

(1) the omission is expressly made sufficient by the law defining the offense; or
(2) a duty to perform the omitted act is otherwise imposed by law.

Unless the omission is expressly made sufficient by the law defining the offense, a duty to perform the omitted act must have been otherwise imposed by law for the omission to have the same standing as a voluntary act for purposes of liability. It should, of course, suffice, as the courts now hold, that the duty arises under some branch of the civil law. If it does, this minimal requirement is satisfied, though whether the omission constitutes an offense depends as well on many other factors. . . .

Consistently with this legal thinking we hold that when the statute provides that an omission to do an act can be the basis for criminal liability if a duty to perform the omitted act has been imposed by law, the legislature intended to distinguish between a legal duty to act and merely a moral duty to act. A duty to act imposed by contract is legally enforceable and, therefore, creates a legal duty. It follows that a failure to perform a duty imposed by contract may be the basis for a charge of criminal homicide if such failure causes the death of another person and all other elements of the offense are present. Because there was evidence in the instant case that Kly's death had been caused by The Pestinakases' failure to provide the food and medical care which they had agreed by oral contract to provide for him, their omission to act was sufficient to support a conviction for criminal homicide. . . .

The Pestinakases argue that, in any event, the Commonwealth failed to prove an enforceable contract requiring them to provide Kly with food and medical attention. It is their position that their contract with Kly required them to provide only a place for Kly to live and a funeral upon his death. This obligation, they contend, was fulfilled. Although we have not been provided with a full and complete record of the trial, it seems readily apparent from the partial record before us, that the evidence was sufficient to create an issue of fact for the jury to resolve. The issue was submitted to the jury on careful instructions by the learned trial judge and does not present a basis entitling The Pestinakases to post-trial relief.

. . . The judgments of sentence must be, as they are, AFFIRMED.

DISSENT

MCEWEN, J.

. . . I must respectfully depart the company of my eminent colleagues who find that the trial court properly instructed the jury that the failure to perform a civil contract, though simple omission *alone,* is sufficient to meet the voluntary act requirements of Section 301 of the Crimes Code. . . .

. . . One of the issues which this Court must now decide is whether The Pestinakases are correct when they argue that the charge to the jury contained error since Pennsylvania law does not permit a finding that a breach, by omission, of a civil contract will suffice as an "act" for purposes of criminal liability where the duty to act arises only by virtue of the contract and not under a statute or other ordinance or regulation. After intense and concerned reflection, I find myself obliged to agree that the trial court erred when it instructed the jury that The Pestinakases could be found guilty of criminal homicide based solely upon a finding of a breach by omission of an oral contract.

The theory of the Commonwealth at trial was that the failure of The Pestinakases to fulfill the alleged civil contract to provide food, shelter, personal and medical care to Mr. Kly was *alone* sufficient to support a finding of first and/or third degree murder.

Section 301(b)(2) of the Crimes Code provides, in relevant part:

> Liability for the commission of any offense may not be based on an *omission unaccompanied by action* unless . . . a duty to perform the omitted act is otherwise *imposed by law.* (emphasis added) 18 Pa.C.S. ß 301(b)(2)

The precise issue thus becomes whether the legislature intended that a "contractual duty" constitutes a "duty imposed by law" for purposes of ascertaining whether conduct is criminal. While I share the desire of the prosecutor and the jury that The Pestinakases must not escape responsibility for their horribly inhuman and criminally culpable conduct, I cling to the view that an appellate court is not free to reshape the intention or revise the language of the Crimes Code. Rather, our constitutional obligation is to implement the intent and comply with the direction of the legislature.

While the Attorney General argues that a finding of criminal responsibility based upon a breach of a contractual duty would be "consistent with principles established in common law," our legislature has, with the enactment of the Crimes Code, abolished common law crimes, 18 Pa.C.S. ß 107(b), and evidenced as well a departure from reliance upon principles of common law in the Crimes Code.

Nor do I find support in Pennsylvania case law for this argument advanced by the Commonwealth. It is true that this Court has upheld convictions for endangering the welfare of children. . . . However, all of the cases which our research has yielded involved, where liability is based upon a failure to act, the parent-child relationship and the statutory imposition of duties upon the parents of minors. . . . In the instant case, where there was no "status of relationship between the parties" except landlord/tenant, a failure to perform a civil contract cannot *alone* sustain a conviction for third degree murder.

Thus, it is that I dissent.

Questions

1. List all the facts relevant to deciding whether the Pestinakases had a legal duty to Joseph Kly.

2. List all of the failures to act and voluntary acts that are relevant to deciding whether the Pestinakases failed to perform a legal duty to Mr. Kly.

3. Summarize the arguments regarding criminal omission of both the majority and dissenting opinions.

4. In your opinion, did the Pestinakases have a legal duty to Joseph Kly? Assuming they did have a legal duty, did they reasonably perform their duty? Back up your answer with facts and arguments in the case excerpt.

Omissions

1. Did She Have a Special Relationship with the Man in Her House?

People v. Oliver, 258 Cal.Rptr. 138 (1989)

FACTS Carol Ann Oliver met Carlos Cornejo in the afternoon when she was with her boyfriend at a bar. She and her boyfriend purchased jewelry from Cornejo. In the late afternoon, when Oliver was leaving the bar to return home, Cornejo got into the car with her, and she drove him home with her. At the time, he appeared to be extremely drunk. At her house, he asked her for a spoon and went into the bathroom. She went to the kitchen, got a spoon, and brought it to him. She knew he wanted the spoon to take drugs. She remained in the living room while Cornejo "shot up" in the bathroom. He then came out and collapsed onto the floor in the living room. She tried but was unable to rouse him. Oliver then called the bartender at the bar where she had met Cornejo. The bartender advised her to leave him and come back to the bar, which Oliver did.

Oliver's daughter returned home at about 5 P.M. that day with two girlfriends. They found Cornejo unconscious on the living room floor. When the girls were unable to wake him, they searched his pockets and found eight dollars. They did not find any wallet or identification.

The daughter then called Oliver on the telephone. Oliver told her to drag Cornejo outside in case he woke up and became violent. The girls dragged Cornejo outside and put him behind a shed so that he would not be in the view of the neighbors. He was snoring when the girls left him there. About a half hour later, Oliver returned home with her boyfriend. She, the boyfriend, and the girls went outside to look at Cornejo. Oliver told the girls that she had watched him "shoot up" with drugs and then pass out.

The girls went out to eat and then returned to check on Cornejo later that evening. He had a pulse and was snoring. In the morning, one of the girls heard Oliver tell her daughter that Cornejo might be dead. Cornejo was purple and had flies around him. Oliver called the bartender at about 6 A.M. and told her she thought Cornejo had died in her backyard. Oliver then told the girls to call the police and she left for work. The police were called.

Oliver was convicted of involuntary manslaughter and appealed. Did Oliver have a "special relationship" with Cornejo that created a legal duty?

DECISION Yes, said the appeals court: We conclude that the evidence of the combination of events which occurred between the time appellant left the bar with Cornejo through the time he fell to the floor unconscious, established as a matter of law a relationship which imposed upon appellant a duty to seek medical aid. At the time appellant left the bar with Cornejo, she observed that he was extremely drunk, and drove him to her home. In so doing, she took him from a public place where others might have taken care to prevent him from injuring himself, to a private place—her home—where she alone could provide care.

2. Did He Have a Legal Duty to His Girlfriend's Baby?

State v. Miranda, 715 A.2d 680 (1998)

FACTS Santos Miranda started living with his girlfriend and her two children in an apartment in September 1992. On January 27, 1993, Miranda was 21 years old, his girlfriend was 16, her son was 2, and her daughter, the victim in this case, born on September 21, 1992, was 4 months old. Although he was not the biological father of either child, Miranda took care of them and considered himself to be their stepfather.

He represented himself as such to the people at Meriden Veteran's Memorial Hospital where, on January 27, 1993, the victim was taken for treatment of her injuries following a 911 call by Miranda that the child was choking on milk. Upon examination at the hospital, it was determined that the victim had multiple rib fractures that were approximately two to three weeks old, two skull fractures that were approximately seven to ten days old, a brachial plexus injury to her left arm, a rectal tear that was actively "oozing blood," and nasal hemorrhages.

The court determined that anyone who saw the child would have had to notice these injuries, the consequent deformities, and her reactions. Indeed, the trial court found that Miranda had been aware of the various bruises on her right cheek and the nasal hemorrhages, as well as the swelling of the child's head; that he knew she had suffered a rectal tear, as well as rib fractures posteriorly on the left and right sides; and that he was aware that there existed a substantial and unjustifiable risk that the child was exposed to conduct that created a risk of death.

The trial court concluded that despite this knowledge, the defendant "failed to act to help or aid [the child] by promptly notifying authorities of her injuries, taking her for medical care, removing her from her circumstances and guarding her from future abuses. As a result of his failure to help her, the child was exposed to conduct which created a risk of death to her, and the child suffered subsequent serious physical injuries. . . ." Did Santos Miranda have a legal duty to "protect health and well-being" of the baby?

DECISION Yes, said the Connecticut Supreme Court: We conclude that, based upon the trial court's findings that the defendant had established a familial relationship with the victim's mother and her two children, had assumed responsibility for the welfare of the children, and had taken care of them as though he were their father, the defendant had a legal duty to protect the victim from abuse. . . .

3. Did the Bystanders Owe Her a Legal Duty?

SOURCE: "37 Who Saw Murder Didn't Call . . . ," by M. Gansberg, March 17, 1964. Copyright 2000 by the New York Times Co. Reprinted with permission.

FACTS For more than half an hour 37 respectable, law-abiding citizens in Queens watched a killer stalk and stab a woman in three separate attacks in Kew Gardens. Twice the sound of their voices and the sudden glow of their bedroom lights interrupted him and frightened him off. Each time he returned, sought her out and stabbed her again.

Not one person telephoned the police during the assault; one witness called after the woman was dead. But Assistant Chief Inspector Frederick M. Lussen, in charge of the borough's detectives and a veteran of 25 years of homicide investigations, is still shocked. He can give a matter of fact recitation of many murders. But the Kew Gardens slaying baffles him—not because it is a murder, but because the "good people" failed to call the police. "As we have reconstructed the crime," he said, "the assailant had three chances to kill this woman during a 35-minute period. He returned twice to complete the job. If we had been called when he first attacked, the woman might not be dead now."

She got as far as a street light in front of a bookstore before the man grabbed her. She screamed. Lights went on in the 10-story apartment house at 82-67 Austin Street, which faces the bookstore. Windows slid open and voices punctured the early morning stillness. Miss Genovese screamed. From one of the upper windows in the apartment house, a man called down: "Let that girl alone!" The assailant looked up at him, shrugged and walked down Austin Street toward a white sedan parked a short distance away.

Miss Genovese struggled to her feet. Lights went out. The killer returned to Miss Genovese, now trying to make her way around the side of the building by the parking lot to get to her apartment. The assailant stabbed her again. "I'm dying!" she shrieked. "I'm dying!" Windows were opened again, and lights went on in many apartments. The assailant got into his car and drove away. Miss Genovese staggered to her feet. A city bus, Q i 10, the Lefferts Boulevard line to Kennedy International Airport, passed. It was 3:35 A.M.

The assailant returned. By then, Miss Genovese had crawled to the back of the building, where the freshly painted brown doors to the apartment house held out hope of safety. The killer tried the first door; she wasn't there. At the second door, 82-62 Austin Street, he saw her slumped on the floor at the foot of the stairs. He stabbed her a third time—fatally.

It was 3:50 by the time the police received their first call, from a man who was a neighbor of Miss Genovese. In two minutes they were at the scene. The neighbor, a 70-year-old woman, and another woman were the only persons on the street. Nobody else came forward.

The man explained that he had called the police after much deliberation. He had phoned a friend in Nassau County for advice and then he had crossed the roof of the building to the apartment of the elderly woman to get her to make the call. "I didn't want to get involved," he sheepishly told the police.

The police stressed how simple it would have been to have gotten in touch with them. "A phone call," said one of the detectives, "would have done it." The police may be reached by dialing "0" for operator or SPring 7-3100.

Today, witnesses from the neighborhood, which is made up of one-family homes in the $35,000 to $60,000 range with the exception of the two apartment houses near the railroad station, find it difficult to explain why they didn't call the police. Lieut. Bernard Jacobs, who handled the investigation by the detectives, said: "It is one of the better neighborhoods. There are few reports of crimes." . . .

The police said most persons had told them they had been afraid to call, but had given meaningless answers when asked what they had feared. "We can understand the reticence of people to become involved in an area of violence," Lieutenant Jacobs said, "but where they are in their homes, near phones, why should they be afraid to call the police?" Witnesses—some of them unable to believe what they had allowed to happen—told a reporter why. A housewife, knowingly if quite casual, said, "We thought it was a lover's quarrel." A husband and wife both said, "Frankly, we were afraid." They seemed aware of the fact that events might have been different. A distraught woman, wiping her hands in her apron, said, "I didn't want my husband to get involved." . . . A man peeked out from a slight opening in the doorway to his apartment and rattled off an account of the killer's second attack. Why hadn't he called the police at the time? "I was tired," he said without emotion. "I went back to bed." It was 4:25 A.M. when the ambulance arrived for the body of Miss Genovese. It drove off. "Then," a solemn police detective said, "the people came out."

Only unreasonable failures to perform legal duties are punishable as criminal omissions. For example, in one case, a sea captain allowed a crew member who had fallen overboard to drown to save other crew members and passengers from a dangerous storm. The court held that failure to try and save the one crew member was not a criminal omission because it was reasonable to allow one person to die to save many others. Nor was it a criminal omission for a baby-sitter who could not swim to fail to dive into deep water to save the child he was watching.

 Go to the Criminal Law 9e website for the full text of the Exploring Further excerpts: www.thomsonedu.com/criminaljustice/samaha.

POSSESSION

Let's start by making clear that possession is *not* action; it's a passive condition. It's only by means of a **legal fiction** (pretending something is a fact when it's not, if there's a "good" reason for pretending) that the principle of *actus reus* includes possession. The list of items that you might "criminally" possess is almost endless. In a detailed and powerful criticism of the expansion of possession crimes, Professor Markus Dubber (2001, 856–57) lists 38 (Table 3.1), "and the list could go on and on." According to Dubber, "millions of people commit one of its variants every day" (856):

> Operating below the radars of policy pundits and academic commentators, as well as under the Constitution, possession does the crime war's dirty work. Possession has replaced vagrancy as the most convenient gateway to the criminal justice system. . . . [It's a] formidable weapon in the war on crime; it expands the scope of policing into the home, it results in harsher penalties and therefore has a far greater incapacitative potential, and it is far less vulnerable to legal challenge [than vagrancy]. (856)

The most common of the many criminal possession crimes are possession of weapons, illegal drugs, and drug paraphernalia. The good reason for pretending possession is an act is the powerful pull of the idea "an ounce of prevention is worth a pound of cure." Better to nip the bud of possession before it grows into an act of doing drugs or shooting someone. Also, most people get possession by their voluntary acts—for example, buying marijuana and putting it in their pocket. So their passive possession is brought about by their active acquisition. But not always. Maybe a student who

TABLE 3.1 Criminal Possession Statutes

1. Air pistols and rifles	20. Graffiti instruments
2. Weapons (including dangerous weapons, instruments, appliances, or substances)	21. Instruments of crime
	22. Noxious materials
3. Ammunition	23. Obscene material
4. Anti-security items	24. Obscene sexual performances by a child
5. Body vests	25. "Premises which [one] knows are being used for prostitution purposes"
6. Burglary tools	
7. Computer-related material	26. Prison contraband
8. Counterfeit trademarks	27. Public benefit cards
9. Drug paraphernalia	28. Slugs
10. Drug precursors	29. Spearfishing equipment
11. Drugs	30. Stolen property
12. Eavesdropping devices	31. Taximeter accelerating devices
13. Embossing machines (to forge credit cards)	32. Tear gas
	33. Toy guns
14. Firearms	34. Unauthorized recordings of a performance
15. Fireworks	35. Undersized catfish (in Louisiana)
16. Forged instruments	36. Usurious loan records
17. Forgery devices	37. Vehicle identification numbers
18. Gambling devices	38. Vehicle titles without complete assignment
19. Gambling records	

Source: Dubber 2001, 856–57.

got a bad grade "planted" the marijuana in my briefcase when I wasn't looking. Or, maybe you put your roommate's Ecstasy in your pocket to take it to the police station and turn it in.

Before we can understand and discuss the passive state of possession as *actus reus*, we need to define two aspects of possession: (1) control of items and substances and (2) awareness of the control.

There are two kinds of possession: actual and constructive possession. **Actual possession** means I've got physical control of banned stuff; it's "on me" (for example, marijuana is in my pocket). **Constructive possession** means I control banned stuff, but it's not on me (it's in my car, my apartment, or other places I control) (American Law Institute 1985, I:2, 24).

As for the awareness aspect, possession can be either "knowing" or "mere." **Knowing possession** means possessors are aware of what they possess. So if you buy crystal meth and know it's crystal meth, you have knowing possession. (Knowing doesn't mean you have to know it's a crime to possess crystal meth, only that you know it's crystal meth.) **Mere possession** means you don't know what you possess. So if you agree to carry your friend's briefcase you don't know is filled with stolen money, you've got mere possession of the money. Most states (except for North Dakota and Washington) require knowing possession. Also, almost all the cases in the court reports are constructive possession cases, and they're almost all drug and/or weapons cases. One of them is an illegal drug possession case, *Miller v. State* (1999).

CASE — *Did He Possess Marijuana and Cocaine?*

Miller v. State
6 S.W.3d 812 (Ark.App. 1999)

HISTORY

James Luther Miller, the defendant-appellant, was convicted by a jury of possession of cocaine and marijuana and sentenced to thirty years' incarceration on the cocaine-possession conviction. He was sentenced to one year's imprisonment in the county jail on the marijuana-possession conviction, and ordered to pay a $1000 fine. Miller appealed. The Court of Appeals, Neal, J., held that: (1) evidence established that defendant constructively possessed marijuana found in vehicle, and (2) evidence did not establish that defendant constructively possessed cocaine found in vehicle. Affirmed part; reversed and dismissed in part.

NEAL, J.

FACTS

At trial, Arkansas State Police Officer Tim Land testified that on February 23, 1997, he came into contact with James Luther Miller, who was a passenger in a vehicle driven by Michael Alexander. Officer Land became suspicious of the vehicle because it approached him from the rear and would not pass his vehicle although he slowed to thirty miles per hour.

Land pulled his car into the median, and as the car passed he noticed that it did not have a license plate. He initiated a stop of the vehicle, and upon approaching the vehicle he smelled the very strong odor of burned marijuana emanating from the vehicle. Land had the driver exit the vehicle, and after noting the odor of burned marijuana and alcohol on his person, administered field sobriety tests, which Alexander failed. Land called for assistance, and Alexander was transported to the county jail for a breathalyzer. According to Land, there were four occupants in the vehicle: Alexander, who was the driver; James Giles, who was sitting in the right front seat; Damon Albert, who was sitting in the rear seat behind the driver; and James Miller (the appellant), who was seated on the right rear seat.

Trooper Land recovered three rolling papers from three of the vehicle's occupants, but could not recall which three occupants possessed the papers. He also stated that he found three rocks of crack cocaine and marijuana in the pouch located on the back of the driver's seat, directly in front of Damon Albert.

The driver of the vehicle, Michael Alexander, testified that on the date in question he asked Miller if he wanted to ride to Hope, Arkansas, with him. He picked up Giles and Albert and took them to a residence in Hope, where they purchased crack cocaine. According to Alexander, Miller did not know that Giles and Albert were purchasing crack, and he did not know about the marijuana until it was smoked. However, Alexander later testified that all of the vehicle's occupants knew that the marijuana was in the vehicle because the marijuana was in the car before the group traveled to Hope.

OPINION

. . . It is not necessary for the State to prove literal physical possession of drugs in order to prove possession. Possession of drugs can be proved by constructive possession. Constructive possession can be implied when the drugs are in the joint control of the accused and another.

However, joint occupancy of a vehicle, standing alone, is not sufficient to establish possession or joint possession. There must be some additional factor linking the accused to the drugs. Other factors to be considered in cases involving automobiles occupied by more than one person are:

1. whether the contraband is in plain view,

2. whether the contraband is found within the accused's personal effects,

3. whether it is found on the same side of the car seat as the accused was sitting or in near proximity to it,

4. whether the accused is the owner of the automobile, or exercised dominion and control over it; and

5. whether the accused acted suspiciously before or during the arrest.

. . . We believe the evidence is sufficient to conclude that the jury had substantial evidence from which it could find that appellant constructively possessed marijuana. By way of analogy, we note that had the officer observed the marijuana in plain view inside of the vehicle, the evidence would be sufficient to compel the conclusion that Miller constructively possessed the marijuana. Here, although the marijuana was not in plain view, we believe that the fact that the police officer smelled marijuana upon approaching the vehicle tends to establish that Miller had knowledge of the presence of the marijuana. It is the knowledge of the existence of the contraband that provides substantial evidence of constructive possession.

Whether the evidence is sufficient to support the conviction of possession of cocaine presents a more difficult question. In *Bond v. State*, 873 S.W.2d 569 (1994), we affirmed a conviction for possession of a controlled substance under facts similar to, but distinguishable from those present in the case at bar. In that case, appellants were stopped by a police officer, who upon approaching the vehicle, smelled alcohol and marijuana. A search of the vehicle revealed a small brass pipe used to smoke marijuana in plain view in the front seat in immediate proximity to both appellants. The arresting officer observed that both appeared to have glassy eyes. In affirming the conviction we utilized the following rationale:

> . . . There are factors in addition to the joint occupancy of the vehicle, from which the jury could find that appellants had joint control and dominion over the contraband. First, as to the small brass pipe, it was found in the front seat in immediate proximity to both appellants. Secondly, *an additional factor, which links both appellants to the marijuana and from which constructive possession could be found, is that the marijuana was in the back seat behind the driver's seat in an area most easily accessible to Joseph the passenger, but also accessible to James, the driver. . . .*

It is the italicized portion of this court's analysis that gives us great cause for concern. This language seems to imply that constructive possession may be proved by merely showing that the defendant was an occupant of a vehicle where illegal contraband is found, in the absence of any additional factor linking the accused to the contraband. However, our case law makes it quite clear that the drugs must be found on the same side of the vehicle as the accused, or in close proximity to the accused.

The highlighted language in *Bond* should be considered in conjunction with the other evidence presented, and not as the sole basis upon which a conviction for constructive possession can be sustained. We note that in *Bond* there was evidence, independent of occupancy of the vehicle, that was sufficient to sustain the conviction. . . .

In the present case, Miller was a rear-seat passenger in his friend's car when the vehicle was stopped by Trooper Land. The contraband found was not in plain view, was not under appellant's exclusive control, and was not found near the seat in which appellant was seated. There was no testimony that appellant acted suspiciously, and, there was no evidence of any contraband found on appellant's person. There was, however, testimony that appellant did not know that there was cocaine in the car until after the police searched the vehicle.

Based upon the evidence presented, we hold that the State did not present sufficient evidence of any factor, other than occupancy, to establish Miller's constructive possession of the cocaine. Miller's conviction for possession of cocaine is reversed and dismissed. His conviction for possession of marijuana is affirmed.

DISSENT

LINKERHART, J.

. . . I would reverse and dismiss Miller's conviction for possession of marijuana. . . . The majority does not set forth any factor linking the appellant to the marijuana. Rather, the majority concludes, "We believe the fact that the police officer smelled marijuana upon approaching the vehicle tends to establish that appellant had knowledge of the presence of marijuana." Certainly, this does not establish that the appellant exercised care, control, or management of the contraband. And most certainly, "mere presence, acquiescence, silence, or knowledge that a crime is being committed, in the absence of a legal duty to act," is not sufficient to establish criminal liability.

This case strongly resembles that of *Kastl v. State*, 303 Ark. 358, 796 S.W.2d 848 (1990), in which the Arkansas Supreme Court found that evidence of beer cans beside the vehicle, beer found in the immediate proximity of the appellant in the vehicle, and the smell of beer on the appellant's person, were not sufficient evidence that the appellant, who was one of five people in the vehicle, constructively possessed the beer.

Relying on our words here, one can easily imagine a "parade of horribles" in which a person who is merely present will stand convicted for merely knowing about the presence of a controlled substance. Insofar as we abide under a just system of laws, this decision cannot stand.

BIRD, J.

I respectfully dissent from the majority opinion in this case because I believe that there was sufficient evidence upon which a jury could find that the appellant was guilty of the crimes of possession of marijuana and cocaine on the basis that he constructively possessed both of those substances.

. . . The contraband was found in the pouch on the back of the driver's seat. Although the contraband was not on the same side of the car as the appellant, it was certainly in close proximity to the other side of the back seat where appellant was seated. . . . Miller was seated in the right rear passenger seat and the contraband, located in the pouch on the back of the driver's seat . . . [was] accessible to him. . . .

Finally, to me, it is contradictory to hold, as the majority does, that, because the police officer smelled the aroma of marijuana smoke coming from the car, the appellant *is* guilty of possession of marijuana, but not guilty of possession of cocaine that was located in exactly the same place in the car as the marijuana. . . . The mere smell of marijuana smoke coming from a vehicle is [not] sufficient to convict a joint occupant of the vehicle of possession of marijuana found in the vehicle. In order to be convicted, the State must prove that the joint occupant was in close proximity to the contraband or that such possession was established by virtue of the existence of one of the other linking factors. In this case, if the appellant was close enough in proximity to the marijuana that the officer smelled to be found guilty of its possession, I fail to see how the majority can say that there was not sufficient evidence to sustain the jury's verdict that appellant was guilty of possession of cocaine that was located in exactly the same place as the marijuana. . . .

Questions

1. Identify the two elements of constructive possession discussed by the court.

2. List the five factors the court identifies that can prove possession in joint occupancy cases.

3. Match the facts of the case to the five factors you listed in (2).

4. Assume you're the prosecutor. Argue that Miller actually and constructively possessed the handgun. Back up your arguments with facts in the case.

5. Assume you're the defense attorney. Argue that Miller didn't physically or constructively possess the gun.

EXPLORING FURTHER

Possession

1. Did He Possess a Loaded Ruger .357 Revolver?

Porter v. State, WL 1919477 (Ark.App. 2003)

FACTS Little Rock Police Officer Beth McNair stopped a vehicle with no license plate on the evening of May 23, 2002. Jermaine Porter was a passenger in the vehicle and was sitting in the back seat on the passenger side. As McNair approached the vehicle, she testified that she observed Porter reaching toward the floor with his left hand. McNair told Porter to keep his left hand where she could see it. As McNair shined her flashlight into the vehicle, she testified that she saw a handgun on Porter's left shoe and that the barrel of the gun (a loaded Ruger .357 revolver) was pointing toward her.

Porter testified that his cousin and his uncle had picked him up at a hotel and that they were taking him to his sister's house. Porter stated that he had only been in the car for approximately 5 minutes when it was stopped, that he did not know that there were any guns inside the vehicle, and that the gun found near his foot was not his. He also denied that he bent over and reached toward the floor, and he testified that there was nothing touching his foot. Porter admitted that the gun may have been found near his foot but explained that it probably "slid back there" from underneath the seat when they were driving up some steep hills.

Did Porter "possess" the revolver?

DECISION Yes, said the Arkansas Court of Appeals. There is substantial evidence in this case supporting the trial court's finding that Porter had possession of the handgun. According to the police officers' testimonies, the handgun was found in plain view on the floorboard of the back seat of the vehicle, the gun was lying on Porter's left foot, it was on the same side of the vehicle as Porter was sitting, and Porter acted suspiciously prior to his arrest by reaching toward the floor with his left hand. The presence of these factors is sufficient to show Porter's knowledge and control of the handgun. Although Porter testified that the gun was not his, that he did not know that there were guns in the vehicle, and that the gun must have "slid back" near his foot when the vehicle went up a steep hill, the trial court specifically stated that it credited the testimony of the State's witnesses. We defer to the trial court in matters of credibility of witnesses, and the trial court is not required to believe the testimony of the accused, as he is the person most interested in the outcome of the trial.

3. Did She Possess Marijuana in Her Boyfriend's House?

State v. Kimberley, 103 S.W.2d (Mo.App. 2003)

FACTS Sometime between 9:30 and 10:00 A.M., officers legally entered an apartment looking for two men who had caused a disturbance earlier that morning. They found Alisha Kimberley lying on the couch, apparently asleep. Marijuana and drug paraphernalia were observed in plain view on the coffee table approximately 2 feet from where Kimberley was lying. No one else was found in the house. The two men who reportedly were part of the original disturbance were never located. A "bong" used for smoking marijuana was found resting on the floor in a corner of a "computer room" in the apartment. Kimberley was a resident of the apartment where the drugs and paraphernalia were found; she shared the apartment with Paul Hoffman, who had earlier run from the apartment and was apprehended. She was charged with possession of marijuana paraphernalia. Did Kimberley possess marijuana paraphernalia?

DECISION Yes, said the Missouri Court of Appeals: The mere presence of the accused on shared premises where contraband is found is not enough circumstantial evidence to show ownership or possession. Mere presence at a place where contraband is found is not enough to create an inference of control. Additional factors are required to prove conscious possession. Some of those factors are routine access to an area where contraband is kept; large quantities of the substance at the scene where the accused is arrested; self-incriminating statements or admissions

showing consciousness of guilt; commingling of contraband with the defendant's personal belongings; and the substance being in public view and easily accessible by the defendant.

The totality of the circumstances must be considered in determining whether additional incriminating circumstances have been proved. She was near the marijuana and paraphernalia, but there was more evidence that Kimberley was guilty of possession. There was an additional item of paraphernalia, a "yellow glass-colored bong," found in a corner, apparently in plain view, in another room (a computer room) to which she had access. Kimberley acknowledged that it was a "large bong" and that it was a "couple feet tall." Kimberley admitted that she recognized the contraband for what it was, and that she knew that marijuana had previously been smoked in the apartment. Hoffman and Kimberley said that the use of the marijuana in the apartment was against Kimberley's wishes; however, the court was not required to believe her testimony.

Because of the presence of the "dug-out," a ceramic pipe, and marijuana on a television tray in very close proximity to Kimberley (and under her apparent control), just about two feet away from Kimberley as she lay on the couch, with some seeds spilled on the floor near the couch (as though used by a person on the couch), in Kimberley's own apartment, with another large item of paraphernalia accessible to her in another room, we cannot say the trial court was being speculative in concluding (beyond a reasonable doubt) that Kimberley possessed the contraband.

The totality of the circumstances was such that a rational fact finder could believe beyond a reasonable doubt that Kimberley knowingly possessed the paraphernalia. It was not necessary for the State to eliminate all theoretical possibilities of her innocence. Accordingly, under our standard of review, we must affirm the conviction.

 Go to the Criminal Law 9e website for the full text of the Exploring Further excerpts: www.thomsonedu.com/criminaljustice/samaha.

SUMMARY

I. Criminal law is primarily concerned with general rules for defining whether a crime has been committed. To do this, we have to answer three questions:

   A. Is there a criminal act of some kind?

   B. Is the act justified?

   C. Is the unjustified act nonetheless excused?

II. The prosecution has to prove five elements of criminal liability beyond a reasonable doubt to convict individual defendants:
   A. Criminal act *(actus reus)*
   B. Criminal intent *(mens rea)*
   C. Concurrence
   D. Attendant circumstances
   E. Result (causing a criminal harm)

III. *Actus reus:* The first principle of criminal liability
   A. *Actus reus* (criminal act) in criminal law requires intent that turns into action.
   B. Why does the law require an act?
      1. Intent alone is impossible to prove.
      2. Intention alone doesn't harm anybody.
      3. It's hard to distinguish daydreaming and fantasy from intent.
   C. The *actus reus* requirement serves several purposes:
      1. It helps prove *mens rea*.
      2. It reserves the harsh sanction of the criminal law for cases of actual danger.
      3. It protects the privacy of individuals.

IV. Voluntary acts: Every crime has to include at least one voluntary act. Why?
   A. Criminal law punishes people.
   B. We can only punish people we can blame.
   C. We can only blame people who are responsible for their acts.
   D. People are only responsible for their voluntary acts.

V. Status
   A. Action describes what we do, status (or condition) denotes who we are.
   B. Status can arise in two ways:
      1. From prior voluntary acts, such as drinking alcohol or using drugs
      2. Being who we are—sex, age, sexual orientation, race, ethnicity
   C. The Constitution bans legislatures from making a crime out of personal condition or status.

VI. Omissions
   A. Failure to act (omissions) can satisfy the *actus reus* requirement only when it's outrageous to fail to do something to help someone in danger.
   B. There are two kinds of criminal omissions:
      1. Failure to report something required by law
      2. Failure to intervene to prevent injuries and death to persons or damage to property
      3. Omissions are *criminal* omissions only if defendants had a legal duty to act.
      4. Legal duties are created in three ways:
         a. Statutes
         b. Contracts
         c. Special relationships

VII. Possession
   A. Possession is *not* action; it's a passive condition.
   B. There are two elements in treating possession as *actus reus:*
      1. Actual or constructive possession
         a. Actual possession is having banned "stuff" on your person.

    b. Constructive possession is having banned "stuff" that isn't on your person but in a place you control.

  2. Awareness of the possession

    a. Knowing possession means that you're aware of what you possess.

    b. Mere possession means you don't know what you possess.

REVIEW QUESTIONS

1. Identify three questions that have to be answered to determine criminal liability.

2. Describe the difference between *actus reus* and *mens rea*.

3. Identify the elements of crime that prosecutors have to prove beyond a reasonable doubt to convict individual defendants.

4. Give an example of an attendant circumstance.

5. What is meant by *concurrence?*

6. Describe the difference between criminal acts and criminal conduct.

7. Identify three purposes the *actus reus* requirement serves.

8. What four rationales are given as to why only voluntary acts qualify as *actus reus?*

9. Identify and describe the two ways status arises.

10. What are the two types of criminal omission? Give an example of each.

11. Identify and give an example of three types of legal duties.

12. Explain the difference between moral and legal duties.

13. Describe the difference between the "Good Samaritan" doctrine and the American bystander rule.

14. What types of failures to perform legal duties are punishable as criminal omissions?

15. Identify and explain the two aspects of the definition of possession.

16. Define the two types of control in possession.

17. Define the two types of awareness in possession.

18. Why does punishing drug addicts violate the U.S. Constitution's Eighth Amendment?

KEY TERMS

The General Principles of Criminal Liability: *Mens Rea*, Concurrence, and Causation

MAIN POINTS

- Most crimes include a mental element.
- It's right and reasonable to punish only those who we can blame for committing crimes.
- The principle of *mens rea* is ancient and highly complex.
- Proving "state of mind" is difficult.
- Subjective and objective fault satisfy the mental element in criminal liability.
- General intent is the minimum requirement for all criminal conduct.
- Specific intent applies to result crimes.
- The Model Penal Code identifies four mental states—purposely, knowingly, recklessly, and negligently.
- Strict liability imposes criminal liability without subjective or objective fault.
- All crimes, except for strict liability offenses, are subject to the principle of concurrence.
- Causation only applies to result crimes; the most prevalent is criminal homicide.
- Proving causation requires proving two kinds of cause: factual and legal.
- Mistake of fact is a defense when it prevents the formation of the mental attitude required by a criminal statute.
- Ignorance of facts or the law is no defense.

George Weller (inset), 89, was convicted of vehicular manslaughter for plowing at freeway speed into a crowded Santa Monica, CA, farmers' market, killing 10 people and injuring 68. During the trial, the defense claimed that Weller mistakenly used the accelerator instead of the brake and los control of the car. The judge concluded, however, that many of Weller's actions were intentional, not accidental, but sentenced him to probation rather than prison because of his failing health.

Was He Guilty?

Police officers stopped Steven Loge for speeding. During a routine search of his automobile, the officers found a nearly empty bottle of beer in a brown paper bag underneath the front passenger seat. Based on this finding, they charged Loge with keeping an open bottle containing intoxicating liquor in an automobile. At trial, Loge testified that the car he was driving belonged to his father and that he, as well as others, had driven it for the past two weeks. He also testified that the open bottle did not belong to him and that he did not know it was in the car.

(STATE V. LOGE 2000)

"I didn't mean to" captures a basic idea about criminal liability: a criminal act (*actus reus*) is necessary, but it's not enough for criminal liability. Most crimes also include a mental element. Why? Because it's right and reasonable to punish only people we can blame. We call this **culpability** or **blameworthiness.** Justice Holmes (1963, 4) put it this way: "Even a dog distinguishes between being stumbled over and being kicked." Recall that criminal conduct consists of both a criminal act *and* criminal intent (Chapters 1 and 3).

Mens rea translated means "evil state of mind," in the singular. In fact, as you'll learn in this chapter, there are several states of mind that can qualify as the mental element. In non–Model Penal Code (MPC) states, these include general intent, specific intent, transferred intent, and constructive intent. The MPC also consists of four states of mind, ranked according to the degree of their blameworthiness— purposely, knowingly, recklessly, and negligently. These are very complicated, but essential, concepts you need to know, not just to get a good grade in your criminal law class but because of their practical importance. They contribute to determining what kind of and how much punishment offenders deserve.

Some kinds of crimes—mostly crimes against persons, such as murder and manslaughter (Chapter 9) and assault, battery, and stalking (Chapter 10)—consist of more than the elements of criminal conduct (*actus reus* + *mens rea*) and circumstantial elements, if any. They also include the element of causing a specific harmful result— death in criminal homicide and bodily or emotional harm in assault, battery, and stalking.

The element of causation consists of two parts. The first is the necessary, but not sufficient, cause in fact—that is, the objective determination that the defendant's act triggered a chain of events that ended as the harmful result, such as death in homicide. The second is when the legal cause, a subjective judgment as to whether it's fair and just to blame the defendant for the result, is coupled with the cause in fact. We'll examine the criteria courts rely on for determining whether it's fair to blame defendants for the result their actions triggered.

THE PRINCIPLE OF *MENS REA*

The **principle of *mens rea*** (the "mental element," also called "mental attitude" or "state of mind," the prosecution has to prove beyond a reasonable doubt) is an ancient idea. "For hundreds of years the books have repeated with unbroken cadence that *actus non facit reum nisi mens sit rea*" ("An act doesn't make the actor guilty, unless her mind is guilty") (Sayre 1932, 974). According to the great medieval jurist Bracton, writing in 1256:

> He who kills . . . without intent to kill should be acquitted, because a crime is not committed unless the intent to injure intervene; and the desire and purpose distinguish evildoing. (quoted in Sayre 1932, 985)

Six hundred years later, the distinguished U.S. criminal law scholar Joel Bishop echoed Bracton: "There can be no crime, large or small, without an evil mind" (Sayre 1932, 974). And, in a 2001 case where *mens rea* was an issue, senior U.S. District Court Judge and scholar Jack Weinstein called the "*actus non facit* . . . maxim the criminal law's 'mantra'" and noted that "Western civilized nations have long looked to the wrongdoer's mind to determine both the propriety and the grading of punishment" (*U.S. v. Cordoba-Hincapie* 2001, 489).

Mens rea isn't just ancient; it's highly complex. "No problem of criminal law . . . has proved more baffling through the centuries than the determination of the precise mental element necessary to convict of any crime" (Sayre 1932, 974). Several reasons account for this bafflement. First, whatever it means, *mens rea* is difficult to discover and then prove in court. Second, courts and legislatures have used so many vague and incomplete definitions of the mental element.

According to the "Commentary on *mens rea*" accompanying the Alabama Criminal Code:

> It would be impossible to review, much less reconcile and make clear and uniform, the myriad of Alabama statutes and cases that have employed or discussed some term of mental culpability. Such mental terms and concepts, while necessarily difficult to articulate, sometimes have been vaguely or only partly defined, or otherwise seem imprecise or inconclusive, unclear or ambiguous, even confusing or contradictory, or over refined with technical, obscure and often subtle, if not dubious, distinctions. (*Burnett v. State* 1999, 575)

Table 4.1 includes a partial list of terms in the Alabama Code before it was reformed along the lines of the states of mind in the MPC. After listing 17, the summary ends, resignedly adding "and scores of others" (575).

Third, the *mens rea* consists of several mental attitudes that range across a broad spectrum, stretching all the way from purposely committing a crime you're well aware is criminal (stealing an iPod from Circuit City) to merely creating risks of criminal conduct or causing criminal harms—risks you're not the slightest bit aware you're creating (driving someone else's car with an open beer bottle you don't even know is in the car).

TABLE 4.1	Mental Attitudes Used in the Alabama Code	
"Intentionally"		"Negligently"
"Willfully"		"With culpable negligence"
"Purposely"		"With gross negligence"
"Designedly"		"With criminal negligence"
"Knowingly"		"Without due caution"
"Deliberately"		"Wickedly"
"Maliciously"		"Unlawfully"
"With premeditation"		"Wrongfully"
"Recklessly"		

We'll discuss these mental attitudes later in the chapter and in Chapters 9–13. For now, it's very important that you understand that intent in criminal law goes way beyond the dictionary definition of *intent*, which refers to acting on purpose or deliberately.

Fourth, a different mental attitude might apply to each of the elements of a crime. So it's possible for one attitude to apply to *actus reus*, another to causation, another to the harm defined in the statute, and still another to attendant circumstance elements (ALI 1985 I:2, 229–33).

As you learn about the *mens rea*, you'll probably be confused by the multiple mental attitudes it includes; by the complexity and uncertainty surrounding the definitions of the multiple attitudes it encompasses; and by the practical problems of matching the attitudes to elements of the offense and then proving each one beyond a reasonable doubt. Maybe you can take some comfort in knowing that courts don't always get the definitions of mental states right and matching them properly. Read this trial judge's instruction to the jury on the difference between "specific" and "general" intent in a sexual assault case:

> A general intent exists when we do things more or less unconsciously. A general intent involves a reflex action. Specific intent, on the other hand, is the act of concentrating, of focusing the mind for some perceptible period. It's a conscious act with the determination of the mind to do the act. Specific intent requires contemplation rather than . . . reflex and the contemplation must precede the act. (*Commonwealth v. Gagne* 2000)

As you'll discover later in the chapter, this definition is dead wrong. The defendant, Richard Gagne, must have thought so, too; he appealed his conviction to the Massachusetts Appeals Court. That court agreed that the trial judge's "instruction on general intent was incorrect" and concluded that "the better practice is to abandon entirely the use of those venerable, but confusing, common law terms." (The "venerable" terms the court was referring to are *general intent* and *specific intent*.) Nonetheless, the court affirmed the conviction, holding that the instruction created "no substantial risk of a miscarriage of justice." I don't think your instructor will be as forgiving toward you as the *Gagne* appeals court was to the trial judge for the jury instruction if you offer this wrong definition on an exam.

Finally, there's the problem of the relationship between mental attitude and **motive.** It's often said that motive is irrelevant to criminal liability; that is, a good motive is no defense and a bad motive can't make legal conduct criminal. So if a wife poisons her husband because he's suffering from the unbearable pain of a terminal bone cancer, she's still guilty of murder. And if she wants him dead because she hates him, and accidentally shoots him while they're deer hunting, she's not guilty even though she wanted him dead and she's glad he's out of the way.

Unfortunately, the relationship between motive and criminal liability is not so simple. The truth is that sometimes motive is relevant and sometimes it's not. Greed, hate, and jealously are always relevant to prove the intent to kill. Compassion may well affect discretionary decisions, such as police decisions to arrest, prosecutors to charge, and judges to sentence, say, mercy killers.

Juries have sometimes refused to convict mercy killers of first-degree murder even though the intent to kill was clearly there (Chapter 9). The murder conviction of Robert Latimer is a good example of this. Latimer could no longer stand the constant pain his 12-year-old daughter, Tracy, was suffering because of her severe and incurable cerebral palsy. She wore diapers, weighed only 38 pounds, and couldn't walk, talk, or feed herself.

So he put Tracy into the cab of his pickup truck on the family farm and pumped exhaust into the cab of the truck. He told the police that he stood by, ready to stop if

Tracy started to cry, but that she simply went quietly "to sleep. My priority was to put her out of her pain." He pleaded not guilty to first-degree murder, but the jury found him guilty of second-degree murder. Despite the verdict of guilty on the lesser charge, many people in the town agreed with an 18-year-old high school student who said Latimer "did what he had to do for his daughter's sake. And that's the way a lot of people in town are feeling" (Farnsworth 1994, A6).

Motive is also important in some defenses. For example, it's a defense to the crime of escaping from prison if a prisoner breaks out to save her life from a rapidly spreading fire (the defense of necessity, Chapter 5). Finally, motive is sometimes an element of a crime itself. For example, one of the attendant circumstances of burglary accompanying the act of breaking and entering someone else's property is "the purpose of committing a crime" once inside (the elements of burglary, Chapter 11).

Let's look more closely at proving the *mens rea*, defining it, and classifying it, and the difficulties and complexities in doing all of these.

Proving "State of Mind"

You can't see a state of mind. Not even the finest instruments of modern technology can find or measure your attitude (Hall 1960, 106). Electroencephalograms can record brain waves, and x-rays can photograph brain tissue, but Chief Justice Brian's words are as true today as they were when he wrote them in 1477: "The thought of man is not triable, for the devil himself knoweth not the thought of man" (Williams 1961, 1). Three hundred years later, Sir William Blackstone put it this way: "A tribunal can't punish what it can't know" (Blackstone 1769, 21).

Confessions are the only direct evidence of mental attitude. Unfortunately, defendants rarely confess their true intentions, so proof of their state of mind usually depends on indirect (circumstantial) evidence. Acts and attendant circumstances are the overwhelming kind of circumstantial evidence. In everyday experience, we rely on what people *do* to tell us what they *intend*. For example, if I break into a stranger's house at night, it's reasonable to infer I'm up to no good. So by observing directly what I do, you can indirectly determine what I intend.

Criminal Intent

The long list of terms used to define the mental element(s) in the Alabama Criminal Code (Table 4.1) before the code was reformed can be reduced to two kinds of fault that satisfy the mental element in criminal liability. One is **subjective fault,** or fault that requires a "bad mind" in the actor. For example, suppose in your state, it's a crime to "receive property you know is stolen." You buy an iPod from another student who you know stole it. The bad state of mind is "knowingly," which is more culpable than "recklessly" and less culpable than "purposely."

Subjective fault is linked frequently with immorality. You can see this connection in expressions in cases and statutes, such as "depravity of will," "diabolic malignity," "abandoned heart," "bad heart," "heart regardless of social duty and fatally bent on mischief," "wicked heart," "mind grievously depraved," or "mischievous vindictive spirit" (Dubber 2002, 50–51). Although these terms were typical of old laws and opinions, they're still in use in non-MPC jurisdictions, as you'll see in some of the case excerpts throughout the book.

The second kind of fault is **objective fault,** which requires no purposeful or conscious bad mind in the actor. For example, suppose it's a crime to "receive property you have reason to believe is stolen." You buy a new iPod in its original package for $10 that you *honestly*, but naively, don't know is stolen. You *should* know it was stolen; a reasonable person *would* know it was stolen, and in fact it *was* stolen. So, even though you had no "bad" mind, you're held accountable because you didn't live up to the norm of the average person.

The third kind of criminal liability isn't on the Alabama list; no-fault liability (called **strict liability**). Suppose a statute reads, "whoever receives stolen property" commits a crime. You buy an iPod for $45 that looks used, but you honestly and reasonably believe it wasn't stolen. It doesn't matter; under this statute, you're liable without either subjective or objective fault.

It's easy enough to define and give examples of these three types of liability. It's also easy to rank them according to the degree of their culpability. Subjective "bad mind" fault is most blameworthy. Objective unreasonable risk creation is less blameworthy; some maintain it shouldn't even qualify as a criminal state of mind. No-fault liability requires the least culpability; it holds people accountable for accidents.

We'll have much more to say about mental fault and no fault shortly (and in the remaining chapters of the book). But now, we have to examine two terms (used by many courts and some statutes) that are the source of most of the uncertainty over what criminal intent means: *general intent* and *specific intent* (LaFave 2003b, 1:352–55).

General Intent: **General intent** is used most commonly in cases to mean the intent to commit any criminal act defined as the *actus reus* in a criminal statute. In that sense, general intent is general because it states the minimum requirement of all crimes—namely, that they have to include a voluntary act, omission, or possession (Chapter 3).

It would be easy and obvious if all courts adopted this definition. But they don't, and that causes confusion. You've already encountered one example in *Commonwealth v. Gagne* in the last section; there the trial court defined general intent as an "unconscious" action or a "reflex," the very opposite of a voluntary act, or "willed muscular contraction" (Chapter 3). For example, some courts define general intent as a "synonym for *mens rea*"; so it includes all levels of both subjective and objective fault.

Another meaning of general intent is the intent to commit a crime at an undetermined time and place with no specific victim in mind. For example, Clifford Hobbs threw a bag of burglar's tools out of his car during a high-speed chase by Des Moines police. He was found guilty of "possession of burglary tools" (*State v. Hobbs* 1961, 239). Hobbs argued that at the time the police apprehended him, he "had no intention of breaking into any place" and appealed his conviction (239). The Iowa Supreme Court disagreed:

> Evidence of the general intent or purpose for which the accused kept and used the tools [is enough], not of present specific intent. . . . It is sufficient to show that defendant had a general intent to use tools or implements for a burglarious purpose, and the intention as to any particular time or place of using the same is not material. . . . (240)

Specific Intent: Some courts limit **specific intent** to the attitude represented by subjective fault, where there's a "bad" mind or will that triggers the act (LaFave 2003b, 1:353–55). It's captured in these adjectives found in most ordinary dictionaries: *deliberate, calculated, conscious, intended, planned, meant, studied, knowing, willful, purposeful, purposive, done on purpose, premeditated, preplanned, preconceived*. We'll have occasion, later in this and the remaining chapters, to define, apply, and grade the degree of blameworthiness of most of these variations of subjective fault.

The most common definition of specific intent is what we might call **general intent "plus,"** where "general intent" refers to the intent to commit the *actus reus* of the crime and "plus" refers to some "special mental element" in addition to the intent to commit the criminal act (LaFave 2003b, 1:354). For example, household burglary is a specific intent crime, because in addition to the intent to commit the household burglary *actus reus*—namely, breaking and entering someone else's house—there's the special mental element, the intent to commit a crime once inside the house (Chapter 11). Similarly, theft is a specific intent crime, because it requires the intent to commit the acts of taking and carrying away someone else's property *plus* the intention to deprive the owner of it permanently (Chapter 11). Sexual assault is not a specific intent crime because it requires the intent only to commit whatever acts of sexual contact or penetration are included in the *actus reus* element of the law.

In *People v. Disimone* (2002), the court affirmed Joseph Disimone's conviction for violating a Michigan statute making it a crime to "offer to vote more than once." In upholding the conviction, the court had to decide whether the law was a general or a specific intent crime.

CASE — *Did He "Offer to Vote" More Than Once?*

People v. Disimone
650 N.W.2d 436 (2002 Mich.App.)

HISTORY

Joseph Disimone, the defendant, was charged with violating a statute providing that a person shall not offer to vote . . . more than once at the same election either in the same or in another voting precinct. The Grand Traverse Circuit Court ruled that a conviction under this statute required the prosecutor to prove that defendant had a specific criminal intent, rather than a general intent, and the prosecutor appealed. The Court of Appeals held that, in proving that defendant made an "offer to vote" within the meaning of statute, the prosecutor was not required to establish that defendant had a specific criminal intent.

WILDER, J.

FACTS

This case involves defendant's voting activity in the November 7, 2000, general election. On that date, defendant went to a voting precinct in Grant Township and presented to the election workers what appeared to be a valid voter registration card that listed him as a Grant Township resident entitled to vote at that location. Defendant's name, however, did not appear on the Grant Township voter registration ledger. Consistent with procedure, one of the election workers, Sue Svec, attempted to contact the township clerk but was unable to immediately reach her after several calls.

Accordingly, because his voter registration card showed him to be a Grant Township resident, the Grant Township election workers permitted defendant to vote. Grant Township records establish that defendant actually voted at that location. Before he was permitted to vote, defendant made a comment to the effect that he could vote at his other voting place. Ms. Svec heard this comment and told him that he "better not." Later, the Grant Township Clerk called the voting precinct and informed Ms. Svec that defendant was not then registered to vote in Grant Township. Ms. Svec then contacted Colfax Township to advise election officials there that defendant had voted in Grant Township and that he should not be permitted to vote in Colfax Township.

At another time during the day of November 7, 2000, defendant also voted at the voting precinct in Colfax Township. According to the testimony of Cynthia Clark, elections chairperson for Colfax Township, sometime after defendant arrived at the Colfax Township voting precinct he expressed confusion about where he was supposed to vote. Ms. Clark checked the voter registration file box for information on defendant. The box contained several records in defendant's name, including the usual card generated and maintained by Colfax Township elections officials to record when a registered voter actually votes in an election, as well as a new registration card that had been sent to the Colfax Township Clerk. In addition, defendant was listed in the Qualified Voter File as a Colfax Township resident. On the basis of this information, Ms. Clark told defendant that he was eligible to vote in Colfax Township and defendant proceeded to vote at the

Colfax Township voting precinct. After he had voted, defendant asked Ms. Clark whether he was permitted to go to Grant Township to vote and she told him he was not.

OPINION

. . . In the circuit court, defendant asserted that M.C.L. ß 168.932a(e) should be construed to require the prosecutor to prove that defendant had a specific criminal intent, and filed a motion to have the jury instructed accordingly. The prosecution . . . challenged the defendant's assertion that an "offer to vote" within the meaning of the act was a specific intent crime. Following a hearing, the circuit court granted defendant's motion. The circuit court first found that defendant could not be convicted under the act unless the evidence established that defendant intended to have two votes counted, and then ruled that the jury would be instructed that they must find defendant had a specific criminal intent in order to convict the defendant. . . . We granted leave to consider the question whether M.C.L. ß 168.932a(e) requires proof of specific or general intent.

. . . Specific intent is defined as a particular criminal intent beyond the act done, whereas general intent is merely the intent to perform the physical act itself. To determine if a criminal statute requires specific intent, this Court looks to the mental state set forth in the statute. . . . Words typically found in specific intent statutes include "knowingly," "willfully," "purposely," and "intentionally." The most common usage of "specific intent" is to designate a special mental element which is required above and beyond any mental state required with respect to the *actus reus* of the crime. . . . A statute that requires a prosecutor to prove that the defendant intended to perform the criminal act creates a general intent crime. A statute that requires proof that the defendant had a particular criminal intent beyond the act done creates a specific intent crime.

. . . We conclude that the trial court erred in finding that the prosecutor was required to prove defendant had a specific criminal intent in order to convict defendant of making an "offer to vote . . . more than once at the same election either in the same or in another voting precinct" in violation of subsection 932a(e). We first note that the Legislature refrained from using the words "knowingly," "willfully," "purposefully" or "intentionally" in reference to the phrase "offer to vote," words typically found in specific intent statutes. In addition, the phrase "offer to vote" does not suggest a legislative design to require the prosecutor to prove defendant had an intent to cause a particular result or a desire that a specific consequence occur as the result of the performance of the prohibited act. . . .

In proving that defendant made an "offer to vote" within the meaning of M.C.L. ß 168.932a(e), the prosecutor is not required to establish that defendant had a specific criminal intent. Because the circuit court construed this provision of subsection 932a(e) as requiring proof of a specific criminal intent, we reverse the circuit court in part and remand for trial. We do not retain jurisdiction.

Questions

1. List Joseph Disimone's acts related to his voting in the 2000 election.

2. Did he intend to make the "bodily movements" involved in voting?

3. Did he "offer to vote more than once at the same election either in the same or in another voting precinct"?

4. Why does the court say that the prosecutor doesn't have to prove that Disimone intended to cause a particular election result?

5. Why would the prosecutor want the crime here to be a general intent crime?

6. Why would the defense want the crime to be a specific intent crime?

The Model Penal Code's (MPC's) Mental Attitudes

Ronald L. Gainer (1988), former deputy attorney general of the United States, wrote the following about the importance of the MPC's defining mental attitudes:

> The Code's provisions concerning culpable mental states introduced both reason and structure to a previously amorphous area of American law. For centuries, the approach to mental components of crimes had been a quagmire of legal refuse, obscured by a thin surface of general terminology denoting wrongfulness. The archaic verbiage suggesting evil and wickedness was replaced by the drafters with concepts of purpose, knowledge, recklessness, and negligence, and the concepts were structured to apply separately to actions, circumstances in which actions took place, and results. (575)

The MPC's culpability provisions were arrived at only after enormous effort and heated debate among some of the leading legal minds of judges, prosecutors, defense attorneys, and professors.

As we look at the MPC's four mental attitudes, we'll discuss how they're ranked according to their degree of culpability and how they're constructed to apply to the elements of act, mental attitude, attendant circumstances, and causing a "bad" result.

From most to least blameworthy, the MPC's four mental states are

1. Purposely

2. Knowingly

3. Recklessly

4. Negligently

The MPC specifies that all crimes requiring a mental element (most minor crimes and a few felonies don't) have to include one of these degrees of culpability. (Recklessness is the default degree of culpability where codes omit one.) The following section from the MPC defines the degrees of culpability:

MPC § 2.02. GENERAL REQUIREMENTS OF CULPABILITY.

1. *Minimum Requirements of Culpability.* . . . [A] person is not guilty of an offense unless he acted purposely, knowingly, recklessly or negligently . . . with respect to each material element of the offense.

2. *Kinds of Culpability Defined*
   a. **Purpose.** A person acts purposely with respect to a material element of an offense when:
      i. if the element involves the nature of his conduct or a result thereof, it is his conscious object to engage in conduct of that nature or to cause such a result;
      ii. [omitted]
   b. **Knowledge.** A person acts knowingly with respect to a material element of an offense when:
      i. if the element involves the nature of his conduct or the attendant circumstances, he is aware that his conduct is of that nature or that such circumstances exist; and
      ii. if the element involves a result of his conduct, he is aware that it is practically certain that his conduct will cause such a result.
   c. **Recklessness.** A person acts recklessly with respect to a material element of an offense when he consciously disregards a substantial and unjustifiable risk that the material element exists or will result from his conduct. The risk must be of such a nature and degree.
   d. **Negligence.** A person acts negligently with respect to a material element of an offense when he should be aware of a substantial and unjustifiable risk that the material element exists or will result from his conduct. The risk must be of such a nature and degree that the actor's failure to perceive it, considering the nature and purpose of his conduct and the circumstances known to him, involves a gross deviation from the standard of care that a reasonable person would observe in the actor's situation. (ALI 1985 1:2, 229)

Purpose: In the MPC, the first and most blameworthy state of mind, purposely committing a crime or causing a criminal result, is roughly the same as the idea in the everyday expression, "You hit me on purpose." Technically, it means having the purpose or "conscious object" to commit crimes. For example, in common-law burglary, the burglar has to break into and enter a house for the very purpose (with the conscious object) of committing a crime after getting inside. In murder, the murderer's purpose (conscious object) has to be to cause the victim's death. The Washington state court of appeals in *State v. Stark* (1992) examined and affirmed Calvin Stark's conviction because he had satisfied the mental element of purpose required by the Washington state assault statute.

State v. Stark

832 P.2d 109 (Wash.App.1992)

HISTORY

Calvin Stark was convicted in the Superior Court, Clallam County, Washington, of two counts of second-degree assault for intentionally exposing his sexual partners to the human immunodeficiency virus (HIV), and he appealed. The Washington Court of Appeals affirmed and remanded the case for resentencing.

PETRICH, CJ.

FACTS

On March 25, 1988, Calvin Stark tested positive for HIV, which was confirmed by further tests on June 25 and on June 30, 1988. From June 30, 1988, to October 3, 1989, the staff of the Clallam County Health Department had five meetings with Stark during which Stark went through extensive counseling about his infection. He was taught about "safe sex," the risk of spreading the infection, and the necessity of informing his partners before engaging in sexual activity with them.

On October 3, 1989, Dr. Locke, the Clallam County Health Officer, after learning that Stark had disregarded this advice and was engaging in unprotected sexual activity, issued a cease and desist order as authorized by RCW 70.24.024(3)(b). Stark did not cease and desist, and, consequently, on March 1, 1990, Dr. Locke went to the County prosecutor's office. . . . The prosecutor . . . had Dr. Locke complete a police report. The State then charged Stark with three counts of assault in the second degree under RCW 9A.36.021(1)(e). [RCW 9A.36.021(1)(e) provides:

> (1) A person is guilty of assault in the second degree if he or she, under circumstances not amounting to assault in the first degree: . . .
> (e) With intent to inflict bodily harm, exposes or transmits human immunodeficiency virus as defined in chapter 70.24 RCW; . . ."

Each count involved a different victim: Count One: The victim and Stark engaged in sexual intercourse on October 27 and October 29, 1989. On both occasions, Stark withdrew his penis from the victim prior to ejaculation. The victim, who could not become pregnant because she had previously had her fallopian tubes tied, asked Stark on the second occasion why he withdrew. He then told her that he was HIV positive.

Count Two: The victim and Stark had sexual relations on at least six occasions between October, 1989, and February, 1990. Stark wore a condom on two or three occasions, but on the others, he ejaculated outside of her body. On each occasion, they had vaginal intercourse. On one occasion Stark tried to force her to have anal intercourse. They also engaged in oral sex. When she told Stark that she had heard rumors that he was HIV positive, he admitted that he was and then gave the victim an AZT pill "to slow down the process of the AIDS."

Count Three: The victim and Stark had sexual relations throughout their brief relationship. It was "almost non-stop with him," "almost every night" during August 1989. Stark never wore a condom and never informed the victim he was HIV positive. When pressed, Stark denied rumors about his HIV status. The victim broke off the relationship because of Stark's drinking, after which Stark told her that he carried HIV and explained that if he had told her, she would not have had anything to do with him.

. . . At the jury trial, the victim in count one testified to her contacts with Stark and the jury received Dr. Locke's deposition testimony regarding the Health Department's contacts with Stark. Stark did not testify. In the bench trial [trial without a jury], Dr. Locke testified. There the State also presented the testimony of one of Stark's neighborhood friends. She testified that one night Stark came to her apartment after drinking and told her and her daughter that he was HIV positive. When she asked him if he knew that he had to protect himself and everybody else, he replied, "I don't care. If I'm going to die, everybody's going to die." The jury found Stark guilty on count one.

A second trial judge found Stark guilty of the second and third counts at a bench trial. On count one, Stark was given an exceptional sentence of 120 months based on his future danger to the community. The standard range for that offense was 13 to 17 months. On counts two and three, Stark was given the low end of the standard range, 43 months each, to be served concurrently, but consecutively to count one.

OPINION

. . . Stark contends that there is insufficient evidence to prove he "exposed" anyone to HIV or that he acted with intent to inflict bodily harm. Since Stark is undisputedly HIV positive, he necessarily exposed his sexual partners to the virus by engaging in unprotected sexual intercourse. The testimony of the three victims supports this conclusion.

The testimony supporting the element of intent to inflict bodily harm includes Dr. Locke's statements detailing his counseling sessions with Stark. With regard to the first victim, we know that Stark knew he was HIV positive, that he had been counseled to use "safe sex" methods, and that it had been explained to Stark that coitus interruptus will not prevent the spread of the virus. While there is evidence to support Stark's position, all the evidence viewed in a light most favorable to the State supports a finding of intent beyond a reasonable doubt. The existence of noncriminal explanations does not preclude a finding that a defendant intended to harm his sexual partners.

With regard to the later victims, we have, in addition to this same evidence, Stark's neighbor's testimony that Stark, when confronted about his sexual practices, said, "I don't care. If I'm going to die, everybody's going to die." We also have the testimony of the victim in count two that Stark attempted to have anal intercourse with her and did have oral sex, both methods the counselors told Stark he needed to avoid.

We affirm the convictions. . . .

Questions

1. Identify all of the facts relevant to determining Stark's mental attitude regarding each of the elements in the assault statute.

2. Using the common-law definition of *specific intent* and the Model Penal Code definitions of *purposely, knowingly, recklessly,* and *negligently,* and relying on the relevant facts, identify Stark's intention with respect to his acts.

3. Is motive important in this case? Should it be?

EXPLORING FURTHER

Purposely

Did He Assault for the Purpose of Ethnic Intimidation?

Commonwealth v. Barnette, 699 N.E.2d 1230 (Mass.App. 1998)

FACTS Maria Acuna was concerned that Aubrey Barnette, who was next door at his sister's house baby-sitting his niece, was going to break her fence. Acuna called through the window to Barnette, asking him to please not trespass and telling him that she would come downstairs to help him out. She did and faced Barnette across the fence. Barnette said:

"You bitch. You don't fit here. What are you doing here, you damn Mexican? Why don't you go back to your country? All of you come and get our jobs and our houses. Get out of here. You don't fit here. I'll kill you and your son." Barnette's tirade continued in the same vein: "I am a black man. I have been living here for seven years. I can go inside your house or anyplace I want to. Because nobody will stop me, you bitch, and I will kill you if you say something. Why don't you just go back to your country?

While standing next to the fence shouting at Acuna, Barnette thrust his fist toward her face so that she "could almost feel the hit of his fist" in her nose and face. Barnette then threw his fingers in a forking motion toward her, coming to within an inch of her eyes.

He was yelling at Acuna so loudly that Acuna's son, Israel Rodriguez, awoke from a nap and came outside to the backyard, pulled his mother away from the fence, and demanded to know from Barnette what was going on. Barnette now attempted to hit Rodriguez with his fists, from the other side of the fence, rattling the gate, trying to enter the backyard, and saying: "You little s__t. Come up here. I'm going to take the f____ing s__t out of you and your mother together. I will beat you both to death."

Acuna and Rodriguez both testified that they felt afraid and threatened by Barnette's rage and determination to hit them. Rodriguez called the police.

Officer Paul Callahan responded to the call and arrived at Acuna's residence to find her and her son visibly upset. In an interview the next day, Barnette admitted that he had said that Acuna should "go back to where she came from."

Did Barnette assault Acuna and Rodriguez "for the purpose of intimidation because of said person's race, color, religion, or national origin?" Yes, said the Massachusetts intermediate court of appeals.

DECISION
In general, a hate crime is "a crime in which the defendant's conduct was motivated by hatred, bias, or prejudice, based on the actual or perceived race, color, religion, national origin, ethnicity, gender, or sexual orientation of another individual or group of individuals." Hate crime laws such as G.L. c. 265, § 39, operate to "enhance the penalty of criminal conduct when it is motivated by racial hatred or bigotry." It is not the conduct but the underlying motivation that distinguishes the crime.

The defendant contends that his outburst at Acuna and Rodriguez was motivated by his anger . . . not . . . by any anti-Mexican sentiment. The defendant believes that the fact that his niece is of Puerto Rican descent demonstrates that he lacks any anti-Hispanic bias or prejudice.

The uncontroverted evidence at trial, however, was that the defendant was shouting specifically anti-Mexican slurs at Acuna and Rodriguez. . . . The trial judge found that the fact that the defendant has an Hispanic niece was not necessarily relevant to whether the victims in the instant case were subjected to racial invective and actions on the part of the defendant. . . .

 Go to the Criminal Law 9e website for the full text of the Exploring Further excerpts: www.thomsonedu.com/criminaljustice/samaha. (Excerpts on "purposely.")

Knowledge: The MPC and many modern statutes identify *knowledge* as the second most blameworthy mental state. *Awareness* (sometimes called by its Latin name **scienter**) is the mental aspect of conduct—you knew what you were doing when you stole your roommate's iPod. Remember, criminal conduct consists of a voluntary act *and* an accompanying mental state. Awareness is also the mental state of the attendant circumstances—you knew the iPod belonged to your roommate. It's not quite the same for result crimes. There, the MPC provides that it's enough for you to be "practically certain" your conduct will cause the result. Professor Markus Dubber (2002) explains why:

> Assuming that I'm blessed with neither omnipotence (allowing me to change day to night) nor prescience (allowing me to see the future), it makes no sense to say that I *know* that what I'm doing will lead to a particular result. . . . A practical certainty . . . [is] the closest thing we ordinary mortals can come to know anything about the future. (65–66)

Knowledge is not the same as purpose or conscious objective. So a surgeon who removes a cancerous uterus to save a pregnant woman's life knowingly kills the fetus in her womb, but killing the fetus wasn't the purpose (conscious object) of the removal. Rather, the death of the fetus is an unavoidable side effect of removing the cancerous uterus.

Similarly, treason, the only crime defined in the U.S. Constitution, requires that traitors provide aid and comfort to enemies, not just knowingly but for the purpose of overthrowing the government. Actors may provide aid and comfort to enemies of the United States knowing their actions are practically certain to contribute to overthrowing the government. But that isn't enough; they have to provide them for the purpose of overthrowing the U.S. government. If their conscious object was to get rich, then they haven't committed treason (*Haupt v. U.S.* 1947). The purpose requirement in treason led to the enactment of other statutes to fill the void—for example, making it a crime to provide secrets to the enemy, an offense that requires only that defendants purposely provide such secrets.

In *State v. Jantzi* (1982), the Oregon Court of Appeals concluded that Pete Jantzi didn't knowingly assault Rex Anderson. The case excerpt will show you just how complicated the application of "knowingly" to the facts of specific cases can get.

CASE | *Did He "Knowingly" Assault with a Knife?*

State v. Jantzi
641 P.2d 62 (1982 Or.App.)

HISTORY

Pete Jantzi was convicted in the Circuit Court, Klamath County, of assault in the second degree, and he appealed. The Court of Appeals held that where defendant knew he had [a] dangerous weapon and that [a] confrontation was going to occur but [he] did not intend to stab victim, defendant acted "recklessly," not "knowingly," and, thus, could be convicted of assault in the third degree rather

than assault in the second degree. Affirmed as modified; remanded for resentencing.

GILLETTE, J.

FACTS

Pete Jantzi, the defendant, testified [and the trial court judge believed] that he was asked to accompany Diane Anderson, who shared a house with defendant and several other people, to the home of her estranged husband, Rex. While Diane was in the house talking with Rex, defendant was using the blade of his knife to let the air out of the tires on Rex's van. Another person put sugar in the gas tank of the van.

While the Andersons were arguing, Diane apparently threatened damage to Rex's van and indicated that someone might be tampering with the van at that moment. Rex's roommate ran out of the house and saw two men beside the van. He shouted and began to run toward the men. Rex ran from the house and began to chase defendant, who ran down a bicycle path. Defendant, still holding his open knife, jumped into the bushes beside the path and landed in the weeds. He crouched there, hoping that Rex would not see him and would pass by. Rex, however, jumped on top of defendant and grabbed his shirt. They rolled over and Rex was stabbed in the abdomen by defendant's knife. Defendant could not remember making a thrusting or swinging motion with the knife; he did not intend to stab Rex.

OPINION

The indictment charged that defendant "did unlawfully and knowingly cause physical injury to Rex Anderson by means of a deadly weapon, to-wit: knife, by stabbing the said Rex Anderson with said knife." ORS 163.175 provides that:

> (1) A person commits the crime of assault in the second degree if [he]: . . .
>> (b) Intentionally or knowingly causes physical injury to another by means of a deadly or dangerous weapon; . . .
> "Knowingly" is defined in ORS 161.085(8):
> "Knowingly" or "with knowledge" when used with respect to conduct or to a circumstance described by a statute defining an offense, means that a person acts with an awareness that [his] conduct is of a nature so described or that a circumstance so described exists."

[According to the commentary to the New York Criminal Code that the Oregon Criminal Code was based on:]

Under the formulations of the Model Penal Code (§ 2.02(2bii)) and the Illinois Criminal Code (ß 4–5(b)), "knowingly" is, in one phase, almost synonymous with "intentionally" in that a person achieves a given result " knowingly" when he "is practically certain" that his conduct will cause that result. This distinction between "knowingly" and "intentionally" in that context appears highly technical or semantic, and the [New York] Revised Penal Law does

not employ the word "knowingly" in defining result offenses. Murder of the common law variety, for example, is committed intentionally or not at all. (Commentary ß 15.05, New York Revised Penal Law)

The trial court . . . [*continued:*] "Basically, the facts of this case are: that Defendant was letting air out of the tires and he has an open knife. He was aware of what his knife is like. He is aware that it is a dangerous weapon. He runs up the bicycle path. He has a very firm grip on the knife, by his own admission, and he knows the knife is dangerous. It is not necessary for the state to prove that he thrust it or anything else. Quite frankly, this could have all been avoided if he had gotten rid of the knife, so he 'knowingly caused physical injury to Rex Anderson.' And, therefore, I find him guilty of that particular charge."

Although the trial judge found defendant guilty of "knowingly" causing physical injury to Anderson, what he described in his findings is recklessness. The court found that defendant knew he had a dangerous weapon and that a confrontation was going to occur. The court believed that defendant did not intend to stab Anderson. The court's conclusion seems to be based on the reasoning that because defendant knew it was possible that an injury would occur, he acted "knowingly." However, a person who "is aware of and consciously disregards a substantial and unjustifiable risk" that an injury will occur acts "recklessly," not "knowingly."

We have authority, pursuant to . . . the Oregon Constitution, to enter the judgment that should have been entered in the court below. Assault in the third degree is a lesser included offense of the crime of assault in the second degree charged in the accusatory instrument in this case. We modify defendant's conviction to a conviction for the crime of assault in the third degree.

Conviction affirmed as modified; remanded for resentencing.

Questions

1. List all of the facts relevant to determining Pete Jantzi's state of mind.

2. State the Oregon statute's mental element for assault.

3. State how, and explain why, Oregon modified the MPC definition of *knowingly.*

4. In your opinion, did Jantzi knowingly assault Rex Anderson? Back up your answer with the facts of the case and the trial and appellate court's opinions.

Recklessness: Awareness is the watchword for *recklessness*, just as it is for knowledge. But there's a critical difference; it's awareness of the *risk* of causing a criminal result, not of causing an *actual* criminal result. Notice that recklessness doesn't apply to conduct crimes for the obvious reason that you have to be aware you're committing a voluntary act (Chapter 3). It *can* refer to attendant circumstances; for instance, you can be aware that a woman you're about to have sex with is under the legal age.

Reckless people know they're creating risks of harm but they don't intend, or at least they don't expect, to cause harm itself. Recklessness (conscious risk creation) isn't as blameworthy as acting purposely or knowingly because reckless defendants don't act for the very purpose of doing harm; they don't even act knowing harm is practically certain to follow. Reckless defendants *do* know they're creating risks of harm. So the blameworthiness of recklessness lies in the probabilities of purpose and knowledge; it lies in certainties—or at least in practical certainties.

Recklessness requires more than awareness of ordinary risks; it requires awareness of "substantial and unjustifiable risks." The MPC proposes that fact finders determine recklessness according to a two-pronged test:

1. Were the defendants *aware* of how substantial and unjustifiable the risks that they disregarded were? Under this prong, notice that even a substantial risk isn't by itself reckless. For example, a doctor who performs life-saving surgery has created a substantial risk. But the risk is justifiable because the doctor took it to save the life of the patient. This prong doesn't answer the important questions of *how* substantial and *how* unjustifiable the risk has to be to amount to recklessness. So the second prong gives guidance to juries.

2. Does the defendant's disregard of risk amount to so "gross a deviation from the standard" that a law-abiding person would observe in that situation? This prong requires juries to make the judgment whether the risk is substantial and unjustifiable enough to deserve condemnation in the form of criminal liability.

This test has both a subjective and an objective component. The first prong of the test is subjective; it focuses on a defendant's actual awareness. The second prong is objective; it measures conduct according to how it deviates from what reasonable people do.

It should be clear to you by now that actual harm isn't the conscious object of reckless wrongdoers. In fact, most reckless actors probably hope they don't hurt anyone. Or, at most, they don't care if they hurt anyone. But the heart of their culpability is that even with the full knowledge of the risks, they act anyway. For example, in one case, a large drug company knew that a medication it sold to control high blood pressure had caused severe liver damage and even death in some patients; it sold the drug anyway. The company's officers, who made the decision to sell the drug, didn't want to hurt anyone (indeed, they hoped no one would die or suffer liver damage). They sought only profit for the company, but they were prepared to risk the deaths of their customers to make a profit (Shenon 1985, A1).

Negligence: Like recklessness, *negligence* is about risk creation. But recklessness is about *consciously* creating risks; negligence is about *unconsciously* (unreasonably) creating risks. Here's an example of a negligent wrongdoer: "OK, so you didn't *mean* to hurt him, and you didn't even *know* the odds were very high you could hurt him, but you *should've* known the odds were high, and you did hurt him." The test for negligence is totally objective—the actors *should* have known, even though in fact they didn't know, they were creating risks. Put another way, a reasonable person would've known she was creating the risk.

For example, a reasonable person would know that driving 50 miles an hour down a crowded street creates a risk of harm. The driver who should know what a reasonable person would know, but doesn't, is negligent. The driver who knows it but drives too fast anyway is reckless.

Negligent defendants, like reckless defendants, have to create substantial and unjustifiable risks—risks that grossly deviate from the ordinary standards of behavior. In *Koppersmith v. State* (1999), the Alabama Court of Appeals wrestled with the difficulty of drawing the line between recklessness and negligence.

CASE — *Did He Kill His Wife Recklessly or Negligently?*

Koppersmith v. State
742 So.2d 206 (Ala.App. 1999)

HISTORY

Gregory Koppersmith, the appellant, was charged with the murder of his wife, Cynthia ("Cindy") Michel Koppersmith. He was convicted of reckless manslaughter, a violation of § 13A-6-3(a)(1), Ala.Code 1975, and the trial court sentenced him to 20 years in prison. The Alabama Court of Appeals reversed and remanded.

BASCHAB, J.

FACTS

Gregory Koppersmith (appellant) and his wife were arguing in the yard outside of their residence. Cindy tried to enter the house to end the argument, but the appellant prevented her from going inside. A physical confrontation ensued, and Cindy fell off of a porch into the yard. She died as a result of a skull fracture to the back of her head.

In a statement he made to law enforcement officials after the incident, the appellant gave the following summary of the events leading up to Cindy's death. He and Cindy had been arguing and were on a porch outside of their residence. Cindy had wanted to go inside the house, but he had wanted to resolve the argument first. As she tried to go inside, he stepped in front of her and pushed her back. Cindy punched at him, and he grabbed her.

When Cindy tried to go inside again, he wrapped his arms around her from behind to stop her. Cindy bit him on the arm, and he "slung" her to the ground. He then jumped down and straddled her, stating that he "had her by the head" and indicating that he moved her head up and down, as if slamming it into the ground. When Cindy stopped struggling, he rolled her over and found a brick covered with blood under her head. The appellant stated that, although Cindy fell near a flowerbed, he did not know there were bricks in the grass.

At trial, the appellant testified that Cindy had tried to go into the house two or three times, but he had stopped her from doing so. During that time, she punched at him

and he pushed her away from him. At one point, he put his arms around her from behind to restrain her, and she turned her head and bit him. When she bit him, he pulled her by her sweater and she tripped. He then "slung" her off of him, and she tripped and fell three to four feet to the ground. He jumped off of the porch and straddled her, grabbing her by the shoulders and telling her to calm down. When he realized she was not moving, he lifted her head and noticed blood all over his hands.

Koppersmith testified that, when he grabbed Cindy from behind, he did not intend to harm her. He also testified that, when he "slung" her away from him off of the porch, he was not trying to hurt her and did not intend to throw her onto a brick. Rather, he stated that he simply reacted after she bit his arm. He also testified that he did not know there were bricks in the yard, that he had not attempted to throw her in a particular direction, and that he was not aware of any risk or harm his actions might cause.

He further testified that, when he grabbed and shook her after she fell, he did not intend to harm her, he did not know there was a brick under her head, and he did not intend to hit her head on a brick or anything else. Instead, he testified that he was trying to get her to calm down.

The medical examiner, Dr. Gregory Wanger, testified that the pattern on the injury to the victim's skull matched the pattern on one of the bricks found at the scene. He stated that, based on the position of the skull fracture and the bruising to the victim's brain, the victim's head was moving when it sustained the injury. He testified that her injuries could have been caused by her falling off of the porch and hitting her head on a brick or from her head being slammed into a brick.

The indictment in this case alleged that the appellant "did, with the intent to cause the death of Cynthia Michel Koppersmith, cause the death of Cynthia Michel Koppersmith, by striking her head against a brick, in violation of § 13A-6-2 of the Code of Alabama. (C.R.11)." Koppersmith requested that the trial court instruct the jury on criminally negligent homicide as a lesser included offense of murder. However, the trial court denied that request, and it instructed the jury only on the offense of reckless manslaughter.

OPINION

Section 13A-6-3(a), Ala.Code 1975, provides that a person commits the crime of manslaughter if he recklessly causes the death of another person. A person acts recklessly with respect to a result or to a circumstance described by a statute defining an offense when he is aware of and consciously disregards a substantial and unjustifiable risk that the result will occur or that the circumstance exists. The risk must be of such nature and degree that disregard thereof constitutes a gross deviation from the standard of conduct that a reasonable person would observe in the situation.

. . . "A person commits the crime of criminally negligent homicide if he causes the death of another person by criminal negligence." §13A-6-4(a), Ala.Code 1975. A person acts with criminal negligence with respect to a result or to a circumstance which is defined by statute as an offense when he fails to perceive a substantial and unjustifiable risk that the result will occur or that the circumstance exists. The risk must be of such nature and degree that the failure to perceive it constitutes a gross deviation from the standard of care that a reasonable person would observe in the situation. A court or jury may consider statutes or ordinances regulating the defendant's conduct as bearing upon the question of criminal negligence.

. . . The only difference between manslaughter under Section 13A-6-3(a)(1) and criminally negligent homicide is the difference between recklessness and criminal negligence. The reckless offender is aware of the risk and "consciously disregards" it. On the other hand, the criminally negligent offender is not aware of the risk created ("fails to perceive") and, therefore, cannot be guilty of consciously disregarding it. The difference between the terms "recklessly" and "negligently" . . . is one of kind, rather than degree. Each actor creates a risk or harm. The reckless actor is aware of the risk and disregards it; the negligent actor is not aware of the risk but should have been aware of it. . . .

Thus, we must determine whether there was any evidence before the jury from which it could have concluded that the appellant did not perceive that his wife might die as a result of his actions. We conclude that there was evidence from which the jury could have reasonably believed that his conduct that caused her to fall was unintentional and that he was not aware he was creating a risk to his wife. He testified that, after she bit him, his reaction—which caused her to fall to the ground—was simply reflexive. He also testified that he did not know there were bricks in the yard. Even in his statement to the police in which he said he was slamming her head against the ground, Koppersmith said he did not know at that time that there was a brick under her head. Finally, he stated that he did not intend to throw her onto a brick or harm her in any way when he "slung" her, and that he did not intend to hit her head on a brick or otherwise harm her when he grabbed and shook her after she had fallen.

Because there was a reasonable theory from the evidence that would have supported giving a jury instruction on criminally negligent homicide, the trial court erred in refusing to instruct the jury on criminally negligent homicide. Thus, we must reverse the trial court's judgment and remand this case for a new trial.

REVERSED AND REMANDED.

Questions

1. List all of the facts relevant to determining Koppersmith's mental state with respect both to his acts and the results of his actions.

2. In your opinion, was Koppersmith reckless or negligent? Support your answer with relevant facts.

3. Is it possible to argue that Koppersmith knowingly or even purposely killed his wife? What facts, if any, support these two states of mind?

 Go to the Criminal Law 9e website to find Exercise 4.1 to learn more about *mens rea*: www.thomsonedu .com/criminaljustice/samaha.

LIABILITY WITHOUT FAULT: STRICT LIABILITY

You've learned that criminal liability depends on at least some degree of blameworthiness, and that's true when we're talking about serious crimes like the cases in the previous culpability sections. But there are enormous numbers of minor crimes where there's liability without either subjective or objective fault. We call this liability without fault **strict liability**, meaning it's based on voluntary action alone. Let's be blunt: Strict liability makes *accidental* injuries a crime. In strict liability cases, the prosecution has to prove only that defendants committed a voluntary criminal act that caused harm. The U.S. Supreme Court has upheld the power of legislatures to create strict liability offenses to protect the "public health and safety," as long as they make clear they're imposing liability without fault (Chapter 3).

Supporters of strict liability make two main arguments. First, there's a strong public interest in protecting public health and safety. Strict liability arose during the industrial revolution when manufacturing, mining, and commerce exposed large numbers of the public to death, mutilation, and disease from poisonous fumes, unsafe railroads, workplaces, and adulterated foods, and other products.

Second, the penalty for strict liability offenses is almost always mild (fines, not jail time).

But strict liability still has its critics. The critics say it's too easy to expand strict liability beyond offenses that seriously endanger the public. They're always wary of making exceptions to blameworthiness, which is central to the *mens rea* principle. It does no good (and probably a lot of harm) to punish people who haven't harmed others purposely, knowingly, recklessly, or at least negligently.

At the end of the day, a criminal law without blameworthiness will lose its force as a stern moral code. The court decided whether Minnesota's legislature created a strict liability open bottle offense in *State v. Loge* (2000).

CASE   *Did He Have to "Know" There Was an Open Bottle in the Car?*

State v. Loge
608 N.W.2d 152 (Minn. 2000)

HISTORY

Steven Loge, the defendant, was convicted in the District Court, Freeborn County, of keeping an opened bottle of intoxicating liquor in an automobile while on a public highway, and he appealed. The Court of Appeals affirmed. The Supreme Court affirmed.

GILBERT, J.

FACTS

Appellant Steven Mark Loge was cited . . . for a violation of Minn. Stat. § 169.122, subd. 3 (1998), which makes it unlawful for the driver of a motor vehicle, when the owner is not present, "to keep or allow to be kept in a motor vehicle when such vehicle is upon the public highway any bottle or receptacle containing intoxicating liquors or 3.2 percent malt liquors which has been opened." Violation of the statute is a misdemeanor.

On September 2, 1997, Loge borrowed his father's pickup truck to go to his evening job. Driving alone on his way home from work, he was stopped by two Albert Lea city police officers on County Road 18 at approximately 8:15 P.M. because he appeared to be speeding. Loge got out

of his truck and stood by the driver's side door. While one officer was talking with Loge, the second officer, who was standing by the passenger side of the truck, observed a bottle, which he believed to be a beer bottle, sticking partially out of a brown paper bag underneath the passenger's side of the seat. He retrieved that bottle, which was open and had foam on the inside. He searched the rest of the truck and found one full, unopened can of beer and one empty beer can. After the second officer found the beer bottle, the first officer asked Loge if he had been drinking.

Loge stated that he had two beers while working and was on his way home. Loge passed all standard field sobriety tests. The officers gave Loge a citation . . . for a violation of the open bottle statute. . . .

[At] the trial . . . Loge testified that the bottle was not his, he did not know it was in the truck and had said that to one of the officers. . . . The trial court found that one of the police officers "observed the neck of the bottle, which was wrapped in a brown paper sack, under the pickup's seat of the truck being operated by defendant." . . . The trial court held that subdivision 3 creates "absolute liability" on a driver/owner to "inspect and determine . . . whether there are any containers" in the motor vehicle in violation of the open bottle law and found Loge guilty. Loge was sentenced to five days in jail, execution stayed, placed on probation for one year, and fined $150 plus costs of $32.50.

Loge appealed the verdict. . . . In a published opinion, the court of appeals affirmed the decision of the trial court. . . . The court of appeals held that proof of knowledge that the bottle was in the truck is not required to sustain a conviction. Loge's petition for further review was granted. The Attorney General then assumed responsibility for this case and filed a respondent's brief in which the Attorney General argues, contrary to the previous position of the state, that there is no knowledge requirement under subdivision 3.

OPINION

Loge is seeking reversal of his conviction because, he argues, the trial court and court of appeals erroneously interpreted subdivision 3 of the open bottle statute not to require proof of knowledge. Minnesota Statutes § 169.122 reads in part:

> *Subdivision 1.* No person shall drink or consume intoxicating liquors or 3.2 percent malt liquors in any motor vehicle when such vehicle is upon a public highway.
>
> *Subdivision 2.* No person shall have in possession while in a private motor vehicle upon a public highway, any bottle or receptacle containing intoxicating liquor or 3.2 percent malt liquor which has been opened, or the seal broken, or the contents of which have been partially removed. . . . This subdivision does not apply to a bottle or receptacle that is in the trunk of the vehicle if it is equipped with a trunk, or that is in another area of the vehicle not normally occupied by the driver and passengers if the vehicle is not equipped with a trunk.
>
> *Subdivision 3.* It shall be unlawful for the owner of any private motor vehicle or the driver, if the owner be not then present in the motor vehicle, to keep or allow to be kept in a motor vehicle when such vehicle is upon the public highway any bottle or receptacle containing intoxicating liquors or 3.2 percent malt liquors which has been opened, or the seal broken, or the contents of which have been partially removed except when such bottle or receptacle shall be kept in the trunk of the motor vehicle when such vehicle is equipped with a trunk, or kept in some other area of the vehicle not normally occupied by the driver or passengers, if the motor vehicle is not equipped with a trunk. A utility compartment or glove compartment shall be deemed to be within the area occupied by the driver and passengers.

. . . An analysis of a statute must begin with a careful and close examination of the statutory language . . . to ascertain and effectuate legislative intent. If the meaning of the statute is "clear and free from all ambiguity, the letter of the law shall not be disregarded under the pretext of pursuing the spirit." . . .

. . . Minn.Stat. § 169.122, subd. 3 . . . establishes liability for . . . a driver when that driver "keeps or *allows* to be kept" [emphasis added] any open bottle containing intoxicating liquor within the area normally occupied by the driver and passengers. These two alternate concepts are separated by the disjunctive "or," not "and." Unlike the use of the word "and," "or" signifies the distinction between two factual situations. We have long held that in the absence of some ambiguity surrounding the legislature's use of the word "or," we will read it in the disjunctive and require that only one of the possible factual situations be present in order for the statute to be satisfied. Accordingly, we limit our opinion to the words "to keep."

. . . In delineating the elements of the crime, we have also held that the legislature is entitled to consider what it deems "expedient and best suited to the prevention of crime and disorder." . . . If knowledge was a necessary element of the open container offense, there would be a substantial, if not insurmountable, difficulty of proof. . . . It is therefore reasonable to conclude that the legislature, weighing the significant danger to the public, decided that proof of knowledge under subdivision 3 was not required.

The legislature has made knowledge distinctions within its traffic statutes that also guide our interpretation. For example, with respect to marijuana in a motor vehicle, the Minnesota legislature has used language similar to the language found in section 169.122, subdivision 3 ("keep or allow to be kept") but added a knowledge requirement. An owner, or if the owner is not present, the driver, is guilty of a misdemeanor if he *"knowingly* keeps or allows to be kept" [emphasis added] marijuana in a motor vehicle. Minn.Stat. § 152.027, subd. 3 (1998). . . . If the legislature had intended section 169.122 to have a knowledge requirement, it could have added the word "knowingly," as the legislature did in section 152.027. . . .

Lastly, Loge argues that an interpretation excluding knowledge as an element could lead to absurd results. While it is true that the legislature does not intend a result that is absurd or unreasonable, we do not believe such a result exists here. Loge's conviction resulted from an officer standing outside the truck observing the open container of beer sticking partially out of a brown bag underneath the seat on the passenger side of the truck Loge was driving. By simply taking control of the truck, Loge took control and charge of the contents of the truck, including the open bottle, even if he did not know the open bottle was in the truck. . . .

AFFIRMED.

DISSENT

ANDERSON, J.

I respectfully dissent. In its effort to reach a correct policy decision, the majority disregards our proper role as interpreters of the law. In doing so, the majority has preempted the legislature's function and assumed the mantle of policymaker.

I agree that under certain circumstances the legislature may provide that criminal liability attach without requiring any showing of intent or knowledge on the part of the person charged. Further, in the context of open containers of alcohol in motor vehicles, there is a credible argument that it is good public policy given the social and economic costs that result from the combination of alcohol and motor vehicles. But, all of that said, the majority's analysis simply does not demonstrate the requisite clear statement of legislative intent necessary to create criminal liability in the absence of a showing of knowledge or intent. . . .

We have stated that when the legislature intends to make an act unlawful and to impose criminal sanctions without any requirement of intent or knowledge, it must do so clearly. . . . Historically, our substantive criminal law is based upon a theory of punishing the vicious will. It postulates a free agent confronted with a choice between doing right and doing wrong and choosing freely to do wrong. . . . § 169.122, subd. 3, simply lacks the requisite clarity to support the imposition of criminal liability without any showing of intent or knowledge. . . .

. . . The majority cannot avoid the implications of the term "allow" because it is convenient to do so. In other contexts, we have held that the inclusion of words like "permit" (a synonym of "allow") clearly indicates a legislative intent to require some level of knowledge or intent. . . .

. . . Under the majority's holding, we now will impose criminal liability on a person, not simply for an act that the person does not know is criminal, but also for an act the person does not even know he is committing. While the district court and the majority seem to assume that everyone who drives a motor vehicle knows that he or she is obligated to search the entire passenger compartment of the vehicle before driving on the state's roads, the law imposes no such requirement.

Most drivers would be surprised to discover that after anyone else used their vehicle—children, friends, spouse—they are criminally liable for any open containers of alcohol that are present, regardless of whether they know the containers are there. This also means that any prudent operator of a motor vehicle must also carefully check any case of packaged alcohol before transport and ensure that each container's seal is not broken. See Minn.Stat. § 169.122 (defining an open bottle as a container that is open, has the contents partially removed, or has the seal broken). Under the majority's interpretation, all of these situations would render the driver criminally liable under Minn.Stat. § 169.122. Without a more clear statement by the legislature that this is the law, I cannot agree with such an outcome.

Questions

1. What words, if any, in the statute indicate a *mens rea* requirement?

2. What *mens rea*, if any, do the words in the statute require?

3. Summarize the arguments that the majority of the court gives to support this as a strict liability offense.

4. What arguments did the dissent give in response to the majority's arguments?

5. Do you agree with the majority or the dissent? Defend your answer.

 Go to the Criminal Law 9e website to find Exercise 4.2, Open Bottle Laws: www.thomsonedu.com/criminaljustice/samaha.

THE PRINCIPLE OF CONCURRENCE

The **principle of concurrence** means that some mental fault has to trigger the *actus reus* in criminal conduct crimes and the cause in bad-result crimes. So all crimes, except strict liability offenses, are subject to the concurrence requirement. In practice, concurrence is an element in all crimes where the mental attitude was formed with purpose, knowledge, recklessness, or negligence. Suppose you and your friend agree to meet at her house on a cold winter night. She's late because her car won't start. So she calls you on her cell phone and tells you to break the lock on her front door so you can wait inside safe from the cold. But once you're inside, you decide to steal her TiVo. Have you committed burglary? No, because in crimes of criminal conduct, the principle of concurrence requires that a criminal intent (*mens rea*) trigger a criminal act (*actus reus*). You decided to steal her TiVo *after* you broke into and entered her house. Burglary requires that the intent to steal set in motion the acts of breaking and entering. That's how concurrence applies to burglary, a crime of criminal conduct.

Now, let's look at an example of concurrence in murder, a bad-result crime. Shafeah hates her sister Nazirah and plans to kill her by running over her with her Jeep Grand Cherokee. Coincidentally, just as Shafeah is headed toward Nazirah in her Cherokee, a complete stranger in a Hummer H1 appears out of nowhere and accidentally runs over and kills Nazirah. Shafeah gets out of her Grand Cherokee, runs over to Nazirah's dead body, and gleefully dances around it. Although definitely a creepy thing to do, Shafeah's not a murderer because her criminal conduct (driving her Cherokee with the intent to kill Nazirah) didn't cause Nazirah's death. Concurrence here means the criminal conduct has to produce the criminal harm; the harm can't be a coincidence (Hall 1960, 185–90; Chapter 11).

We'll say no more about concurrence, either here or in the remaining chapters. Not because it's not important. Quite the contrary, it's critical to criminal liability. But it's never an issue, at least not in real cases—not in the thousands of appellate court cases I've read over the years. And from what lawyers and trial judges I've known tell me, it's never an issue in the cases they try and decide. It's mentioned, as it's mentioned in this section, but that's the end of it. So for your purposes, know what it is, know it's a critical element, and that's enough.

THE PRINCIPLE OF CAUSATION

The **principle of causation** is about *attribution* (also called "imputation"). It's when the law holds an actor accountable for the results of her conduct. So causation only applies to bad-result crimes, the most prominent being criminal homicide (Chapter 9), but there are others, such as causing bodily harm in assault, damage to property in malicious mischief, and destruction of property in arson. Like all elements of crime, prosecutors have to prove causation beyond a reasonable doubt. Proving causation requires proving two kinds of cause:

1. *Factual cause* (also called "but for" cause) of death, other bodily harm, and damage to and destruction of property.

2. *Legal cause* (also called "proximate" cause) of death, other bodily harm, and damage to and destruction of property.

Factual ("But For") Cause

Factual cause is an empirical question of fact that asks whether an actor's conduct triggered a series of events that ended in causing death, or other bodily harm; damage to property; or destruction of property. In the cases and statutes, factual cause usually goes by the name **"but for" cause**, or if you want to be fancy and use its Latin name, *sine qua non* cause. "But for" cause means, if it weren't for an actor's conduct, the result wouldn't have occurred.

Put another way, an actor's conduct triggered a chain of events that, sooner or later, ended in death or injury to a person or damage to and/or destruction of property. For example, I push a huge smooth round rock down a hill with a crowd at the bottom because I want to watch the crowd panic and scatter. The people see the rock and, to my delight, they scatter. Unfortunately, the rock hits and kills two people who couldn't get out of its path. My push is the cause in fact (the "but for") that kills the two people at the bottom. If I hadn't pushed the rock, they'd be alive. The MPC, Section 2.03(1) puts it this way: "Conduct is the cause of a result when it is an antecedent but for which the result in question would not have occurred."

Legal ("Proximate") Cause

Proving factual cause in almost all real cases is as easy as the no-brainer example of pushing the rock. But proving "but for" cause isn't enough. The prosecution has to prove legal (proximate) cause, too. "But for" cause is necessary, but it's not enough to prove my push *legally* caused the deaths. Factual cause is an objective, empirical question of fact; that's why we call it factual cause. **Proximate cause** is a subjective question of fairness that appeals to the jury's sense of justice. It asks, "Is it fair to blame the defendant for this harm?" If the harm is accidental enough or far enough removed from the defendant's triggering act, there's a reasonable doubt about the justice of blaming the defendant, and there's no proximate cause.

Take our pushing the rock example. Change the facts: On the way down the hill, the rock runs into a tree and lodges there. A year later, a mild earthquake shakes the rock free and it finishes its roll by killing the victims at the bottom.

Now, the no-brainer isn't a no-brainer anymore. Why? Because something else, facts in addition to my pushing, contributed to the deaths. We call this "something else" an **intervening cause,** and now we've got our proximate cause problem: Is it fair to punish me for something that's not entirely my fault? As with factual cause, most legal (proximate) cause cases don't create problems, but the ones that do are serious crimes involving death, mutilation, injury, and property destruction and damage.

How do we (and the jury or judge in nonjury cases) determine whether it's fair to attribute the cause of a result to a defendant's conduct? The common law, criminal codes, and the MPC have used various and highly intricate, elaborate devices to help fact finders decide the proximate cause question. For our purposes, they're not too helpful. The best way to understand how fact finders and judges answer the fairness question is to look at how they decided the fairness of imputing results to actors' conduct in some real cases. *Commonwealth v. McCloskey* (2003) and some of the interesting "Exploring Further: Causation" cases should help you understand proximate cause better.

CASE · *Did Her Conduct Cause the Deaths?*

Commonwealth v. McCloskey
835 A.2d 801 (Pa.Super 2003)

HISTORY

Judith Claire McCloskey, Defendant, was convicted in the Court of Common Pleas, Northampton County, Criminal Division, of three counts of involuntary manslaughter. She was sentenced to three consecutive terms of four (4) to eighteen (18) months in prison, for an aggregate term of one to four and one-half years. She appealed. The Superior Court, No. 3292 EDA 2002, affirmed the judgment of sentence.

BECK, J.

FACTS

On April 28, 2001, one of McCloskey's daughters, 17-year-old Kristen, hosted a party in the basement of McCloskey's home. McCloskey's other daughter, 14-year-old Kelly, also invited guests to her home that night. The Commonwealth presented over two dozen teenagers, all of whom were present at the party, to testify about the events. Their testimony, in its entirety, established the following.

Two 18-year-old boys, with the help of a 56-year-old man, brought two kegs of beer to McCloskey's home. Kristen charged party guests $5.00, for which each guest received a plastic cup to use for beer. As the evening progressed, there were in excess of 40 people at the party, all of them under age 21. As many as 20 cars were parked around the house. The teenagers drank beer and played drinking games throughout the evening, from approximately 8:00 P.M. until 11:00 P.M. Several party guests observed 19-year-old Christopher Mowad drinking heavily and exhibiting signs of intoxication.

McCloskey knew that a party was planned and, according to witnesses, assisted in getting ice and blankets ready for the kegs. McCloskey testified at trial that she thought the party was just a get-together to discuss the upcoming prom. McCloskey was at home for the entire party, but she stayed upstairs and did not venture into the basement, except to open the door on one or more occasions to tell the teens to turn down the music. Witnesses also testified that McCloskey called down to the basement to request assistance in finding her "bowl," *i.e.*, marijuana pipe. Throughout the evening, several teens made their way upstairs to the first floor where McCloskey watched television and drank beer with her boyfriend. Party guests moved in and out of the kitchen, Kelly's bedroom and the bathroom, all of which were on the first floor. Some guests arrived at the party and left again through the front door, passing McCloskey on their way and, at times, speaking to her. More than one teenager testified that they chatted with McCloskey while they (the teens) were drinking beer.

A large number of teenage witnesses testified that they not only attended the April 28th drinking party, but also drank alcohol at McCloskey's home on prior occasions. They told the jury that they did not hide this fact from McCloskey, but instead drank in her presence, and were never reprimanded by her or prevented from doing so. The testimony, on the whole, established that McCloskey's home was a place where the teenagers regularly drank alcohol without fear of repercussion.

At some point in the evening, Kimberly Byrne (18 years old) and cousins Courtney Kiefer (17 years old) and Bryan Kiefer (18 years old) left the party and went to a nearby field. About twenty minutes later, a neighbor contacted police because she was concerned about the number of people and cars on the rural road near McCloskey's home. Courtney Kiefer called Mowad, who was still at the party. Mowad informed her that the police had arrived and he was leaving. He ran out of McCloskey's home, avoided the police and drove his Isuzu Rodeo to the field. There, he picked up the three teens and drove back toward McCloskey's residence to see what happened.

The foursome rode past McCloskey's house, observed police there and talked about how lucky they were not to have been caught. But later, while driving around, Mowad sideswiped another vehicle and, in an effort to elude the driver, sped away. He lost control of the car and drove off the road. The vehicle flipped over several times before coming to rest on its roof. All four teenagers were ejected. Mowad, Byrne and Bryan Kiefer died as a result of blunt force trauma to their heads, necks and chests. Courtney Kiefer, the only survivor, sustained multiple serious injuries, including head trauma, and required extended hospitalization. Mowad's blood alcohol content was .20%.

Meanwhile, Plainfield Police Officer Vincent A. Tomaro had responded to the call at McCloskey's house and observed people leaving from the rear of the home. Officer Tomaro entered the home with McCloskey's permission and proceeded to the basement where he discovered, and

confiscated, the kegs of beer. McCloskey told Officer Tomaro that she was unaware of the beer. The officer requested back-up assistance and began to interview McCloskey's daughter and other teenagers at the scene.

Party guests who were 18 years old or older were permitted to leave the premises if their preliminary breath tests registered negative. Police contacted the parents of teens under the age of 18. Those parents either came to retrieve the teens or permitted them to stay at McCloskey's house.

Later that morning, some teenagers still at McCloskey's home, and another who reappeared there, observed McCloskey when she received the news of the fatal crash. In response to learning that the teens were dead, McCloskey stated: "I'm f_ _ _ed."

OPINION

Involuntary manslaughter is defined as follows:

> A person is guilty of involuntary manslaughter when as a direct result of the doing of an unlawful act in a reckless or grossly negligent manner, or the doing of a lawful act in a reckless or grossly negligent manner, he causes the death of another person. 18 Pa.C.S.A. ß 2504(a).

Thus, involuntary manslaughter requires (1) a mental state of either recklessness or gross negligence and (2) a causal nexus between the conduct of the accused and the death of the victim. McCloskey insists that both elements are lacking in this case.

[The court's discussion of mental state is omitted.]

Causation

McCloskey next claims that the Commonwealth failed to prove causation. She argues that Mowad's voluntary act of drinking to excess, his decision to drive, the fact that he was speeding when he lost control of his vehicle and all of the occupants' choices to refrain from wearing seatbelts were their own "tragic decisions," causing their deaths.

. . . In order to impose criminal liability, causation must be direct and substantial. . . . Criminal causation has come to involve a case-by-case social determination; *i.e., is it just or fair under the facts of the case to expose the defendant to criminal sanctions. In other words, was the defendant's conduct so directly and substantially linked to the actual result as to give rise to the imposition of criminal liability or was the actual result so remote and attenuated that it would be unfair to hold the defendant responsible for it?* [emphasis added]. . . .

Our review of the facts in this case leads us to conclude that McCloskey's "furnishing" of alcohol to minors, including Mowad, "started the chain of causation" that led to the death of three teens. The record supports the finding that McCloskey knew the party guests, all of whom were under age 21 and some of whom were as young as 14, were drinking beer in her home. She allowed them to do so for several hours without interruption, supervision or comment. The teens came and went throughout the evening in their cars, nearly twenty of which were parked on McCloskey's property at some point.

We conclude that the occurrence of a fatal automobile accident following a teenager's unlimited consumption of alcohol at a wholly unsupervised teenage beer party is neither "remote" nor "attenuated." Further, we are convinced that it is not "unfair" or "unjust" to hold McCloskey responsible under these facts, despite the existence of other factors that combined with McCloskey's conduct to achieve the tragic result here. We reiterate, this is not a case where McCloskey simply failed to supervise a teen party in her home at which beer was secretly being served. McCloskey "furnished" the alcohol to the minors under the plain language of the statute. The tragic and all too familiar outcome of her conduct warrants the criminal responsibility imposed.

Contrary to her assertions, McCloskey was not prosecuted for involuntary manslaughter based on an incident caused by "adolescent foolhardiness." Appellant's Brief at 21. Rather, she was brought to trial because she "started the chain of causation" that led to the death of three teens. Her outrageous conduct, in knowing the teens were consuming alcohol, interacting with them as they drank and allowing the illegal and unsupervised behavior to continue into the night, is the source of her culpability. . . . Judgment of sentence affirmed.

Questions

1. List all the facts relevant to whether Judith McCloskey was the factual cause of the deaths of Christopher Mowad (19 years old), Kimberly Byrne (18 years old), and Bryan Kiefer (18 years old).

2. List facts that indicate intervening causes and whether, in your opinion, a jury could reasonably find they were dependent or independent causes.

3. Is it just or fair under the facts of the case to expose McCloskey to criminal sanctions? In other words, was the defendant's conduct so directly and substantially linked to the actual result as to give rise to the imposition of criminal liability, or was the actual result so remote and attenuated that it would be unfair to hold the defendant responsible for it? Back up your answer with the facts you listed in questions 1–3 and with arguments from the court's opinion.

4. Is there any merit in McCloskey's argument that "Mowad's voluntary act of drinking to excess, his decision to drive, the fact that he was speeding when he lost control of his vehicle and all of the occupants' choices to refrain from wearing seatbelts were their own 'tragic decisions,' causing their deaths"? Defend your answer.

Causation

1. Were His Actions in the Drag Race the Legal Cause of Death?

Velazquez v. State, 561 So.2d 347 (Fla.App. 1990)

FACTS At about 2:30 A.M., Isaac Alejandro Velazquez met the deceased Adalberto Alvarez at a Hardee's restaurant in Hialeah, Florida. The two had never previously met but in the course of their conversation agreed to "drag race" each other with their automobiles. They accordingly left the restaurant and proceeded to set up a quarter-mile drag race course on a nearby public road that ran perpendicular to a canal alongside the Palmetto Expressway in Hialeah; a guardrail and a visible stop sign stood between the end of this road and the canal.

The two men began their drag race at the end of this road and proceeded away from the canal in a westerly direction for a quarter mile. Upon completing the course without incident, the deceased Alvarez suddenly turned his automobile 180 degrees around and proceeded east toward the starting line and the canal; Velazquez did the same and followed. Alvarez led and attained an estimated speed of 123 mph; he was not wearing a seat belt and subsequent investigation revealed that he had a blood alcohol level between .11 and .12.

Velazquez, who had not been drinking, trailed Alvarez the entire distance back to the starting line and attained an estimated speed of 98 mph. As both drivers approached the end of the road, they applied their brakes, but neither could stop. Alvarez, who was about a car length ahead of Velazquez, crashed through the guardrail first and was propelled over the entire canal, landing on its far bank; he was thrown from his car upon impact, was pinned under his vehicle when it landed on him, and died instantly from the resulting injuries.

Velazquez also crashed through the guardrail but landed in the canal where he was able to escape from his vehicle and swim to safety uninjured. Velazquez was charged with vehicular homicide.

Were his actions in participating in the drag race the legal (proximate) cause of Alvarez's death?

DECISION No, according to the appeals court: In unusual cases like this one, whether certain conduct is deemed the legal cause of a certain result is ultimately a policy question. The question of legal causation thus blends into the question of whether we are willing to hold a defendant responsible for a prohibited result. Or, stated differently, the issue is not causation; it is responsibility. In my opinion, policy considerations are against imposing responsibility for the death of a participant in a race on the surviving racer when his sole contribution to the death is the participation in the activity mutually agreed upon.

2. Who Legally Caused His Death?

People v. Kibbe, 362 N.Y.S.2d 848 (1974)

FACTS Barry Kibbe and a companion, Roy Krall, met George Stafford in a bar on a cold winter night. They noticed Stafford had a lot of money and was drunk. When Stafford asked them for a ride, they agreed, having already decided to rob him. "The three men entered Kibbe's automobile and began the trip toward Canandaigua. Krall drove the car while Kibbe demanded that Stafford turn over any money he had. In the course of an exchange, Kibbe slapped Stafford several times, took his money, then compelled him to lower his trousers and to take off his shoes to be certain that Stafford had given up all his money. When they were satisfied that Stafford had no more money on his person, the defendants forced him to exit the Kibbe vehicle.

As he was thrust from the car, Stafford fell onto the shoulder of the rural two-lane highway on which they had been traveling. His trousers were still down around his ankles, his shirt was rolled up toward his chest, he was shoeless, and he had also been stripped of any outer clothing. Before the defendants pulled away, Kibbe placed Stafford's shoes and jacket on the shoulder of the highway. Although Stafford's eyeglasses were in Kibbe's vehicle, the defendants, either through inadvertence or perhaps by specific design, did not give them to him before they drove away.

Michael W. Blake, a college student, was driving at a reasonable speed when he saw Stafford in the middle of the road with his hands in the air. Blake could not stop in time to avoid striking Stafford and killing him.

Did Kibbe and his companion or Blake legally cause Stafford's death?

DECISION Yes, Kibbe and his companion legally caused Stafford's death: To be a sufficiently direct cause of death so as to warrant the imposition of a criminal penalty . . . , it will suffice if it can be said beyond a reasonable doubt, as indeed it can be here said, that the ultimate harm is something which should have been foreseen as being reasonably related to the acts of the accused. . . . We conclude that Kibbe and his companion's activities were a sufficiently . . . proximate . . . cause of the death of George Stafford so as to warrant the imposition of criminal sanctions. In engaging in what may properly be described as a despicable course of action, Kibbe and Krall left a helplessly intoxicated man without his eyeglasses in a position from which, because of these attending circumstances, he could not extricate himself and whose condition was such that he could not even protect himself from the elements.

. . . Under the conditions surrounding Blake's operation of his truck (i.e., the fact that he had his low beams on as the two cars approached; that there was no artificial lighting on the highway; and that there was insufficient time in which to react to Stafford's presence in his lane), we do not think it may be said that any . . . intervening wrongful act occurred to relieve the defendants from the directly foreseeable consequences of their actions.

3. Did He Cause the Drowning?

People v. Armitage, 239 Cal.Rptr. 515 (Cal.App. 1987)

FACTS David Armitage and his friend, Peter Maskovich, after an evening of drinking, wound up racing Armitage's small aluminum boat on the Sacramento River while both of them were intoxicated. The boat contained no personal flotation devices. They had the motor wide open, were zigzagging, and had no running lights on at the time. They were using loud and vulgar language and were operating the boat very fast and erratically.

Some time around 3 A.M., Armitage came to James Snook's door; he was soaking wet and appeared quite intoxicated. He reported that he had flipped his boat over in the river and had lost his buddy. He said that at first he and his buddy had been hanging onto the overturned boat, but that his buddy swam for shore and he did not know whether he had made it. As it turned out, Maskovich did not make it; he drowned in the river. Armitage also stated that he told the victim to hang onto the boat, but his friend ignored his warning and started swimming for the shore.

Was Armitage's conduct the proximate cause of Maskovich's drowning? Yes, said the California Court of Appeals.

DECISION In order to be guilty of felony drunk boating the defendant's act or omission must be the proximate cause of the ensuing injury or death. Armitage asserts that after his boat flipped over he and the victim were holding on to it and the victim, against his advice, decided to abandon the boat and try to swim to shore. According to Armitage, the victim's fatally reckless decision should exonerate him from criminal responsibility for his death. Armitage claims that the victim's attempt to swim ashore . . . constituted a break in the natural and continuous sequence arising from the unlawful operation of the boat.

The claim cannot hold water. . . . If an intervening cause is a normal and reasonably foreseeable result of defendant's original act the intervening cause . . . will not relieve defendant of liability. . . . An unreflective act in response to a peril created by defendant will not break a causal connection. In such a case, the actor has a choice, but his act is nonetheless unconsidered. When defendant's conduct causes panic an act done under the influence of panic or extreme fear will not negate causal connection unless the reaction is wholly abnormal.

Here Armitage, through his misconduct, placed the intoxicated victim in the middle of a dangerous river in the early morning hours clinging to an overturned boat. The fact that the panic stricken victim recklessly abandoned the boat and tried to swim ashore was not a wholly abnormal reaction to the perceived peril of drowning. Just as "detached reflection cannot be demanded in the presence of an uplifted knife" (*Brown v. United States* (1921) 256 U.S. 335, 343 HOLMES, J.), neither can caution be required of a drowning man. Having placed the inebriated victim in peril, defendant cannot obtain exoneration by claiming the victim should have reacted differently or more prudently.

. . . The evidence establishes that defendant's acts and omissions were the proximate cause of the victim's death.

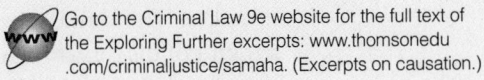Go to the Criminal Law 9e website for the full text of the Exploring Further excerpts: www.thomsonedu .com/criminaljustice/samaha. (Excerpts on causation.)

IGNORANCE AND MISTAKE

"The trail leads plainly to *mens rea*," the great scholar of criminal law Professor Jerome Hall replied to the question, "Why should we punish anyone who commits crime because of ignorance or mistake?" (Hall 1960, 360):

> Ignorance and mistake are words of ancient mintage which have been discussed in all ages by the wise and the prudent, by realists and idealists, and many others. We need not here review this vast literature, but we may note certain widely accepted conclusions. . . . Knowledge exists; and the contrary of that is ignorance. . . . Likewise . . . , mistakes also occur. (361)

You've probably heard the old saying, "Ignorance of the law is no defense." You probably haven't heard that "mistake of fact *is* a defense." As you probably suspect, the reality of ignorance and mistake in criminal law is more complicated than these sayings appear.

We'll get into the complications shortly, but before we do, let's be clear about the difference between "ignorance" and "mistake." When you're *ignorant* of the facts or the law, you don't know what they are. Put another way, **ignorance of the law** is an absence of knowledge about facts or law. When you're *mistaken* about the law or facts, you're wrong about them. You *believe* they're one thing when they're really another.

Mistake of Fact

Professor Hall (1960) breaks down **mistake of facts** into five elements:

1. Facts exist.

2. Facts differ from impressions (opinions, judgments, and beliefs) of facts.

3. Impressions of facts either fit or don't fit the facts.

4. Mistakes of fact are accepted as true—for a while.

5. Later, the mistakes are recognized.

Hall (362) gives this example. In the evening light, a person looks at an object in the distance; she believes it's a man. As she gets closer, she decides it's a tree, recognizing her initial impression was mistaken. The next morning she discovers she was twice mistaken—it's really a tree stump.

The rationale for the mistake of fact defense is the ethical principle that moral obligation depends not on the facts as they actually are, but on what you believe they are (Hall 363).

In one famous old case (*Levett's* Case 1638), strange noises awakened the defendant in the middle of the night. Thinking it was a burglar about to attack him, he ran his sword through a curtain he believed the burglar was hiding behind. He was mistaken. The intruder wasn't a burglar; she wasn't even an intruder. She was Frances, a friend of his servant who had permission for Frances to visit. The court held it wasn't manslaughter "for he did . . . without intention of hurt to the said Frances." So the "trail" of Levett's acquittal "leads directly to the *mens rea*. We can't blame him because he had no *mens rea*."

Mistake of fact is a defense whenever the mistake prevents the formation of any fault-based mental attitude by purpose, knowledge, recklessness, or negligence. There's a great debate over whether to call mistake a defense (*General v. State* 2002). On one side are those who say what the defendant did was wrong, but her mistake excused her; they call mistake a "defense of excuse" (Chapter 6).

The other side says the mistake prevented the formation of a culpable state of mind; they say there's no crime at all because the mental element is missing. It's impossible to have a defense to conduct that's not *criminal* conduct. They're not really defenses, in the sense that they either justify or excuse criminal liability. Instead, mistakes raise a reasonable doubt about the mental element required for criminal conduct.

Mistakes sometimes are called a "failure of proof" defense because defendants present the evidence of mistake. We'll see, in Chapter 6, other examples of defenses that can be called either defenses of excuse or failures of proof of mental attitude. We won't get into the details of why, or whether, to treat mistakes as a defense of excuse or as a failure of proof here. But note that the debate isn't just an academic mental exercise; it has important procedural and other consequences (LaFave 2003a, 282–83).

To simplify matters for you, we'll follow the MPC's approach, which is that mistake matters when it prevents the formation of a mental attitude required by a criminal statute. To decide whether a mistake negates the mental element, we need to know what mental element the statute requires. Suppose it's a crime in your state for a bartender to sell alcoholic beverages to anyone under 21 for the purpose of supplying a minor with an alcoholic beverage. You're a bartender; you believe the customer you just sold to is 21 because he showed you a driver's license with a birth date more than 22 years prior to today's date. He's really 18. Your mistake negates the mental element— purpose.

Suppose the statute says "recklessly supplies anyone under 21." You look at another customer's license; the date looks altered, but you're not sure. You say, "This date looks like it's been changed, but what the hell, I feel like living dangerously tonight" and sell her an orange blossom martini. She's 19. You're guilty, because you created a "substantial and unjustifiable risk" that she was under 21.

One final and important point about mistake of fact; it doesn't work with strict liability crimes. Why? There's no mental element in strict liability offenses. In other words, the trail of mistake doesn't have to (in fact, it can't) lead to fault. To follow through with the bartender example, suppose the statute makes it a crime "to sell any alcoholic beverage to a person under 21." There's no mental element to negate, so it doesn't matter whether you sold it purposely, knowingly, recklessly, or negligently.

Ignorance of the Law

To bar ignorance or mistake of law from negating the mental element "seems to hold morally innocent people criminally liable, upon an obvious fiction—that everyone is presumed to know the law" (Hall 1960, 376).

Why does mistake of fact, but not ignorance of the law, negate the mental element? The answer lies in the differences between the two propositions. One difference is that "law is 'about' facts; it gives distinctive meaning to facts" (376). For example, if Jesse kills his father, that's a fact. But whether the killing is a "murder" depends on a legal rule, such as a statute that defines murder as "intentionally causing the death of another person."

Second, the meanings of "ignorance of the law" and "mistake of fact" differ. Knowledge of facts is based on perception gained from our senses; knowledge of legal propositions is more intellectual. Perception of facts is relatively certain, because we assume that facts objectively exist; mistakes about facts are due to "excitement, negligence, poor conditions of observation, intoxication, and the like" (377).

Knowledge of the law can't be that certain. Most of the time, the "law is unavoidably vague. . . . It is therefore possible to disagree infinitely" about the meaning of laws (382). One aspect of the principle of legality not directly discussed in Chapter 1 is that the debate over what the law means and how it applies to individual criminal defendants has to take place in courts. Professor Hall lists three elements required by the *principle of legality:*

1. Rules of law express objective meanings.

2. Only authorized "competent" officials, after following established procedures, are allowed to declare what the objective meanings are.

3. Only these official declarations are binding; that is, only these official interpretations are the law. (383)

Allowing a defendant to avoid criminal liability by demonstrating that she has a different interpretation of the law contradicts all three of the propositions just listed. The principle of legality rejects this contradiction. Our legal order is (at least in principle) based on opposing "objectivity to subjectivity, judicial process to individual opinion, official to lay, and authoritative to non-authoritative declarations of what the law is. This is the rationale of ignorance of the law is no excuse" (382).

That's the *process* rationale behind preventing ignorance of the law from negating the mental element of crime. There's also an ethical rationale. Criminal law represents moral principles that are contradicted by allowing ignorance of the law to negate an element of criminal liability. Criminal law is an *objective* morality that an individual's moral judgment can't override the moral judgment expressed in the criminal law. That would allow the individual's moral judgment to trump community moral values. Criminal laws are an expression of the community's values.

The process and moral rationales can be reduced to a single proposition—criminal laws can't be ignored or contradicted by allowing defendants to plead that their ignorance or mistake of law negated the mental element of a crime.

SUMMARY

I. The principle of *mens rea* is not only ancient but highly complex.
    A. Most crimes include both a criminal act (*actus reus*) and a mental element.
    B. There are five reasons for confusion involving the mental element of a crime:
        1. *Mens rea* is difficult to discover and then to prove in court.
        2. Courts and legislatures have used so many vague and incomplete definitions of the mental element.
        3. *Mens rea* consists of several mental attitudes that range across a broad spectrum.

4. Different mental attitudes might apply to each of the elements of a crime.
5. There's a problem with the relationship between mental attitude and motive.

II. Proving state of mind is difficult.
A. Confessions are the only direct evidence of mental attitude.
B. Defendants rarely confess their true intentions, so proof of their state of mind depends on indirect (circumstantial) evidence.

III. Criminal intent requires proof of a mental element.
A. There are two kinds of fault that satisfy the mental element in criminal liability:
   1. Subjective fault, which requires a "bad mind" in the actor and is linked with immorality
   2. Objective fault, which requires no purposeful or conscious "bad mind" in the actor
B. A third type of criminal liability, known as "no-fault liability," requires neither subjective nor objective fault.

IV. *General intent* is defined several ways.
A. In most cases, it means the intent to commit at the minimum any criminal act defined as the *actus reus* in a criminal statute.
B. Some courts define *general intent* as a synonym for *mens rea* and includes both subjective and objective fault.
C. It's also defined as the intent to commit a crime at an undetermined time and place with no specific victim in mind.

V. *Specific intent* refers to a deliberate act.
A. Some courts limit specific intent to the attitude represented by subjective fault where there is a "bad mind" or will.
B. The most common definition of *specific intent* is "general intent 'plus,'" where the "plus" refers to a special mental element beyond the intent to commit the criminal act.

VI. Ranked in order of the degree of culpability, the four Model Penal Code mental states are
A. *Purpose* Acting purposely to commit a crime or having the conscious object to commit crime
B. *Knowledge* Awareness but without the very purpose or conscious object of causing harm
C. *Recklessness* Consciously creating risks of substantial and unjustifiable harm, without the intent to cause harm
D. *Negligence* Unconsciously, but unreasonably, creating risks of substantial and unjustifiable harms

VII. *Strict liability* is liability without fault.
A. Strict liability is based on voluntary action alone.
B. Strict liability makes accidental injuries a crime.

VIII. All crimes, except strict liability offenses, are subject to the concurrence requirement.
A. The *principle of concurrence* means that some mental fault has to trigger the *actus reus*.
B. Concurrence is an element in all crimes where the mental attitude is formed with purpose, knowledge, recklessness, or negligence.

IX. The principle of causation applies to result crimes.
  A. *Factual cause,* also called "'but for' cause," means that if it weren't for an actor's conduct, a certain result wouldn't have occurred.
  B. Legal, or proximate, cause is a subjective question, which asks, "Is it fair to blame the defendant for the harm he caused?"
  C. Intervening causes contribute indirectly to causing harmful results.

X. Mistake of fact may be a defense.
  A. Mistakes are a wrong interpretation of law or facts.
  B. Mistake of fact is a defense whenever the mistake prevents the formation of any fault-based mental attitude.
  C. Mistake of fact doesn't apply to strict liability crimes, because there's no mental element in strict liability offenses.

XI. Ignorance of the law isn't a defense.
  A. Ignorance is an absence of knowledge about facts or law.
  B. Ignorance of the law isn't a defense to negate the mental element.
  C. Criminal laws are an expression of the community's values and wouldn't hold true if individual moral judgment could override such values.

REVIEW QUESTIONS

1. Describe the history behind the principle of *mens rea.*

2. Why is *mens rea* complex?

3. What's the difference between *mental attitude* and *motive?* Give an example of each.

4. Why is it hard to prove the "state of mind"?

5. Identify and describe three types of fault. Give an example of each.

6. What's the difference between *general intent* and *specific intent?* Give an example of each.

7. What is meant by *general intent "plus"?* Give an example.

8. State the minimum requirement of culpability.

9. Identify and describe the MPC's four kinds of culpability. Give an example of each.

10. What is meant by the mental element *conscious object?* Give an example.

11. What's the difference between the mental states of *purpose* and *knowledge?* Give an example of each.

12. How does awareness in recklessness differ from that in knowledge?

13. Identify and describe the two prongs of the Model Penal Code's test of recklessness. Which prong is subjective? Which prong is objective?

14. Identify and describe the difference between *recklessness* and *negligence.* Give an example of each.

15. Define *strict liability.* List the arguments for and against it.

16. Identify and describe two kinds of cause that need to be proven in proving causation. Give an example of each.

17. Why does mistake of fact, but not ignorance of the law, negate the mental element?

18. Professor Hall identifies three elements required by the principle of legality. Identify and describe the three elements.

KEY TERMS

culpability, p. 106
blameworthiness, p. 106
principle of *mens rea*, p. 106
motive, p. 108
subjective fault, p. 109
objective fault, p. 109
strict liability, p. 110
general intent, p. 110

specific intent, p. 110
general intent "plus," p. 111
purpose, p. 113
knowledge, p. 113
recklessness, p. 113
negligence, p. 113
scienter, p. 116
strict liability, p. 120

principle of concurrence, p. 123
principle of causation, p. 124
factual cause, p. 124
"but for" cause, p. 124
proximate cause, p. 125
intervening cause, p. 125
ignorance of the law, p. 129
mistake of facts, p. 129

Defenses to Criminal Liability: Justifications

MAIN POINTS

- Defendants who plead justification admit they're responsible for committing crimes but contend they're right under the circumstances.
- Defendants who plead excuse admit they're wrong but contend that, under the circumstances, they're not responsible.
- The heart of self-defense is necessity.
- Use of deadly force in self-defense is limited to preventing imminent death or serious bodily injury to yourself or others.
- There's no duty to retreat from your own home if retreating threatens your personal safety.
- The right to defend your home sometimes includes the right to use deadly force.
- The choice-of-evils defense justifies choosing to commit a lesser crime to avoid an imminent threat of harm from a greater crime.
- The heart of the defense of consent is the high value placed on individual autonomy in a free society.

5

Susan Polk at trial for the murder of her husband in Martinez, CA. Polk claimed that she acted in self-defense when she fatally stabbed her husband, a man who had been her therapist when she was a teenager. But prosecutors claimed that Susan Polk planned the violent death to put an end to a bitter divorce and custody battle. Ultimately, the jury found her guilty of second-degree murder.

Did He Shoot in Self-Defense?

Canty approached Goetz, possibly with Allen beside him, and said to Goetz, "Give me five dollars." Goetz stated that he knew from the smile on Canty's face that they wanted to "play with me." Although he was certain that none of the youths had a gun, he had a fear, based on prior experiences, of being "maimed." Goetz then established "a pattern of fire," deciding specifically to fire from left to right. His stated intention at that point was to "murder [the four youths], to hurt them, to make them suffer as much as possible." When Canty again requested money, Goetz stood up, drew his weapon, and began firing, aiming for the center of the body of each of the four. Goetz recalled that the first two he shot "tried to run through the crowd [but] they had nowhere to run." Goetz then turned to his right to "go after the other two." Cabey "tried pretending that he wasn't with [the others]" by standing still, holding

(continued)

on to one of the subway hand straps, and not looking at Goetz. Goetz nonetheless fired his fourth shot at him. He then ran back to the first two youths to make sure they had been "taken care of." Seeing that they had both been shot, he spun back to check on the other two. Goetz noticed that the youth who had been standing still was now sitting on a bench and seemed unhurt. As Goetz told the police, "I said, '[y]ou seem to be all right, here's another,'" and he fired the shot which severed Cabey's spinal cord. Goetz added that "if I was a little more under self-control . . . I would have put the barrel against his forehead and fired." He also admitted that "if I had had more [bullets], I would have shot them again, and again, and again."

(PEOPLE V. GOETZ 1986)

Proving *criminal conduct* (a criminal act and a criminal mental attitude) is necessary to hold individuals accountable for the crimes they commit. But it's not enough. It's the first of three necessary requirements; remember the overall analysis of criminal liability. First, we have to answer the questions asked in Chapters 3 and 4, "Was there criminal conduct?" If there wasn't, the inquiry is over, and the defendant walks. If there was, we have to answer the question of this chapter, "Was the criminal conduct justified?" If it was, the conduct was legal, the inquiry ends, and the defendant walks. If it wasn't justified, we have to go on to answer the third question, asked in Chapter 6, "Was the unjustified conduct excused?" If it wasn't, the defendant is criminally accountable for her criminal conduct. If it was, the defendant *may*, or may not, walk.

In practice, the principles of justification and excuse comprise numerous individual defenses to criminal liability; we'll discuss some of them. But first, let's explain the difference between justification and excuse. In the **justification defenses,** defendants admit they were responsible for their acts but claim what they did was right (justified) under the circumstances. The classic justification is self-defense; kill or be killed. "I killed her; I'm responsible for killing her; but under the circumstances it was right to kill her." So even if the government proves all the elements in the crime beyond a reasonable doubt, the defendant walks because she's not blameworthy.

In the **excuse defenses,** defendants admit what they did was *wrong* but claim that, under the circumstances, they weren't *responsible* for what they did. The classic excuse is insanity. "What I did was wrong, but I was too insane to know or control what I did. So, under the circumstances, I'm not responsible for what I did."

Most justifications and excuses are **affirmative defenses,** which operate like this: Defendants have to "start matters off by putting in some evidence in support" of their justification or excuse (LaFave and Scott, 1986, 52). We call this the **burden of production.** Why put this burden on defendants? Because "We can assume that those who commit crimes are sane, sober, conscious, and acting freely. It makes sense, therefore, to make defendants responsible for injecting these extraordinary circumstances into the proceedings" (52).

The amount of evidence required "is not great; some credible evidence" is enough. In some jurisdictions, if defendants meet the burden of production, they also have the **burden of persuasion,** meaning they have to prove their defenses by a **preponderance of the evidence,** defined as more than 50 percent. In other jurisdictions, once defendants meet the burden of production, the burden shifts to the government to prove defendants weren't justified or excused (Loewy 1987, 192–204).

AFFIRMATIVE DEFENSES AND PROVING THEM

Most defenses are **perfect defenses,** meaning defendants are acquitted. The defense of insanity is different. Defendants who successfully plead insanity don't "walk"—at least not right away. Special hearings are held to determine if these defendants are still insane. Most hearings decide they are, and so they're sent to maximum-security hospitals to be confined there until they regain their sanity; in most serious crimes, that's never (Chapter 6).

Evidence that doesn't amount to a perfect defense might amount to an **imperfect defense;** that is, defendants are guilty of lesser offenses. For example, in *Swann v. U.S.* (1994), Ted Swann and Steve Crawford got into an argument while shooting baskets. Crawford's ball hit Swann in the stomach, where he had recently been stabbed. Crawford ordered Swann off the court. When Swann instead walked past him, ignoring the order, Crawford said, "You think you stabbed up now, just watch." Then, placing his hands to his side, Crawford appeared to be reaching for his back pocket. Swann, who had seen a bulge in Crawford's pocket, thought that he was reaching for a gun to kill him. Swann pulled his own gun from his waistband and shot Crawford twice in the head (929).

The court ruled that Swann was entitled to a jury instruction on imperfect defense that would reduce the murder charge to manslaughter, because there was enough evidence for a jury to conclude that

> Swann's belief that he was in imminent danger and that he had to use deadly force to repel that danger was in fact actually and honestly held but was in one or both respects objectively unreasonable. (930)

Even when the evidence doesn't add up to an imperfect defense, it might still show mitigating circumstances that convince judges or juries that defendants don't deserve the maximum penalty for the crime they're convicted of. For example, words, however insulting, can't reduce murder to manslaughter in most states, but they might mitigate death to life without parole. So when a Black man killed a White man in a rage brought on by the White man's relentless taunting, "nigger, nigger," the killing was still murder but the taunting mitigated the death penalty to life without parole (Chapter 9).

Let's now look at some justification defenses: self-defense, the defense of others, the defense of home and property, the choice-of-evils defense, and consent.

SELF-DEFENSE

If you use force to protect yourself, your home or property, or the people you care about, you've violated the rule of law, which our legal system is deeply committed to (Chapter 1). According to the rule of law, the government has a monopoly on the use of force; so when you use force, you're "taking the law into your own hands." With that great monopoly on force goes the equally great responsibility of protecting individuals who are banned from using force themselves.

But, sometimes, the government isn't, or can't be, there to protect you when you need it. So **necessity**—the heart of the defense of justification—allows "self-help" to kick in. Self-defense is a grudging concession to necessity. It's only good before the law when three circumstances come together: the necessity is great, it exists "right now," and it's for prevention only. Preemptive strikes aren't allowed; you can't use force to prevent an attack that's going to take place tomorrow or even this afternoon. Retaliation isn't allowed either; you can't use it to "pay back" an attack that took place last year or even this morning. In short, preemptive strikes come too soon and retaliation too late; they both fail the necessity test. Individuals have to rely on conventional means to prevent future attacks, and only the state can punish past attacks (Fletcher 1988, 18–19).

To learn more about the justification of self-defense, we'll examine the elements of self-defense. Then, we'll look at if and when claims of self-defense are justifiable when it's possible to retreat to escape harm.

Elements

When can we ignore the government's monopoly on force and take the law into our own hands to defend ourselves? The law of self-defense says four elements have to be present:

1. *Unprovoked attack* The defender didn't start or provoke the attack.

2. *Imminent danger* The defender honestly and reasonably believes the unprovoked attack is going to happen "right now."

3. *Necessity* The defender honestly and reasonably believes there's a need to use force to defend against the attack.

4. *Reasonable force* The defender uses only the amount of force she reasonably believes is necessary to repel the attack.

Unprovoked Attack Self-defense is available only against *unprovoked* attacks. So self-defense isn't available to an **initial aggressor;** someone who provokes an attack can't then use force to defend herself against the attack she provoked. With one exception: according to the **withdrawal exception,** if attackers completely withdraw from attacks they provoke, they can defend themselves against an attack by their initial victims. In a classic old case, *State v. Good* (1917, 1006), a son threatened to shoot his father with a shotgun. The father went to a neighbor's, borrowed the neighbor's shotgun, and came back. The son told him to "stop." When the father shot, the son turned and ran and the father pursued him. The son then turned and shot his father, killing him. The trial court failed to instruct the jury on the withdrawal exception. The Supreme Court of Missouri reversed because the trial judge's instruction

> ignores and excludes the defendant's right of self-defense. Although he may have brought on the difficulty with the intent to kill his father, still, if he was attempting to withdraw from the difficulty, and was fleeing from his father in good faith for the purpose of such

withdrawal, and if his father, knowing that defendant was endeavoring to withdraw from such conflict, pursued defendant and sought to kill him, or do him some great bodily harm, then the defendant's right of self-defense revived. (1007)

Imminent Danger, Necessity, and Reasonable Force   What does **imminent danger** of attack mean? Simply put, it means, "The time for defense is right now!" How much and what kind of defense? Only the *amount* of force the imminent danger *reasonably* demands. And against what kind of attacks? The best-known cases involve individuals who need to kill to save their own lives, but self-defense is broader than that. It also includes killing someone who's about to kill a member of your family—or any innocent person for that matter.

Necessity doesn't limit you to killing someone who's going to kill. You can also kill an attacker whom you reasonably believe is right now going to hurt you or someone else badly enough to send you or them to the hospital for the treatment of serious injury. This is what *serious* (sometimes called "grievous") bodily injury means in most self-defense statutes.

Some self-defense statutes go even further. They allow you to kill someone you reasonably believe is about to commit a serious felony against you that doesn't threaten either your life or serious bodily injury. These felonies usually include rape, sodomy, kidnapping, and armed robbery. But the list also almost always includes home burglary and, sometimes, even personal property (discussed in "In the Defense of Home and Property" later).

What kind of belief does self-defense require? Is it enough that you honestly believe the imminence of the danger, the need for force, and the amount of force used? No. Almost all statutes require that your belief also be reasonable; that is, a reasonable person in the same situation would have believed the imminence of the attack, the need for force, and the amount of force used were necessary to repel an attack. In the 1980s' sensational "New York Subway Vigilante case," the New York Court of Appeals examined these elements as applied to the defense against armed robbery provision in New York's self-defense statute (Fletcher 1988, 18–27).

CASE   *Did He Shoot in Self-Defense?*

People v. Goetz
497 N.E.2d 41 (N.Y. 1986)

HISTORY

Bernhard Goetz, the defendant, was indicted for criminal possession of a weapon, attempted murder, assault, and reckless endangerment. The Supreme Court, Trial Term, New York County, dismissed the indictment and the People appealed. The Supreme Court, Appellate Division affirmed, and the People appealed. The Court of Appeals reversed and dismissed, and reinstated all the counts of the indictment.

WACHTLER, CJ.

FACTS

On Saturday afternoon, December 22, 1984, Troy Canty, Darryl Cabey, James Ramseur, and Barry Allen boarded an IRT express subway train in the Bronx and headed south toward lower Manhattan. The four youths rode together in the rear portion of the seventh car of the train. Two of the four, Ramseur and Cabey, had screwdrivers inside their coats, which they said were to be used to break into the coin boxes of video machines.

Bernhard Goetz boarded this subway train at 14th Street in Manhattan and sat down on a bench toward the rear section of the same car occupied by the four youths. Goetz was carrying an unlicensed .38 caliber pistol loaded with five rounds of ammunition in a waistband holster. The train left the 14th Street station and headed toward Chambers Street.

Canty approached Goetz, possibly with Allen beside him, and stated, "Give me five dollars." Neither Canty nor any of the other youths displayed a weapon. Goetz responded by standing up, pulling out his handgun and firing four shots in rapid succession. The first shot hit Canty in the chest; the second struck Allen in the back; the third went through Ramseur's arm and into his left side; the fourth was fired at Cabey, who apparently was then standing in the corner of the car, but missed, deflecting instead off of a wall of the conductor's cab.

After Goetz briefly surveyed the scene around him, he fired another shot at Cabey, who then was sitting on the end bench of the car. The bullet entered the rear of Cabey's side and severed his spinal cord.

All but two of the other passengers fled the car when, or immediately after, the shots were fired. The conductor, who had been in the next car, heard the shots and instructed the motorman to radio for emergency assistance. The conductor then went into the car where the shooting occurred and saw Goetz sitting on a bench, the injured youths lying on the floor or slumped against a seat, and two women who had apparently taken cover, also lying on the floor.

Goetz told the conductor that the four youths had tried to rob him. While the conductor was aiding the youths, Goetz headed toward the front of the car. The train had stopped just before the Chambers Street station and Goetz went between two of the cars, jumped onto the tracks and fled.

Police and ambulance crews arrived at the scene shortly thereafter. Ramseur and Canty, initially listed in critical condition, have fully recovered. Cabey remains paralyzed and has suffered some degree of brain damage.

On December 31, 1984, Goetz surrendered to police in Concord, New Hampshire, identifying himself as the gunman being sought for the subway shootings in New York nine days earlier.

Later that day, after receiving *Miranda* warnings, he made two lengthy statements, both of which were tape recorded with his permission. In the statements, which are substantially similar, Goetz admitted that he had been illegally carrying a handgun in New York City for three years. He stated that he had first purchased a gun in 1981 after he had been injured in a mugging. Goetz also revealed that twice between 1981 and 1984 he had successfully warded off assailants simply by displaying the pistol.

According to Goetz's statement, the first contact he had with the four youths came when Canty, sitting or lying on the bench across from him, asked, "How are you?" to which he replied, "Fine." Shortly thereafter, Canty, followed by one of the other youths, walked over to the defendant and stood to his left, while the other two youths remained to his right, in the corner of the subway car.

Canty then said, "Give me five dollars." Goetz stated that he knew from the smile on Canty's face that they

wanted to "play with me." Although he was certain that none of the youths had a gun, he had a fear, based on prior experiences, of being "maimed."

Goetz then established "a pattern of fire," deciding specifically to fire from left to right. His stated intention at that point was to "murder [the four youths], to hurt them, to make them suffer as much as possible." When Canty again requested money, Goetz stood up, drew his weapon, and began firing, aiming for the center of the body of each of the four.

Goetz recalled that the first two he shot "tried to run through the crowd [but] they had nowhere to run." Goetz then turned to his right to "go after the other two." One of these two "tried to run through the wall of the train, but . . . he had nowhere to go." The other youth (Cabey) "tried pretending that he wasn't with [the others]," by standing still, holding on to one of the subway hand straps, and not looking at Goetz. Goetz nonetheless fired his fourth shot at him.

He then ran back to the first two youths to make sure they had been "taken care of." Seeing that they had both been shot, he spun back to check on the latter two. Goetz noticed that the youth who had been standing still was now sitting on a bench and seemed unhurt. As Goetz told the police, "I said, 'you seem to be all right, here's another,'" and he then fired the shot which severed Cabey's spinal cord. Goetz added that "if I was a little more under self-control . . . I would have put the barrel against his forehead and fired." He also admitted that "if I had had more [bullets], I would have shot them again, and again, and again."

After waiving extradition, Goetz was brought back to New York and arraigned on a felony complaint charging him with attempted murder and criminal possession of a weapon. The matter was presented to a Grand Jury in January 1985, with the prosecutor seeking an indictment for attempted murder, assault, reckless endangerment, and criminal possession of a weapon. Neither the defendant nor any of the wounded youths testified before this Grand Jury.

On January 25, 1985, the Grand Jury indicted defendant on one count of criminal possession of a weapon in the third degree (Penal Law § 265.02), for possessing the gun used in the subway shootings, and two counts of criminal possession of a weapon in the fourth degree (Penal Law § 265.01), for possessing two other guns in his apartment building. It dismissed, however, the attempted murder and other charges stemming from the shootings themselves.

Several weeks after the Grand Jury's action, the People, asserting that they had newly available evidence, moved for an order authorizing them to resubmit the dismissed charges to a second Grand Jury. Supreme Court, Criminal Term, after conducting an in camera [in the judge's chambers] inquiry, granted the motion. Presentation of the case to the second Grand Jury began on March 14, 1985. Two of the four youths, Canty and Ramseur, testified. Among the other witnesses were four passengers from the seventh car of the subway who had seen some portions of the incident.

Goetz again chose not to testify, though the tapes of his two statements were played for the grand jurors, as had been done with the first Grand Jury.

On March 27, 1985, the second Grand Jury filed a 10-count indictment, containing four charges of attempted murder (Penal Law §§ 110.00, 125.25 [1]), four charges of assault in the first degree (Penal Law § 120.10[1]), one charge of reckless endangerment in the first degree (Penal Law § 120.25), and one charge of criminal possession of a weapon in the second degree (Penal Law § 265.03 [possession of a loaded firearm with intent to use it unlawfully against another]).

Goetz was arraigned on this indictment on March 28, 1985, and it was consolidated with the earlier three-count indictment.

On October 14, 1985, Goetz moved to dismiss the charges contained in the second indictment, alleging, among other things, that the . . . prosecutor's instructions to that Grand Jury on the defense of justification were erroneous and prejudicial to the defendant so as to render its proceedings defective.

On November 25, 1985, while the motion to dismiss was pending before Criminal Term, a column appeared in the *New York Daily News* containing an interview which the columnist had conducted with Darryl Cabey the previous day in Cabey's hospital room. The columnist claimed that Cabey had told him in this interview that the other three youths had all approached Goetz with the intention of robbing him.

The day after the column was published, a New York City police officer informed the prosecutor that he had been one of the first police officers to enter the subway car after the shootings, and that Canty had said to him, "We were going to rob [Goetz]." The prosecutor immediately disclosed this information to the court and to defense counsel, adding that this was the first time his office had been told of this alleged statement and that none of the police reports filed on the incident contained any such information. . . .

In an order dated January 21, 1986 . . . the court, after inspection of the Grand Jury minutes . . . held . . . that the prosecutor, in a supplemental charge elaborating upon the justification defense, had erroneously introduced an objective element into this defense by instructing the grand jurors to consider whether Goetz's conduct was that of a "reasonable man in [Goetz's] situation."

The court . . . concluded that the statutory test for whether the use of deadly force is justified to protect a person should be wholly subjective, focusing entirely on the defendant's state of mind when he used such force. It concluded that dismissal was required for this error because the justification issue was at the heart of the case. . . . [We disagree.]

OPINION

Penal Law article 35 recognizes the defense of justification, which "permits the use of force under certain circumstances." One such set of circumstances pertains to the use of force in defense of a person, encompassing both self-defense and defense of a third person (Penal Law § 35.15).

Penal Law § 35.15(1) sets forth the general principles governing all such uses of force: A person may . . . use physical force upon another person when and to the extent he *reasonably* believes such to be necessary to defend himself or a third person from what he *reasonably* [emphasis added] believes to be the use or imminent use of unlawful physical force by such other person.

Section 35.15(2) sets forth further limitations on these general principles with respect to the use of "deadly physical force": A person may not use deadly physical force upon another person under circumstances specified in subdivision one unless

a. He reasonably believes that such other person is using or about to use deadly physical force . . . *or* [emphasis added]

b. He reasonably believes that such other person is committing or attempting to commit a kidnapping, forcible rape, forcible sodomy or robbery.

Section 35.15(2)(a) further provides, however, that even under these circumstances a person ordinarily must retreat if he knows that he can with complete safety as to himself and others avoid the necessity of [using deadly physical force] by retreating.

Thus, consistent with most justification provisions, Penal Law § 35.15 permits the use of deadly physical force only where requirements as to triggering conditions and the necessity of a particular response are met. As to the triggering conditions, the statute requires that the actor "reasonably believes" that another person either is using or about to use deadly physical force or is committing or attempting to commit one of certain enumerated felonies, including robbery.

As to the need for the use of deadly physical force as a response, the statute requires that the actor "reasonably believes" that such force is necessary to avert the perceived threat. While the portion of section 35.15(2)(b) pertaining to the use of deadly physical force to avert a felony such as robbery does not contain a separate "retreat" requirement, it is clear from reading subdivisions (1) and (2) of section 35.15 together, as the statute requires, that the general "necessity" requirement in subdivision (1) applies to all uses of force under section 35.15, including the use of deadly physical force under subdivision (2)(b).

Because the evidence before the second Grand Jury included statements by Goetz that he acted to protect himself from being maimed or to avert a robbery, the prosecutor correctly chose to charge the justification defense in section 35.15 to the Grand Jury. The prosecutor properly instructed the grand jurors to consider whether the use of deadly physical force was justified to prevent either serious physical injury or a robbery, and, in doing so, to separately analyze the defense with respect to each of the charges. He elaborated upon the prerequisites for the use of deadly physical force essentially by reading or paraphrasing the language in Penal Law § 35.15. The defense does not contend that he committed any error in this portion of the charge.

When the prosecutor had completed his charge, one of the grand jurors asked for clarification of the term "reasonably believes." The prosecutor responded by instructing the grand jurors that they were to consider the circumstances of the incident and determine "whether the defendant's conduct was that of a reasonable man in the defendant's situation." It is this response by the prosecutor—and specifically his use of "a reasonable man"—which is the basis for the dismissal of the charges by the lower courts. As expressed repeatedly in the Appellate Division's plurality opinion, because section 35.15 uses the term "he reasonably believes," the appropriate test, according to that court, is whether a defendant's beliefs and reactions were "reasonable to him."

Under that reading of the statute, a jury which believed a defendant's testimony that he felt that his own actions were warranted and were reasonable would have to acquit him, regardless of what anyone else in defendant's situation might have concluded.

Such an interpretation defies the ordinary meaning and significance of the term "reasonably" in a statute, and misconstrues the clear intent of the Legislature, in enacting section 35.15, to retain an objective element as part of any provision authorizing the use of deadly physical force.

Penal statutes in New York have long codified the right recognized at common law to use deadly physical force, under appropriate circumstances, in self-defense. These provisions have never required that an actor's belief as to the intention of another person to inflict serious injury be *correct* in order for the use of deadly force to be justified, but they have uniformly required that the belief comport with an *objective notion of reasonableness*. [emphasis added]. . . .

The plurality below agreed with defendant's argument that the change in the statutory language from "reasonable ground," used prior to 1965, to "he reasonably believes" in Penal Law § 35.15 evinced a legislative intent to conform to the subjective standard. . . .

We cannot lightly impute to the Legislature an intent to fundamentally alter the principles of justification to allow the perpetrator of a serious crime to go free simply because that person believed his actions were reasonable and necessary to prevent some perceived harm. To completely exonerate such an individual, no matter how aberrational or bizarre his thought patterns, would allow citizens to set their own standards for the permissible use of force. It would also allow a legally competent defendant suffering from delusions to kill or perform acts of violence with impunity, contrary to fundamental principles of justice and criminal law.

We can only conclude that the Legislature retained a reasonableness requirement to avoid giving a license for such actions. . . . Statutes or rules of law requiring a person to act "reasonably" or to have a "reasonable belief" uniformly prescribe conduct meeting an objective standard measured with reference to how "a reasonable person" could have acted. . . .

Goetz . . . argues that the introduction of an objective element will preclude a jury from considering factors such as the prior experiences of a given actor and thus, require it to make a determination of "reasonableness" without regard to the actual circumstances of a particular incident. This argument, however, falsely presupposes that an objective standard means that the background and other relevant characteristics of a particular actor must be ignored. To the contrary, we have frequently noted that a determination of reasonableness must be based on the "circumstances" facing a defendant or his "situation." Such terms encompass more than the physical movements of the potential assailant.

As just discussed, these terms include any relevant knowledge the defendant had about that person. They also necessarily bring in the physical attributes of all persons involved, including the defendant. Furthermore, the defendant's circumstances encompass any prior experiences he had which could provide a reasonable basis for a belief that another person's intentions were to injure or rob him or that the use of deadly force was necessary under the circumstances.

Accordingly, a jury should be instructed to consider this type of evidence in weighing the defendant's actions. The jury must first determine whether the defendant had the requisite beliefs under section 35.15, that is, whether he believed deadly force was necessary to avert the imminent use of deadly force or the commission of one of the felonies enumerated therein. If the People do not prove beyond a reasonable doubt that he did not have such beliefs, then the jury must also consider whether these beliefs were reasonable. The jury would have to determine, in light of all the "circumstances," as explicated above, if a reasonable person could have had these beliefs.

The prosecutor's instruction to the second Grand Jury that it had to determine whether, under the circumstances, Goetz's conduct was that of a reasonable man in his situation was thus essentially an accurate charge. . . .

The order of the Appellate Division should be REVERSED, and the dismissed counts of the indictment reinstated.

Questions

1. Consider the following:
   a. New York tried Goetz for attempted murder and assault. The jury acquitted him of both charges. The jury said Goetz "was justified in shooting the four men with a silver-plated .38-caliber revolver he purchased in Florida." They did convict him of illegal possession of a firearm, for which the court sentenced Goetz to one year in jail.
   b. Following the sentencing, Goetz told the court: "This case is really more about the deterioration of society than it is about me. . . . I believe society needs to be protected from criminals."
   c. Criminal law professor George Fletcher followed the trial closely. After the acquittal, he commented:

The facts of the Goetz case were relatively clear, but the primary fight was over the moral interpretation of the facts. . . . I am not in the slightest bit convinced that the four young men were about to mug Goetz. If he had said, "Listen buddy, I wish I had $5, but I don't," and walked to the other side of the car the chances are 60–40 nothing would have happened. Street-wise kids like that are more attuned to the costs of their behavior than Goetz was. (quoted in Roberts 1989)

If Professor Fletcher is right, was Goetz justified in shooting?

2. Under what circumstances can people use deadly force, according to the New York statutes cited in the opinion?

3. Do you agree with those circumstances?

4. Would you add more? Remove some? Which ones? Why?

5. Were Goetz's shots a preemptive strike? Retaliation? Necessary for self-protection? Explain.

 Go to the Criminal Law 9e website to learn more about Bernhard Goetz in "The Rest of the Story": www.thomsonedu.com/criminaljustice/samaha.

Present Danger   We've talked now about danger from imminent attack, but what about this case? A battered wife who's been beaten repeatedly over a period of years shoots her husband while he's asleep. (She can escape by driving away.) The danger of being beaten again, and maybe even killed, is real and it's not going to go away (*People v. Williams* 1965, 753). But it's not imminent, because it's not going to happen right now. Let's call it **present danger** (danger you reasonably believe is always hanging over you).

In most states, unlike imminent danger, present danger doesn't justify taking the law into your hands. Why? Because you don't have to; you've got time to escape or call the police. In *State v. Stewart* (1988), the Kansas Supreme Court rejected the argument that present danger satisfied the imminent danger requirement in battered woman cases.

CASE | *Was She in Imminent or Present Danger?*

State v. Stewart
763 P.2d 572 (Kans. 1988)

HISTORY

Peggy Stewart, the defendant, was charged with murder in the first degree of her husband, Mike Stewart. The Butler District Court trial jury found Stewart not guilty. The prosecution appealed with a question reserved. The Kansas Supreme Court sustained the appeal.

[The state can't appeal an acquittal, because a jury's verdict of not guilty is final. But the state can appeal questions of law that came up during the trial. In these cases, the state can appeal even though the jury acquitted. That's what's happening here. The state is appealing the legal question: What's the definition of imminent danger? Whatever the answer to the legal question is, Peggy Stewart's acquittal was final.]

LOCKETT, J.

FACTS

Following an annulment from her first husband and two subsequent divorces in which she was the petitioner, Peggy Stewart married Mike Stewart in 1974. Evidence at trial disclosed a long history of abuse by Mike against Peggy and her two daughters from one of her prior marriages.

Laura, one of Peggy's daughters, testified that early in the marriage Mike hit and kicked Peggy, and that after the first year of the marriage Peggy exhibited signs of severe psychological problems. Subsequently, Peggy was hospitalized and diagnosed as having symptoms of paranoid schizophrenia; she responded to treatment and was soon released. It appeared to Laura, however, that Mike was encouraging Peggy to take more than her prescribed dosage of medication.

In 1977, two social workers informed Peggy that they had received reports that Mike was taking indecent liberties with her daughters. Because the social workers did not want Mike to be left alone with the girls, Peggy quit her job. In 1978, Mike began to taunt Peggy by stating that Carla, her 12-year-old daughter, was "more of a wife" to him than Peggy.

Later, Carla was placed in a detention center, and Mike forbade Peggy and Laura to visit her. When Mike finally allowed Carla to return home in the middle of summer, he forced her to sleep in an un–air-conditioned room with the windows nailed shut, to wear a heavy flannel nightgown, and to cover herself with heavy blankets. Mike would then wake Carla at 5:30 A.M. and force her to do all the housework.

Peggy and Laura were not allowed to help Carla or speak to her. When Peggy confronted Mike and demanded that the situation cease, Mike responded by holding a shotgun to Peggy's head and threatening to kill her. Mike once kicked Peggy so violently in the chest and ribs that she required hospitalization. Finally, when Mike ordered Peggy to kill and bury Carla, she filed for divorce. Peggy's attorney in the divorce action testified in the murder trial that Peggy was afraid for both her and her children's lives.

One night, in a fit of anger, Mike threw Carla out of the house. Carla, who was not yet in her teens, was forced out of the home with no money, no coat, and no place to go. When the family heard that Carla was in Colorado, Mike refused to allow Peggy to contact or even talk about Carla.

Mike's intimidation of Peggy continued to escalate. One morning, Laura found her mother hiding on the school bus, terrified and begging the driver to take her to a neighbor's home. That Christmas, Mike threw the turkey dinner to the floor, chased Peggy outside, grabbed her by the hair, rubbed her face in the dirt, and then kicked and beat her.

After Laura moved away, Peggy's life became even more isolated. Once, when Peggy was working at a cafe, Mike came in and ran all the customers off with a gun because he wanted Peggy to go home and have sex with him right that minute.

He abused both drugs and alcohol and amused himself by terrifying Peggy, once waking her from a sound sleep by beating her with a baseball bat. He shot one of Peggy's pet cats and then held the gun against her head and threatened to pull the trigger. Peggy told friends that Mike would hold a shotgun to her head and threaten to blow it off and indicated that one day he would probably do it.

In May 1986, Peggy left Mike and ran away to Laura's home in Oklahoma. It was the first time Peggy had left Mike without telling him. Because Peggy was suicidal, Laura had her admitted to a hospital. There, she was diagnosed as having toxic psychosis as a result of an overdose of her medication. On May 30, 1986, Mike called to say he was coming to get her. Peggy agreed to return to Kansas.

Peggy told a nurse she felt like she wanted to shoot her husband. At trial, she testified that she decided to return with Mike because she was not able to get the medical help she needed in Oklahoma.

When Mike arrived at the hospital, he told the staff that he "needed his housekeeper." The hospital released Peggy to Mike's care, and he immediately drove her back to Kansas. Mike told Peggy that all her problems were in her head and he would be the one to tell her what was good for her, not the doctors. Peggy testified that Mike threatened to kill her if she ever ran away again.

As soon as they arrived at the house, Mike forced Peggy into the house and forced her to have oral sex several times.

The next morning, Peggy discovered a loaded .357 magnum. She testified she was afraid of the gun. She hid the gun under the mattress of the bed in a spare room. Later that morning, as she cleaned house, Mike kept making remarks that she should not bother because she would not be there long, or that she should not bother with her things because she could not take them with her. She testified she was afraid Mike was going to kill her.

Mike's parents visited Mike and Peggy that afternoon. Mike's father testified that Peggy and Mike were affectionate with each other during the visit. Later, after Mike's parents had left, Mike forced Peggy to perform oral sex.

After watching television, Mike and Peggy went to bed at 8:00 P.M. As Mike slept, Peggy thought about suicide and heard voices in her head repeating over and over, "Kill or be killed." At this time, there were two vehicles in the driveway and Peggy had access to the car keys.

About 10:00 P.M., Peggy went to the spare bedroom and removed the gun from under the mattress, walked back to the bedroom, and killed her husband while he slept. She then ran to the home of a neighbor, who called the police.

When the police questioned Peggy regarding the events leading up to the shooting, Peggy stated that things had not gone quite right that day and that when she got the chance she hid the gun under the mattress. She stated that she shot Mike to "get this over with, this misery and this torment."

When asked why she got the gun out, Peggy stated to the police:

I'm not sure exactly what . . . led up to it . . . and my head started playing games with me and I got to thinking about things and I said I didn't want to be by myself again. . . . I got the gun out because there had been remarks made about me being out there alone. It was as if Mike was going to do something again like had been done before. He had gotten me down here from McPherson one time and he went and told them that I had done something and he had me put out of the house and was taking everything I had. And it was like he was going to pull the same thing over again.

Two expert witnesses testified during the trial. The expert for the defense, psychologist Marilyn Hutchinson, diagnosed Peggy as suffering from "battered woman syndrome," or post-traumatic stress syndrome. Dr. Hutchinson testified that Mike was preparing to escalate the violence in retaliation for Peggy's running away. She testified that loaded guns, veiled threats, and increased sexual demands are indicators of the escalation of the cycle.

Dr. Hutchinson believed Peggy had a repressed knowledge that she was in a "really grave lethal situation." The State's expert, psychiatrist Herbert Modlin, neither subscribed to a belief in the battered woman syndrome nor to a theory of learned helplessness as an explanation for why women do not leave an abusive relationship. Dr. Modlin testified that abuse such as repeated forced oral sex would not be trauma sufficient to trigger a post–traumatic stress disorder. He also believed Peggy was erroneously diagnosed as suffering from toxic psychosis. He stated that Peggy was unable to escape the abuse because she suffered from schizophrenia, rather than the battered woman syndrome.

At defense counsel's request, the trial judge gave an instruction on self-defense to the jury. The jury found Peggy not guilty.

OPINION

. . . K.S.A. 21-3211 . . . provides:

A person is justified in the use of force against an aggressor when and to the extent it appears to him and he reasonably believes that such conduct is necessary to defend himself or another against such aggressor's imminent use of unlawful force.

The traditional concept of self-defense has posited onetime conflicts between persons of somewhat equal size and strength. When the defendant claiming self-defense is a victim of long-term domestic violence, such as a battered spouse, such traditional concepts may not apply. Because of the prior history of abuse, and the difference in strength and size between the abused and the abuser, the accused in such cases may choose to defend during a momentary lull in the abuse, rather than during a conflict. However, in order to warrant the giving of a self-defense instruction, the facts of the case must still show that the spouse was in imminent danger close to the time of the killing.

A person is justified in using force against an aggressor when it appears to that person and he or she reasonably believes such force to be necessary. A reasonable belief implies both an honest belief and the existence of facts which would persuade a reasonable person to that belief. A self-defense instruction must be given if there is any evidence to support a claim of self-defense, even if that evidence consists solely of the defendant's testimony.

Where self-defense is asserted, evidence of the deceased's long-term cruelty and violence towards the defendant is admissible. In cases involving battered spouses, expert evidence of the battered woman syndrome is relevant to a determination of the reasonableness of the defendant's perception of danger. . . .

In order to instruct a jury on self-defense, there must be some showing of an imminent threat or a confrontational circumstance involving an overt act by an aggressor. There is no exception to this requirement where the defendant has suffered long-term domestic abuse and the victim is the abuser. In such cases, the issue is not whether the defendant believes homicide is the solution to past or future problems with the batterer, but rather whether circumstances surrounding the killing were sufficient to create a reasonable belief in the defendant that the use of deadly force was necessary.

In recent Kansas cases where battered women shot their husbands, the women were clearly threatened in the moments prior to the shootings. *State v. Hundley*, 693 P.2d 475, involved a severely abused wife, Betty Hundley. . . . On the day of the shooting, Carl threatened to kill her. That night he forcibly broke into Betty's motel room, beat and choked her, painfully shaved her pubic hair, and forced her to have intercourse with him. Thereafter, he pounded a beer bottle on the nightstand and demanded that Betty get him some cigarettes. Betty testified that he had attacked her with beer bottles before. She pulled a gun from her purse and demanded that Carl leave. When Carl saw the gun he stated: "You are dead, bitch, now." Betty fired the gun and killed Carl. . . .

Here, however, there is an absence of imminent danger to defendant: Peggy told a nurse at the Oklahoma hospital of her desire to kill Mike. She later voluntarily agreed to return home with Mike when he telephoned her. She stated that after leaving the hospital Mike threatened to kill her if she left him again. Peggy showed no inclination to leave. In fact, immediately after the shooting, Peggy told the police that she was upset because she thought Mike would leave her. Prior to the shooting, Peggy hid the loaded gun. The cars were in the driveway and Peggy had access to the car keys. After being abused, Peggy went to bed with Mike at 8 P.M. Peggy lay there for two hours, then retrieved the gun from where she had hidden it and shot Mike while he slept.

Under these facts, the giving of the self-defense instruction was erroneous. Under such circumstances, a battered woman cannot reasonably fear imminent life threatening danger from her sleeping spouse. . . .

One additional issue must be addressed. . . . The Kansas County and District Attorney Association contends the instruction given by the trial court improperly modified the law of self-defense to be more generous to one suffering from the battered woman syndrome than to any other defendant relying on self-defense. We agree and believe it is necessary to clarify [our prior decisions]. . . .

The trial judge gave the instruction . . .

A person is justified in the use of force against an aggressor when and to the extent it appears to him and he reasonably believes that such conduct is necessary to defend himself or another against such aggressor's imminent use of unlawful force.

Such justification requires both a belief on the part of the defendant and the existence of facts that would persuade a reasonable person to that belief.

The trial judge then added the following:

You must determine, from the viewpoint of the defendant's mental state, whether the defendant's belief in the need to defend herself was reasonable in light of her subjective impressions and the facts and circumstances known to her.

. . . The statement that the reasonableness of defendant's belief in asserting self-defense should be measured from the defendant's own individual subjective viewpoint conflicts with prior law. Our test for self-defense is a two pronged one. We first use a subjective standard to determine whether the defendant sincerely and honestly believed it necessary to kill in order to defend. We then use an objective standard to determine whether defendant's belief was reasonable—specifically, whether a reasonable person in defendant's circumstances would have perceived self-defense as necessary. In . . . cases involving battered spouses, "the objective test is how a reasonably prudent battered wife would perceive the aggressor's demeanor."

The appeal is sustained.

DISSENT

HERD, J.

. . . We have a well-established rule that a defendant is entitled to a self-defense instruction if there is any evidence to support it, even though the evidence consists solely of the defendant's testimony. It is for the jury to determine the sincerity of the defendant's belief she needed to act in self-defense, and the reasonableness of that belief in light of all the circumstances. . . .

It is evident . . . [Stewart] met her burden of showing some competent evidence that she acted in self-defense, thus making her defense a jury question. She testified she acted in fear for her life, and Dr. Hutchinson corroborated this testimony. The evidence of Mike's past abuse, the escalation of violence, his threat of killing her should she attempt to leave him, and Dr. Hutchinson's testimony that Peggy was indeed in a "lethal situation" more than met the minimal standard of "any evidence" to allow an instruction to be given to the jury.

Peggy introduced much uncontroverted evidence of the violent nature of the deceased and how he had brutalized her throughout their married life. . . .

Psychologist Marilyn Hutchinson qualified as an expert on the battered woman syndrome and analyzed the uncontroverted facts for the jury. She concluded Peggy was a victim of the syndrome and reasonably believed she was in imminent danger. . . .

The majority implies its decision is necessary to keep the battered woman syndrome from operating as a defense in and of itself. It has always been clear the syndrome is not a defense itself. Evidence of the syndrome is admissible only because of its relevance to the issue of self-defense. . . . The expert testimony explains how people react to circumstances in which the average juror has not been involved. It assists the jury in evaluating the sincerity of the defendant's belief she was in imminent danger requiring self-defense and whether she was in fact in imminent danger.

Dr. Hutchinson explained to the jury at Peggy's trial the "cycle of violence" which induces a state of "learned helplessness" and keeps a battered woman in the relationship. She testified Peggy was caught in such a cycle. The cycle begins with an initial building of tension and violence, culminates in an explosion, and ends with a "honeymoon."

The woman becomes conditioned to trying to make it through one more violent explosion with its battering in order to be rewarded by the "honeymoon phase," with its expressions of remorse and eternal love and the standard promise of "never again."

After all promises are broken time after time and she is beaten again and again, the battered woman falls into a state of learned helplessness where she gives up trying to extract herself from the cycle of violence. She learns fighting back only delays the honeymoon and escalates the violence. If she tries to leave the relationship, she is located and returned and the violence increases. She is a captive. She begins to believe her husband is omnipotent, and resistance will be futile at best.

It is a jury question to determine if the battered woman who kills her husband as he sleeps fears he will find and kill her if she leaves, as is usually claimed. Under such circumstances the battered woman is not under actual physical attack when she kills but such attack is imminent, and as a result she believes her life is in imminent danger. She may kill during the tension-building stage when the abuse is apparently not as severe as it sometimes has been, but nevertheless has escalated so that she is afraid the acute stage to come will be fatal to her. She only acts on such fear if she has some survival instinct remaining after the husband-induced "learned helplessness." . . .

It was Dr. Hutchinson's opinion Mike was planning to escalate his violence in retaliation against Peggy for running away. She testified that Mike's threats against Peggy's life, his brutal sexual acts, and Peggy's discovery of the loaded gun were all indicators to Peggy the violence had escalated and she was in danger. Dr. Hutchinson believed Peggy had a repressed knowledge she was in what was really a gravely lethal situation. She testified Peggy was convinced she must "kill or be killed." The majority claims permitting a jury to consider self-defense under these facts would permit anarchy. This underestimates the jury's ability to recognize an invalid claim of self-defense. . . .

The majority bases its opinion on its conclusion Peggy was not in imminent danger, usurping the right of the jury to make that determination of fact. The majority believes a person could not be in imminent danger from an aggressor merely because the aggressor dropped off to sleep. This is a fallacious conclusion. For instance, picture a hostage situation where the armed guard inadvertently drops off to sleep and the hostage grabs his gun and shoots him. The majority opinion would preclude the use of self-defense in such a case.

. . . The jury in homicide cases where a battered woman ultimately kills her batterer is entitled to all the facts about the battering relationship in rendering its verdict. The jury also needs to know about the nature of the cumulative terror under which a battered woman exists and that a batterer's threats and brutality can make life-threatening danger imminent to the victim of that brutality even though, at the moment, the batterer is passive.

Where a person believes she must kill or be killed, and there is the slightest basis in fact for this belief, it is a question for the jury as to whether the danger was imminent. I confess I am an advocate for the constitutional principle that in a criminal prosecution determination of the facts is a function of the jury, not the appellate court.

Questions

1. How does the court define *imminent*?

2. Can battered women ever be in imminent danger when their husbands are sleeping?

3. Should we have a special battered woman's defense of justification?

4. Should we expand the definition of *imminent*? Or change the requirement from imminent to present, or continuing, danger?

5. Why does the court talk about putting the power of capital punishment into the hands of battered wives?

6. Consider the following comment:

> Retaliation, as opposed to defense, is a common problem in cases arising from wife battering and domestic violence. The injured wife waits for the first possibility of striking against a distracted or unarmed husband. The man may even be asleep when the wife finally reacts.
>
> . . . Retaliation is the standard case of "taking the law into your own hands." There is no way, under the law, to justify killing a wife batterer or a rapist in retaliation or revenge, however much sympathy there may be for the wife wreaking retaliation. Private citizens cannot act as judge and jury toward each other. They have no authority to pass judgment and to punish each other for past wrongs. (Fletcher 1988, 21–22)

Do you agree with the statement? Explain your answer.

7. In your opinion, was Peggy Stewart's act one of self-defense, a preemptive strike, or retaliation? Back up your answer with facts in the case.

EXPLORING FURTHER

Imminent Danger

Was She in *Imminent* Danger?

State v. Hundley, 693 P.2d 475 (Kans. 1985)

FACTS The married life of Carl and Betty Hundley had been a tumultuous one. They had been married approximately ten years. During that time, Carl had subjected Betty to much abuse. He had knocked out several of her teeth, broken her nose at least five times, and threate... to cut her eyeballs out and her head off. Carl had kicked Betty down the stairs on numerous occasions and had repeatedly broken her ribs.

Mrs. Hundley suffered from diabetes and, as part of his abuse, Carl prevented Betty from taking her required dosage of insulin on numerous occasions by hiding it or diluting the insulin with water. Needless to say, Betty Hundley went into diabetic comas on those occasions. In November 1982, approximately six weeks prior to Carl's death, Betty had been in the hospital for unknown causes. When she was discharged she went to live with Carl. He reacted in his usual manner by knocking her down, kicking her, and choking her into unconsciousness. This was all Carl's violence Betty could take. She moved to the Jayhawk Junior Motel. As in typical wife-beating cases, her moving did not eliminate the problem. Carl then started a pattern of constant harassment. He would call her night and day to threaten her life and those of her family. She was so frightened she started carrying a gun.

On January 13, 1983, the day of the shooting, Betty had seen Carl early in the day, at which time Carl told Betty he was going to come over and kill her. That night she heard a thumping on her motel door while she was in the bathroom. By the time Betty got out of the bathroom Carl had broken the door lock and entered the room. His entry was followed by violence. Betty was hit and choked and her life was again threatened. Carl then forced Betty to shower with him, during which time he shaved her pubic hair in a rough and violent fashion, nicking and cutting her. After that crude episode, Carl forced Betty to submit to sexual intercourse with him.

Even after that, Carl continued to threaten Betty. She was sobbing and afraid. He pounded a beer bottle on the nightstand and threw a dollar bill toward the window, demanding she get him some cigarettes. Betty testified Carl had hit her with beer bottles many times in the past. Therefore, feeling threatened by the beer bottle, she went to her purse, pulled out the gun and demanded Carl leave. When he saw the gun, Carl laughed tauntingly and said, "You are dead bitch, now!" As he reached for the beer bottle, Betty shut her eyes and fired her gun. She fired it again and again. There were five spent shells in the gun when it was seized. At the time of the shooting, the deceased had his back to Betty and was paying attention to the beer bottle. She was not physically blocked from going to the door.

The autopsy revealed two gunshot wounds in the body of the deceased. It also appeared the gun had been fired from a distance greater than two feet from the body of the victim. A blood sample revealed the deceased's body had .17 alcohol content. The deceased weighed 160 pounds. Appellant testified he weighed 220 pounds.

. . . The defense called fifteen witnesses, other than appellant, who testified about the violent nature of the deceased and the numerous occasions on which he brutalized appellant.

Can the jury consider a husband's violent history toward his battered wife?

es, said the Kansas Supreme Court.

... a textbook case of the battered wife, which is ically similar to hostage and prisoner of war attered women are terror-stricken people ...se mental state is distorted and bears a marked resemblance to that of a hostage or a prisoner of war. The horrible beatings they are subjected to brainwash them into believing there is nothing they can do. They live in constant fear of another eruption of violence. They become disturbed persons from the torture.

... An aggressor who is customarily armed and gets involved in a fight may present an imminent danger, justifying the use of force in self-defense, even though the aggressor is unarmed on the occasion. In other words, the law of self-defense recognizes one may reasonably fear danger but be mistaken. . . .

 Go to the Criminal Law 9e website to find the full text of the Exploring Further excerpts: www.thomsonedu .com/criminaljustice/samaha. (Excerpts on imminent danger.)

Retreat

What if you can avoid an attack by escaping? Do you have to retreat? Or can you stand your ground and fight back? The majority rule is the **stand-your-ground rule;** it says that if you didn't start the fight, you can stand your ground and kill. The minority rule, the **retreat rule,** says you have to retreat but only if you reasonably believe that backing off won't unreasonably put you in danger of death or serious bodily harm. Of course, you have to believe *reasonably* that you're in danger of death or serious bodily harm.

Different values underlie these rules. The retreat rule puts a premium on human life and discourages injuring or killing another person (even an assailant). The stand-your-ground rule (we used to call it the "true man rule"; *State v. Kennamore* 1980, 858) is based on the belief that retreat forces innocent people to take a cowardly or humiliating position. Most states follow the stand-your-ground rule.

States that require retreat have carved out an exception to the retreat doctrine. According to this exception, when you're attacked in your home, you can stand your ground and use deadly force to fend off an unprovoked attack but only if you reasonably believe the attack threatens death or serious bodily injury.

The Second Circuit U.S. District Court of Appeals dealt with retreat and the castle (your home) exception in *U.S. v. Peterson* (1973).

C A S E *Did He Have to Retreat?*

U.S. v. Peterson
483 F.2d 1222 (2nd Cir. 1973)

HISTORY

Bennie Peterson, the defendant, was convicted before the United States District Court for the District of Columbia of manslaughter, and he appealed. The District of Columbia Court of Appeals affirmed.

ROBINSON III, J.

FACTS

Charles Keitt, the deceased, and two friends drove in Keitt's car to the alley in the rear of Peterson's house to remove the windshield wipers from Peterson's wrecked car. (The car was characterized by some witnesses as "wrecked" and by others as "abandoned." The testimony left it clear that its condition was such that it could not be operated.)

While Keitt was doing so, Peterson came out of the house into the backyard to protest. After a verbal exchange, Peterson went back into the house, obtained a pistol, and very shortly returned to the yard. In the meantime, Keitt had reseated himself in his car, and he and his companions were about to leave.

Upon his reappearance in the yard, Peterson paused briefly to load the pistol. "If you move," he shouted to Keitt, "I will shoot." He walked to a point in the yard slightly inside a gate in the rear fence and, pistol in hand, said, "If you come in here I will kill you."

Keitt alighted from his car, took a few steps toward Peterson and exclaimed, "What the hell do you think you are going to do with that?" (There was abundant evidence that Keitt was intoxicated or nearly so. His companions readily admitted to a considerable amount of drinking earlier that day, and an autopsy disclosed that he had a .29% blood-alcohol content.)

Keitt then made an about-face, walked back to his car and got a lug wrench. With the wrench in a raised position, Keitt advanced toward Peterson, who stood with the pistol pointed toward him. Peterson warned Keitt not to "take another step" and, when Keitt continued onward, shot him in the face from a distance of about ten feet. Death was apparently instantaneous.

Shortly thereafter, Peterson left home and was apprehended 20-odd blocks away.

Peterson did not testify or offer any evidence, but the Government introduced a statement which he had given the police after his arrest, in which he related a somewhat different version.

Keitt had removed objects from his car before, and on the day of the shooting he had told Keitt not to do so. After the initial verbal altercation, Keitt went to his car for the lug wrench, so he, Peterson, went into his house for his pistol. When Keitt was about ten feet away, he pointed the pistol "away of his right shoulder"; adding that Keitt was running toward him, Peterson said he "got scared and fired the gun. He ran right into the bullet." "I did not mean to shoot him," Peterson insisted, "I just wanted to scare him."

At trial, Peterson moved for a judgment of acquittal on the ground that . . . the evidence was insufficient to support a conviction. The trial judge denied the motion. After receiving instructions . . . the jury returned a verdict finding Peterson guilty of manslaughter. Judgment was entered conformably with the verdict, and this appeal followed.

OPINION

. . . Peterson's . . . position is that . . . his act was one of self-preservation.

. . . The Government, on the other hand, has contended from the beginning that Keitt's slaying fell outside the bounds of lawful self-defense. The questions remaining for our decision inevitably track back to this basic dispute. . . .

Necessity is the pervasive theme of the . . . conditions which the law imposes on the right to kill or maim in self-defense. There must have been a threat, actual or apparent, of the use of deadly force against the defender. The threat must have been unlawful and immediate. The defender

must have believed that he was in imminent peril of death or serious bodily harm, and that his response was necessary to save himself therefrom.

These beliefs must not only have been honestly entertained, but also objectively reasonable in light of the surrounding circumstances. It is clear that no less than a concurrence of these elements will suffice.

Here the parties' opposing contentions focus on . . . the defendant's failure to utilize a safe route for retreat from the confrontation. . . . At no time did Peterson endeavor to retreat from Keitt's approach with the lug wrench.

The judge instructed the jury that if Peterson had reasonable grounds to believe and did believe that he was in imminent danger of death or serious injury, and that deadly force was necessary to repel the danger . . . Peterson was entitled to stand his ground and use such force as was reasonably necessary under the circumstances to save his life and his person from pernicious bodily harm.

But, the judge continued, if Peterson could have safely retreated but did not do so, that failure was a circumstance which the jury might consider, together with all others, in determining whether he went further in repelling the danger, real or apparent, than he was justified in going.

Peterson contends that this imputation of an obligation to retreat was error, even if he could safely have done so. He points out that at the time of the shooting he was standing in his own yard, and argues he was under no duty to move. We are persuaded . . . that in the circumstances presented here, the trial judge did not err in giving the instruction challenged.

Within the common law of self-defense there developed the rule of "retreat to the wall," which ordinarily forbade the use of deadly force by one to whom an avenue for safe retreat was open. . . .

In a majority of American jurisdictions, contrary to the common law rule, one may stand his ground and use deadly force whenever it seems reasonably necessary to save himself. While the law of the District of Columbia on this point is not entirely clear, it seems allied with the strong minority adhering to the common law. . . . This court, adverting to necessity as the soul of homicidal self-defense, [has] declared that "no necessity for killing an assailant can exist, so long as there is a safe way open to escape the conflict." . . .

That is not to say that the retreat rule is without exceptions. . . . The doctrine of retreat was never intended to enhance the risk to the innocent; its proper application has never required a faultless victim to increase his assailant's safety at the expense of his own.

A slight variant of the same consideration is the principle that there is no duty to retreat from an assault producing an imminent danger of death or grievous bodily harm. "Detached reflection cannot be demanded in the presence of an uplifted knife," nor is it "a condition of immunity that one in that situation should pause to consider whether a reasonable man might not think it possible to fly with safety or to disable his assailant rather than to kill him."

The trial judge's charge to the jury incorporated each of these limitations on the retreat rule. Peterson, however, invokes another, the so-called "castle" doctrine. It is well settled that one who through no fault of his own is attacked in his home is under no duty to retreat. The oft-repeated expression that "a man's home is his castle" reflected the belief in olden days that there were few if any safer sanctuaries than the home. The "castle" exception, moreover, has been extended by some courts to encompass the occupant's presence within the curtilage outside his dwelling. Peterson reminds us that when he shot to halt Keitt's advance, he was standing in his yard and so, he argues, he had no duty to endeavor to retreat.

Despite the practically universal acceptance of the "castle" doctrine . . . it is clear . . . it was inapplicable here. The right of self-defense . . . cannot be claimed by the aggressor in an affray so long as he retains that unmitigated role. . . . Any rule of no-retreat which may protect an innocent victim of the affray would . . . [is] unavailable to the party who provokes or stimulates the conflict. Accordingly, the law is well settled that the "castle" doctrine can be invoked only by one who is without fault in bringing the conflict on.

That, we think, is the critical consideration here. . . . By no interpretation of the evidence could it be said that Peterson was blameless in the affair. And while, of course, it was for the jury to assess the degree of fault, the evidence well nigh dictated the conclusion that it was substantial.

The only reference in the trial judge's charge intimating an affirmative duty to retreat was the instruction that a failure to do so, when it could have been done safely, was a factor in the totality of the circumstances which the jury might consider in determining whether the force which he employed was excessive. We cannot believe that any jury was at all likely to view Peterson's conduct as irreproachable.

We conclude that for one who, like Peterson, was hardly entitled to fall back on the "castle" doctrine of no retreat, that instruction cannot be just cause for complaint. . . .

The judgment of conviction appealed from is accordingly AFFIRMED.

Questions

1. List all of the facts relevant to deciding whether Bennie Peterson shot and killed Charles Keitt in self-defense.

2. Apply both the retreat and stand-your-ground rules to the facts of the case. Is Peterson guilty under both, one, or neither? Defend your answer.

3. Does the castle exception apply to the facts of the case? Rely on the specific facts in the case to back up your answer.

4. Do you favor the retreat or the stand-your-ground rule of self-defense? Why?

5. Exactly where would you draw the line in the castle exception? Or would you abolish the exception? Explain your answer.

Retreat

Did He Have to Retreat from His Own Apartment?

State v. Quarles, 504 A.2d 473 (R.I. 1986)

FACTS Quarles saw Pinto in a bar talking with a man he didn't recognize. After Pinto refused to leave with Quarles, he walked back to their common residence in Newport. About ten minutes later Pinto walked into the house and informed Quarles that he had one week to find another place to live. Quarles agreed to leave in a week and went upstairs to their bedroom and began to undress. Pinto followed him upstairs and started to choke him. He punched her to get her to release him.

Infuriated, she told him to get out "tonight." Quarles called her a "tramp" and indicated that he wouldn't put up with her antics any longer. Pinto went downstairs into the kitchen. After Quarles dressed, he followed her downstairs. When he entered the kitchen, Pinto swung a 9-inch kitchen knife at him. He stepped back and wrestled the knife out of her hands.

Quarles conceded that at this point he could have left the house with the knife under his control. But Pinto suddenly grabbed his arm and struggled with him in an attempt to regain control over the knife. During the ensuing affray, in the early morning hours of October 5, Pinto was fatally stabbed by Quarles. Quarles claims that the stabbing occurred when Pinto grabbed his arm and drew the knife toward herself. When he withdrew the knife and saw blood on it, he realized that there had been a stabbing. He insists that Pinto's wound was self-inflicted.

Did he have to retreat from his co-occupant in their joint residence?

DECISION Yes, said the Rhode Island appeals court:

> We are of the opinion that a person assailed in his or her own residence by a co-occupant is not entitled under the guise of self-defense to employ deadly force and kill his or her assailant. The person attacked is obligated to attempt retreat if he or she is aware of a safe and available avenue of retreat.
>
> The right of self-defense is born of necessity and should terminate when the necessity is no more. Thus, the obligation to attempt retreat exists where one is assaulted in his or her own living quarters by his or her co-occupant.

 Go to the Criminal Law 9e website to find the full text of the Exploring Further excerpt: www.thomsonedu.com/criminaljustice/samaha. (Excerpts on retreat.)

 Go to the Criminal Law 9e website to find Exercise 5-1 to learn more about self-defense in your state.

THE DEFENSE OF OTHERS

Historically, self-defense meant protecting yourself and the members of your immediate family. Although several states still require a special relationship, the trend is in the opposite direction. Many states have abandoned the special-relationship requirement altogether, replacing it with the defense of anyone who needs immediate protection from attack.

Several states that retain the requirement have expanded it to include lovers and friends. The "others" have to have the right to defend themselves before someone else can claim the defense. This is important in cases involving abortion rights protestors. In *State v. Aguillard* (1990, 674), protestors argued they had the right to prevent abortions by violating the law because they were defending the right of unborn children to live. In rejecting the defense of others, the court said:

> The "defense of others" specifically limits the use of force or violence in protection of others to situations where the person attacked would have been justified in using such force or violence to protect himself. In view of *Roe v. Wade* and the provisions of the Louisiana abortion statute, defense of others as justification for the defendants' otherwise criminal conduct is not available in these cases. Since abortion is legal in Louisiana, the defendants had no legal right to protect the unborn by means not even available to the unborn themselves. (676)

IN THE DEFENSE OF HOME AND PROPERTY

The right to use force to defend your home is deeply rooted in the common-law idea that "a man's home is his castle." As early as 1604, Sir Edward Coke, the great common-law judge, in his report of *Semayne's Case*, wrote:

> The house of everyone is to him his castle and fortress, as well for his defense against injury and violence, as for his repose; and although the life of a man is a thing precious and favored in law . . . if thieves come to a man's house to rob him, or murder, and the owner or his servants kill any of the thieves in defense of himself and his house, it is not felony and he shall lose nothing. (*State v. Mitcheson* 1977, 1122)

The most impassioned statement of the supreme value placed on the sanctity of homes came from the Earl of Chatham during a debate in the British Parliament in 1764:

> The poorest man may in his cottage bid defiance to all the forces of the Crown. It may be frail; its roof may shake; the wind may blow through it; the storm may enter; the rain may enter; but the King of England may not enter; all his force dares not cross the threshold of the ruined tenement. (Hall 1991, 2:4)

Don't let the Earl of Chatham's moving words lure you into thinking you can *automatically* kill an intruder to defend the sanctity of your home. Sir William Blackstone (1769), in his eighteenth-century *Commentaries* (the best-known—and often the only known—law book to American lawyers at that time), argues the right is broad but limited. He writes:

> If any person attempts . . . to break open a house in the nighttime . . . and shall be killed in such attempt, the slayer shall be acquitted and discharged. This reaches not to . . . the breaking open of any house in the daytime, unless it carries with it an attempt of robbery. (180)

You can see that the defense was limited to nighttime invasions, except for breaking into homes to commit daytime robberies. Many modern statutes limit the use of deadly force to cases where it's reasonable to believe intruders intend to commit crimes of violence (like homicide, assault, rape, and robbery) against occupants. Some go further and include all felonies. A few include *all* offenses. The most extreme is the Colorado "make my day law," which provides:

USE OF DEADLY PHYSICAL FORCE AGAINST AN INTRUDER

(1) The general assembly hereby recognizes that the citizens of Colorado have a right to expect absolute safety within their own homes.

(2) . . . Any occupant of a dwelling is justified in using any degree of physical force, including deadly physical force, against another person when that other person has made an unlawful entry into the dwelling, and when the occupant has a reasonable belief that such other person has committed a crime in the dwelling in addition to the uninvited entry, or is committing or intends to commit a crime against a person or property in addition to the uninvited entry, and when the occupant reasonably believes that such other person might use any physical force, no matter how slight, against any occupant.

(3) Any occupant of a dwelling using physical force, including deadly physical force, in accordance with the provisions of subsection (2) of this section shall be immune from criminal prosecution for the use of such force.

(4) Any occupant of a dwelling using physical force, *including deadly physical force*, in accordance with the provisions of subsection (2) of this section shall be immune from any civil liability for injuries or death resulting from the use of such force (Section 18-1-704.5). [Emphasis added]

Statutes also vary as to the area the use of deadly force covers. Most require entry into the home itself. This doesn't include the **curtilage**, the area immediately surrounding the home. Many require entry into an occupied home. This means you can't set some automatic device to shoot whoever trips the switch when you're not home.

The Maryland Court of Appeals dealt with the limits on the use of deadly force to protect your home in the tragic case of *Law v. State* (1974).

CASE | *Was He Justified in Killing to Protect His Home?*

Law v. State
318 A.2d 859 (Md.App. 1974)

HISTORY

James Law, the defendant, was convicted in the Circuit Court, Charles County, of murder and assault with intent to murder and he appealed. He was sentenced to 10 years in prison.

The Court of Special Appeals reversed and remanded.

LOWE, J.

FACTS

When James Cecil Law, Jr., purchased a thirty-nine dollar shotgun for "house protection," he could not possibly have conceived of the ordeal it would cause him to undergo. Mr. Law, a 32-year-old black man, had recently married and moved to a predominantly white middle-class neighborhood. Within two weeks, his home was broken into and a substantial amount of clothing and personal property was taken.

The investigating officer testified that Mr. Law was highly agitated following the burglary and indicated that he would take the matter into his own hands. The officer quoted Mr. Law as saying: "I will take care of the job. I know who it is." The officer went on to say that Law told him " . . . he knew somebody he could get a gun from in D.C. and he was going to kill the man and he was going to take care of it." Two days later he purchased a 12-gauge shotgun and several "double ought" shells.

The intruder entered the Laws' home between 6:30 and 9:00 in the evening by breaking a windowpane in the kitchen door which opened onto a screened back porch. The intruder then apparently reached in and unlocked the door. Law later installed "double locks" which required the use of a key both inside and outside. He replaced the glass in the door window in a temporary manner by holding it in place with a few pieces of molding, without using the customary glazing compound to seal it in.

One week after the break-in a well-meaning neighbor saw a flickering light in the Laws' otherwise darkened house and became suspicious. Aware of the previous burglary, he reported to the police that someone was breaking into the Laws' home. Although the hour was 8:00 P.M., Mr. Law and his bride had retired for the evening. When the police arrived, a fuse of circumstances ignited by fear exploded into a tragedy of errors.

The police did not report to or question the calling neighbor. Instead they went about routinely checking the house seeking the possible illegal point of entry. They raised storm windows where they could reach them and shook the inside windows to see if they were locked. They shined flashlights upon the windows out of reach, still seeking evidence of unlawful entry. Finding none, two officers entered the back screened porch to check the back door, whereupon they saw the windowpane which appeared to have been temporarily put in place with a few pieces of molding. These officers apparently had not known of the repair or the cause of damage.

Upstairs Mr. and Mrs. Law heard what sounded like attempts to enter their home. Keenly aware of the recent occurrence, Mr. Law went downstairs, obtained and loaded his newly acquired shotgun and, apparently facing the rear door of the house, listened for more sounds.

In the meantime, the uniformed officers found what they thought to be the point of entry of a burglar, and were examining the recently replaced glass. While Officer Adams held the flashlight on the recently replaced pane of glass, Officer Garrison removed the molding and the glass, laid them down and stated that he was going to reach in and unlock the door from the inside to see if entry could be gained. Officer Adams testified that they "were talking in a tone a little lower than normal at this point."

Officer Adams stated that Officer Garrison then tested the inside lock, discovered it was a deadlock and decided no one could have gotten in the door without a key. A law enforcement student, riding with Officer Garrison that evening, testified that he then heard a rattling noise and someone saying "if there was somebody here, he's still in there." As Officer Garrison removed his hand from the window he was hit by a shotgun blast which Law fired through the door. Officer Garrison was dead on arrival at the hospital.

Officer Potts, the officer next to arrive at the scene, saw Officer Adams running to his car to call for reinforcements. He heard another shot and Officer Adams yell "they just shot at me." The tragedy of errors had only begun. The officers, having obtained reinforcements and apparently believing they had cornered a burglar, subjected the house to a fusillade of gunfire evidenced by over forty bullet holes in the bottom of the kitchen door and the police department transcription of a telephone conversation during the ensuing period of incomprehensible terror.

Mr. Law testified that while he stood listening to the sounds and voices at the door, fearful that someone was about to come in ". . . the gun went off, like that, and when it went off like that it scared me and I was so scared because I had never shot a shotgun before and then I heard a voice on the outside say that someone had been shot." Mr. Law was not able to hear who had been shot but he then ". . . hollered up to my wife, call a police officer, I think I shot a burglar."

His wife called the police and most of her conversation was recorded. The appellant, James Cecil Law, Jr. was found guilty of murder in the second degree and of assault with intent to murder. He was convicted by a jury in the Circuit Court for Charles County following removal from Prince George's County. Judge James C. Mitchell sentenced him to concurrent ten-year terms.

OPINION

. . . There is a dearth of Maryland authority upon the question of what constitutes justifiable homicide in the defense of one's home. . . . The defense of habitation is explained by text writers . . . as an extension of the right of self-defense. The distinction between the defense of home and the defense of person is primarily that in the former there is no duty to retreat. "A man in his own house was treated as 'at the wall' and could not, by another's assault, be put under any duty to flee therefrom." The regal aphorism that a man's home is his castle has obscured the limitations on the right to preserve one's home as a sanctuary from fear of force or violence. . . .

> . . . If an assault on a dwelling and an attempted forcible entry are made under circumstances which would create a reasonable apprehension that it is the design of the assailant to commit a felony or to inflict on the inhabitants injury which may result in loss of life or great bodily harm, and that the danger that the design will be carried into effect is imminent, a lawful occupant of the dwelling may prevent the entry even by the taking of the intruder's life.

The felonies the prevention of which justifies the taking of a life "are such and only such as are committed by forcible means, violence, and surprise such as murder, robbery, burglary, rape or arson." . . . It is "essential that killing is necessary to prevent the commission of the felony in question. If other methods would prevent its commission, a homicide is not justified; all other means of preventing the crime must first be exhausted." The right thus rests upon real or apparent necessity. It is this need for caution in exercising the right that has been relegated to obscurity.

The position espoused by appellant typifies the misunderstanding of the extent of the right to defend one's home against intrusion. He says:

> The defendant is not required to act as a reasonable, prudent and cautious individual, nor was he required to limit his force to only that that was required under the circumstances—not when the defendant was in his own home, and believed he was being set upon, or about to

be set upon by would be robbers or burglars who were in the act of breaking into his home at the time.

The judgment which must usually be made precipitously under frightening conditions nevertheless demands a certain presence of mind and reasonableness of judgment. . . .

> A man may repel force by force in defense of his person, habitation, or property against one who manifestly intends and endeavors, by violence or surprise, to commit a known felony, such as murder, rape, robbery, arson, burglary, and the like, upon either. In these cases he is not obliged to retreat, but may pursue his adversary until he has secured himself from all danger; and if he kill him in so doing it is called justifiable self-defense; as, on the other hand, the killing by such felon of any person so lawfully defending himself will be murder. *But a bare fear of any of these offenses, however well grounded, as that another lies in wait to take away the party's life, unaccompanied with any overt act indicative of such an intention, will not warrant in killing that other by way of prevention. . . .*" [My italics]

Judgments REVERSED; case REMANDED for a new trial.

[The court reversed and remanded the case because the conviction was based on a coerced confession banned by Miranda v. Arizona.*]*

Questions

1. Exactly how does the court define the defense of *habitation?*

2. List all of the facts relevant to deciding whether James Cecil Law is entitled to the defense.

3. Assume that you're the prosecutor. Argue that Law was not justified in killing the officer. Rely on the court's definition and the facts of the case to back up your arguments.

4. Now, assume that you're the defense lawyer. Argue that Law was justified in killing the officer. Rely on the court's definition and the facts of the case to back up your arguments.

5. When the case was remanded and the court on remand rejected Law's defense of home defense, the court commented on the mitigating circumstances that might reduce his punishment:

> We think the evidence . . . fairly generated an issue of mitigation. At the time of the homicide, appellant and his bride of a few weeks were alone in the bedroom in their darkened house. Two weeks before the homicide their house had been burglarized. They heard noises outside. Appellant got out of bed, nude, and went downstairs to investigate the matter. He continued to hear noises like someone was "trying to get in."
>
> He obtained from the living room his shotgun, purchased for "home protection" after his house

had been burglarized two weeks before. He heard a noise on his back porch, "a fiddling around with the door." There were curtains on the back door and he could see no figures on the darkened back porch. He felt that there were burglars on his porch, and "then I heard the scraping of a window pane." He next heard a voice say, "let's go in." At that time he was in the living room, "standing there with my shotgun shaking . . ." because he was scared. In appellant's words, "at that time the gun went off." He said he didn't know how the gun went off; he could have pulled the trigger intentionally or accidentally; he didn't know. When the gun went off, it was held about waist high pointed toward the back door.

> The single shotgun blast went through the door killing police officer Garrison, who at that time was attempting to gain entrance to the house. The blast narrowly missed police officer Adams who was standing beside officer Garrison. The two officers had gone to the house in response to a call from appellant's next door neighbor who, unknown to appellant or his wife, had earlier called the police to report a suspected burglary attempt at appellant's house.

> The State conceded in closing argument that appellant did not knowingly shoot a police officer and that "he probably thought he shot a burglar or whatever that was outside." Although by far the most common form of mitigation is that of a hot-blooded response to legally adequate provocation, this is not the only form of mitigation that will negate malice and will reduce what might otherwise be murder to manslaughter. . . . For example, if one man kills another intentionally, under circumstances beyond the scope of innocent homicide, the facts may come so close to justification or excuse that the killing will be classed as voluntary manslaughter rather than murder. (*Law v. State*, 349 A.2d 295 [Md.App. 1975])

Do you think that this is evidence of mitigation or of justifiable homicide in the defense of home? Explain your answer.

EXPLORING FURTHER

In the Defense of Home and Property

1. Was "Outside the Front Door" Part of the "Home"?

People v. Guenther 740 P.2d 971 (Colo. 1987)

FACTS When neighbors pounded on David and Pam Guenther's door, and Pam went outside and got into a struggle with one of the neighbors, David shot and killed two neighbors standing outside the front door with four shots from a Smith and Wesson .357 Magnum 6-inch revolver. The Guenthers lived in Colorado after the state passed its "make my day" law quoted on p. 154.

Was David Guenther justified in shooting his neighbors standing outside his front door?

DECISION No, said the Colorado Supreme Court:

> In accordance with the explicit terms of the statute, we hold that section 18-1-704.5 provides the home occupant with immunity from prosecution only for force used against one who has made an unlawful entry into the dwelling, and that this immunity does not extend to force used against non-entrants. . . .

2. Was the "Booby Trap" Justifiable Deadly Force?

Falco v. State, 407 So.2d 203 (Fla. 1981)

FACTS A youth, Richard Brush, Jr., entered Carmine Falco's home from a side bathroom window—without Falco's consent and in the course of the commission of a burglary. (The day before this entry, the appellant's home either had been burglarized or an attempt had been made. It had been broken into and reported to the police a number of times in the immediate past.) Brush had already illegally entered the appellant's bathroom and was opening the bathroom door to move into the living room, when he was mortally wounded by a bullet from a .22-caliber rifle positioned on a chair in the living room. No one was present at the time of Brush's entry. To activate the gun, it would have been necessary to have entered into the residence in the same manner as did Brush and to thereafter move from one interior room to another. The rifle was not attached to any exterior door or window, nor to any main entry into Falco's home. It was aimed so that the bullet would enter the bathroom door at 3 feet, 1 inch above the floor and would exit at 3 feet, 2 inches above the floor. Richard Brush, Jr., was 5 feet, 7 inches tall.

Was the spring gun a justified use of deadly force?

DECISION No, said the Florida Supreme Court:

Appellant (Falco) erroneously presumes that the use of a deadly mechanical device, such as a trap gun, in defense of any property is a justifiable use of force based on a reasonable belief of its necessity. We agree with the state's argument that the use of such a device is fundamentally unnecessary and unjustifiable.

A trap gun or spring gun is absolutely incapable of exercising discretion or reason. Rather, it sentences its victim to death or great bodily injury in a split second explosion of deadly force. Such arbitrary brutality should necessarily be prohibited under any circumstance. . . .

Allowing persons, at their own risk, to employ deadly mechanical devices imperils the lives of children, firemen and policemen acting within the scope of their employment, and others. *Where the actor is present, there is always the possibility he will realize that deadly force is not necessary, but deadly mechanical devices are without mercy or discretion.* Such devices "are silent instrumentalities of death. They deal death and destruction to the innocent as well as the criminal intruder without the slightest warning. The taking of human life (or infliction of great bodily injury) by such means is brutally savage and inhuman."

Although a "forcible felony" includes burglary in Florida . . . , a defendant is not protected from liability merely by the fact that the intruder's conduct is such as would justify the defendant, were he present, in believing that the intrusion threatened death or serious bodily injury. There is ordinarily the possibility that the defendant, were he present, would realize the true state of affairs and recognize the intruder as one whom he would not be justified in killing or wounding.

 Go to the Criminal Law 9e website to find the full text of the Exploring Further excerpts: www.thomsonedu .com/criminaljustice/samaha. (Excerpts on defense of home and property.)

 Go to the Criminal Law 9e website to find Exercise 5-2 to learn more about the defense of home in your state: www.thomsonedu.com/criminaljustice/samaha.

Homes are special places; they're not in the same category as our "stuff." Can you use force to protect your "stuff"? Not deadly force. But you can use the amount of nondeadly force you reasonably believe is necessary to prevent someone from taking your stuff. You also can run after and take back what someone has just taken from you. But, as with all the justifications based on necessity, you can't use force if there's time to call the police.

NECESSITY ("CHOICE OF EVILS")

At the heart of the **choice-of-evils defense** is the necessity to prevent imminent danger; so it's like all the defenses we've discussed up to now. The justifications based on the necessity of defending yourself, other people, and your home aren't controversial. Why?

Because we see the attackers as evil and the defenders as good. (Don't forget—legally, it's always evil to take the law into our own hands, even if it's a necessary lesser evil and therefore justified.) However, in the general choice-of-evils defense, the line between good and evil isn't always drawn as clearly as it is in self-defense and defense of home.

The choice-of-evils defense, also called the **general principle of necessity,** has a long history in the law of Europe and the Americas. And, throughout that history, the defense has generated heated controversy. The great 13th-century jurist of English and Roman law Bracton declared that what "is not otherwise lawful, necessity makes lawful." Other distinguished English commentators, such as Sir Francis Bacon, Sir Edward Coke, and Sir Matthew Hale in the 16th and 17th centuries, agreed with Bracton. The influential 17th-century English judge Hobart expressed the argument this way: "All laws admit certain cases of just excuse, when they are offended in letter, and where the offender is under necessity, either of compulsion or inconvenience."

On the other side of the debate, the distinguished 19th-century English historian of criminal law Judge Sir James F. Stephen believed that the defense of necessity was so vague that judges could interpret it to mean anything they wanted. In the mid-1950s, the distinguished professor of criminal law Glanville Williams (1961) wrote: "It is just possible to imagine cases in which the expediency of breaking the law is so overwhelmingly great that people may be justified in breaking it, but these cases cannot be defined beforehand" (724–25).

Early cases record occasional instances of defendants who successfully pleaded the necessity defense. In 1500, a prisoner successfully pleaded necessity to a charge of prison break; he was trying to escape a fire that burned down the jail. The most common example in the older cases is destroying houses to stop fires from spreading. In 1912, a man was acquitted on the defense of necessity when he burned a strip of the owner's heather to prevent a fire from spreading to his house (Hall 1960, 425).

The most famous case of imminent necessity is *The Queen v. Dudley and Stephens* (1884). Dudley and Stephens, two adults with families, and Brooks, an 18-year-old man without any family responsibilities, were lost in a lifeboat on the high seas. They had no food or water, except for two cans of turnips and a turtle they caught in the sea on the fourth day. After twenty days (the last eight without food), perhaps a thousand miles from land and with virtually no hope of rescue, Dudley and Stephens—after failing to get Brooks to cast lots—told him that, if no rescue vessel appeared by the next day, they were going to kill him for food. They explained to Brooks that his life was the most expendable because they each had family responsibilities and he didn't.

The following day, no vessel appeared. After saying a prayer for him, Dudley and Stephens killed Brooks, who was too weak to resist. They survived on his flesh and blood for four days, when they were finally rescued. Dudley and Stephens were prosecuted, convicted, and sentenced to death for murder. They appealed, pleading the defense of necessity.

Lord Coleridge, in this famous passage, rejected the defense of necessity:

> The temptation to act . . . here was not what the law ever called necessity. Nor is this to be regretted. Though law and morality are not the same, and many things may be immoral

which are not necessarily illegal, yet the absolute divorce of law from morality would be of fatal consequence; and such divorce would follow if the temptation to murder in this case were to be held by law an absolute defense of it. It is not so. . . .

To preserve one's life is generally speaking a duty, but it may be the plainest and the highest duty to sacrifice it. War is full of instances in which it is a man's duty not to live, but to die. The duty, in case of shipwreck, of a captain to his crew, of the crew to the passengers, of soldiers to women and children . . . ; these duties impose on men the moral necessity, not of the preservation, but of the sacrifice of their lives for others. . . . It is not correct, therefore, to say that there is any absolute or unqualified necessity to preserve one's own life. . . .

It is not needful to point out the awful danger of admitting the principle contended for.

Who is to be the judge of this sort of necessity? By what measure of the comparative value of lives to be measured? Is it to be strength, or intellect, or what? It is plain that the principle leaves to him who is to profit by it to determine the necessity which will justify him in deliberately taking another's life to save his own. In this case, the weakest, the youngest, the most unresisting, was chosen. Was it more necessary to kill him than one of the grown men? The answer must be "No"—"So spake the Fiend, and with necessity, The tyrant's plea, executed his devilish deeds." It is not suggested that in this particular case, the deeds were "devilish," but it is quite plain that such a principle once admitted might be made the legal cloak for unbridled passion and atrocious crime.

Lord Coleridge sentenced them to death but expressed his hope that Queen Victoria would pardon them. The queen didn't pardon them, but she almost did—she commuted their death penalty to 6 months in prison.

The crux of the choice-of-evils defense is proving the defendant made the right choice, the only choice—namely, the necessity of choosing now to do a lesser evil to avoid a greater evil. The Model Penal Code choice-of-evils provision contains three elements laid out in three steps:

1. Identify the evils.

2. Rank the evils.

3. Choose the lesser evil to avoid the greater evil that's on the verge of happening. (ALI 1985, 1:2, 8–22)

Simply put, the choice-of-evils defense justifies choosing to commit a lesser crime to avoid the harm of a greater crime. The choice of the lesser evil has to be both imminent and necessary. Those who choose to do the lesser evil have to believe reasonably their only choice is to cause the lesser evil that's going to happen right now.

The Model Penal Code (ALI 1985, 1:2, 8) lists all of the following "right" choices:

1. Destroying property to prevent spreading fire

2. Violating a speed limit to get a dying person to a hospital

3. Throwing cargo overboard to save a sinking vessel and its crew

4. Dispensing drugs without a prescription in an emergency

5. Breaking into and entering a mountain cabin to avoid freezing to death

The right choice is life, safety, and health over property. Why? Because according to our values, life, safety, and health always trump property interests (ALI 1985, 12).

The MPC doesn't leave the ranking of evils to individuals; it charges legislatures or judges and juries at trial with the task. Once an individual has made the "right" choice, she's either acquitted, or it's a mitigating circumstance that can lessen the punishment. The U.S. Court of Appeals applied the choice-of-evils defense to illegal immigration in *U.S. v. Aguilar et al.*

Was Smuggling, Transporting, and Harboring Illegal Immigrants a Lesser Evil?

U.S. v. Aguilar et al.
883 F.2d 662 (CA9, 1989)

HISTORY

Defendants were convicted before the U.S. District Court for the District of Arizona, of violations of the immigration laws, arising from their participation in a "sanctuary movement" aimed at the smuggling, transporting, and harboring of Central American refugees. On defendants' appeal, a unanimous three-judge panel of the U.S. 9th Court of Appeals held that the defendants were not entitled to a necessity defense based on allegations that the INS frustrated legal means of obtaining refugee status, and affirmed the convictions.

CYNTHIA HOLCOMB HALL, J.

FACTS

I

Appellants were convicted of masterminding and running a modern-day underground railroad that smuggled Central American natives across the Mexican border with Arizona. Beginning in Mexico, various appellants directed illegal aliens to several Arizona churches that operated as self-described sanctuaries. From Arizona, appellants sent many of these illegal aliens to Chicago, Illinois, where they were subsequently dispersed throughout the United States to so-called safe houses. Appellants were sentenced to varying terms of probation; none received jail terms.

A Appellants sought and received extensive media coverage of their efforts on behalf of Central American aliens. Eventually, the INS accepted appellants' challenge to investigate their alien smuggling and harboring activities. The INS infiltrated the sanctuary movement with several undercover informers and agents who tape recorded some meetings. . . .

On March 19, 1982, appellant John M. Fife, in an interview published by a Tucson, Arizona, newspaper, announced that he and his church, the Southside Presbyterian Church, "can no longer cooperate with or defy the law covertly as we have done." He challenged the United States government to arrest him as a felon in violation of the immigration laws. Indeed, Fife wrote to the Attorney General of the United States on March 23, 1982, to protest "the current administration of United States law [which] prohibits us from sheltering these refugees from Central America."

The following day, several hundred people rallied at the Federal Building in Tucson to protest the government's failure to grant political asylum to Central American aliens. The protesters then marched to Fife's church and, once there, Fife hosted a news conference at which he introduced a person he described as an undocumented Salvadoran alien who was staying at the church.

. . . On December 12, 1982, the CBS television program 60 Minutes broadcast a segment featuring James A. Corbett, one of the defendants. Before a national television audience, Corbett boasted of having smuggled 250 to 300 illegal aliens from Central America. Later that same month, Fife was featured in a Tucson newspaper article, and again in a February 7, 1983, article. Corbett was interviewed for an article appearing on August 1, 1983 in a Phoenix newspaper. Noting that stepped-up INS border enforcement efforts had proven more effective, Corbett stated that the sanctuary movement had advised aliens to cross the border at different points.

B The government initiated an undercover investigation of appellants' smuggling activities on March 27, 1984, when undercover agent Jesus Cruz ("Cruz") contacted appellant Ramon Dagoberto Quinones at Quinones' church office in Nogales, Sonora, Mexico. Cruz told Quinones that he supported the sanctuary movement and that he wished to volunteer. Cruz next met Quinones on April 16, 1984, when he accompanied Quinones to the Mexican federal prison in Nogales, where Mexico detains Central Americans who have violated Mexican immigration laws. Quinones introduced Cruz to Maria del Socorro Pardo Viuda de Aguilar ("Aguilar"), and the three entered the prison to meet with Central Americans who Mexico was set to deport.

Quinones counseled the Nogales prisoners that if they planned to reattempt their journey to the United States, they should contact certain persons in Mexico who would instruct them on how to avoid Mexican immigration authorities. Quinones also told the prisoners that if they should reach the United States border they should avoid INS officials. He said that if they were apprehended by INS officials, they should lie and claim to be Mexican citizens, as this would avoid their formal deportation to Central America.

From this introduction to the sanctuary movement, Cruz quickly became appellants' trusted and valued colleague. Cruz met Philip M. Conger on May 3, 1984, in Nogales, Mexico. Cruz accompanied Conger as he drove the Rodriguez family to a hilltop overlooking the United States border. Once there, Conger identified a hole in the border fence and the steeples of the Sacred Heart Church, where he advised the family to go. Conger assured the family that the church would provide them sanctuary. Conger also asked Cruz to give the family a brief history of Mexico so that they could pretend to be Mexicans if apprehended. The family made their way to the church later that week.

Cruz also became involved in Aguilar's and Quinones's plan to smuggle Julio and Ana Benavidez, both Salvadoran citizens, into the United States. On Aguilar's orders, Cruz obtained an envelope from Quinones which contained an immigration document. Cruz gave Aguilar this document, and she instructed Ana to memorize the name, age, and address of the person identified on the document. Aguilar dressed Ana to look like the person portrayed on the document. Cruz, Aguilar, and Ana then went to the Nogales Port of Entry where Aguilar walked 13-year-old Ana through the checkpoint.

[The Court related numerous similar smuggling stories omitted here.]

C Because of their considerable contribution to the sanctuary movement, Cruz, agent Nixon, and another undercover informer, Soloman Graham, were invited to join meetings of the movement's inner circle at the Southside Church. They attended such a meeting at the church on August 27, 1984. Appellants Fife, Conger, and Corbett participated, along with several other sanctuary movement members.

The discussion initially focused on a group of four Salvadoran children and a woman, Elba Teresa, who were in Mexico City, Mexico, and sought assistance crossing the United States border. Fife expressed concern that if these aliens were not moved promptly, it would interfere with their efforts to smuggle 23 Guatemalans across the border. Corbett suggested that innovative methods were necessary to aid the Guatemalans, such as concealing them in cars or using remote border crossing points. Conger suggested using a border graveyard in Douglas, Arizona. Finally, Fife stated that they had to sell or trade four vehicles because they operated in border areas so frequently that the INS probably linked them to smuggling.

Cruz attended another meeting on September 4, 1984, with Fife, Conger, Nicgorski, Peggy Hutchison and Corbett. Conger said that he had an argument with Quinones about smuggling the 23 Guatemalans who, in any event, already had made their way independently to Colorado. On September 10, 1984, Cruz was invited to attend his third meeting at the Southside Church. Conger, Fife, Hutchison, and others were present. The topic of discussion was how to smuggle the Elba Teresa group across the Mexican border. They debated who amongst them was most qualified to go to Mexico City to assist the aliens, but no decision was reached. Hutchison opposed sending two new recruits to the sanctuary movement, as they were too inexperienced.

Hutchison and Fife subsequently brought the Elba Teresa group across the border. On October 29, 1984, Cruz and Graham were at Nicgorski's apartment in Phoenix when the group arrived. Nicgorski asked them to drive the group to Canoga Park, California. A sanctuary worker from Seattle, Washington, came along and covered most of the trip's expenses. Cruz attended his last meeting at the Southside Church on November 26, 1984. Nicgorski, Conger, Hutchison, and others discussed plans to smuggle three separate groups of Central Americans across the border.

II

On January 10, 1985, the government filed an indictment that ultimately led to the conviction of appellants. Along with the indictment, the government brought a motion . . . that sought to exclude evidence that appellants believed that the 1980 Refugee Act entitled the Central American aliens to enter or reside in the United States lawfully. The government contended that appellants' sincere belief that the aliens were refugees under the Refugee Act would not, as a matter of law, negate the specific intent that appellants had to bring the aliens surreptitiously into the United States without INS inspection. According to the government, the mere fact that appellants sought to transport the aliens into the United States without inspection satisfied the specific intent requirement under 8 U.S.C. ß 1324 (1982). Consequently, pressed the government, "whatever status to which the [appellants] concluded these aliens were entitled under the Refugee Act is irrelevant."

On October 28, 1985, the district court granted the government's . . . motion. The lower court excluded from trial "evidence of [appellants'] belief that those aliens involved in the charges were refugees" based on their interpretation of the immigration laws. . . .

OPINION

As a matter of law, a defendant must establish the existence of four elements to be entitled to a necessity defense:

(1) that he was faced with a choice of evils and chose the lesser evil;

(2) that he acted to prevent imminent harm;

(3) that he reasonably anticipated a causal relation between his conduct and the harm to be avoided; and

(4) that there were no other legal alternatives to violating the law.

The . . . test is stated in the conjunctive; thus, if defendants' offer of proof is deficient with regard to any of the four elements, the district judge must grant the motion to preclude evidence of necessity.

In the present case, appellants' offer was legally deficient in at least one respect: They failed to establish that there were no other legal alternatives. The proffer emphasizes that the INS continuously has frustrated the present legal way of obtaining refugee status. In addition, the immigration judges purportedly deny the due process rights of those granted an asylum hearing and make incorrect determinations of credibility concerning the danger faced in the aliens' homelands. Defendants thus made the following decision:

Given this information regarding the almost automatic deportation of refugees who applied for asylum, religious workers realized that their religious beliefs precluded them from presenting the refugees whose lives were in danger, [sic] to the INS. Their goal was to protect those from danger, and the results of the asylum process had demonstrated that that process was not only futile, but also extremely dangerous to those who filed and lost.

According to defendants, they established the sanctuary movement only after trying "all these other methods" and concluding that there was "no other safe alternative." The only "other methods" referred to in the proffer were "attempts at working with and through the INS." After purportedly finding that the proper legal channels were futile, appellants resorted to an underground movement.

As the district judge correctly concluded, however, appellants failed to appeal to the judiciary to correct any alleged improprieties by the INS and the immigration courts. In fact, by successfully suing the INS, Salvadorans already have effected changes in INS detention and asylum procedures involving Salvadorans in California.

Appellants of course do not dispute this; rather, they conclude that "to the extent the legal alternative of a civil suit could be pursued, it was." In the meantime, they continue, many years had passed between filing of the complaint and granting of the permanent injunction, and newly arriving refugees needed immediate help.

This argument overlooks the potential for a provisional remedy, such as was provided soon after the complaint was filed in *Orantes-Hernandez v. Smith.* Moreover, to the extent that aliens were arriving prior to the filing of a class action, appellants themselves could have initiated an action on behalf of the aliens, seeking initial provisional relief and ultimate permanent relief. Since this legal alternative nullifies the existence of necessity for all the underlying crimes stated in section 1324, appellants claim of district court error fails.

The appellants have advanced numerous arguments in challenging their convictions for violating the United States immigration laws. We have reviewed each challenge carefully and conclude that none has merit. Accordingly, the judgment is AFFIRMED.

Questions

1. Identify and summarize the four elements of the necessity defense, as the court defines them.
2. Who has the burden to prove the elements?
3. Why did the court discuss only one element?
4. Summarize the court's reasons for rejecting that element.
5. Based on the discussion of the elements of "choice of evils" in the text, were the other elements proven?

Back up your answer with facts from the case and points made in the discussion of necessity in the text preceding the case excerpt.

EXPLORING FURTHER

Choice of Evils

1. Was Violating the Marijuana Law a Lesser Evil?

State v. Ownbey 996 P.2d 510 (Ore.App. 2000)

DEITS, C.J.

FACTS Jack Ownbey is a veteran of the Vietnam War. He has been diagnosed with Post–Traumatic Stress Syndrome (PTSD). In his defense to the charges against him, Ownbey intended to show that "his actions in growing marijuana and possessing marijuana were as a result of medical necessity or choice of evils."

ORS 161.200, codifies that defense in Oregon. It provides:

(2) Unless inconsistent with . . . some other provision of law, conduct which would otherwise constitute an offense is justifiable and not criminal when:
 (a) That conduct is necessary as an emergency measure to avoid an imminent public or private injury; and
 (b) The threatened injury is of such gravity that, according to ordinary standards of intelligence and morality, the desirability and urgency of avoiding the injury clearly outweigh the desirability of avoiding the injury sought to be prevented by the statute defining the offense in issue.

(3) The necessity and justifiability of conduct under subsection (1) of this section shall not rest upon considerations pertaining only to the morality and advisability of the statute, either in its general application or with respect to its application to a particular class of cases arising thereunder.

Was Ownbey entitled to the defense of necessity?

DECISION No, according to the Oregon Court of Appeals:

. . . Ownbey fails to recognize . . . that the defense of necessity is available only in situations wherein the legislature has not itself, in its criminal statute, made a determination of values. If the legislature has not made such a value judgment, the defense would be available. However, when, as here, the legislature has already balanced the competing values that would be presented in a choice-of-evils defense and made a choice, the court is precluded from reassessing that judgment.

2. Was Speeding the Lesser Evil?

People v. Dover, 790 P.2d 834 (Colo. 1990)

FACTS The prosecution proved beyond a reasonable doubt by the use of radar readings that James Dover was driving 80 miles per hour in a 55 mile-per-hour zone. However, the court also found that the defendant, who is a lawyer, was not guilty on the grounds that his speeding violation was justified because he was late for a court hearing in Denver as a result of a late hearing in Summit County, Colorado.

A Colorado statute, § 42-4-1001(8)(a) provides:

> The conduct of a driver of a vehicle which would otherwise constitute a violation of this section is justifiable and not unlawful when: It is necessary as an emergency measure to avoid an imminent public or private injury which is about to occur by reason of a situation occasioned or developed through no conduct of said driver and which is of sufficient gravity that, according to ordinary standards of intelligence and morality, the desirability and urgency of avoiding the injury clearly outweigh the desirability of avoiding the consequences sought to be prevented by this section.

Was Dover justified in speeding because of necessity?

DECISION No, said the Colorado Supreme Court:

> In this case, the defendant did not meet the foundational requirements of § 42-4-1001(8)(a). He merely testified that he was driving to Denver for a "court matter" and that he was late because of the length of a hearing in Summit County. No other evidence as to the existence of emergency as a justification for speeding was presented. The defendant did not present evidence as to the type or extent of the injury that he would suffer if he did not violate § 42-4-1001(1). He also failed to establish that he did not cause the situation or that his injuries would outweigh the consequences of his conduct.

3. Was Burglary the Lesser Evil?

State v. Celli, 263 N.W.2d 145 (S.D. 1978)

FACTS On a cold winter day, William Celli and his friend, Glynis Brooks, left Deadwood, South Dakota, hoping to hitchhike to Newcastle, Wyoming, to look for work. The weather turned colder, they were afraid of frostbite, and there was no place of business open for them to get warm. Their feet were so stiff from the cold that it was difficult for them to walk.

They broke the lock on the front door, and entered the only structure around, a cabin. Celli immediately crawled into a bed to warm up, and Brooks tried to light a fire in the fireplace. They rummaged through drawers to look for matches, which they finally located, and started a fire. Finally, Celli came out of the bedroom, took off his wet moccasins, socks, and coat; placed them near the fire; and sat down to warm himself. After warming up somewhat they checked the kitchen for edible food. That morning, they had shared a can of beans but had not eaten since. All they found was dry macaroni, which they could not cook because there was no water.

A neighbor noticed the smoke from the fireplace and called the police. When the police entered the cabin, Celli and Brooks were warming themselves in front of the fireplace. The police searched them but turned up nothing belonging to the cabin owners.

Did Celli and his friend choose the lesser of two evils?

DECISION The trial court convicted Celli and Brooks of fourth-degree burglary. The appellate court reversed on other grounds, so, unfortunately for us, the court never got to the issue of the defense of necessity.

 Go to the Criminal Law 9e website to find the full text of the Exploring Further excerpts: www.thomsonedu.com/ criminaljustice/samaha. (Excerpts on choice of evils.)

CONSENT

Now we turn to a justification that has nothing to do with necessity. At the heart of the **defense of consent** is the high value placed on individual autonomy in a free society. If mentally competent adults want to be crime victims, so the argument for the justification of consent goes, no paternalistic government should get in their way.

Consent may make sense in the larger context of individual freedom and responsibility, but the criminal law is hostile to consent as a justification for committing crimes. For all the noise about choice, you know already that except for the voluntary act requirement (discussed in Chapter 3), there are many examples of crimes where choice is either a total fiction or very limited. We've seen some major examples in the chapters so far. There's the rule of lenity discussed in Chapter 1; the void-for-vagueness doctrine discussed in Chapter 2; and the mental state of negligence and the absence of mental fault in strict liability discussed in Chapter 4.

Individuals can take their own lives and inflict injuries on themselves, but in most states they can't authorize others to kill them or beat them. Let's look at how confined choice is in the defense of consent and examine some of the reasons. Here's an example from the Alabama Criminal Code:

ALABAMA CRIMINAL CODE (1977) SECTION 13A-2-7

(a) *In general.* The consent of the victim to conduct charged to constitute an offense or to the result thereof is a defense if such consent negatives a required element of the offense or precludes the infliction of the harm or evil sought to be prevented by the law defining the offense.

(b) *Consent to bodily harm.* When conduct is charged to constitute an offense because it causes or threatens bodily harm, consent to such conduct or to the infliction of such harm is a defense only if:

(1) The bodily harm consented to or threatened by the conduct consented to is not serious; or
(2) The conduct and the harm are reasonably foreseeable hazards of joint participation in a lawful athletic contest or competitive sport.

(c) Ineffective consent. Unless otherwise provided by this Criminal Code or by the law defining the offense, assent does not constitute consent if:

(1) It is given by a person who is legally incompetent to authorize the conduct; or
(2) It is given by a person who by reason of immaturity, mental disease or defect, or intoxication is manifestly unable and known by the actor to be unable to make a reasonable judgment as to the nature or harmfulness of the conduct; or
(3) It is given by a person whose consent is sought to be prevented by the law defining the offense; or
(4) It is induced by force, duress or deception.

In most states, the law recognizes only four exceptions that allow the defense of consent as a justification:

1. No serious injury results from the consensual crime.

2. The injury happens during a sporting event.

3. The conduct benefits the consenting person, such as when a doctor performs surgery.

4. The consent is to sexual conduct. (Fletcher 1978, 770)

Fitting into one of these four exceptions is necessary, but it's not enough to entitle defendants to the defense. They also have to prove the consent was voluntary, knowing, and authorized. *Voluntary consent* means consent was the product of free will, not of force, threat of force, promise, or trickery. Forgiveness after the commission of a crime doesn't qualify as voluntary consent. *Knowing consent* means the person consenting understands what she's consenting to; she's not too young or insane to understand. *Authorized consent* means the person consenting has the authority to give consent; I can't give consent for someone else whom I'm not legally responsible for. The court dealt with the sporting event exception in *State v. Shelley* (1997).

State v. Shelley
929 P.2d 489 (Wash.App. 1997)

HISTORY

Jason Shelley was convicted in the Superior Court, King County, of second-degree assault, arising out of an incident in which Shelley intentionally punched another basketball player during a game. Shelley appealed. The Court of Appeals affirmed the conviction.

GROSSE, J.

FACTS

On March 31, 1993, Jason Shelley and Mario Gonzalez played "pickup" basketball on opposing teams at the University of Washington Intramural Activities Building (the IMA). Pickup games are not refereed by an official; rather, the players take responsibility for calling their own fouls.

During the course of three games, Gonzalez fouled Shelley several times. Gonzalez had a reputation for playing overly aggressive defense at the IMA. Toward the end of the evening, after trying to hit the ball away from Shelley, he scratched Shelley's face and drew blood. After getting scratched, Shelley briefly left the game and then returned.

Shelley and Gonzalez have differing versions of what occurred after Shelley returned to the game. According to Gonzalez, while he was waiting for play in the game to return to Gonzalez's side of the court, Shelley suddenly hit him. Gonzalez did not see Shelley punch him. According to Shelley's version of events, when Shelley rejoined the game, he was running down the court and he saw Gonzalez make "a move towards me as if he was maybe going to prevent me from getting the ball." The move was with his hand up "across my vision." Angry, he "just reacted" and swung. He said he hit him because he was afraid of being hurt, like the previous scratch. He testified that Gonzalez continually beat him up during the game by fouling him hard.

A week after the incident, a school police detective interviewed Shelley and prepared a statement for Shelley to sign based on the interview. Shelley reported to the police that Gonzalez had been "continually slapping and scratching him" during the game. Shelley "had been getting mad" at Gonzalez and the scratch on Shelley's face was the "final straw."

As the two were running down the court side by side, "I swung my right hand around and hit him with my fist on the right side of his face." Shelley asserted that he also told the detective that Gonzalez waved a hand at him just before Shelley threw the punch and that he told the detective that he was afraid of being injured.

Gonzalez required emergency surgery to repair his jaw. Broken in three places, it was wired shut for six weeks. His treating physician believed that a "significant" blow caused the damage.

During the course of the trial, defense counsel told the court he intended to propose a jury instruction that: "A person legally consents to conduct that causes or threatens bodily harm if the conduct and the harm are reasonably foreseeable hazards of joint participation in a lawful, athletic contest or competitive sport."

Although the trial court agreed that there were risks involved in sports, it stated that "the risk of being intentionally punched by another player is one that I don't think we ever do assume." The court noted, "In basketball . . . you consent to a certain amount of rough contact. If they were both going for a rebound and Mr. Shelley's elbow or even his fist hit Mr. Gonzalez as they were both jumping for the rebound and Mr. Gonzalez's jaw was fractured in exactly the same way . . . then you would have an issue."

Reasoning that "our laws are intended to uphold the public peace and regulate behavior of individuals," the court ruled "that as a matter of law, consent cannot be a defense to an assault." The court indicated that Shelley could not claim consent because his conduct "exceeded" what is considered within the rules of that particular sport:

> Consent is a contact that is contemplated within the rules of the game and that is incidental to the furtherance of the goals of that particular game. If you can show me any rule book for basketball at any level that says an intentional punch to the face in some way is a part of the game, then I would take another . . . look at your argument. I don't believe any such rule book exists.

Later, Shelley proposed jury instructions on the subject of consent:

> An act is not an assault, if it is done with the consent of the person alleged to be assaulted. It is a defense to a charge of second degree assault occurring in the course of an athletic contest if the conduct and the harm are reasonably foreseeable hazards of joint participation in a lawful athletic contest or competitive sport.

The trial court rejected these, and Shelley excerpted. The trial court did instruct the jury about self-defense.

OPINION

First, we hold that consent is a defense to an assault occurring during an athletic contest. This is consistent with the law of assault as it has developed in Washington. A person is guilty of second-degree assault if he or she "intentionally assaults another and thereby recklessly inflicts substantial bodily harm."

One common law definition of assault recognized in Washington is "an unlawful touching with criminal intent." At the common law, a touching is unlawful when the person touched did not give consent to it, and [it] was either harmful or offensive. As our Supreme Court stated in *State v. Simmons*, "where there is consent, there is no assault." The State argues that because *Simmons* was a sexual assault case, the defense of consent should be limited to that realm. We decline to apply the defense so narrowly.

Logically, consent must be an issue in sporting events because a person participates in a game knowing that it will involve potentially offensive contact and with this consent the "touchings" involved are not "unlawful." The rationale that courts offer in limiting [consent as a defense] is that society has an interest in punishing assaults as breaches of the public peace and order, so that an individual cannot consent to a wrong that is committed against the public peace.

Urging us to reject the defense of consent because an assault violates the public peace, the State argues that this principle precludes Shelley from being entitled to argue the consent defense on the facts of his case. In making this argument, the State ignores the factual contexts that dictated the results in the cases it cites in support. When faced with the question of whether to accept a school child's consent to hazing or consent to a fight, *People v. Lenti*, 253 N.Y.S.2d 9 (1964), or a gang member's consent to a beating, *Helton v. State*, 624 N.E.2d 499, 514 (Ind.Ct.App.1993), courts have declined to apply the defense. Obviously, these cases present "touchings" factually distinct from "touchings" occurring in athletic competitions.

If consent cannot be a defense to assault, then most athletic contests would need to be banned because many involve "invasions of one's physical integrity." Because society has chosen to foster sports competitions, players necessarily must be able to consent to physical contact and other players must be able to rely on that consent when playing the game. This is the view adopted by the drafters of the Model Penal Code:

There are, however, situations in which consent to bodily injury should be recognized as a defense to crime. . . .

There is . . . the obvious case of participation in an athletic contest or competitive sport, where the nature of the enterprise often involves risk of serious injury. Here, the social judgment that permits the contest to flourish necessarily involves the companion judgment that reasonably foreseeable hazards can be consented to by virtue of participation.

The more difficult question is the proper standard by which to judge whether a person consented to the particular conduct at issue. The State argues that "when the conduct in question is not within the rules of a given sport, a victim cannot be deemed to have consented to this act." The trial court apparently agreed with this approach.

Although we recognize that there is authority supporting this approach, we reject a reliance on the rules of the games as too limiting. Rollin M. Perkins in *Criminal Law* explains:

The test is not necessarily whether the blow exceeds the conduct allowed by the rules of the game. Certain excesses and inconveniences are to be expected beyond the formal rules of the game. It may be ordinary and expected conduct for minor assaults to occur. However, intentional excesses beyond those reasonably contemplated in the sport are not justified.

Instead, we adopt the approach of the Model Penal Code which provides:

(4) *Consent to Bodily Injury*. When conduct is charged to constitute an offense because it causes or threatens bodily injury, consent to such conduct or to the infliction of such injury is a defense if: . . .

(c) the conduct and the injury are reasonably foreseeable hazards of joint participation in a lawful athletic contest or competitive sport or other concerted activity not forbidden by law.

The State argues the law does not allow "the victim to 'consent' to a broken jaw simply by participating in an unrefereed, informal basketball game." This argument presupposes that the harm suffered dictates whether the defense is available or not. This is not the correct inquiry. The correct inquiry is whether the conduct of defendant constituted foreseeable behavior in the play of the game.

Additionally, the injury must have occurred as a byproduct of the game itself. . . . In *State v. Floyd*, a fight broke out during a basketball game and the defendant, who was on the sidelines, punched and severely injured several opposing team members. . . . The defense did not apply because the statute "contemplated a person who commits acts during the course of play. . . ." There is a "continuum, or sliding scale, grounded in the circumstances under which voluntary participants engage in sport . . . which governs the type of incidents in which an individual volunteers (i.e., consents) to participate." The New York courts provide another example. In a football game, while tackling the defendant, the victim hit the defendant. After the play was over and all of the players got off the defendant, the defendant punched the victim in the eye. . . . Initially it may be assumed that the very first punch thrown . . . in the course of the tackle was consented to by defendant. The act of tackling an opponent in the course of a football game may often involve "contact" that could easily be interpreted to be a "punch." Defendant's response after the pileup to complainant's initial act of "aggression" cannot be mistaken. . . . This was not a consented to act. *People v. Freer*, 381 N.Y.S.2d 976, 978 (1976).

. . . The State may argue that the defendant's conduct exceeded behavior foreseeable in the game. Although in "all sports players consent to many risks, hazards and blows," there is "a limit to the magnitude and dangerousness of a blow to which another is deemed to consent."

This limit, like the foreseeability of the risks, is determined by presenting evidence to the jury about the nature of the game, the participants' expectations, the location where the game has been played, as well as the rules of the game.

Here, taking Shelley's version of the events as true, the magnitude and dangerousness of Shelley's actions were beyond the limit. There is no question that Shelley lashed out at Gonzalez with sufficient force to land a substantial blow to the jaw, and there is no question but that Shelley intended to hit Gonzalez. There is nothing in the game of basketball, or even rugby or hockey, that would permit consent as a defense to such conduct. Shelley admitted to an assault and was not precluded from arguing that the assault justified self-defense; but justification and consent are not the same inquiry. . . .

We AFFIRM.

Questions

1. According to the court, why can participants in a sport consent to conduct that would otherwise be a crime?

2. Why should they be allowed to consent to such conduct when in other situations, such as those enumerated in the Exploring Further cases that follow, they can't consent?

3. Should individuals be allowed to knowingly and voluntarily consent to the commission of crimes against themselves? Why or why not?

4. Why was Shelley not allowed the defense of consent in this case?

5. Do you agree with the court's decision? Relying on the relevant facts in the case, defend your answer.

EXPLORING FURTHER

Consent

1. Is Shooting BB Guns a Sport?

State v. Hiott, 987 P.2d 135 (Wash.App. 1999)

FACTS Richard Hiott and his friend Jose were playing a game of shooting at each other with BB guns. During the game, Jose was hit in the eye and lost his eye as a result. Richard was charged with third-degree assault. His defense was consent. Was he entitled to the defense?

DECISION No, said the Washington Court of Appeals:

Hiott argues that . . . the game they were playing "is within the limits of games for which society permits consent." Hiott compares the boys' shooting of BB guns at each other to dodgeball, football, rugby, hockey, boxing, wrestling, "ultimate fighting," fencing, and "paintball." We disagree.

The games Hiott uses for comparison, although capable of producing injuries, have been generally accepted by society as lawful athletic contests, competitive sports, or concerted activities not forbidden by law. And these games carry with them generally accepted rules, at least some of which are intended to prevent or minimize injuries. In addition, such games commonly prescribe the use of protective devices or clothing to prevent injuries.

Shooting BB guns at each other is not a generally accepted game or athletic contest; the activity has no generally accepted rules; and the activity is not characterized by the common use of protective devices or clothing.

Moreover, consent is not a valid defense if the activity consented to is against public policy. Thus, a child cannot consent to hazing, a gang member cannot consent to an initiation beating, and an individual cannot consent to being shot with a pistol. . . . Assaults . . . are breaches of the public peace. And we consider shooting at another person with a BB gun a breach of the public peace and, therefore, against public policy.

2. Can She Consent to Being Assaulted?

State v. Brown, 364 A.2d 27 (N.J. 1976)

FACTS Mrs. Brown was an alcoholic. On the day of the alleged crime she had been drinking, apparently to her husband Reginald Brown's displeasure. Acting according to the terms of an agreement between the defendant Reginald Brown and his wife, he punished her by beating her severely with his hands and other objects.

Brown was charged with atrocious assault and battery. He argued he wasn't guilty of atrocious assault and battery because he and Mrs. Brown, the victim, had an understanding to the effect that if she consumed any alcoholic beverages (and/or became intoxicated), he would punish her by physically assaulting her. The trial court refused the defense of consent.

Was Mr. Brown justified because of Mrs. Brown's consent?

DECISION No, said the New Jersey appellate court:

The laws . . . are simply and unequivocally clear that the defense of consent cannot be available to a defendant charged with any type of physical assault that causes appreciable injury. If the law were otherwise, it would not be conducive to a peaceful, orderly and healthy society. . . .

This court concludes that, as a matter of law, no one has the right to beat another even though that person may ask for it. Assault and battery cannot be consented to by a victim, for the State makes it unlawful and is not a party to any such agreement between the victim and perpetrator. To allow an otherwise criminal act to go unpunished because of the victim's consent would not only threaten the security of our society but also might tend to detract from the force of the moral principles underlying the criminal law. . . .

Thus, for the reasons given, the State has an interest in protecting those persons who invite, consent to and permit others to assault and batter them. Not to enforce these laws which are geared to protect such people would seriously threaten the dignity, peace, health and security of our society.

3. Can He Consent to Being Shot?

State v. Fransua, 510 P.2d 106 (N.Mex.App. 1973)

FACTS Daniel Fransua and the victim were in a bar in Albuquerque. Fransua had been drinking heavily that day and the previous day. Sometime around 3:00 P.M., after an argument, Fransua told the victim he'd shoot him if he had a gun. The victim got up, walked out of the bar, went to his car, took out a loaded pistol, and went back in the bar. He came up to Fransua, laid the pistol on the bar, and said, "There's the gun. If you want to shoot me, go ahead." Fransua picked up the pistol, put the barrel next to the victim's head, and pulled the trigger, wounding him seriously.

Was the victim's consent a justification that meant Fransua wasn't guilty of aggravated battery?

DECISION No, said the New Mexico Court of Appeals:

It is generally conceded that a state enacts criminal statutes making certain violent acts crimes for at least two reasons: One reason is to protect the persons of its citizens; the second, however, is to prevent a breach of the public peace. While we entertain little sympathy for either the victim's absurd actions or the defendant's equally unjustified act of pulling the trigger, we will not permit the defense of consent to be raised in such cases.

Whether or not the victims of crimes have so little regard for their own safety as to request injury, the public has a stronger and overriding interest in preventing and prohibiting acts such as these. We hold that consent is not a defense to the crime of aggravated battery, irrespective of whether the victim invites the act and consents to the battery.

 Go to the Criminal Law 9e website to find the full text of the Exploring Further excerpts: www.thomsonedu.com/criminaljustice/samaha. (Excerpts on consent.)

SUMMARY

I. Affirmative defenses and proving them
  A. Proving that their criminal conduct wasn't justified is the second necessary requirement to hold individuals accountable for their crimes.
  B. In justification defenses, defendants admit they were responsible for their acts but claim what they did was right under the circumstances.
  C. In excuse defenses, defendants admit what they did was wrong but claim that, under the circumstances, they weren't responsible for what they did.

II. Court proceedings and justified and excused conduct
  A. Most justifications and excuses are affirmative defenses, in which defendants present some evidence in support of their arguments. This is called the "burden of production."
  B. In some jurisdictions, if defendants meet the burden of production, they also have the "burden of persuasion," meaning they have to prove their defenses by a preponderance, or more than 50 percent, of the evidence.
  C. Most justifications and excuses are *perfect defenses*, meaning defendants are acquitted. (Defendants who plead insanity don't walk free; they're held in maximum-security hospitals until they regain their sanity.)
  D. Evidence that doesn't amount to a perfect defense might amount to an imperfect defense; that is, the defendants are guilty of lesser offenses.

III. Self-defense
  A. According to the rule of law, the government has a monopoly on the use of force, so when you use force, you're "taking the law into your own hands."

B. Self-defense is only justifiable under three circumstances—when it's reasonable to believe:
1. The necessity is great.
2. It's imminent, meaning it exists "right now."
3. It's for prevention only.
C. Preemptive strikes and retaliation fail the necessity test.
D. The law of self-defense boils down into four elements:
1. *Unprovoked attack*
   a. Self-defense is available only against unprovoked attacks.
   b. It's not available to an initial aggressor, with one exception.
   c. The withdrawal exception states that if attackers completely withdraw from attacks they provoke, they can defend themselves against an attack by their initial victims.
2. *Imminent danger*
   a. *Imminent danger* means an honest and reasonable belief that "The time for defense is right now!"
   b. Present danger doesn't justify taking the law into your own hands because the attack isn't imminent.
3. *Necessity* The defender honestly and reasonably believes there's a need to defend against the attack right now.
4. *Reasonable force* The defender uses only the amount of force reasonably necessary to repel the attack.
E. The retreat rule says that people have to retreat only if they honestly and reasonably believe that backing off won't unreasonably put them in danger of death or serious bodily harm, with one exception, when they're attacked at home ("castle exception").
F. Most states follow the stand-your-ground rule, which says that if you didn't start the fight, you can stand your ground and kill your attacker, if you honestly and reasonably believe it's necessary to do.

IV. The defense of "others"
A. Historically, *self-defense* meant protecting yourself and the members of your immediate family.
B. Many states have expanded this protection to anyone who needs immediate protection from attack.
C. However, "others" have to have the right to defend themselves before someone else can claim the defense.

V. In the defense of home and property
A. The right to defend your home is an extension of the right of self-defense.
B. Many modern statutes limit the use of deadly force to cases where it's reasonable to believe intruders intend to commit crimes of violence against occupants.
C. The defense of the home doesn't include the *curtilage* (the area immediately surrounding the house).

VI. Necessity ("choice of evils")
A. The heart of the choice-of-evils defense is choosing to commit a lesser crime to avoid a greater crime.
B. Making the choice to commit a lesser evil has to be both imminent and necessary.

C. The Model Penal Code choice-of-evils provision contains three elements laid out in three steps:
   1. Identify the evils.
   2. Rank the evils.
   3. Choose the lesser evil to avoid the greater evil that's on the verge of happening.

VII. Consent
   A. If mentally competent adults want to be crime victims, so the argument goes, no paternalistic government should get in their way.
   B. In most states, the law recognizes consent as a justification only under four conditions:
      1. No serious injury results from the consensual crime.
      2. The injury happened during a sporting event.
      3. The conduct benefits the consenting person.
      4. The consent is to sexual conduct.
   C. Defendants also have to prove the consent was voluntary, knowing, and authorized.

REVIEW QUESTIONS

1. Identify five types of justification defenses.

2. What's the difference between justification defenses and excuse defenses?

3. How does taking the law into your own hands violate the rule of law?

4. Explain how affirmative defenses work.

5. How do perfect defenses and imperfect defenses differ?

6. Why aren't preemptive strike and retaliation protected by the justification of self-defense?

7. Identify and define the four elements of self-defense.

8. Identify the three circumstances that have to come together to make a good claim of self-defense.

9. Define *initial aggressor* and how the withdrawal exception relates to it.

10. Why does present danger void the justification of self-defense? Give an example.

11. Identify the values behind the retreat doctrine and the stand-your-ground doctrine.

12. What requirement has to be met before a person can claim the right to defend someone else against an attacker?

13. Explain the history behind the right to defend your home and property.

14. In what area of the home is it not justified to use deadly force?

15. Identify arguments for and against the choice-of-evils defense.

16. Identify the three elements in the choice-of-evils defense.

17. Identify and rank the five choices of evil listed in the Model Penal Code.

18. List four limits to the defense of consent.

19. Identify the three elements in the defense of consent.

KEY TERMS

Defenses to Criminal Liability: Excuse

MAIN POINTS

- Defendants who plead an excuse defense admit what they did was wrong but argue that, under the circumstances, they weren't responsible for their actions.
- The defense of insanity excuses criminal liability when it seriously damages defendants' capacity to control their acts and/or capacity to reason and understand the wrongfulness of their conduct.
- Few defendants plead the insanity defense, and those who do rarely succeed.
- Insanity isn't the equivalent of mental disease or defect.
- The right-wrong test focuses on defects in reason or cognition.
- The volitional incapacity test focuses on defects in self-control or will.
- The substantial capacity test focuses on reason *and* self-control.
- The product-of-mental-illness test focuses on criminal acts resulting from mental disease.
- Current trends favor shifting the burden of proof for insanity to defendants.
- Diminished capacity and diminished responsibility apply only to homicide.
- Juvenile court judges can use their discretion to transfer a juvenile to adult criminal court.
- It's sometimes OK to excuse people who harm innocent people to save themselves.
- Voluntary intoxication is no excuse for committing a crime; involuntary intoxication is.
- Entrapment is used in all societies, even though it violates a basic purpose of government in free societies—to prevent crime, not to encourage it.
- Despite the immense criticism of them, syndrome excuses should be taken seriously.

© Associated Press

Prosecutor Kaylynn Williford with a poster showing the deceased children of Andrea Yates. Yates, originally sentenced to life in prison in 2002 after a jury found her guilty of capital murder for drowning each of her five children in a bathtub, obtained a retrial on appeal. At the retrial the jury found her not guilty by reason of insanity, and Yates will remain confined in a Texas state mental hospital for at least another year.

Was He Too Young to Commit Burglary?

In July 1990, K. R. L., who was then 8 years and 2 months old, was playing with a friend behind a business building in Sequim, WA. Catherine Alder, who lived near the business, heard the boys playing, and she instructed them to leave because she believed the area was dangerous. Alder said that K. R. L.'s response was belligerent, the child indicating that he would leave "in a minute." Losing patience with the boys, Alder said, "No, not in a minute, now; get out of there, now." The boys then ran off. Three days later, during daylight hours, K. R. L. entered Alder's home without her permission. He pulled a live goldfish from her fishbowl, chopped it into several pieces with a steak knife, and "smeared it all over the counter." He then went into Alder's bathroom and clamped a "plugged in" hair curling iron onto a towel.

(STATE V. K. R. L. 1992)

In Chapter 5, you learned that defendants who plead defenses of justification accept responsibility for their actions but claim that, under the circumstances (necessity and consent), they were right. In this chapter, you'll learn about defendants who plead excuse. They admit what they did was wrong but claim that, under the circumstances, they weren't responsible for what they did. The best-known excuse is insanity, but there are others.

Some defenses in this chapter can be viewed within either of two theories. One theory is that they're defenses that excuse criminal conduct the prosecution has proved beyond a reasonable doubt. Remember our three-step analysis of criminal liability:

1. Was there criminal conduct? (Chapters 3 and 4)
2. If there was criminal conduct, was it justified? (Chapter 5)
3. If it wasn't justified, was it excused? (That's where we are now.)

Chronologically, the first theory occurs in Step 3. The prosecution has proved its case beyond a reasonable doubt; next, the defendant hasn't proved that her conduct was justified, but now, she claims she's excused. Legally, she's pleading an affirmative defense. In affirmative defenses of excuse, defendants have to carry some of the burden of proving they have an excuse that will relieve them of criminal responsibility. We'll examine this later on in the "Burden of Proof" section.

Chronologically, the second theory, the **failure-of-proof theory** of excuse, comes during step 1, proving criminal conduct. At this stage, defendants don't have any burden to prove their conduct wasn't criminal, but they can raise a reasonable doubt about the prosecution's case. Here, they can present evidence that something about their mental capacity shows they couldn't form the state of mind required by the mental element in the crime they're charged with committing. If they're successful, they negate the mental element. In other words, there's no proven criminal conduct. So these so-called failure-of-proof defenses aren't really defenses at all. Defenses justify or excuse criminal conduct; logically, of course, you can't (and, practically, you don't need to) justify or excuse conduct that's not criminal.

In this chapter, we'll look at insanity, diminished capacity, age, duress, intoxication, entrapment, and syndrome defenses. We'll note when appropriate how these excuse defenses fit in with either of the theories presented here.

INSANITY

Thanks to CNN, in 1994 the whole world knew that Lorena Bobbitt walked out of a mental hospital after she successfully pleaded "not guilty by reason of insanity" for cutting off her husband's penis with a kitchen knife. By contrast, no one knew that John Smith, who drove a Greyhound bus out of the New York City Port Authority bus terminal in 1980, crashed, and was acquitted "by reason of insanity," is still locked up in the Manhattan Psychiatric Center on Ward's Island in New York City. For a brief moment in 1994, CNN may have made "Lorena Bobbitt" a household name throughout the world, whereas no one but the lawyers, doctors, and hospital staff probably knows of John Smith. But Smith's case is hands-down the more typical insanity defense case; Bobbitt's is extremely rare (Perlin 1989–90; Sherman 1994, 24).

The insanity defense attracts a lot of public and scholarly attention, but the public badly misunderstands the way the defense actually works (Table 6.1). Keep in mind that **insanity** is a legal concept, not a medical term. What psychiatry calls "mental illness" may or may not be legal insanity. Mental disease is legal insanity only when the disease affects a person's reason and/or will.

Insanity excuses criminal liability only when it seriously damages the person's capacity to act and/or reason and understand. This means that if defendants were so mentally diseased they couldn't form a criminal intent and/or control their actions, we can't blame them for what they did. Psychiatrists testify in courts to help juries decide whether defendants are legally insane, not to prove defendants are mentally ill.

The verdict "guilty but mentally ill," used by several states, makes this point clear. In this verdict, juries can find defendants sane but mentally ill when they committed crimes. These defendants receive criminal sentences and go to prison, where they're treated for their mental illness while they're being punished for their crimes.

Contrary to widespread belief, few defendants plead the insanity defense (only a few thousand a year). The few who do plead insanity hardly ever succeed. According to an eight-state study funded by the National Institute of Mental Health (American Psychiatric Association 2003):

> The insanity defense was used in less than one percent of the cases in a representative sampling of cases before those states' county courts. The study showed that only 26 percent of those insanity pleas were argued successfully. Most studies show that in approximately 80 percent of the cases where a defendant is acquitted on a "not guilty by reason of insanity" finding, it is because the prosecution and defense have agreed on the appropriateness of the plea before trial. That agreement occurred because both the defense and prosecution agreed that the defendant was mentally ill and met the jurisdiction's test for insanity.

The few who "succeed" don't go free. In a noncriminal proceeding, called a **civil commitment,** courts have to decide if defendants who were insane when they committed their crimes are still insane. If they are—and courts almost always decide they are—they're locked up in maximum-security prisons called "hospitals." And like John Smith, and unlike Lorena Bobbitt, they stay there for a long time—until they're no longer "mentally ill and dangerous"—often for the rest of their lives.

It might be used only rarely, but the insanity defense stands for the important proposition—familiar to you by now—that we can only blame people who are responsible. For those who aren't responsible, retribution is out of order. There are four tests of insanity:

1. *Right-wrong test (the* M'Naghten *rule)* The rule in 28 jurisdictions (*Clark v. Arizona* 2006, slip opinion, majority 9)

TABLE 6.1

Popular Myths and Empirical Realities about the Insanity Defense

Myth	Reality
1. The insanity defense is overused.	All empirical analyses are consistent: "the public, legal profession and—specifically—legislators 'dramatically' and 'grossly' overestimate both the frequency and the success rate of the insanity plea."
2. The use of the insanity defense is limited to murder cases.	In one jurisdiction where the data have been closely studied, slightly fewer than one-third of the successful insanity pleas entered over an 8-year period were reached in cases involving a victim's death. Further, individuals who plead insanity in murder cases are no more successful at being found "Not Guilty by Reason of Insanity" (NGRI) than persons charged with other crimes.
3. There is no risk to the defendant who pleads insanity.	Defendants who asserted an insanity defense at trial and who were ultimately found guilty of their charges served significantly longer sentences than defendants tried on similar charges who didn't assert the insanity defense.
4. NGRI acquittees are quickly released from custody.	Of all the individuals found NGRI over an 8-year period in one jurisdiction, only 15 percent had been released from all restraints; 35 percent remained in institutional custody; and 47 percent were under partial court restraint following conditional release.
5. NGRI acquittees spend much less time in custody than do defendants convicted of the same offenses.	NGRI acquittees actually spend almost double the amount of time that defendants convicted of similar charges spend in prison settings and often face a lifetime of post-release judicial oversight.
6. Criminal defendants who plead insanity are usually faking.	Of 141 individuals found NGRI in one jurisdiction over an 8-year period, there was no dispute that 115 were schizophrenic (including 38 of the 46 cases involving a victim's death), and in only 3 cases was the diagnostician unable to specify the nature of the patient's mental illness.
7. Criminal defense attorneys employ the insanity defense plea solely to "beat the rap."	First, the level of representation afforded to mentally disabled defendants is frequently substandard. Second, the few studies that have been done paint an entirely different picture: lawyers may enter an insanity plea to obtain immediate mental health treatment for their client, as a plea-bargaining device to ensure that their client ultimately receives mandatory mental health care, and to avoid malpractice litigation. Third, the best available research suggests that jury biases exist relatively independent of lawyer functioning and are generally "not induced by attorneys."

Source: Perlin 1997, 648–55.

2. *Volitional incapacity (irresistible impulse)* The rule in a few jurisdictions (LaFave 2003b, 389)

3. *Substantial capacity test (the MPC test)* The majority rule until John Hinckley attempted to murder President Reagan in 1981. It's still the rule in 14 jurisdictions (*Clark v. Arizona* 2006, slip opinion, majority, 10) but not in federal courts, where it was abolished in 1984 and replaced with the right-wrong test

4. *Product test* (Durham *rule*) Followed only in New Hampshire

All four tests look at defendants' mental capacity, but they differ in what they're looking *for*. The right-wrong test focuses exclusively on *reason*—psychologists call it "cognition"—that is, on the capacity to tell right from wrong. The other tests focus on either reason or will. *Will*—psychologists call it "volition"—popularly means "willpower"; in the insanity tests it refers to defendants' power to control their actions.

The Right-Wrong Test

The **right-wrong test** depends on defendants' mental capacity to know right from wrong. It's also known as the ***M'Naghten* rule** after a famous 1843 English case. Daniel M'Naghten suffered the paranoid delusion that the prime minister, Sir Robert Peel, had masterminded a conspiracy to kill him. M'Naghten shot at Peel in a delusion of self-defense but killed Peel's secretary, Edward Drummond, by mistake. Following his trial for murder, the jury returned a verdict of "not guilty by reason of insanity."

On appeal, in *M'Naghten's Case* (1843), England's highest court, the House of Lords, created the two-pronged right-wrong test, or the *M'Naghten* rule, of insanity. The test consists of two elements:

1. The defendant had a mental disease or defect at the time of the crime, *and*

2. The disease or defect caused the defendant not to know either
    a. The nature and the quality of his or her actions, *or*
    b. That what he or she was doing was wrong.

Several terms in the test need defining, because there's a lot of back and forth in the courts about just what the terms mean. Statutes often don't give the courts much guidance, leaving the courts to legislate judicially on the matter. Nevertheless, we can say this much. *Mental disease* means psychosis, mostly the paranoia from which M'Naghten suffered, and schizophrenia. It doesn't include personality disorders, such as psychopathic and sociopathic personalities that lead to criminal or antisocial conduct. *Mental defect* refers to mental retardation or brain damage severe enough to make it impossible to know what you're doing or to know that it's wrong.

In most states, *know* means simple awareness: cognition. Some states require more—that defendants understand or "appreciate" (grasp the true significance of) their actions. Other states don't define the term, leaving juries to define it by applying it to the facts of specific cases as they see fit. The *nature and quality of the act* means you don't know what you're doing (ALI 1985 1:2, 174–76). (To use an old law school example, "If a man believes he's squeezing lemons when in fact he's strangling his wife," he doesn't know the "nature and quality of his act.")

Deciding the meaning of *wrong* has created problems. Some states require that defendants didn't know their conduct was legally wrong; others say it means morally wrong. In *People v. Schmidt* (1915), Schmidt confessed to killing Anna Aumuller by slitting her throat. He pleaded insanity, telling physicians who examined him that

> he had heard the voice of God calling upon him to kill the woman as a sacrifice and atonement. He confessed to a life of unspeakable excesses and hideous crimes, broken, he said, by spells of religious ecstasy and exaltation. In one of these moments, believing himself, he tells us, in the visible presence of God, he committed this fearful crime. (325)

The trial judge instructed the jury that Schmidt had to know that slitting Aumuller's throat was legally wrong. The New York Court of Appeals disagreed: "We are unable to accept the view that the word 'wrong' . . . is to receive such a narrow construction." The court of appeals recommended this as a suitable instruction:

> Knowledge of the nature and quality of the act has reference to its physical nature and quality, and that knowledge that it is wrong refers to its moral side; that to know that the act is wrong, the defendant must know that it is "contrary to law, and contrary to the

accepted standards of morality, and then he added . . . that it must be known to be contrary to the laws of God and man." (336)

In *State v. Odell* (2004), the Minnesota Supreme Court upheld Darren Odell's murder conviction, because there was enough evidence to prove he knew it was wrong to kill his father.

CASE | *Did He Know It Was Wrong to Kill His Father?*

State v. Odell
676 N.W.2d 646 (Minn. 2004)

HISTORY

Darren Paul Odell (appellant) was indicted on one count of first-degree murder under Minn.Stat. ß 609.185(a)(1) (2002) as a result of the shooting death of his father, Dennis Raymond Odell. At trial, appellant pleaded not guilty and not guilty by reason of mental illness under Minn.Stat. ß 611.026 (2002), commonly referred to as the *M'Naghten* rule, which has long been part of Minnesota law. [The statute provides:]

> No person shall be . . . excused from criminal liability except upon proof that at the time of committing the alleged criminal act the person was laboring under such a defect of reason, from one of these causes, as not to know the nature of the act, or that it was wrong.

A defendant who pleads not guilty by reason of mental illness is afforded a bifurcated trial under Minn. R.Crim. P. 20.02, subd. 6(2). The first phase of the trial determines whether the state has met its burden of proof as to the defendant's guilt. If the defendant is found guilty, the second phase determines whether the defendant has sustained the burden of establishing the mental illness defense.

Appellant waived his right to a jury trial and at the conclusion of the guilt phase of the trial, the court found that appellant acted with premeditation and intent to kill his father. This finding was not appealed. After the mental illness phase, the trial court found that appellant failed to sustain his burden in proving a mental illness defense and sentenced him to life in prison. On direct appeal, appellant contests the trial court's ruling with respect to the *M'Naghten* rule.

GILBERT, J.

FACTS

On Sunday, April 23, 2000, appellant attended Easter dinner at his great aunt's house. While his father was seated at the dining room table, appellant retrieved a 9mm Beretta handgun from his truck. When he returned, appellant waited until some of the guests cleared the dining room area. While two guests remained seated beside his father, appellant fired three bullets into his father's chest, which resulted in fatal wounds. Immediately following the shooting, appellant fled the crime scene, but returned shortly thereafter and peacefully surrendered himself to police. On appeal, appellant admits to shooting his father, but challenges the trial court's decision as to his mental illness.

At trial, extensive evidence relevant to appellant's mental state was introduced. In phase two of the trial, the court found the following doctors, who evaluated appellant, qualified to render expert witness testimony: Dr. James H. Gilbertson was called to testify for the defense, Dr. Dallas D. Erdmann was appointed by the court, and Drs. Michael G. Farnsworth and Kristine Kienlen were called to testify for the state.

On May 1, 2001, Drs. Erdmann and Farnsworth examined appellant to determine whether he was competent to proceed to trial. Both doctors concluded that as a result of appellant's mental illness, he was incapable of understanding the proceedings or participating in his defense. Thereafter, appellant was committed to the Minnesota Security Hospital in St. Peter, Minnesota for treatment. In the fall of 2002, Odell was found competent to proceed to trial.

After initial interviews with appellant, all four doctors agreed that appellant did not qualify for the *M'Naghten* defense. Although Drs. Gilbertson and Erdmann diagnosed appellant as suffering from schizophrenia at the time of the murder, both believed appellant understood the nature and wrongfulness of shooting his father, yet elected to engage in the criminal behavior regardless of the consequences. Drs. Farnsworth and Kienlen agreed that appellant was suffering from a mental illness at the time of the shooting and concluded, as Drs. Gilbertson and Erdmann did, that appellant did not satisfy the *M'Naghten* rule, that is, appellant understood the nature and wrongfulness of his acts.

Following the first set of mental evaluations, appellant's sister, while cleaning appellant's house, found a popcorn tin containing several post-it notes and other writings apparently authored by appellant. The contents of the notes and writings contained bizarre references to celebrities Reba McIntyre and Elvis Presley, and numerology, but did not reference appellant's relationship with or animus toward his father. Subsequently, counsel stipulated to and the trial court granted appellant's request to be reexamined.

Based on a review of the post-it notes, updated medical reports, and a second interview with appellant, Drs. Gilbertson and Erdmann revised their opinions and concluded that appellant did not know it was morally wrong to kill his father. Therefore, Drs. Gilbertson and Erdmann believed appellant met the requirements of the *M'Naghten* rule. However, Dr. Farnsworth did not waver from his original conclusion that, at the time of the offense, appellant knew the nature and wrongfulness of the act and did not have the *M'Naghten* defense available to him. Dr. Kienlen did not prepare a second report, but testified at trial that after reviewing the post-it notes, medical records, and a videotape of Dr. Farnsworth's second interview with appellant, she saw no reason to deviate from her initial opinion that appellant did not have the *M'Naghten* defense available to him.

OPINION

The *M'Naghten* rule requires that in order to be excused from criminal liability by reason of insanity, a defendant must show that he either did not know the nature of his act or that the act was wrong. A defendant must prove mental illness at the time of the crime by a preponderance of the evidence.

The narrow question before this court is whether the evidence presented at trial was sufficient to prove, by a preponderance of the evidence, that appellant did not understand the wrongfulness of his acts on April 23, 2000. The parties do not dispute that appellant suffered from a mental illness at the time of the offense. Further, it is undisputed that appellant knew that he was shooting his father and that such a shooting would result in his father's death. Therefore, appellant concedes that he knew the nature of his actions.

On appeal, this Court conducts a rigorous review of the record to determine whether the evidence, direct and circumstantial, viewed most favorably to support a finding of guilt, was sufficient to permit the trial court to reach its conclusion. When reviewing a defendant's challenge to sufficiency of evidence, this court cannot retry facts, but must assume the fact-finder—here, the trial court—believed the state's witnesses and disbelieved any contradictory evidence. This court has held that the issue of legal mental illness is a question for the finder of fact to resolve. Broad deference is granted to the fact-finder in determining the appropriate weight to assign expert psychiatric testimony."

In the trial court's extensive findings of fact and verdict, it carefully considered the evidence presented by all four experts and determined the believability and weight to be given to each expert's testimony. Accordingly, the court decided to give greater weight to the opinions of Drs. Farnsworth and Kienlen because their reports were more consistent with appellant's behavior and belief system.

The court could not reconcile the opinions of Drs. Gilbertson and Erdmann with several facts of the case; namely, that on April 23, 2000, immediately before and after the murder, appellant was able to communicate and interact with others normally. Further, the court questioned some of the underpinnings of Dr. Erdmann's revised analysis and found that in his first and second opinions Dr. Erdmann had relied on similar facts to support divergent conclusions. Finally, the court concluded that appellant had proved by a preponderance of the evidence that, at the time of the murder, he was suffering from a severe mental illness, but that appellant had failed to prove that because of his mental illness he did not understand the nature of his act or that the act constituting the offense was wrong.

Upon a rigorous review of the record, noting the broad deference granted to the fact-finder in determining the appropriate weight to assign expert psychiatric testimony and viewing the evidence most favorably to support a finding of guilt, we hold that sufficient evidence existed to support the trial court's conviction of appellant.

Affirmed.

Questions

1. State the elements in Minnesota's version of the right-wrong test.

2. List all the facts relevant to each element of the test.

3. Summarize the court's arguments for its decision.

4. In your opinion, was Darren Odell entitled to the defense of insanity, according to the Minnesota statute? Back up your answer with facts and arguments in the case excerpt.

5. Now, read the more detailed version of the case that appeared in *City Pages* (Hawkins 2003). Assume Hawkins's version to be true.

    Darren Odell had just about finished Easter dinner when he killed his father. There had been ham, of course, and potatoes, and some kind of salad with whipped cream in it, he later told detectives. Just before 6:00 P.M., while his relatives were eating dessert, Odell left the dining room to get the gun he had hidden in his pickup, and more ice for his Pepsi. "I like Pepsi with ice just because it's watered down a little bit," he explained afterward. "I watch my health and that now. I usually don't drink a can of pop straight."

    It was Sunday, April 23, 2000, and Darren had been thinking about killing his father for more than two years. Several times he'd brought the gun to family gatherings at his great-aunt's house in Blaine. But the time never seemed right.

Sometimes there were too many people in the way who might get injured; sometimes his three-year-old niece was present, and he didn't want to upset her.

Dennis Odell had arrived at the Easter gathering with a card for Darren signed "Love, Dad." Darren later said he knew his father was trying hard to do something nice, but he didn't believe the words on the card. "His eyes were kind of teary," Darren commented later. "He knew he wasn't handling it right, not making things better."

After he got his gun, Darren retrieved a few cubes of ice from his aunt's freezer and poured the rest of his Pepsi into his glass, which was resting on the kitchen table. Instead of picking up the drink, though, he walked to the dining room and fired four shots into his father's chest.

Darren walked back into the kitchen, turned and looked at the people still seated at the dinner table, and left the house. He drove away, but ended up just circling the block. When the police came, he lay down in the driveway, told the officers where to find his gun, and suggested they take the spare magazine of ammunition out of his back pocket.

He was equally cooperative at the police station, although he seemed to think that the interrogation was a formality. "It feels like a ton of bricks off me," he explained to the detectives. "I can go back out there now and just leave, live a normal life again, without having to deal with my dad and all. Do you think I'll have to go to trial for this? I just would like to go home and really not deal with anything anymore. Just start over."

Odell did not get to go home that day. It quickly became clear that he was so severely mentally ill he couldn't even stand trial. He was sent to a state psychiatric hospital, where he was kept on heavy medication for the next two and a half years. At first, the doctors who evaluated his mental health were convinced that he knew right from wrong and should eventually be tried. . . .

As Odell flitted in and out of sanity, and as the new evidence regarding the strength of his delusions was uncovered, a small army of psychiatrists and psychologists examined and re-examined him. In the end, all would agree that Odell suffered from chronic paranoid schizophrenia and that he killed his father because he believed the two were locked in a contest for survival. But they wouldn't be able to agree whether Odell was legally insane. . . .

Darren Odell may well have known that his actions would be seen as wrong. On one hand, he took a number of steps to make sure that no one else would be hurt during the shooting, and that his niece wouldn't have to see the killing. He even bought a silencer to spare everyone's ears. He practiced regularly at a target range. After he shot his father, he waited for the police. . . .

In May 1998 Darren bought a gun, a 9mm Beretta, and took up target practice. From the start, he said, he was concerned about causing injury to anyone but his father. He used earplugs and bought a silencer. He would head right home after visiting the shooting range so that there would be no chance the weapon might be stolen and used.

Several times over the years he loaded the gun and took it to his aunt's house for family get-togethers. But there were always too many people milling around, he later said, too many children he didn't want to see the shooting.

That Easter, when Darren realized he had a clear shot at Dennis from his aunt's kitchen doorway and the kids were outside, he paced back and forth in the kitchen trying to decide whether the moment had really arrived. Eventually, he concluded that it had. He aimed carefully because he wanted his father to die as quickly as possible. "I hit him point-blank, in the heart I believe," Darren Odell told police. "I know it was a painful death, but I thought it could have been more painful if he was hit in the head or if he suffered a long time.

"It's difficult for me to talk about, 'cause I love my dad so, so much when I was growin' up and that," he continued. "Inside I feel terrible. But I suffered enough emotionally and physically and I sure wasn't gonna have my dad put me back down into, you know, into a place or mental institution or something again for anything." . . .

Odell was to find himself back in a psychiatric ward within a couple of weeks, however. Separate experts had been retained by the prosecution, defense, and court. . . . The experts . . . concluded that Odell knew that shooting his father was wrong, and that he did not meet the legal definition of insanity. . . .

Did Hawkins's version of the facts in the case change your mind? Explain your answer.

The Irresistible Impulse Test

Just because you know something is wrong, even if you fully appreciate its wrongfulness, doesn't mean you can stop yourself from doing it. I used to be fat. I knew and fully appreciated the wrongfulness of overeating. I can remember so many times *knowing* those french fries were really bad for me, but I just couldn't stop myself from shoving them in. According to the **irresistible impulse test,** we can't blame or deter people who because of a mental disease or defect lose their self-control and can't bring their actions into line with what the law requires.

A few jurisdictions have responded to criticism that the insanity defense should look at the effect of mental disease on reason *and* will. These jurisdictions supplement the right-wrong test with a test that takes volition into account.

According to the test, even if defendants know what they're doing and know it's wrong, they can qualify for a verdict of not guilty by reason of insanity if they suffer from a mental disease that damages their volition (willpower). In 1877, the court in *Parsons v. State* spelled out the application of the right-wrong test with its irresistible impulse supplement:

1. At the time of the crime, was the defendant afflicted with "a disease of the mind"?

2. If so, did the defendant know right from wrong with respect to the act charged? If not, the law excuses the defendant.

3. If the defendant did have such knowledge, the law will still excuse her if two conditions concur:
   a. If the mental disease caused the defendant to so far lose the power to choose between right and wrong and to avoid doing the alleged act that the disease destroyed his free will *and*
   b. If the mental disease was the sole cause of the act

Some critics say the irresistible impulse supplement doesn't go far enough. First, they argue that it should include not just sudden impulses but also conduct "characterized by brooding and reflection." Second, they claim the irresistible requirement implies defendants have to lack *total* control over their actions. In practice, however, juries do acquit defendants who have *some* control. Sometimes, statutes don't use the phrase at all; for example, Georgia's Criminal Code (2006, Title 17, Section 16-3-3) provides:

> A person shall not be found guilty of a crime when, at the time of the act, . . . because of mental disease, injury, or congenital deficiency, [he] acted as he did because of a delusional compulsion as to such act which overmastered his will to resist committing the crime.

But more critics say the test goes too far. By allowing people who lack self-control to escape punishment, the test cripples both retribution and deterrence. They point to the high-profile case of John Hinckley, Jr., acquitted because the jury found him insane when, in 1981, he attempted to assassinate President Ronald Reagan to get actress Jodie Foster's attention. Shortly after Hinckley's trial, Harvard criminal law professor Charles Nesson (1982) wrote:

> To many Mr. Hinckley seems like a kid who had a rough life and who lacked the moral fiber to deal with it. This is not to deny that Mr. Hinckley is crazy but to recognize that there is a capacity for craziness in all of us. Lots of people have tough lives, many tougher than Mr. Hinckley's, and manage to cope. The Hinckley verdict let those people down. For anyone who experiences life as a struggle to act responsibly in the face of various temptations to let go, the Hinckley verdict is demoralizing, an example of someone who let himself go and who has been exonerated because of it. (29)

After Hinckley's attempt to kill President Reagan, the federal government and several states abolished the irresistible impulse defense on the ground that juries can't distinguish between irresistible impulses beyond the power to control and those that aren't. The federal statute (U.S. Code 2003) abolishing the irresistible impulse test in federal cases provides as follows:

> It is an affirmative defense to a prosecution under any Federal statute that, at the time of the commission of the acts constituting the offense, the defendant, as a result of a severe mental disease or defect, was unable to appreciate the nature and quality or the wrongfulness of his acts. Mental disease or defect does not otherwise constitute a defense.

The Substantial Capacity Test

The **substantial capacity test,** adopted in the MPC, is supposed to remove the objections to both the right-wrong test and its irresistible impulse supplement while preserving the legal nature of both tests. It emphasizes both of the qualities in insanity that affect culpability: reason and will (Schlopp 1988).

As the name of the test indicates, defendants have to lack *substantial*, not complete, mental capacity. The substantial capacity element clears up the possibility that "irresistible" in irresistible impulse means *total* lack of knowledge and/or control. So people who can tell right from wrong only modestly and/or who have only a feeble will to resist are insane. Most substantial capacity test states follow the MPC's (ALI 1985 [3]) definition of substantial capacity:

> A person is not responsible for criminal conduct if at the time of such conduct as a result of mental disease or defect he lacks substantial capacity either to appreciate the criminality [wrongfulness] of his conduct or to conform his conduct to the requirements of law. (163)

The use of *appreciate* instead of *know* makes clear that intellectual awareness by itself isn't enough to create culpability; affective or emotional components of understanding are required. The phrase *conform his conduct* removes the requirement of a "sudden" lack of control. In other words, the code provision eliminates the suggestion that losing control means losing it on the spur of the moment, as the "impulse" in irresistible impulse test can be read to mean. The MPC's definition of "mental disease or defect" excludes psychopathic personalities, habitual criminals, and antisocial personalities from the defense.

The California Supreme Court dropped the right-wrong test after more than a century of use; replaced it with the MPC substantial capacity test; and applied it retroactively, all in a single case, *People v. Drew* (1978).

CASE   *Did He Lack "Substantial Capacity" to Appreciate the Wrongfulness of His Acts?*

People v. Drew
583 P.2d 1318 (Cal. 1978)

HISTORY

Ronald Jay Drew, defendant, was charged with battery on a peace officer and related offenses, and pled not guilty and not guilty by reason of insanity. The jury, Superior Court, Imperial County, found Drew guilty as charged, and also found him sane. Drew was sentenced to prison on the battery charge. The California Supreme Court reversed and remanded for a new trial on the issue raised by Drew's plea of not guilty by reason of insanity.

Note: California's procedure for insanity defense cases is a two-stage (bifurcated) trial. The first is to determine guilt, and the second is to determine sanity.

TOBRINER, J.

FACTS

Guilt Stage

Defendant Drew, a 22-year-old man, was drinking in a bar in Brawley during the early morning of October 26, 1975. He left $5 on the bar to pay for drinks and went to the men's room. When he returned, the money was missing. Drew accused one Truman Sylling, a customer at the bar, of taking the money. A heated argument ensued, and the bartender phoned for police assistance.

Officers Guerrero and Bonsell arrived at the bar. When Guerrero attempted to question Sylling, Drew interfered to continue the argument. Bonsell then asked Drew to step outside. Drew refused. Bonsell took Drew by the hand, and he and Officer Schulke, who had just arrived at the bar, attempted to escort Drew outside. Drew broke away from the officers and struck Bonsell in the face. Bonsell struck his head against the edge of the bar and fell to the floor. Drew fell on top of him and attempted to bite him, but was restrained by Guerrero and Schulke. Drew continued to resist violently until he was finally placed in a cell at the police station.

Charged with battery on a peace officer (Pen. Code, ß 243), obstructing an officer (Pen. Code, ß 148), and disturbing the peace (Pen. Code, ß 415), Drew pled not guilty and not guilty by reason of insanity. At the guilt trial, Drew testified on his own behalf; he denied striking Bonsell and maintained that the officer's injuries were accidental. Bonsell's testimony, however, was corroborated by Guerrero and Sylling. The jury found Drew guilty as charged.

Sanity Stage

Two court-appointed psychiatrists testified at the sanity trial. Dr. Otto Gericke, former Medical Director at Patton State Hospital, testified that Drew was committed to that hospital for nine months in 1972 after Drew was found incompetent to stand trial on an unspecified charge. He examined him on that occasion; again on February 1, 1976, to determine Drew's competency to stand trial on the instant charge; and a third time on June 6, 1976, on the question of Drew's sanity.

Dr. Gericke described Drew's condition as one of latent schizophrenia, characterized by repeated incidents of assaultive behavior and by conversing with inanimate objects and nonexistent persons; this condition could be controlled by medication but if left untreated would deteriorate to paranoid schizophrenia. Relying upon his examinations and Drew's medical history at Patton State Hospital, Dr. Gericke concluded that Drew was unable to appreciate the difference between right and wrong at the time he attacked Officer Bonsell.

The second witness, Dr. Ethel Chapman, was a staff psychiatrist at Patton State Hospital. She also examined Drew under court appointment in February and June of 1976, and was acquainted with him from his stay at the hospital in 1972. She concurred with Dr. Gericke's diagnosis of his condition, adding the observation that his symptoms would be aggravated by the ingestion of alcohol, and joined in Dr. Gericke's conclusion that Drew did not understand that his assault upon Officer Bonsell was wrong.

The prosecution presented no evidence at the sanity trial. Nevertheless the jury, instructed that the defendant has the burden of proving insanity under the *M'Naghten* test, found him sane. The court thereupon sentenced Drew to prison on the battery conviction. He appeals from the judgment of conviction.

OPINION

. . . Although the Legislature has thus provided that "insanity" is a defense to a criminal charge, it has never attempted to define that term. The task of describing the circumstances under which mental incapacity will relieve a defendant of criminal responsibility has become the duty of the judiciary. Since . . . 1864, the California courts have followed the *M'Naghten* rule to define the defense of insanity. . . .

> . . . To establish a defence on the ground of insanity, it must be clearly proved that, at the time of committing the act, the party accused was labouring under such a defect of reason, from disease of the mind, as not to know the nature and quality of the act he was doing; or, if he did know it, that he did not know he was doing what was wrong. (*M'Naghten's Case*, 8 Eng. Rep. 718, 722)

Although an advisory opinion, and thus most questionable authority, this language became the basis for the test of insanity in all American states except New Hampshire.

Despite its widespread acceptance, the deficiencies of *M'Naghten* have long been apparent. Principal among these is the test's exclusive focus upon the cognitive capacity of the defendant. . . . The *M'Naghten* rules fruitlessly attempt to relieve from punishment only those mentally diseased persons who have no cognitive capacity. This formulation does not comport with modern medical knowledge that an individual is a mentally complex being with varying degrees of awareness. It also fails to attack the problem presented in a case wherein an accused may have understood his actions but was incapable of controlling his behavior. . . .

M'Naghten's exclusive emphasis on cognition would be of little consequence if all serious mental illness impaired the capacity of the affected person to know the nature and wrongfulness of his action. . . . Current psychiatric opinion, however, holds that mental illness often leaves the individual's intellectual understanding relatively unimpaired, but so affects his emotions or reason that he is unable to prevent himself from committing the act. The annals of this court are filled with illustrations of the above statement: the deluded defendant in *People v. Gorshen*, 51 Cal.2d 716, who believed he would be possessed by devilish visions unless he killed his foreman; the schizophrenic boy in *People v. Wolff, supra*, 61 Cal.2d 795, who knew that killing his mother was murder but was unable emotionally to control his conduct despite that knowledge; the defendant in *People v. Robles* (1970) 2 Cal.3d 205, suffering from organic brain damage, who mutilated himself and killed others in sudden rages. To ask whether such a person knows or understands that his act is "wrong" is to ask a question irrelevant to the nature of his mental illness or to the degree of his criminal responsibility.

Secondly, *M'Naghten*'s single-track emphasis on the cognitive aspect of the personality recognizes no degrees of incapacity. Either the defendant knows right from wrong or he does not. . . . But such a test is grossly unrealistic. . . . As the commentary to the American Law Institute's Model Penal Code observes, "The law must recognize that when there is no black and white it must content itself with different shades of gray." In short, *M'Naghten* purports to channel psychiatric testimony into the narrow issue of cognitive capacity, an issue often unrelated to the defendant's illness or crime. . . .

In our opinion the continuing inadequacy of *M'Naghten* as a test of criminal responsibility cannot be cured by further attempts to interpret language dating from a different era of psychological thought, nor by the creation of additional concepts designed to evade the limitations of *M'Naghten*. It is time to recast *M'Naghten* in modern language, taking account of advances in psychological knowledge and changes in legal thought.

The definition of mental incapacity appearing in section 4.01 of the American Law Institute's Model Penal Code represents the distillation of nine years of research, exploration, and debate by the leading legal and medical minds of the country. It specifies that

A person is not responsible for criminal conduct if at the time of such conduct as a result of mental disease or defect he lacks substantial capacity either to appreciate the criminality [wrongfulness] of his conduct or to conform his conduct to the requirements of law.

The American Law Institute takes no position as to whether the term "criminality" or the term "wrongfulness" best expresses the test of criminal responsibility; we prefer the term "criminality." . . .

Adhering to the fundamental concepts of free will and criminal responsibility, the American Law Institute test restates *M'Naghten* in language consonant with current legal and psychological thought. . . .

In the opinion of most thoughtful observers . . . the ALI test is a significant improvement over *M'Naghten*. The advantages may be briefly summarized. First, the ALI test adds a volitional element, the ability to conform to legal requirements, which is missing from the *M'Naghten* test.

Second, it avoids the all-or-nothing language of *M'Naghten* and permits a verdict based on lack of substantial capacity. Third, the ALI test is broad enough to permit a psychiatrist to set before the trier of fact a full picture of the defendant's mental impairments and flexible enough to adapt to future changes in psychiatric theory and diagnosis. Fourth, by referring to the defendant's capacity to "appreciate" the wrongfulness of his conduct the test confirms . . . that mere verbal knowledge of right and wrong does not prove sanity. Finally, by establishing a broad test of nonresponsibility, including elements of volition as well as cognition, the test provides the foundation on which we can order and rationalize the convoluted and occasionally inconsistent law of diminished capacity. . . .

. . . Although we have today rejected the *M'Naghten* rule, we must nevertheless determine whether the jury's verdict based on that rule is supported by the record. We therefore explain our conclusion that on the present record a jury instructed under the *M'Naghten* rule could reasonably reject the opinions of psychiatric witnesses; finding that Drew had thus failed to prove his lack of understanding of the nature or wrongfulness of his act, the jury accordingly could return a verdict of sanity.

Drew relies on the fact that both court-appointed psychiatrists testified that he was unaware of the wrongfulness of his assault. The jurors, however, are not automatically required to render a verdict which conforms to the expert opinion. . . . However impressive this seeming unanimity of expert opinion may at first appear, our inquiry on this just as on other factual issues is necessarily limited at the appellate level to a determination whether there is substantial evidence in the record to support the jury's verdict of sanity . . . under the law of this state. It is only in the rare case when the evidence is uncontradicted and entirely to the effect that the accused is insane that a unanimity of expert testimony could authorize upsetting a jury finding to the contrary. Indeed we have frequently upheld on appeal verdicts which find a defendant to be sane in the face of contrary unanimous expert opinion. . . .

. . . In the present case the jurors might well note that both experts were unfamiliar with Drew's conduct during the four years following his release from Patton State Hospital, and that their subsequent examinations of him were relatively brief. More significantly, the jurors could note that although both psychiatrists stated an opinion that Drew did not appreciate the wrongfulness of his act, nothing in their testimony explained the reasoning which led to this opinion. Although the psychiatric testimony described Drew's repeated aggressive acts, and diagnosed his condition as one of latent schizophrenia, neither psychiatrist explained why that behavior and diagnosis would lead to the conclusion that Drew was unable to appreciate the wrongfulness of his aggressive acts.

The prosecution presented no evidence at the sanity trial. Defendant, however, has the burden of proof on the issue of insanity; if neither party presents credible evidence on that issue the jury must find him sane. Thus the question on appeal is not so much the substantiality of the evidence favoring the jury's finding as whether the evidence contrary to that finding is of such weight and character that the jury could not reasonably reject it. Because the jury could reasonably reject the psychiatric opinion that Drew was insane under the *M'Naghten* test on the ground that the psychiatrists did not present sufficient material and reasoning to justify that opinion, we conclude that the jury's verdict cannot be overturned as lacking support in the trial record. . . .

. . . It is not surprising that in view of the fact that we had not then endorsed the ALI test of mental incapacity neither witnesses nor counsel structured their presentation at trial in terms of the ALI test, and the court did not instruct the jury on that standard. The record on appeal, nevertheless, adduces substantial evidence of incapacity under the ALI criteria. . . .

. . . In view of the absence of prosecution evidence on the insanity issue, we conclude that if the case had been tried under the ALI standard and the jury instructed accordingly, it probably would have returned a verdict finding Drew insane. The trial court's failure to employ the ALI test therefore constitutes prejudicial error. . . .

The judgment is reversed and the cause remanded for a new trial on the issue raised by defendant's plea of not guilty by reason of insanity. Bird, C. J., Mosk, J., and Newman, J., concurred.

DISSENT

RICHARDSON, J.

I respectfully dissent. My objection to the majority's approach may be briefly stated. I believe that a major change in the law of the type contemplated by the majority should be made by the Legislature. Although variously phrased, this has been the consistent, firm, and fixed position of this court for many years for reasons equally as applicable today as when first expressed.

[*Justice Richardson reviews numerous cases to support his claim.*] . . .

. . . The majority now proposes to abandon both deference to legislative interest and a carefully constructed accretion of California law and opt for an entirely different standard. Suddenly, "The task of describing the circumstances under which mental illness will relieve a defendant of criminal responsibility *has become the duty of the judiciary.*" . . . *Why* has it now become our duty? . . . Frankly, and I say this with complete respect, there is only one explanation for this judicial U-turn, namely,

impatience. The majority, wearied of waiting, and browsing among the varied offerings at a judicial smorgasbord, has picked the ALI formulation. There may be merit in the choice, but a decision to adopt it or any other proposed test and thereby abandon the carefully structured California rule, already a substantial "recast" of the original *M'Naghten* rule and "*an integral part of the legislative scheme,*" should be preceded by a much more extensive factual investigation and analysis than we are able to perform. . . .

. . . We are not equipped to pick and choose the best among the various alternatives that are available, and we should leave the task to those who are so equipped. A legislative committee aided by staff can conduct hearings and studies, question experts, and develop a policy consensus on the questions of fact or mixed questions of fact and law that are involved. . . . Such a legislative inquiry doubtless will reveal that the ALI test is not without its critics. Indeed, in its desire to abandon the modified California test, the majority accepts a proposed new rule which may well create an entirely new set of problems. . . .

Clark, J., and Manuel, J., concurred.

CLARK, J.,

Today's majority opinion shatters California's intricate and enlightened system of criminal responsibility, replacing it with a vague behavioral test to be determined by court psychiatrists. The venerable equations of right versus wrong, good versus evil, go down in favor of an experiment determining criminal conduct by probing a defendant's metaphysical thought process. Worse, the majority orders its new rule to apply retroactively, requiring retrial of dozens, if not hundreds, of criminal cases. . . .

Questions

1. Summarize the majority's criticisms of the right-wrong test.
2. Summarize the majority's reasons for adopting the substantial capacity test.
3. Summarize the dissent's criticisms of the majority's decision.
4. Which test would you adopt? Defend your answer.
5. In your opinion, was Drew insane under the right-wrong test? Back up your answer with the facts from the excerpt.
6. In your opinion, was Drew insane under the substantial capacity test? Back up your answer with the facts from the excerpt.

The Product-of-Mental-Illness Test

As the science of psychiatry and psychology advanced, the right-wrong test generated increasing criticism. One line of criticism began in the 1950s, when many social reformers thought that Freudian psychology could cure individual and social "diseases." *Durham v. U.S.* (1954) reflects the influence of that psychology. According to the court:

> The science of psychiatry now recognizes that a man is an integrated personality and that reason, which is only one element in that personality, is not the sole determinant of his conduct. The right-wrong test, which considers knowledge or reason alone, is therefore an inadequate guide to mental responsibility for criminal behavior. (871)

Based on these insights, the U.S. Circuit Court for the District of Columbia replaced the right-wrong test with the **product-of-mental-illness test,** also known as the *Durham* rule. According to this "new" test (New Hampshire adopted it in 1871), acts that are the "products" of mental disease or defect excuse criminal liability. So, with this test, the court stretched the concept of insanity beyond the purely intellectual knowledge examined by the right-wrong test into deeper areas of cognition and will.

Disillusionment with Freudian psychology, a major shift in public opinion from rehabilitation to punishment, and the anger and disgust following the verdict in John Hinckley's trial for attempting to kill President Reagan prompted the U.S. Congress to replace the product test with the right-wrong test. That legislation did away with the product test in the District of Columbia, where *Durham* was decided. Only two states, New Hampshire and Maine, ever adopted the product test. Maine abandoned the test. That leaves the product test in effect only in New Hampshire, where it was created in 1871.

One reason the product test never took hold in the states is because, critics say, it misses the point of mental illness in the defense of insanity. They maintain that the product test makes insanity the equivalent of mental illness. But in the eyes of the criminal law, mental illness is only a tool to help juries decide whether the illness has impaired mental capacity enough to relieve persons of criminal responsibility. Two articulate defenders of the right-wrong test (Livermore and Meehl 1967) put their criticism of the product test this way:

> It is always necessary to start any discussion of *M'Naghten* by stressing that the case does not state a test of psychosis or mental illness. Rather, it lists conditions under which those who are mentally diseased will be relieved from criminal responsibility. Thus, criticism of *M'Naghten* based on the proposition that the case is premised on an outdated view of mental disease is inappropriate. The case can only be criticized justly if it is based on an outdated view of the mental conditions that ought to preclude application of criminal sanction. (800)

The Burden of Proof

The defense of insanity not only poses definition problems but also gives rise to difficulties in application. States vary as to who has to prove insanity and how convincingly they have to do so. The Hinckley trial made these questions the subject of heated debate and considerable legislative reform in the 1980s.

Federal law required the government to prove Hinckley's sanity beyond a reasonable doubt. So if Hinckley's lawyers could raise a doubt in jurors' minds about his sanity, the jury had to acquit him. That means that even though the jury thought Hinckley was sane, if they weren't convinced beyond a reasonable doubt that he was, they had to acquit him.

And that's just what happened: The jury *did* believe Hinckley was sane but had their doubts, so they acquitted him. In 1984, the federal Comprehensive Crime Control Act (*Federal Criminal Code and Rules* 1988, § 17[b]) shifted the burden of proof from the government having to prove sanity beyond a reasonable doubt to defendants having to prove they were insane by clear and convincing evidence.

Most states don't follow the federal standard; they call insanity an affirmative defense. As an affirmative defense, sanity and, therefore, responsibility are presumed. The practical reason for the presumption saves the government the time and effort to prove sanity in the vast number of cases where insanity isn't an issue. In that sense, it's like concurrence: it's necessary but practically never an issue (*Clark v. Arizona* 2006, slip opinion majority, 26).

To overcome the sanity presumption, the defense has the burden to offer some evidence of insanity. If they do, the burden shifts to the government to prove sanity. States differ as to how heavy the government's burden to prove sanity is. Some states require proof beyond a reasonable doubt; some require clear and convincing evidence; and some require a preponderance of the evidence.

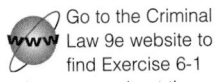 Go to the Criminal Law 9e website to find Exercise 6-1 to learn more about the insanity defense: www.thomsonedu.com/criminaljustice/samaha.

There's a trend in favor of shifting the burden to defendants and making that burden heavier. This is both because Hinckley's trial generated antagonism toward the insanity defense and because of growing hostility toward rules that the public believes coddle criminals (ALI 1985 [3], 226; Perlin 1989–90).

DIMINISHED CAPACITY

Diminished capacity is an unfortunate term. First, it's not an affirmative defense in the sense that it excuses criminal conduct. It's a failure-of-proof defense (discussed at the beginning of the chapter), "a rule of evidence that allows the defense to introduce evidence to negate . . . specific intent" in a very narrow set of cases—mostly premeditation in first-degree murder. "It is an attempt to prove that the defendant, incapable of the requisite intent of the crime charged, is innocent of that crime but may well be guilty of a lesser one" (*State v. Phipps* 1994, 143)—second-degree murder instead of first degree.

Second, diminished *capacity* isn't the same as **diminished *responsibility***, with which it's often confused. Diminished responsibility is a defense of excuse; it's a variation on the defendant's argument, "What I did was wrong, but under the circumstances I'm not responsible." In diminished responsibility, the defendant argues, "What I did was wrong, but under the circumstances I'm *less* responsible." According to *State v. Phipps* (1994; excerpted later in the "Syndromes" section):

> A defendant pleading diminished responsibility does not seek relief from punishment by justification or excuse, but seeks to be punished for a lesser offense which he generally admits committing. In contrast, diminished capacity focuses on a defendant's capacity to commit a specific intent crime, and, if established, does not excuse punishment, but results in punishment instead for the general intent crime defendant was capable of committing. Evidence to demonstrate such a lack of specific intent is not equivalent to evidence to establish diminished responsibility. (144)

Most states reject diminished capacity of either type. California is one example. The legislature abolished diminished capacity, mostly because of public hostility to it:

> The defense of diminished capacity is hereby abolished. In a criminal action . . . evidence concerning an accused person's . . . mental illness, disease, or defect shall not be admissible to show or negate capacity to form the particular purpose, intent, motive, malice

aforethought, knowledge, or other mental state required for the commission of the crime charged. . . . (California Penal Code 2003, § 25)

The statute didn't eliminate diminished capacity altogether. It provided that "diminished capacity or of a mental disorder may be considered by the court only at the time of sentencing."

In practice, diminished capacity and diminished responsibility apply only to homicide. Most of the cases involve reducing first- to second-degree murder. In a very few cases, defendants are allowed to introduce evidence to reduce murder to manslaughter. In other words, diminished capacity and responsibility are very rare issues in criminal law (LaFave 2003a, 453). How often do defendants succeed in reducing their liability when they're allowed to introduce "diminishment" evidence? Unfortunately, we don't know.

 AGE

The common law divided children into three categories for the purpose of deciding their capacity to commit crimes:

1. *Under 7* Children had no criminal capacity.

2. *Ages 7–14* Children were presumed to have no criminal capacity, but the presumption could be overcome.

3. *Over 14* Children had the same capacity as adults.

Today, statutes decide when young people can be convicted of crimes. These statutes come in several varieties, and they vary as to the age of capacity to commit crimes. One type of statute identifies a specific age, usually 14, but sometimes as young as 10 and as old as 18. These statutes usually provide that children under the specified age are subject to juvenile delinquency proceedings, even very young children. Another type of statute grants exclusive jurisdiction to juvenile courts up to a certain age but makes exceptions for a list of serious crimes. A third type of statute simply states that juvenile court jurisdiction is not exclusive (LaFave 2003a, 487).

All states have established juvenile justice systems to handle juvenile delinquency. One kind of delinquency, and the one we're concerned with here, is conduct that violates the criminal law. Most juvenile court statutes place no lower age limit on delinquency; they all place an upper age limit, almost always 18. Don't misunderstand this to mean that *all* juvenile cases will be handled in juvenile court. Every state has a statute that provides for the transfer of juveniles to adult criminal court. The technical term for this transfer is *waiver* to adult criminal court, meaning the juvenile court gives up its jurisdiction over the case and turns it over to the adult criminal court.

The shift from the philosophy of rehabilitation to retribution has led to more juveniles at younger ages being tried as adults. Here are a few examples illustrating this trend:

In New York, two fifteen-year-old private school students stand accused of savagely slashing to death a forty-four-year-old real estate agent and dumping his body in the lake at midnight in Central Park. In New Jersey, a fifteen-year-old awaits trial for the murder, sexual assault, and robbery of an eleven-year-old who had been going door to door collecting for his school's PTA fundraiser. In Mississippi, a sixteen-year-old slit the throat of his own mother before going to Pearl High School to hunt down the girl who had just broken up with him—killing her, killing another girl, and wounding seven of his high school classmates. In Arizona, three teenagers (out of a believed ten), ages thirteen, fourteen, and sixteen, face prosecution for the eighteen-hour abduction and gang rape of a fourteen-year-old. In California, three Satan-worshipping high school students, ages fifteen, sixteen, and seventeen, stand charged with drugging, raping, torturing, and murdering a fifteen-year-old, reportedly in hopes that a virgin sacrifice would earn them "a ticket to hell." (Gordon 1999, 193–94)

Waivers come in three varieties: judicial, prosecutorial, and legislative. By far, the most common is **judicial waiver;** that's when a juvenile court judge uses her discretion to transfer a juvenile to adult criminal court. Most states have adopted the criteria for making the waiver decision approved by the U.S. Supreme Court (*Kent v. U.S.* 1966) for the District of Columbia. These include:

1. The seriousness of the offense
2. Whether the offense was committed in an aggressive, violent, premeditated, willful manner
3. Whether the offense was against a person
4. The amount of evidence against the juvenile
5. The sophistication and maturity of the juvenile
6. The prior record of the juvenile
7. The threat the juvenile poses to public safety (LaFave 2003a, 490)

In *State v. K. R. L.* (1992), the Washington State Supreme Court grappled with the capacity of an 8-year-old boy to form criminal intent.

CASE   *Was He Too Young to Commit Burglary?*

State v. K. R. L.

840 P.2d 210 (Wash.App. 1992)

HISTORY

K. R. L., an eight-year-old boy, was convicted of residential burglary by the Superior Court, Clallam County, and he appealed. The Court of Appeals reversed.

ALEXANDER, J.

FACTS

In July 1990, K. R. L., who was then 8 years and 2 months old, was playing with a friend behind a business building in Sequim. Catherine Alder, who lived near the business, heard the boys playing and she instructed them to leave because she believed the area was dangerous. Alder said that K. R. L.'s response was belligerent, the child indicating that he would leave "in a minute." Losing patience with the boys, Alder said "no, not in a minute, now, get out of there now." The boys then ran off. Three days later, during daylight hours, K. R. L. entered Alder's home without her permission. He proceeded to pull a live goldfish from her fishbowl, chopped

it into several pieces with a steak knife and "smeared it all over the counter." He then went into Alder's bathroom and clamped a "plugged in" hair curling iron onto a towel.

Upon discovering what had taken place, Alder called the Sequim police on the telephone and reported the incident.

A Sequim police officer contacted K. R. L.'s mother and told her that he suspected that K. R. L. was the perpetrator of the offense against Alder. K. R. L.'s mother confronted the child with the accusation and he admitted to her that he had entered the house. She then took K. R. L. to the Sequim Police Department where the child was advised of his constitutional rights by a Sequim police officer.

This took place in the presence of K. R. L.'s mother who indicated that she did not believe "he really understood." K. R. L. told the police officer that he knew it was wrong to enter Alder's home. The statement given by K. R. L. to the officer was not offered by the State to prove guilt. Initially, the State took the position that K. R. L. fully understood those rights and that he had made a free and voluntary waiver of rights. Defense counsel objected to the admission of the statements and eventually the State withdrew its offer of the evidence, concluding that the evidence was cumulative in that K. R. L.'s admissions were already in evidence through the testimony of his mother.

K. R. L. was charged in Clallam County Juvenile Court with residential burglary, a class B felony. Residential burglary is defined in RCW 9A.52.025 as:

A person is guilty of residential burglary if, with intent to commit a crime against a person or property therein, the person enters or remains unlawfully in a dwelling. . . .

At trial, considerable testimony was devoted to the issue of whether K. R. L. possessed sufficient capacity to commit that crime. The juvenile court judge heard testimony in that regard from K. R. L.'s mother, Catherine Alder, two school officials, a Sequim policeman who had dealt with K. R. L. on two prior occasions as well as the incident leading to the charge, one of K. R. L.'s neighbors and the neighbor's son.

K. R. L.'s mother, the neighbor, the neighbor's son, and the police officer testified to an incident that had occurred several months before the alleged residential burglary.

This incident was referred to by the police officer as the "Easter Candy Episode." Their testimony revealed that K. R. L. had taken some Easter candy from a neighbor's house without permission. As a consequence, the Sequim police were called to investigate. K. R. L. responded to a question by the investigating officer, saying to him that he "knew it was wrong and he wouldn't like it if somebody took his candy."

The same officer testified to another incident involving K. R. L. This was described as the "joyriding incident," and it occurred prior to the "Easter Candy Episode." It involved K. R. L. riding the bicycles of two neighbor children without having their permission to do so. K. R. L. told the police officer that he "knew it was wrong" to ride the bicycles.

The assistant principal of K. R. L.'s elementary school testified about K. R. L.'s development. He said that K. R. L. was of "very normal" intelligence. K. R. L.'s first grade teacher said that K. R. L. had "some difficulty" in school. He said that he would put K. R. L. in the "lower age academically."

K. R. L.'s mother testified at some length about her son and, in particular, about the admissions he made to her regarding his entry into Alder's home. Speaking of that incident, she said that he admitted to her that what he did was wrong "after I beat him with a belt, black and blue." She also said that her son told her "that the Devil was making him do bad things."

The juvenile court rejected the argument of K. R. L.'s counsel that the State had not presented sufficient evidence to show that K. R. L. was capable of committing a crime. It found him guilty, saying:

From my experience in my eight, nine years on the bench, it's my belief that the so-called juvenile criminal system is a paper tiger and it's not going to be much of a threat to Mr. [K. R. L.], so I don't think that for that reason there is a whole lot to protect him from.

OPINION

There is only one issue—did the trial court err in concluding that K. R. L. had the capacity to commit the crime of residential burglary? RCW 9A.04.050 speaks to the capability of children to commit crimes and, in pertinent part, provides:

Children under the age of eight years are incapable of committing crime. Children of eight and under twelve years of age are presumed to be incapable of committing crime, but this presumption may be removed by proof that they have sufficient capacity to understand the act or neglect, and to know that it was wrong.

This statute applies in juvenile proceedings.

Because K. R. L. was 8 years old at the time he is alleged to have committed residential burglary, he was presumed incapable of committing that offense. The burden was, therefore, on the State to overcome that presumption and that burden could only be removed by evidence that was "clear and convincing." Thus, on review we must determine if there is evidence from which a rational trier of fact could find capacity by clear and convincing evidence.

There are no reported cases in Washington dealing with the capacity of 8-year-old children to commit crimes. That is not too surprising in light of the fact that up to age 8, children are deemed incapable of committing crimes. Two cases involving older children are, however, instructional.

In *State v. Q.D.* . . . our Supreme Court looked at a case involving a child who was charged with committing indecent liberties. In concluding that there was clear and convincing circumstantial evidence that the child understood the act of indecent liberties and knew it to be wrong, the court stressed the fact that the child was only 3 months shy of age 12, the age at which capacity is presumed to exist. The court also placed stock in the fact that the defendant used stealth in committing the offense as well as the fact that she had admonished the victim, a 2-year-old child whom she had been babysitting, not to tell what happened.

In another case, *State v. S. P.*, 746 P.2d 813 (1987), Division One of this court upheld a trial judge's finding that a child, S. P., had sufficient capacity to commit the crime of indecent liberties. In so ruling, the court noted that

(1) S. P. was 10 years of age at the time of the alleged acts;
(2) S. P. had had sexual contact with two younger boys during the prior year;
(3) in treatment for the earlier incident, S. P. acknowledged that sexual behavior was wrong;
(4) S. P. was aware that if convicted on the present charge, detention could result; and
(5) experts concluded that S. P. had an extensive knowledge of sexual terms and understood the wrongfulness of his conduct toward the victims.

None of the factors that the courts highlighted in the two aforementioned cases is present here. Most notably, K. R. L. is considerably younger than either of the children in the other two cases. In addition, we know almost nothing about what occurred when K. R. L. went into Alder's home. Furthermore, there was no showing that he used "stealth" in entering Alder's home. We know only that he entered her home in daylight hours and that while he was there he committed the act.

Neither was there any showing that K. R. L. had been previously treated for his behavior, as was the case in *State v. S. P.*

The State emphasizes the fact that K. R. L. appeared to appreciate that what he did at Alder's home and on prior occasions was wrong. When K. R. L. was being beaten "black and blue" by his mother, he undoubtedly came to the realization that what he had done was wrong. We are certain that this conditioned the child, after the fact, to know that what he did was wrong. That is a far different thing than one appreciating the quality of his or her acts at the time the act is being committed.

In arguing that it met its burden, the State placed great reliance on the fact that K. R. L. had exhibited bad conduct several months before during the so-called "Easter Candy" and "Joyriding" incidents. Again, we do not know much about these incidents, but it seems clear that neither of them involved serious misconduct and they shed little light on whether this child understood the elements of the act of burglary or knew that it was wrong. . . .

Here, we have a child of very tender years—only two months over 8 years. While the State made a valiant effort to show prior bad acts on the part of the child, an objective observer would have to conclude that these were examples of behavior not uncommon to many young children.

Furthermore, there was no expert testimony in this case from a psychologist or other expert who told the court anything about the ability of K. R. L. to know and appreciate the gravity of his conduct. Although two school officials testified, one of them said K. R. L. was of an age lower than 8, "academically." In short, there is simply not enough here so that we can say that in light of the State's significant burden, there is sufficient evidence to support a finding of capacity.

REVERSED.

Questions

1. Was the trial judge or the supreme court of Washington right in the ruling on the capacity of K. R. L. to form criminal intent? Back up your answer with facts from the case.

2. Did K. R. L. know what he was doing intellectually yet not sufficiently appreciate what he was doing? What facts support this conclusion?

3. Should it matter whether he appreciated what he did as long as he knew what he did was wrong? Explain your answer.

EXPLORING FURTHER

The Excuse of Age

Was He Too Old to Be Responsible?

FACTS A prosecutor was faced with the question of whether the other end of the age spectrum, old age, should affect the capacity to commit crimes:

> You have this married couple, married for over 50 years, living in a retirement home. The guy sends his wife out for bagels and while the wife can still get around she forgets and brings back onion rolls. Not a capital offense, right?
>
> Anyway, the guy goes berserk and he axes his wife; he kills the poor woman with a Boy Scout–type axe! What do we do now? Set a high bail? Prosecute? Get a conviction and send the fellow to prison? You tell me! We did nothing. The media dropped it quickly and, I hope, that's it. (Cohen 1985, 9)

Youth doesn't always excuse criminal conduct; it can also make the consequences worse. For example, 17-year-old Miguel Muñoz (*People v. Muñoz* 1960) was convicted of possessing a switchblade under a New York City ordinance that prohibited youths under 21 from carrying such knives. Had Muñoz been over 21, what he did wouldn't have been a crime.

 Go to the Criminal Law 9e website to find the full text of the Exploring Further excerpt: www.thomsonedu.com/criminaljustice/samaha. (Excerpt on the excuse of age.)

 DURESS

"Sometimes people are forced to do what they do," writes Professor Hyman Gross (1978). What if what they're forced to do is a crime? Should they be excused? The **defense of duress** is about answering these questions. According to Professor Gross, "It seems that the compulsion ought to count in their favor. After all, we say, such a person wasn't free to do otherwise—he couldn't help himself" (276). On the other hand, he continues:

> There are times . . . when we ought to stand firm and run the risk of harm to ourselves instead of taking a way out that means harm to others. In such a situation we must expect to pay the price if we cause harm when we prefer ourselves, for then the harm is our fault even though we did not mean it and deeply regret it. (276)

Let's take a closer look at the problem of duress and its elements.

The Problem of Duress

Professor Gross's comments strike at the heart of the problem of duress: It's hard to blame someone who's forced to commit a crime, but should we excuse people who harm innocent people to save themselves? The positions taken by three of the last two centuries' great authorities on criminal law show how different the answers can be. At one extreme is a historian of the criminal law and judge, Sir James Stephen (1883a, 108), who maintained that duress is never an excuse for crime. (Stephen did say duress should mitigate the punishment.) At the other extreme is Professor Glanville Williams (1961, 755). Author of a highly respected treatise on criminal law, he says the law should excuse individuals if they're so "in thrall[ed] to some power" the law can't control their choice. Professor Jerome Hall (1960, 448), author of yet another distinguished treatise, took the middle position that duress shouldn't excuse the most serious crimes, but it should be an excuse when the choice is either commit a minor crime or face imminent death.

The Elements of Duress

There are four elements in the defense of duress. The definitions of the elements vary from state to state:

1. *Threats amounting to duress* Death threats are required in some states. Threats of "serious bodily injury" qualify in several states. Others don't specify what threats qualify.

2. *Immediacy of the threats* In some states, the harm has to be "instant." In others, "imminent" harm is required. In Louisiana, duress is an excuse only if the defendant reasonably believed the person making the threats would "immediately carry out the threats if the crime were not committed."

3. *Crimes the defense applies to* In the majority of states, duress isn't a defense to murder. In other states, it's a defense to all crimes. Some states are silent on the point.

4. *Degree of belief regarding the threat.* Most states require a reasonable belief the threat is real. Others demand the threat actually be real. Some say nothing on the point.

DURESS STATUTES

NEW YORK PENAL CODE, § 40.00

In any prosecution for an offense, it is an affirmative defense that the defendant engaged in the proscribed conduct because he was coerced to do so by the use or threatened imminent use of unlawful physical force upon him or a third person, which force or threatened force a person of reasonable firmness in his situation would have been unable to resist.

ALABAMA PENAL CODE, SECTION 13A-3-30 (A)

It is a defense to prosecution that the actor engaged in the proscribed conduct because he was compelled to do so by the threat of imminent death or serious physical injury to himself or another. . . .

(d) The defense provided by this section is unavailable in a prosecution for:
    (1) murder; or
    (2) any killing of another under aggravated circumstances.

MINNESOTA CRIMINAL CODE, § 609.08 (3)

When any crime is committed or participated in by two or more persons, any one of whom participates only under compulsion by another engaged therein, who by threats creates a reasonable apprehension in the mind of such participator that in case of refusal that participator is liable to instant death, such threats and apprehension constitute duress which will excuse such participator from criminal liability.

INTOXICATION

Johnny James went quietly to his death by lethal injection . . . inside the Texas prison system's Huntsville Unit. His crimes were grisly. He abducted two women, forced them to have sex with each other, and then shot them both in the head. One died, but the other lived to identify him at trial. The Texas courts turned a deaf ear to James's plea that he was too drunk to know what he was doing when he abducted, raped, and shot his victims.

According to Professor George Fletcher (1978), the defense of intoxication is "buffeted between two conflicting principles":

1. *Accountability* Those who get drunk should take the consequences of their actions. Someone who gets drunk is liable for the violent consequences.

2. *Culpability* Criminal liability and punishment depend on blameworthiness. (846) The common-law approach focused on the first principle:

   As to artificial, voluntarily contracted madness, by drunkenness or intoxication, which, depriving men of their reason, puts them in a temporary frenzy; our law looks upon this as an aggravation of the offense, rather than as an excuse for any criminal misbehavior. (Blackstone 1769, 25–26)

The Johnny James case is only one dramatic example that the common-law principle is alive and well today. John Gibeaut, who wrote about the James case in the article "Sobering Thoughts" (Gibeaut 1997), notes the contemporary emphasis on accountability in the subtitle: "Legislatures and courts increasingly are just saying no to intoxication as a defense or mitigating factor." Section § 13-03 of the Arizona Criminal Code (2003) is a typical accountability statute:

   Temporary intoxication resulting from the voluntary ingestion, consumption, inhalation or injection of alcohol, an illegal substance under chapter 34 of this title or other psychoactive substances or the abuse of prescribed medications does not constitute insanity and is not a defense for any criminal act or requisite state of mind.

Between November 1996 and May 1997, at least ten states introduced bills similar to the Arizona statute. According to a member of the Prosecution Function Committee of the American Bar Association's Criminal Justice Section, "The fight goes back to the ancient struggle over just how much free will one has" (Gibeaut 1997, 57).

What we have said so far applies only to *voluntary* intoxication. Involuntary intoxication is an excuse to criminal liability in all states. Involuntary intoxication includes cases in which defendants don't know they are taking intoxicants or know but are forced to take them. In *People v. Penman* (1915), a man took what his friend told him were "breath perfumer" pills; in fact, they were cocaine tablets. While under their influence, he killed someone. The court allowed the defense of intoxication.

Involuntary intoxication applies only under extreme conditions. According to one authority (Hall 1960), "a person would need to be bound hand and foot and the liquor literally poured down his throat, or . . . would have to be threatened with immediate serious injury" (540). In another case, *Burrows. v. State* (1931), where the defendant claimed involuntary intoxication, an 18-year-old man was traveling with an older man across the desert. The older man insisted that the young man drink some whiskey with him.

When he said no, the older man got abusive. Afraid that the older man would throw him out of the car in the middle of the desert without any money, he drank the whiskey, got drunk, and killed the older man. The court rejected his defense of involuntary intoxication, because the older man had not compelled the youth "to drink against his will and consent."

The reason the law excuses involuntary intoxication and not voluntary intoxication is that we can blame voluntarily intoxicated persons and hold them accountable for their actions. Why? They chose to put themselves in a state where they either didn't know or couldn't control what they were doing.

We can't blame involuntarily intoxicated persons for their actions. Why not? Because people forced or tricked into an intoxicated state didn't choose to put themselves out of control. (Review Chapter 3 where we discussed voluntarily induced involuntary conditions or acts qualifying as *actus reus*.)

Alcohol isn't the only intoxicant covered by the defense of intoxication. In most states, it includes all "substances" that disturb mental and physical capacities. In *State v. Hall* (1974), Hall's friend gave him a pill, telling him it was only a "little sunshine" to make him feel "groovy." In fact, the pill contained LSD (lysergic acid diethylamide). A car picked up Hall while he was hitchhiking. The drug caused Hall to hallucinate that the driver was a rabid dog, and, under this sad delusion, Hall shot and killed the driver. The court said that criminal responsibility recognizes no difference between alcohol and other intoxicants.

ENTRAPMENT

Ancient tyrants and modern dictators alike have relied on secret agents as a law enforcement tool. From the days of Henry VIII to the era of Hitler and Stalin, to Slobodan Milosevic and Saddam Hussein in our own time, the world's police states have relied on persuading people to commit crimes, so they could catch and then crush their opponents.

But government persuasion isn't only a dictator's tool. All societies rely on it, even though it violates a basic purpose of government in free societies. The great Victorian British Prime Minister William Gladstone was referring to this purpose when he advised government to make it easy to do right and difficult to do wrong. Persuading people to commit crimes also flies in the face of the entreaty of the Lord's Prayer to "lead us not into temptation, but deliver us from evil" (Carlson 1987).

For a long time, U.S. courts rejected the idea that **entrapment** (government agents getting people to commit crimes they wouldn't otherwise commit) excused criminal liability. In *Board of Commissioners v. Backus* (1864), the New York Supreme Court explained why:

> Even if inducements to commit crime could be assumed to exist in this case, the allegation of the defendant would be but the repetition of the pleas as ancient as the world, and first interposed in Paradise: "The serpent beguiled me and I did eat." That defense was overruled by the great Lawgiver, and whatever estimate we may form, or whatever judgment

pass upon the character or conduct of the tempter, this plea has never since availed to shield crime or give indemnity to the culprit, and it is safe to say that under any code of civilized, not to say Christian ethics, it never will. (42)

The court in *People v. Mills* (1904) summed up the acceptance of entrapment this way:

We are asked to protect the defendant, not because he is innocent, but because a zealous public officer exceeded his powers and held out a bait. The courts do not look to see who held out the bait, but to see who took it. (791)

The earlier attitude was based on indifference to government encouragement to commit crimes. After all, "once the crime is committed, why should it matter what particular incentives were involved and who offered them?" However, attitudes have shifted from indifference to both a "limited sympathy" toward entrapped defendants and a growing intolerance of government inducements to entrap otherwise law-abiding people (Marcus 1986).

The practice of entrapment arose because of the difficulty in enforcing laws against consensual crimes, such as drug offenses, pornography, official wrongdoing, and prostitution. There's no constitutional right not to be entrapped. Entrapment is an affirmative defense created by statutes; that is, defendants have to show some evidence they were entrapped. If they do this, the burden shifts to the prosecution to prove defendants were not entrapped. The jury—or the judge in trials without juries—decides whether officers in fact entrapped defendants. The courts have adopted two types of tests for entrapment; one is subjective and the other objective.

The Subjective Test

The majority of state and all federal courts have adopted a subjective test of entrapment. The **subjective test of entrapment** focuses on the predisposition of defendants to commit crimes. According to the test, the defense has to prove the government pressured the defendants to commit crimes they wouldn't have committed without the pressure.

The crucial question in the subjective test is, "Where did the criminal intent originate?" If it originated with the defendant, then the government didn't entrap the defendant. If it originated with the government, then the government did entrap the defendant.

For example, in a leading U.S. Supreme Court entrapment case, *Sherman v. U.S.* (1958), Kalchinian, a government informant and undercover agent, met Sherman in a drug treatment center. He struck up a friendship with Sherman and eventually asked Sherman to get him some heroin. Sherman (a heroin addict) refused. Following weeks of persistent begging and pleading, Sherman finally gave in and got Kalchinian some heroin. The police arrested Sherman.

The U.S. Supreme Court found that the intent originated with the government. According to the Court, Sherman was hardly predisposed to commit a drug offense given that he was seriously committed to a drug treatment program to cure his addiction.

After defendants present some evidence that the government persuaded them to commit crimes they wouldn't have committed otherwise, the government can prove disposition to commit the crimes in one of the following ways:

1. Defendants' prior convictions for similar offenses

2. Defendants' willingness to commit similar offenses

3. Defendants' display of criminal expertise in carrying out the offense

4. Defendants' readiness to commit the crime

Consensual crimes, especially drug offenses, are the usual target of law enforcement inducement tactics, but some police departments have also used them to combat street muggings. In *Oliver v. State* (1985) and *DePasquale v. State* (1988), the Nevada Supreme Court dealt with two street mugging decoy cases operating in an area of Las Vegas with a high population of "street people."

CASE — *Were They Entrapped?*

Oliver v. State
703 P.2d 869 (Nev. 1985)

HISTORY

Ernest Oliver was convicted of larceny from the person in the Eighth Judicial District Court and sentenced to 10 years in prison. He appealed. The Supreme Court reversed.

GUNDERSON, J.

FACTS

On the night of Oliver's arrest, three policemen undertook to conduct a "decoy operation" near the intersection of Main and Ogden in Las Vegas. That corner is in a downtown area frequented by substantial numbers of persons commonly characterized as "street people," "vagrants," and "derelicts." It appears Oliver, a black man, is one of these.

Disguised as a vagrant in an old Marine Corps jacket, the decoy officer slumped against a palm tree, pretending to be intoxicated and asleep. His associates concealed themselves nearby. The decoy prominently displayed a ten-dollar bill, positioning it to protrude from the left breast pocket of his jacket. This was done, the decoy later testified, "to provide an opportunity for a dishonest person to prove himself." Oliver, who had the misfortune to come walking down the street, saw the decoy and evidently felt moved to assist him. Shaking and nudging the decoy with his foot, Oliver attempted to warn the decoy that the police would arrest him if he did not move on. The decoy did not respond, and Oliver stepped away. Up to this point, Oliver had shown no predisposition whatever to commit any criminal act.

Then, Oliver saw the ten-dollar bill protruding from the decoy's pocket. He reached down and took it. "Thanks, home boy," he said. Thereupon, he was arrested by the decoy and the two other officers. Following the trial, a jury convicted Oliver of larceny from the person, and he has been sentenced to ten years imprisonment.

OPINION

Oliver's counsel contends he was entrapped into committing the offense in question. We agree. . . . Government agents or officers may not employ extraordinary temptations or inducements. They may not manufacture crime.

We have repeatedly endorsed the following concept: Entrapment is the seduction or improper inducement to commit a crime for the purpose of instituting a criminal prosecution, but if a person in good faith and for the purpose of detecting or discovering a crime or offense, furnishes the opportunity for the commission thereof by one who has the requisite criminal intent, it is not entrapment.

Thus, because we discern several facts which we believe combined to create an extraordinary temptation, which was inappropriate to apprehending merely those bent on criminal activity, we feel constrained to reverse Oliver's conviction. We note, first of all, that the decoy portrayed himself as completely susceptible and vulnerable. He did not respond when Oliver attempted to wake him, urging him to avoid arrest by moving to another location. Moreover, the decoy displayed his ten-dollar bill in a manner calculated to tempt any needy person in the area, whether immediately disposed to crime or not.

In the case of Oliver, the police succeeded in tempting a man who apparently did not approach the decoy with larceny in mind, but rather to help him. Even after being lured into petty theft by the decoy's open display of currency and apparent helplessness, Oliver did not go on to search the decoy's pockets or to remove his wallet.

On this record, then, we think the activities of the officers, however well intentioned, accomplished an impermissible entrapment. . . . Through the state's own witnesses at trial, Oliver's counsel established a prima facie showing that Oliver's criminal act was instigated by the state. There was no countervailing evidence whatever. Accordingly, on this record, we must conclude as a matter of law that Oliver was entrapped, and we reverse his conviction.

DePasquale v. State

757 P.2d 367 (1988)

HISTORY

Vincent DePasquale was convicted of larceny from person in the Eighth Judicial District Court, Clark County and sentenced to ten years in prison. He appealed and the Nevada Supreme Court affirmed.

YOUNG, J.

FACTS

Four officers on the LVMPD's S.C.A.T. Unit (Street Crime Attack Team) were performing a decoy operation near the intersection of Fremont Street and Casino Center Blvd. in Las Vegas on April 30, 1983, at 11:45 P.M. Officer Debbie Gautwier was the decoy, and Officers Shalhoob, Young, and Harkness were assigned to "back-up." Officer Gautwier was dressed in plain clothes and was carrying a tan shoulder bag draped over her left shoulder.

Within one of the side, zippered pockets of the bag, she had placed a $5 bill and $1 bill wrapped with a simulated $100 bill. The money, including the numbers of the simulated $100 bill, were exposed so as to be visible to persons near by; however, the zipper was pulled tight against the money so as to require a concentrated effort to remove it.

Officer Young, also in plain clothes, was standing approximately six to seven feet away from Officer Gautwier (the decoy), near the entrance of the Horseshoe Club, when Randall DeBelloy approached Officer Gautwier from behind and asked if he could borrow a pen. Officer Gautwier stated that she did not have a pen, and DeBelloy retreated eight to ten feet. Within a few seconds he approached a second time, asking for a piece of paper. Again the response was "no." During these approaches Officer Young observed DeBelloy reach around Officer Gautwier toward the exposed cash.

DeBelloy again retreated eight to ten feet from Officer Gautwier. He then motioned with his hand to two men who were another eight to ten feet away, and the trio huddled together for 15 to 30 seconds. As DeBelloy talked with the two men, he looked up and over in the direction of Officer Gautwier. Vincent DePasquale was one of the two men who joined DeBelloy in this huddle.

While this trio was conversing, Officer Gautwier had been waiting for the walk signal at the intersection. When the light changed, she crossed Fremont Street and proceeded southbound on the west sidewalk of Casino Center Blvd. DePasquale and DeBelloy followed her, 15 to 20 feet behind. After crossing the street, Officer Gautwier looked back briefly and saw DeBelloy following her.

DePasquale was four to seven feet behind DeBelloy and to his right.

As they walked in this formation, DePasquale yelled out, "Wait lady, can I talk to you for a minute." As Officer Gautwier turned to her right in response—seeing DePasquale whom she identified in court—DeBelloy took a few quick steps to her left side, took the money with his right hand and ran.

DeBelloy was arrested, with the marked money in his possession, by Officers Harkness and Shalhoob. DePasquale was arrested by Officers Gautwier and Young. Both were charged with larceny from the person and convicted by a jury.

OPINION

DePasquale argues that he was entrapped, that the district court erred in its instruction to the jury on the law of entrapment, that the evidence fails to support the verdict, and that the sentence of ten years is disproportionate and, therefore, cruel and unusual.

Upon these facts, the decoy simply provided the opportunity to commit a crime to anyone who succumbed to the lure of the bait. . . . Entrapment encompasses two elements:

(1) an opportunity to commit a crime is presented by the state

(2) to a person not predisposed to commit the act.

Thus, this subjective approach focuses upon the defendant's predisposition to commit the crime. . . . [In the] present case, the cash, although exposed, was zipped tightly to the edge of a zippered pocket, not hanging temptingly from the pocket of an unconscious derelict. Admittedly, the money was exposed; however, that attraction alone fails to cast a pall over the defendant's predisposition. The exposed valuables (money) were presented in a realistic situation, an alert and well-dressed woman walking on the open sidewalks in the casino area.

The fact that the money was exposed simply presented a generally identified social predator with a logical target. These facts suggest that DePasquale was predisposed to commit this crime. Furthermore, the fact that DePasquale had no contact with the decoy but rather succumbed to the apparent temptation of his co-defendant to systematically stalk their target, evidences his predisposition. . . .

Lastly, DePasquale complains that his sentence was disproportionate to the crime and, therefore, cruel and unusual punishment. . . . A sentence is unconstitutional if it is so disproportionate to the crime for which it is inflicted that it shocks the conscience and offends fundamental notions of human dignity. . . . While the punishment authorized in Nevada is strict, it is not cruel and unusual. . . .

Accordingly, we AFFIRM the judgment of conviction.

Questions

1. State the test for entrapment according to Nevada law.

2. What facts led the court to conclude that Oliver was entrapped but DePasquale wasn't?

EXPLORING FURTHER

Entrapment

1. Was the Use of a Sexual Relationship Entrapment?

U.S. v. Simpson, 813 F.2d 1462 (CA9 1987)

FACTS Miller, an undercover agent for the FBI, acting on instruction by the FBI, pretended to be a close personal friend of Simpson's for a period of over five months. During that time, Miller had sex with him on a regular basis. After developing the relationship, she asked Simpson to sell drugs to some "friends" who, unknown to Simpson, were also FBI agents. Was the target entrapped?

DECISION No, said the Ninth Circuit Court of Appeals:

Simpson argues that Miller's use of sex to deceive him into believing she was an intimate friend just so she could lure him into selling heroin to undercover FBI agents constituted an outrageous invasion of his constitutionally protected realms of privacy and autonomy. Although we do not necessarily condone this investigatory tactic, we hold that the government's conduct was not so shocking as to violate the due process clause. (1465)

 Go to the Criminal Law 9e website to find the full text of the Exploring Further excerpts: www.thomsonedu.com/criminaljustice/samaha. (Excerpts on entrapment.)

The Objective Test

A minority of courts follow an **objective test of entrapment.** The objective test focuses not on the predisposition of defendants but instead on the actions that government agents take to induce individuals to commit crimes. According to the objective test, if the intent originates with the government and their actions would tempt an "ordinarily law-abiding" person to commit the crime, the court should dismiss the case even if the defendant was predisposed to commit the crime. This test is a prophylactic rule aimed to deter "unsavory police methods" (ALI 1985 1:2, 406–7).

SYNDROMES

Since the 1970s, a range of syndromes, describing affected mental states, has led to novel defenses in criminal law. *Webster* defines a **syndrome** as "a group of symptoms or signs typical of a disease, disturbance, or condition." Law professor and famous defense attorney Alan Dershowitz (1994) has written a book about these novel defenses. Its title, *The Abuse Excuse and Other Cop-Outs, Sob Stories, and Evasions of Responsibility,* makes clear his opinion of them.

Dershowitz's book includes discussions of the policeman's love, fear, chronic brain, and holocaust syndromes. He worries these excuses are "quickly becoming a license to kill and maim" (3). His is probably a needless worry because defendants rarely plead these excuses, and, except for a few notorious cases picked up by television, the newspapers, and the Internet, defendants rarely succeed when they do plead syndromes and other "abuse excuses."

Some syndromes are (and should be) taken seriously as excuses. For example, some women have claimed the battered woman syndrome to justify killing spouses in self-defense, even though they weren't in imminent danger (Chapter 7). Occasionally, women also have used the premenstrual syndrome (PMS) to excuse their crimes. In a New York case, Shirley Santos called the police, telling them, "My little girl is sick." The medical team in the hospital emergency room diagnosed the welts on her little girl's legs and the blood in her urine as the results of child abuse. The police arrested Santos, who explained, "I don't remember what happened. . . . I would never hurt my baby. . . . I just got my period" (Press and Clausen 1982, 111).

At a preliminary hearing, Santos asserted PMS as a complete defense to assault and endangering the welfare of a child, both felonies. She admitted beating her child but argued that she had blacked out because of PMS; hence, she couldn't have formed the intent to assault or endanger her child's welfare. After lengthy plea bargaining, the prosecutor dropped the felony charges, and Santos pleaded guilty to the misdemeanor of harassment. She received no sentence, not even probation or a fine, even though her daughter spent 2 weeks in the hospital from the injuries. The plea bargaining prevented a legal test of the PMS defense in this case. Nevertheless, the judge's leniency suggests that PMS affected the outcome informally.

There are three obstacles to proving the PMS defense (Carney and Williams 1983):

1. Defendants have to prove that PMS is a disease; little medical research exists to prove that it is.

2. The defendant has to suffer from PMS; rarely do medical records document the condition.

3. The PMS has to cause the mental impairment that excuses the conduct; too much skepticism still surrounds PMS to expect ready acceptance that it excuses criminal conduct.

The Vietnam War led to another syndrome defense, post–traumatic stress syndrome (PTS). Many of the war's combat soldiers suffered emotional and mental casualties that were often more lasting and serious than their physical wounds. PTS is another defense that can be treated either as a failure to prove the mental element, so there's no criminal conduct at all, or as an affirmative excuse defense ("What I did was wrong, but I'm not responsible because my PTS made me do it.")

In *State v. Phipps* (1994), when a Gulf War veteran killed his wife's boyfriend, the Tennessee Court of Criminal Appeals ruled that PTS could negate premeditation and purpose to kill.

CASE | *Is Post–Traumatic Stress Syndrome an Excuse?*

State v. Phipps
883 S.W.2d 138 (Tenn.App. 1994)

HISTORY

David Phipps, Defendant, was convicted of first-degree murder of his wife's boyfriend following a trial in the Circuit Court, Henry County. Defendant appealed. The Court of Criminal Appeals reversed and remanded for new trial.

WHITE, J.

FACTS

In the fall of 1990, the appellant, David Phipps, a career soldier, was sent to Saudi Arabia as part of the forces in Desert Shield and Desert Storm. His military occupational specialty was that of a nuclear-chemical/biological-chemical warfare coordinator with an emphasis on decontamination. He was responsible for providing appropriate chemical measures and counter-measures and served in a front line unit that was one of the first to enter Iraq. Appellant received a bronze star for his exemplary service in Desert Storm.

Within a month of appellant's return to the States, his wife informed him that she had been living with Michael Presson while he was overseas and that she wanted a divorce. She then moved her possessions out of their home. Marcie Phipps continued to communicate with appellant, visited him occasionally to discuss financial matters, shared meals, and had sexual relations with him. Appellant accompanied her to a trial in which she was a plaintiff. Appellant implored her to move back home, but she refused. Approximately a week after his wife left him, appellant attempted suicide.

At approximately 4:45 A.M. on June 1st, several of the victim's neighbors were awakened by the sounds of a struggle. The neighbors heard cries for help, grunting, and moaning. In the dark, one neighbor saw "something" being dragged across the yard to a vehicle. In response to a disturbance call at 4:51 A.M., Officer Damon Lowe, a Henry County deputy sheriff, went to the scene. He found a white Oldsmobile Cutlass parked in the driveway and a white male, the appellant, sitting on the driver's side. The keys were in the ignition. The victim, who was still alive, was lying on the back seat of the car. He appeared to have been brutally and savagely beaten.

When the deputy found appellant in the car, his pants, shirt, and shoes were covered with blood, he was sweating profusely, and he appeared to be very exhausted. He was wearing a knife in a sheath. At first, the appellant said that as he was driving down the road he saw a fight and had stopped to take the injured man to the emergency room. A few minutes later, he told the officer that he thought the man's name was David Presson and that his wife had been living with Presson.

The appellant did not deny beating Presson to death. He testified that he went to the house to wait for his wife to return from work in the hope that he could convince her to leave Presson and come back to him. However, at some point, he approached the house carrying the knapsack. According to the appellant, Presson was watching television. The appellant knocked on the screen door and entered. Presson jumped up, threw a glass at the appellant, and ran out a side door.

Presson went to his car and Phipps thought he was going to leave. However, Presson returned to the house with a stick in his hand. Presson told Phipps that Marcie was no longer his and to leave. According to Phipps, Presson threatened him with the stick. Phipps grabbed the stick and a struggle ensued. Although Phipps said that he had no clear memory of the events that followed, he had no doubt that he struck many blows to the body and head of Presson. He remembered moving the body and being in the car with the body.

On cross-examination, Richard Hixson testified that two weeks before the murder, he, the appellant and a third party had discussed a murder in which the body was hidden in the woods and burned.

Four experts testified as to the appellant's mental state. Dr. Samuel Craddock and Dr. Jackson B. White testified for the state and Dr. William D. Kenner and Dr. Patricia

Auble testified for the appellant. All four experts agreed that David Phipps was competent to stand trial and that he was not legally insane at the time of the murder. However, all four experts also agreed that the appellant was suffering from major depression and post–traumatic stress syndrome.

The appellant testified to his experiences during Operation Desert Storm which included his killing a young Iraqi soldier outside the camp and the suicide of an officer. Soldiers who served with the defendant testified to the constant tension created by being on the front line and the anxiety caused by Iraqi Scud attacks. They also recounted two incidents in which the appellant had behaved in an unusual manner. In addition to failing to report to his superiors the incident with the young Iraqi, appellant threw his gun into the sand when ordered to remain in Iraq after the rest of his unit moved out. Witnesses viewed those actions as totally out of character for the appellant who was considered an outstanding soldier with an exemplary military record.

Dr. Craddock testified that appellant's depression was "of a sufficient level to significantly affect his thinking, reasoning, judgment, and emotional well-being," and that the "components of his post–traumatic stress disorder may have lessened his threshold or made him more sensitive to defending himself and protecting himself and increased the likelihood of him over-reacting to a real or perceived threat." Dr. White, the other state expert, agreed that appellant's anxiety was sufficient to significantly affect his thinking and reasoning.

Dr. Kenner, testifying for the defense, stated that while the defendant was not insane, he was unable to make a calculated decision to murder someone. While Dr. Auble, a psychologist, expressed no opinion on appellant's ability to formulate intent, she agreed with the other three experts that the appellant was suffering from major depression, severe anxiety, and post–traumatic stress syndrome.

All experts expressed the opinion that the appellant was truthful and that he was not dissembling or faking any symptoms.

OPINION

. . . At trial, the appellant did not deny committing the murder, nor did he plead insanity. His theory of defense was that at the time of the killing he could not and did not formulate the specific intent required to commit first-degree murder.

After giving . . . instructions on the elements of first-degree murder, including premeditation and deliberation, second-degree murder, and voluntary manslaughter, [the court] issued the following instruction:

> The defendant contends that he was suffering from mental conditions known as post traumatic stress disorder, and major depression at the time of the commission of the criminal offense giving rise to this case.

I charge you that post traumatic stress disorder and major depression are not defenses to a criminal charge. Insanity may be a defense, however, the defendant makes no claim that he was insane at the time of the killing giving rise to this case.

. . . The essence of appellant's defense was that at the time of the killing he lacked the requisite mental state for first-degree murder. In support of that defense he offered expert and lay testimony which, without contradiction, indicated that he was suffering from post–traumatic stress syndrome and major depression. The court instructed the jury that the evidence offered did not constitute a defense and refused to instruct the jury, as appellant requested, that the evidence could be considered on the issue of proof of requisite mental state.

. . . Appellant contends that the jury instruction given by the trial court which stated that post–traumatic stress syndrome and major depression were not defenses to a criminal offense in effect precluded the jury from considering the expert testimony relating to his mental state on the element of intent. We agree.

. . . Although the trial court correctly instructed the jury on the elements of first-degree murder, second-degree murder, and voluntary manslaughter, the comment on the nonexistence of the "defense" of post–traumatic stress disorder did not clearly reflect the state of the law in Tennessee. Moreover, it suggested that the evidence was impertinent. As such it served to exclude from jury consideration defendant's theory of the case.

Appellant did not rely on an insanity defense or on any affirmative defense. The cornerstone of appellant's case was that he did not have the requisite intent to commit first-degree murder. Virtually all of his testimony was directed toward negating the specific intent element of first-degree murder. While those schooled in the law may be able to discern the difference between considering expert testimony on defendant's mental condition as a complete defense to the charge and considering it to determine whether the requisite mental state has been proved, that subtlety would be lost on most jurors absent clear instructions.

DISSENT

CORNELIUS, SJ.

In my opinion the direct evidence overwhelmingly established a most brutal and atrocious homicide. The evidence points unerringly to this having been an intentional, deliberately premeditated killing of another human being.

Questions

1. State the exact rule the court adopted regarding post–traumatic stress syndrome.

2. Summarize the court's arguments for admitting evidence of post–traumatic stress syndrome.

3. List all the evidence supporting the claim that David Phipps suffered from post–traumatic stress syndrome.

4. Assume you're the prosecutor, and argue Phipps had the specific intent to kill his wife's boyfriend.

5. Assume you're the defense attorney, and argue Phipps didn't have the specific intent to kill his wife's boyfriend.

6. Now, assume you're a juror. Would you vote to convict or acquit? Defend your answer.

SUMMARY

I. Insanity

   A. The public badly misunderstands the way the insanity defense actually works.

   B. Insanity is a legal concept, and it excuses criminal liability only when it seriously damages the person's capacity to act and/or reason and understand.

   C. Few defendants plead the insanity defense, and those that do hardly ever succeed.

   D. If defendants are still insane after committing their crime, they are locked up in maximum-security prisons called "hospitals."

   E. There are four tests of insanity:

      1. The right-wrong test (*M'Naghten* rule)

         a. The right-wrong test depends on defendants' mental capacity to know right from wrong.

b. The test requires that two elements be met:
(1) The defendant had a mental disease or defect at the time of the crime.
(2) The disease or defect caused the defendant not to know either the nature and the quality of his or her actions or that what he or she was doing was wrong.

2. Volitional incapacity test (irresistible impulse): According to the irresistible impulse test, even if defendants know what they're doing and know it's wrong, they can qualify for a verdict of not guilty by reason of insanity if they suffer from a mental disease that damages their willpower (volition).

3. Substantial capacity test (MPC)
a. In the substantial capacity test, defendants have to lack substantial, not complete, mental capacity.
b. The substantial capacity test emphasizes both of the qualities in insanity that affect culpability: reason and will.
c. The MPC's definition of *mental disease or defect* excludes psychopathic personalities, habitual criminals, and antisocial personalities from the insanity defense

4. Product-of-mental-illness test (*Durham* rule)
a. According to the *Durham* rule, acts that are the "products" of mental disease or defect excuse criminal liability.
b. Following John Hinckley's successful insanity defense for the attempt to assassinate President Reagan, legislators did away with the product test.
c. Many critics say that the product-of-mental-illness test misses the point of mental illness in the defense of insanity.

F. Burden of proof
1. States vary as to who has to prove insanity and how convincingly they have to do so.
2. The federal Comprehensive Crime Control Act shifted the burden of proof from the government having to prove sanity beyond a reasonable doubt to defendants having to prove they were insane by clear and convincing evidence.

II. Diminished Capacity
A. Diminished capacity is an attempt to prove the defendant is guilty of a lesser crime by negating specific intent.
B. Diminished capacity isn't the same as diminished responsibility.
C. Diminished capacity and diminished responsibility only apply to homicide.

III. Age
A. The common law divided children into three categories for the purpose of determining their capacity to commit crimes:
1. *Under 7* Children had no criminal capacity.
2. *Ages 7–14* Children were presumed to have no criminal capacity, but the presumption could be overcome.
3. *Over 14* Children had the same capacity as adults.
B. Today, statutes decide when young people can be convicted of crimes.
1. One type of statute identifies a specific age, usually 14, but sometimes as young as 10 and as old as 18.
2. Another type of statute grants exclusive jurisdiction to juvenile courts up to a certain age but makes exceptions for a list of serious crimes.

3. A third type of statute simply states that juvenile court jurisdiction isn't exclusive.
C. Waivers from a juvenile court to adult criminal court come in three varieties:
1. Judicial
2. Prosecutorial
3. Legislative
D. Grounds for waivers include:
1. The seriousness of the offense
2. Whether the offense was committed in an aggressive, violent, premeditated, willful manner
3. Whether the offense was against a person
4. The amount of evidence against the juvenile
5. The sophistication and maturity of the juvenile
6. The prior record of the juvenile
7. The threat the juvenile poses to public safety

IV. Duress
A. The debate on whether to excuse people who harm innocent people to save themselves because they are forced to commit a crime is the heart of duress.
B. There are four elements in the defense of duress, which vary from state to state:
1. *Threats amounting to duress* Death threats are required in some states, whereas threats of serious bodily injury qualify in other states.
2. *Immediacy of the threats* Some states require that the harm has to be instant, whereas other states require that the harm has to be imminent.
3. *Crimes the defense applies to* In most states, duress isn't a defense to murder, whereas in other states it's a defense to all crimes.
C. *The degree of belief regarding the threat* Most states require a reasonable belief the threat is real, whereas others demand the threat actually be real.

V. Intoxication
A. The defense of intoxication is stuck between two conflicting principles:
1. *Accountability* Those who get drunk should take the consequences of their actions.
2. *Culpability* Criminal liability and punishment depend on blameworthiness.
B. The defense of intoxication only applies to involuntary intoxication and only under extreme conditions.
C. Alcohol is not the only intoxicant covered by the defense of intoxication; it includes all "substances" that disturb mental and physical capacities.

VI. Entrapment
A. All societies rely on entrapment, even though it violates a basic purpose of government in free societies.
B. The modern practice of entrapment arose because of the difficulty in enforcing laws against drug offenses, pornography, official wrongdoing, and prostitution.
C. Entrapment is an affirmative defense, and defendants have to show that they were entrapped.
D. The courts have adopted two types of tests for entrapment:
1. The majority of state and federal courts have adopted a subjective test of entrapment. According to the subjective test, the defense has to prove the

government pressured the defendants to commit crimes they wouldn't have committed without pressure.

    2. The objective test focuses not on the predisposition of the defendants but on the actions that government agents take to induce individuals to commit crimes.

VII. Syndromes

    A. Despite being seen as an excuse to kill or maim, some syndromes are and should be taken seriously.

    B. Syndromes include:

        1. Battered woman syndrome

        2. Premenstrual syndrome

        3. Post–traumatic stress syndrome

REVIEW QUESTIONS

1. Explain the difference between the defenses of justification and excuses.

2. Explain why "insanity" is a legal concept and not a medical term.

3. When does insanity excuse criminal liability?

4. Explain the verdict "guilty but mentally ill."

5. State the success rate of those who actually plead insanity.

6. Identify the four tests of the insanity defense, and contrast the meaning of mental capacity in each.

7. State, describe, and give an example of the two elements of the right-wrong test.

8. Define the following terms in the right-wrong test: *mental disease, mental defect, know,* and *wrong.*

9. What do critics say about the irresistible impulse test?

10. State, explain, and give an example of the elements of the substantial capacity test.

11. Why did the product-of-mental-illness test never take a strong hold in criminal courts?

12. Explain the history behind who has the burden of proving insanity. What are current-day trends?

13. Explain the difference between *diminished capacity* and *diminished responsibility.* To what types of crimes does each term apply?

14. Identify the three categories of age the common law applied to divide children's levels of culpability.

15. Identify seven criteria judges use to waive a judicial proceeding into adult criminal court.

16. Identify the positions taken on duress by three of the last two centuries' great authorities on criminal law.

17. Identify and explain the four elements of duress and how they differ from state to state.

18. Explain both types of intoxication and when it's an excuse to criminal liability.

19. Identify and explain the two tests courts use to determine if someone was entrapped.

20. Define *syndromes* and their importance in excuses to criminal liability.

21. Identify three types of syndromes.

22. What are three obstacles to proving premenstrual syndrome (PMS) defense?

KEY TERMS

failure-of-proof theory, p. 174
insanity, p. 175
civil commitment, p. 175
right-wrong test (*M'Naghten* rule), p. 177
irresistible impulse test, p. 181

substantial capacity test, p. 182
product-of-mental-illness test, p. 186
diminished capacity, p. 187
diminished responsibility, p. 187
judicial waiver, p. 189

defense of duress, p. 191
entrapment, p. 194
subjective test of entrapment, p. 195
objective test of entrapment, p. 198
syndrome, p. 198

Parties to Crime and Vicarious Liability

MAIN POINTS

- Participants before and during the commission of crimes are guilty of the crime itself.
- Participants after the commission of crimes are guilty of a separate, less serious offense.
- The core idea of accessory liability is that it's not as blameworthy to help someone else escape prosecution and punishment as it is to participate in the crime itself.
- Vicarious liability has to be created by statute.
- Vicarious liability can apply either to enterprises (mainly business) or to individuals.

The Scream 1893, by Edvard Munch 1863–1944 Norwegian. Tempera and pastel on board. National Gallery, Oslo, Norway. ©2007 The Munch Museum/The Munch-Ellingsen Group/Artists Rights Society (ARS) New York.

7

A Norwegian court sentenced three men to between four and eight years in prison for their role in the theft of Edvard Munch's iconic masterpiece, The Scream. After a six-week trial, Björn Hoen, 37, was found guilty of planning the robbery and sentenced to seven years in prison. His accomplices fared similarly: Petter Tharaldsen, 34, who drove the getaway car, was jailed for eight years, and Petter Rosenvinge, 38, was sentenced to four years.

Was the Fraternity Guilty of Prostitution and Selling Alcohol to Minors?

Zeta Chi fraternity, a New Hampshire corporation at the University of New Hampshire in Durham, held a "rush" at its fraternity houses. In order to encourage people to attend the rush, Zeta Chi hired two female strippers to perform at the event. Fraternity brothers encouraged guests to give the strippers dollar bills so that they would continue to perform. Andrew Strachan, a nineteen-year-old guest at the fraternity party, at some point during the evening, learned that beer was available from a soda machine. He made his way to an apartment in another part of the fraternity house where the machine was located, waited in line with three or four other people, and purchased three to five cans of beer.

(STATE V. ZETA CHI FRATERNITY 1997)

The principle of *actus reus* stands on the fundamental idea that we punish people for what they do, not for who they are. The principle of *mens rea* stands on the fundamental idea that we can only punish people we can blame. This chapter affirms another basic idea of our criminal law: that one person can be liable for someone else's crimes. This liability arises in two ways:

1. When an actor is liable for someone else's *conduct* (**complicity**)
2. When the *relationship* between two parties makes one party criminally liable for another party's conduct (**vicarious liability**)

In this chapter, we'll look more closely at parties to crimes and vicarious liability.

PARTIES TO CRIME

"Two heads are better than one." "The whole is greater than the sum of its parts." These popular sayings express the positive side of teamwork, an ordinary phenomenon under ordinary circumstances. When, under extraordinary circumstances, teamwork turns malicious, then "teamwork" can become "complicity" in criminal law. A group of young men playing football generates no criminal liability; a gang rape—teamwork turned malicious—is aggravated rape. *Complicity* establishes when you can be criminally liable for someone else's conduct. It applies criminal liability to accomplices and accessories because they *participate* in crimes.

Vicarious liability establishes when a party can be criminally liable because of a relationship. Vicarious liability transfers the criminal conduct of one party to another because of their *relationship*. By far the most common relationships are business relationships, such as employer-employee, corporation-manager, buyer-seller, producer-consumer, and service provider–recipient. But vicarious liability can also arise in other situations, such as making the owner of a car liable for the driver's traffic violations and holding parents liable for their children's crimes.

At common law, there were four parties to crime:

1. *Principals in the first degree* Persons who actually commit the crime
2. *Principals in the second degree* Persons present when the crime is committed and who help commit it (lookouts and getaway drivers)
3. *Accessories before the fact* Persons not present when the crimes are committed but who help before the crime is committed (for example, someone who provided a weapon used in a murder)
4. *Accessories after the fact* Persons who help after the crime is committed (harboring a fugitive)

These distinctions used to be important because of the common-law rule that the government couldn't try accomplices until principals in the first degree were convicted. This ban on trying accomplices before these principals were convicted applied even if there was absolute proof of guilt. Why? Probably because, during that time, all felonies were capital offenses. But as the number of capital crimes shrank, so did the need for the complicated law of principals and accessories.

Today, there are two parties to crime:

1. **Accomplices** Participants before and during the commission of crimes
2. **Accessories** Participants after crimes are committed

Participation before and during the Commission of a Crime

All participants before and during the commission of a crime (accomplices) are prosecuted for the crime itself (accomplices to murder are prosecuted as murderers). So participation before and during a crime (accomplice liability) is a very serious business, because the punishment for being an accomplice is the same as for the person who actually committed the crime. Participation after crimes are committed (accessory liability) is prosecuted as a separate, minor offense (accessory to murder). Accessories are punished for misdemeanors, a much less serious offense because accessories are looked at as obstructors of justice, not as felons.

We need to clear up a problem before we get further into accomplice liability. Accomplices are often confused with co-conspirators (Chapter 8), because both accomplice and conspiracy cases have more than one participant, but they're two completely different crimes. *Conspiracy* is an agreement to commit some other crime. A conspiracy to commit murder is not murder; it's the lesser offense of agreeing to commit murder (Chapter 8). Participating in a murder is the crime of murder itself. For example, two people agree to commit a murder. At this point, they've committed conspiracy to murder. Now they go to a gun shop, buy a gun, and drive together to the victim's house. One acts as a lookout while the other shoots the victim, who dies instantly. They drive away together. They're both murderers. They've committed two separate crimes—the less serious crime of conspiracy to commit murder and the crime of murder.

The rule that the crime of conspiracy and the crime the conspirators agree to commit are separate offenses is called the ***Pinkerton* rule.** The name comes from a leading U.S. Supreme Court case, *Pinkerton v. U.S* (1946). The two Pinkerton brothers conspired to evade taxes. They were found guilty of both conspiracy to evade taxes and tax evasion itself. According to Justice Douglas, who wrote the opinion for the Court, "It has been long and consistently recognized by the Court that the commission of the . . . offense and a conspiracy to commit it are separate and distinct offenses (643)."

Accomplice Actus Reus   You'll usually see words borrowed from the old common law of principals and accessories to define accomplice *actus reus* in modern accomplice statutes. The use of words such as *aid, abet, assist, counsel, procure, hire,* or *induce* is widespread.

The meaning of these words boils down to this core idea: The actor took "some positive act in aid of the commission of the offense." How much aid is enough? It's not always easy to decide, but here are a few acts that definitely qualify:

- Providing guns, supplies, or other instruments of crime
- Serving as a lookout
- Driving a getaway car
- Sending the victim to the principal
- Preventing warnings from getting to the victim (ALI 1953, 43)

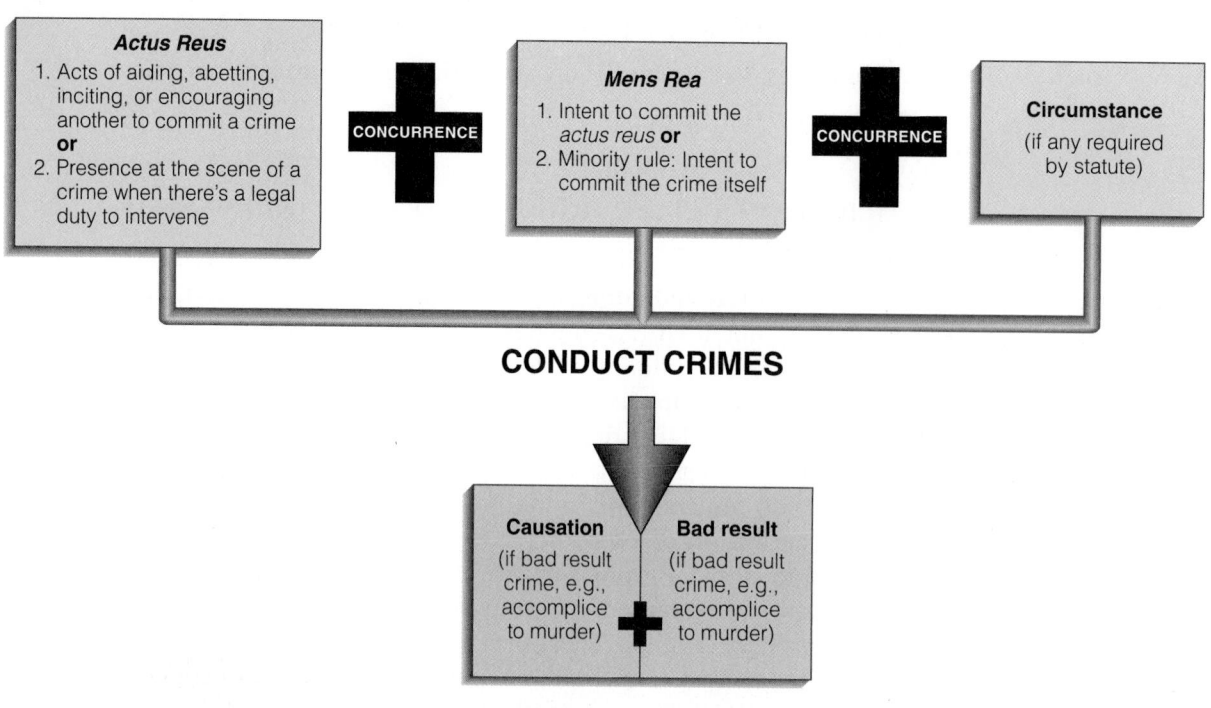

Elements of Accomplice

Words are also acts that can amount to accomplice *actus reus* if they encourage and approve the commission of the crime.

Mere presence at the scene of a crime isn't enough to satisfy the accomplice *actus reus* requirement. According to the **mere presence rule,** even presence at the scene of a crime followed by flight is not enough action to satisfy the *actus reus* requirement of accomplice liability. For example, in *Bailey v. U.S.* (1969), Bailey spent most of the afternoon shooting craps with another man. Then, when a man carrying cash walked by, Bailey's craps partner pulled a gun and robbed the man with the cash. Both Bailey and the other man fled the scene. Bailey was caught; the other man never was. The court held that although flight from the scene of a crime can be taken into account, it's not enough to prove accomplice *actus reus*. According to the court:

> We no longer hold tenable the notion that "the wicked flee when no man pursueth, but the righteous are as bold as a lion." The proposition that "one flees shortly after a criminal act is committed or when he is accused of something does so because he feels some guilt concerning the act" is not absolute as a legal doctrine "since it is a matter of common knowledge that men who are entirely innocent do sometimes fly from the scene of a crime through fear of being apprehended as guilty parties or from an unwillingness to appear as witnesses." (1114)

There's one major exception to the mere presence rule: When defendants have a legal duty to act, presence alone is enough to satisfy the *actus reus* requirement. In *State v. Walden* (1982), George Hoskins beat Aleen Walden's one-year-old son Lamont "repeatedly over an extended period of time," with a leather belt, until he was bloody. Walden "looked on the entire time the beating took place but did not say anything or do anything to stop the 'Bishop' [Hoskins] from beating Lamont or to otherwise deter such conduct (783)."

A jury found Walden guilty as an accomplice to assault. On appeal, the court said that

> the trial court properly allowed the jury . . . to consider a verdict of guilty of assault . . . upon a theory of aiding and abetting, solely on the ground that the defendant was present when her child was brutally beaten. . . . A person who so aids or abets under another in the commission of a crime is equally guilty with that other person as a principal. (787)

One final point about accomplice *actus reus:* Actions taken after crimes are committed aren't themselves accomplice *actus reus*, but juries can use participation after the crime to prove defendants participated before or during the commission of the crime. In the grisly murder case, *State v. Ulvinen* (1981), the Minnesota Supreme Court dealt with these issues in connection with Helen Ulvinen's participation in her son David's murder of his wife Carol:

1. Words of encouragement before and during the commission of the crime

2. Accomplices not present when the crime was committed

3. Inferring participation before and during the commission of the crime from actions to help after the commission of the crime

CASE | *Was She an Accomplice to Murder?*

State v. Ulvinen
313 N.W.2d 425 (Minn. 1981)

HISTORY

Helen Ulvinen was convicted of first-degree murder pursuant to Minn. Stat. § 609.05, subd. 1 (1980), which imposes criminal liability on one who "intentionally aids, advises, hires, counsels, or conspires with or otherwise procures" another to commit a crime. The Minnesota Supreme Court reversed.

OTIS, J.

FACTS

Carol Hoffman, Helen Ulvinen's (appellant's) daughter-in-law, was murdered late on the evening of August 10th or the very early morning of August 11th by her husband, David Hoffman. She and David had spent an amicable evening together playing with their children, and when they went to bed David wanted to make love to his wife.

However, when she refused him he lost his temper and began choking her. While he was choking her, he began to believe he was "doing the right thing" and that to get "the evil out of her" he had to dismember her body.

After his wife was dead, David called down to the basement to wake his mother, asking her to come upstairs to sit on the living room couch. From there she would be able to see the kitchen, bathroom, and bedroom doors and could stop the older child if she awoke and tried to use the bathroom.

Mrs. Ulvinen didn't respond at first but after being called once, possibly twice more, she came upstairs to lie on the couch. In the meantime, David had moved the body to the bathtub. Mrs. Ulvinen was aware that while she was in the living room her son was dismembering the body but she turned her head away so that she could not see.

After dismembering the body and putting it in bags, Hoffman cleaned the bathroom, took the body to Weaver Lake, and disposed of it. On returning home, he told his mother to wash the cloth covers from the bathroom toilet and tank, which she did. David fabricated a story about Carol leaving the house the previous night after an argument, and Helen agreed to corroborate it. David phoned the police with a missing person report and during the ensuing searches and interviews with the police, he and his mother continued to tell the fabricated story.

On August 19, 1980, David confessed to the police that he had murdered his wife. In his statement, he indicated that not only had his mother helped him cover up the crime but she had known of his intent to kill his wife that night. After hearing Hoffman's statement the police arrested Mrs. Ulvinen and questioned her with respect to her part in the cover up [sic]. Police typed up a two-page statement, which she read and signed. The following day a detective questioned her further regarding events surrounding the crime, including her knowledge that it was planned.

Mrs. Ulvinen's relationship with her daughter-in-law had been a strained one. She moved in with the Hoffmans on July 26, two weeks earlier to act as a live-in babysitter for their two children. Carol was unhappy about having her move in and told friends that she hated Helen, but she told both David and his mother that they could try the arrangement to see how it worked.

On the morning of the murder, Helen told her son that she was going to move out of the Hoffman residence because "Carol had been so nasty to me." In his statement to the police, David reported the conversation that morning as follows:

. . . Sunday morning I went downstairs and my mom was in the bedroom reading the newspaper and she had tears in her eyes, and she said in a very frustrated voice, "I've got to find another house." She said, "Carol don't want me here," and she said, "I probably shouldn't have moved in here." And I said then, "Don't let what Carol said hurt you. It's going to take a little more period of readjustment for her." Then, I told mom that I've got to do it tonight so that there can be peace in this house.

Q: What did you tell your mom that you were going to have to do that night?

A: I told my mom I was going to have to put her to sleep.

Q: Dave, will you tell us exactly what you told your mother that morning, to the best of your recollection?

A: I said I'm going to have to choke her tonight, and I'll have to dispose of her body so that it will never be found. That's the best of my knowledge.

Q: What did your mother say when you told her that?

A: She just—she looked at me with very sad eyes and just started to weep. I think she said something like "it will be for the best." David spent the day fishing with a friend of his. When he got home that afternoon he had another conversation with his mother. She told him at that time about a phone conversation Carol had had in which she discussed taking the children and leaving home. David told the police that during the conversation with his mother that afternoon he told her "Mom, tonight's got to be the night."

Q: When you told your mother, "Tonight's got to be the night," did your mother understand that you were going to kill Carol later that evening?

A: She thought I was just kidding her about doing it. She didn't think I could. . . .

Q: Why didn't your mother think that you could do it?

A: . . . Because for some time I had been telling her I was going to take Carol scuba diving and make it look like an accident.

Q: And she said?

A: And she always said, "Oh, you're just kidding me." . . .

Q: But your mother knew you were going to do it that night?

A: I think my mother sensed that I was really going to do it that night.

Q: Why do you think your mother sensed you were really going to do it that night?

A: Because when I came home and she told me what had happened at the house, and I told her, "Tonight's got to be the night," I think she said, again I'm not certain, that "it would be the best for the kids."

OPINION

. . . It is well-settled in this state that presence, companionship, and conduct before and after the offense are circumstances from which a person's participation in the criminal intent may be inferred. The evidence is undisputed that appellant was asleep when her son choked his wife. She took no active part in the dismembering of the body but came upstairs to intercept the children, should they awake, and prevent them from going into the bathroom.

She cooperated with her son by cleaning some items from the bathroom and corroborating David's story to prevent anyone from finding out about the murder. She is insulated by statute from guilt as an accomplice after-the-fact for such conduct because of her relation as a parent of the offender. (See Minn. Stat. § 609.495, subd. 2 (1980).)

The jury might well have considered appellant's conduct in sitting by while her son dismembered his wife so shocking that it deserved punishment. Nonetheless, these subsequent actions do not succeed in transforming her behavior prior to the crime to active instigation and encouragement. Minn.Stat. § 609.05, subd. 1 (1980) implies a high level of activity on the part of an aider and abettor in the form of conduct that encourages another to act. Use of terms such as "aids," "advises," and "conspires" requires something more of a person than mere inaction to impose liability as a principal.

The evidence presented to the jury at best supports a finding that appellant passively acquiesced in her son's plan to kill his wife. The jury might have believed that David told his mother of his intent to kill his wife that night and that she neither actively discouraged him nor told anyone in time to prevent the murder. Her response that "it would be the best for the kids" or "it will be the best" was not, however, active encouragement or instigation. There is no evidence that her remark had any influence on her son's decision to kill his wife.

Minn.Stat. § 609.05, subd. 1 (1980), imposes liability for actions which affect the principal, encouraging him to take a course of action which he might not otherwise have taken. The state has not proved beyond a reasonable doubt that appellant was guilty of anything but passive approval.

However morally reprehensible it may be to fail to warn someone of their impending death, our statutes do not make such an omission a criminal offense. We note that mere knowledge of a contemplated crime or failure to disclose such information without evidence of any further involvement in the crime does not make that person liable as a party to the crime under any state's statutes. . . .

David told many people besides appellant of his intent to kill his wife but no one took him seriously. He told a co-worker, approximately three times a week that he was going to murder his wife, and confided two different plans for doing so. Another co-worker heard him tell his plan to cut Carol's air hose while she was scuba diving, making her death look accidental, but did not believe him. Two or three weeks before the murder, David told a friend of his that he and Carol were having problems and he expected Carol "to have an accident sometime." None of these people has a duty imposed by law, to warn the victim of impending danger, whatever their moral obligation may be. . . .

Her conviction must be reversed.

Questions

1. List all the facts (including words) surrounding Mrs. Ulvinen's behavior before or during the murder that might make her an accomplice.

2. List all the facts after the murder that a jury could infer proved Mrs. Ulvinen participated before or during the murder itself.

3. According to the court, why isn't Mrs. Ulvinen guilty of murder?

4. Do you agree with the court that however morally reprehensible her behavior, she nonetheless was not an accomplice? Defend your answer.

Accomplice Mens Rea

> MY FRIEND STEVE: Lend me your gun.
>
> ME: What for?
>
> STEVE: So I can rob the grocery store.
>
> ME: OK. But only if you give me half the take.

My intent is clear in this scenario (as it is in most complicity cases): My purpose in lending Steve my gun is to help him rob the grocery store, and I definitely want the robbery to succeed. So we can say my mental attitude is "purposely"; I'm acting for the very purposes of (1) helping Steve and (2) committing a robbery. Cases like this scenario don't give courts much trouble. Others do—like *knowingly* helping someone who is going to commit a crime but not for the very purpose of benefiting from the criminal venture, such as in these examples:

- I lease an apartment to someone I know is going to use it for prostitution.

- A gun dealer sells me a gun she knows I'm going to use to shoot someone.

- A telephone company provides service to a customer it knows is going to use it for illegal gambling.

- A farmer leases 200 acres of farmland to a renter he knows is going to grow marijuana for sale. (ALI 1985 I:2, 316)

Early court decisions ruled that knowingly helping someone was enough to prove the mental element required for accomplice liability. In one Fourth Circuit U.S. Court of Appeals case, *Backun v. U.S.* (1940), Max Backun sold silver he knew was stolen to Zucker. But Backun didn't sell the silver for the purpose of sharing any profits with Zucker. Still, according to the court, knowingly selling the stolen property was good enough:

> Guilt . . . depends, not on having a stake in the outcome of crime . . . but on aiding and assisting the perpetrators; and those who make a profit by furnishing to criminals, whether by sale or otherwise, the means to carry on their nefarious undertakings aid them just as truly as if they were actual partners with them, having a stake in the fruits of their enterprise.
>
> To say that the sale of goods is a normally lawful transaction is beside the point. The seller may not ignore the purpose for which the purchase is made if he is advised of that purpose, or wash his hands of the aid that he has given the perpetrator of a felony by the plea that he has merely made a sale of merchandise. One who sells a gun to another

knowing that he is buying it to commit a murder, would hardly escape conviction as an . . . [accomplice] to the murder by showing that he received full price for the gun; and no difference in principle can be drawn between such a case and any other case of a seller who knows that the purchaser intends to use the goods which he is purchasing in the commission of felony. (637)

In another very famous federal case, *U.S. v. Peoni* (1938, 401), decided by the well-known and enormously respected Judge Learned Hand, the outcome was the opposite. Joseph Peoni sold counterfeit money to Dorsey in the Bronx. Dorsey was caught trying to pass the fake money in Brooklyn. Peoni was indicted as an accomplice to Dorsey.

At the trial, the prosecution relied on the words "aids, abets, counsels, commands, induces, or procures" in the U.S. Criminal Code's accomplice statute. The prosecution argued that Peoni knew Dorsey possessed counterfeit money and that knowledge was enough to convict him.

The jury convicted Peoni, but, on appeal, Judge Hand didn't buy the prosecution's argument. According to Judge Hand, if someone were suing Peoni for damages, knowledge would be good enough, but, this was a criminal case, where all the words in the statute

demand that he in some sort associate himself with the venture, that he participate in it as in something that he wishes to bring about, that he seek by his action to make it succeed. All the words used—even the most colorless, "abet"—carry an implication of purposive attitude towards it. (402)

U.S. v. Peoni is cited over and over again as defining the *mens rea* of accomplice liability. If only it were that clear, but it's not. In a 2002 survey of only federal court cases, Assistant U.S. Attorney Baruch Weiss (2002) cited "a few examples" illustrating the confusion:

Is simple knowledge enough? Yes, said the Supreme Court . . . in 1870; no, said Judge Learned Hand in . . . 1938; yes, implied the Supreme Court in 1947; no, said the Supreme Court in 1949; yes, if it is accompanied by an act that substantially facilitates the commission of the underlying offense, said the Supreme Court in 1961; usually, said the Second Circuit in 1962; only if knowledge is enough for the underlying offense, said the Second Circuit in another case in 1962; sometimes, said the Seventh Circuit in 1985; always, implied the Seventh Circuit in 1995; no, said the Second Circuit in 1995 and the Seventh Circuit in 1998. (1351–52)

Further confusion arises because both recklessness and negligence can satisfy the *mens rea* requirement. For example, if participants can predict that aiding and abetting one crime might reasonably lead to another crime, they're guilty of both. The court dealt with this problem in *People v. Poplar* (1970).

CASE · *Did He Have Accomplice* Mens Rea?

People v. Poplar
173 N.W.2d 732 (1970)

HISTORY

Marathon Poplar, the defendant, was charged as an aider and abettor of breaking and entering and of assault with intent to commit murder. He moved for a directed verdict on both charges, claiming that there wasn't enough evidence to submit the case to the jury. The motions were denied. Poplar was found guilty on both counts by a jury in the Circuit Court, Genesee. The Court of Appeals affirmed.

GILLIS, J.

FACTS

Alfred Williams and Clifford Lorrick broke into and entered the Oak Park recreation building in Flint in the early morning of December 3, 1964. When the manager of the building discovered the two men, Williams shot him in the face with a shotgun. Poplar, the defendant, allegedly acted as a lookout. Williams was tried as a codefendant and was convicted, along with this defendant, of breaking and entering and of assault with intent to commit murder.

Lorrick pled guilty to breaking and entering on January 25, 1965, and testified for the prosecution at defendant's trial. He stated that he met defendant and Williams in a bar the night before the breaking and entering and left with them and two others. The five men allegedly drove around for a while before stopping to pick up some tools.

They then took the tools and placed them in back of the bowling alley. An unsuccessful attempt to enter was made at that time. The group continued to drive around and during that time a shotgun that was in the car accidentally discharged, blowing a hole in the windshield. Just before the actual breaking and entering, the defendant, after getting out of the car with Lorrick and Williams, proceeded to a house directly across from the bowling alley. Lorrick testified that defendant went to see if anybody was watching.

Poplar took the stand and testified that he was in no way involved in the plans of Lorrick and Williams. He stated that the purpose of his going to the house across the street was to seek a friend who he thought would help him find employment.

OPINION

. . . It [was not] error for the trial court to deny defendant's motion for directed verdict on the issue of whether defendant (Poplar) aided and abetted in the breaking and entering by acting as a lookout. The circumstances leading up to the offense, coupled with Lorrick's testimony, present sufficient evidence which, if believed by the jury, would support a conviction under the statute.

. . . A more difficult question is whether Poplar may be found guilty, as an aider and abettor, of assault with intent to commit murder. Where a crime requires the existence of a specific intent, an alleged aider and abettor cannot be held as a principal unless he himself possessed the required intent or unless he aided and abetted in the perpetration of the crime knowing that the actual perpetrator had the required intent. . . . It is the knowledge of the wrongful purpose of the actor plus the encouragement provided by the aider and abettor that makes the latter equally guilty. Although the guilt of the aider and abettor is dependent upon the actor's crime, the criminal intent of the aider and abettor is presumed from his actions with knowledge of the actor's wrongful purpose.

There was no evidence that Poplar harbored any intent to commit murder. Therefore, knowledge of the intent of Williams to kill the deceased is a necessary element to constitute Poplar a principal. This, however, may be established either by direct or circumstantial evidence from which knowledge of the intent may be inferred.

A typical case of this kind is one where, as here, a crime not specifically within the common intent and purpose is committed during an escape. Convictions for aiding and abetting such crimes have been carefully scrutinized. . . . Whether the crime committed was fairly within the scope of the common unlawful enterprise is a question of fact for the jury.

In the present case, the evidence tends to show that the gun with which the victim was shot was removed from the trunk of the car to the front seat. It is not clear whether Poplar was present when the gun was moved but he was aware of its presence inside the car. Since the record also fails to reveal whether or not defendant knew that the gun was taken into the bowling alley, the question is whether it was proper for the jury to infer from the circumstantial evidence that the defendant entertained the requisite intent to render him liable as a principal for assault with intent to commit murder.

In our opinion the jury could reasonably infer from the defendant's knowledge of the fact that a shotgun was in the car that he was aware of the fact that his companions might use the gun if they were discovered committing the burglary or in making their escape. If the jury drew that inference, then it could properly conclude that the use of the gun was fairly within the scope of the common unlawful enterprise and that the defendant was criminally responsible for the use by his confederates of the gun in effectuating their escape.

AFFIRMED.

Questions

1. List all of the facts relevant to determining Poplar's mental state.

2. On the basis of these facts, did Poplar intend to kill? Did he do so knowingly? Recklessly? Negligently?

3. According to the Court, what's the *mens rea* required for accomplice liability?

4. In light of Poplar's *mens rea*, does it make sense to hold him criminally liable for breaking and entering and assault with intent to murder? Defend your answer.

EXPLORING FURTHER

Accomplice Mens Rea

1. Did He Have the "Mens Rea" of an Accomplice to Criminal Homicide?

Lewis et al. v. State, 251 S.W.2d 490 (Ark. 1952)

FACTS Harry Wren was driving his friend Steve Lewis's car. On the way from Atkins to Morrilton, they purchased 12 cans of beer and drank a considerable amount of beer and gin from 7 P.M. until immediately before colliding head on with another car. Occupants of both automobiles were seriously injured, and Mrs. Pounds, driver of the other car, died from her injuries 3 days later. Was Lewis guilty of criminal homicide?

DECISION The court said yes:

If the owner of a dangerous instrumentality like an automobile knowingly puts that instrumentality in the immediate control of a careless and reckless driver, sits by his side, and permits him without protest so recklessly and negligently to operate the car as to cause the death of another, he is as much responsible as the man at the wheel.

2. Can He Intend to Commit "Negligent" Homicide?

State v. Foster, 522 A.2d 277 (Conn. 1987)

FACTS Michael Foster believed Bill had raped his girlfriend. Foster beat up Bill. He, then, handed his friend Otha a knife, telling him to keep Bill from leaving until he returned with his girlfriend to verify the rape. After Foster left, Otha got nervous and stabbed Bill, who died from the stab wounds. Was Foster an accomplice to negligent homicide?

DECISION Yes, said the court. Even though Foster didn't intend to kill Bill, he was negligent with respect to the death; he should've foreseen that Otha, armed with a knife, might have stabbed Bill.

 Go to the Criminal Law 9e website for the full text of the Exploring Further excerpts: www.thomsonedu.com/criminaljustice/samaha. (Excerpts on accomplice *mens rea*.)

Participation after the Commission of a Crime

At common law, accessories after the fact were punished like accomplices; that is, they were treated as if they'd committed the crime itself. So if you gave a burglar a place to hide after he'd committed burglary, you were guilty of burglary, too. But accessories aren't really burglars; they don't come on the scene until the burglary is over. That's why they used to be called "accessories after the fact." And (so the thinking goes), it's not as bad to help someone who's already committed a crime as it is to help her commit the crime in the first place.

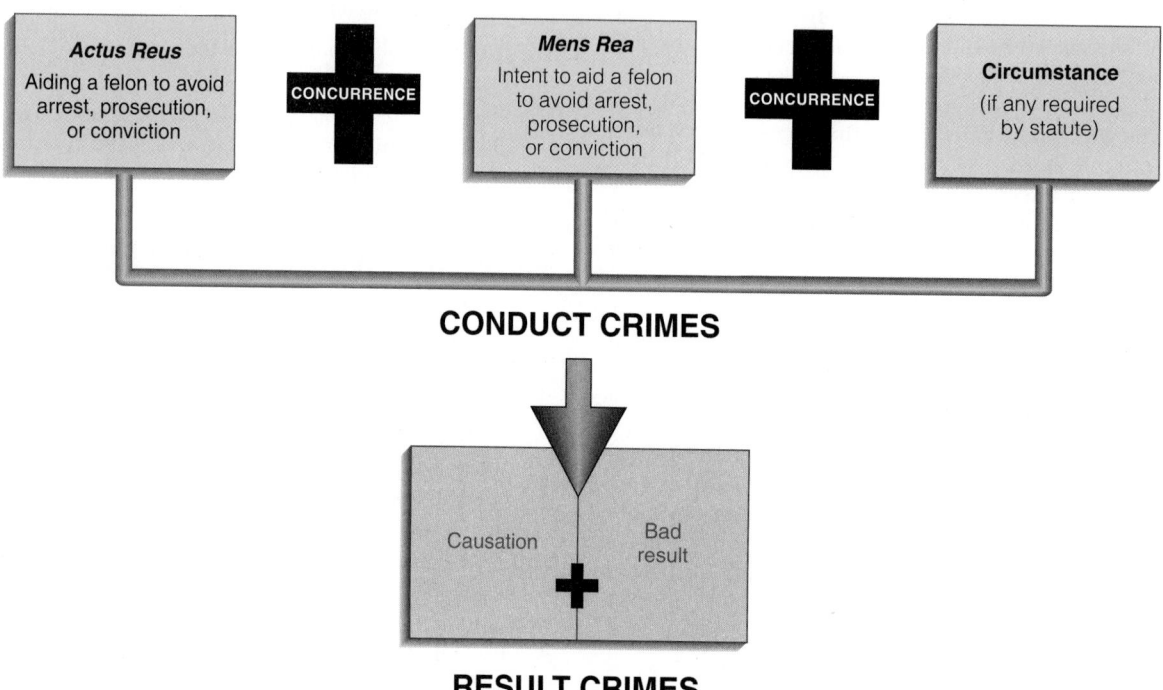

Elements of Accessory-after-the-Fact Liability

Modern statutes have reduced the punishment to fit this less serious offense. Accessory after the fact (now called simply, "accessory") is a separate offense, usually a misdemeanor. Sometimes, it's even got a different name, such as "obstructing justice," "interfering with prosecution," and "aiding in escape."

Most accessory-after-the-fact statutes have four elements, one *actus reus*, two *mens rea*, and one circumstance element:

1. The accessory personally aided the person who committed the crime (the *actus reus* element).

2. The accessory knew the felony was committed (*mens rea* element).

3. The accessory aided the person who committed the crime for the purpose of hindering the prosecution of that person (*mens rea* element).

4. Someone besides the accessory actually committed a felony (the circumstance element).

The Supreme Court of Louisiana dealt with these elements under Louisiana's accessory-after-the-fact statute in the bizarre case of *State v. Chism* (1983).

CASE — *Was He an Accessory after the Fact?*

State v. Chism
436 So.2d 464 (La. 1983)

HISTORY

Brian Chism (Defendant) was convicted before the First Judicial District Court, Caddo Parish, of being an accessory after the fact, and was sentenced to three years in parish prison, with three and one-half years suspended, and defendant appealed. The Louisiana Supreme Court affirmed the conviction, vacated the sentence, and remanded the case for resentencing.

DENNIS, J.

FACTS

On the evening of August 26, 1981 in Shreveport, Tony Duke gave the defendant, Brian Chism, a ride in his automobile. Brian Chism was impersonating a female, and Duke was apparently unaware of Chism's disguise. After a brief visit at a friend's house the two stopped to pick up some beer at the residence of Chism's grandmother.

Chism's one-legged uncle, Ira Lloyd, joined them, and the three continued on their way, drinking as Duke drove the automobile. When Duke expressed a desire to have sexual relations with Chism, Lloyd announced that he wanted to find his ex-wife Gloria for the same purpose. Shortly after midnight, the trio arrived at the St. Vincent Avenue Church of Christ and persuaded Gloria Lloyd to come outside. As Ira Lloyd stood outside the car attempting to persuade Gloria to come with them, Chism and Duke hugged and kissed on the front seat as Duke sat behind the steering wheel.

Gloria and Ira Lloyd got into an argument, and Ira stabbed Gloria with a knife several times in the stomach and once in the neck. Gloria's shouts attracted the attention of two neighbors, who unsuccessfully tried to prevent Ira from pushing Gloria into the front seat of the car alongside Chism and Duke. Ira Lloyd climbed into the front seat also, and Duke drove off. One of the bystanders testified that she could not be sure but she thought she saw Brian's foot on the accelerator as the car left.

Lloyd ordered Duke to drive to Willow Point, near Cross Lake. When they arrived, Chism and Duke, under Lloyd's direction, removed Gloria from the vehicle and placed her on some high grass on the side of the roadway, near a wood line. Ira was unable to help the two because his wooden leg had come off. Afterwards, as Lloyd requested, the two drove off, leaving Gloria with him.

There was no evidence that Chism or Duke protested, resisted, or attempted to avoid the actions which Lloyd ordered them to take. Although Lloyd was armed with a knife, there was no evidence that he threatened either of his companions with harm.

Duke proceeded to drop Chism off at a friend's house, where he changed to male clothing. He placed the blood-stained women's clothes in a trash bin. Afterward, Chism went with his mother to the police station at 1:15 A.M. He gave the police a complete statement, and took the officers to the place where Gloria had been left with Ira Lloyd. The police found Gloria's body in some tall grass several feet from that spot.

An autopsy indicated that stab wounds had caused her death. Chism's discarded clothing disappeared before the police arrived at the trash bin.

OPINION

According to Louisiana statute 14:25:

> An accessory after the fact is any person who, after the commission of a felony, shall harbor, conceal, or aid the offender, knowing or having reasonable ground to believe that he has committed the felony, and with the intent that he may avoid or escape from arrest, trial, conviction, or punishment. . . .
>
> Whoever becomes an accessory after the fact shall be fined not more than five hundred dollars, or imprisoned, with or without hard labor, for not more than five years, or both; provided that in no case shall his punishment be greater than one-half of the maximum provided by law for a principal offender. La.R.S. 14:25

Chism appealed from his conviction and sentence and argues that the evidence was not sufficient to support the judgment. Consequently, in reviewing the defendant's assigned error, we must determine whether, after viewing the evidence in the light most favorable to the prosecution, any rational trier of fact could have found beyond a reasonable doubt that

(a) a completed felony had been committed by Ira Lloyd before Brian Chism rendered him the assistance described below; *and*

(b) Chism knew or had reasonable grounds to know of the commission of the felony by Lloyd; *and*

(c) Chism gave aid to Lloyd personally under circumstances that indicate either that he actively desired that the felon avoid or escape arrest, trial conviction, or punishment or that he believed that one of these consequences was substantially certain to result from his assistance.

There was clearly enough evidence to justify the finding that a felony had been completed before any assistance was rendered to Lloyd by the defendant. The record vividly demonstrates that Lloyd fatally stabbed his ex-wife before she was transported to Willow Point and left in the high grass near a wood line. Thus, Lloyd committed the felonies of attempted murder, aggravated battery, and simple kidnapping, before Chism aided him in any way. A person cannot be convicted as an accessory after the fact to a murder because of aid given after the murderer's acts but before the victim's death, but under these circumstances the aider may be found to be an accessory after the fact to the felonious assault. . . .

The evidence overwhelmingly indicates that Chism had reasonable grounds to believe that Lloyd had committed a felony before any assistance was rendered. In his confessions and his testimony Chism indicates that the victim was bleeding profusely when Lloyd pushed her into the vehicle, that she was limp and moaned as they drove to Willow Point, and that he knew Lloyd had inflicted her wounds with a knife.

The Louisiana offense of accessory after the fact deviates somewhat from the original common-law offense in that it does not require that the defendant actually know that a completed felony has occurred. Rather, it incorporates an objective standard by requiring only that the defendant render aid "knowing or having reasonable grounds to believe" that a felony has been committed.

The closest question presented is whether any reasonable trier of fact could have found beyond a reasonable doubt that Chism assisted Lloyd under circumstances that indicate that either Chism actively desired that Lloyd would avoid or escape arrest, trial, conviction, or punishment, or that Chism believed that one of these consequences was substantially certain to result from his assistance.

. . . In this case we conclude that . . . a trier of fact reasonably could have found that Chism acted with at least a general intent to help Lloyd avoid arrest because:

(1) Chism did not protest or attempt to leave the car when his uncle, Lloyd, shoved the mortally wounded victim inside;

(2) he did not attempt to persuade Duke, his would-be lover, to exit out the driver's side of the car and flee from his uncle, whom he knew to be one-legged and armed only with a knife;

(3) he did not take any of these actions at any point during the considerable ride to Willow Point;

(4) at their destination, he docilely complied with Lloyd's directions to remove the victim from the car and leave Lloyd with her, despite the fact that Lloyd made no threats and that his wooden leg had become detached;

(5) after leaving Lloyd with the dying victim, he made no immediate effort to report the victim's whereabouts or to obtain emergency medical treatment for her;

(6) before going home or reporting the victim's dire condition he went to a friend's house, changed clothing and discarded his own in a trash bin from which the police were unable to recover them as evidence;

(7) he went home without reporting the victim's condition or location;

(8) and he went to the police station to report the crime only after arriving home and discussing the matter with his mother.

The defendant asserted . . . that he helped to remove the victim from the car and to carry her to the edge of the bushes because he feared that his uncle would use the knife on him. . . . However, fear as a motivation to help his uncle is inconsistent with some of Chism's actions after he left his uncle. Consequently, we conclude that despite Chism's testimony, the trier of fact could have reasonably found that he acted voluntarily and not out of fear when he aided Lloyd and that he did so under circumstances indicating that he believed that it was substantially certain to follow from his assistance that Lloyd would avoid arrest, trial, conviction, or punishment.

For the foregoing reasons, it is also clear that the judge's verdict was warranted. . . . There is evidence in this record from which a reasonable trier of fact could find a defendant guilty beyond a reasonable doubt. Therefore, we affirm the defendant's conviction.

We note, however, that the sentence imposed by the trial judge is illegal. The judge imposed a sentence of three years. He suspended two and one-half of years of the term. The trial judge has no authority to suspend part of a sentence in a felony case. The correct sentence would have been a suspension of all three years of the term, with a six-month term as a condition of two years probation. We therefore vacate the defendant's sentence and remand the case for resentencing.

Conviction AFFIRMED; sentence vacated; REMANDED.

DISSENT

DIXON, CJ.

I respectfully dissent from what appears to be a finding of guilt by association. The majority lists five instances of inaction, or failure to act, by defendant:

(1) did not protest or leave the car;

(2) did not attempt to persuade Duke to leave the car;

(3) did neither (1) nor (2) on ride to Willow Point;

(5) made no immediate effort to report crime or get aid for the victim;

(7) failed to report victim's condition or location after changing clothes.

The three instances of defendant's action relied on by the majority for conviction were stated to be:

(4) complying with Lloyd's direction to remove the victim from the car and leave the victim and Lloyd at Willow Point;

(6) changing clothes and discarding bloody garments; and

(8) discussing the matter with defendant's mother before going to the police station to report the crime.

None of these actions or failures to act tended to prove defendant's intent, specifically or generally, to aid defendant avoid arrest, trial, conviction or punishment.

Questions

1. Identify the elements of accessory-after-the-fact according to the Louisiana statute.

2. List all the facts stated by the court, and then match them to each of the elements of the statute.

3. Summarize the court's conclusions regarding the evidence of each of the elements.

4. Do you agree with the court that Chism is guilty of being an accessory-after-the-fact? Back up your answer with facts in the case.

5. Summarize the reasons the dissent couldn't go along with the majority. Do you agree with the dissent? Defend your answer.

EXPLORING FURTHER

Participation after the Commission of a Crime

1. Was He an Accessory after the Fact to Grand Larceny?

Dunn v. Commonwealth, WL 147448 (Va.App. 1997)

FACTS On two separate occasions, Charles Lee Dunn was a passenger in a car when two grand larcenies occurred. He claimed he didn't know the others in the car planned to break into cars and didn't participate in the thefts of stereo equipment and CDs. He admitted that, after the first theft on September 4, he voluntarily went with the others when they sold the equipment, and he received a small piece of crack cocaine from the proceeds. Regarding one of the offenses, he testified that he took no active part in the theft and was taken home immediately thereafter.

The Commonwealth's evidence included testimony from the investigating officer, Detective Ramsey, that appellant (Dunn) told him that he knew the purpose of going to the location of the first offense was "to take equipment belonging to Mr. Roberts. It was known there was equipment in his car."

As to the September 7, 1995 offense, Ramsey testified that Dunn said:

> The three of them went to a location near Mr. Jackson's house. Mr. Dunn waited in the car, and Mr. Walker and Mr. Kraegers approached Mr. Jackson's vehicle. They entered the vehicle through an unlocked door and took stereo equipment from the vehicle, brought it back to the car. [Appellant] states that they put the speaker box in the trunk, put the amp and a CD player in the car, and he says, I think they got some CDs. That equipment was also taken to the city and traded for crack cocaine which they all used, and that property has not been recovered.

Ramsey stated that Dunn admitted to participating and taking the property to the city in exchange for crack cocaine.

Was Dunn an accessory after the fact?

DECISION Yes, said the Virginia Court of Appeals:

> While Dunn contends that the evidence failed to establish he did anything other than ride in a car with

friends, the trial court was not required to accept his explanation.

Dunn admitted to Ramsey that he knew the others intended to steal on both occasions; he smoked crack cocaine purchased with the money received from disposing of the goods; and he went out with the code-fendants three days after the first larceny occurred.

Under the facts of this case, the Commonwealth's evidence was sufficient to prove beyond a reasonable doubt that appellant was an accessory after the fact to the two grand larcenies. Affirmed.

 Go to the Criminal Law 9e website for the full text of the Exploring Further excerpts (see excerpts on participation after the commission of a crime) and to find Exercise 7-1, Learn about Elements of Accomplice Liability in your state: www.thomsonedu.com/criminaljustice/samaha.

VICARIOUS LIABILITY

As noted earlier, *vicarious liability* transfers the *actus reus* and the *mens rea* of one party to another because of their *relationship*. Most vicarious liability involves business relationships, such as employer-employee, manager-corporation, buyer-seller, producer-consumer, and service provider–recipient. But it can also apply to other enterprises, like the college fraternity in the next case excerpt, and relationships between individuals, such as making the owner of a car liable for the driver's traffic violations and holding parents liable for their children's crimes.

In this section, we'll examine the differences between enterprise and individual vicarious liabilities.

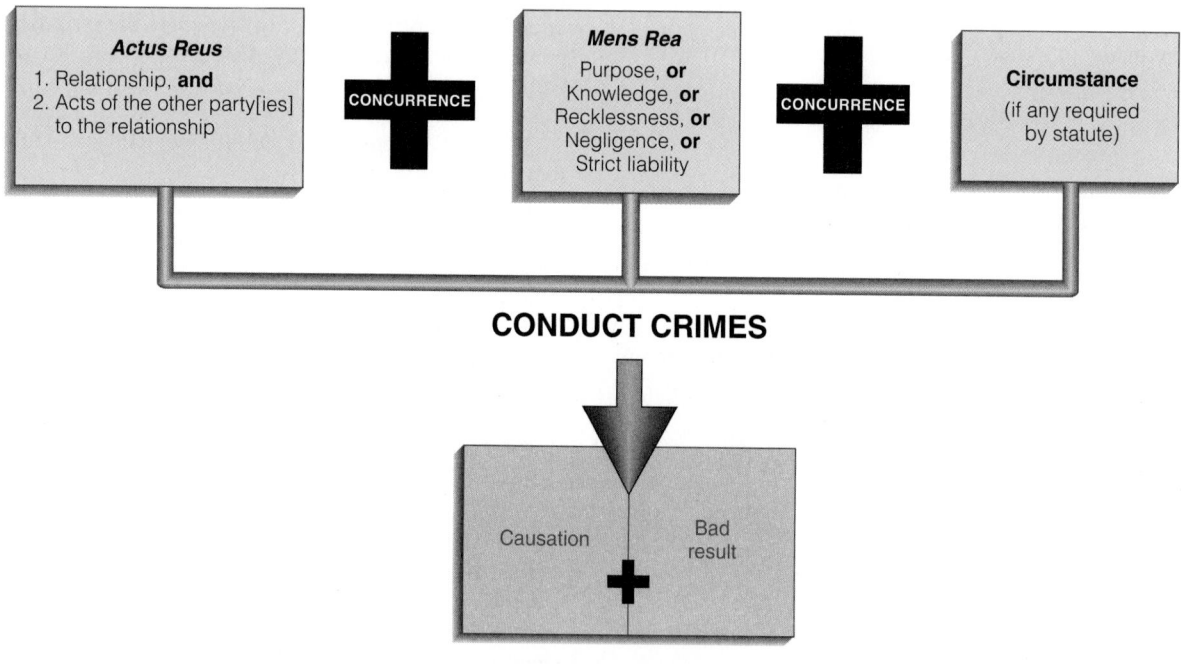

Elements of Vicarious Liability

Enterprise Vicarious Liability

Successfully applying vicarious liability to convict and punish individuals for business crimes is difficult under any circumstances. Pinpointing responsibility for corporate crimes is especially difficult, because, frequently, many people are involved in a decision that leads to criminal conduct or causes a criminal result.

This problem increases with the complexity of corporate structures. The larger and more spread out the business, the harder it is to identify just who's responsible for actions taken in the name of the corporation. It's also hard (sometimes impossible) to prove the mental element. A corporation can't have a state of mind because it can't think, so prosecutors have to rely on two doctrines to prove corporate criminal liability:

1. *Strict liability* Removes the mental element

2. *Vicarious liability* Attaches the intent of managers and agents to the corporation

Although vicarious and strict liability often work together to impose criminal liability, they're very different ideas: strict liability *eliminates* the *mens rea;* vicarious liability *transfers* the *actus reus* and *mens rea* of an employee to the corporation (Fisse 1986, 23–54).

Criminal punishment that's based on a relationship, especially when there's no fault as in strict vicarious liability, raises constitutional questions. Some courts have ruled that putting someone in jail based on vicarious liability violates the fundamental fairness required by due process (Chapter 2). Other courts have gone so far as to declare that even fining someone based on vicarious liability violates due process if noncriminal measures are enough to control harmful business practices. Fundamental fairness is also involved, because stockholders, "most of whom ordinarily had nothing to do with the offense and were powerless to prevent it," wind up actually paying the fines.

The issue of whether vicarious liability is effective is also problematic. Fines probably don't deter officers or other agents who don't have to pay them. Because businesses treat fines as just another business expense, the deterrent effect is further weakened. Finally, officers don't suffer a stigma if their actions are looked at as just violating "regulations" as opposed to committing "real crimes." Quite the contrary: officers can boost their reputation for "shrewd business" practices by breaking the rules to turn a profit.

The New Hampshire Supreme Court upheld a verdict finding a university fraternity, a corporation, guilty of prostitution and selling alcohol to a minor in *State v. Zeta Chi Fraternity* (1997).

CASE · *Was Zeta Chi Guilty of Prostitution and Selling Alcohol to Minors?*

State v. Zeta Chi Fraternity
686 A.2d. 530 (N.H. 1997)

HISTORY

Defendant, a college fraternity, was convicted, following trial in the Superior Court, Strafford County, of selling alcohol to a person under the age of 21 and of prostitu-

tion. Defendant appealed. The Supreme Court affirmed the convictions.

HORTON, J.

FACTS

On February 21, 1994, the defendant, a New Hampshire corporation and fraternity at the University of New

Hampshire in Durham, held a "rush" at its fraternity house to attract new members. In order to encourage people to attend the rush, the defendant hired two female strippers to perform at the event. Fraternity brothers encouraged guests to give the strippers dollar bills so that they would continue to perform. The brothers also told guests that the more money the strippers were given, the more that they would do. One of the members of the fraternity was providing change for larger bills. As part of the performance, the dancers lay on a mattress brought out by members of the fraternity and simulated oral sex on each other. At one point, a guest gave five dollars to one of the strippers who sat on the guest's lap. When a brother moved the dancer along, the guest complained that he had given five dollars. The stripper took the guest to the mattress and pushed his head into her crotch. Two witnesses testified at trial that they saw guests being led to the mattress after they gave money, at which point the guests then performed oral sex on the dancer.

In addition, Andrew Strachan, a nineteen-year-old guest at the fraternity party, testified that at some point during the evening he learned that beer was available from a soda machine. He made his way to an apartment in another part of the fraternity house where the machine was located, waited in line with three or four other people, and purchased three to five cans of beer. Strachan also testified that he noticed someone making change for the machine. The fraternity's secretary testified that the fraternity members voted not to provide alcohol at the rush and that they moved the vending machine that contained beer to a separate apartment in another part of the fraternity house for the rush. He also testified, however, that the fraternity had control over the vending machine and its proceeds and that only fraternity members would have an interest in making change for the machine.

OPINION

I. Sufficiency of Evidence

A. ILLEGAL SALE OF ALCOHOL The defendant . . . argues that the State failed to prove that the defendant caused alcohol to be sold to Strachan. See RSA 179:5:

I. No licensee, salesperson, direct shipper, common carrier, delivery agent, nor any other person, shall sell or give away or cause or allow or procure to be sold, delivered or given away any liquor or beverage to a person under the age of 21 or to an intoxicated individual. . . .

II. No licensee, manager or person in charge of a licensed premises shall allow or permit any individual, who is under the age of 21, to possess or consume any liquor or beverage on the licensed premises.

The defendant asserts that because the fraternity voted not to provide beer at the rush and the soda machine was moved from the main area in the fraternity house to a

separate apartment at the back of the house, the defendant did not have control over the machine, and, therefore, could not have caused the sale of alcohol from the machine.

Essentially, the defendant is arguing that the individuals responsible for making the beer available for sale to Strachan were not acting on behalf of the corporation or within the scope of their authority.

We begin by noting that the only defendant in this case is a corporate entity. A corporation is a jural person, but not a person in fact. It is an artificial creature, acting only through agents. . . . A corporation may be held criminally liable for criminal acts performed on its behalf by agents or employees acting within the scope of their authority or employment. The criminal conduct need not have been performed, authorized, ratified, adopted or tolerated by the corporation's directors, officers or other high managerial agents in order to be chargeable to the corporation.

In fact, a corporation can be convicted for actions of its agents even if it expressly instructed the agents not to engage in the criminal conduct. The agents, however, must have been acting within the scope of their actual or apparent authority. Express authority exists when the principal explicitly manifests its authorization for the agent to act. Implied authority is the reasonable incident or construction of the terms of express authority or results from acquiescence by the principal in a course of dealing by the agent. Apparent authority, on the other hand, exists where the principal so conducts itself as to cause a third party to reasonably believe that the agent is authorized to act.

It is the rare case in which the corporate leadership explicitly authorizes its agents to engage in criminal conduct. Of necessity, the proof of authority to so act must rest on all the circumstances and conduct in a given situation and the reasonable inferences to be drawn therefrom.

Evidence at trial indicates that the defendant had control over the apartment in which the vending machine was located, even though it had voted to make the apartment separate from the fraternity house. More importantly, however, witnesses testified that the defendant had control over the soda machine; that only the defendant had an interest in the proceeds from the machine; that only fraternity members had keys to the apartment in which the machine was located; that someone was making change for the machine; and that no one would have an interest in making change except a member of the fraternity. We believe that from these facts the jury could reasonably have found that an agent of the defendant sold beer from the vending machine and that this agent was acting on behalf of the corporation and within the scope of his authority.

The defendant next argues that the evidence was insufficient for the jury to find that the defendant acted recklessly, the *mens rea* charged in the indictment. Because the defendant is a corporation, its mental state depends on the knowledge of its agents. The corporation is considered to have acquired the collective knowledge of its employees and is held responsible for their failure to act accordingly.

A person acts recklessly with respect to a material element of an offense when he is aware of and consciously disregards a substantial and unjustifiable risk that the material element exists or will result from his conduct. The risk must be of such a nature and degree that, considering the circumstances known to him, its disregard constitutes a gross deviation from the conduct that a law-abiding person would observe in the situation.

In this case, the jury could reasonably have found that the defendant acted recklessly from the facts that about 150 guests, many of them under the age of twenty-one, were at the rush party that had been widely publicized on campus; that it was the defendant's vending machine; that only fraternity members had keys to the apartment in which the machine was located; that party guests gained access to the machine; that someone was making change; and that a number of people were waiting in line to use the machine.

B. PROSTITUTION . . . The defendant . . . contends that the State failed to prove that the defendant knowingly allowed the prostitution and that if prostitution occurred, the individuals who allowed it were not acting within the scope of their authority.

We will first address the issue of agency. As noted above, in the context of corporate criminal liability, the corporation acts through its agents and those agents must be acting within the scope of either their actual or apparent authority in order for the corporation to be liable for their actions. The defendant asserts that because the members of the fraternity announced that guests were not allowed to touch the dancers and that, if the dancer stayed too long with one guest, members of the fraternity would move her along, this indicated the lack of actual or apparent authority.

Whether an agent has acted within his actual or apparent authority . . . is a question for the trier of fact. Apparent authority can result when the principal fails to disapprove of the agent's act or course of action so as to lead the public to believe that his agent possesses authority to act . . . in the name of the principal. In this case, there was testimony that the guests were told that if they paid more money the dancers would do more; that on more than one occasion guests were led to the mattress that was brought into the room by the brothers to perform oral sex in exchange for money; and that at least one guest performed oral sex on the dancer for "quite a while." From these facts the jury could reasonably have found that members of the fraternity acted within the scope of their authority and on behalf of the corporation in allowing oral sex to be performed in exchange for money.

The defendant argues that the State failed to prove the requisite mens rea with regard to the prostitution charge, that is, that the defendant knowingly permitted oral sex to occur at the party. See RSA 645:2, I(e). "A person acts knowingly with respect to conduct or to a circumstance that is a material element of an offense when he is aware that his conduct is of such nature or that such circumstances exist." The defendant argues that the material element to which the "knowingly" mens rea applies is permission. The defendant contends that there was no opportunity for the defendant to manifest its lack of permission before the oral sex occurred because the dancer's actions were unexpected.

Based on the facts of this case, the defendant's argument is without merit. As noted above, because the defendant is a corporation, and a corporation acts through its agents, the knowledge obtained by the agents of the corporation acting within the scope of their agency is imputed to the corporation. There was testimony that several guests performed oral sex on the dancer and that on at least one occasion it occurred for several minutes. Moreover, the fraternity president testified that he "was very well in control" of the party. Therefore, even if the first act caught members of the fraternity by surprise, the jury could reasonably have inferred that the defendant knowingly permitted oral sex to occur from the defendant's failure to prevent the subsequent conduct. A corporation is not insulated from criminal liability merely because it published instructions and policies which are violated by its employee; the corporation must place the acts outside the scope of an employee's employment by adequately enforcing its rules.

Convictions affirmed.

Questions

1. State the elements of vicarious liability according to New Hampshire law.

2. List all the facts relevant to deciding whether Zeta Chi, through its officers, was acting within its authority in each of the crimes.

3. Summarize the court's arguments upholding the trial court's conviction in each of the offenses.

4. In your opinion, was Zeta Chi guilty of selling alcohol to a minor? Of prostitution? Back up your answer with facts and arguments from the court's opinion.

Individual Vicarious Liability

Most cases of vicarious liability are like *State v. Zeta Chi*; they impose liability on various types of corporations. But not all cases. Sometimes, individuals are vicariously liable for their agents' actions. At common law, superiors weren't liable for their agent's crimes committed during the agency relationship. "Vicarious liability for another's criminal conduct or failure to prevent another's criminal conduct can be delineated by statute; it cannot be created by the courts" (*State v. Tomaino* 1999, 1194). Most common are cases of employees' crimes, committed within the scope of their employment but without the approval or knowledge of their employers.

Because vicarious liability requires a statute, the issue in most vicarious liability statutes is interpreting whether the statute actually imposes vicarious liability. In *State v. Tomaino* (1999), the Ohio Court of Appeals interpreted the Ohio "disseminating harmful matter to juveniles" statute not to include vicarious liability.

C A S E   *Was the Owner Liable for the Clerk Renting "Pornos" to a Minor?*

State v. Tomaino
733 N.E.2d 1191 (Ohio App. 1999)

HISTORY

Peter Tomaino, the owner of an adult video store, was convicted in the Court of Common Pleas, Butler County, of disseminating matter harmful to juveniles. He appealed. The Court of Appeals reversed and remanded.

WALSH, J.

FACTS

Peter Tomaino, Appellant, owns VIP Video, a video sales and rental store in Millville, Ohio. VIP Video's inventory includes only sexually oriented videotapes and materials. On October 13, 1997, Carl Frybarger, age thirty-seven, and his son Mark, age seventeen, decided that Mark should attempt to rent a video from VIP. Mark entered the store, selected a video, and presented it to the clerk along with his father's driver's license and credit card.

The purchase was completed and the Frybargers contacted the Butler County Sheriff's Department. After interviewing Mark and his father, Sergeant Greg Blankenship, supervisor of the Drug and Vice Unit, determined that Mark should again attempt to purchase videos at VIP Video with marked money while wearing a radio transmitter wire.

On October 14, 1997, Mark again entered the store. A different clerk was on duty. Following Blankenship's instructions, Mark selected four videos and approached the clerk. He told her that he had been in the store the previous day and that he was thirty-seven. Mark told the clerk that he

had used a credit card on that occasion and that he was using cash this time and thus did not have his identification with him. The clerk accepted the cash ($100) and did not require any identification or proof of Mark's age. It is this video transaction that constitutes the basis of the indictment.

The clerk, Billie Doan, was then informed by Blankenship that she had sold the videos to a juvenile and that she would be arrested. Doan said that she needed to call appellant and made several unsuccessful attempts to contact appellant at different locations.

The grand jury indicted appellant Tomaino and Doan on two counts. Count One charged the defendants with recklessly disseminating obscene material to juveniles and Count Two charged the defendants with disseminating matter that was harmful to juveniles.

OPINION

Billie Doan was tried separately from appellant. Appellant moved to dismiss the indictment against him. During pretrial proceedings, appellant argued that criminal liability could not be imputed to him based on the actions of the clerk. The state moved to amend the bill of particulars to provide that appellant "recklessly failed to supervise his employees and agents." The trial court denied appellant's motion to dismiss and the case against appellant proceeded to a jury trial on August 25, 1998. Mark and Carl Frybarger and Blankenship testified on behalf of the state; the defense presented no evidence. Counsel for appellant made a motion for acquittal pursuant to Crim.R. 29 at the close of the state's case. The trial court overruled the motion.

The state argued that appellant was reckless by not having a sign saying "no sales to juveniles." Appellant argued in part that he was not liable for the clerk's actions. The jury was instructed that in order to convict they must find beyond a reasonable doubt that appellant, recklessly and with knowledge of its character or content, sold to a juvenile any material that was obscene (Count One) and harmful to a juvenile (Count Two).

The jury was also instructed on the definitions of knowingly and recklessly and on the definitions of obscene material and of material harmful to juveniles. The jury found appellant not guilty on Count One (disseminating obscene material) and guilty on Count Two (disseminating matter harmful to juveniles).

Following the verdict, appellant moved for both a judgment of acquittal and a new trial. Appellant again argued that he could not be held criminally liable for the acts of another and that there was no evidence that he had recklessly provided material harmful to a juvenile. The trial court denied both motions. . . . The court stated that the jury could find that appellant was the owner of the store and thus had knowledge of the character or content of the material being sold in his store. The court also stated that appellant "did not implement any policies, plans or procedures to prohibit entrance of juveniles into his store or the sale of material to juveniles."

. . . Appellant argues that . . . no statute imposed criminal liability for his actions or inactions. Having carefully reviewed the state's arguments, we must agree, although we hold that the court erred in its instructions to the jury rather than in denying the motion for acquittal.

Appellant was convicted of disseminating matter harmful to juveniles. R.C. 2907.31 provides in relevant part:

(A) No person, with knowledge of its character or content, shall recklessly do any of the following:
  (1) Sell, deliver, furnish, disseminate, provide, exhibit, rent, present to a juvenile any material or performance that is obscene or harmful to juveniles."

. . . Ohio has no common law offenses. . . . Criminal liability is rigidly and precisely limited to those situations that the General Assembly has specifically delineated by statute. In R.C. 2901.21, the legislature has further provided that a person is not guilty of an offense unless both of the following apply:

(1) His liability is based on conduct which includes either a voluntary act, or an omission to perform an act or duty which he is capable of performing;

(2) He has the requisite degree of culpability for each element as to which a culpable mental state is specified by the section defining the offense.

. . . Vicarious liability for another's criminal conduct or failure to prevent another's criminal conduct can be delineated by statute; it cannot be created by the courts. Statutes defining offenses are to be strictly construed against the state and liberally construed in favor of the accused. The elements of a crime must be gathered wholly from the statute. . . . Liability based on ownership or operation of a business may . . . be specifically imposed by statute. For instance, the owner of premises used for gambling—even if he is not present while gambling occurs—can be criminally liable under the statute prohibiting operating a gambling house. Such premises-oriented liability is specifically imposed by the statute, which provides in part that "no person being the . . . owner of premises, shall . . . recklessly permit such premises to be used or occupied for gambling." R.C. 2915.03.

. . . It is undisputed that the clerk furnished the video to the minor and that appellant was not present. Because we find that a plain reading of the disseminating matter harmful to juveniles statute requires personal action by a defendant . . . and does not by its terms impose vicarious or premises oriented liability, the jury was not correctly instructed in this case. . . .

Judgment reversed and cause remanded.

Questions

1. State the elements of the Ohio statutes relevant to Peter Tomaino's liability for Billie Doan's acts.

2. Summarize the events that led to Tomaino's prosecution.

3. Summarize the state's arguments in favor of Tomaino's vicarious liability.

4. Summarize Tomaino's arguments against his vicarious liability for Billie Doan's acts.

5. Summarize the Ohio Court of Appeals reasons for rejecting vicarious liability under the Ohio statute referred to in (1).

6. In your opinion, should Peter Tomaino be liable for Billie Doan's acts? Back up your answer with facts from the case and the arguments from the state, Tomaino, and the court.

Virtually all vicarious liability statutes involve the employer-employee relationship. But not all do; for example, in some states and municipalities, registered vehicle owners are liable for some traffic violations involving their vehicles, regardless of who violated the law. So if you let your friend drive your car to go shopping, and he didn't feed the parking meter, you're liable for paying the fine.

Another nonbusiness relationship subject to vicarious criminal liability is parents' criminal liability for their kids' crimes. For example, in 1995, Salt Lake City enacted an ordinance that made it a crime for parents to fail to "supervise and control their children." By 1997, 17 states and cities had adopted one of these parental responsibility laws.

The idea of holding parents responsible for their children's crimes is nothing new. Contributing to the delinquency of a minor is an old offense. Contributing-to-the-delinquency-of-minors statutes mandate that the acts of minor children were done at the direction or with the consent of their parents. So, in one case, a father was found guilty for "allowing his child to violate a curfew ordinance," and, in another, a mother was convicted for "knowingly" permitting her children "to go at large in violation of a valid quarantine order."

One disturbing case involved the Detroit suburb of St. Clair Shores, which has an ordinance making it a crime to fail to "exercise reasonable control" to prevent children from committing delinquent acts. Alex Provenzino, 16, committed a string of seven burglaries. The local police ordered his parents to "take control" of Alex. When his father tried to discipline him, Alex "punched his father." When he tried to restrain him, Alex escaped by pressing his fingers into his father's eyes. When Alex tried to attack him with a golf club, his father called the police. The parents were charged with, but acquitted of, both vicariously committing the seven burglaries and failing to supervise their son (Siegel 1996, A1).

Traditional parental responsibility statutes aren't the same as vicarious liability. Parental responsibility statutes are based on parents' *acts* and *omissions;* vicarious liability statutes are based on the parent-child *relationship.* Vicarious liability statutes grew out of public fear, frustration, and anger over juvenile violence and parents' failure to control their kids. However, there are only a few cases in the appellate courts based on these vicarious liability statutes that make the crimes of kids the crimes of their parent solely on the basis of the parent-child relationship (DiFonzo 2001). One of these rare cases is *State v. Akers* (1979), where the New Hampshire Supreme Court dealt with a state statute making parents liable for their children's illegal snowmobile driving.

| CASE | *Are the Parents Guilty of Illegal Snowmobiling?* |

State v. Akers
400 A.2d 38 (N.H. 1979)

HISTORY

Parent defendants were found guilty of violating a snowmobile statute which makes parents vicariously liable for the acts of their children simply because they occupy the status of parents. The parents waived all right to an appeal de novo [*new trial*] to superior court. The parents objected to the constitutionality of the parent responsibility statute. The New Hampshire Supreme Court sustained the objections.

GRIMES, J.

FACTS

The defendants are fathers whose minor sons were found guilty of driving snowmobiles in violation of RSA 269-C:6—a II (operating on public way) and III (reasonable speed) (Supp.1977). RSA 269-C:24 IV, which pertains to the operation and licensing of off Highway Recreational Vehicles (OHRV), provides that "(t)he parents or guardians or persons assuming responsibility will be responsible for any damage incurred or for any violations of this chapter by any person under the age of 18." Following a verdict of guilty for violating RSA 269-C:24 IV the two defendants waived all right to an appeal de novo to the superior court and all questions of law were reserved and transferred by the District Court to the New Hampshire Supreme Court.

OPINION

The defendants argue that (1) RSA 269-C:24 IV, the statute under which they were convicted, was not intended by the legislature to impose criminal responsibility, and (2) if in fact the legislative intention was to impose criminal responsibility, then the statute would violate N.H.Const. pt. 1, art. 15 and U.S.Const. amend. XIV, § 1.

. . . The language of RSA 269-C:24 IV, "parents . . . will be responsible . . . for any violations of this chapter by any person under the age of 18," clearly indicates the legislature's intention to hold the parents criminally responsible for the OHRV violations of their minor children. It is a general principle of this State's Criminal Code that "(a) person is not guilty of an offense unless his criminal liability is based on conduct that includes a voluntary Act or the voluntary omission to perform an act of which he is physically capable." RSA 269-C:24 IV seeks to impose criminal liability on parents for the acts of their children without basing liability on any voluntary act or omission on the part of the parent. Because the statute makes no reference at all to parental conduct or acts it seeks to impose criminal responsibility solely because of their parental status contrary to the provisions of RSA 626:1.

The legislature has not specified any voluntary acts or omissions for which parents are sought to be made criminally responsible and it is not a judicial function to supply them. It is fundamental to the rule of law and due process that acts or omissions which are to be the basis of criminal liability must be specified in advance and not Ex post facto. N.H.Const. pt. 1, art. 23.

It is argued that liability may be imposed on parents under the provisions of RSA 626:8 II(b), which authorizes imposing criminal liability for conduct of another when "he is made accountable for the conduct of such other person by the law defining the offense." This provision comes from the Model Penal Code § 2.04(2)(b). The illustrations of this type of liability in the comments to the Code all relate to situations involving employees and agents, and no suggestion is made that it was intended to authorize imposing vicarious criminal liability on one merely because of his status as a parent.

Without passing upon the validity of statutes that might seek to impose vicarious criminal liability on the part of an employer for acts of his employees, we have no hesitancy in holding that any attempt to impose such liability on parents simply because they occupy the status of parents, without more, offends the due process clause of our State constitution.

Parenthood lies at the very foundation of our civilization. The continuance of the human race is entirely dependent upon it. It was firmly entrenched in the Judeo-Christian ethic when "in the beginning" man was commanded to "be fruitful and multiply." Genesis I. Considering the nature of parenthood, we are convinced that the status of parenthood cannot be made a crime. This, however, is the effect of RSA 269-C:24 IV. Even if the parent has been as careful as anyone could be, even if the parent has forbidden the conduct, and even if the parent is justifiably unaware of the activities of the child, criminal liability is still imposed under the wording of the present statute.

There is no other basis for criminal responsibility other than the fact that a person is the parent of one who violates the law. One hundred and twenty seven years ago the justices of this court in giving their opinions regarding a proposed law that would have imposed vicarious criminal liability on an employer for acts of his employee stated, "(b)ut this does not seem to be in accordance with the spirit of our Constitution . . ." Because the net effect of the statute is to punish parenthood, the result is forbidden by substantive due process requirements of N.H.Const. pt. 1, art. 15.

Exceptions sustained.

DISSENT

BOIS, J.

The majority read RSA 269-C:24 IV in isolation. They conveniently ignore RSA 626:8 (Criminal Liability for Conduct of Another), which provides in subsection II that "(a) person is legally accountable for the conduct of another person when: (b) he is made accountable for the conduct of such other person by the law defining the offense. . . ." RSA 269-C:24 IV is such a law. Imposing criminal liability based on status for certain violations of a *mala prohibitum* nature does not offend constitutional requirements.

Even if I were to accept the majority's conclusion that the vicarious imposition of criminal liability on parents of children who have committed an OHRV [Off Highway Recreational Vehicles] violation under RSA ch. 269-C is constitutionally impermissible, I would still uphold the validity of RSA 269-C:24 IV. A closer reading of this State's Criminal Code belies the majority's reasoning that RSA 269-C:24 IV holds parents of minor offenders criminally responsible for their children's offenses solely on the basis of their parental status. RSA 626:1 I, enunciating the fundamental principle of the Criminal Code, states that all criminal liability must be based on a "voluntary act" or "voluntary omission." When RSA 269-C:24 IV is read in conjunction with RSA 626:1 I, a parental conviction can result only when the State shows beyond a reasonable doubt that a minor child has committed a violation under a provision of chapter 269-C, and that his parent voluntarily performed or omitted to perform an act such as participating in the minor's conduct, or entrusting, or negligently allowing his minor child to operate an OHRV.

When RSA 269-C:24 IV is construed to require a voluntary act or voluntary omission in accordance with RSA 626:1 I, there are no due process infirmities, either under N.H.Const. pt. 1, art. 15 or U.S. Const. amend. XIV, § 1. Culpable intent is not required to impose criminal penalties for minor infractions. "It is well settled in this jurisdiction that the Legislature may declare criminal a certain act or omission to act without requiring it to be done with intent." When the legislature imposes criminal responsibility without requiring intent, we will override it only when such imposition violates concepts of fundamental fairness.

In the present case, there is a demonstrable public interest to assure the safe operation of OHRVs, and the minor penalties imposed upon violators of RSA 269-C:24 IV are insubstantial. In such circumstances, we will not second guess the wisdom of the legislature.

Public welfare offenses requiring no criminal intent have also been held consistent with the due process requirements of U.S. Const. amend. XIV, § 1. "There is wide latitude in the lawmakers to declare an offense and to exclude elements of knowledge and diligence from its definition." "In vindicating its public policy . . . a State in punishing particular acts may provide that 'he who shall do them shall do them at his peril. . . .'"

Questions

1. Exactly what does the New Hampshire statute prohibit?

2. Summarize all of the arguments of the majority and dissenting opinions. Which side do you agree with? Defend your answer.

3. Apart from the legal and constitutional arguments, do you think it's good public policy to make parents criminally liable for their children's crimes? Defend your answer.

SUMMARY

I. Two types of liability for someone else's crimes
    A. Parties to crime (complicity) establishes when you can be held liable for others' crimes.
    B. Vicarious liability establishes which types of relationships can create criminal liability.

II. Parties to crime
    A. Four types of parties to crime at common law
        1. Principals in the first degree actually commit the crime.
        2. Principals in the second degree are present when the crimes are committed.
        3. Accessories before the fact:
            a. Help before the crime is committed
            b. Aren't present when the crime is committed
        4. Accessories after the fact help after the crime is committed.
    B. Participation before and during the commission of a crime (accomplices)
        1. Accomplices are prosecuted for committing the crime itself (helping a murderer is murder).
        2. Accomplice *actus reus*
            a. The core idea is that the accomplice took some positive act to help commit a crime.
            b. Words can be accomplice *actus reus*.
            c. Presence at the crime scene isn't enough unless there's a duty (parent to minor child).
            d. Actions after the crime can be relevant to prove *actus reus*.
        3. Accomplice *mens rea*
            a. "Purposely" clearly qualifies as accomplice *mens rea*.

b. Jurisdictions vary and sometimes are confused as to whether knowledge, recklessness, or negligence qualify.

   C. Participation after the commission of a crime (accessory)

      1. Accessory is a separate lesser offense than accomplice liability.

      2. Elements of accessory after the fact

         a. The accessory personally helped the person who committed the felony (*actus reus* element).

         b. The accessory knew a felony was committed (*mens rea* element).

         c. The accessory helped for the purpose of hindering prosecution (*mens rea* element).

         d. Someone other than the accessory actually committed a felony (circumstance element).

III. Vicarious liability

   A. Vicarious liability bases liability on a relationship between a person who commits the crime and someone else.

   B. Corporate vicarious liability

      1. Pinpointing responsibility is difficult because of the complexity of organizations and the number of people making decisions.

      2. Constitutional and policy questions

         a. Due process issues

            (1) Liability is based on relationship and not acts and/or intent.

            (2) Is it fair to shareholders, who usually pay the fines?

         b. Policy question—is there a deterrent effect?

   C. Individual vicarious liability

      1. There was no common-law vicarious liability.

      2. Vicarious liability is created by statute.

      3. Vicarious liability statutes hold the owner of a car responsible for the actions of others who drive his or her car.

      4. Should there be parental responsibility for kids' crimes?

         a. Constitutional question—Does holding parents responsible based solely on the parent-child relationship violate due process?

         b. Policy goals

            (1) Protect the public from violent juveniles.

            (2) Get parents to control their kids.

REVIEW QUESTIONS

1. Identify the basic idea of criminal law reflected in complicity (parties to crime) and vicarious liability.

2. Identify the two ways criminal liability for someone else's crimes arises.

3. Explain the basic difference between complicity (parties to crime) and vicarious liability.

4. Explain the differences between accomplice and accessory liability.

5. What's the thinking behind punishing accomplice and accessory liability differently?

6. Identify and give examples of the core idea of accomplice *actus reus*.

7. When does presence at the scene of a crime satisfy the *actus reus* requirement of accomplice liability?

8. What does participation after crimes are committed have to do with participation before and during the commission of crimes?

9. Explain and give examples of the trouble accomplice *mens rea* creates for courts.

10. List the four elements of accessory liability, and identify whether each is an *actus reus, mens rea,* or circumstance element.

11. Explain why conviction and punishment on the basis of vicarious liability is difficult to obtain in corporate crimes.

12. List and summarize the objections to vicarious liability for corporate crimes.

13. Identify the two doctrines prosecutors rely on to prove corporate liability.

14. Describe and explain why vicarious liability for traffic offenses was created.

15. Identify and explain how vicarious traffic liability statutes are written to give owners a way out of liability.

16. Explain the difference between traditional parental responsibility statutes and parents' vicarious liability for their kids' crimes.

17. Identify two reasons for the creation of vicarious liability of parents for their kids' crimes.

KEY TERMS

complicity, p. 208
vicarious liability, p. 208

accomplices, p. 209
accessories, p. 209

Pinkerton rule, p. 209
mere presence rule, p. 210

80025 75540

Inchoate Crimes: Attempt, Conspiracy, and Solicitation

MAIN POINTS

- Inchoate offenses punish people for crimes they haven't finished committing.
- Inchoate offenses require some action but not enough to complete the crime intended.
- Liability for criminal attempt offenses is based on two rationales: preventing dangerous conduct and neutralizing dangerous people.
- The *mens rea* of inchoate crimes is *always* the purpose or specific intent to commit a specific crime.
- The *actus reus* of attempt is an action that's beyond mere preparation but not enough to complete the crime.
- Legal impossibility is a defense to attempt liability; factual impossibility isn't.
- Voluntary and complete abandonment of an attempt in progress is a defense to attempt liability in some states.
- Punishing conspiracy and solicitation to commit a crime is based on nipping in the bud the special danger of group criminality.

© Dennis Van Tine/Landov

How close to completing a crime is close enough to satisfy the criminal act requirement of attempt actus reus? If officers interrupted a bank robber at this Citibank, for example, at what point in the robbery do you think the robber would need to be to meet attempt actus reus?

Did He Attempt to Murder His Wife?

Ralph Damms and his estranged wife Marjory were parked in a restaurant parking lot. Ralph asked Marjory how much money she had with her, and she said "a couple of dollars." Ralph then requested to see Marjory's checkbook; she refused to give it to him. They quarreled. Marjory opened the car door and started to run around the restaurant building screaming, "Help!" Ralph pursued her with the pistol in his hand. Marjory's cries for help attracted the attention of the persons inside the restaurant, including two officers of the State Traffic Patrol who were eating lunch. One officer rushed out of the front door and the other the rear door. In the meantime, Marjory had run nearly around three sides of the building. In seeking to avoid colliding with a child that was in her path, she turned, slipped, and fell. Ralph crouched down, held the pistol at her head, and pulled the trigger; but nothing happened. He then exclaimed, "It won't fire. It won't fire".

(STATE V. DAMMS 1960)

We all know that a man who chases his wife around a restaurant parking lot and shoots her in the head and kills her with the loaded gun in his hand when she trips and falls commits murder. However, what about the same man who does the same thing, but unbeknown to him, the gun isn't loaded? When he pulls the trigger and nothing happens, he yells, "It won't fire! It won't fire!" What crime is that? That's what this chapter is about—criminal liability for trying to commit crimes, **criminal attempts;** for making agreements with someone else to commit crimes, **criminal conspiracy;** and for trying to get someone else to commit a crime, **criminal solicitation.**

We call these three crimes **inchoate offenses.** The word *inchoate* comes from the Latin "to begin." Each inchoate offense has its own elements, but they all share two elements: the *mens rea* of purpose or specific intent [Chapter 4]) and the *actus reus* of taking some steps toward accomplishing the criminal purpose—but not enough steps to complete the intended crime.

Just to keep your bearings about where you are in the grand scheme of the criminal law—and in your book—with regard to the general part (criminal conduct, justification, and excuse) and the special part (specific crimes) of criminal law, the inchoate offenses stand partly in the general and partly in the special part. Unlike the general part, they're specific crimes, such as attempted robbery. But, like the general part, they apply to many crimes, such as the mental attitude of specific intent or purpose and the voluntary acts that fall short of completing the intended crime. That's why the Model Penal Code calls them **"offenses of general application"** (Dubber 2002, 142).

Incomplete criminal conduct poses the dilemma whether to punish someone who's done no harm or to set free someone who's determined to commit a crime. The doctrine of inchoate crimes asks the question: How far should criminal law go to prevent crime by punishing people who haven't accomplished their criminal purpose?

Creating criminal liability for uncompleted crimes flies in the face of the notion that free societies punish people for what they have done, not for what they might do. On the other hand, the doctrine of inchoate crimes reflects the widely held belief that "an ounce of prevention is worth a pound of cure." The law of inchoate crimes resolves the dilemma by three means:

1. Requiring a specific intent or purpose to commit the crime or cause a harm
2. Requiring some action to carry out the purpose
3. Punishing inchoate crimes less severely than completed crimes (ALI 1985, 3:293–98; Perkins and Boyce 1982, 611–58)

ATTEMPT

Failure is an unwelcome part of everyday life, but in criminal law, we hope for failure. Criminal attempt is probably the best-known failure in criminal law. So we're relieved when a would-be murderer shoots at someone and misses the target, and we're happy when a store detective interrupts an aspiring thief just about to steal a CD from a bin in Wal-Mart.

In this section, we'll look at how the history of attempt law has evolved over more than two thousand years, rationales for attempt law, the elements of criminal attempt, and how failures to complete crimes because of either impossibility or voluntary abandonment are treated within the law.

History

> [One who] has a purpose and intention to slay another and only wounds him should be regarded as a murderer. (Plato, Laws, 360 B.C.)

> For what harm did the attempt cause, since the injury took no effect? (Henry of Bracton, about 1300; Bracton 1968–77, 3:21)

These two quotes, almost a thousand years apart, underscore how long philosophers and judges have struggled with how the criminal law should respond to criminal attempts. Until the 1500s, the English common law sided with Bracton; in attempts, "a miss was as good as a mile" (Hall 1960, 560). There were a few cases of attempted murder in the 1300s that adopted Plato's view, captured in the maxim "the intent shall be taken for the deed." One was a servant who cut his master's throat and ran off with his goods and the other a lover who attacked the husband and left him for dead (Hall 1960, 561). But according to the great scholar of medieval English law, Maitland, "the adoption of this perilous saying was but a momentary aberration" provoked by excessive leniency in these "murderous assaults that which did not cause death" (560).

Modern attempt law began in 1500s England out of frustration with this "excessive leniency" in a violent society where tempers were short and hot, and everyone was armed. The famous royal court (a special court of the monarch not bound by common-law rules) that met in the Star Chamber started punishing a wide range of potential harms, hoping to nip violence in the bud. Typical cases included lying in wait, threats, challenges, and even words that "tended to challenge." Surviving records are full of efforts to punish budding violence that too often erupted into serious injury and death (Elton 1972, 170–71).

In the early 1600s, the English common-law courts began to develop a doctrine of attempt law. Stressing the need to prevent the serious harms spawned by dueling, Francis Bacon maintained that "all the acts of preparation should be punished." He argued for this criminal attempt principle:

> I take it to be a ground infallible: that wheresoever an offense is capital, or matter of felony, though it be not acted, there the combination or acting tending to the offense is punishable. . . . Nay, inceptions and preparations in inferior crimes, that are not capital have likewise been condemned. (Samaha 1974; 1981, 189)

By the late 1700s, the English common-law courts had created a full-fledged law of attempt. In the great case of *Rex v. Scofield* (1784), a servant put a lighted candle in his master's house, intending to burn the house down. The house didn't burn, but the servant was punished anyway. According to the court, "the intent may make an act, innocent in itself, criminal; nor is the completion of an act, criminal in itself, necessary to constitute criminality." By the 1800s, common-law attempt was well defined:

> All attempts whatever to commit indictable offenses, whether felonies or misdemeanors . . . are misdemeanors, unless by some special statutory enactment they are subjected to special punishment. (Stephen 1883, 2:224)

Some jurisdictions still follow the common law of attempt. In 1979, a Maryland appeals court judge confidently wrote that "the common law is still alive and well in Maryland," and that the common law of attempt "still prospers on these shores" (*Gray v. State* 1979, 854). As of July 2006, no cases in Maryland had disputed this claim.

Rationales

Why do we punish people who haven't hurt anyone? There are two old and firmly entrenched rationales. One focuses on dangerous acts (*actus reus*), the other on dangerous persons (*mens rea*). The **dangerous act rationale** looks at how close defendants came to completing their crimes. The **dangerous person rationale** concentrates on how fully defendants have developed their criminal purpose.

Both rationales measure dangerousness according to actions, but they do so for different reasons. The dangerous act rationale aims at preventing harm from dangerous conduct, so its concern is how close to completion the crime was. The dangerous person rationale aims at neutralizing dangerous people, so it looks at how developed the defendant's criminal purpose was (Brodie 1995, 237–38).

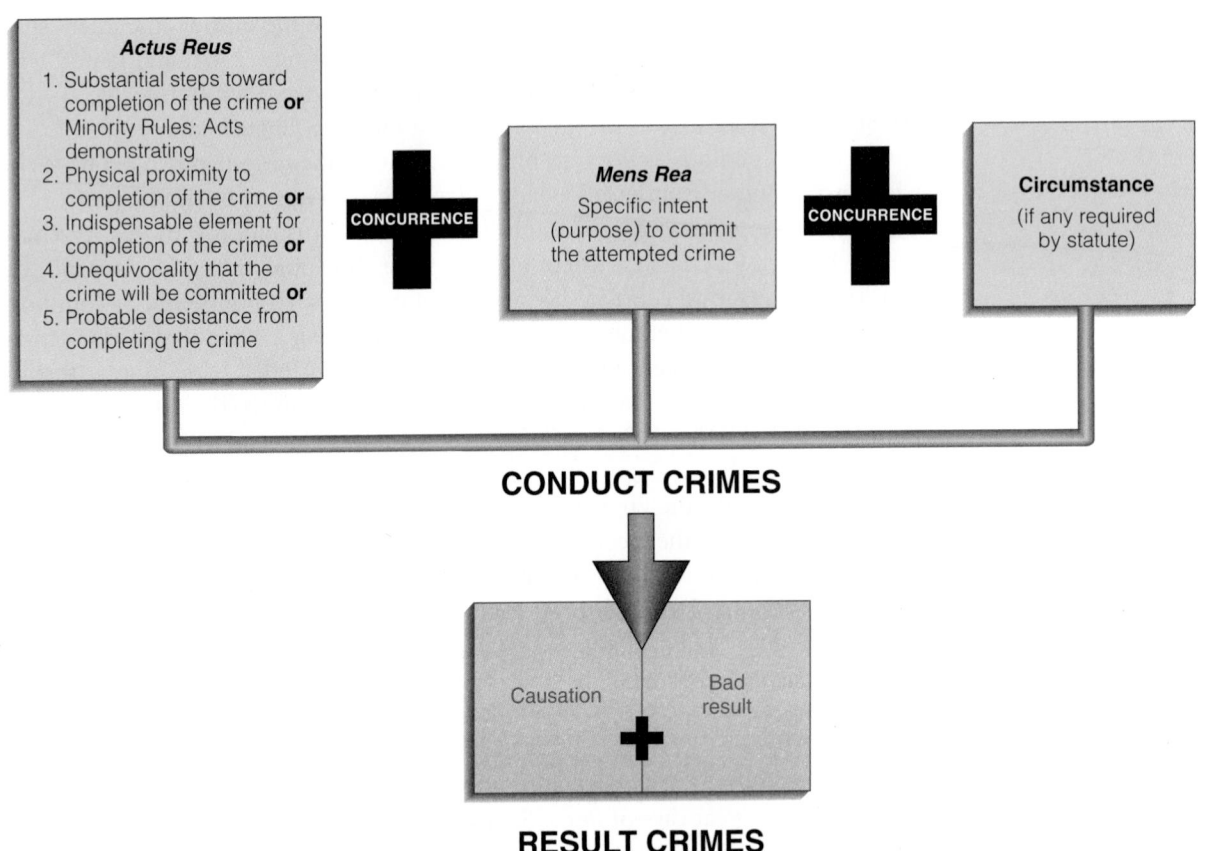

Elements of Attempt Liability

Elements

The crime of attempt consists of two elements: (1) intent or purpose to commit a specific crime and (2) an act, or acts, to carry out the intent. There are two types of attempt statutes, general and specific. Alabama's attempt statute is typical of the general type: "A person is guilty of an attempt to commit a crime if, with the intent to commit a specific offense, he does any overt act towards the commission of such offense" (Alabama Criminal Code 1975). Specific attempt statutes define attempts in terms of specific crimes, such as attempted murder, attempted robbery, and attempted rape in separate statutes. Let's look at each of the two elements the prosecution has to prove beyond a reasonable doubt in criminal attempts, *mens rea* and *actus reus*.

Go to the Criminal Law 9e website to find Exercise 8.1, Elements of Attempt Liability in Your State: www.thomsonedu.com/criminaljustice/samaha.

Attempt Mens Rea

Attempt is a crime of purpose. Attempt means to try, and you can't try to do something you don't specifically intend to do. As one authority put it:

> To attempt something . . . necessarily means to seek to do it, to make a deliberate effort in that direction. [Specific] intent is inherent in the notion of attempt; it is the essence of the crime. An attempt without intent is unthinkable; it cannot be. (Enker 1977, 847)

So when it comes to **attempt *mens rea*,** you don't have to worry about the difficult task of figuring out whether it was knowing, reckless, negligent, or strict liability. All attempt crimes require *purpose* to engage in criminal conduct or cause a criminal result.

U.S. Supreme Court Justice and legal philosopher Oliver Wendell Holmes (1963), in his classic, *The Common Law*, criticized the view that there can be no attempt without specific intent:

> Acts should be judged by their tendency, under the known circumstances, not by the actual intent which accompanies them. It may be true that in the region of attempts, as elsewhere, the law began with cases of actual intent, as these cases were the most obvious ones. But it cannot stop with them, unless it attaches more importance to the etymological meaning of the word attempt than to the general principles of punishment. (54–55)

Despite the weight of Justice Holmes's views, having the purpose to act or to bring about a specific result remains the linchpin of the criminal attempt mental attitude. The Michigan Court of Appeals examined, and rejected, the defendant's claim that he didn't intend to rob the Alpine Party Store—he was only joking.

CASE | *Did He Intend to Rob the Store?*

People v. Kimball

311 N.W.2d 343 (1981 Mich.App.)

HISTORY

James Kimball, Defendant, was charged with and convicted of attempted unarmed robbery, at a bench trial conducted in early August of 1979. He was sentenced to a prison term of from 3 to 5 years and appeals by leave granted. Reversed and remanded.

MAHER, J.

There is really very little dispute as to what happened on May 21, 1979, at the Alpine Party Store near Suttons Bay, Michigan. Instead, the dispute at trial centered on whether what took place amounted to a criminal offense or merely a bad joke.

FACTS

James Kimball (defendant) went to the home of a friend, Sandra Storey, where he proceeded to consume a large amount of vodka mixed with orange juice. Defendant was still suffering from insect stings acquired the previous day so he also took a pill called "Eskaleth 300," containing 300 milligrams of Lithium, which Storey had given him. After about an hour, the pair each mixed a half-gallon container of their favorite drinks (vodka and orange juice, in the defendant's case), and set off down the road in Storey's '74 MGB roadster. At approximately 8:15 or 8:30 in the evening, defendant (who was driving) pulled into the parking lot of the Alpine Party Store. Although he apparently did not tell Storey why he pulled in, defendant testified that the reason for the stop was to buy a pack of cigarettes.

Concerning events inside the store, testimony was presented by Susan Stanchfield, the clerk and sole employee present at the time. She testified that defendant came in and began talking to and whistling at the Doberman Pinscher guard dog on duty at the time. She gave him a "dirty look," because she didn't want him playing with the dog. Defendant then approached the cash register, where Stanchfield was stationed, and demanded money. Stanchfield testified that she thought the defendant was joking, and told him so, until he demanded money again in a "firmer tone."

STANCHFIELD: "By his tone I knew he meant business; that he wanted the money."

PROSECUTION: "You felt he was serious?"

STANCHFIELD: "I knew he was serious."

Stanchfield then began fumbling with the one dollar bills until defendant directed her to the "big bills." Stanchfield testified that as she was separating the checks from the twenty dollar bills defendant said "I won't do it to you; you're good looking and I won't do it to you this time, but if you're here next time, it won't matter."

A woman then came in (Storey) who put a hand on defendant's shoulder and another on his stomach and directed him out of the store. Stanchfield testified that she called after the defendant, saying that she would not call the police if he would "swear never to show your face around here again." To this defendant is alleged to have responded: "You could only get me on attempted anyway." Stanchfield then directed a customer to get the license plate number on defendant's car while she phoned the owner of the store.

Defendant also testified concerning events inside the store. He stated that the first thing he noticed when he walked in the door was the Doberman Pinscher. When he whistled the dog came to him and started licking his hand. Defendant testified that while he was petting the dog Stanchfield said "watch out for the dog; he's trained to protect the premises."

DEFENDANT: Well, as soon as she told me that the dog was a watchdog and a guarddog (sic), I just walked up in front of the cash register and said to Sue (Stanchfield) I said, "I want your money."

I was really loaded and it just seemed to me like it was kind of a cliché because of the fact that they've got this big bad watchdog there that's supposed to watch the place and there I was just petting it, and it was kind of an open door to carry it a little further and say hey, I want all your money because this dog isn't going to protect you. It just kind of happened all at once.

She said I can't quote it, but something to the effect that if this is just a joke, it's a bad joke, and I said, "Just give me your big bills."

Then she started fumbling in the drawer, and before she pulled any money out of the drawer I don't know whether she went to the ones or the twenties I said as soon as she went toward the drawer to actually give me the money, I said, "Hey, I'm just kidding," and something to the effect that you're too good-looking to take your money.

And she said, "Well, if you leave right now and don't ever come back, I won't call the police," and I said, "Okay, okay," and I started to back up.

And Sandy (Storey) I mean I don't know if I was stumbling back or stepping back, but I know she grabbed me, my arm, and said, "Let's go," and we turned around and left, and that was it.

Both Stanchfield and the defendant testified that there were other people in the store during the time that defendant was in the store, but the testimony of these people revealed that they did not hear what was said between Stanchfield and the defendant.

Storey testified that she remained in the car while defendant went into the store but that after waiting a reasonable time she went inside to see what was happening. As she approached the defendant she heard Stanchfield say "just promise you will never do that again and I won't take your license number." She then took defendant's arm, turned around, gave Stanchfield an "apologetic smile," and took defendant back to the car.

Once in the car, defendant told Storey what had happened in the store, saying "but I told her (Stanchfield) I was only kidding." Defendant and Storey then drove to a shopping center where defendant was subsequently arrested.

OPINION

The general attempt statute, under which defendant was prosecuted, provides in part as follows:

Any person who shall attempt to commit an offense prohibited by law, and in such attempt shall do any act towards the commission of such offense, but shall fail in the perpetration, or shall be intercepted or prevented in the execution of the same, when no express provision is made by law for the punishment of such attempt, shall be punished. . . . M.C.L. ß 750.92; M.S.A. ß 28.287.

The elements of an attempt are

(1) the specific intent to commit the crime attempted and

(2) an overt act going beyond mere preparation towards the commission of the crime.

Considering the second element first, it is clear that in the instant case defendant committed sufficient overt acts. As the trial court noted, there was evidence on every element of an unarmed robbery except for the actual taking of money. From the evidence presented, including the evidence of defendant's intoxication, the question of whether defendant undertook these acts with the specific intent to commit an unarmed robbery is a much closer question. After hearing all the evidence, however, the trial court found that defendant possessed the requisite intent and we do not believe that finding was clearly erroneous. . . . REVERSED AND REMANDED.

[The court reversed and remanded because the trial court didn't allow the defendant to prove that he voluntarily abandoned his attempt to rob the store. Abandonment is discussed later in the chapter.]

Questions

1. Summarize Susan Stanchfield's version and then James Kimball's version of what happened in the Alpine Party Store.

2. If you were a juror, which version would you believe? Explain your answer.

3. List the all the facts relevant to deciding whether Kimball specifically intended to rob the store.

4. Did Kimball specifically intend to rob the store? Back up your answer with the relevant facts and portions of the opinion.

EXPLORING FURTHER

Attempt Mens Rea

1. Did He Intend to Kill or to Injure Her?

State v. Harrell, 811 So.2d 1015 (La.App., 2002)

FACTS Defendant Thaddeus Harrell, who had blood all over his hands, told Deputy Joseph Ortego, who was responding to a disturbance call, that he had just "beat up his old lady." After handcuffing Harrell, Deputy Ortego went into the apartment and discovered the victim, lying face down on the ground in a large pool of blood, unconscious, but breathing. The apartment was in disarray, with furniture overturned, things broken and blood splattered everywhere, including the walls.

Deputy Ortego called for an ambulance, and the victim was transported to Charity Hospital, where she was treated for massive facial injuries. She had three facial lacerations: a 3-centimeter laceration below the right eye involving the corner of the eye and tear duct system, a 4-centimeter laceration above the left eye to the forehead with the bone showing, and a 2-centimeter laceration on her lower lip. She also sustained massive facial fractures, including a blowout fracture of her right eye socket and nasal fractures.

Was Harrell guilty of attempted murder?

DECISION The trial court said yes. The Louisiana Appeals court agreed:

. . . First or second degree attempted murder requires a specific intent to kill. Specific intent is that state of mind which exists when the circumstances indicate that the offender actively desired the prescribed criminal consequences to follow his act or failure to act. . . .

. . . Although . . . [Harrell] testified that he never intended to kill his wife, his specific intent to kill can be inferred from his actions and the extent and severity of the victim's injuries. Defendant first hit his wife outside of the apartment and continued to beat her when they went inside the apartment. . . . Dr. Lala Dunbar, the attending emergency room physician and director of the Medical Emergency Room at Charity Hospital, testified that the victim's beating was among the worst cases that she had seen in her 16 years in the emergency room at Charity Hospital. . . .

We find that the severity of the victim's injuries demonstrates the Defendant's specific intent to kill. Thus, the State proved the essential elements of the charged offense, attempted second degree murder, beyond a reasonable doubt.

2. Did She Shoot with the Intent to Kill?

People v. Moreland, WL 459026, (Cal.App. 2 Dist. 2002)

FACTS At approximately 10:20 P.M. on May 23, 1999, Mauricio Licea and his wife, Ana, parked their car in the parking lot of a Ralph's grocery store. Mauricio went into the store while Ana waited in the car. Mauricio returned to the car a few minutes later. As he opened the driver's side door to get in the car, the defendant (Lashun Pamela Moreland) approached him. Mauricio got in the car and shut the door. Moreland stood outside next to the car, knocked on the driver's side window, and said something. Mauricio tried to ignore her.

Moreland pulled a gun, pointed it at Mauricio, and motioned for him to open the door. Mauricio did not comply. Moreland then put her hand in the driver's side wing window opening and opened the door. Simultaneously, a man, identified as codefendant Hafez Hakeem, opened the car's rear door and got in the back seat. Hakeem pointed a gun at Ana's head, and Moreland pointed her gun at Mauricio's head.

Hakeem and Moreland took several items from Mauricio and Ana, including Mauricio's watch, Ana's engagement ring, cash, and a receipt from a market named Numero Uno. Moreland yelled at Mauricio, who did not speak English. Still, Mauricio tried to explain to Moreland that he had nothing left for her to take.

Hakeem struck Mauricio in the back of his head with the gun. Mauricio tried to get out of the car, raising his hands to his shoulders. Moreland pulled the trigger of her gun in rapid succession. Her gun did not fire during the first couple of attempts, but it then did so, hitting Mauricio twice in his abdomen and once in a finger. After the shooting, Moreland and Hakeem ran away. . . .

Mauricio suffered extensive damage to his intestines as a result of the shooting. He underwent two surgeries, was hospitalized for 20 days, and had to wear colostomy bags for 8 months. . . .

Did Moreland shoot Mauricio Licea for the purpose of killing him?

DECISION Yes, according to the appeals court: Moreland and her cohort robbed Mauricio and Ana Licea at gunpoint while they were seated in their car.

> During the robbery, defendant pointed a gun at Mauricio's head. When Mauricio tried to exit the car, defendant fired point-blank at Mauricio in rapid succession. Although defendant's first few attempts were ineffectual, apparently because her gun misfired, she succeeded in shooting Mauricio twice in his abdomen and once in his finger. A bullet was discovered inside of Mauricio's car.

> The foregoing reasonably supports a determination that defendant specifically intended to kill Mauricio when she shot him. That the evidence might support a different inference, i.e., that defendant panicked and in her panic she fired the gun without intending to kill Mauricio, is immaterial. On appeal, we are required to determine the legal sufficiency of the evidence and not to reweigh the evidence or second-guess the reasonable inferences reached by the trier of fact.

 Go to the Criminal Law 9e website to find the full text of the Exploring Further excerpts: www.thomsonedu. com/criminaljustice/samaha. (Excerpts on attempt *mens rea*.)

Attempt Actus Reus   You're sitting in your apartment, planning in detail when, how, and where you're going to kill your boyfriend and your best friend because they cheated on you with each other. You decide to do it tonight with your roommate's gun. You get up, go to her room, get the gun, pick up your car keys, and go to your car. Then, the enormity of what you're going to do hits you. You say to yourself, "What's wrong with me? What am I doing? I can't kill them." You go back and turn on the TV.

I don't believe anyone would think you committed attempted murder. Why? First, because, as we learned in Chapters 3 and 4, we don't punish people for their *bare* intentions. Justice Holmes in a famous passage wrote, "There is no law against a man's intending to commit a murder the day after tomorrow" (1963, 54). Of course, there's more than bare intention in our example. You got the gun, picked up your car keys, and went to your car. But we have a deeply entrenched rule that *preparing* to carry out your intention to commit a crime doesn't qualify as attempt *actus reus*.

But what if you went into her room, took the gun, loaded it, got your car keys, got in your car, and drove to your boyfriend's apartment. When he answered the door, you took out the gun, and pulled the trigger, but your hands were shaking so much you missed? I believe everybody would think you committed attempted murder. Why? Because you did everything you could to kill them. This version of the example represents the strictest rule of **attempt *actus reus*** called the **last proximate act rule.** Proximate means that your acts brought you as close as possible to completing the crime.

Most real cases aren't so easy. They fall somewhere between mere intent and "all but the last act" necessary to complete the crime. The toughest question in attempt law is, "How close to completing a crime is close enough to satisfy the criminal act requirement of attempt *actus reus?*" The general answer is somewhere on a continuum between preparation and the last proximate act.

This general answer is so general it's useless as a guide for deciding (and for us, understanding) real cases. So courts and attempt statutes have established tests to help decide when defendants' acts have taken them further than just getting ready to attempt and brought them close enough to completing crimes to qualify as attempt *actus reus*.

The tests reflect the focus of the two theories of attempt: dangerous conduct and dangerous people. Proximity tests focus on dangerous conduct; they look at what *remains* for actors to do before they hurt society by completing the crime. Other tests focus on dangerous people; they look at what actors have already *done* to demonstrate that they're a danger to society, not just in this crime but, more important, crimes they may commit in the future if they're not dealt with now. We'll look at three proximity tests of dangerous conduct: physical proximity, dangerous proximity, and indispensable element. Then, we'll examine two dangerous people tests: unequivocality (also called *res ipsa loquiter*) and substantial steps.

Before we examine the tests, it's important that you understand that the tests aren't mutually exclusive. As you work your way through the tests, don't look at them as conflicting definitions of the one single "true" test. Instead, think of them as efforts to describe more definitely the acts that are enough to fall within the spectrum between the end of preparation and short of the completed crime. Also, you should avoid thinking of one test as meaning closer in time to the completed crime than the others. That *might* be true (as in dangerous proximity), but it doesn't *have* to be. It can also mean more in quantity and quality (as when an indispensable element is present). Finally, *enough* and, as some courts say, *sufficient*, are "weasel" words, meaning they're purposely ambiguous to allow for variations in particular crimes and facts in specific cases.

Usually, courts in a jurisdiction adopt one test to determine if there are enough acts to satisfy the *actus reus* element in attempt. Others don't. According to the Florida Court of Appeals, "It does not appear that Florida has ever expressly adopted one of the . . . approaches." It went on to note that "adopting one approach to the exclusion of the others may not be advisable" (*State v. Hudson* 1999, 1000). Why isn't it advisable? So courts can use the tests as flexible instruments that best fit the countless variations in facts among individual cases. Now, let's look at the tests.

The **proximity tests** ask, "Were the defendant's acts close enough to the intended crime to count as the criminal act in the attempt?" Before we can answer that, we have to answer the question, "How close is close enough?" No cases or statutes have limited attempt *actus reus* to the last proximate act. Of course, "all but the last proximate act" satisfies the proximity test. The problem with this strict test is that it excludes dangerous conduct that falls short of the last proximate act that should be included. For example, the first dose of poison in a case of intended killing by small doses of poison wouldn't satisfy the last proximate act test for attempted murder *actus reus*. But the first dose *should* qualify as the *actus reus* (LaFave 2003a, 590).

Some courts have adopted broader proximity tests to help judges decide whether the facts that juries find the prosecution has proven beyond a reasonable doubt are enough to satisfy the *actus reus*. That is, they help to decide whether the defendant's acts fall within the spectrum between preparation, which clearly doesn't, and the last proximate act, which clearly does, satisfy the proximity test. Let's look at two of these broader proximity tests: the dangerous proximity to success and indispensable element tests.

The **dangerous proximity to success test** (also called the **physical proximity test**) asks whether defendants have come "dangerously close" to completing the crime. In Justice Holmes's words, "there must be a dangerous proximity to success" (*Hyde v. U.S.* 1912, 388). This test focuses on what actors still have to do to carry out their purpose to commit crimes, not on what they've already done to commit them. For example, if you plan to rob a bank messenger, and you're driving around checking out places where you think she might be, but you haven't found her yet, have you attempted to rob her? No, according to the court that decided the famous case of *People v. Rizzo* (1927):

> These defendants had planned to commit a crime, and were looking around the city for an opportunity to commit it, but the opportunity fortunately never came. Men would not be

guilty of attempt at burglary if they planned to break into a building while they were hunting about the streets for the building not knowing where it was. Neither would a man be guilty of an attempt to commit murder if he armed himself and started out to find the person he intended to kill but could not find him. So here these defendants were not guilty of an attempt to commit robbery . . . when they had not found or reached the presence of the person they intended to rob. (888)

The **indispensable element test** asks whether defendants have reached a point where they've gotten control of everything they need to complete the crime. For example, a drug dealer can't attempt to sell "Ecstasy" until she gets some Ecstasy, even if she has a customer right there, ready, and waiting to buy it. Once she's got the Ecstasy, she's close (proximate) enough to completing the crime to satisfy the attempt criminal act requirement.

Now, let's turn to two dangerous person tests that look at what defendants have already *done*, not at what they still have to do: the unequivocality and substantial steps tests.

The **unequivocality test,** also called the *res ipsa loquiter* test ("the act speaks for itself"), examines whether an ordinary person who saw the defendant's acts without knowing her intent would believe she was determined to commit the intended crime. Notice, it's the "intended" crime, not any crime. Here's a frequently used example to describe the test:

It is as though a cinematograph film, which had so far depicted the accused person's act without stating what was his intention, had been suddenly stopped, and the audience were asked to say to what end those acts were directed. If there is only one reasonable answer to this question then the accused has done what amounts to an "attempt" to attain that end. (Turner 1934, 238)

Walter Lee Stewart passed the "stop the film test." In *State v. Stewart* (1988, 50), the facts were that

Scott Kodanko was waiting for a bus on a Saturday afternoon after leaving work. He was alone in a three-sided plexiglas bus shelter open to the street in downtown Milwaukee. Two men, Mr. Moore and Walter Lee Stewart, the defendant, entered the bus shelter while a third man, Mr. Levy, remained outside.

Moore and the defendant stood one to two feet from Kodanko. Kodanko was in a corner of the shelter, his exit to the street blocked by the two men. Moore asked Kodanko if he wanted to buy some cigarettes. Kodanko responded that he did not. Moore then said, "Give us some change." When Kodanko refused, the defendant said "Give us some change, man." The defendant repeated this demand in an increasingly loud voice three to four times. Kodanko still refused to give the two men change. The defendant then reached into his coat with his right hand at about the waist level, whereupon Moore stated something to the effect of "put that gun away." At that point Levy, who had been waiting outside the bus shelter, entered and said to the defendant and Moore "Come on, let's go." Levy showed Kodanko some money, stating, "I don't want your money, I got lots of money." (45–46)

According to the court:

If the defendant had been filmed in this case and the film stopped just before Levy entered the bus stop and the three men departed, we conclude that a trier of fact could find beyond a reasonable doubt that the defendant's acts were directed toward robbery. The film would show the defendant demanding money and appearing to reach for a gun. This evidence is sufficient to prove that the defendant had taken sufficient steps for his conduct to constitute an attempted robbery. (50)

The distinguished Professor Glanville Williams (1961) criticizes the unequivocality test because it "would acquit many undoubted criminals" (630).

The **probable desistance test** is another dangerous person test that focuses on how far defendants have gone, not on what's left for them to do to complete the crime. According to the test, defendants have gone far enough toward completing the crime

CHAPTER 8/INCHOATE CRIMES: ATTEMPT, CONSPIRACY, AND SOLICITATION that it's unlikely they'll turn back. Former prosecutor Robert Skilton provides us with this excellent description of probable desistance:

> The defendant's conduct must pass that point where most . . . [people], holding such an intention as the defendant holds, would think better of their conduct and desist. All of us, or most of us, at some time or other harbor what may be described as a criminal intent to effect unlawful consequences. Many of us take some steps—often slight enough in character—to bring the consequences about; but most of us, when we reach a certain point, desist, and return to our roles as law-abiding citizens. The few who do not and pass beyond that point are, if the object of their conduct is not achieved, guilty of a criminal attempt. (Skilton 1937, 309–10)

The Model Penal Code's **substantial steps test** (also called the **"MPC test"**) was designed to accomplish three important goals:

1. Replace (or at least drastically reform) the proximity and unequivocality tests with a clearer and easier-to-understand-and-apply test

2. Draw more sharply (and push back further toward preparation) the line between preparation and beginning to attempt the crime

3. Base the law of attempt firmly on the theory of neutralizing dangerous persons, not just on preventing dangerous conduct

In line with these goals, the MPC's attempt *actus reus* includes two elements: (1) "substantial steps" toward completing the crime and (2) steps that "strongly corroborate the actor's criminal purpose." In other words, the code requires that attempters take enough steps toward completing the crime not to show that a crime is about to occur but to prove that the attempters are determined to commit it.

To sharpen the line between preparation and attempt, push it back closer to preparation, and make clear the commitment to neutralizing dangerous people, the code lists seven acts (most of which would qualify as mere preparation in traditional attempt statutes) that can amount to "substantial steps" if they strongly corroborate the actor's criminal purpose to commit the intended crime:

1. Lying in wait, searching for, or following the contemplated victim of the crime

2. Enticing, or seeking to entice, the contemplated victim of the crime to go to the place contemplated for its commission

3. Reconnoitering ["casing"] the place contemplated for the commission of the crime

4. Unlawful entry of a structure, vehicle, or enclosure in which it is contemplated that the crime will be committed

5. Possession of materials to be employed in the commission of the crime that are specially designed for such unlawful use or that can serve no lawful purpose of the actor under the circumstances

6. Possession, collection, or fabrication of materials to be employed in the commission of the crime, at or near the place contemplated for its commission, if such possession, collection, or fabrication serves no lawful purpose of the actor under the circumstances

7. Soliciting an innocent agent to engage in conduct constituting an element of the crime (ALI 1985, 3:296)

Borrowing from indecent liberties statutes (which make it a crime to lure minors into cars or houses for sex), the Model Penal Code provides that enticement satisfies the *actus reus* of criminal attempt. The drafters of the MPC say that enticement clearly demonstrates the intent to commit a crime—so enticers are dangerous enough to punish.

The MPC provides that reconnoitering—popularly called "casing a joint"—satisfies attempt *actus reus*, because "scouting the scene of a contemplated crime" clearly signals the intent to commit the crime. By their unlawful entries, intruders also demonstrate their criminal purpose.

The unlawful entry provision is particularly useful in two types of cases: entries to commit sex offenses and entries to steal. In one case (*Bradley v. Ward* 1955), two defendants entered a car intending to steal it, but they got out when the owner unexpectedly came back to the car. According to the court, the defendants hadn't attempted to steal the car. But under the MPC's "unlawful entry" provision, they wouldn't have been so lucky.

In most states, collecting, possessing, or preparing materials used to commit crimes is preparation, not attempt. So courts have found that buying a gun to murder someone, making a bomb to blow up a house, and collecting tools for a burglary are preparations, not attempts. Although these activities aren't criminal attempts, in many criminal codes it's a crime to possess items and substances like burglary tools, illegal drugs, drug paraphernalia, and concealed weapons (Chapter 3). Under the MPC (ALI 1985, 3:337–46), these possessions can be acts of attempt, but only if they "strongly corroborate" a purpose to commit a crime. Why? Because, according to the MPC's *Reporter*, people who carry weapons and burglary tools with them with the clear intent to commit crimes are dangerous enough to punish.

The MPC provides that bringing weapons, equipment, and other materials to the scene of a crime can qualify as attempt *actus reus*. Examples include bringing guns to a robbery, explosives to an arson, or a ladder to a burglary. But the items have to be plainly instruments of crime. A potential robber who brings a gun to a bank is bringing an instrument of robbery; a would-be forger who brings a ballpoint pen into a bank isn't (ALI 1985, 3:337).

Preparation isn't criminal attempt, but some states have created less serious preparation offenses. In Nevada, preparing to commit arson is a crime. Preparing to manufacture illegal substances is an offense in other states. These statutes are aimed at balancing the degree of threatening behavior and the dangerousness of persons against the remoteness in time and place of the intended harm (ALI, 1985, 2:344–45).

Young v. State (1985) adopts and then applies the MPC's substantial steps test to Raymond Young's acts in leading up to what the prosecution believed was Young's attempt to rob a bank.

CASE · *Did He Take Substantial Steps to Rob the Bank?*

Young v. State
493 A.2d 352 (Md. 1985)

HISTORY

Raymond Alexander Young, Defendant, was convicted before the Circuit Court for Prince George's County, of attempted armed robbery. He was sentenced to 20 years, and he appealed. The Court of Special Appeals affirmed the conviction and sentence, and Young petitioned for certiorari. The Maryland Court of Appeals (Maryland's highest court) affirmed his conviction.

ORTH, J.

The offense of criminal attempt has long been accepted as a part of the criminal law of Maryland. . . . [The court defined elements of the offense as:]

1) a specific intent to do a criminal act and

2) some act in furtherance of that intent going beyond mere preparation.

[A statute provides that] the sentence of a person who is convicted of an attempt to commit a crime may not exceed the maximum sentence for the crime attempted. . . .

Such was the posture of the law of Maryland regarding criminal attempts when Raymond Alexander Young, also known as Morris Prince Cunningham and Prince Alexander Love, was found guilty by a jury in the Circuit Court for Prince George's County. . . . In imposing sentence the court said:

> Young is 41 years old. He has been a crime wave up and down the East Coast from New York to Tennessee. Now he stopped in Maryland, and look what he did here.
>
> He is a violent criminal. Now I am sorry he doesn't have this consciousness of right or wrong. And I don't understand why he can't learn it, because he has had a chance to reflect in prison. But I have to take him off the street for the safety of people.
>
> It appears from the transcript of the sentencing proceedings that at the time Young was sentenced upon the convictions here reviewed he was also sentenced upon convictions rendered at a separate trial of armed robbery and the use of a handgun in a crime of violence to 20 years and 15 years respectively to run concurrently, but consecutively to the sentences imposed in this case.

FACTS

Several banks in the Oxon Hill–Fort Washington section of Prince George's County had been held up. The Special Operations Division of the Prince George's Police Department set up a surveillance of banks in the area. In the early afternoon of 26 November 1982 the police team observed Young driving an automobile in such a manner as to give rise to a reasonable belief that he was casing several banks. They followed him in his reconnoitering.

At one point when he left his car to enter a store, he was seen to clip a scanner onto his belt. The scanner later proved to contain an operable crystal number frequency that would receive Prince George's County uniform patrol transmissions. At that time Young was dressed in a brown waist-length jacket and wore sunglasses.

Around 2:00 P.M. Young came to rest at the rear of the Fort Washington branch of the First National Bank of Southern Maryland. Shortly before, he had driven past the front of the Bank and parked in the rear of it for a brief time.

He got out of his car and walked hurriedly beside the Bank toward the front door. He was still wearing the brown waist-length jacket and sunglasses, but he had added a blue knit stocking cap pulled down to the top of the sunglasses, white gloves and a black eye patch. His jacket collar was turned up. His right hand was in his jacket pocket and his left hand was in front of his face. As one of the police officers observing him put it, he was "sort of duck[ing] his head."

It was shortly after 2:00 P.M. and the Bank had just closed. Through the windows of his office the Bank Manager saw Young walking on the "landscape" by the side of the Bank toward the front door. Young had his right hand in his jacket pocket and tried to open the front door with his left hand. When he realized that the door was locked and the Bank was closed, he retraced his steps, running past the windows with his left hand covering his face. The Bank Manager had an employee call the police.

Young ran back to his car, yanked open the door, got in, and put the car in drive "all in one movement almost," and drove away. The police stopped the car and ordered Young to get out. Young was in the process of removing his jacket; it fell over the car seat and partially onto the ground. The butt of what proved to be a loaded .22 caliber revolver was sticking out of the right pocket of the jacket. On the front seat of the car were a pair of white surgical gloves, a black eye patch, a blue knit stocking cap, and a pair of sunglasses. Young told the police that his name was Morris P. Cunningham. As Young was being taken from the scene, he asked "how much time you could get for attempted bank robbery."

OPINION

A criminal attempt requires specific intent; the specific intent must be to commit some other crime. . . . [The court concluded that the] . . . evidence is most compelling . . . is more than legally sufficient to establish beyond a reasonable doubt that Young had the specific intent to commit an armed robbery as charged. . . .

The determination of the overt act which is beyond mere preparation in furtherance of the commission of the intended crime is a most significant aspect of criminal attempts. If an attempt is to be a culpable offense serving as the basis for the furtherance of the important societal interests of crime prevention and the correction of those persons who have sufficiently manifested their dangerousness, the police must be able to ascertain with reasonable assurance when it is proper for them to intervene.

It is not enough to say merely that there must be "some overt act beyond mere preparation in furtherance of the crime" as the general definition puts it.

The definition does, however, highlight the problem as to what "proximity to completion person must achieve before he can be deemed to have attempted to commit a crime." In solving this problem the interest of society and the rights of the individual must be kept in balance. Thus, the importance of the determination of the point at which the police may properly intervene is readily apparent. There is no dispute that there must be some overt act to trigger police action. . . . Bad thoughts do not constitute a crime, and so it is not enough that a person merely have intended and prepared to commit a crime. There must also be an act, and not any act will suffice.

What act will suffice to show that an attempt itself has reached the stage of a completed crime has persistently troubled the courts. They have applied a number of approaches in order to determine when preparation for the commission of a crime has ceased and the actual attempt to commit it has begun.

[The court surveys here the proximity, probable desistance, unequivocality, and MPC substantial capacity tests discussed in your text just prior to this excerpt.] . . .

Each of these approaches is not without advantages and disadvantages in theory and in application, as is readily apparent from a perusal of the comments of various text writers and of the courts. We believe that the preferable approach is one bottomed on the "substantial step" test as is that of Model Penal Code. We think that using a "substantial step" as the criterion in determining whether an overt act is more than mere preparation to commit a crime is clearer, sounder, more practical and easier to apply to the multitude of differing fact situations which may occur. Therefore, in formulating a test to fix the point in the development of events at which a person goes further than mere unindictable preparation and becomes guilty of attempt, we eliminate from consideration the "Proximity Approach," the "Probable Desistance Approach" and the "Equivocality Approach."
. . . Convinced that an approach based on the "substantial step" test is the proper one to determine whether a person has attempted to commit a crime, and that ß 110.00 of the Md. Proposed Criminal Code best expressed it, we adopt the provisions of that section.

[With a few modifications, the court's adoption tracks the excerpted parts of the MPC provision in your text.]

This language follows ß 5.01(1)(c) of the Model Penal Code, but . . . eliminates failure to consummate the intended crime as one of the essential elements of a criminal attempt. Thus, the State is not required to prove beyond a reasonable doubt that the crime was not in fact committed. Furthermore, the elimination of failure as a necessary element makes attempt available as a compromise verdict or a compromise charge.

When the facts and circumstances of . . . [this] case . . . are considered in the light of the overt act standard which we have adopted, it is perfectly clear that the evidence was sufficient to prove that Young attempted the crime of armed robbery as charged.

As we have seen, the police did not arrive on the scene after the fact. They had the advantage of having Young under observation for some time before his apprehension. They watched his preparations. They were with him when he reconnoitered or cased the banks.

His observations of the banks were in a manner not usual for law-abiding individuals and were under circumstances that warranted alarm for the safety of persons or property. Young manifestly endeavored to conceal his presence by parking behind the Bank which he had apparently selected to rob. He disguised himself with an eye patch and made an identification of him difficult by turning up his jacket collar and by donning sunglasses and a knit cap which he pulled down over his forehead. He put on rubber surgical gloves. Clipped on his belt was a scanner with a police band frequency. Except for the scanner, which he had placed on his belt while casing the

Bank, all this was done immediately before he left his car and approached the door of the Bank.

As he walked towards the Bank he partially hid his face behind his left hand and ducked his head. He kept his right hand in the pocket of his jacket in which, as subsequent events established, he was carrying, concealed, a loaded handgun, for which he had no lawful use or right to transport. He walked to the front door of the Bank and tried to enter the premises.

When he discovered that the door was locked, he ran back to his car, again partially concealing his face with his left hand. He got in his car and immediately drove away. He removed the knit hat, sunglasses, eye patch and gloves, and placed the scanner over the sun visor of the car. When apprehended, he was trying to take off his jacket. His question as to how much time he could get for attempted bank robbery was not without significance.

It is clear that the evidence which showed Young's conduct leading to his apprehension established that he performed the necessary overt act toward the commission of armed robbery, which was more than mere preparation.

Even if we assume that all of Young's conduct before he approached the door of the Bank was mere preparation, on the evidence, the jury could properly find as a fact that when Young tried to open the bank door to enter the premises, that act constituted a "substantial step" toward the commission of the intended crime. It was strongly corroborative of his criminal intention.

One of the reasons why the substantial step approach has received such widespread favor is because it usually enables the police to intervene at an earlier stage than do the other approaches. In this case, however, the requisite overt act came near the end of the line. Indeed, it would qualify as the necessary act under any of the approaches—the proximity approach, the probable desistance approach or the equivocality approach. It clearly met the requirements of the substantial step approach. Since Young, as a matter of fact, could be found by the jury to have performed an overt act which was more than mere preparation, and was a substantial step towards the commission of the intended crime of armed robbery, it follows as a matter of law that he committed the offense of criminal attempt.

We think that the evidence adduced showed directly, or circumstantially, or supported a rational inference of, the facts to be proved from which the jury could fairly be convinced, beyond a reasonable doubt, of Young's guilt of attempted armed robbery as charged. Therefore, the evidence was sufficient in law to sustain the conviction. We so hold.

JUDGMENTS OF THE COURT OF SPECIAL APPEALS AFFIRMED; COSTS TO BE PAID BY APPELLANT.

Questions

1. List all of Young's acts that the court recites in the excerpt
2. Mark on your list the following points that you believe show:

a. When, if at all, Young formed the intent to commit the robbery
b. When, if at all, Young's preparation began and ended
c. When, if at all, Young's acts were enough to satisfy the *actus reus* requirement for attempted armed robbery

Explain your answers.

3. Which of the tests for *actus reus* discussed in the text do Young's acts pass? Back up your answers with the facts you listed in (1).

EXPLORING FURTHER

Attempt Actus Reus

1. Did He Take "Substantial Steps" Toward Escaping?

Commonwealth v. Gilliam, 417 A.2d 1203 (Pa.Sup. 1980)

FACTS A guard at Dallas State Correctional Institution discovered that the bars of the window in Richard Gilliam's cell had been cut and were being held in place by sticks and paper.

The condition of the bars was such that they could be removed manually at will. The same guard observed that a shelf hook was missing from its place in the cell. A subsequent search revealed vise grips concealed inside the appellant's mattress, and two knotted extension cords attached to a hook were found in a box of clothing. At trial, evidence showed that the hook had been fashioned from the missing shelf hook. The vise grips were capable of cutting barbed wire of the type located along the top of the fence that was the sole barrier between the appellant's cell window and the perimeter of the prison compound. Inspection of the cell immediately before it was assigned to Gilliam as its sole occupant had disclosed bars intact and the shelf hooks in place. Did Gilliam commit the crime of attempted escape?

DECISION The Pennsylvania Superior court said yes, because Gilliam had taken substantial steps by not only gathering the tools for his escape but also sawing through the bars. According to the court, "the substantial step [MPC] test broadens the scope of attempt liability by concentrating on the acts the defendant has done and does not . . . focus on the acts remaining to be done before actual commission of the crime."

2. Did They Get "Very Near" to Robbing the Clerk?

People v. Rizzo, 158 N.E. 888 (N.Y.App. 1927)

FACTS Charles Rizzo, Anthony J. Dorio, Thomas Milo, and John Thomasello were driving through New York City looking for a payroll clerk they intended to rob. While they were still looking for their victim, the police apprehended and arrested them. They were tried and convicted of attempted robbery. Rizzo appealed. Did their acts add up to attempt *actus reus*?

DECISION The trial court said yes. The New York Court of Appeals (New York's highest court), reversed:

The Penal Law, § 2, prescribes that:

An act, done with intent to commit a crime, and tending but failing to effect its commission, is "an attempt to commit that crime." The word "tending" is very indefinite. It is perfectly evident that there will arise differences of opinion as to whether an act in a given case is one tending to commit a crime. "Tending" means to exert activity in a particular direction. Any act in preparation to commit a crime may be said to have a tendency towards its accomplishment.

The procuring of the automobile, searching the streets looking for the desired victim, were in reality acts tending toward the commission of the proposed crime.

The law, however, had recognized that many acts in the way of preparation are too remote to constitute the crime of attempt. The line has been drawn between those acts which are remote and those which are proximate and near to the consummation. The law must be practical, and therefore considers those acts only as tending to the commission of the crime which are so near to its accomplishment that in all reasonable probability the crime itself would have been committed, but for timely interference. The cases which have been before the courts express this idea in different language, but the idea remains the same. The act or acts must come or advance very near to the accomplishment of the intended crime.

3. "Preparation" or "All But the Last Act"?

Commonwealth v. Peaslee, 59 N.E. 55 (Mass. 1901)

FACTS Lincoln Peaslee had made and arranged combustibles in a building he owned so they were ready to be lighted and, if lighted, would have set fire to the building and its contents.

He got within a quarter of a mile of the building, but his would-be accomplice refused to light the fire. Did Peaslee attempt to commit arson?

DECISION According to the court, he didn't: "A mere collection and preparation of materials in a room, for the purpose of setting fire to them, unaccompanied by any present intent to set the fire, would be too remote and not all but 'the last act' necessary to complete the crime."

 Go to the Criminal Law 9e website to find the full text of the Exploring Further Excerpts: www.thomsonedu.com/criminaljustice/samaha. (Excerpts on attempt *actus reus*.)

Impossibility

To avoid paying customs, a man sneaks an antique book past customs. What he doesn't know is there's an exception in the law for antique books. Has he attempted to evade customs laws? A woman stabs her battering husband repeatedly, thinking he's asleep. In fact, he died of a heart attack 2 hours before she stabs him. Has she committed attempted murder? The would-be customs evader isn't guilty; the battered woman is.

The first scenario is an example of **legal impossibility.** A legal impossibility occurs when actors intend to commit crimes, and do everything they can to carry out their criminal intent, but the criminal law doesn't ban what they did. So even though he wanted to evade customs laws, and did all he could to commit the crime of tax evasion, it's legally impossible to commit a crime that doesn't exist. If the law were different, he'd be guilty; but it isn't, so legal impossibility is a defense to criminal liability.

Stabbing an already dead victim is an example of **factual impossibility.** A factual impossibility occurs when actors intend to commit a crime and try to but some fact or circumstance—an **extraneous factor**—interrupts them to prevent the completion of the crime. The woman intended to murder her battering husband. She did all she could to commit it by stabbing him; if the facts had been different—that is, if her victim had been alive—she would've murdered him.

Legal impossibility requires a different law to make the conduct criminal; factual impossibility requires different facts to complete the crime. In most jurisdictions, legal impossibility is a defense to criminal attempt; factual impossibility is not. The main reason for the difference is that to convict someone for conduct the law doesn't prohibit, no matter what the actor's intentions, violates the principle of legality—no crime without a law, no punishment without a crime (see Chapter 1). Factual impossibility, on the other hand, would allow chance to determine criminal liability. A person who's determined to commit a crime, and who does enough to succeed in that determination, shouldn't escape responsibility and punishment because of a stroke of good luck (Dutile and Moore 1979, 181).

The Wisconsin Supreme Court addressed the issue of factual impossibility in *State v. Damms* (1960).

CASE — *Was the Unloaded Gun a "Factual Impossibility"?*

State v. Damms
100 N.W.2d 592 (Wis. 1960)

HISTORY

The defendant Ralph Damms was charged by information with the offense of attempt to commit murder in the first degree. The jury found the defendant guilty as charged, and the defendant was sentenced to imprisonment in the state prison at Waupun for a term of not more than ten years. Damms appealed to the Wisconsin Supreme Court. The Supreme Court affirmed the conviction.

CURRIE, J.

FACTS

The alleged crime occurred on April 6, 1959, near Menomonee Falls in Waukesha county. Prior to that date Marjory Damms, wife of the defendant, had instituted an action for divorce against him and the parties lived apart.

She was thirty-nine years and he thirty-three years of age. Marjory Damms was also estranged from her mother, Mrs. Laura Grant.

That morning, a little before eight o'clock, Damms drove his automobile to the vicinity in Milwaukee where he knew Mrs. Damms would take the bus to go to work. He saw her walking along the sidewalk, stopped, and induced her to enter the car by falsely stating that Mrs. Grant was ill and dying. They drove to Mrs. Grant's home. Mrs. Damms then discovered that her mother was up and about and not seriously ill. Nevertheless, the two Damms remained there nearly two hours conversing and drinking coffee. Apparently it was the intention of Damms to induce a reconciliation between mother and daughter, hoping it would result in one between himself and his wife, but not much progress was achieved in such direction.

At the conclusion of the conversation, Mrs. Damms expressed the wish to phone for a taxicab to take her to work. Damms insisted on her getting into his car, and said he would drive her to work. They again entered his car, but instead of driving south towards her place of employment, he drove in the opposite direction. Some conversation was had in which he stated that it was possible for a person to die quickly and not be able to make amends for anything done in the past, and referred to the possibility of "judgment day" occurring suddenly.

Mrs. Damms' testimony as to what then took place is as follows: "When he was telling me about this being judgment day, he pulled a cardboard box from under the seat of the car and brought it up to the seat and opened it up and took a gun out of a paper bag. He aimed it at my side and he said, 'This is to show you I'm not kidding.' I tried to quiet him down. He said he wasn't fooling. I said if it was just a matter of my saying to my mother that everything was all right, we could go back and I would tell her that."

They did return to Mrs. Grant's home and Mrs. Damms went inside and Damms stayed outside. In a few minutes he went inside and asked Mrs. Damms to leave with him. Mrs. Grant requested that they leave quietly so as not to attract the attention of the neighbors. They again got into the car, and this time drove out on Highway 41 towards Menomonee Falls. Damms stated to Mrs. Damms that he was taking her "up North" for a few days, the apparent purpose of which was to effect a reconciliation between them.

As they approached a roadside restaurant, he asked her if she would like something to eat. She replied that she wasn't hungry but would drink some coffee. Damms then drove the car off the highway beside the restaurant and parked it with the front facing, and in close proximity to, the restaurant wall.

Damms then asked Mrs. Damms how much money she had with her and she said "a couple of dollars." He then requested to see her checkbook and she refused to give it to him. A quarrel ensued between them. Mrs. Damms opened the car door and started to run around the restaurant building screaming, "Help!" Damms pursued her with the pistol in his hand.

Mrs. Damms cries for help attracted the attention of the persons inside the restaurant, including two officers of the State Traffic Patrol who were eating their lunch. One officer rushed out of the front door and the other the rear door. In the meantime, Mrs. Damms had run nearly around three sides of the building. In seeking to avoid colliding with a child, who was in her path, she turned, slipped and fell. Damms crouched down, held the pistol at her head, and pulled the trigger, but nothing happened. He then exclaimed, "It won't fire. It won't fire."

Damms testified that at the time he pulled the trigger the gun was pointing down at the ground and not at Mrs. Damms' head. However, the two traffic patrol officers both testified that Damms had the gun pointed directly at her head when he pulled the trigger. The officers placed Damms under arrest. They found that the pistol was unloaded. The clip holding the cartridges, which is inserted in the butt of the gun to load it, they found in the cardboard box in Damms' car together with a box of cartridges.

That afternoon, Damms was questioned by a deputy sheriff at the Waukesha county jail, and a clerk in the sheriff's office typed out the questions and Damms' answers as they were given. Damms later read over such typed statement of questions and answers, but refused to sign it. In such statement Damms stated that he thought the gun was loaded at the time of the alleged attempt to murder. Both the deputy sheriff and the undersheriff testified that Damms had stated to them that he thought the gun was loaded. On the other hand, Damms testified at the trial that he knew at the time of the alleged attempt that the pistol was not loaded.

OPINION

The two questions raised on this appeal are:

(1) Did the fact, that it was impossible for the accused to have committed the act of murder because the gun was unloaded, preclude his conviction of the offense of attempt to commit murder?

(2) Assuming that the foregoing question is answered in the negative, does the evidence establish the guilt of the accused beyond a reasonable doubt?

Sec. 939.32(2), Stats., provides as follows:

An attempt to commit a crime requires that the actor have an intent to perform acts and attain a result which, if accomplished, would constitute such crime and that he does acts toward the commission of the crime which demonstrate unequivocally, under all the circumstances, that he formed that intent and would commit the crime *except for the intervention of* another person or *some other extraneous factor*. (emphasis added)

The issue with respect to the first of the aforestated two questions boils down to whether the impossibility of accomplishment due to the gun being unloaded falls within the statutory words, "except for the intervention of . . . some other extraneous factor." We conclude that it does.

Prior to the adoption of the new criminal code by the 1955 legislature the criminal statutes of this state had separate sections making it an offense to assault with intent to do great bodily harm, to murder, to rob, and to rape, etc. The new code did away with these separate sections by creating sec. 939.32, Stats., covering all attempts to commit a battery or felony, and making the maximum penalty not to exceed one-half the penalty imposed for the completed crime, except that, if the penalty for a completed crime is life imprisonment, the maximum penalty for the attempt is thirty years imprisonment.

In an article in 1956 *Wisconsin Law Review*, by assistant attorney general Platz, who was one of the authors of the new criminal code, explaining such code, he points out that "attempt" is defined therein in a more intelligible fashion than by using such tests as "beyond mere preparation," "*locus poenitentiae*" (the place at which the actor may repent and withdraw), or "dangerous proximity to success." Quoting the author:

> Emphasis upon the dangerous propensities of the actor as shown by his conduct, rather than upon how close he came to succeeding, is more appropriate to the purposes of the criminal law to protect society and reform offenders or render them temporarily harmless.

[The court reviewed cases from other states and criminal treatises by well-known scholars on the question of impossibility.] . . .

Sound public policy would seem to support the majority view that impossibility not apparent to the actor should not absolve him from the offense of attempt to commit the crime he intended. An unequivocal act accompanied by intent should be sufficient to constitute a criminal attempt. Insofar as the actor knows, he has done everything necessary to insure the commission of the crime intended, and he should not escape punishment because of the fortuitous circumstance that by reason of some fact unknown to him it was impossible to effectuate the intended result.

It is our considered judgment that the fact, that the gun was unloaded when Damms pointed it at his wife's head and pulled the trigger, did not absolve him of the offense charged, if he actually thought at the time that it was loaded.

We do not believe that the further contention raised in behalf of the accused, that the evidence does not establish his guilt of the crime charged beyond a reasonable doubt, requires extensive consideration on our part.

The jury undoubtedly believed the testimony of the deputy sheriff and undersheriff that Damms told them on the day of the act that he thought the gun was loaded. This is also substantiated by the written statement constituting a transcript of his answers given in his interrogation at the county jail on the same day.

The gun itself, which is an exhibit in the record, is the strongest piece of evidence in favor of Damms' present contention that he at all times knew the gun was unloaded. Practically the entire bottom end of the butt of the pistol is open. Such opening is caused by the absence of the clip into which the cartridges must be inserted in order to load the pistol. This readily demonstrates to anyone looking at the gun that it could not be loaded. Because the unloaded gun with this large opening in the butt was an exhibit which went to the jury room, we must assume that the jury examined the gun and duly considered it in arriving at their verdict.

We are not prepared to hold that the jury could not come to the reasonable conclusion that, because of Damms' condition of excitement when he grabbed the gun and pursued his wife, he so grasped it as not to see the opening in the end of the butt which would have unmistakably informed him that the gun was unloaded. Having so concluded, they could rightfully disregard Damms' testimony given at the trial that he knew the pistol was unloaded.

Judgment affirmed.

DISSENT

DIETERICH, J.

I disagree with the majority opinion in respect to their interpretations and conclusions of sec. 939.32(2), Stats.

The issue raised on this appeal: Could the defendant be convicted of murder, under sec. 939.32(2), Stats., when it was impossible for the defendant to have caused the death of anyone because the gun or pistol involved was unloaded?

Sec. 939.32(2), Stats., provides:

> *An attempt* to commit a crime *requires* that *the actor* have an *intent* to *perform acts* and *attain a result* which, *if accomplished*, would constitute such crime and that *he does acts* toward the commission of the crime which *demonstrate unequivocally*, under all the circumstances, that he *formed* that *intent* and would *commit* the crime *except for the intervention of another person or some other extraneous factor*. (emphasis added)

In view of the statute, the question arising under sec. 939.32(2), is whether the impossibility of accomplishment due to the pistol being unloaded falls within the statutory words "*except for the intervention of . . . or some other extraneous factor*," it does not.

In interpreting the statute we must look to the ordinary meaning of words. Webster's New International Dictionary defines "extraneous" as not belonging to or dependent upon a thing, . . . originated or coming from without.

The plain distinct meaning of the statute is: A person must form an intent to commit a particular crime and this intent must be coupled with sufficient preparation on his part and with overt acts from which it can be determined clearly, surely and absolutely the crime would be committed except for the intervention of some independent thing or something originating or coming from someone or something over which the actor has no control.

As an example, if the defendant actor had formed an intent to kill someone, had in his possession a loaded pistol, pulled the trigger while his intended victim was within range and the pistol did not fire because the bullet or cartridge in the chamber was defective or because someone unknown to the actor had removed the cartridges or bullets or because of any other thing happening which happening or thing was beyond the control of the actor, the actor could be guilty under sec. 339.32(2), Stats.

But when as in the present case (as disclosed by the testimony) the defendant had never loaded the pistol, although having ample opportunity to do so, then he had never completed performance of the act essential to kill someone, through the means of pulling the trigger of the pistol. This act, of loading the pistol, or using a loaded pistol, was dependent on the defendant himself. It was in no way an extraneous factor since by definition an extraneous factor is one which originates or comes from without.

Under the majority opinion the interpretations of the statute are if a person points an unloaded gun (pistol) at someone, knowing it to be unloaded and pulls the trigger, he can be found guilty of an attempt to commit murder. This type of reasoning I cannot agree with.

He could be guilty of some offense, but not attempt to commit murder. If a person uses a pistol as a bludgeon and had struck someone, but was prevented from killing his victim because he (the actor) suffered a heart attack at that moment, the illness would be an extraneous factor within the statute and the actor could be found guilty of attempt to commit murder, provided the necessary intent was proved.

In this case, there is no doubt that the pistol was not loaded. The defendant testified that it had never been loaded or fired. The following steps must be taken before the weapon would be capable of killing. . . .

A. To load pistol requires pulling of slide operating around barrel toward holder or operator of pistol.

B. After pulling slide to rear, safety latch is pushed into place by operator of pistol to hold pistol in position for loading.

C. A spring lock is located at one side of opening of magazine located at the bottom grip or butt of gun.

D. This spring is pulled back and the clip is inserted into magazine or bottom of pistol and closes the bottom of the grip or butt of the pistol.

E. The recoil or release of the safety latch on the slide loads the chamber of the pistol and it is now ready to fire or be used as a pistol.

The law judges intent objectively. It is impossible to peer into a man's mind particularly long after the act has been committed.

Viewing objectively the physical salient facts, it was the defendant who put the gun, clip and cartridges under the car seat. It was he, same defendant, who took the pistol out of the box without taking clip or cartridges. It is plain he told the truth—he knew the gun would not fire, nobody else knew that so well. In fact his exclamation was "It won't fire. It won't fire." The real intent showed up objectively in those calm moments while driving around the county with his wife for two hours, making two visits

with her at her mother's home, and drinking coffee at the home. He could have loaded the pistol while staying on the outside at his mother-in-law's home on his second trip, if he intended to use the pistol to kill, but he did not do this required act.

The majority states:

> The gun itself, which is an exhibit in the record, is the strongest piece of evidence in favor of Damms' present contention that he at all times knew the gun was unloaded. Practically the entire bottom end of the butt of the pistol is open. . . . This readily demonstrates to anyone looking at the gun that it could not be loaded.

They are so correct.

The defendant had the pistol in his hand several times before chasing his wife at the restaurant and it was his pistol. He, no doubt, had examined this pistol at various times during his period of ownership—unless he was devoid of all sense of touch and feeling in his hands and fingers it would be impossible for him not to be aware or know that the pistol was unloaded. He could feel the hole in the bottom of the butt, and this on at least two separate occasions for he handled the pistol by taking it out of the box and showing it to his wife before he took her back to her mother's home the second time, and prior to chasing her at the restaurant.

Objective evidence here raises reasonable doubt of intent to attempt murder. It negatives intent to kill. The defendant would have loaded the pistol had he intended to kill or murder or used it as a bludgeon. . . .

The Assistant Attorney General contends and states in his brief:

> In the instant case, the failure of the attempt was due to lack of bullets in the gun but a loaded magazine was in the car. If defendant had not been prevented by the intervention of the two police officers, or possibly someone else, or conceivably by the flight of his wife from the scene, he could have returned to the car, loaded the gun, and killed her. Under all the circumstances the jury were justified in concluding that that is what he would have done, but for the intervention.

If that conclusion is correct, and juries are allowed to convict persons based on speculation of what *might* have been done, we will have seriously and maybe permanently, curtailed the basic rights of our citizenry to be tried only on the basis of proven facts. I cannot agree with his contention or conclusion.

The total inadequacy of the means (in this case the unloaded gun or pistol) in the manner intended to commit the overt act of murder, precludes a finding of guilty of the crime charged under sec. 939.32(2), Stats.

Questions

1. List all the facts relevant to deciding whether Ralph Damms intended to murder Marjory Damms.

2. List all the facts relevant to deciding whether Damms had taken enough steps to attempt to murder Marjory Damms according to the Wisconsin statute.

3. Summarize the majority's arguments that the unloaded gun was an extraneous factor, a stroke of luck Damms shouldn't benefit from.

4. Summarize the dissent's arguments that the unloaded gun was not an extraneous factor but an impossibility that prevents Damms from attempting to murder Marjorie Damms.

5. In your opinion, is the majority or dissent right? Explain your answer in terms of what effect impossibility should have on liability for criminal attempt.

6. Should it matter why the gun was unloaded? Explain your answer.

7. What if Damms knew the gun was unloaded? Should he still be guilty of attempted murder? Explain your answer.

8. Is the Wisconsin rule punishing attempts that are about half the actions needed to complete the crime a good idea?

9. Some states punish attempts at the same level as completed crimes because people bent on committing crimes shouldn't benefit at all from a stroke of luck. Do you agree? Defend your answer with arguments from the case excerpt and the text.

EXPLORING FURTHER

Impossibility

1. Was It "Legally Impossible" to Commit "Child Enticement"?

State v. Robins, 646 N.W. 2d 287 (Wis. 2002)

FACTS Beginning on January 31, 2000, Brian Robins, using the screen name "WI4kink," had a series of online conversations with "Benjm13," initially in an Internet chat room known as "Wisconsin M4M."

["M4M" meant either Male for Male or Men for Men.]

Unbeknown to Robins, "Benjm13" was Thomas Fassbender, a 42-year-old DOJ agent posing online as a 13-year-old boy named Benjamin living in Little Chute, Wisconsin. The subject of "Benjamin's" age came up within the first twelve minutes of the first online conversation between Robins and Benjm13. Benjamin told Robins that he was 13 years old.

The initial and subsequent online conversations and emails between Robins and Benjm13 centered on explicit sexual matters (including, among other things, oral sex, masturbation, ejaculation, and penis size) and were recorded by Fassbender. . . .

[The court here included several of these communications.]

According to the Wisconsin criminal code:

An attempt to commit a crime requires that the actor have an intent to perform acts and attain a result which, if accomplished, would constitute such crime and that the actor does acts toward the commission of the crime which demonstrate unequivocally, under all the circumstances, that the actor formed that intent and would commit the crime except for the intervention of another person or some other extraneous factor. Wis. Stat. § 939.32(3).

Robins moved to dismiss the charge because, he argued, he was being charged with a crime that didn't exist because of a legal impossibility—there was no child. Should the motion to dismiss be granted?

DECISION No, said the trial court and the Wisconsin Supreme Court, which was faced with a bunch of child enticement cases with similar facts involving stings catching both older men looking for boys and those looking for girls:

We reject Robins' argument that the case should be overruled. . . . The extraneous factor that intervened to make the crime an attempted rather than completed child enticement is the fact that "Benjm13" was an adult government agent rather than a 13-year-old boy.

That there may be or could have been other intervening factors does not make this an impermissible prosecution for an "attempt to attempt a crime." . . .

We conclude . . . that the crime of attempted child enticement contrary to Wis. Stat. § 948.07 may be charged where the extraneous factor that intervenes to make the crime an attempted rather than completed child enticement is the fact that, unbeknownst to the defendant, the "child" is fictitious.

2. Was It "Impossible" to Receive a Stolen Harley-Davidson That Wasn't Stolen?

State v. Kordas, 528 N.W.2d 483 (Wis. 1995)

FACTS Michael Kordas was charged with buying a Harley-Davidson motorcycle from an undercover police officer. The police had modified the cycle and made misrepresentations about the cycle to Kordas so that it appeared to be stolen when, in fact, it actually "had been provided to the Milwaukee Police Department for educational purposes."

The undercover officer gave Kordas certain information about the motorcycle that signaled that it was stolen. Specifically, the undercover officer represented that the motorcycle in question was a 1988 Harley DynaGlide, although Harley did not begin making that model until 1991, which Kordas later acknowledged knowing at the time.

In addition, the vehicle identification number on the motorcycle had been altered in an obvious way, again a fact that Kordas later acknowledged knowing at the time he examined the motorcycle prior to purchasing it. Kordas bought the motorcycle, was given what was purported to be title to it, and took it with him in a van before he was stopped and arrested by backup officers working on the undercover operation. The complaint indicates that Kordas made additional admissions to the police upon his arrest indicating his knowledge that the motorcycle was stolen.

In fact, however, the motorcycle was not stolen. Did he attempt to receive a stolen Harley-Davidson?

DECISION Yes, according to the trial court:

> Here, the allegations are that Kordas had the requisite intent but his actions even after they were fully executed did not constitute the crime and therefore it was an "attempt." But there was no "intervention of another person or some other extraneous factor" which prevented the ultimate commission of the acts which the defendant intended. Instead, the intended acts were completed but the results were not criminal because of the legal status of the property in question.

So the trial court dismissed the complaint of attempt to receive stolen property because it was a legal impossibility. The Wisconsin Supreme Court disagreed:

> The trial court based its conclusion on the view that "there was no 'intervention of . . . some other extraneous factor' which prevented the ultimate commission"

of receiving stolen property. We disagree. Indeed, an extraneous factor did intervene—the fact, beyond Kordas's knowledge or control, that the motorcycle was not stolen property. But for that factor, Kordas allegedly would have committed the crime of receiving stolen property. Because of that factor, Kordas allegedly committed only the attempt to receive stolen property.

According to the allegations in the amended complaint, Kordas "did in fact possess the necessary criminal intent to commit" the crime of receiving stolen property.

The extraneous factor—that the motorcycle was not stolen—was unknown to him and had no impact on his intent. Thus, the legal "impossibility not apparent to [Kordas] should not absolve him from the offense of attempt to commit the crime he intended." Accordingly, we reverse the order dismissing the amended criminal complaint and remand to the trial court for further proceedings.

 Go to the Criminal Law 9e website to find the full text of the Exploring Further excerpts: www.thomsonedu .com/criminaljustice/samaha. (Excerpts on impossibility.)

Abandonment

We know from the last section that those bent on committing crimes who've taken steps to carry out their criminal plans can't escape criminal liability just because an outside force or person interrupted them. But what about people who clearly intend to commit crimes, take enough steps to carry out their intent, and then change their mind and voluntarily abandon the scheme? Should the law benefit those who themselves are the force that intercepts the crimes they wanted to commit and are marching toward completing? The answer depends on which jurisdiction they're in.

A little more than half the states and the U.S. government accept the affirmative **defense of voluntary abandonment** to attempt liability (*People v. Kimball* 1981, 347). Recall that *affirmative defense* means defendants have to produce some evidence of abandonment, and then the government has to prove beyond a reasonable doubt that the defendants didn't voluntarily abandon.

Michigan has a typical voluntary abandonment provision:

> It is an affirmative defense . . . that, under circumstances manifesting a voluntary and complete renunciation of his criminal purpose, the actor avoided the commission of the offense attempted by abandoning his criminal effort. . . .
>
> A renunciation is not "voluntary and complete" within the meaning of this chapter if it is motivated in whole or in part by either of the following:
>
> (a) A circumstance which increases the probability of detection or apprehension of the defendant or another participant in the criminal operation or which makes more difficult the consummation of the crime.

(b) A decision to postpone the criminal conduct until another time or to substitute another victim or another but similar objective. (*People v. Kimball*, 346–48)

According to the Model Penal Code, voluntary abandonment means

a change in the actor's purpose not influenced by outside circumstances, what may be termed repentance or change of heart. Lack of resolution or timidity may suffice. A reappraisal by the actor of the criminal sanctions hanging over his conduct would presumably be a motivation of the voluntary type as long as the actor's fear of the law is not related to a particular threat of apprehension or detection. (ALI 1985, 3:356)

Supporters of the voluntary abandonment defense favor it for two reasons. First, those who voluntarily renounce their criminal attempts in progress (especially during the first acts following preparation) aren't the dangerous people the law of attempt is designed to punish; they probably weren't even bent on committing the crime in the first place. Second, at the very end of the progress to completing the crime, it prevents what we most want—the harm the completed crime is about to inflict on victims.

This defense encourages would-be criminals to give up their criminal designs by the promise of escaping punishment. Opponents say the defense encourages bad people to take the first steps to commit crimes because they know they can escape punishment (Moriarity 1989, 1).

The court in *Le Barron v. State* denied David Le Barron's defense that he voluntarily abandoned his plan to rape Jodean Randen.

CASE — *Did He Voluntarily Abandon His Attempt to Rape?*

Le Barron v. State
145 N.W.2d 79 (Wis. 1966)

HISTORY

David Le Barron was convicted of attempted rape and sentenced to not more than fifteen years in prison. He appealed. The Wisconsin Supreme Court affirmed the conviction.

CURRIE, J.

FACTS

On March 3, 1965 at 6:55 P.M., the complaining witness, Jodean Randen, a housewife, was walking home across a fairly well-traveled railroad bridge in Eau Claire, Wisconsin. She is a slight woman whose normal weight is 95 to 100 pounds. As she approached the opposite side of the bridge she passed a man who was walking in the opposite direction.

The man turned and followed her, grabbed her arm and demanded her purse. She surrendered her purse and at the command of the man began walking away as fast as she could. Upon discovering that the purse was empty, he caught up with her again, grabbed her arm and told her that if she did not scream he would not hurt her.

He then led her—willingly, she testified, so as to avoid being hurt by him—to the end of the bridge. While walking he shoved her head down and warned her not to look up or do anything and he would not hurt her.

On the other side of the bridge along the railroad tracks there is a coal shack. As they approached the coal shack he grabbed her, put one hand over her mouth, and an arm around her shoulder and told her not to scream or he would kill her. At this time Mrs. Randen thought he had a knife in his hand.

He then forced her into the shack and up against the wall. As she struggled for her breath he said, "You know what else I want," unzipped his pants and started pulling up her skirt. She finally succeeded in removing his hand from her mouth, and after reassuring him that she would not scream, told him she was pregnant and pleaded with him to desist or he would hurt her baby.

He then felt her stomach and took her over to the door of the shack, where in the better light he was able to ascertain that, under her coat, she was wearing maternity clothes. He thereafter let her alone and left after warning her not to scream or call the police, or he would kill her.

OPINION

The material portions of the controlling statutes provide:

§ 944.01(1), Stats. Any male who has sexual intercourse with a female he knows is not his wife, by force and against her will, may be imprisoned not more than 30 years.

§ 939.32(2), Stats. An attempt to commit a crime requires that the actor have an intent to perform acts and attain a result which, if accomplished, would constitute such crime and that he does acts toward the commission of the crime which demonstrate unequivocally, under all the circumstances, that he formed that intent and would commit the crime except for the intervention of another person or some other extraneous factor.

The two statutory requirements of intent and overt acts which must concur in order to have attempt to rape are as follows:

(1) The male must have the intent to act so as to have intercourse with the female by overcoming or preventing her utmost resistance by physical violence, or overcoming her will to resist by the use of threats of imminent physical violence likely to cause great bodily harm;

(2) the male must act toward the commission of the rape by overt acts which demonstrate unequivocally, under all the circumstances, that he formed the intent to rape and would have committed the rape except for the intervention of another person or some other extraneous factor.

The thrust of defendant's argument, that the evidence was not sufficient to convict him of the crime of attempted rape, is two-fold: first, defendant desisted from his endeavor to have sexual intercourse with complainant before he had an opportunity to form an intent to accomplish such intercourse by force and against her will; and, second, the factor which caused him to desist, viz., the pregnancy of complainant, was intrinsic and not an 'extraneous factor' within the meaning of sec. 939.32(2), Stats.

It is difficult to consider the factor of intent apart from that of overt acts since the sole evidence of intent in attempted rape cases is almost always confined to the overt acts of the accused, and intent must be inferred therefrom. In fact, the express wording of sec. 939.32(2), Stats. recognizes that this is so.

We consider defendant's overt acts, which support a reasonable inference that he intended to have sexual intercourse with complainant by force and against her will, to be these:

(1) He threatened complainant that he would kill her if she refused to cooperate with him;

(2) he forced complainant into the shack and against the wall; and

(3) he stated, 'You know what else I want,' unzipped his pants, and started pulling up her skirt.

The jury had the right to assume that defendant had the requisite physical strength and weapon (the supposed knife) to carry out the threat over any resistance of complainant.

We conclude that a jury could infer beyond a reasonable doubt from these overt acts of defendant that he intended to have sexual intercourse with defendant by force and against her will. The fact that he desisted from his attempt to have sexual intercourse as a result of the plea of complainant that she was pregnant, would permit of the opposite inference. However, such desistance did not compel the drawing of such inference nor compel, as a matter of law, the raising of a reasonable doubt to a finding that defendant had previously intended to carry through with having intercourse by force and against complainant's will. . . .

The argument that the pregnancy . . . which caused defendant's desistance does not qualify as an "extraneous factor" . . . is in conflict with our holding in *State v. Damms*.

[See case excerpt under "Impossibility."]

. . . Particularly significant is this statement in the opinion:

An unequivocal act accompanied by intent should be sufficient to constitute a criminal attempt. Insofar as the actor knows, he has done everything necessary to insure the commission of the crime intended, and he should not escape punishment because of the fortuitous circumstance that by reason of some fact unknown to him it was impossible to effectuate the intended result.

The unloaded condition of the gun was every bit as much a part of the intrinsic fact situation in the *Damms* Case as was complainant's pregnancy in the instant case. We determine that such pregnancy constituted the intervention of an "extraneous factor" within the meaning of sec. 939.32(2), Stats.

AFFIRMED.

Questions

1. List all the facts relevant to deciding whether Le Barron had the intent to rape Jodean Randen.

2. At what point, if any, did his acts cross the line from preparation to the *actus reus* of attempt under Wisconsin law?

3. Describe the details surrounding Le Barron's decision to abandon the attempted rape of Randen.

4. Why did Le Barron abandon his attempt to rape Randen? Because he believed it was morally wrong to rape a pregnant woman? Or did the pregnancy simply repel him sexually? Does it matter? Explain your answer.

5. Is Le Barron equally dangerous, whichever reason led to interrupting the rape? Explain.

6. The court said a jury could have concluded Randen's pregnancy was either an extraneous factor he couldn't benefit from or an intrinsic factor that caused Le Barron to renounce voluntarily his intention to rape. If you were a juror, how would you have voted on whether the pregnancy was an extraneous or an intrinsic factor?

Abandonment

Did He Voluntarily Abandon His Attempt to Murder?

People v. Johnson 750 P.2d 72 (Colo.App. 1987)

PIERCE, J.

FACTS Following a fight with a friend outside a bar where the two had been drinking, defendant, Floyd Johnson, walked a mile to his house, retrieved his .22 rifle and ten cartridges, walked back to the bar, and crawled under a pickup truck across the street to wait for the friend. Defendant testified that he, at first, intended to shoot the friend to "pay him back" for the beating he had received in their earlier altercation.

When the owner of the pickup arrived, defendant obtained his keys, instructed him to sit in the pickup, and gave him one or more bottles of beer. Defendant then crawled back under the pickup to resume his wait for his friend. The police were alerted by a passerby and arrested defendant before his friend emerged from the bar. There was also testimony that while he was lying under the pickup truck, defendant sobered up somewhat and began to think through his predicament. He testified that he changed his mind and removed the shells from the rifle, placing them in his pocket. By that time there were two persons in the pickup truck, and he began a discussion with them, telling them his name and address and inviting them to his residence to have a party. The three of them were still there drinking and conversing when the police arrived, at which time the rifle was found to be unloaded and the shells were still in the defendant's pocket.

Did Johnson voluntarily abandon his attempt to murder his friend?

DECISION The trial court refused Johnson's request for an instruction on the affirmative defense of abandonment or renunciation. The Court of Appeals reversed and sent the case back to the trial court for a new trial:

> Under the circumstances in this case, there was sufficient evidence to warrant an instruction on the affirmative defense of abandonment or renunciation. Had the tendered instruction been given and the defendant's testimony and other evidence been accepted by the jury, the outcome of this trial could well have been otherwise.

 Go to the Criminal Law 9e website to find the full text of the Exploring Further excerpt: www.thomsonedu.com/criminaljustice/samaha. (Excerpt on abandonment.)

CONSPIRACY

The core of conspiracy is an agreement to commit a crime.

> It's this agreement that gives rise to criminal liability, by transforming a lonely criminal thought hatched in the mind of a single, powerless, individual into an agreement with another person, I reveal myself as one of those persons who suffer from an abnormal disposition to engage in criminal conduct, by distinguishing myself from those untold millions who harbor criminal thoughts, but never share them with others, never mind act on them in any way. But my decision to seek out likeminded protocriminals, and to join hands with them in the pursuit of a common criminal goal is symptomatic of my extraordinary dangerousness. By combining forces with another similarly dangerous person, I multiply my already considerable dangerousness through the magic of cooperation. (Dubber 2002, 163)

Conspiracy, the crime of agreeing with one or more people to commit a crime, is further removed from actually committing a crime than attempts to commit crimes. In fact, "one can become guilty of conspiracy long before his act has come so dangerously

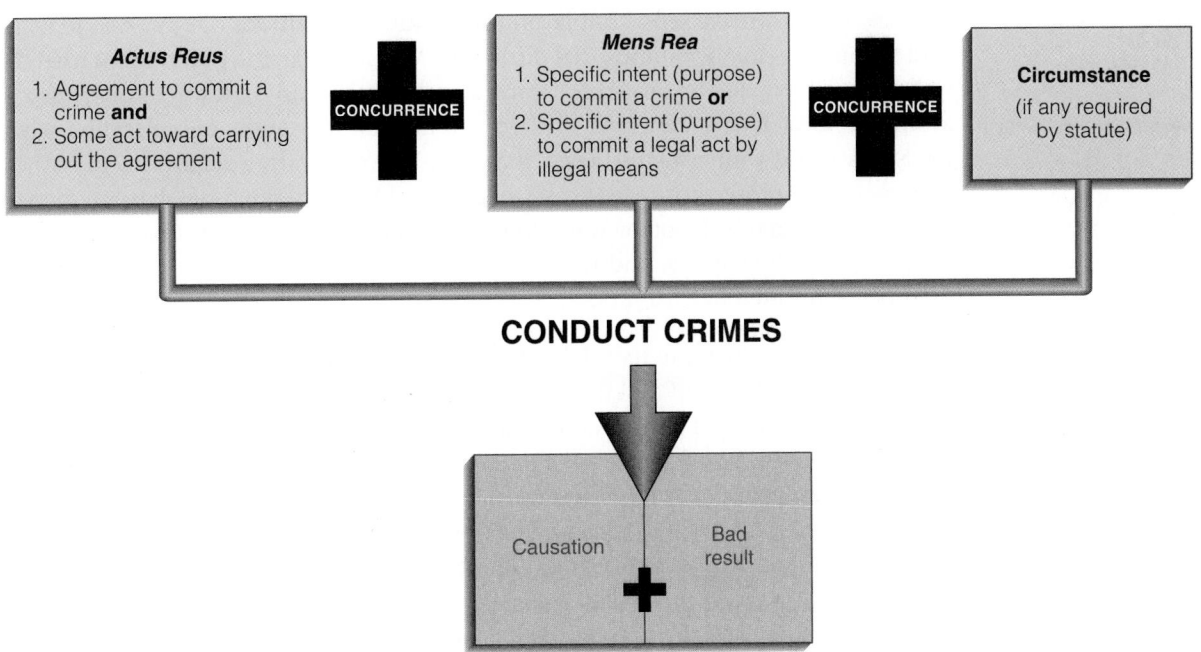

CONDUCT CRIMES

RESULT CRIMES

Elements of Conspiracy

near to completion as to make him criminally liable for the attempted crime" (Sayre 1921–22, 399).

There are two public policy justifications for attaching criminal liability to actions further away from completion than attempts:

1. Conspiracy works hand in hand with attempts to nip criminal purpose in the bud.

2. Conspiracy strikes at the special danger of group criminal activity. (ALI 1985, 3:377–78)

In this section, we'll look at what's necessary to prove the *actus reus* and *mens rea* of conspiracy, how the law treats the parties to conspiracies, how large-scale conspiracies differ, and how the law limits the definition of the criminal objective of a conspiracy.

Conspiracy *Actus Reus*

Conspiracy *actus reus* consists of two parts: (1) *an agreement to commit a crime* (in all states) and (2) an overt act in furtherance of the agreement (in about half the states). Let's look at each part.

The Agreement   The heart of the crime of conspiracy is the act of agreement between two or more people to commit a crime. The agreement doesn't have to be a signed written contract. It's "not necessary to establish that the defendant and his coconspirators signed papers, shook hands, or uttered the words 'we have an agreement'" (*State v. Vargas* 2003, 208–9). Facts and circumstances that point to an unspoken understanding between the conspirators are good enough to prove the conspirators agreed to commit a crime. This rule makes sense because conspirators rarely put their agreements in writing.

The rule may make sense, but it can lead to vague definitions of *agreement* that can lead to injustice. In one famous trial during the Vietnam War, the government tried the well-known baby doctor turned war protestor, Dr. Benjamin Spock, for conspiracy to avoid the draft law. Videotapes showed several hundred spectators clapping while Dr. Spock urged young men to resist the draft. Spurred on by antagonism to antiwar protestors, the prosecutor in the case made the ridiculous assertion that any person seen clapping on the videotape was a co-conspirator. According to the prosecutor, these people were aiding Spock, and that made them parties to a conspiracy to violate the draft law (Mitford 1969, 70–71).

The Overt Act   In about half the states, the agreement itself satisfies the *actus reus* of conspiracy. The other half and the federal courts require the act of agreeing to commit a crime plus another act to further the agreement; the second act is called the **overt act.** Why the requirement of an "overt act"? To verify the firmness of the agreement. The overt act doesn't have to amount to much. In the words of the American Law Institute's commentator (1985 ,[3] 387), it may "be of very small significance." And according to the U.S. Supreme Court Justice Oliver Wendell Holmes (*Hyde v. U.S.* 1912):

> if the overt act is required, it does not matter how remote the act may be from accomplishing the [criminal] purpose, if done to effect it; that is, I suppose, in furtherance of it in any degree. (388)

The U.S. Ninth Circuit Court of Appeals found the agreement plus an overt act missing in a charge that Cody Garcia, a member of the "Bloods" gang conspired to assault three rival "Crips" with a deadly weapon that there was no evidence Garcia fired.

CASE | *Did He "Agree" to Assault Three Crips Members with a Deadly Weapon?*

U.S. v. Garcia
151 F.3d 1243 (CA9 1998)

HISTORY

Leon Garcia, also known as Cody Garcia, Defendant, was convicted in the United States District Court for the District of Arizona, of conspiracy to assault with a dangerous weapon, and was sentenced to 60 months in prison. Defendant appealed. The Court of Appeals reversed and remanded.

REINHARDT, J.

One evening, a confrontation broke out between rival gangs at a party on the Pasqua Yaqui Indian reservation. The resultant gunfire injured four young people, including appellant Cody Garcia. Two young men involved in the shooting, Garcia and Noah Humo, were charged with conspiracy to assault three named individuals with dangerous weapons. A jury acquitted Humo but convicted Garcia. Because there is no direct evidence of an agreement to commit the criminal act which was the alleged

object of the conspiracy, and because the circumstances of the shootings do not support the existence of an agreement, implicit or explicit, the government relied heavily on the gang affiliation of the participants to show the existence of such an agreement. We hold that gang membership itself cannot establish guilt of a crime, and a general agreement, implicit or explicit, to support one another in gang fights does not provide substantial proof of the specific agreement required for a conviction of conspiracy to commit assault. The defendant's conviction therefore rests on insufficient evidence, and we reverse.

FACTS

The party at which the shootings occurred was held in territory controlled by the Crips gang. The participants were apparently mainly young Native Americans. While many of the attendees were associated with the Crips, some members of the Bloods gang were also present. Appellant Cody Garcia arrived at the party in a truck driven by his uncle, waving a red bandanna (the Bloods claim the color red and the Crips the color blue) out the truck window and calling out his gang affiliation: "ESPB Blood!" Upon arrival, Garcia began "talking smack" to (insulting) several Crips members. Prosecution witnesses testified that Garcia's actions suggested that he was looking for trouble and issuing a challenge to fight to the Crips at the party.

Meanwhile, Garcia's fellow Bloods member Julio Baltazar was also "talking smack" to Crips members, and Blood Noah Humo bumped shoulders with one Crips member and called another by a derogatory Spanish term. Neither Baltazar nor Humo had arrived with Garcia, nor is there any indication that they had met before the party to discuss plans or that they were seen talking together during the party.

At some point, shooting broke out. Witnesses saw both Bloods and Crips, including Garcia and Humo, shooting at one another. Baltazar was seen waving a knife or trying to stab a Crip. The testimony at trial does not shed light on what took place immediately prior to the shooting, other than the fact that one witness heard Garcia ask, "Who has the gun?" There is some indication that members of the two gangs may have "squared off" before the shooting began. No testimony establishes whether the shooting followed a provocation or verbal or physical confrontation.

Four individuals were injured by the gunfire: the defendant, Stacy Romero, Gabriel Valenzuela, and Gilbert Baumea. Stacy Romero who at the time was twelve years old was the cousin both of Garcia's co-defendant Humo and his fellow Blood, Baltazar. No evidence presented at trial established that any of the injured persons was shot by Garcia, and he was charged only with conspiracy. The government charged both Garcia and Humo with conspiracy to assault Romero, Valenzuela, and Baumea with dangerous weapons under 18 U.S.C. ß ß 371, 113(a)(3) and 1153. . . .

After a jury trial, . . . Garcia was convicted of conspiracy to assault with a dangerous weapon and sentenced to 60 months in prison. He appeals on the ground that there was insufficient evidence to support his conviction.

OPINION

In order to prove a conspiracy, the government must present sufficient evidence to demonstrate both an overt act and an agreement to engage in the specific criminal activity charged in the indictment. While an implicit agreement may be inferred from circumstantial evidence, proof that an individual engaged in illegal acts with others is not sufficient to demonstrate the existence of a conspiracy. Both the existence of and the individual's connection to the conspiracy must be proven beyond a reasonable doubt. Even though a defendant's connection to the conspiracy may be slight, the connection must nonetheless be proven beyond a reasonable doubt.

The government claims that it can establish the agreement to assault in two ways: first, that the concerted provocative and violent acts by Garcia, Humo and Baltazar are sufficient to show the existence of a prior agreement; and second, that by agreeing to become a member of the gang, Garcia implicitly agreed to support his fellow gang members in violent confrontations.

However, no inference of the existence of any agreement could reasonably be drawn from the actions of Garcia and other Bloods members on the night of the shooting. An inference of an agreement is permissible only when the nature of the acts would logically require coordination and planning.

The government presented no witnesses who could explain the series of events immediately preceding the shooting, so there is nothing to suggest that the violence began in accordance with some prearrangement. The facts establish only that perceived insults escalated tensions between members of rival gangs and that an ongoing gang-related dispute erupted into shooting. Testimony presented at trial suggests more chaos than concert. Such evidence does not establish that parties to a conspiracy worked together understandingly, with a single design for the accomplishment of a common purpose.

Given that this circumstantial evidence fails to suggest the existence of an agreement, we are left only with gang membership as proof that Garcia conspired with fellow Bloods to shoot the three named individuals. The government points to expert testimony at the trial by a local gang unit detective, who stated that generally gang members have a "basic agreement" to back one another up in fights, an agreement which requires no advance planning or coordination. This testimony, which at most establishes one of the characteristics of gangs but not a specific objective of a particular gang—let alone a specific agreement on the part of its members to accomplish an illegal objective—is insufficient to provide proof of a conspiracy to commit assault or other illegal acts.

Recent authority in this circuit establishes that "membership in a gang cannot serve as proof of intent, or of the facilitation, advice, aid, promotion, encouragement or instigation needed to establish aiding and abetting." In overturning the state conviction of a gang member that rested on the theory that the defendant aided and abetted a murder by "fanning the fires of gang warfare," . . . *Mitchell v. Prunty*, 107 F.3d. 1337, expressed concern that allowing a conviction on this basis would "smack of guilt by association." The same concern is implicated when a conspiracy conviction is based on evidence that an individual is affiliated with a gang which has a general rivalry with other gangs, and that this rivalry sometimes escalates into violent confrontations.

. . . Acts of provocation such as "talking smack" or bumping into rival gang members certainly does not prove a high level of planning or coordination. Rather, it may be fairly typical behavior in a situation in which individuals who belong to rival gangs attend the same events. At most, it indicates that members of a particular gang may be looking for trouble, or ready to fight. It does not demonstrate a coordinated effort with a specific illegal objective in mind.

Conspiracy requires proof of both an intention and agreement to accomplish a specific illegal objective. The fact that gang members attend a function armed with weapons may prove that they are prepared for violence, but without other evidence it does not establish that they have made plans to initiate it. And the fact that more than one member of the Bloods was shooting at rival gang members also does not prove a prearrangement—the Crips, too, were able to pull out their guns almost immediately, suggesting that readiness for a gunfight requires no prior agreement. Such readiness may be a sad commentary on the state of mind of many of the nation's youth, but it is not indicative of a criminal conspiracy.

Finally . . . allowing a general agreement among gang members to back each other up to serve as sufficient evidence of a conspiracy would mean that any time more than one gang member was involved in a fight it would constitute an act in furtherance of the conspiracy and all gang members could be held criminally responsible—whether they participated in or had knowledge of the particular criminal act, and whether or not they were present when the act occurred. Indeed, were we to accept fighting the enemy as an illegal objective, all gang members would probably be subject to felony prosecutions sooner rather than later, even though they had never personally committed an improper act. This is contrary to fundamental principles of our justice system. There can be no conviction for guilt by association. . . .

Because of these concerns, evidence of gang membership cannot itself prove that an individual has entered a criminal agreement to attack members of rival gangs. Moreover, here the conspiracy allegation was even more specific: the state charged Garcia with conspiracy to assault three specific individuals—Romero, Baumea and Valenzuela—with deadly weapons. Even if the testimony presented by the state had sufficed to establish a general conspiracy to assault Crips, it certainly did not even hint at a conspiracy to assault the three individuals listed in the indictment. Of course, a more general indictment would not have solved the state's problems in this case. In some cases, when evidence establishes that a particular gang has a specific illegal objective such as selling drugs, evidence of

gang membership may help to link gang members to that objective. However, a general practice of supporting one another in fights, which is one of the ordinary characteristics of gangs, does not constitute the type of illegal objective that can form the predicate for a conspiracy charge. . . .

Because the government introduced no evidence from which a jury could reasonably have found the existence of an agreement to engage in any unlawful conduct, the evidence of conspiracy was insufficient as a matter of law. A contrary result would allow courts to assume an ongoing conspiracy, universal among gangs and gang members, to commit any number of violent acts, rendering gang members automatically guilty of conspiracy for any improper conduct by any member. We therefore reverse Garcia's conviction and remand to the district court to order his immediate release. As a result of this decision, Garcia is not subject to retrial. He has already served over a year in prison.

REVERSED AND REMANDED.

Questions

1. State the two parts of the element of agreement in conspiracy, according to the Court of Appeals.

2. Summarize the government's evidence and arguments that supports the conclusion that Garcia was part of an agreement to assault Romero, Valenzuela, and Baumea with dangerous weapons.

3. Summarize the reasons the court rejected the government's arguments and ordered that Garcia should go free.

4. In your opinion, was there an agreement to assault Romero, Valenzuela, and Baumea with dangerous weapons? Back up your answer with relevant facts and arguments from the case excerpt.

5. According to the court, what "fundamental principle of our justice system" would the government's definition of *agreement* violate? Do you agree? Explain your answer.

Conspiracy *Mens Rea*

Conspiracy *mens rea* wasn't defined clearly at common law, and most modern legislatures haven't made it any clearer. This leaves the courts to define it. The courts in turn have taken imprecise, widely divergent, and inconsistent approaches to the *mens rea* problem. According to former Supreme Court Justice Robert Jackson, "The modern crime of conspiracy is so vague that it almost defies definition" (*Krulewitch v. U.S.* 1949, 445–46).

Authorities frequently call conspiracy a specific-intent crime. But what does that mean? Does it mean that conspiracy involves intent to enter an agreement to commit a crime? Or does conspiracy also have to include an intent to attain a specific *criminal objective?* A **criminal objective** is the criminal goal of an agreement to commit a crime. For example, if two men agree to burn down a building, they intend to commit arson. But if they don't intend to hurt anyone and someone dies, did they also conspire to commit murder? Not if the conspiracy *mens rea* means the specific intent to achieve a particular criminal objective. This example demonstrates an important distinction between, on one hand, the intent to make agreements and, on the other hand, the intent to achieve a criminal objective. If the objective is to commit a specific crime, it has to satisfy that crime's *mens rea*. So conspiring to take another's property isn't conspiring to commit larceny unless the conspirators intended to deprive permanently the owner of possession (Chapter 11).

Courts further complicate conspiracy *mens rea* by not clarifying whether it requires purpose. Consider cases involving suppliers of goods and services, such as doctors who order drugs from pharmaceutical companies that they then use or sell illegally. At what point do the suppliers become co-conspirators, even though they haven't agreed specifically to supply drugs for illegal distribution?

Do prosecutors have to prove the suppliers agreed specifically to further the buyers' criminal purposes? Most courts say yes, even though that kind of proof is difficult to obtain, because as we've already seen, conspirators aren't foolish enough to put proof of their crimes in writing. So purpose has to be inferred from circumstances surrounding the agreement, such as quantities of sales, the continuity of the supplier-recipient relationship, the seller's initiative, a failure to keep records, and the relationship's clandestine nature. Some argue that knowing, or conscious, wrongdoing ought to satisfy the conspiracy *mens rea* (*Direct Sales Co. v. U.S.* 1943).

Parties

The traditional definition of conspiracy includes the attendant circumstance element that agreements involve "two or more parties agreeing or combining to commit a crime (ALI 1985, 3:398). Most modern statutes have replaced this traditional definition with a **unilateral approach** that doesn't require that all conspirators agree—or even know— the other conspirators. For example, if one of two conspirators secretly has no intention to go through with the agreement, the other conspirator is still a party.

When there's more than one party, failure to convict one party doesn't prevent conviction of other parties to the conspiracy. Typically, statutes are similar to the Illinois Criminal Code (*Illinois Criminal Law and Procedure* 1988), which provides:

> It shall not be a defense to conspiracy that the person or persons with whom the accused is alleged to have conspired
>
> 1. Has not been prosecuted or convicted, *or*
> 2. Has been convicted of a different offense, *or*
> 3. Is not amenable to justice, *or*
> 4. Has been acquitted, *or*
> 5. Lacked the capacity to commit an offense. (chap. 38, § 8-4)

Large-Scale Conspiracies

The relationship of parties to conspiracies can get intricate, particularly when they involve large operations. Most of these large-scale conspiracies fall into two major patterns: "wheel" and "chain" conspiracies. In **wheel conspiracies,** one or more defendants participate in every transaction. These participants make up the hub of the wheel conspiracy. Others participate in only one transaction; they are the spokes in the wheel. In **chain conspiracies,** participants at one end of the chain may know nothing of those at the other end, but every participant handles the same commodity at different points, such as manufacture, distribution, and sale.

Chain conspiracies often involve the distribution of some commodity, such as illegal drugs. In one famous old case still relevant today, *U.S. v. Bruno* (1939), smugglers brought narcotics into New York, middlemen purchased the narcotics, and two groups of "retailers" (one operating in New York and the other in Louisiana) bought narcotics from middlemen.

Criminal Objective

Conspiracy is an agreement but an agreement to do what? In the old days, the criminal objective was defined to cover a broad spectrum. The objective could be as narrow as an agreement to commit a felony or as broad as agreements to

- Commit "any crime."
- Do "anything unlawful."
- Commit "any act injurious to the public health, or for the perversion of or obstruction of justice, or due administration of the laws (ALI 1985, 3:395).
- Do even "lawful things by unlawful means."

In most modern statutes, the criminal objective is almost always limited to agreements to commit crimes.

The often vague definitions of the elements in conspiracy offer considerable opportunity for prosecutorial and judicial discretion. At times, this discretion borders on abuse, leading to charges that conspiracy law is unjust. First, a general criticism is that conspiracy law punishes conduct too far remote from the actual crime. Second, labor organizations, civil liberties groups, and large corporations charge that conspiracy is a weapon against their legitimate interests of, respectively, collective bargaining and strikes, dissent from accepted points of view and public policies, and profit making.

Critics say that when prosecutors don't have enough evidence to convict for the crime itself, they turn, as their last hope, to conspiracy. Conspiracy's vague definitions greatly enhance the chance for a guilty verdict. Not often mentioned, but extremely important, is that intense media attention to conspiracy trials can lead to abuse. This happened in the conspiracy trials of Dr. Benjamin Spock, the Chicago Eight, and others involving radical politics during the 1960s.

It also occurred in the Watergate conspiracy trials involving President Nixon's associates during the 1970s, in the alleged conspiracies surrounding the sale of arms to Iran for hostages and the subsequent alleged diversion of funds during the 1980s, and in the early 2000s' alleged conspiracy of Osama bin Laden's chauffer and the various alleged conspiracies of officials in the White House.

Several states have made efforts to overcome these criticisms by defining conspiracy elements more narrowly. The definitions of agreement or combination (two or more parties combining to commit crimes) are no longer as vague as they once were.

The Model Penal Code has adopted the overt act requirement (acts in furtherance of the act of agreement), and about half the states are following that lead. Those states have refined *mens rea* to include only purposeful conduct—that is, a specific intent to carry out the objective of the agreement or combination. Knowledge, recklessness, and negligence are increasingly attacked as insufficient culpability for an offense as remote from completion as conspiracy. Furthermore, most recent legislation restricts conspiratorial objectives to criminal ends. Phrases such as "unlawful objects," "lawful objects by unlawful means," and "objectives harmful to public health, morals, trade, and commerce" are increasingly regarded as too broad and, therefore, unacceptable.

On the other hand, the Racketeer Influenced and Corrupt Organizations Act (RICO) (Chapter 11) demonstrates the continued vitality of conspiracy law. RICO reflects the need for effective means to meet the threat posed by organized crime. It imposes enhanced penalties for "all types of organized criminal behavior, that is, enterprise criminality—from simple political to sophisticated white collar schemes to traditional Mafia-type endeavors" (Blakely and Gettings 1980, 1013–14).

Racketeering activity includes any act chargeable under state and federal law, including murder, kidnapping, bribery, drug dealing, gambling, theft, extortion, and securities fraud. Among other things, the statute prohibits using income from a "pattern of racketeering activity" to acquire an interest in or establish an enterprise affecting interstate commerce; conducting an enterprise through a pattern of racketeering; or conspiring to violate these provisions.

RICO's drafters intended the statute to "break the back of organized crime." According to conservative columnist William Safire (1989), the racketeers they had in mind were "loan sharks, drug kingpins, prostitution overlords, and casino operators who hired murderers and arsonists to enforce and extort—you know, the designated bad guys who presumably did not deserve the rights of due process that should protect all of us (19)." Now, however, aggressive prosecutors use RICO against white-collar crime. Rudolf Giuliani, when he was a U.S. Attorney, for example, caused Drexel Burnham Lambert to plead guilty to several counts of securities violations to avoid RICO prosecution, which would not only have resulted in harsher legal penalties for these white-collar criminals but also attached the label of "racketeer" to them (19).

SOLICITATION

Suppose I want to murder my wife, but I'm afraid to do it. If I ask a friend to kill her and she does, we're both murderers. If she tries to kill her and fails because her gun isn't loaded, then we've committed attempted murder. If she agrees to kill her and buys the gun but doesn't follow through, we've committed conspiracy to commit murder.

But what if I try to get my friend to kill my wife by offering her $5000, and she turns me down? That's a crime, too—**solicitation**, the crime of trying to get someone else to commit a crime. There's disagreement about whether solicitation to commit a crime is dangerous enough to be a crime.

Those in the "not-dangerous-enough" group make two arguments to support their position. First, solicitation isn't dangerous enough conduct because an independent moral agent (the person solicited) stands between solicitors and their criminal objectives. Second, solicitors aren't dangerous enough people. They prove it by turning to someone else to do what they're too timid to do themselves.

Those in the "dangerous enough" group have their own arguments. First, they say solicitation is just another form of the danger created by group participation in crime, only more removed from the completed crime than conspiracy—kind of like an attempted conspiracy. Second, solicitors are intelligent, artful masters at manipulating others to do their dirty work.

We'll look at the elements of solicitation—the *actus reus*, *mens rea*, and the attendant circumstance of the criminal objective of the solicitation.

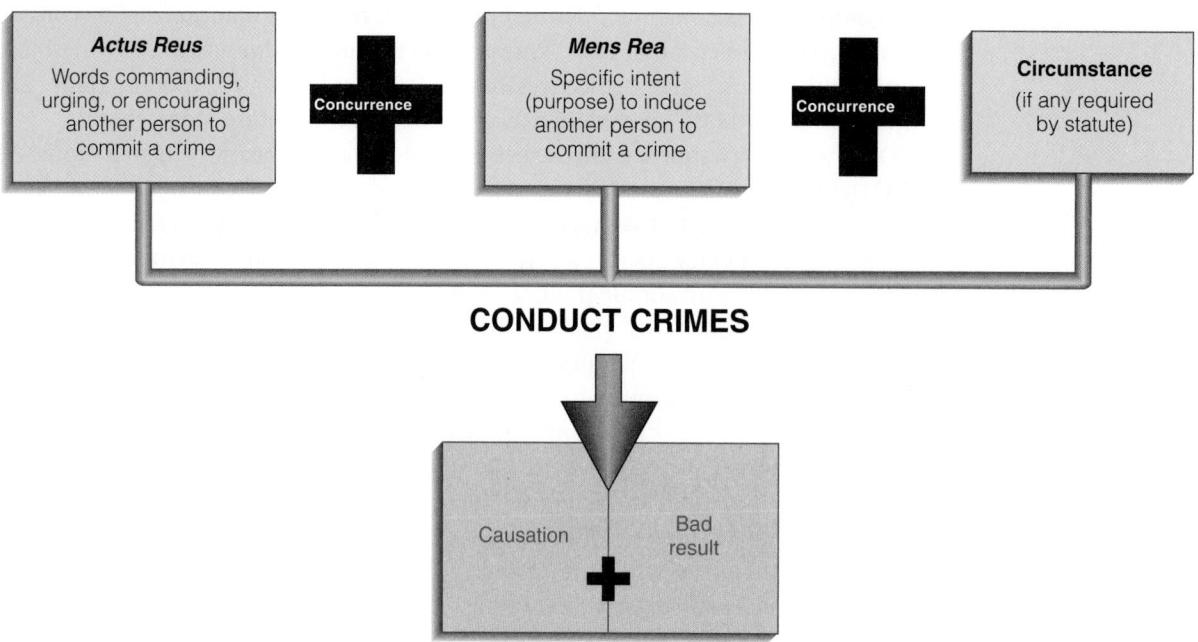

CONDUCT CRIMES

RESULT CRIMES

Elements of Solicitation

Solicitation *Actus Reus*

The criminal act in criminal solicitation consists of words, but the law only imprecisely tells us what words qualify as **solicitation** *actus reus.* Courts agree that statements that merely favor committing a crime aren't enough to qualify as criminal acts. So someone who says, "I think it'd be great if someone killed that terrorist" hasn't solicited murder.

There has to be some kind of inducement to commit a crime. The typical words we see in the statutes and court opinions are like the ones we saw in accomplice liability (Chapter 7): *advises, commands, counsels, encourages, entices, entreats, importunes, incites, induces, instigates, procures, requests, solicits,* or *urges.* In other words, the criminal act in solicitation consists of the *effort* to get another to commit a crime, whether or not the solicitation ever ripens into a completed crime (LaFave and Scott 1986, 419).

Does the solicitor have to address the words to precise individuals? Not necessarily. Soliciting audiences is precise enough. One speaker was convicted for urging his audience to commit murder and robbery. Even the inducement that doesn't reach its object qualifies. So if I send a letter to my hoped-for collaborator, offering her $30,000 to kill my enemy, I've solicited murder even if the letter gets lost in the mail (*State v. Schleifer* 1923).

Solicitation *Mens Rea*

Solicitation is a specific-intent crime; that is, it's a crime of purpose. The **solicitation mens rea** requires words that convey that their purpose is to get someone to commit a specific crime. If I urge my friend who works in an expensive jewelry shop to take a gold chain for me, I've solicited her to steal the chain. If, on the other hand, I ask another friend who works in a clothing shop to get a coat for me to use for the evening, and I plan to return the coat the next morning before anyone knows it's missing, I haven't solicited her to steal the coat because I don't intend to steal the coat, only to use it for the night (Chapter 11).

Criminal Objective

Some statutes restrict the circumstance element of the criminal objective to committing *felonies*—in some cases, to committing *violent* felonies. In other jurisdictions, it's a crime to solicit another to commit *any* crime, whether it's a felony, misdemeanor, or violation.

Furthermore, solicitation doesn't have to include an inducement to commit a *criminal* act at all. For example, suppose a robber urges a friend to borrow money and lend it to him for a plane ticket to escape from the jurisdiction. The robber has solicited escape or aiding and abetting a robbery. Although borrowing money isn't a crime, and lending money to a robber isn't by itself a crime, both escape and aiding and abetting robbers are crimes. Someone who urges another to commit those crimes has committed the crime of solicitation.

The New Mexico Court of Appeals dealt with criminal solicitation in *State v. Cotton* (1990).

CASE *Did He Solicit His Wife to Bribe or Intimidate a Witness?*

State v. Cotton
790 P.2d 1050 (N.M.App. 1990)

HISTORY

James Cotton, Defendant, was convicted in the District Court, Eddy County, of criminal solicitation, and he appealed. The Court of Appeals reversed and remanded.

DONNELLY, J.

FACTS

In 1986, defendant, together with his wife Gail, five children, and a stepdaughter, moved to New Mexico. A few months later, defendant's wife and children returned to Indiana. Shortly thereafter, defendant's fourteen-year-old stepdaughter moved back to New Mexico to reside with him. In 1987, the Department of Human Services investigated allegations of misconduct involving defendant and his stepdaughter. Subsequently, the district court issued an order awarding legal and physical custody of the stepdaughter to the Department, and she was placed in a residential treatment facility in Albuquerque.

In May 1987, defendant was arrested and charged with multiple counts of criminal sexual penetration of a minor and criminal sexual contact of a minor. While in the Eddy County Jail awaiting trial on those charges defendant discussed with his cellmate, James Dobbs, and Danny Ryan,

another inmate, his desire to persuade his stepdaughter not to testify against him. During his incarceration defendant wrote numerous letters to his wife; in several of his letters he discussed his strategy for defending against the pending criminal charges.

On September 23, 1987, defendant addressed a letter to his wife. In that letter he requested that she assist him in defending against the pending criminal charges by persuading his stepdaughter not to testify at his trial. The letter also urged his wife to contact the stepdaughter and influence her to return to Indiana or that she give her money to leave the state so that she would be unavailable to testify. After writing this letter defendant gave it to Dobbs and asked him to obtain a stamp for it so that it could be mailed later.

Unknown to defendant, Dobbs removed the letter from the envelope, replaced it with a blank sheet of paper, and returned the sealed stamped envelope to him. Dobbs gave the original letter written by defendant to law enforcement authorities, and it is undisputed that defendant's original letter was never in fact mailed nor received by defendant's wife.

On September 24 and 26, 1987, defendant composed another letter to his wife. He began the letter on September 24 and continued it on September 26, 1987. In this letter defendant wrote that he had revised his plans and that this letter superseded his previous two letters. The letter stated that he was arranging to be released on bond; that his wife should forget about his stepdaughter for a while and not come to New Mexico; that defendant would request that the court permit him to return to Indiana to obtain employment; that his wife should try to arrange for his stepdaughter to visit her in Indiana for Christmas; and that his wife should try to talk the stepdaughter out of testifying or to talk her into testifying favorably for defendant. Defendant also said in the letter that his wife should "warn" his stepdaughter that if she did testify for the state "it won't be nice . . . and she'll make [New Mexico] news," and that, if the stepdaughter was not available to testify, the prosecutor would have to drop the charges against defendant.

Defendant secured his release on bail on September 28, 1987, but approximately twenty-four hours later was rearrested on charges of criminal solicitation. . . . At the time defendant was rearrested, law enforcement officers discovered and seized from defendant's car, two personal calendars, and other documents written by defendant. It is also undisputed that the second letter, was never mailed to defendant's wife.

Following a jury trial, defendant was convicted on two counts of criminal solicitation. A third count of criminal solicitation was dismissed by the state prior to trial.

OPINION

The charges of criminal solicitation were alleged to have occurred on or about September 23, 1987. Count I of the amended criminal information alleged that defendant committed the offense of criminal solicitation by soliciting another person "to engage in conduct constituting a felony, to-wit: Bribery or Intimidation of a Witness (contrary to Sec. 30-24-3, NMSA 1978)." Count II alleged that defendant committed the offense of criminal solicitation by soliciting another "to engage in conduct constituting a felony, to-wit: Custodial Interference (contrary to Sec. 30-4-4, NMSA 1978)."

The offense of criminal solicitation as provided in NMSA 1978, Section 30-28-3 (Repl. Pamp. 1984), is defined in applicable part as follows:

A. Except as to bona fide acts of persons authorized by law to investigate and detect the commission of offenses by others, a person is guilty of criminal solicitation if, with the intent that another person engage in conduct constituting a felony, he solicits, commands, requests, induces, employs or otherwise attempts to promote or facilitate another person to engage in conduct constituting a felony within or without the state.

Defendant contends that the record fails to contain the requisite evidence to support the charges of criminal solicitation against him because defendant's wife, the intended solicitee, never received the two letters. In reviewing this position, the focus of our inquiry necessarily turns on whether or not the record contains proper evidence sufficient to establish each element of the alleged offenses of criminal solicitation beyond a reasonable doubt.

. . . On appeal, we view the testimony and evidence in the light most favorable to the state, resolving all conflicts therein and indulging all permissible inferences therefrom in favor of the verdict. The evidence may be direct or circumstantial. However, evidence supporting a criminal conviction must be based on logical inference and not upon surmise or conjecture.

The state's brief-in-chief states that "neither of these letters actually reached Mrs. Cotton, but circumstantial evidence indicates that other similar letters did reach her during this period." The state also argues that under the express language of Section 30-28-3(A), where defendant is shown to have the specific intent to commit such offense and "otherwise attempts" its commission, the offense of criminal solicitation is complete. The state reasons that even in the absence of evidence indicating that the solicitations were actually communicated to or received by the solicitee, under our statute, proof of defendant's acts of writing the letters, attempts to mail or forward them, together with proof of his specific intent to solicit the commission of a felony constitutes sufficient proof to sustain a charge of criminal solicitation. We disagree.

The offense of criminal solicitation, as defined in Section 30-28-3 by our legislature, adopts in part, language defining the crime of solicitation as set out in the Model Penal Code promulgated by the American Law Institute. . . . As enacted by our legislature, however, Section 30-28-3 specifically omits that portion of the Model Penal Code subsection declaring that an uncommunicated solicitation to commit a crime may constitute the offense of criminal solicitation. The latter omission, we conclude, indicates an implicit legislative intent that the offense of solicitation requires some form of actual communication from the defendant to either an intermediary or the person intended to be solicited, indicating the subject matter of the solicitation. . . .

Defendant's convictions for solicitation are reversed and the cause is remanded with instructions to set aside the convictions for criminal solicitation.

Questions

1. State the elements of solicitation according to the New Mexico statute.

2. List all the facts relevant to deciding whether James Cotton satisfied the act and mental elements of solicitation according to the statute.

3. In your opinion, should solicitation include an attendant circumstance element requiring that the solicitation be communicated to the person being solicited? Explain your answer, taking into account the arguments for and against having a crime of solicitation.

SUMMARY

I. Inchoate crimes
A. *Inchoate* comes from the Latin verb "to begin."
B. Inchoate crimes are separate crimes of starting but not finishing any other crime.
C. Whether to make it a crime to start but not finish committing a crime poses a dilemma:
  1. Is the law punishing someone who has done no harm or setting free someone who is determined to do harm?
  2. The dilemma of criminal attempt law is resolved through three requirements:
    a. Requiring specific intent
    b. Requiring some action
    c. Punishing inchoate crimes less severely than completed crimes
D. Inchoate offenses include:
  1. *Attempt* Trying to commit a crime
  2. *Conspiracy* Agreeing to commit a crime
  3. *Solicitation* Trying to get someone else to commit a crime
E. All inchoate offenses are crimes of purpose (specific intent).

II. Attempt
A. Attempt is the crime of trying but failing to commit a crime.
B. There are two rationales for criminal attempt law:
  1. Prevent harm from dangerous conduct (focuses on how close to completion the crime is).
  2. Neutralize dangerous people (focuses on how developed the criminal purpose is).
  3. Both (1) and (2) look at actions taken to measure the danger.
C. The *mens rea* of attempt is always purpose or specific intent.
D. The *actus reus* of attempt
  1. Asks how much action is enough?
    a. Preparation isn't enough to qualify as the *actus reus* of attempt.
    b. The toughest problem in criminal attempt is drawing the line between preparation and attempt *actus reus.*
  2. Tests help draw the line between preparation and the act of attempt.
    a. Tests reflect the focus of the dangerous *conduct* and dangerous *people.*
    b. Proximity tests focus on dangerous conduct; they look at what remains to be done to complete the crime. The tests ask, "Were the defendant's acts close enough to the intended crime to count as the criminal act in the attempt?"
      (1) Dangerous proximity to success tests require that defendants get very close to, but not to, the very last act before completing the crime.
      (2) Indispensable element tests focus on whether defendants have control of what they need to complete the crime (possess drugs in attempted drug sale).

   (3) Unequivocality tests ("act speaks for itself;" "stop the film") examine whether an ordinary person who saw the defendant's acts without knowing her intent would believe she was determined to commit the intended crime.

   (4) Probable desistance tests

    (a) Probable desistance focuses on how much defendants have already done to demonstrate that they're dangerous people.

    (b) The defendant's conduct has to pass that point where most people would think better of their conduct and stop and go back to being law-abiding citizens.

   (5) "Substantial steps" (Model Penal Code) test

    (a) Substantial steps tests focus on what's already done, not what's left to do. The test looks for enough acts to demonstrate the actor is dangerous.

    (b) *Definition* The test looks for substantial steps that "strongly corroborate" the defendants' criminal purpose.

 E. The impossibility of completing the crime

  1. Legal impossibility is a defense to criminal attempt; factual impossibility isn't.

  2. Legal impossibility

   a. Defendants intend to commit a crime, do everything they can to complete the crime, but what they intend and do isn't a crime (e.g., intending to smuggle antique books into the country without paying customs, but they don't know that bringing these books into the country isn't illegal).

   b. You can't punish someone for a crime that doesn't exist.

  3. Factual impossibility

   a. Defendants intend to commit a crime and take all the steps necessary to complete it, but a fact makes it impossible (e.g., standing over a victim pulling the trigger of a gun the defendant believes is loaded but it's not).

   b. People bent on committing crimes shouldn't benefit from a stroke of luck.

 F. Abandonment

  1. Complete and voluntary abandonment of attempts is an affirmative defense in about half the states.

  2. Arguments in favor of the abandonment defense

   a. People who voluntarily and completely give up their criminal attempts aren't dangerous.

   b. We want to encourage people who are just about to hurt someone or their property to give up their plans.

  3. An argument against the defense of abandonment is that it encourages bad people to take the early steps in committing crimes, because they know they won't be punished.

III. Conspiracy

 A. Agreeing to commit crimes (criminal conspiracy) is further removed from completed crimes than trying to commit them (criminal attempt).

 B. Justifications for the conspiracy law

  1. It works hand in hand with attempts to nip in the bud criminal purpose.

  2. It strikes at the special danger of group criminal activity.

C. Conspiracy *actus reus*
 1. An agreement to commit a crime is the heart of the crime of conspiracy.
  a. It doesn't have to be in writing.
  b. An unspoken understanding inferred from facts and circumstances is good enough to prove agreement.
 2. Half the states require an "overt act" in addition to the act of agreement.
  a. The purpose is to verify the firmness of the agreement.
  b. The act doesn't have to amount to much; it can be of "very small significance."
D. Conspiracy *mens rea*
 1. It's a crime of purpose (specific intent).
 2. This can mean intent to make the agreement or intent to achieve the criminal objective.
E. Parties to conspiracy
 1. *Traditional* Two or more individuals agree to commit crimes.
 2. *Unilateral approach* Not all the conspirators had to agree to commit a crime as long as the defendant believes they did.
F. Large-scale conspiracies are of two types: wheel and chain.
 1. *Wheel conspiracies* These break down into two types:
  a. *Hub* Conspirators who participate in all transactions
  b. *Spokes* Conspirators who only participate in one transaction
 2. *Chain conspiracies* Participants at one end of the chain don't know anything of participants at the other end, but they all handle the same illegal commodity at different points (manufacture, distribution, sale).
G. The criminal objective of conspiracy
 1. Traditionally, it included everything from treason to disturbing the peace.
 2. States have made some effort to limit the reach of conspiracy:
  a. It requires an overt act in addition to an act of agreement.
  b. This applies to criminal objectives only.

IV. Solicitation
A. *Definition* The crime of trying to get someone else to commit a crime
B. Arguments against criminal solicitation law
 1. The act of soliciting isn't dangerous enough to punish, because an independent moral force (the person solicited) stands between the solicitation and its objective.
 2. Solicitors aren't dangerous enough people, and they prove it by needing someone else to do their dirty work.
C. Arguments for criminal solicitation law
 1. Solicitation is another form of the danger of group criminality.
 2. Solicitors are smart masters at manipulating others to do their dirty work.
D. Solicitation *actus reus* requires words that actually try to get someone to commit a crime (not just approve the commission of the crime).
E. Solicitation *mens rea* requires purpose or specific intent to get someone to commit a specific crime.
F. The objective of criminal solicitation varies from limiting it to violent felonies in some jurisdictions to including all crimes in other jurisdictions.

REVIEW QUESTIONS

1. Why are attempt, conspiracy, and solicitation called "inchoate offenses"?

2. What do all the inchoate crimes have in common?

3. Identify and explain the dilemma caused by the inchoate crimes; then identify the three means by which it's resolved.

4. Explain the significance of the quotes from Plato and Bracton.

5. Briefly summarize the history of criminal attempt law.

6. Identify and explain the difference between the two theories of attempt law.

7. List, define, and give an example of the two elements of criminal attempts.

8. Identify and describe two types of criminal attempt statutes.

9. Identify the two theories of attempt that each of the tests of attempt *actus reus* relate to.

10. What problem are the "indispensable element" and "dangerous proximity" tests supposed to solve in criminal attempt law, and how are they each supposed to solve it?

11. What problems is the "unequivocality test" supposed to correct in criminal attempt law, and how is it supposed to correct them?

12. Summarize the probable desistance test.

13. State the elements of the MPC "substantial steps" test of attempt *actus reus*.

14. List the seven examples of "substantial steps" in the MPC that can satisfy the requirements of attempt *actus reus*.

15. Explain the difference between factual and legal impossibility, give an example of each, and explain why they have different consequences in liability for criminal attempt.

16. Summarize the arguments for and against the defense of voluntary abandonment.

17. Identify the two public policy justifications for the crime of conspiracy.

18. Identify, explain, and give an example of the two parts of conspiracy *actus reus*.

19. Explain what *specific intent* means in conspiracy.

20. State the traditional definition of *parties to conspiracies,* and then identify and state the modern definition that replaced it.

21. Define and give an example of the "objective" in criminal conspiracy.

22. List the criticisms of criminal conspiracy definitions, and describe efforts to overcome these criticisms.

23. Summarize the arguments for and against making it a crime to try to get someone else to commit a crime.

24. Identify and give an example of the elements of criminal solicitation.

KEY TERMS

Crimes Against Persons I: Criminal Homicide

MAIN POINTS

- Criminal homicide is different from all other crimes because of the finality of its result: the death of the victim.
- Most of the law of criminal homicide is about grading the seriousness of the offense.
- Grading murder into first and second degree is important because only first-degree murders qualify for the death penalty.
- Most criminal homicide statutes apply to corporations, but prosecutions are rare.
- The heart of voluntary manslaughter is an intentional, sudden killing triggered by an adequate provocation.
- Provocation isn't an excuse for criminal homicide; it only reduces the seriousness of the crime and the punishment to allow for human frailty.

© Lee Celano/Reuters/Landov

9

What kind and amount of punishment should be inflicted on people who kill other people? Should we kill them? Lock them up for the rest of their lives? Lock them up for a certain number of years? Fine them? All of these options are provided for in the state and federal criminal codes, and they vary not only from one criminal homicide to another but also from state to state, sometimes drastically.

Did He Murder His Wife?

Schnopps and his wife were having marital problems. Among the problems was that his wife was having an affair with a man at work. Schnopps found out about the affair. Mrs. Schnopps moved out of the house, taking their children with her. Schnopps asked his wife to come to their home and talk over their marital difficulties. Schnopps told his wife that he wanted his children at home, and that he wanted the family to remain intact. Schnopps cried during the conversation and begged his wife to let the children live with him and to keep their family together. His wife replied, "No, I am going to court, you are going to give me all the furniture, you are going to have to get the Hell out of here, you won't have nothing." Then, pointing to her crotch, she said, "You will never touch this again, because I have got something bigger and better for it." On hearing those words, Schnopps claims that his mind went blank, and that he went "berserk." He went to a cabinet and got out a pistol he had bought and loaded the day before, and he shot his wife and himself. Schnopps survived the shooting, but his wife died. ◉

(COMMONWEALTH V. SCHNOPPS 1983)

"**D**eath is different," the U.S. Supreme Court said about capital punishment. Killing is different, too—it's the most serious of all crimes. In 1769, Blackstone, the great 18th-century commentator on the criminal law, introduced his chapter on homicide with words that are pretty close to describing the crimes you'll be learning about in this chapter:

> Of crimes injurious to . . . persons . . . the most . . . important is the offence of taking away that life, which is the immediate gift of the great creator; and which therefore no man can be entitled to deprive . . . another of. . . . The subject therefore of the present chapter will be, the offense of homicide or destroying the life of man, in its several stages of guilt, arising from the particular circumstances of mitigation or aggravation. (4:177)

Of course, raping, assaulting, and kidnapping harm people, too; but however awful they may be, they leave their victims alive (Chapter 10). And crimes against homes and property (Chapter 11)—crimes against public order and morals—also hurt their victims and society (Chapter 12), but these are injuries to worldly things. According to the distinguished professor of criminal law George P. Fletcher (1978):

> Killing another human being is not only a worldly deprivation; in the Western conception of homicide, killing is an assault on the sacred, natural order. In the Biblical view, the person who slays another was thought to acquire control over the blood—the life force—of the victim. The only way that this life force could be returned to God, the origin of all life, was to execute the slayer himself. In this conception of crime and punishment, capital execution for homicide served to expiate the desecration of the natural order. (235–36)

CRIMINAL HOMICIDE IN CONTEXT

To put criminal homicide in the context of the crimes you'll be studying throughout the rest of the book, they're very rare events. In 2004, there were 16,000 murders and attempted murders reported to the FBI compared with 1,367,009 total violent felonies and attempted violent felonies reported. The total number of all crimes and attempts in the FBI Index of serious crimes (homicide, forcible rape, robbery, aggravated assault, burglary, theft, motor vehicle theft, and arson) was 11,695,264, compared with the 16,000 criminal homicides and attempted homicides (FBI 2005).

These numbers aren't meant to diminish the seriousness of killing another person—an act that stands alone in its awfulness. But there are more reasons why we study criminal homicide. Much of what you've learned in the earlier chapters grew out of the law of criminal homicide. This is especially true of the mental element, or *mens rea*, and the justification of self-defense.

But there's more: the three-step analysis of criminal liability—(1) criminal conduct, (2) without justification, and (3) excuse—grew out of the great work on the law of criminal homicide written by the principal drafter of the Model Penal Code (MPC),

Professor Herbert Wechsler at Columbia Law School (Michael and Wechsler 1937; Dubber and Kelman 2005, 846).

Most of the law of homicide is devoted to answering questions like: Is this murder first or second degree? Is that killing murder or manslaughter? Is this manslaughter voluntary or involuntary? Students ask: "Does it really matter?" Certainly not to the victim—who's already and always dead! But it does make a big practical difference. Why? Because the punishment for criminal homicide depends on the degree of murder or the type of manslaughter committed.

Three elements of criminal homicide—*actus reus*, *mens rea*, and special mitigating and aggravating circumstances—are used to define the kinds and grade the seriousness of the criminal homicides you'll learn about in this chapter. Defining what kind of criminal homicide a particular killing is and grading its seriousness will make you think about deep philosophical questions regarding crime and punishment. This is good and proper.

But there's more than a purely philosophical question here. There's the practical question of the kind and amount of punishment to inflict on people who kill other people. Should we kill them? Lock them up for the rest of their lives? Lock them up for a certain number of years? Fine them? All of these are provided for in the state and federal criminal codes. And they vary not only from one criminal homicide to another but also from state to state, sometimes drastically. For the most striking example, first-degree murder is the only crime you can die for, and in non–death penalty states, it's the only crime for which you can get life in prison without a chance of parole.

As you read the chapter, keep in focus both the moral or ethical dimension *and* the practical dimension of criminal homicide and their importance in shaping the definition, grading, and punishment of how and why one person kills another.

In this chapter, we'll look at murder and manslaughter. We'll examine the history of murder law; the elements of murder and manslaughter—namely, the *actus reus*, the *mens rea*, and the circumstance elements; and how the elements affect the punishment of the various kinds of murder and manslaughter. Then, we'll turn to the lesser offense of criminally negligent homicide, or manslaughter. Before we do, we begin with the very important question of the meaning of "person" or "human being" for the purposes of homicide law.

THE MEANING OF "PERSON" OR "HUMAN BEING"

Killing another "person" is central to criminal homicide liability because it defines who's a victim. Person seems like a simple concept to understand. However, it raises deep philosophical questions and hot controversy. We won't get deeply into the broad controversy, except as a preliminary matter to understanding the elements of criminal homicide. The definition of person for purposes of criminal homicide presents problems at both ends of the life cycle—when life begins and when it ends. When life begins tells us when a potential victim becomes a real victim; when life ends tells us when a real victim is no longer a victim.

When Does Life Begin?

Throughout most of its history, homicide law has followed the **born-alive rule.** According to that rule, to be a person, and therefore a homicide victim, a baby had to be "born alive" and capable of breathing and maintaining a heartbeat on its own. There have been only a few exceptions to the rule; *People v. Chavez* (1947) was one.

Josephine Chavez, an unmarried woman about 21 years old, was charged with murdering her second newborn during its birth. She "knew the baby was going to be born" while she was sitting on the toilet. She didn't call for help. "It came out rather slow. Next, the head was out, and it sort of dropped out real fast." She knew from her first baby's birth that the placenta had to be removed and so, after the baby was in the toilet "a little while," she expelled the placenta by putting pressure on her stomach. She didn't notice whether the baby's head was under water, because the afterbirth fell over its head. It took two to three minutes for the placenta to come out.

Then, she removed the baby from the toilet, picking it up by the feet, and cut the cord with a razor blade. She testified that the baby was limp and made no cry; that she thought it was dead; and that she made no attempt to tie the cord as she thought there was no use. She then laid the baby on the floor and proceeded to take further care of herself and clean up the room.

The baby remained on the floor about fifteen minutes, after which she wrapped it in a newspaper and placed it under the bathtub to hide it from her mother. She then returned to bed and the next day went about as usual, going to a carnival that evening. On the next day, April 1, her mother discovered the body of the infant under the bathtub (92–95).

Chavez was convicted of manslaughter. She appealed to the California Court of Appeals. According to the court, in the opinion affirming the conviction:

> A viable child *in the process of being born* is a human being within the meaning of the homicide statutes, whether or not the process has been fully completed. . . . It would be a mere fiction to hold that a child is not a human being because the process of birth has not been fully completed, when it has reached that state of viability when the destruction of the life of its mother would not end its existence and when, if separated from the mother naturally or by artificial means, it will live and grow in the normal manner. . . .
>
> We have no hesitation in holding that the evidence is sufficient here to support the implied finding of the jury that this child was born alive and became a human being within the meaning of the homicide statutes. . . . The evidence is sufficient to support a finding, beyond a reasonable doubt, that a live child was actually born here, and that it died because of the negligence of the appellant in failing to use reasonable care in protecting its life, having the duty to do so. This baby was completely removed from its mother and even the placenta was removed. (94–95)

But in *Keeler v. Superior Court* (1970, discussed in Chapter 1), the California Supreme Court refused to push back the definition of *person* to include fetuses before the birth process. Keeler was convicted of manslaughter for causing the death of his wife's unborn fetus by kicking her in the stomach.

Some states that follow the "born alive" common-law rule have held that deaths due to prenatal injuries can be prosecuted as criminal homicide if the fetus dies after it's born alive. For example, in *State v. Cotton* (2000), Lawrence Cotton accidentally shot his girlfriend, L. W., in the back of the head. L. W. was $8^1/_2$ months pregnant at the time. Although L. W. died shortly after arriving at the hospital, her daughter was delivered alive. But the fatal injury to L. W. had so decreased the blood supply to the baby that the infant died the following day (920).

Cotton was convicted on two counts of reckless homicide, one for L. W. and one for the infant. Cotton argued that the cause of death, his accidental shot that killed his girlfriend, occurred before the fetus was born. The Arizona Court of Appeals rejected Cotton's argument:

> That the shooting in this case occurred while the infant was in utero does not preclude her post-birth status as a "person" for purposes of Arizona's homicide statutes. While the homicide statutes require that the victim be a "person," they do not limit the nature or timing of the injury that causes the death of the "person." (922)

Because the infant here was undeniably a "person" at the time of her death a day after the shooting, it is irrelevant that the injuries that led to her death were inflicted while she was still in utero. (923)

About half the states have filled the gap in the "born alive" rule by passing two types of statutes. One type revises existing homicide statutes to include persons and fetuses as potential homicide victims. California passed this kind of statute to overturn *Keeler* by adding just three words to its murder statute, which before *Keeler* read "Murder is the unlawful killing of a human being with malice aforethought." Since *Keeler*, it reads, "Murder is the unlawful killing of a human being, *or a fetus*, with malice aforethought" (emphasis added; California Penal Code 2006, § 187(a)).

Other state legislatures have created the new crime of **feticide,** specifically directed at the killing of fetuses. These statutes vary as to when in the development of the fetus criminal liability attaches. Some say it's at viability; some say at "quickening"; some specify the number of weeks. Seven states say criminal liability attaches at "conception" or "fertilization" (LaFave 2003a, 729).

When Does Life End?

It used to be easy to define death: when the heart and breathing stop. Not any more. Determining when life ends has become increasingly complex as organ transplants and sophisticated artificial life support mechanisms make it possible to maintain vital life signs.

Still, to kill a dying person, to accelerate a person's death, or to kill a "worthless" person is clearly homicide under current law. In *State v. Fiero* (1979, 77–78) a doctor who removed a vital organ too soon committed criminal homicide. And anyone who kills another by purposely disconnecting a respirator has also committed criminal homicide.

The concept of brain death has complicated the simple definition as when the heart and breathing stop. This complication has implications not just for medicine and morals but also for criminal law. If artificial supports alone maintain breathing and the heartbeat while brain waves remain minimal or flat, brain death has occurred. The Uniform Brain Death Act provides that an individual who has suffered irreversible cessation of all brain functions, including those of the brain stem, is dead (ALI 1985, 2:1, 10–11).

More difficult cases involve individuals with enough brain functions to sustain breathing and a heartbeat but nothing more, such as patients in a deep coma. They may breathe and their hearts may beat on their own, but are they alive according to the criminal law? Troubling cases arise in which patients in a deep coma have been described by medical specialists as "vegetables" but regain consciousness and live for a considerable time afterward, such as the Minneapolis police officer who was shot and written off for dead after more than a year in a deep coma. He regained consciousness and lived for several more years.

MURDER

The common law divided homicides into two kinds, and so do modern criminal codes, the MPC, and this chapter. The two kinds are:

1. *Murder* Killing a person *with* "malice aforethought," which we'll define and discuss in this section

2. *Manslaughter* Killing a person *without* malice aforethought, which we'll discuss in the "Manslaughter" section

According to Blackstone, writing in 1769, *malice aforethought* was the "grand criterion, which now distinguishes murder from other killing" (188–89). These two

 Go to the Criminal Law 9e website to find Exercise 9.1 and learn how state criminal codes classify criminal homicides: www .thomsonedu.com/ criminaljustice/samaha.

divisions were in turn divided into several kinds of murder and manslaughter, and, eventually, some special kinds of homicide, such as vehicular homicide (which we'll discuss later in the chapter), were added.

A long history of criminal homicides preceded the publication of Blackstone's classic work in 1769; we'll look at a little bit of it in this section. We'll also examine the elements of murder, the kinds and degrees of murder, first-degree murder, second-degree murder, and corporation murder.

The History of Murder Law

Our modern law of criminal homicide took centuries to develop. Over several centuries, the English common-law judges had developed two broad kinds of homicide, criminal and noncriminal. By the 1550s, the common-law judges, with the help of a growing number of statutes, had further divided criminal homicide into murder and manslaughter and noncriminal homicide into justifiable and excusable homicide (Chapters 5 and 6).

By 1700, the English common and statute laws of homicide and the American colonies' law recognized three kinds of homicide:

1. *Justifiable homicide* Self-defense (Chapter 5), capital punishment, and law enforcement use of deadly force

2. *Excusable homicide* Killings done by someone "not of sound memory and discretion" (insane and immature) (Chapter 6)

3. *Criminal homicide* All homicides that are neither justified nor excused

Eventually, these laws further divided criminal homicide into murder and manslaughter. We'll examine manslaughter later in the chapter. For now, let's concentrate on murder.

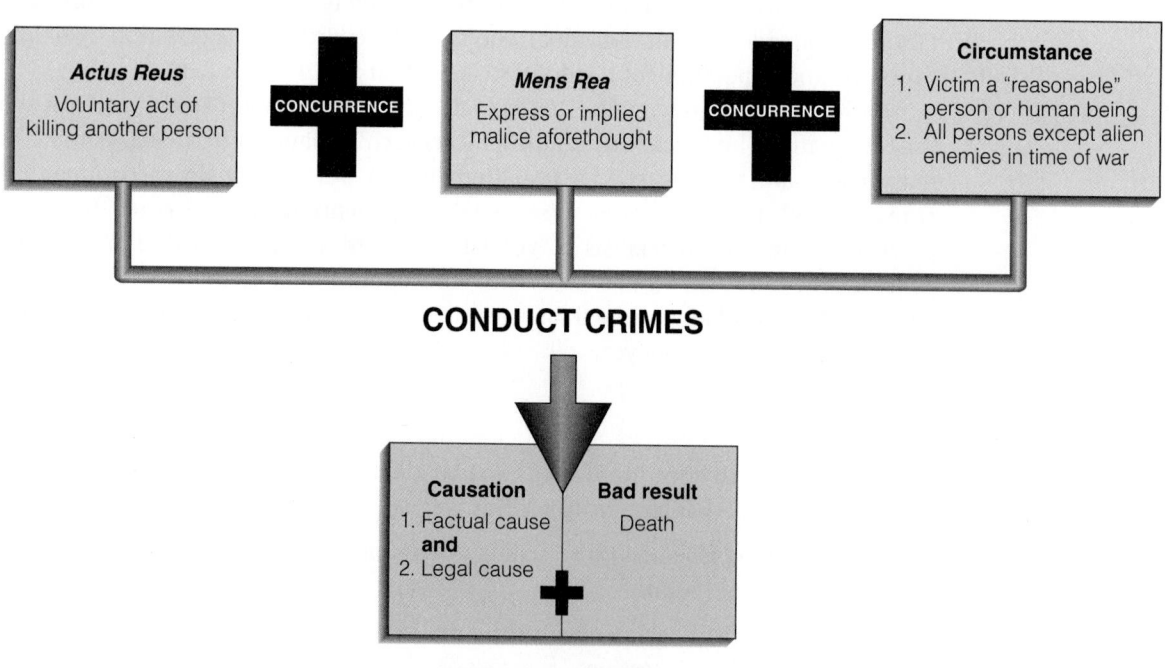

Elements of Common-Law Murder

In the early 1600s, Sir Edward Coke wrote that common-law murder occurred

when a person, of sound memory and discretion, unlawfully killeth any reasonable creature in being and under the king's peace, with malice aforethought, either express or
implied. (Blackstone 1769, 4:195, quoting from Coke 1628 *Institutes*, 3:47)

Let's look at how Blackstone defined those elements of common-law murder
in 1769:

1. *"Sound memory and discretion"* excused "lunatics and infants" from criminal
   liability.

2. *Unlawfully* meant killing without justification (Chapter 5) or excuse (Chapter 6).

3. *Killeth* included causing death by "poisoning, striking, starving, drowning, and
   a thousand other forms of death, by which human nature may be overcome." (196)

4. *Reasonable creature in being* was someone already born alive and breathing at the
   time of the killing. (198)

5. *Under the king's peace* meant: "To kill an alien, a Jew, or an outlaw, who are all
   under the king's . . . protection, is as much murder as to kill the most regular
   Englishman; except he be an alien enemy in time of war." (198)

6. *With malice aforethought, express or implied.*

Let's look more closely at the mental element—killing with **malice aforethought.**
At first, *malice* meant with specific intent or killing on purpose and probably with some
amount of spite, hate, or bad will. *Aforethought* meant the acts were planned in advance
of the killing. The English homicide statutes in the 1550s defined *murder* as killing
someone intentionally by "poison" or "lying in wait," classic examples of acts planned
in advance. So the only kind of murder was intentional, premeditated killing—in other
words, killing with malice aforethought.

After that, the judges invented new kinds of murder. First, they added intentional
(malicious) killings that weren't premeditated. These included sudden killings during
the heat of passion, "unreasonably" provoked by the victim's conduct. We'll discuss
"unreasonably" provoked when we get to voluntary manslaughter, but it's enough for
now to think of it this way: If a reasonable person would've cooled off between the
provocation and the killing, the killing was murder even though it wasn't premeditated. For example, suppose someone doesn't like casual touching. As she's leaving her
criminal law class, a student in the class comes up, puts his arm around her, and says,
"Boring class, huh?" Very offended, she pulls away, saying "Back off, jerk." He responds
with, "Oh, come on, I'm just being friendly" and approaches her again. She pulls out
her gun and shoots him; he dies. She was "unreasonably" provoked.

Next, the judges added *unintended* killings if they occurred during the commission
of felonies. For example, an arsonist set fire to a house when she believed no one was
at home. Unfortunately, someone was at home, and he burned to death. She didn't
intend to kill him, and because she didn't intend to kill him, obviously she couldn't
have planned to kill him before she set fire to the house.

Then came **depraved heart murder,** defined as extremely reckless killings. Recall
here the definition of *recklessness* (Chapter 4): knowingly creating a substantial and
unjustifiable risk. In the case of a depraved heart murder, the risk is of death. For example, a roofer on a tall building, without bothering to look, throws a heavy board onto
a busy street below; the board kills three people. He didn't intend to kill them, but he
knew he was creating a high risk that the board would kill someone, and he threw it
anyway. These are extremely reckless killings, or depraved heart murders.

The judges took one last step further away from the premeditated, intentional killing requirement. They created **intent-to-cause-serious-bodily-injury murder.** No intent to kill was required when a victim died following acts triggered by the intent to inflict serious bodily injury short of death. Suppose a parent has a 17-year-old son who regularly drinks heavily, cuts school, and steals to buy alcohol; he's just generally out of control. Talking to him, grounding him, taking away his car, sending him to counseling—nothing works. So his father, angry and frustrated, decides to "beat him within an inch of his life." He does, and his son dies. He commits an intent-to-cause-serious-bodily-injury murder.

"Serious bodily injury" has a technical meaning. Some states define it by statute. Here's Tennessee's (Tennessee Criminal Code 2005, 39-11-106(a)(34)) definition, which is similar to other states' definitions:

> "Serious bodily injury" means bodily injury which involves:
>
> (A) A substantial risk of death;
>
> (B) Protracted unconsciousness;
>
> (C) Extreme physical pain;
>
> (D) Protracted or obvious disfigurement; or
>
> (E) Protracted loss or substantial impairment of a function of a bodily member, organ or mental faculty.

Throughout the centuries when judges were expanding the definition of murder to include these very different kinds of killings, they continued to call all of them by the same name—"killing another with malice aforethought." But they added the critical phrase "express or implied." **"Express" malice aforethought** was reserved for killings that fit the original meaning of murder—intentional killings planned in advance. According to Blackstone (1769):

> Express malice is when one, with a sedate deliberate mind and formed design, doth kill another, which formed design is evidenced by external circumstances discovering that inward intention; as lying in wait, antecedent menaces, former grudges, and concerted schemes to do him some bodily harm. (199)

"Implied" malice aforethought referred to the four additional kinds of murder we just discussed:

1. Intentional killings without premeditation or reasonable provocation

2. Unintentional killings during the commission of felonies

3. Depraved heart killings

4. Intent to inflict grievous bodily harm killings

The Elements of Murder

Murder is a result crime. Recall that result crimes consist of criminal conduct that causes a criminal harm (Chapter 3). Therefore, proving murder requires proof beyond a reasonable doubt of these elements:

1. *Actus reus*, the act of killing

2. *Mens rea*, purpose or knowledge, or extreme recklessness

3. Causation, the act caused

4. Death

5. Attendant circumstances, if there are any

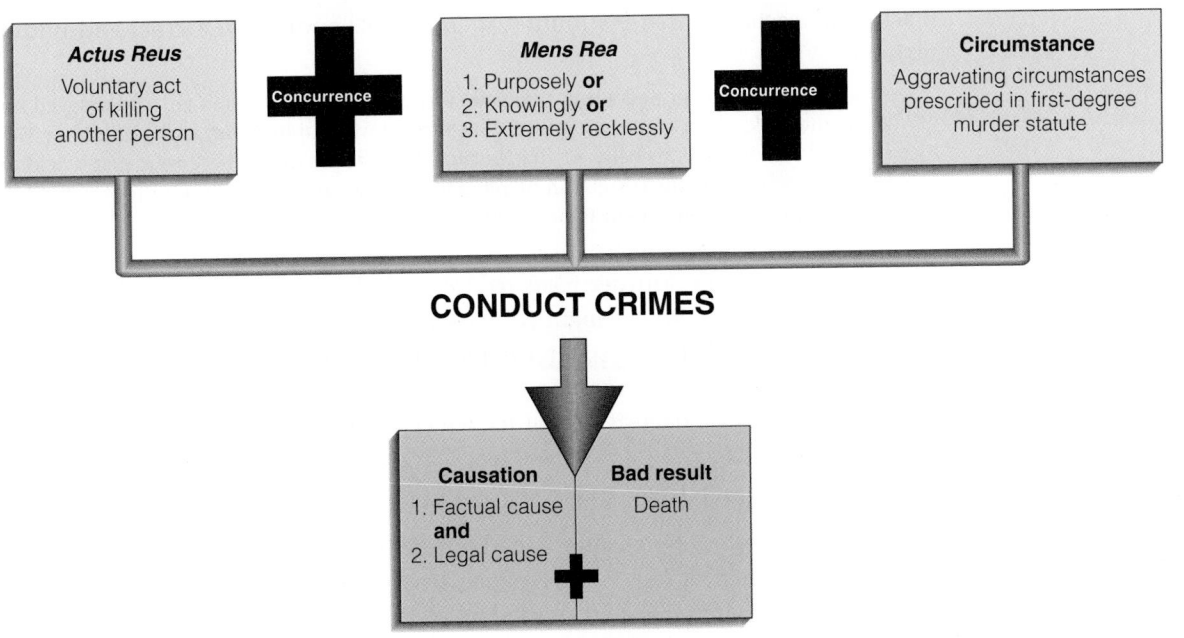

Elements of Murder

Before we go any further, it's important for you to keep in mind throughout the following discussion that the required criminal acts, mental attitudes, tests of causation, and attendant circumstances vary from state to state. So if you're interested in finding out what the elements of murder (or any of the specific kinds of homicide or any of the crimes in the rest of the book) are in your state, you can find them online free. (One of the several links to your state's code is http://www.law.cornell.edu/topics/state_statutes2.html#criminal_code.)

Now, let's turn to the elements of murder. We won't discuss causation here because Chapter 4 covers all you need to know about it. As for the result, the death of a person, we said all that was necessary in the "Meaning of 'Person'" section earlier. And we'll leave the discussion of the circumstance element to the places in the text where there is a circumstance. Let's look at how the general principles of *actus reus* and *mens rea* apply to the criminal act and mental attitude elements of criminal homicide.

Murder Actus Reus   "Killing" or "causing death" is the heart of **murder** *actus reus*, and it's easy to define. We can't improve much on Blackstone's (1769) words here: "The killing may be by poisoning, striking, starving, drowning, and a thousand other forms by which human nature can be overcome" (196). It can also result from failures to act—such as a husband who stands by and watches his blind wife, whom he hates, walk off the edge of a cliff—or by words—such as a wife who sneaks up behind her husband, whom she hates, who is standing at the edge of the Grand Canyon and yells, "Boo!" causing him to fall over the edge.

Notice that *how* the murderer kills someone doesn't matter in most cases. But it can be a circumstance element in first-degree murder or an aggravating circumstance in death penalty cases. Even though there were no degrees of murder at the time,

Blackstone teaches us that it's murder if "one beats another in a cruel and unusual manner":

> As when a park keeper tied a boy, that was stealing wood, to a horse's tail and dragged him along the park; when a master corrected his servant with an iron bar; and a school master stamped on his scholar's belly, so that each of the sufferers died. These were justly held to be murders because, the correction being excessive and such as could not proceed but from a bad heart, it was equivalent to an act of slaughter. (199–200)

Murder Mens Rea   **Murder** *mens rea* can include every state of mind included in the concept of malice aforethought (discussed in the last section). In the language of the Model Penal Code (discussed in Chapter 4), purpose, knowledge, and recklessness can qualify as the mental element in murder. We'll have more to say about the mental element in each of the degrees of murder, which we'll turn to now.

The Kinds and Degrees of Murder

The English judges never *formally* divided murder into degrees. All murders, in fact all felonies, except theft of less than 12 pence, were capital offenses. But the judges had enormous discretion to free all convicted felons by means of "benefit of clergy," a practice that began with a rule that allowed priests to be tried only in ecclesiastical courts. To get transferred from the common law to the ecclesiastical courts, priests had to prove they were clerics by reading a passage from the Bible. This was a reliable test because only clerics could read. Eventually, "reading the book" became a pure formality; the passage in the "book" convicted felons had to "read" was always the same few words, and the ability to read spread beyond the clergy.

This was a formality the judges manipulated to mitigate *informally* the harshness of the common law, which mandated that all felons, from cold-blooded murderers to petty thieves, should hang. By the reign of Henry VIII (1509–37), successful pleas of clergy were so widely granted by the judges that Parliament enacted a form of mandatory sentencing to curb judicial discretion; it banned the plea in all cases of premeditated murder (Samaha 1974). The list of "nonclergyable" offenses would grow in the centuries that followed.

Dividing murder into degrees was a continuation of the idea that not all felons—in this case, not all murderers—should be executed. In the new United States, degrees of murder were created, not by judges but by legislatures. Pennsylvania was the first state to depart from the common law, enacting a statute in 1794 that divided murder into first and second degrees. The Pennsylvania statute provided that

> all murder, which shall be perpetrated by means of poison, lying in wait, or by any other kind of willful, deliberate or premeditated killing, or which shall be committed in the perpetration, or attempt to perpetrate any arson, rape, robbery or burglary shall be deemed murder in the first degree; and all other kinds of murder shall be deemed murder in the second degree. (Pennsylvania Laws 1794, chap. 257, §§ 1–2)

So under the statute, premeditated intent-to-kill murders and some felony murders were capital offenses, just as they were under the old common law. And they still are. All other murders (depraved heart and intent to cause serious bodily injury) were second-degree murders, just as they were under the old law. *Sometimes*, they still are. The MPC doesn't use the degrees, but, since its publication in 1960, state criminal codes have increasingly used the MPC's scheme of dividing murder according to mental attitude—purpose, knowing, and extreme recklessness.

Most states quickly followed Pennsylvania's example. Behind this quick adoption of the statutes was the first of many waves of opposition to the death penalty throughout

U.S. history. Three results followed, results which profoundly influenced the criminal law you're studying in this book:

(1) the gradual peeling away of layers of criminal homicides that were thought not to deserve the death penalty;

(2) the emergence of more detailed grading schemes placing various types of criminal homicide along the spectrum of available criminal punishments; and

(3) the development of various justifications and excuses making certain homicides non-criminal. (Low 1990, 335)

Today, most states divide homicide into two degrees, and a few divide it into three degrees. We'll look at first-degree and second-degree murder.

First-Degree Murder

Almost all states that divide murder into degrees establish two kinds of first-degree murder: (1) premeditated, deliberate, intent-to-kill murders and (2) felony murders. First-degree murder is the only crime today in which the death penalty can be imposed (Chapter 2). Because of a series of U.S. Supreme Court cases, death penalty cases are complicated proceedings. So we need to look at first-degree murder and the death penalty before we go further.

The Death Penalty   The death penalty is discretionary in all states in which the penalty is authorized. To guide judges' and juries' decisions whether to execute or sentence to life in prison a person convicted of first-degree murder, the U.S. Supreme Court, in a series of decisions since the 1970s, has completely revised the procedures for imposing capital punishment. The matter is highly complicated, and the Court's cases haven't always made it clear just what's required, but here's a list of the main practices the Constitution bans, requires, and allows:

1. *Mandatory death sentences are banned.* States can't require the death penalty in *all* first-degree murders.

2. *Unguided discretionary death penalty decisions are banned.* Judges and juries can't impose the death penalty without a list of specific criteria for and against the death penalty to guide their decision.

3. *Mitigating factors are required.* States can't limit the range of mitigating factors that might favor life imprisonment instead of death.

4. *Additional aggravating factors are allowed.* Jurors and/or judges are allowed to consider factors in favor of death not specifically included in statutory lists of aggravating factors.

Most states have adopted the MPC's two recommended procedures—bifurcation and the criteria for guiding the decision to impose the death sentence in **capital cases.** (We define *capital cases* as death penalty cases in death penalty states and "mandatory life sentence without parole" cases in non–death penalty states.) **Bifurcation** mandates that the death penalty decision be made in two phases: a trial to determine guilt and a second separate proceeding, after a finding of guilt, to consider the aggravating factors for, and mitigating factors against, capital punishment. At the penalty phase, prosecutors get the opportunity to present evidence not presented at the trial phase, and defendants can offer evidence in mitigation.

The **criteria for decision** must be limited by the criteria established and announced *before* the decision to sentence the defendant to death. Juries, or judges where state law authorizes judges to decide, have to consider aggravating *and* mitigating factors before making their decision. They can't actually impose the death penalty unless they find

> one of the aggravated circumstances . . . and further finds that there are no mitigating circumstances sufficiently substantial to call for leniency. (ALI 1985, Art. 210.6)

The list of aggravating circumstances is:

1. The murder was committed by a convict under sentence of imprisonment.

2. The defendant was previously convicted of another murder or of a felony involving the use or threat of violence to the person.

3. At the time the murder was committed, the defendant also committed another murder.

4. The defendant knowingly created a great risk of death to many persons.

5. The murder was committed while the defendant was engaged or was an accomplice in the commission, or an attempt to commit, or flight after committing or attempting to commit, robbery, rape or deviate sexual intercourse by force or threat of force, arson, burglary, or kidnapping.

6. The murder was committed for the purpose of avoiding or preventing a lawful arrest or effecting an escape from lawful custody.

7. The murder was committed for pecuniary gain.

8. The murder was especially heinous, atrocious, or cruel, manifesting exceptional depravity.

The list of mitigating factors is

1. The defendant has no significant history of criminal activity.

2. The murder was committed while the defendant was under the influence of extreme mental or emotional disturbance.

3. The victim was a participant in the defendant's homicidal conduct or consented to the homicidal act.

4. The murder was committed under circumstances which the defendant believed to provide a moral justification or extenuation for his conduct.

5. The defendant was an accomplice in a murder committed by another person and his participation in the homicidal act was relatively minor.

6. The defendant acted under duress or under the domination of another person.

7. At the time of the murder, the capacity of the defendant to appreciate the criminality [wrongfulness] of his conduct or to conform his conduct to the requirements of law was impaired as a result of mental disease or defect or intoxication.

8. The defendant was a young age at the time of the crime.

First-Degree Murder Mens Rea   "All murder which is perpetrated by . . . willful, deliberate, and premeditated killing . . . is murder of the first degree" (California Penal Code 2006, ß 189). This is a broad, even vague, definition of first-degree murder often found in criminal codes.

Most courts say that "premeditated" and "deliberate" mean something more than the intent to kill. In other words, they refine the mental attitude of the MPC's "purposely" and "knowingly" and the common law's "specific intent." Judges understand that the purpose of the refinement is to distinguish between murders so awful that they deserve the harshest punishment the law allows from murders that don't deserve the worst punishment.

But just what the refinement consists of varies greatly, and there's often disagreement, sometimes among judges on the same court, not just on the definitions but whether they apply to the facts of the case they're deciding. Unfortunately, some courts blur the line between intentional killings and the more refined deliberate, premeditated intentional killings. The result is that there's no meaningful difference between first- and second-degree murder. This is serious business, not just theoretically but practically, too; it could mean, literally, the difference between life and death.

"Willful" rarely comes up in the appellate cases today, so we can fairly assume it means what one judge instructing the jury in a murder trial just after the Civil War said: "Many cases have been decided under this clause, in all of which it has been held that the *intention* to kill is the essence of the offense. Therefore, if an intention to kill exists, it is willful" (*Commonwealth v. Drum* 1868, 6).

The same isn't true of "deliberate" and "premeditated. They're frequently issues in the cases, and the courts define them differently, sometimes radically so. We can start with a few simple definitions just to give you the general idea of what willful, deliberate, premeditated killing means. Professor LaFave (2003a) describes the thought process the mental attitude refers to:

It has been suggested that for premeditation the killer asks himself the question, "Shall I kill him?" The intent to kill aspect of the crime is found in the answer, "Yes I shall." The deliberation part of the crime requires a thought like, "Wait, what about the consequences? Well, I'll do it anyway." (766)

Professor LaFave acknowledges what the cases amply demonstrate:

It is not easy to give a meaningful definition to the words "premeditate" and "deliberate" as they are used in connection with first degree murder. Perhaps the best that can be said of "deliberation" is that it requires a cool mind that is capable of reflection, and of "premeditation" that it requires that one with the cool mind did in fact reflect, at least for a short period of time before killing. (766–67)

Justice Agnew of the Supreme Court of Pennsylvania summed up the mental attitude about as well as any in his colorful instruction to the jury in the murder trial of a youth, William Drum, who fatally stabbed another youth, David Mohigan, who had attacked Drum the week before the fatal stabbing (*Commonwealth v. Drum* 1868).

A life has been taken. The unfortunate David Mohigan has fallen into an untimely grave; struck down by the hand of violence; and it is for you to determine whose was that hand, and what its guilt. The prisoner is in the morning of life; as yet so fresh and fair. As you sat and gazed into his youthful face, you have thought, no doubt, most anxiously thought, is his that hand? Can he, indeed, be a murderer? This, gentlemen, is the solemn question you must determine upon the law and the evidence. . . . (5)

In this case we have to deal . . . with that kind of murder in the first degree described as "willful, deliberate, and premeditated." Many cases have been decided under this clause, in all of which it has been held that the *intention* to kill is the essence of the offence.

Therefore, if an intention to kill exists, it is willful; if this intention be accompanied by such circumstances as evidence a mind fully conscious of its own purpose and design, it is deliberate; and if sufficient time be afforded to enable the mind fully to frame the design to kill, and to select the instrument, or to frame the plan to carry this design into execution, it is premeditated.

The law fixes upon no length of time as necessary to form the intention to kill, but leaves the existence of a fully formed intent as a fact to be determined by the jury, from all the facts and circumstances in the evidence. (6)

. . . It is equally true both in fact and from experience, that *no* time is too short for a wicked man to frame in his mind his scheme of murder, and to contrive the means of accomplishing it."

But this expression must be qualified, lest it mislead. It is true that such is the swiftness of human thought, that no time is so short in which a wicked man may not form a design to kill, and frame the means of executing his purpose; yet this suddenness is opposed to premeditation, and a jury must be well convinced upon the evidence that there was time to deliberate and premeditate.

The law regards, and the jury must find, the actual intent; that is to say, the fully formed purpose to kill, with so much time for deliberation and premeditation, as to convince them that this purpose is not the immediate offspring of rashness and impetuous temper, and that the mind has become fully conscious of its own design. If there be time to frame in the mind, fully and consciously, the intention to kill, and to select the weapon or means of death, and to think and know beforehand, though the time be short, the use to be made of it, there is time to deliberate and to premeditate.

Blackstone (1769) called "willful, premeditated, deliberate killings" the "grand criterion" of murder because they reflect "the dictate of a wicked, depraved, and malignant heart" (199).

Modern court opinions display a far broader spectrum of definitions. At one extreme are those that fit the definitions of the original "grand criterion"—killings planned in advance and then committed in "cold blood" that we've just reviewed. A good example is *People v. Anderson* (1968).

We have repeatedly pointed out that the legislative classification of murder into two degrees would be meaningless if "deliberation" and "premeditation" were construed as requiring no more reflection than may be involved in the mere formation of a specific intent to kill. A verdict of murder in the first degree (on a theory of a willful, deliberate, and premeditated killing) is proper only if the slayer killed as a result of careful thought and weighing of considerations; as a deliberate judgment or plan; carried on coolly and steadily. (948)

States that adopt this **specific-intent-plus-real-premeditation-deliberation definition** rely on three categories of evidence to prove murders really were premeditated and deliberate:

Category 1. Facts about how and what defendant did prior to the actual killing which show that the defendant was engaged in activity directed toward, and explicable as intended to result in, the killing—what may be characterized as planning activity;

Category 2. Facts about the defendant's prior relationship and/or conduct with the victim from which the jury could reasonably infer a "motive" to kill the victim, which inference of motive, together with facts of type (1) or (3), would in turn support an inference that the killing was the result of "a pre-existing reflection and careful thought and weighing of considerations rather than mere unconsidered or rash impulse hastily";

Category 3. Facts about the nature of the killing from which the jury could infer that the manner of killing was so particular and exacting that the defendant must have intentionally killed according to a preconceived design to take his victim's life in a particular way for a reason which the jury can reasonably infer from facts of type (1) or (2). (949)

Table 9.1 highlights cases that demonstrate each of the three categories.

At the other extreme are courts that define "willful, premeditated, deliberate" killing as the equivalent of the specific intent to kill. A good example is *Macias v. State* (1929):

There need be no appreciable space of time between the intention to kill and the act of killing. They may be as instantaneous as successive thoughts of the mind. It is only necessary that the act of killing be preceded by a concurrence of will, deliberation, and premeditation on the part of the slayer, and, if such is the case, the killing is murder in the first degree. (715)

TABLE 9.1 **Proving Premeditated, Deliberate Intent**

Category 1	Category 2	Category 3
• *U.S. v. Blue Thunder* (1979). Brought the murder weapon, a knife, to the murder scene • *People v. Kemp* (1961). Entered the house through a bedroom window • *U.S. v. Downs* (1995). Arranged to meet the victim at home when no one would be home	• *State v. Crawford* (1996). Prior threats to kill the victim • *State v. Thomas* (1999). Starving the child to death would conceal a prior killing • *State v. Hamlet* (1984). Victim had bragged about knocking out the defendant in a prior fight	• *U.S. v. Treas-Wilson* (1993) Precise and fatal injury; 4-inch incision severing esophagus, trachea, and large neck veins • *People v. Steele* (2002). Stabbed victim eight times in the chest • *State v. Taylor* (2002). Eight blows to the head with a heavy object

There's considerable criticism in court decisions and among commentators that this **equivalent-of-specific-intent definition** renders the difference between first- and second-degree murder meaningless. That's serious because it means there's no real difference between capital murder that can lead to execution in death penalty states or to life in prison without the chance of parole in non–death penalty states.

In *Byford v. State* (2000), the Nevada Supreme Court affirmed 20-year-old Robert Byford's death sentence because he intentionally, with premeditation and deliberation, killed Monica Wilkins and because the aggravating circumstance outweighed the mitigating circumstances present in the case.

CASE   *Was He Guilty of Capital Murder?*

Byford v. State
994 P.2d 700 (Nev. 2000)

HISTORY

Robert Byford, Defendant, and a codefendant were convicted in the Eighth Judicial District Court, Clark County, of first-degree murder with use of deadly weapon and were sentenced to death, and they appealed. The Supreme Court reversed and remanded for retrial. On remand, defendant was again convicted in the Eighth Judicial District Court, Clark County, of first-degree murder with use of deadly weapon and was again sentenced to death. Defendant appealed. The Supreme Court affirmed.

SHEARING, J.

FACTS

Byford, Williams, and two teenage girls were visiting Smith at his parents' residence in Las Vegas on March 8, 1991. Byford was twenty years old, Williams seventeen,

and Smith nineteen. Monica Wilkins, who was eighteen, called and told Smith she would pay him for a ride home from a local casino. Smith drove his jeep to pick Wilkins up, accompanied by Williams and one of the girls. After Smith picked up Wilkins and her friend, Jennifer Green, he asked Wilkins for gas money. Wilkins had Smith stop at a Burger King so that she could get some money. Williams went inside the store to see what was taking her so long, and Wilkins told him that she had gotten another ride. Smith and Williams were upset with Wilkins, and after they drove away, Williams fired a handgun out the window of the jeep.

Smith testified that Wilkins had angered him, Williams, and Byford before because she had invited them to her apartment to party but then left with other men. Byford and Williams had talked about "getting rid of her" because she was always "playing games with our heads." Smith participated in the talk but took the threats as jokes.

Later that night, Smith, Williams, and Byford were together at Smith's house when Wilkins called again for a ride home. Accompanied by Byford and Williams, Smith drove to pick her up. Smith then drove all four of them to the desert outside of town to find a party that Byford heard was taking place. Wilkins told the other three that she had taken LSD earlier and was hallucinating. Smith drove to the usual area for parties, but they found no party. They then stopped so that everyone could urinate. Wilkins walked up a ravine to do so.

Smith testified to the following. As Wilkins finished, Byford handed Williams a handgun and said he "couldn't do it." Smith asked Byford what he was doing with the gun, and Byford told Smith to "stay out of it." Williams then shot Wilkins in the back three to five times. She screamed and fell to the ground. Wilkins got up, walked to Williams, and asked him why he had shot her. He told her that he had only shot around her. Wilkins walked up out of the ravine but then felt the back of her neck, saw that she was bleeding, and again confronted Williams.

Williams told her that he shot her because she was "a bitch." He then walked behind her and shot her again repeatedly. Wilkins screamed and fell to the ground again. Byford then took the gun from Williams, said that he would "make sure the bitch is dead," and fired two shots into her head. Byford then got a can of gasoline from the jeep and poured it on Wilkins. Byford tried to hand a lighter to Smith and get him to light the gasoline, but Smith refused. Byford called him a "wussie" and lit the body. As it burned, the three drove off. As they returned to Las Vegas, Byford pointed the handgun at Smith and threatened to kill him if he ever told anyone.

Smith further testified that about a week after the murder, Byford and Williams had him drive them back to the desert to bury the body. An inmate who was incarcerated in jail with Byford and Williams after their arrest also testified that the two told him about this trip back to the body. They told the inmate that the body was decomposing and had maggots on it. Byford and Williams rolled the corpse into the ravine and partly covered it with a few shovelfuls of dirt.

After about two more weeks, the body was discovered by target shooters. Las Vegas Metropolitan Police Department investigators collected sixteen .25 caliber shell casings at the site; ballistic testing showed that all were fired from the same weapon. Ten .25 caliber bullets were recovered; five were in the body. Three bullets were in the chest and abdomen, and two were in the head. Either of the bullets in the head would have been fatal. The body was partly eaten by coyotes or wild dogs. Other bullets could have been lost from the body due to this eating or the burning and decomposition of the body. The burning appeared to be postmortem.

In mid-April 1991, Byford's friend, Billy Simpson, was visiting Byford's residence. When the two came upon a dead rabbit covered with maggots, Byford told Simpson that he had seen maggots on a human body before. That same night, Simpson and his brother Chad observed Byford and Williams engage in "play acting" in which Williams acted as if he shot Byford with a gun, Byford fell and then stood back up, and Williams opened his eyes

wide and pretended to reload and shoot him again. Byford and Williams explained that they had shot and killed Wilkins in the desert and then burned her body.

In the spring or summer of 1991, Byford conversed with two girls in a city park. He admitted to them that he and Williams had shot and killed a girl in the desert and then burned her body. He told them that he wanted to see what would happen when someone under the influence of "acid" was shot. In August 1991, Byford told another friend that he was a "bad person" and "had done evil things" because he had shot and killed someone in order to know what it felt like to kill someone.

After the police investigation led to Byford and Williams, Byford asked his girlfriend to provide an alibi for him by telling the police that on the night of the murder they had been on the phone all night.

Neither Byford nor Williams testified. However, Williams introduced, over Byford's objection, Byford's testimony from the first trial. The gist of that prior testimony was that Smith and Wilkins were boyfriend and girlfriend, that they argued that night, that Smith shot Wilkins, and that Byford and Williams only aided Smith in concealing the crime. The testimony also included Byford's admission that he had a prior felony conviction for attempted possession of a stolen vehicle. In closing argument, the prosecutor referred to Byford as a convicted felon.

The jury found Byford and Williams guilty of first-degree murder with the use of a deadly weapon.

At the penalty hearing, the State called Marian Wilkins, the mother of the victim, to testify on the impact of losing her daughter. A probation officer testified that Byford had violated his probation conditions in 1991 and been placed under house arrest. Byford violated house arrest in 1992 by removing his transmitter bracelet and absconding. The officer also described Byford's juvenile record, which included burglary in 1984 and carrying a concealed weapon in 1987. A detention officer testified that in 1994 Byford was disciplined for fighting with another inmate at the Clark County Detention Center; the officer considered Byford to be a behavioral problem for the Center.

Two of Byford's aunts testified to Byford's good character growing up, as did his sister. Byford's mother also testified on his behalf and described him as a good boy and a caring son. Byford and his father had often got in conflicts, and his father was "heavy-handed" in disciplining him. Byford was very close to his grandfather. When his grandfather died, he became angry and withdrawn and quit attending church. Byford's mother was raising Byford's son. Byford talked with his son on the phone and was a good influence on him.

Thomas Kinsora, a Ph.D. in clinical neuropsychology, testified for Byford. Byford was diagnosed with attention deficit disorder as a child. He had conflicts with and anger toward his father for the latter's abuse of alcohol and emotional distance. Byford lost interest in school and immersed himself in alcohol and marijuana after his grandfather's death. He later used methamphetamines heavily for a time. After testing Byford, Dr. Kinsora concluded that the results were largely unremarkable and that Byford was not psychopathic.

Byford spoke briefly in allocution and said that he was sorry for his part in Wilkins's death.

In Byford's case, jurors found one mitigating circumstance: possible substance abuse. The jury found two aggravating circumstances: the murder was committed by a person under sentence of imprisonment and involved torture or mutilation of the victim. Byford received a sentence of death. In Williams's case, jurors found six mitigating circumstances. One aggravating circumstance was found: the murder involved torture or mutilation of the victim. Williams received a sentence of life imprisonment without possibility of parole.

OPINION

The Instructions Defining the Mens Rea *Required for First-Degree Murder*

The jury in this case was instructed:

> Premeditation is a design, a determination to kill, distinctly formed in the mind at any moment before or at the time of the killing.
>
> Premeditation need not be for a day, an hour or even a minute. It may be as instantaneous as successive thoughts of the mind. For if the jury believes from the evidence that the act constituting the killing has been preceded by and has been the result of premeditation, no matter how rapidly the premeditation is followed by the act constituting the killing, it is willful, deliberate and premeditated murder.

We will refer to this as the *Kazalyn* instruction because it first appears in this court's case law in *Kazalyn v. State*.

Byford argues that this instruction is improper because it mandates a finding of willful, deliberate, and premeditated murder based only on the existence of premeditation. Although we reject this argument as a basis for any relief for Byford, we recognize that it raises a legitimate concern which this court should address.

We conclude that the evidence in this case is clearly sufficient to establish deliberation and premeditation on Byford's part. Byford and Williams had talked of "getting rid" of the victim on prior occasions. On the night of the murder, Byford handed the gun to Williams, saying that he (Byford) "couldn't do it," and told Smith to "stay out of it." Thus, it is evident that Byford and Williams discussed shooting the victim before doing so.

Williams and Byford then calmly and dispassionately shot the victim in the absence of any provocation, confrontation, or stressful circumstances of any kind. Williams first shot her several times and then, after a passage of some time, shot her several more times. Byford watched this transpire, and when the victim was helpless on the ground, he took the gun from Williams, said that he would make sure she was dead, and shot her in the head twice.

This evidence was sufficient for the jurors to reasonably find that before acting to kill the victim Byford weighed the reasons for and against his action, considered its consequences, distinctly formed a design to kill, and did not act simply from a rash, unconsidered impulse.

The *Kazalyn* instruction, however, does raise a concern which we will now consider. NRS 200.030(1)(a) provides in relevant part that murder perpetrated by "willful, deliberate and premeditated killing" is first-degree murder. In this regard, willful means intentional. Therefore, willful first-degree murder requires that the killer actually intend to kill. Not every murder requires an intent to kill. For example, murder can also exist when a killer acts with a reckless disregard for human life amounting to "an abandoned and malignant heart." However, such a murder would not constitute willful first-degree murder.

In addition to willfulness, the statutory provision in question requires deliberation and premeditation. These are the truly distinguishing elements of first-degree murder under this provision. But the jurisprudence of Nevada, like that of other states, has shown a trend toward a confusion of premeditation and deliberation. We therefore take this opportunity to adhere to long-established rules of law and abandon the modern tendency to muddle the line between first-and second-degree murder.

The *Kazalyn* instruction and some of this court's prior opinions have underemphasized the element of deliberation. The neglect of "deliberate" as an independent element of the *mens rea* for first-degree murder seems to be a rather recent phenomenon. Before *Kazalyn*, it appears that "deliberate" and "premeditated" were both included in jury instructions without being individually defined but also without "deliberate" being reduced to a synonym of "premeditated." We did not address this issue in our *Kazalyn* decision, but later the same year, this court expressly approved the *Kazalyn* instruction, concluding that "deliberate" is simply redundant to "premeditated" and therefore requires no discrete definition. . . . This court went so far as to state that "the terms premeditated, deliberate and willful are a single phrase, meaning simply that the actor intended to commit the act and intended death as the result of the act."

We conclude that this line of authority should be abandoned. By defining only premeditation and failing to provide deliberation with any independent definition, the *Kazalyn* instruction blurs the distinction between first- and second-degree murder. [The] further reduction of premeditation and deliberation to simply "intent" unacceptably carries this blurring to a complete erasure. . . . It is clear from the statute that *all three elements*, willfulness, deliberation, and premeditation, must be proven beyond a reasonable doubt before an accused can be convicted of first degree murder. . . . In order to establish first-degree murder, the premeditated killing must also have been done deliberately, that is, with coolness and reflection. . . .

Accordingly, we set forth the following instructions for use by the district courts in cases where defendants are charged with first-degree murder based on willful, deliberate, and premeditated killing.

Murder of the first degree is murder which is perpetrated by means of any kind of willful, deliberate, and premeditated killing. All three elements—willfulness, deliberation, and premeditation—must be proven beyond a reasonable doubt before an accused can be convicted of first-degree murder.

Willfulness is the intent to kill. There need be no appreciable space of time between formation of the intent to kill and the act of killing.

Deliberation is the process of determining upon a course of action to kill as a result of thought, including weighing the reasons for and against the action and considering the consequences of the action.

A deliberate determination may be arrived at in a short period of time. But in all cases the determination must not be formed in passion, or if formed in passion, it must be carried out after there has been time for the passion to subside and deliberation to occur. A mere unconsidered and rash impulse is not deliberate, even though it includes the intent to kill.

Premeditation is a design, a determination to kill, distinctly formed in the mind by the time of the killing.

Premeditation need not be for a day, an hour, or even a minute. It may be as instantaneous as successive thoughts of the mind. For if the jury believes from the evidence that the act constituting the killing has been preceded by and has been the result of premeditation, no matter how rapidly the act follows the premeditation, it is premeditated.

The law does not undertake to measure in units of time the length of the period during which the thought must be pondered before it can ripen into an intent to kill which is truly deliberate and premeditated. The time will vary with different individuals and under varying circumstances.

The true test is not the duration of time, but rather the extent of the reflection. A cold, calculated judgment and decision may be arrived at in a short period of time, but a mere unconsidered and rash impulse, even though it includes an intent to kill, is not deliberation and premeditation as will fix an unlawful killing as murder of the first degree.

The Aggravating Circumstance of Torture or Mutilation

. . . NRS 200.033(8) provides as an aggravating circumstance that "[t]he murder involved torture or the mutilation of the victim." Establishing either torture or mutilation is sufficient to support the jury's finding of this aggravating circumstance.

In discussing torture, we have held that NRS 200.033(8) requires that the murderer must have intended to inflict pain beyond the killing itself. . . .

. . . Evidence indicated that Byford and Williams resented Wilkins because of perceived slights they had received from her. Thus revenge of a sort appears to have been their primary reason for shooting her. After shooting her in the back, Williams lied to Wilkins—who was under the influence of LSD—denying that he had shot her and telling her that he had only shot around her. When she realized she had been shot and asked why, he said because she was "a bitch" and then walked behind her and shot her again repeatedly. We conclude that the jury could have reasonably found that this behavior had a vengeful, sadistic purpose and was intended to inflict pain beyond the killing itself and therefore constituted torture. Byford, of course, was equally culpable of this torture: a person who aids and abets an act constituting an offense is a principal and subject to the same punishment as one who directly commits the act. . . . Our case law . . . tends to support the conclusion that the aggravating circumstance set forth in NRS 200.033(8) includes postmortem mutilation. More important, this conclusion is consistent with the statutory language. Although a victim who has died cannot be tortured, mutilation can occur after death. By including both terms as a basis for the aggravator, the statute penalizes egregious behavior whether it occurs before or after a victim's death. We agree with the State's assertion that the legislative intent in making mutilation an aggravating circumstance "was to discourage the desecration of a fellow human being's body." We therefore take this opportunity to expressly hold that mutilation, whether it occurs before or after a victim's death, is an aggravating circumstance under NRS 200.033(8).

Postmortem mutilation occurred here when Byford set the body on fire. Therefore, the evidence in this case supports a finding of both torture and mutilation.

Review of the Death Sentence under NRS 177.055

Byford contends that his death sentence is excessive, arguing as follows. Smith's testimony was the State's primary evidence of the murder, and that testimony showed that Williams was more culpable in murdering Wilkins. The penalty hearing evidence also showed that Williams had caused a great deal of trouble while in prison between the first and second trials. Byford asserts that he has been "an exemplary prisoner" during his years of imprisonment and was only twenty at the time of the murder. Yet he was sentenced to death while Williams received a sentence less than death.

The record indeed shows that Williams took the initiative in murdering Wilkins and has caused worse disciplinary problems as an inmate. But Byford overlooks the fact that his criminal record prior to the murder was worse than Williams's. Because Byford was on probation at the time of the murder, the jury found an additional aggravating circumstance in his case, for a total of two, versus one for Williams. And the jury found only one mitigating circumstance in Byford's case, versus six for Williams. One was Williams's youth: he was younger than Byford, only seventeen, at the time of the murder. Finally, the evidence showed that Byford fired two fatal shots into the victim's head when she was completely helpless, threatened to kill Smith if he told, and took the initiative in concealing the crime. Thus, Byford's culpability in the murder was comparable to Williams's.

We conclude that Byford's death sentence is not excessive and that there is no evidence it was imposed under the influence of passion, prejudice, or any arbitrary factor. We affirm Byford's conviction and sentence of death.

Questions

1. How does the court define the terms *willful, deliberate,* and *premeditated?*

2. Sort and arrange the facts of the case according to the definitions of the three terms in (1).

3. Nevada's criminal code defines first-degree murder as killing "perpetrated by means of poison, lying in wait or torture, or by any other kind of willful, deliberate and premeditated killing." In your opinion, did Robert Byford commit first-degree murder?

4. Assuming Byford is guilty of first-degree murder, should he be sentenced to death? Consider the list of aggravating and mitigating circumstances in the "Death Penalty" section (page 284). Nevada has a similar list. Which items on the list might apply to him? Explain your answer, based on the facts in the case.

EXPLORING FURTHER

First-Degree Murder

1. Did He Premeditate and Deliberately Kill His Wife?

State v. Thompson 65 P. 3d 420 (Ariz. 2003)

FACTS On May 17, 1999, Thompson shot and killed his wife, Roberta Palma. Several days before the shooting, Palma had filed for divorce, and Thompson had discovered that she was seeing someone else. Just a week before the shooting, Thompson moved out of the couple's home. As he did so, Thompson threatened Palma that, "[i]f you divorce me, I will kill you."

Thompson returned to the couple's neighborhood the morning of May 17. He was seen walking on the sidewalk near the home and his car was spotted in a nearby alley. Two witnesses reported that a man dragged a woman by the hair from the front porch into the home. That same morning, police received and recorded a 911 call from the house. The tape recorded a woman's screams and four gunshots. The four gunshots span nearly 27 seconds. Nine seconds elapsed between the first shot and the third, and there was an 18-second delay between the third shot and the fourth.

Police arrived shortly after the call and found Palma dead from gunshot wounds. A jury found Thompson guilty of first-degree murder, and the judge sentenced him to life in prison without the possibility of parole. Thompson appealed.

Did Thompson premeditate and deliberately kill Palma?

DECISION Yes, said the Arizona Supreme Court. According to the court:

the State presented overwhelming evidence that Thompson actually reflected on his decision to kill his wife, including evidence of threats to kill her a week before the murder, the time that elapsed between each gunshot, and the victim's screams as recorded on the 9-1-1 tape between each gunshot.

2. Did He Premeditate and Deliberately Kill Her?

State v. Snowden 313 P.2d 706 (Idaho 1957)

FACTS Ray Snowden had been playing pool and drinking in a Boise poolroom early in the evening. With a companion, one Carrier, he visited a club near Boise, then went to nearby Garden City. There the two men visited a number of bars, and defendant had several drinks. Their last stop was the HiHo Club. Witnesses related that while defendant was in the HiHo Club he met and talked to Cora Lucyle Dean. The defendant himself said he hadn't been acquainted with Mrs. Dean prior to that time, but he had "seen her in a couple of the joints up town." He danced with Mrs. Dean while at the HiHo Club. Upon departing from the tavern, the two left together.

In statements to police officers, that were admitted in evidence, defendant Snowden said after they left the club Mrs. Dean wanted him to find a cab and take her back to Boise, and he refused because he didn't feel he should pay her fare. After some words, he related: "She got mad at me so I got pretty hot and I don't know whether I back handed her there or not. And, we got calmed down and decided to walk across to the gas station and call a cab."

They crossed the street, and began arguing again. Defendant said: "She swung and at the same time she kneed me again. I blew my top." Defendant said he pushed the woman over beside a pickup truck which was standing near a business building. There he pulled his knife—a pocket knife with a two-inch blade—and cut her throat.

The body, which was found the next morning, was viciously and sadistically cut and mutilated. An autopsy surgeon testified the voice box had been cut, and that this would have prevented the victim from making any intelligible outcry. There were other wounds inflicted while she was still alive—one in her neck, one in her abdomen, two in the face, and two on the back of the neck. The second neck wound severed the spinal cord and caused death.

There were other wounds all over her body, and her clothing had been cut away. The nipple of the right breast was missing. There was no evidence of a sexual attack on the victim; however, some of the lacerations were around the breasts and vagina of the deceased. A blood test showed Mrs. Dean was intoxicated at the time of her death.

Defendant took the dead woman's wallet. He hailed a passing motorist and rode back to Boise with him. There he went to a bowling alley and changed clothes. He dropped his knife into a sewer, and threw the wallet away. Then he went to his hotel and cleaned up again. He put the clothes he had worn that evening into a trash barrel.

Did Snowden premeditate and deliberately kill Cora Dean?

DECISION Yes, said the Idaho Supreme Court:

> The principal argument of the defendant pertaining to . . . [premeditation] is that the defendant did not have sufficient time to develop a desire to take the life of the deceased, but rather this action was instantaneous and a normal reaction to the physical injury which she had dealt him. . . .

In the present case, the trial court had no other alternative than to find the defendant guilty of willful, deliberate, and premeditated killing with malice aforethought in view of the defendant's acts in deliberately opening up a pocket knife, next cutting the victim's throat, and then hacking and cutting until he had killed Cora Lucyle Dean and expended himself. The full purpose and design of defendant's conduct was to take the life of the deceased. . . .

The trial court could have imposed life imprisonment, or, as in the instant case, sentenced the defendant to death. . . . To choose between the punishments of life imprisonment and death there must be some distinction between one homicide and another. This case exemplifies an abandoned and malignant heart and sadistic mind, bent upon taking human life.

 Go to the Criminal Law 9e website to find the full text of the Exploring Further excerpts: www.thomsonedu .com/criminaljustice/samaha. (Excerpts on first-degree murder.)

Not everyone agrees that premeditated, deliberate killings, even if they're truly planned and committed in cold blood, are the worst kind of murders. According to the 19th-century English judge and criminal law reformer James F. Stephen (1883):

> As much cruelty, as much indifference to the life of others, a disposition at least as dangerous to society, probably even more dangerous, is shown by sudden as by premeditated murders. The following cases appear to me to set this in a clear light. A man, passing along the road, sees a boy sitting on a bridge over a deep river and, out of mere wanton barbarity, pushes him into it and so drowns him. A man makes advances to a girl who repels him. He deliberately but instantly cuts her throat. A man civilly asked to pay a just debt pretends to get the money, loads a rifle and blows out his creditor's brains. In none of these cases is there premeditation unless the word is used in a sense as unnatural as "afore-thought" in "malice aforethought," but each represents even more diabolical cruelty and ferocity than that which is involved in murders premeditated in the natural sense of the word. (94)

First-Degree Murder Actus Reus As you've already learned, how a murderer kills doesn't matter most of the time. As Blackstone taught us in 1769 (in the quote earlier), "The killing may be by poisoning, striking, starving, drowning, and a thousand other forms by which human nature can be overcome." But **first-degree murder** *actus reus* can be critical when it comes to deciding whether to sentence a person convicted of first-degree murder to death—or to prison for life without parole in states without the death penalty—or a lesser penalty. Killing by means of "heinous, atrocious, or cruel" acts, meaning especially brutal murders or torture murders intended to cause lingering death, appears on the list of aggravating factors that qualifies a murderer for the death penalty.

The Florida Supreme Court applied the state's "heinous, atrocious, or cruel" aggravating circumstance provision to approve the death penalty for Richard Henyard, who was convicted of first-degree murder in a grisly killing during a carjacking and rape in *Henyard v. State* (1996).

Henyard v. State

689 So.2d 239 (Fla. 1996)

HISTORY

Richard Henyard, Defendant, was convicted in the Circuit Court, Lake County, of sexual battery, kidnapping, and murder. Defendant appealed. The Supreme Court affirmed.

PER CURIAM

[Per curiam *means "by the court." It means it's an opinion for the whole court, not an opinion written by an individual judge. It's a brief, usually unanimous, decision rendered without elaborate discussion.*]

FACTS

Around 10 P.M. on January 30, Lynette Tschida went to the Winn Dixie store in Eustis. She saw Richard Henyard and a younger man sitting on a bench near the entrance of the store. When she left, Henyard and his companion got up from the bench; one of them walked ahead of her and the other behind her. As she approached her car, the one ahead of her went to the end of the bumper, turned around, and stood. Ms. Tschida quickly got into the car and locked the doors. As she drove away, she saw Henyard and the younger man walking back towards the store.

At the same time, the eventual survivor and victims in this case, Ms. Lewis and her daughters, Jasmine, age 3, and Jamilya, age 7, drove to the Winn Dixie store. Ms. Lewis noticed a few people sitting on a bench near the doors as she and her daughters entered the store. When Ms. Lewis left the store, she went to her car and put her daughters in the front passenger seat. As she walked behind the car to the driver's side, Ms. Lewis noticed Alfonza Smalls coming towards her.

As Smalls approached, he pulled up his shirt and revealed a gun in his waistband. Smalls ordered Ms. Lewis and her daughters into the back seat of the car, and then called to Henyard. Henyard drove the Lewis car out of town as Smalls gave him directions.

The Lewis girls were crying and upset, and Smalls repeatedly demanded that Ms. Lewis "shut the girls up." As they continued to drive out of town, Ms. Lewis beseeched Jesus for help, to which Henyard replied, "This ain't Jesus, this is Satan." Later, Henyard stopped the car at a deserted location and ordered Ms. Lewis out of the car. Henyard raped Ms. Lewis on the trunk of the car while her daughters remained in the back seat. Ms. Lewis attempted to reach for the gun that was lying nearby on the trunk.

Smalls grabbed the gun from her and shouted, "You're not going to get the gun, bitch." Smalls also raped Ms. Lewis on the trunk of the car. Henyard then ordered her to sit on the ground near the edge of the road. When she hesitated, Henyard pushed her to the ground and shot her in the leg.

Henyard shot her at close range three more times, wounding her in the neck, mouth, and the middle of the forehead between her eyes. Henyard and Smalls rolled Ms. Lewis's unconscious body off to the side of the road, and got back into the car. The last thing Ms. Lewis remembers before losing consciousness is a gun aimed at her face. Miraculously, Ms. Lewis survived and, upon regaining consciousness a few hours later, made her way to a nearby house for help. The occupants called the police and Ms. Lewis, who was covered in blood, collapsed on the front porch and waited for the officers to arrive.

As Henyard and Smalls drove the Lewis girls away from the scene where their mother had been shot and abandoned, Jasmine and Jamilya continued to cry and plead: "I want my Mommy," "Mommy," "Mommy." Shortly thereafter, Henyard stopped the car on the side of the road, got out, and lifted Jasmine out of the back seat while Jamilya got out on her own. The Lewis girls were then taken into a grassy area along the roadside where they were each killed by a single bullet fired into the head. Henyard and Smalls threw the bodies of Jasmine and Jamilya Lewis over a nearby fence into some underbrush.

Later that evening, Bryant Smith, a friend of Smalls, was at his home when Smalls, Henyard, and another individual appeared in a blue car. Henyard bragged about the rape, showed the gun to Smith, and said he had to "burn the bitch" because she tried to go for his gun.

Henyard was found guilty by the jury of three counts of armed kidnapping in violation of section 787.01, Florida Statutes (1995), one count of sexual battery with the use of a firearm in violation of section 794.011(3), Florida Statutes (1995), one count of attempted first-degree murder in violation of sections 782.04(1)(a)(1) and 777.04(1), Florida Statutes (1995), one count of robbery with a firearm in violation of section 812.13(2)(a), Florida Statutes (1995), and two counts of first-degree murder in violation of section 782.04(1)(a), Florida Statutes (1995).

After a penalty phase hearing, the jury recommended the death sentence for each murder by a vote of 12 to 0. The trial court followed this recommendation and sentenced Henyard to death. The court found in aggravation:

(1) the defendant had been convicted of a prior violent felony;

(2) the murder was committed in the course of a felony;

(3) the murder was committed for pecuniary gain; the murder was especially heinous, atrocious or cruel, see section 921.141(5)(h).

The court found Henyard's age of eighteen at the time of the crime as a statutory mitigating circumstance, and accorded it "some weight." The trial court also found that the defendant was acting under an extreme emotional disturbance and his capacity to conform his conduct to the requirements of law was impaired, and accorded these mental mitigators "very little weight."

As for nonstatutory mitigating circumstances, the trial court found the following circumstances but accorded them "little weight":

(1) the defendant functions at the emotional level of a thirteen-year-old and is of low intelligence;

(2) the defendant had an impoverished upbringing;

(3) the defendant was born into a dysfunctional family;

(4) the defendant can adjust to prison life; and (5) the defendant could have received eight consecutive life sentences with a minimum mandatory fifty years.

Finally, the trial court accorded "some weight" to the nonstatutory mitigating circumstance that Henyard's codefendant, Alfonza Smalls, could not receive the death penalty as a matter of law. The court concluded that the mitigating circumstances did not offset the aggravating circumstances.

OPINION

. . . Henyard contends that the trial court erred in allowing Ms. Lewis to testify during the penalty phase that Henyard, upon hearing Ms. Lewis' prayers to Jesus, stated, "You might as well stop calling Jesus, this ain't Jesus this is Satan." Henyard claims his statement is not relevant to prove the existence of any aggravating circumstance. We disagree.

Under Florida law, the heinous, atrocious, or cruel aggravating circumstance may be proven in part by evidence of the infliction of "mental anguish" which the victim suffered prior to the fatal shot. In this case, Ms. Lewis testified that she was sitting in the back seat between her daughters, that her girls were quiet at the time Henyard made the statement at issue, and that Henyard spoke loudly enough for all to hear. Ms. Lewis explained that neither child had trouble hearing and she believed her daughters heard Henyard's statement.

Thus, Henyard's statement, which the trial court characterized as the "harbinger" of the agonizing events to come, was relevant to show the mental anguish inflicted upon the Lewis girls before they were killed, and as evidence of the heinous, atrocious and cruel aggravating circumstance. Consequently, we find that the trial court properly admitted the statement into evidence during the penalty phase of Henyard's trial. . . .

Henyard contends that the trial court erred in finding the heinous, atrocious, or cruel aggravating circumstance in this case because each child was killed with a single gunshot,

and "if the victims were adults, heinous, atrocious, [or] cruel would not be present on this record." We disagree.

We have previously upheld the application of the heinous, atrocious, or cruel aggravating factor based, in part, upon the intentional infliction of substantial mental anguish upon the victim. Moreover, "fear and emotional strain may be considered as contributing to the heinous nature of the murder, even where the victim's death was almost instantaneous."

In this case, the trial court found the heinous, atrocious or cruel aggravating factor to be present based upon the entire sequence of events, including the fear and emotional trauma the children suffered during the episode culminating in their deaths and, contrary to Henyard's assertion, not merely because they were young children. Thus, we find the trial court properly found that the heinous, atrocious, or cruel aggravating factor was proved beyond a reasonable doubt in this case.

The sentencing order reads in pertinent part: After shooting Ms. Lewis, Henyard and Smalls rolled Ms. Lewis' unconscious body off to the side of the road. Henyard got back into Ms. Lewis' car and drove a short distance down the deserted road, whereupon Henyard stopped the car.

Jasmine and Jamilya, who had been in continual close approximation and earshot of the rapes and shooting of their mother, were continuing to plead for their mother; "I want my Mommy," "Mommy," "Mommy." After stopping the car, Henyard got out of Ms. Lewis' vehicle and proceeded to lift Jasmine out of the back seat of the car, Jamilya got out without help. Then both of the pleading and sobbing sisters, were taken a short distance from the car, where they were then executed, each with a single bullet to the head.

. . . Accordingly, we affirm Henyard's convictions and the imposition of the sentences of death in this case.

Questions

1. How does the court define "heinous, atrocious, and cruel"?

2. List the facts in the case that are relevant to deciding whether this was a "heinous, atrocious, and cruel" murder.

3. Summarize the arguments in favor of and against classifying this as a "heinous, cruel, and atrocious" murder.

EXPLORING FURTHER

First-Degree Murder Actus Reus

1. Was Beating Him to Death with a Baseball Bat Atrocious First-Degree Murder?

Commonwealth v. Golston, 249, 366 N.E.2d 744 (Mass. 1977)

FACTS About 2 P.M. on Sunday, August 24, 1975, a white man about 34 years old came out of a store and walked toward his car. Siegfried Golston, a 19-year-old African American man, tiptoed up behind the victim and hit him on the head with a baseball bat. A witness testified to the sound made by Golston's blow to the victim's head: "Just like you hit a wet, you know, like a bat hit a wet baseball; that's how it sounded." Golston then went into a building, changed his clothes, and crossed the street to the store, where he worked. When asked why he had hit the man, Golston replied, "For kicks." The victim later died. Was this "atrocious murder," a form of first-degree murder that qualified Golston for the death penalty?

DECISION According to the court, it was:

> There was evidence of great and unusual violence in the blow, which caused a four-inch cut on the side of the skull. . . . There was also evidence that after he was struck the victim fell to the street, and that five minutes later he tried to get up, staggered to his feet and fell again to the ground. He was breathing very hard and a neighbor wiped vomit from his nose and mouth. Later, according to the testimony, the defendant said he did it, "For kicks." There is no requirement that the defendant know that his act was extremely atrocious or cruel, and no requirement of deliberate premeditation. A murder may be committed with extreme atrocity or cruelty even though death results from a single blow. Indifference to the victim's pain, as well as actual knowledge of it and taking pleasure in it, is cruelty; and extreme cruelty is only a higher degree of cruelty.

2. Was Killing Him by Multiple Stabbings Heinous First-Degree Murder?

Duest v. State, 462 So.2d 446 (Fla. 1985)

FACTS On February 15, 1982, Lloyd Duest, carrying a knife in the waistband of his pants, boasted that he was going to a gay bar to "roll a fag." Duest was later seen at a predominantly gay bar with John Pope. Pope and Duest left the bar and drove off in Pope's gold Camaro. Several hours later, Pope's roommate returned home and found the house unlocked, the lights on, the stereo on loud, and blood on the bed. The sheriff was contacted. Upon arrival, the deputy sheriff found Pope on the bathroom floor in a pool of blood with multiple stab wounds. Duest was found and arrested on April 18, 1982. He was tried and found guilty of first-degree murder. In accordance with the jury's advisory recommendation, the trial judge imposed the death sentence. Duest argued that this was not a particularly heinous or atrocious killing. Was it?

DECISION Yes, the court wrote:

> We disagree with the defendant. The evidence presented at trial shows that the victim received eleven stab wounds, some of which were inflicted in the bedroom and some inflicted in the bathroom. The medical examiner's testimony revealed that the victim lived some few minutes before dying.

 Go to the Criminal Law 9e website to find the full text of the Exploring Further excerpts: www.thomsonedu .com/criminaljustice/samaha. (Excerpts on first-degree murder *actus reus*.)

Second-Degree Murder

As you learned earlier in the chapter, the reason for creating first- and second-degree murders, beginning with Pennsylvania in 1794, was to separate murders that deserved the death penalty from those that didn't. The point was to *limit* capital punishment without *eliminating* it. But dividing murders into capital and noncapital murders wasn't, and still isn't, the only way to divide murders between first-, second-, and in a few states, third-degree murder.

Another way to divide murder is between intentional and unintentional murders. Unintentional murders, which are **second-degree murders,** include the "implied malice" crimes created by the common-law judges but which still exist in common-law states and by statute: felony murders, intent-to-inflict-serious-bodily-injury murders, and depraved heart murders. Intent-to-inflict-serious-bodily-injury murders are indistinguishable from depraved heart murders; in fact, they're treated as a subset of depraved heart murders, so we won't discuss them. We'll concentrate on depraved heart and felony murders.

Depraved Heart Murders   Depraved heart murders are unintentional but extremely reckless murders. Recall that the reckless mental attitude consists of consciously creating a substantial risk of criminal harm, in this case death. (There are also reckless manslaughters, which are difficult to distinguish from depraved heart murders. You'll encounter some in the "Manslaughter" section.) For now, let's put the difference crudely: reckless manslaughter is killing very recklessly, and reckless murder is killing very, very, very recklessly.

In addition to unintentional second-degree felony murders (there are first-degree felony murders, too), which we'll discuss later, there are other second-degree murders. Sometimes, second-degree murder is treated as a default murder category, meaning it includes all murders that aren't first-degree murders. Some state statutes make this default definition explicit. Michigan's statute (Michigan Criminal Code 2006, § 750.317) is a good example. After defining first-degree murder, the Michigan second-degree murder section provides:

> All other kinds of murder shall be murder of the second degree, and shall be punished by imprisonment in the state prison for life, or any term of years, in the discretion of the court trying the same.

Other states have specific depraved heart second-degree murder statutes. California's provision reads, "Malice is implied, when . . . the circumstances attending the killing show an abandoned and malignant heart" (quoted in *People v. Protopappas* 1988, 922). In *Protopappas*, the California Court of Appeals affirmed Dr. Tony Protopappas's conviction for three depraved heart second-degree murders.

CASE — Did He Kill Them with a "Depraved Heart"?

People v. Protopappas
201 Cal.App.3d 152 (Cal.App. 1988)

Court of Appeal, Fourth District, Division 3, California

HISTORY

Tony Protopappas, a licensed dentist and oral surgeon, was convicted in the Superior Court, Orange County, of the second-degree murder of three of his patients and he appealed. The Court of Appeal affirmed.

WALLIN, J.

FACTS

Protopappas opened his Costa Mesa dental clinic in 1974. By September of 1982, he employed a staff of five dentists, many dental assistants, and two office managers. He was the only dentist at the clinic licensed to administer general anesthesia and was solely responsible for injecting the initial doses of drugs used for general anesthesia of patients. He personally standardized these initial doses or "setups," which were prepared daily by his assistants. The staff dentists were also given standardized instructions on how to maintain patients under anesthesia.

Kim Andreassen

At a frail 85 pounds, 24-year-old Kim Andreassen went to Protopappas's clinic with her mother on September 21, 1982. Although she was not experiencing any pain or problems with her teeth, she decided to have an initial examination after Protopappas finished her mother's evaluation. Andreassen told Protopappas she suffered from lupus (a multisystem disease inhibiting normal growth), total kidney failure requiring thrice weekly dialysis, high blood pressure, anemia, a heart murmur, and chronic seizure disorder. Andreassen also told Protopappas she was taking anticoagulants, high blood pressure medication, and phenobarbital. After the examination, Protopappas told her she needed a root canal, three fillings, and a crown. He recommended local anesthesia to perform the work. Andreassen protested, refusing to have any work done unless she was asleep. Protopappas warned her that, because of her poor health, there was a very high risk she could die under general anesthesia.

Andreassen returned to the clinic with her mother on September 28. The office manager, who had contacted Andreassen's general physician, informed Protopappas she was not to be placed under general anesthesia even for a short time. Andreassen was given preoperative medications to be taken 30 minutes before her next appointment. Protopappas was later heard telling the office manager of his reluctance to sedate Andreassen intravenously, saying, "I don't want to do that because that's a death for sure."

Having failed to take her premedication as directed, Andreassen arrived at the clinic for treatment between 12 noon and 1 P.M. on September 30. She then took the medication. Around 2 P.M., Protopappas began an intravenous

(I.V.) setup. At Andreassen's suggestion, he started it in her foot because of her collapsed veins. He administered his standard doses of drugs at 10 to 20 second intervals. He also gave her a local anesthetic. By the time he finished administering the drugs, Andreassen was asleep.

Protopappas began the scheduled treatment. Within 5 to 20 minutes, Andreassen's lips turned purple, her face pale blue, and her pulse became irregular. Protopappas administered oxygen and her lip color returned to normal. At one point, upon getting restless and opening her eyes, she was given brevital. When an assistant noticed Andreassen was taking very shallow breaths followed by big deep breaths, he directed Protopappas's attention to the irregular breathing. Protopappas responded, "Maybe that's normal for her because she is so ill."

[An expert in the field of anesthesiology testified the breathing pattern exhibited by Andreassen is known as Cheynes-Stokes respiration. It is a symptom of severe toxicity and a terminal type of respiration.]

He completed the dental work. Andreassen was breathing normally when he left the room at 4:30 P.M.

Ten to fifteen minutes later her breathing became shallow and irregular, her pulse became weak, and her face turned blue. The attending assistant gave her oxygen, and when Andreassen did not respond, she called another dentist, Dr. Brown, to help. He observed that Andreassen had gone into respiratory collapse and immediately placed an oxygen mask on her face. Two to three minutes later, Protopappas arrived and gave her oxygen. When she failed to respond, he left the room to get additional medication. Either Protopappas or his assistant brought in narcan, a medication to reverse the effects of the drugs she had received. Protopappas administered the narcan. Fire department paramedics were called shortly thereafter.

When the paramedics arrived, Andreassen was not breathing, her pupils did not respond to light, she had no pulse, and she was blue. Protopappas was holding a disposable oxygen mask over her face. He reported the patient had been in this condition for 20 minutes, and he did not have any positive pressure oxygen equipment. A disposable oxygen mask does not supply oxygen to a patient who is not breathing. By contrast, positive pressure oxygen equipment will deliver oxygen to a patient under pressure and will breathe for the patient who is not breathing. Despite the efforts of the paramedics, Andreassen was clinically dead when she arrived at the hospital.

The coroner concluded the general anesthesia resulted in critical cardiac arrest with the disseminated lupus being a significant contributing factor. Two anesthesiologists and two oral surgeons testifying as expert witnesses opined that she died of a massive drug overdose.

One oral surgeon stated the amount of drugs given were massive amounts for anyone, "let alone a sickly 88 pound girl." He further explained the combination of drugs administered did not make any sense. "It is not a regimen to sedate a patient. It is illogical. It is—I don't know anybody who does this kind of thing for sedation or anesthesia. It is a use of multiple depressant agents. You never know which agent is doing what. You have no way of knowing where the patient is with regard to response to any of these medications. It is crazy. It is really an illogical approach to treating people."

Dr. Frank McCarthy, chair of the anesthesiology department at the University of Southern California's dental school, testified that Andreassen's irregular breathing was symptomatic of severe toxicity and should have been interpreted as urgent and life threatening. He concluded Protopappas did not recognize or respond to Andreassen's Cheynes-Stokes breathing. Moreover, his delay in calling the paramedics endangered her life and, without effective cardio-pulmonary resuscitation (CPR) after her heart stopped, she suffered brain death.

Protopappas testified in his own defense. He felt the deep cavity in Andreassen's tooth needed a root canal or the lupus would cause infection to spread and would become life threatening. He did not put her under general anesthesia but used conscious sedation instead. In his opinion Andreassen's irregular breathing did not present an emergency and, having felt a pulse, he did not feel CPR was necessary. When she failed to respond to the administration of oxygen and narcan, however, he put a local anesthetic under her tongue with a drug to stimulate the heart.

Patricia Craven

[Thirteen-year-old Patricia Craven died shortly after Kim Andreassen under similar circumstances. Details are omitted here.]

Cathryn Jones

While Craven remained in a coma, 31-year-old Cathryn Jones arrived at the Protopappas clinic on February 11, 1983. She had had a pituitary tumor removed nine months earlier and was suffering from periodontitis, bone loss, and abscess formation around a great number of her teeth. On Protopappas's advice, she decided to have her teeth removed.

[Jones also died from the same causes under similar circumstances as Kim Andreassen and Patricia Craven. Details are omitted here.]

OPINION

. . . The Legislature has provided little guidance in defining implied malice. The only statutory description of the requisite mental state appears in Penal Code section 188:

Malice is implied, when . . . the circumstances attending the killing show an abandoned and malignant heart.

. . . The entire thrust of the prosecution's case was that Protopappas knew his procedures threatened his patients' lives. The prosecutor carefully and repeatedly emphasized Protopappas's subjective awareness in closing argument:

The first element of implied malice on these facts is that the killing results from somebody intentionally doing acts which are dangerous. We clearly have that in every instance here. Utterly no dispute about it. Those acts are deliberately done by a person who knows that his conduct endangers the life of another. And the second thing, acts with what the law calls conscious disregard for life. . . .

And you have implied malice under these facts because you have Tony Protopappas intentionally injecting potentially lethal drugs into people to do dental work. He knows that this conduct will endanger the life of his patient if he doesn't do it with great care. He has actual personal knowledge of the specific risk faced by each victim in this case, over and above his general knowledge that he possessed of the dangerousness of what he was doing. He knew in each particular case that there were specific, special risks posed to each victim by what he was doing, and he acted with conscious disregard of the lives of Kim Andreassen and Patricia Craven and Cathryn Jones. . . .

Protopappas . . . contends there is insufficient evidence of implied malice to sustain the convictions for second degree murder and seeks modification to involuntary manslaughter. He concedes he may have been inept, but emphasizes there is little precedent for implying malice from his failure to provide proper medical treatment. His case does appear to be one of second impression. The issue presented, whether a licensed provider of health services designed, presumably, to improve the patient's health, can be held for murder when life is unintentionally lost as a result of his efforts, has rather startling implications.

The most troubling aspect of this case is that Protopappas has been convicted of murder for acts committed as a practicing, licensed dentist under circumstances where there can be no doubt he did not truly intend to kill anyone. Dying patients would be bad for business; and nothing shines through this record quite so brightly as Protopappas's enthusiasm for making money—lots of it.

Certainly every reasonable dentist or physician examining this opinion would agree Protopappas was grossly negligent in each of these three homicides, but where is the evidence of the malice necessary to justify a murder conviction? For the benefit of the concerned dental or medical professional, the answer to that question is simple: This case is highly unusual and, hopefully, unlikely to recur; for it is the health care equivalent of shooting into a crowd or setting a lethal mantrap in a dark alley. . . .

Malice may be implied when a person, knowing that his conduct endangers the life of another, nonetheless acts deliberately with conscious disregard for life. . . . Implied malice contemplates a subjective awareness of a higher degree of risk than does gross negligence, and involves an element of wantonness which is absent in gross negligence. . . . A finding of implied malice depends upon a determination that the defendant actually appreciated the risk involved, i.e., a subjective standard. It is an element of viciousness—an extreme indifference to the value of human life. The question is whether there was substantial evidence Protopappas's treatment of his patients was aggravated, culpable, gross, or reckless neglect incompatible with a proper regard for human life (involuntary manslaughter) or involved such a high degree of probability that it would result in death that it constituted a wanton disregard for human life making it second degree murder.

Was there substantial evidence Protopappas knew his conduct endangered Kim Andreassen's life and that he nonetheless acted deliberately in conscious disregard of her life? Protopappas agrees there was some evidence he was aware of the risk of death, but argues it was not substantial. He emphasizes that a review of the entire record discloses he was not acting with wanton disregard for his patient's well being. He would not have consciously and deliberately jeopardized a dental practice he had successfully developed over many years.

Moreover, he had used his standardized methods on many patients and none of them had died before Andreassen. Even Andreassen's treatment proceeded normally until after the work was completed. Finally, he concludes the evidence of an overdose is insufficient because anesthesiologists disagree on the quantity of drugs constituting an overdose for a particular patient.

This argument is unavailing as it relies on evidence and inferences not accepted by the jury. The evidence, viewed in the light most favorable to the prosecution, supports the jury's finding Protopappas was subjectively aware of the risk and acted with wanton disregard for Andreassen's life. He knew there was a very high probability Andreassen would die. He told Andreassen, her mother, and many of his staff she probably would not survive the treatment under general anesthesia because of her extremely poor health. He not only knew how sick she was but also that her treating physician had only authorized a local anesthetic and a small amount of muscle relaxant. Nevertheless, he administered a quantity of drugs that would be massive for anyone, "let alone a sickly 88 pound girl."

If the initial dosage of anesthetic were not substantial evidence of Protopappas's conscious disregard for Andreassen's life, then the jury could add to it his indifference to the difficulty she thereafter experienced. He observed her irregular breathing and did nothing. When she finally turned blue, had only a weak pulse, and exhibited very shallow and irregular breathing, he put a disposable oxygen mask over her mouth. Although he at least recognized the emergency at that point, he failed to call the paramedics immediately or begin CPR. The jury could find he exhibited all the elements of implied malice including wantonness, an extreme indifference to Andreassen's life, and subjective awareness of the very high probability of her death. . . .

. . . These are the acts of "a person who knows that his conduct endangers the life of another and who acts with conscious disregard for life." Moreover, to understand how these facts support a finding of second degree murder . . . , it is essential to recall the broad meaning of the somewhat elusive term "malice aforethought." As one leading text explains,

> In ordinary conversation the word "malice" conveys some notion of hatred, grudge, ill-will, or spite, but no such limitation is incorporated in the legal concept of "malice aforethought." Many murders are committed to satisfy a feeling of hatred or grudge, it is true, but this crime may be perpetrated without the slightest trace of personal ill-will." (Perkins & Boyce, Criminal Law (3d ed. 1982) p. 58, fns. omitted.)

This is clearly the law of California. Professors Perkins and Boyce supply a number of examples to illustrate the point: the mother who kills an illegitimate infant out of shame even though she may be filled with maternal love; a mercy killing carried out at the victim's own request; shooting a person with the intent to wound, but not to kill, without justification or provocation; unlawfully attempting to destroy property by explosion where the risk to life is great and which results in an unintended death, despite precautions to prevent injuries to others; carrying a bomb into a place where it poses a danger to life and death results, notwithstanding the perpetrator's desire to avoid detonation or injury; and shooting into inhabited dwellings, automobiles, or trains.

Protopappas's conduct is not meaningfully distinguishable from any of the acts described above. No reasonable person, much less a dentist trained in the use of anesthesia, could have failed to appreciate the grave risk of death posed by the procedures he utilized. It was not a question of whether a fatality would occur, only a question of when; and ultimately there were three of them.

The judgment is affirmed.

Questions

1. List all the facts relevant to Dr. Tony Protopappas's mental attitude.

2. According to the court, what's the mental element required for depraved heart murder?

3. Recall the mental attitudes discussed in Chapter 4: purposely, knowingly, recklessly, and negligently. Which one does the California depraved heart statute, as defined by the court, most closely resemble? Explain your answer.

4. In your opinion, is Dr. Protopappas guilty of murder? If so, what degree—first or second degree? Explain your answer.

5. If he's not guilty, should he be guilty of some lesser degree of criminal homicide? Give a preliminary answer now; then, when we get to manslaughter, you can give a more informed answer.

Second-Degree Murder

Did He Intend to Kill?

People v. Thomas, 272 N.W.2d 157 (Mich.App. 1978)

HOLBROOK, JR. J.

FACTS The victim, a 19-year-old male "catatonic schizophrenic," was at the time of his death a resident of Oak Haven, a religious practical training school. When it appeared he was not properly responding to ordinary treatment, defendant, the work coordinator at Oak Haven, obtained permission from the victim's parents to discipline him if such seemed necessary. Thereafter defendant, together with another supervisor at Oak Haven, took decedent to the edge of the campus, whereupon decedent's pants were taken down, following which he was spanked with a rubber hose. Such disciplinary session lasted approximately 15 to 30 minutes. During a portion thereof decedent's hands were tied behind his back for failure to cooperate.

Following the disciplinary session, defendant testified that the young man improved for awhile but then commenced to backslide. Defendant again received permission from decedent's parents to subject him to further discipline.

On September 30, 1976, defendant again took decedent to the approximate same location, removed his pants, bound his hands behind him with a rope looped over a tree limb and proceeded to beat him with a doubled-over rubber hose. This beating lasted approximately 45 minutes to an hour. While the evidence conflicted, it appears that the victim was struck between 30 to 100 times. The beating resulted in severe bruises ranging from the victim's waist to his feet. Decedent's roommate testified that decedent had open bleeding sores on his thighs. . . .

Could Thomas be guilty of second-degree murder?

DECISION Yes, said the Michigan Court of Appeals:

> Malice or intent to kill may be inferred from the acts of the defendant. . . . The intent to kill may be implied where the actor actually intends to inflict great bodily harm or the natural tendency of his behavior is to cause death or great bodily harm. In the instant case defendant's savage and brutal beating of the decedent is amply sufficient to establish malice. He clearly intended to beat the victim and the natural tendency of defendant's behavior was to cause great bodily harm.

 Go to the Criminal Law 9e website to find the full text of the Exploring Further excerpt: www.thomsonedu .com/criminaljustice/samaha. (Excerpt on second-degree murder.)

Felony Murder   Unintentional deaths that occur during the commission of some felonies are called **felony murder** in most states. What felonies? States vary widely, but the most common are criminal sexual conduct, kidnapping, robbery, arson, and burglary. What degree of murder is this? Here, too, states vary. In some states, it's first degree; in others, it's second degree. Maryland's felony murder statute (Maryland Criminal Code 2006, § 2-201) provides:

(a) A murder is in the first degree if it is:

> (4) committed in the perpetration of or an attempt to perpetrate:
>
>> (i) arson in the first degree;
>>
>> (ii) burning a barn, stable, tobacco house, warehouse, or other outbuilding that:
>>
>>> 1. is not parcel to a dwelling; and
>>>
>>> 2. contains cattle, goods, wares, merchandise, horses, grain, hay, or tobacco;
>>
>> (iii) burglary in the first, second, or third degree;
>>
>> (iv) carjacking or armed carjacking;
>>
>> (v) escape in the first degree from a State correctional facility or a local correctional facility;
>>
>> (vi) kidnapping . . . ;
>>
>> (vii) mayhem;
>>
>> (viii) rape;
>>
>> (ix) robbery . . . ;
>>
>> (x) sexual offense in the first or second degree;
>>
>> (xi) sodomy; . . .

(b) (1) A person who commits a murder in the first degree is guilty of a felony and on conviction shall be sentenced to:

> (i) death;
>
> (ii) imprisonment for life without the possibility of parole; or
>
> (iii) imprisonment for life.

Let's look briefly at felony murder *mens rea*, rationales for felony murder statutes, third-party exceptions to these rules, and the dangerous-to-life circumstance element of felony murder.

Felony murder mens rea: Felony murder doesn't require the intent either to kill or to inflict serious bodily harm. In fact, most felony murderers don't want to kill or injure their victims (not necessarily because they're nice people but because they don't want to qualify for the death penalty or some other severe penalty for murder).

How can these unintended deaths be murder? One answer is that the specific intent to commit the underlying felony substitutes for the intent to kill. Why? Take this example. If a robber fires a gun during the robbery and kills a convenience store clerk without the intent to kill, the intent to rob is blameworthy enough to satisfy the *mens rea* of felony murder.

Another answer, and probably the most common, is that felony murder is a strict liability crime, so it doesn't require a fault-based state of mind. This is an inaccurate and misleading answer. If you go back to our discussion of states of mind in Chapter 4, you'll find that most felony murders turn out to be at least negligent, or more likely

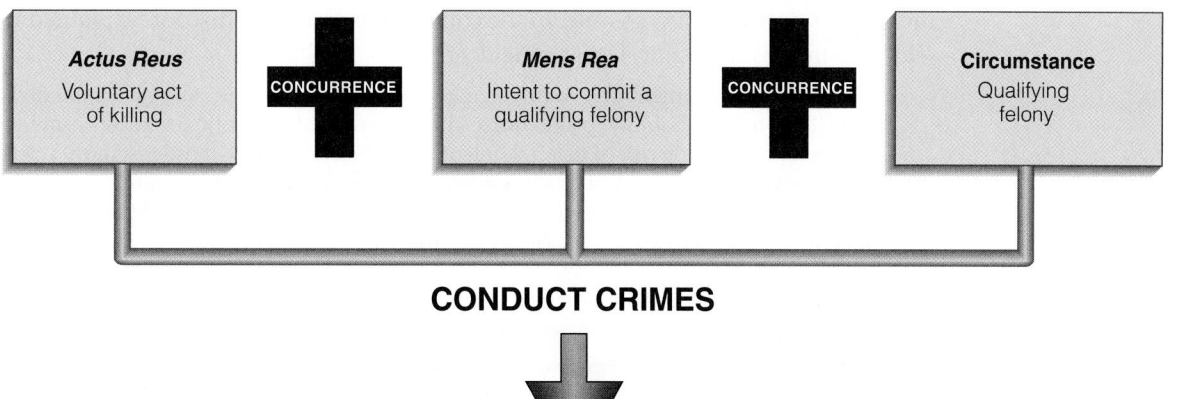

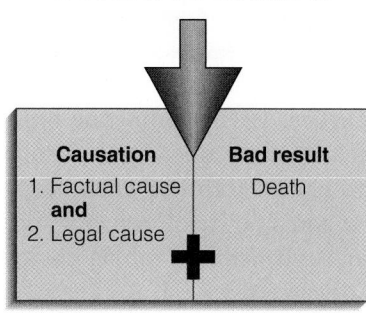

RESULT CRIMES

Elements of Felony Murder

reckless, with respect to causing death. Most of the actual felony murder cases bear this out.

Even without reading a lot of cases, just ask yourself how many robbers don't know they're creating a substantial risk of killing their victims, and of those few remaining who don't actually know they're creating the high risk, shouldn't they be aware of it? So the best way to put it is that most felony murderers specifically intend ("purposely," or "with the conscious object" in MPC language) to commit the underlying felony, knowing full well they're creating substantial and unjustifiable risks that someone will die while they're committing that felony (Simons 1997, 1121–22).

Rationales: Felony murder laws have three rationales:

1. *Deter offenders* The added threat of a murder conviction is supposed to prevent would-be felons from committing felonies that can lead to death.

2. *Reduce violence* The threat of a murder conviction is intended to curtail the use of violence during the commission of felonies by inducing felons to act more carefully during robberies and other felonies with risks of injury and death.

3. *Punish wrongdoers* People who intentionally commit felonies connected with high risks of death or injury deserve the most punishment available.

Empirical research hasn't demonstrated that the rule either deters dangerous felons or reduces the number of deaths during the commission of felonies. Four states—Ohio, Hawaii, Michigan, and Kentucky—have abolished felony murder.

Other states have restricted felony murder to deaths that were foreseeable during the commission of the underlying felony. In *State v. Noren* (1985), during a robbery, Monte Noren punched his victim three times in the head so hard that Noren's knuckles bled. The victim was extremely drunk, which Noren knew. The court decided that the victim's death was foreseeable. In the course of its opinion, the court explained why felony murder is limited to foreseeable deaths:

> The statutory requirement that death be a probable consequence of a felony is intended to limit felony-murder liability to situations where the defendant's conduct creates some measure of foreseeable risk of death. Under the predecessor felony-murder statute, a defendant committed murder when death resulted from the commission of any felony. This rule was modified because it imposed severe criminal sanctions without considering the moral culpability of the defendant. . . . [Therefore,] the acts causing death must be inherently dangerous to life.
>
> We apply this test to felony-murder because it requires a high degree of foreseeability, thereby implicitly requiring greater culpability than lesser grades of homicide. Our supreme court applied this standard under the predecessor felony-murder statute when it stated that the act constituting the felony must be in itself dangerous to life.

Third-party exception: What if someone besides the felon—say the victim, police officers, a co-felon, or a bystander—causes someone's death during a felony? Some states have a **third-party exception** to the felony murder rule. In *Campbell v. State* (1982), a cabdriver and a police officer shot and killed one of two men attempting to rob the driver. The court held the robber couldn't be found guilty of felony murder under the third-party exception.

Some states have created a **resisting-victim exception** to the third-party exception. In *State v. O'Dell* (1984), a felony assault victim shot and killed one of his attackers. The court ruled that the surviving attacker could be found guilty of felony murder under the resisting-victim exception.

Dangerous-to-life circumstance: Many states include a circumstance element that limits felony murder to deaths that occur during the commission of other "dangerous felonies." Some states accomplish this by providing specifically for it in their murder statutes. In Kansas, first-degree felony murder is defined as the "killing of a human being . . . in the commission of, attempt to, or flight from an *inherently dangerous felony*" (emphasis added; Kansas Criminal Code 2005-6, 21-3401).

Other states name a category of felony that *implies* danger to life. For example, under Iowa's murder statute, it's first-degree murder to kill "another person while participating in a *forcible* felony" (emphasis added; Iowa Criminal Code 1999, ß 707.2).

Most statutes specifically list the felonies that the state recognizes as dangerous to life. The Maryland felony murder statute (quoted on page 300) is a typical example.

The determination of whether felonies are dangerous arises in at least two situations. One is where statutes, such as the Kansas statute, use the term *inherently dangerous* without defining it. The other situation is when the statute includes a first-degree felony murder statute and a catchall second-degree murder statute that provides that "all murders not first degree are second degree murders." The next case excerpt, *State v. Stuart*, examines this problem, first, as to whether felony murder is included in the catchall phrase and, second, as to which felonies are "dangerous to life."

Before we get to the excerpt, you need to understand the two approaches courts take when they decide whether the felony being committed when the killing occurred was "dangerous" to life. The first is the **inherently dangerous felony approach.** In this approach, courts look at the felony in the abstract; that is, they look at the elements of the felony without looking at how it was carried out in the specific case before them to determine whether the elements amount to a dangerous felony. If a felony *can* be committed in a way that's *not* dangerous to life, even if it was committed in a dangerous way in the case before the court, then it's not inherently dangerous.

In *People v. Phillips* (1966), Dr. Marvin Phillips fraudulently convinced 8-year-old Linda Epping's parents that he could cure Linda's advanced virulent eye cancer by using chiropractic procedures. She died, and Phillips was convicted of felony murder based on the felony of fraud. The California Supreme Court reversed because fraud isn't an inherently dangerous felony, even though in this case it resulted in Linda Epping's tragic death.

The other approach is the **case-by-case approach,** where the facts and circumstances surrounding the way the felony was committed in the particular case, not the elements of the crime in the abstract, may be considered to determine whether it was dangerous to human life.

In *State v. Harrison* (1977), Frank Harrison and Emmett Cunejo, were driving around in Gallup, New Mexico. They had two rifles, a handgun, and ammunition with them to go prairie dog hunting. They stopped and picked up Susan Brown walking along the road. They drove to a remote area known as the Hog's Back near Gallup. Having been told to "take a walk," Cunejo left Harrison and Mrs. Brown in the car and practiced shooting with one of the rifles far from the car.

Cunejo returned after some time, picked up a beer and more ammunition, left, returned, got in the back seat, noticed the handgun, and picked it up. He pulled the trigger a few times, thinking the gun was unloaded. A shot went off and instantly killed Mrs. Brown, who was in the front seat with Harrison. Harrison and Cunejo panicked. They spent the next few days trying to dispose of the body, getting drunk, and destroying evidence. They ran a roadblock and hit a car in the process, whereupon they threw the cadaver out of the car. They were arrested shortly thereafter. Harrison was convicted of false imprisonment and felony murder and was sentenced to 1 to 5 years for the false imprisonment and to death for the murder (1322).

In adopting the case-by-case test, the New Mexico Supreme Court held:

> One who is perpetrating a felony which seems not of itself to involve any element of human risk, may resort to a dangerous method of committing it, or may make use of dangerous force to deter others from interfering. If the dangerous force thus used results in death, the crime is murder just as much as if the danger was inherent in the very nature of the felony itself. (1324)

The Rhode Island Supreme Court adopted the case-by-case approach in *State v. Stewart* (1995) and found that Tracy Stewart was guilty of second-degree felony murder of her infant son Travis, based on the felony of allowing him to suffer from lack of food and dehydration.

CASE | *Did She Commit an "Inherently Dangerous" Felony?*

State v. Stewart
663 A.2d 912 (R.I. 1995)

HISTORY

Twenty-year-old Tracy Stewart was convicted in the Superior Court, Providence County, of second-degree

felony murder. She appealed. The Supreme Court affirmed the conviction.

WEISBERGER, CJ.

FACTS

On August 31, 1988, twenty-year-old Tracy Stewart gave birth to a son, Travis Young (Travis). Travis's father was

Edward Young, Sr. (Young). Stewart and Young, who had two other children together, were not married at the time of Travis's birth. Travis lived for only fifty-two days, dying on October 21, 1988, from dehydration.

During the week prior to Travis's death, Stewart, Young, and a friend, Patricia McMasters (McMasters), continually and repeatedly ingested cocaine over a two- to three-consecutive-day period at the apartment shared by Stewart and Young. The baby, Travis, was also present at the apartment while Stewart, Young, and McMasters engaged in this cocaine marathon. Young and McMasters injected cocaine intravenously and also smoked it while Stewart ingested the cocaine only by smoking it. The smoked cocaine was in its strongest or base form, commonly referred to as "crack." When the three exhausted an existing supply of cocaine, they would pool their money and Young and McMasters would go out and buy more with the accumulated funds.

The primary source of funds from which the three obtained money for this cocaine spree was Stewart's and McMasters's Aid to Families with Dependent Children (AFDC) checks. Stewart and McMasters had each just received the second of their semimonthly AFDC checks. They both cashed their AFDC checks and gave money to Young, which he then used to purchase more cocaine.

After all the AFDC funds had been spent on cocaine and the group had run out of money, McMasters and Young committed a robbery to obtain additional money to purchase more cocaine.

The cocaine binge continued uninterrupted for two to three days. McMasters testified that during this time neither McMasters nor Stewart slept at all. McMasters testified that defendant was never far from her during this entire two- to three-day period except for the occasions when McMasters left the apartment to buy more cocaine. During this entire time, McMasters saw defendant feed Travis only once. Travis was in a walker, and defendant propped a bottle of formula up on the walker, using a blanket, for the baby to feed himself. McMasters testified that she did not see defendant hold the baby to feed him nor did she see defendant change Travis's diaper or clothes during this period.

Ten months after Travis's death defendant (Stewart) was indicted on charges of second-degree murder, wrongfully causing or permitting a child under the age of eighteen to be a habitual sufferer for want of food and proper care (hereinafter sometimes referred to as "wrongfully permitting a child to be a habitual sufferer"), and manslaughter.

The second-degree-murder charge was based on a theory of felony murder. The prosecution did not allege that defendant intentionally killed her son but rather that he had been killed during the commission of an inherently dangerous felony, specifically, wrongfully permitting a child to be a habitual sufferer. Moreover, the prosecution did not allege that defendant intentionally withheld food or care from her son. Rather the state alleged that because of defendant's chronic state of cocaine intoxication, she may have realized what her responsibilities were but

simply could not remember whether she had fed her son, when in fact she had not.

At defendant's trial both the prosecution and the defense presented expert medical witnesses who testified concerning what they believed to be the cause of Travis's death. The experts for both sides agreed that the cause of death was dehydration, but they strongly disagreed regarding what caused the dehydration. The prosecution expert witnesses believed that the dehydration was caused by insufficient intake of food and water, that is, malnutrition. The defense expert witnesses, conversely, believed that the dehydration was caused by a gastrointestinal virus known as gastroenteritis which manifested itself in an overwhelming expulsion of fluid from the baby's body.

The defendant was found guilty of both second-degree murder and wrongfully permitting a child to be a habitual sufferer. A subsequent motion for new trial was denied.

This appeal followed. . . .

OPINION

. . . Rhode Island's murder statute, § 11231, enumerates certain crimes that may serve as predicate felonies [felonies murder can be based on] to a charge of first-degree murder. A felony that is not enumerated in § 11231 can, however, serve as a predicate felony to a charge of second-degree murder. Thus the fact that the crime of wrongfully permitting a child to be a habitual sufferer is not specified in § 11231 as a predicate felony to support a charge of first-degree murder does not preclude such crime from serving as a predicate to support a charge of second-degree murder.

In Rhode Island, second-degree murder has been equated with common-law murder. At common law, where the rule is unchanged by statute, "homicide is murder if the death results from the perpetration or attempted perpetration of an inherently dangerous felony." To serve as a predicate felony to a charge of second-degree murder, a felony that is not specifically enumerated in § 11231 must therefore be an inherently dangerous felony.

The defendant contends that wrongfully permitting a child to be a habitual sufferer is not an inherently dangerous felony and cannot therefore serve as the predicate felony to a charge of second-degree murder. In advancing her argument, defendant urges this court to adopt the approach used by California courts to determine if a felony is inherently dangerous. This approach requires that the court consider the elements of the felony "in the abstract" rather than look at the particular facts of the case under consideration. With such an approach, if a statute can be violated in a manner that does not endanger human life, then the felony is not inherently dangerous to human life.

Moreover, the California Supreme Court has defined an act as "inherently dangerous to human life when there is 'a high probability that it will result in death.'"

The defendant urges this court to adopt the method of analysis employed by California courts to determine if a felony is inherently dangerous to life. . . . We decline defendant's invitation to adopt the California approach in determining whether a felony is inherently dangerous to life and thus capable of serving as a predicate to a charge of second-degree felony murder. We believe that the better approach is for the trier of fact to consider the facts and circumstances of the particular case to determine if such felony was inherently dangerous in the manner and the circumstances in which it was committed, rather than have a court make the determination by viewing the elements of a felony in the abstract. We now join a number of states that have adopted this approach. . . .

The proper procedure for making such a determination is to present the facts and circumstances of the particular case to the trier of fact and for the trier of fact to determine if a felony is inherently dangerous in the manner and the circumstances in which it was committed.

This is exactly what happened in the case at bar. The trial justice instructed the jury that before it could find defendant guilty of second-degree murder, it must first find that wrongfully causing or permitting a child to be a habitual sufferer for want of food or proper care was inherently dangerous to human life "in its manner of commission." This was a proper charge. By its guilty verdict on the charge of second-degree murder, the jury obviously found that wrongfully permitting a child to be a habitual sufferer for want of food or proper care was indeed a felony inherently dangerous to human life in the circumstances of this particular case. . . .

. . . We are of the opinion that the evidence offered by the state was sufficient to prove beyond a reasonable doubt each of the elements of second-degree felony murder, including that the crime of wrongfully permitting a child to be a habitual sufferer was an inherently dangerous felony in its manner of commission. . . .

The theory of felony murder is that a defendant does not have to have intended to kill. . . . The intent to commit the underlying felony will be imputed to the homicide. . . .

The defendant claims that the evidence presented at trial failed to establish that she intentionally committed the crime of wrongfully permitting a child to be a habitual sufferer. She claims that absent an intent to commit this felony, it cannot serve as a predicate to support a charge of second-degree felony murder because there would then be no intent to be imputed from the underlying felony to the homicide.

We agree with defendant that intent to commit the underlying felony is a necessary element of felony murder. However, we believe the circumstances surrounding the events preceding Travis's death support a finding that defendant did indeed intentionally permit her son to be a habitual sufferer for want of food or proper care.

The defendant's addiction to and compulsion to have cocaine were the overriding factors that controlled virtually every aspect of her life. She referred to the extended periods that she was high on cocaine as "going on a mission." Although she was receiving public assistance and did not have much disposable income, she nevertheless spent a great deal of money on cocaine, including her

AFDC money. She shoplifted and traded the stolen merchandise for cocaine. She stole food because she had used the money that she should have been using to purchase food to purchase cocaine. The compulsion to have cocaine at any cost took precedence over every facet of defendant's life including caring for her children.

Although defendant did not testify at trial, she did testify before the grand jury. A redacted tape of her grand jury testimony was admitted into evidence and played for the jury at trial. During the days preceding Travis's death, defendant had been on a two- to three-day cocaine binge, a "mission," as she referred to it. Her grand jury testimony indicated that she knew that during such periods she was unable to care for her children properly.

The defendant testified that whenever she would go on a mission, her mother, who lived only a few houses away, would take and care for the children. This testimony evinced a knowledge on the part of defendant that she was incapable of properly caring for her children during these periods of extended cocaine intoxication.

In addition, defendant was prone to petit mal seizures, which were exacerbated by her cocaine use. During such seizures she would "black out" or "go into a coma state." She testified before the grand jury that she was aware that taking cocaine brought on more seizures and that the weekend before Travis died she had in fact blacked out and "went into a coma state."

Despite her grand jury testimony to the contrary, Travis remained with defendant at her apartment during the entire two- to three-day binge. He died two or three days later. The defendant's repeated voluntary and intentional ingestion of crack cocaine while her seven-week-old son was in her care, in addition to her testimony that she knew that she was incapable of properly caring for her children during these extended periods of cocaine intoxication, support a finding that she intentionally permitted her son to be a habitual sufferer for want of food and proper care.

We make the distinction between a finding that defendant intentionally deprived her son of food and proper care, which even the state does not allege, and a finding that defendant intentionally permitted her son to be a habitual sufferer for want of food or proper care, which we find to be supported by the evidence adduced at trial. . . .

Two or three days after the cocaine binge had ended, defendant went to McMasters's apartment and informed her that Travis had died that morning. The defendant was carrying a bag containing cans of baby formula and asked McMasters if she knew where she (defendant) could exchange the unused formula for cocaine. McMasters told defendant that she did not know where the formula could be exchanged for cocaine but suggested that she take it to a local supermarket to get a cash refund.

McMasters then accompanied defendant to a supermarket in Pawtucket where they attempted to return the formula for cash. They were unsuccessful in this attempt, however, because they did not have a receipt for the formula and store policy dictated that no cash refunds be given for returns without a receipt for the merchandise.

The defendant told the assistant store manager that her baby had just died, and the manager gave defendant $20 out of his own pocket because he felt sorry for her. The defendant used this $20 to purchase cocaine. The defendant and McMasters then went to McMasters's apartment and smoked cocaine. . . .

In order for the crime of wrongfully permitting a child to be a habitual sufferer to serve as a predicate felony to a charge of second-degree felony murder, the accused must have . . . intentionally caused or permitted her son to be a habitual sufferer for want of food or proper care. . . .

. . . We believe that the [trial judge's] instructions requiring that the jury find that defendant had no legal justification or no legal excuse for causing her son to be a habitual sufferer and also requiring that the jury find that defendant knew or was aware beforehand that causing or permitting her son to be a habitual sufferer for want of food or proper care was likely to endanger his life, were the functional equivalent to an instruction requiring the jury to find that defendant intentionally caused or permitted her son to be a habitual sufferer.

This failure to distinguish between intent . . . and knowledge is probably of little consequence in many areas of the law, as often there is good reason for imposing liability whether the defendant desired or merely knew of the practical certainty of the results. The distinction between acting purposely and knowingly is inconsequential for most purposes of liability; acting knowingly is ordinarily sufficient. . . .

For the foregoing reasons the defendant's appeal is denied and dismissed, and the judgment of conviction is AFFIRMED.

Questions

1. Explain California's approach of determining an "inherently dangerous felony" in the abstract.

2. Why did the Rhode Island court reject the California approach?

3. What test did the Rhode Island court use in determining whether the felony of wrongfully permitting a child to suffer is inherently dangerous?

4. In your opinion, which is the better test? Why?

5. List all of the evidence in this case relevant to determining whether Tracy Stewart was guilty of felony murder.

6. Assume you're a defense attorney in California. Relying on the relevant evidence you listed in (5), argue that Stewart is not guilty of felony murder.

7. Assume you're a prosecutor in Rhode Island. Relying on the evidence in (5), argue that Stewart is guilty of felony murder.

8. Assume you're a defense attorney in Rhode Island. Relying on the evidence in (5), argue that there's a reasonable doubt as to whether Stewart is guilty of felony murder.

EXPLORING FURTHER

Felony Murder

Was Fraud a Felony "Inherently Dangerous to Human Life"?

People v. Phillips, 414 P.2d 353 (Cal. 1966)

FACTS Linda Epping died on December 29, 1961, at the age of 8, from a rare and fast-growing form of eye cancer. Linda's mother first observed a swelling over the girl's left eye in June of that year. The doctor whom she consulted recommended that Linda be taken to Dr. Straatsma, an ophthalmologist at the UCLA Medical Center.

On July 10th Dr. Straatsma first saw Linda; on July 17th the girl, suffering great pain, was admitted to the center. Dr. Straatsma performed an exploratory operation and the resulting biopsy established the nature of the child's affliction. Dr. Straatsma advised Linda's parents that her only hope for survival lay in immediate surgical removal of the affected eye. The Eppings were loath to permit such surgery, but on the morning of July 21st Mr. Epping called the hospital and gave his oral consent. The Eppings arrived at the hospital that afternoon to consult with the surgeon.

While waiting they encountered a Mrs. Eaton who told them that defendant had cured her son of a brain tumor without surgery. Mrs. Epping called defendant at his office. According to the Eppings, defendant repeatedly assured them that he could cure Linda without surgery. They testified that defendant urged them to take Linda out of the hospital, claiming that the hospital was "an experimental place," that the doctors there would use Linda as "a human guinea pig" and would relieve the Eppings of their money as well.

The Eppings testified that in reliance upon defendant's statements they took Linda out of the hospital and placed her under defendant's care. They stated that if defendant had not represented to them that he could cure the child without surgery and that the UCLA doctors were only interested in experimentation, they would have proceeded with the scheduled operation. The prosecution introduced medical testimony which tended to prove that if Linda had undergone surgery on July 21st her life would have been prolonged or she would have been completely cured.

Defendant treated Linda from July 22 to August 12, 1961. He charged an advance fee of $500 for three months' care as well as a sum exceeding $200 for pills and medicines.

On August 13th Linda's condition had not improved; the Eppings dismissed defendant. Later the Eppings sought to cure Linda by means of a Mexican herbal drug known as yerba mansa and, about the 1st of September, they placed her under the care of the Christian Science movement. They did not take her back to the hospital for treatment. . . . Was Phillips guilty of felony murder?

DECISION The jury said yes. No, ruled the California Supreme Court:

> Only such felonies as are in themselves "inherently dangerous to human life" can support the application of the felony murder rule. We have ruled that in assessing such peril to human life inherent in any given felony "we look to the elements of the felony in the abstract, not the particular 'facts' of the case."

> We have thus recognized that the felony murder doctrine expresses a highly artificial concept that deserves no extension beyond its required application. Indeed the rule itself has been abandoned by the courts of England, where it had its inception. It has been subjected to severe and sweeping criticism. No case to our knowledge in any jurisdiction has held that because death results from a course of conduct involving a felonious perpetration of a fraud, the felony murder doctrine can be invoked. . . .

 Go to the Criminal Law 9e website to find the full text of the Exploring Further excerpt: www.thomsonedu.com/criminaljustice/samaha. (Excerpt on felony murder.)

Corporation Murder

Can corporations commit murder? Yes, according to a few prosecutors who've prosecuted corporations for murder (Cullen, Maakestad, and Cavender 1987). Probably the most publicized corporate murder case involved the deaths of three young women who were killed on an Indiana highway in 1978 when their Ford Pinto exploded after being struck from behind by another vehicle.

The explosion followed several other similar incidents involving Pintos that led to grisly deaths. Published evidence revealed that Ford may have known that the Pinto gas tanks weren't safe but took the risk that they wouldn't explode and injure or kill anyone. Following the three young women's deaths, the state of Indiana indicted Ford Motor Company for reckless homicide, charging that Ford had recklessly authorized, approved, designed, and manufactured the Pinto and allowed the car to remain in use with defectively designed fuel tanks. These tanks, the indictment charged, killed the three young women in Indiana. For a number of reasons not related directly to whether corporations can commit murder, the case was later dismissed.

In another case that drew wide public attention during the 1980s, Autumn Hills Convalescent Centers, a corporation that operated nursing homes, went on trial for charges that it had murdered an 87-year-old woman by neglect. David Marks, a Texas assistant attorney general, said, "From the first day until her last breath, she was unattended to and allowed to lie day and night in her own urine and waste."

The case attracted attention because of allegations that as many as sixty elderly people had died from substandard care at the Autumn Hills nursing home near Galveston, Texas. The indictment charged that the company had failed to provide nutrients, fluids, and incontinent care for the woman, Mrs. Breed, and neglected to turn and reposition her regularly to combat bedsores. One prosecution witness testified that Mrs. Breed's bed was wet constantly and the staff seldom cleaned her. The corporation defended against the charges, claiming that Mrs. Breed had died from colon cancer, not improper care (Reinhold 1985, 17).

Most state criminal codes apply to corporate criminal homicide in the same way that they apply to other crimes committed for the corporation's benefit. Specifically, both corporations and high corporate officers acting within the scope of their authority and for the benefit of a corporation can commit murder. In practice, however, prosecutors rarely charge corporations or their officers with criminal homicide, and convictions rarely follow.

The reluctance to prosecute corporations for murder, or for any homicide requiring the intent to kill or inflict serious bodily injury, is due largely to the hesitation to view corporations as persons. Although, theoretically, the law clearly makes that possible, in practice, prosecutors and courts have drawn the line at involuntary manslaughter, a crime whose *mens rea* is negligence and occasionally recklessness.

As for corporate executives, the reluctance to prosecute stems from vicarious liability and the questions it raises about culpability (see Chapter 4). It has been difficult to attribute deaths linked with corporate benefit to corporate officers who were in charge generally but didn't order or authorize a killing, didn't know about it, or even didn't want it to happen.

Only in outrageous cases that receive widespread public attention, such as the Pinto and nursing home cases, do prosecutors risk acquittal by trying corporations and their officers for criminal homicide. In these cases, prosecutors aren't hoping to win the case in traditional terms, meaning to secure convictions. Business law professor William J. Maakestad says, "At this point, success of this type of corporate criminal prosecution is defined by establishing the legitimacy of the case. If you can get the case to trial, you have really achieved success" (Lewin 1985, D2).

People v. O'Neil (1990) involved one of the few prosecutions of a corporation and its officers for murder.

CASE   *Did They "Murder" Their Employee?*

People v. O'Neil
550 N.E.2d 1090 (Ill.App. 1990)

HISTORY

Following a joint bench trial [trial by a judge without a jury], Steven O'Neil, Charles Kirschbaum, and Daniel Rodriguez, agents of Film Recovery Systems, Inc. (Film Recovery), were convicted of the murder of Stefan Golab, a Film Recovery employee, from cyanide poisoning stemming from conditions in Film Recovery's plant in Elk Grove Village, Illinois. Corporate defendants Film Recovery and its sister corporation Metallic Marketing Systems, Inc. (Metallic Marketing), were convicted of involuntary manslaughter in the same death.

O'Neil, Kirschbaum, and Rodriguez each received sentences of 25 years' imprisonment for murder. O'Neil and Kirschbaum were also each fined $10,000 with respect to the murder convictions. Corporate defendants Film Recovery and Metallic Marketing were each fined $10,000 with respect to the convictions for involuntary manslaughter.

The defendants appealed, and the appellate court reversed the convictions.

LORENZ, J.

FACTS

. . . In 1982, Film Recovery occupied premises at 1855 and 1875 Greenleaf Avenue in Elk Grove Village. Film Recovery was there engaged in the business of extracting, for resale, silver from used x-ray and photographic film. Metallic Marketing operated out of the same premises on Greenleaf Avenue and owned 50% of the stock of Film Recovery. The recovery process was performed at Film Recovery's plant located at the 1855 address and involved "chipping" the film product and soaking the granulated pieces in large open bubbling vats containing a solution of water and sodium cyanide. The cyanide solution caused silver contained in the film to be released. A continuous flow system pumped the silver laden solution into polyurethane tanks which contained electrically charged stainless steel plates to which the separated silver adhered. The plates were removed from the tanks to another room where the accumulated silver was scraped off. The remaining solution was pumped out of the tanks and the granulated film, devoid of silver, shoveled out.

On the morning of February 10, 1983, shortly after he disconnected a pump on one of the tanks and began to stir the contents of the tank with a rake, Stefan Golab became dizzy and faint. He left the production area to go rest in the lunchroom area of the plant. Plant workers present on that day testified Golab's body had trembled and he had foamed at the mouth. Golab eventually lost consciousness and was taken outside of the plant. Paramedics summoned to the plant were unable to revive him. Golab was pronounced dead upon arrival at Alexian Brothers Hospital.

The Cook County medical examiner performed an autopsy on Golab the following day. Although the medical examiner initially indicated Golab could have died from cardiac arrest, he reserved final determination of death pending examination of results of toxicological laboratory tests on Golab's blood and other body specimens. After receiving the toxicological report, the medical examiner determined Golab died from acute cyanide poisoning through the inhalation of cyanide fumes in the plant air.

Defendants were subsequently indicted by a Cook County grand jury. The grand jury charged defendants O'Neil, Kirschbaum, Rodriguez, Pett, and Mackay with murder, stating that, as individuals and as officers and high managerial agents of Film Recovery, they had, on February 10, 1983, knowingly created a strong probability of Golab's death.

The indictment stated the individual defendants failed to disclose to Golab that he was working with substances containing cyanide and failed to advise him about, train him to anticipate, and provide adequate equipment to protect him from, attendant dangers involved.

The grand jury charged Film Recovery and Metallic Marketing with involuntary manslaughter stating that, through the reckless acts of their officers, directors, agents, and others, all acting within the scope of their employment, the corporate entities had, on February 10, 1983, unintentionally killed Golab. Finally, the grand jury charged both individual and corporate defendants with reckless conduct as to 20 other Film Recovery employees based on the same conduct alleged in the murder indictment, but expanding the time of that conduct to "on or about March 1982 through March 1983."

Proceedings commenced in the circuit court in January 1985 and continued through the conclusion of trial in June of that year. In the course of the 24-day trial, evidence from 59 witnesses was presented, either directly or through stipulation of the parties. That testimony is contained in over 2,300 pages of trial transcript. The parties also presented numerous exhibits including photographs, corporate documents and correspondence, as well as physical evidence.

On June 14, 1985, the trial judge pronounced his judgment of defendants' guilt. The trial judge found that "the mind and mental state of a corporation is the mind and mental state of the directors, officers and high managerial personnel because they act on behalf of the corporation for both the benefit of the corporation and for themselves." Further, "if the corporation's officers, directors and high managerial personnel act within the scope of their corporate responsibilities and employment for their benefit and for the benefit of the profits of the corporation, the corporation must be held liable for what occurred in the work place." Defendants filed timely notices of appeal,

the matters were consolidated for review, and arguments were had before this court in July 1987. . . .

OPINION

The Criminal Code of 1961 defines murder as follows:

> A person who kills an individual without lawful justification commits murder if, in performing the acts which cause the death: He knows that such acts create a strong probability of death or great bodily harm to that individual. (Ill.Rev.Stat.1981, ch. 38, par.9-1(a)(2).)

Involuntary manslaughter is defined as:

> A person who unintentionally kills an individual without lawful justification commits involuntary manslaughter if his acts whether lawful or unlawful which cause the death are such as are likely to cause death or great bodily harm to some individual, and he performs them recklessly. (Ill.Rev.Stat.1981, ch. 38, par. 9-3(a).)

Reckless conduct is defined as:

> A person who causes bodily harm to or endangers the bodily safety of an individual by any means, commits reckless conduct if he performs recklessly the acts which cause the harm or endanger safety, whether they otherwise are lawful or unlawful. (Ill.Rev.Stat.1981, ch. 38, par. 12-5(a).)

. . . In Illinois, a corporation is criminally responsible for offenses "authorized, requested, commanded, or performed by the board of directors or by a high managerial agent acting within the scope of his employment." A high managerial agent is defined as "an officer of the corporation, or any other agent who has a position of comparable authority for the formulation of corporate policy or the supervision of subordinate employees in a managerial capacity." (Ill.Rev.Stat. 1981, ch. 38, par. 5-4(c)(2).) Thus, a corporation is criminally responsible whenever any of its high managerial agents possess the requisite mental state and is responsible for a criminal offense while acting within the scope of his employment. . . .

Evidence at trial indicated Golab died after inhaling poisonous cyanide fumes while working in a plant operated by Film Recovery and its sister corporation Metallic Marketing where such fumes resulted from a process employed to remove silver from used X-ray and photographic film. The record contains substantial evidence regarding the nature of working conditions inside the plant. Testimony established that air inside the plant was foul smelling and made breathing difficult and painful. Plant workers experienced dizziness, nausea, headaches, and bouts of vomiting.

There is evidence that plant workers were not informed they were working with cyanide. Nor were they informed of the presence of, or danger of breathing, cyanide gas.

Ventilation in the plant was poor. Plant workers were given neither safety instruction nor adequate protective clothing.

Finally, testimony established that defendants O'Neil, Kirschbaum, and Rodriguez were responsible for operating the plant under those conditions. For purposes of our disposition, we find further elaboration on the evidence unnecessary.

Moreover, although we have determined evidence in the record is not so insufficient as to bar retrial, our determination of the sufficiency of the evidence should not be in any way interpreted as a finding as to defendants' guilt that would be binding on the court on retrial.

REVERSED and REMANDED.

Questions

1. List all the evidence for and against the corporation's and the individuals' liability for murder and involuntary manslaughter.

2. Why did the court reverse and remand the case?

3. On remand, would you find the defendants guilty of murder? Explain your answer.

4. Do you agree that it's inconsistent to find that the corporation had one state of mind and the individuals another?

5. Consider the following remarks made after the convictions in the original trial (Greenhouse 1985, 1):
   a. Following the conviction in the original trial, then attorney Richard M. Daley said the verdicts meant that employers who knowingly expose their workers to dangerous conditions leading to injury or even death can be held criminally responsible for the results of their actions.
   b. Ralph Nader, consumer advocate lawyer, said:
      The public is pretty upset with dangerously defective products, bribery, toxic waste, and job hazards. The polls all show it. The verdict today will encourage other prosecutors and judges to

take more seriously the need to have the criminal law catch up with corporate crime.
   c. Professor John Coffee, Columbia Law School, said, "When you threaten the principal adequately, he will monitor the behavior of his agent."
   d. A California deputy district attorney put it more bluntly: "A person facing a jail sentence is the best deterrent against wrongdoing."
   e. Joseph E. Hadley, Jr., a corporate lawyer who specializes in health and safety issues, said the decision would not send shockwaves through the corporate community:
      I don't think corporate America should be viewed as in the ballpark with these folks. This was a highly unusual situation, but now people see that where the egregious situation occurs, there could be a criminal remedy.
   f. Robert Stephenson, a lawyer defending another corporation, said, "I don't believe these statutes [murder and aggravated battery] were ever meant to be used in this way."
   g. Utah's governor, Scott M. Matheson, refused to extradite Michael T. McKay, a former Film Recovery vice president then living in Utah, because he was an "exemplary citizen who should not be subjected to the sensational charges in Illinois."

Which of the statements best describes what you think is proper policy regarding prosecutions of corporate executives for murder? Defend your answer.

 Go to the Criminal law 9e website to find Exercise 9.2 and learn more about murder: www.thomsonedu.com/criminaljustice/samaha.

MANSLAUGHTER

Manslaughter, like murder, is an ancient common-law crime created by judges, not by legislators. According to the 18th-century commentator Blackstone (1769):

> Manslaughter is . . . the unlawful killing of another . . . which may be either voluntarily upon a sudden heat, or involuntarily . . . where one had no intent to do another any personal mischief. (191–92)

Blackstone's definition is more than three centuries old, but it goes straight to *mens rea*—the heart of manslaughter, as it is in most murder classifications: "Was it intentional (voluntary) or unintentional (involuntary)?

Voluntary Manslaughter

> If upon a sudden quarrel two persons fight, and one of them kills the other, this is [voluntary] manslaughter. And, so it is, if they upon such an occasion go out and fight in a field, for this is one continued act of passion and the law pays that regard to human frailty, as not to put a hasty and a deliberate act upon the same footing with regard to guilt. So also a man be greatly

provoked, as by pulling his nose, or other great indignity, and immediately kills the aggressor, though this is not excusable, since there is no absolute necessity for doing so to preserve himself, yet neither is it murder for there is no previous malice. (Blackstone 1769, 191)

Blackstone's description of voluntary manslaughter in the late 1700s is an excellent way to begin our discussion of voluntary manslaughter. **Voluntary manslaughter** is about letting your anger get the better of you in the worst possible way—killing another person. Criminal law aims to bridle passions and build self-control, but it also recognizes the frailty of human nature.

The law of voluntary manslaughter takes into account both the seriousness of this felony and human frailty. So although a sudden intentional killing in anger is a very serious felony, it's not the most serious; that's reserved for murder. Let's be clear that the law of voluntary manslaughter doesn't reward individuals who give in to their rages by letting them walk; it punishes them severely, but it punishes them less than they'd get for murder.

Adequate Provocation Voluntary manslaughter (like all criminal homicides) consists of the elements of *actus reus, mens rea,* causation, and death. But it has one element not present in murder, and one we haven't discussed; this is the circumstance element of **adequate provocation.** In voluntary manslaughter, adequate provocation is the trigger that sets off the sudden killing of another person.

But not everyone who flies into a rage and suddenly kills someone has committed voluntary manslaughter instead of murder. Adequate provocation has to be both objective and subjective. First, the defendant herself must be provoked; that's the subjective aspect. Second, the provocation has to be reasonable; that's the objective aspect.

The Maryland Court of Appeals puts it this way:

> For a provocation to be "adequate," it must be "calculated to inflame the passion of a *reasonable* person and tend to cause *that person* to act for the moment from passion rather than reason." (emphasis added)

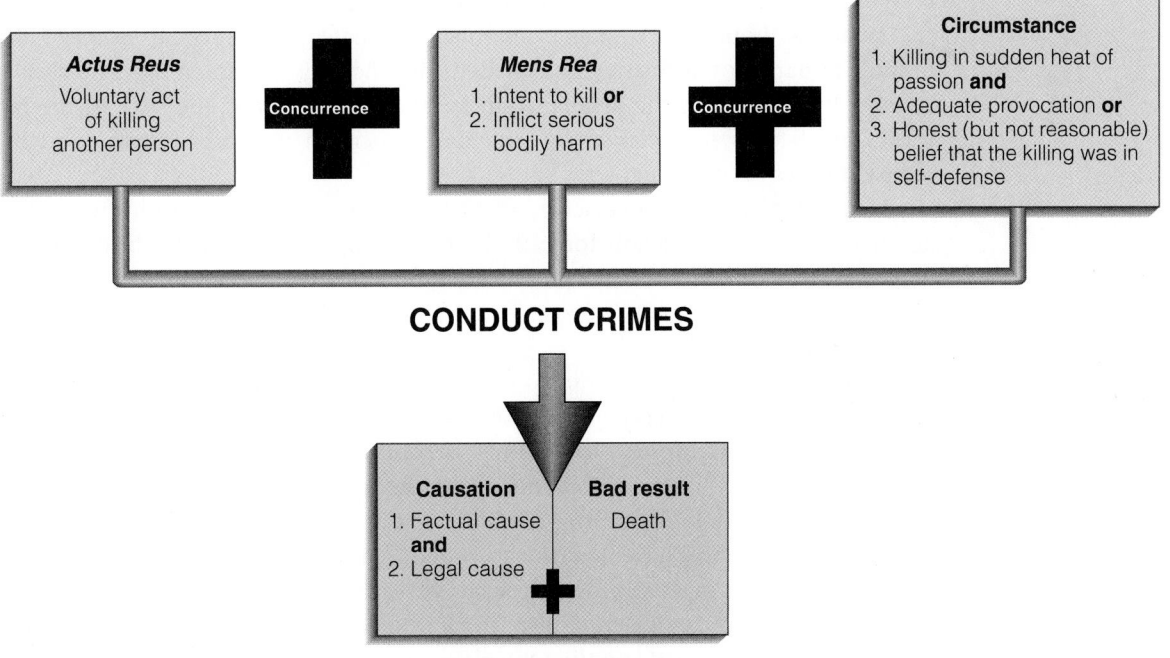

Elements of Voluntary Manslaughter

That describes one aspect of "adequacy." There is another, which flows from the requirement that the passion be that of a reasonable person; the provocation must be one the law is prepared to recognize as minimally sufficient, in proper circumstances, to overcome the restraint normally expected from reasonable persons. There are many "slings and arrows of outrageous fortune" that people either must tolerate or find an alternative way, other than homicide, to redress. (*Dennis v. State* 1995, 695)

Of course, reasonable persons, however great the provocation, would never kill someone except in self-defense (Chapter 4). That's why voluntary manslaughter isn't a *justifiable* homicide; it's only a lesser version of intentional murder. Professor LaFave (2003a), in his treatise widely cited in appellate court cases like the ones you're reading in the case excerpts, recommends that we call *reasonable* provocation, *understandable* provocation.

What is really meant by "reasonable provocation" is provocation which causes a reasonable man to lose his normal self-control; and although a reasonable man who had thus lost control over himself would not kill, yet his homicidal reaction is at least understandable. Therefore, one who reacts to the provocation should not be guilty of murder. But neither should he be not guilty at all. So, his conduct falls into the intermediate category of voluntary manslaughter. (777)

The common law (and many states today) recognized four reasonable provocations:

1. Mutual combat (fighting)

2. Assault and battery (Chapter 10)

3. Trespass (Chapter 11)

4. Adultery

Only *serious* fights are adequate provocation; scuffles aren't. Some batteries—but not all offensive touching (see Chapter 10)—are adequate provocation. Being pistol whipped on the head, being struck hard in the face by fists, or enduring "staggering" body blows qualify. Being slapped or shoved doesn't.

Assault without body contact is *sometimes* adequate provocation. In *Beasley v. State* (1886), a man shot at Beasley and missed him. Beasley was so enraged he shot his attacker in the back as the assailant ran away. The court ruled the shot in the back wasn't justified as self-defense, but the initial incident was provocative enough to reduce murder to manslaughter.

Insulting gestures by themselves aren't adequate provocation, but if they indicate an intent to attack with deadly force, they are. So "flipping someone the bird" isn't adequate provocation, but waving a gun around in a threatening manner can be.

Trespassing is adequate provocation only if the trespassers invade the home and threaten someone with death.

Voluntary manslaughter requires killing in the "sudden heat of passion" with no "cooling off" period (Perkins and Boyce 1982, 95–96). Whether the actual time between the provocation and the killing—seconds, hours, or even days—qualifies as the "sudden heat of passion" depends upon the facts of the individual case. Courts apply an **objective test of cooling-off time;** that is, would a reasonable person under the same circumstances have had time to cool off? If defendants had a reasonable time for their murderous rages to subside, the law views their killings as murders even if they would've been adequate if they'd taken place immediately following the provocations.

Blackstone (1769, 191) applied the objective test to this example (given earlier): If two persons "upon a sudden quarrel" start fighting indoors, it's voluntary manslaughter "if they upon such an occasion go out and fight in a field, for this is one continued act of passion and the law pays that regard to human frailty, as not to put a hasty and a deliberate act upon the same footing with regard to guilt." Using the same objective test, the time for cooling off may be considerable.

In a famous old case, *State v. Flory* (1929), Flory's wife told him her father had raped her. The court ruled that Flory's passion hadn't reasonably cooled even after he walked all night to his father-in-law's house and killed him the next day! The court said the heinous combination of incest and rape was more than enough to keep a reasonable person in a murderous rage for at least several days.

Causation   To prove voluntary manslaughter, the prosecution has to prove that the provocation caused the passion and the killing. Suppose Sonny intends to kill his wife Carly because she lied to him. He goes to her bedroom, finds her in bed with his worst enemy, and shoots her to death. Is it voluntary manslaughter or murder? It's murder, because Carly's lie, not her adultery, provoked Sonny to kill her.

Provocation by Words   It's often said that words are never adequate provocation. That was true when the rule was created in the days of the common law. It's still the rule in most states but not everywhere. Section 609.20 of the Minnesota Criminal Code provides:

> **609.20 MANSLAUGHTER IN THE FIRST DEGREE**
>
> Whoever does any of the following is guilty of manslaughter in the first degree and may be sentenced to imprisonment for not more than 15 years or to payment of a fine of not more than $30,000, or both:
>
> (1) intentionally causes the death of another person in the heat of passion provoked by such words or acts of another as would provoke a person of ordinary self-control under like circumstances, provided that the crying of a child does not constitute provocation.

There are signs, besides Minnesota statute, that the bright-line rule, "words can *never* provoke," isn't as bright as it used to be. Some cases are adopting a more flexible rule that "words can *sometimes* amount to adequate provocation" (LaFave 2003a, 780–81). A few states, such as California and Pennsylvania, have adopted the **"last-straw" rule** (also called "long smoldering" or "slow burn" rule) of adequate provocation. It's defined as "a smoldering resentment or pent-up rage resulting from earlier insults or humiliating events culminating in a triggering event that, by itself, might be insufficient to provoke the deadly act (*Dennis v. State* 1995, 689).

Probably the most significant development is the adoption by several states of the Model Penal Code (MPC) **extreme mental or emotional disturbance** manslaughter provision:

> **SECTION 210.3 MANSLAUGHTER**
>
> Criminal homicide constitutes manslaughter when:
>   (a) it is committed recklessly; or
>   (b) a homicide which would otherwise be murder is committed under the influence of extreme mental or emotional disturbance for which there is reasonable explanation or excuse. The reasonableness of such explanation or excuse shall be determined from the viewpoint of the person in the actor's situation under the circumstances as he believes them to be. (ALI 1985, *Model Penal Code*)

Other states, probably most, continue to follow the words-can-never-provoke rule. Maryland is one. In *Dennis v. State* (1995), for example, the Maryland Court of Appeals rejected the last-straw rule. John Patrick Dennis married his high school sweetheart Robin when she became pregnant with their child. According to Dennis, he worked hard to support his family, but they ran into money problems because of Robin's illegal drug use and spending habits. Robin moved out of their house, and in with her boyfriend, Dantz. After learning that Robin and Dantz did drugs in front of their son, Dennis became really agitated. He went to confront them at Dantz's. When he got there, he saw Robin and Dantz through the window; they were hugging, and maybe getting "sexual." Dennis claims to have blacked out at that point. Robin called the police, screaming that Dantz was dead (690).

Dennis was convicted of voluntary manslaughter. The trial court rejected his claim that he was adequately provoked. He appealed. The Court of Appeals affirmed, rejecting the last-straw rule, and held that "rejected taunts and verbal assaults" aren't "adequate provocation, even when taking on their humiliating and enraging character from antecedent events" (689).

Provocation by Intimates According to the common-law **paramour rule,** a husband who caught his wife in the act of adultery had adequate provocation to kill: "There could be no greater provocation than this." Some state statutes went further than the common-law rule; they called paramour killings justifiable homicide. In the early days, the rule was only available to husbands. Today, it applies to both.

Many cases have held that it's voluntary manslaughter for a spouse to kill the adulterous spouse, the paramour, or both, if the killing took place in the first heat of passion following the sight of the adultery.

Many voluntary manslaughter cases in states that have adopted these reforms, which are aimed at expanding the reach of common law "adequate" provocation to include the definitions we've just discussed, *don't* involve "sordid affairs and bedside confrontations." According to Professor Victoria Nourse (1997), significant numbers of cases in her empirical study of states who've adopted the MPC extreme mental or emotional disturbance manslaughter provision (quoted earlier)

> involved no sexual infidelity whatsoever, but only the desire of the killer's victim to leave a miserable relationship. Reform has permitted juries to return a manslaughter verdict in cases where the defendant claims passion because the victim left, moved the furniture out, planned a divorce, or sought a protective order (1332).
>
> Even infidelity has been transformed under reform's gaze into something quite different from the sexual betrayal we might expect—it is the infidelity of a fiancé who danced with another, of a girlfriend who decided to date someone else, and of the divorcee found pursuing a new relationship months after the final decree. (1332–33)

Commonwealth v. Schnopps (1983) involved dancing, an affair, and a spouse who wanted to leave. The court wasn't "reform" minded; it rejected the spouse's arguments of adequate provocation and found him guilty of first-degree murder.

CASE   *Did He Commit First-Degree Murder?*

Commonwealth v. Schnopps
459 N.E.2d 98 (Mass. 1983)

HISTORY

George Schnopps, the defendant, was convicted before the Superior Court, Berkshire County, Massachusetts, of first-degree murder of his estranged wife and of unlawfully carrying a firearm. At a retrial, the defendant, Schnopps, again was convicted of first-degree murder, and he appealed again. The Massachusetts Supreme Judicial Court affirmed.

ABRAMS, J.

FACTS

On October 13, 1979, George Schnopps fatally shot his wife of fourteen years. The victim and Schnopps began having marital problems approximately six months earlier when Schnopps became suspicious that his wife was seeing another man. Schnopps and his wife argued during this period over his suspicion that she had a relationship with a particular man, whom Schnopps regarded as a "bum." On a few occasions Schnopps threatened to harm his wife with scissors, with a knife, with a shotgun, and with a plastic pistol.

A few days prior to the slaying, Schnopps threatened to make his wife suffer as "she had never suffered before." However, there is no evidence that Schnopps physically harmed the victim prior to October 13.

On October 12, 1979, while at work, Schnopps asked a coworker to buy him a gun. He told the coworker he had been receiving threatening telephone calls. After work, Schnopps and the coworker went to Pownal, Vermont, where the coworker purchased a .22 caliber pistol and a box of ammunition for the defendant. Schnopps purchased a starter pistol to scare the caller if there was an attempted break-in. Schnopps stated he wanted to protect himself and his son, who had moved back with him.

Schnopps and his coworker had some drinks at a Vermont bar. The coworker instructed Schnopps in the use of the .22 caliber pistol. Schnopps paid his coworker for the gun and the ammunition. While at the bar Schnopps told the coworker that he was "mad enough to kill." The coworker asked Schnopps "if he was going to get in any trouble with the gun." Schnopps replied that "a bullet was too good for her, he would choke her to death." Schnopps testified that his wife had left him three weeks prior to the slaying. He claims that he first became aware of problems in his fourteen-year marriage at a point about six months before the slaying. According to Schnopps, on that occasion he took his wife to a club to dance, and she spent the evening dancing with a coworker.

On arriving home, Schnopps and his wife argued over her conduct. She told him that she no longer loved him and that she wanted a divorce. Schnopps became very upset. He admitted that he took out his shotgun during the course of this argument, but he denied that he intended to use it.

During the next few months, Schnopps argued frequently with his wife. Schnopps accused her of seeing another man, but she steadfastly denied the accusations. On more than one occasion Schnopps threatened his wife with physical harm. He testified he never intended to hurt his wife but only wanted to scare her so that she would end the relationship with her coworker.

One day in September 1979, Schnopps became aware that the suspected boyfriend used a "signal" in telephoning Schnopps' wife. Schnopps used the signal, and his wife answered the phone with "Hi, Lover." She hung up immediately when she recognized Schnopps' voice. That afternoon she did not return home. Later that evening, she informed Schnopps by telephone that she had moved to her mother's house and that she had the children with her.

On that day she moved to her mother's home and took their three children with her. (The children were two daughters, age thirteen and age four, and a son, age eleven.)

On October 6, the son returned to his father's home. She told Schnopps she would not return to their home. Thereafter she "froze me out," and would not talk to him. During this period, Schnopps spoke with a lawyer about a divorce and was told that he had a good chance of getting custody of the children, due to his wife's "desertion and adultery."

On the day of the slaying, Schnopps told a neighbor he was going to call his wife and have her come down to pick up some things. He said he was thinking of letting his wife have the apartment. This was the first time Schnopps indicated he might leave the apartment. He asked the neighbor to keep the youngest child with her if his wife brought her so he could talk with his wife. Schnopps had asked his wife to come to their home and talk over their marital difficulties.

Schnopps told his wife that he wanted his children at home, and that he wanted the family to remain intact. Schnopps cried during the conversation, and begged his wife to let the children live with him and to keep their family together.

His wife replied, "No, I am going to court, you are going to give me all the furniture, you are going to have to get the Hell out of here, you won't have nothing." Then, pointing to her crotch, she said, "You will never touch this again, because I have got something bigger and better for it."

Schnopps said that these words "cracked" him. He explained that everything went "around" in his head, that he saw "stars." He went "toward the guns in the dining room." He asked his wife, "Why don't you try" (to salvage the marriage). He told her, "I have nothing more to live for," but she replied, "Never, I am never coming back to you."

The victim jumped up to leave and Schnopps shot her. He was seated at that time. He told her she would never love anyone else. After shooting the victim, Schnopps said, "I want to go with you," and he shot himself.

Shortly before 3 P.M., Schnopps called a neighbor and said he had shot his wife and also had tried to kill himself. Schnopps told the first person to arrive at his apartment that he shot his wife "because of what she had done to him."

Neighbors notified the police of the slaying. On their arrival, Schnopps asked an officer to check to see if his wife had died. The officer told him that she had, and he replied, "Good." A police officer took Schnopps to a hospital for treatment of his wounds. The officer had known Schnopps for twenty-nine years. Schnopps said to the officer that he would not hurt a fly. The officer advised Schnopps not to say anything until he spoke with a lawyer.

Schnopps then said, "The devil made me do it." The officer repeated his warning at least three times. Schnopps said that he "loved his wife and his children." He added, "Just between you and I, . . . I did it because she was cheating on me." The victim died of three gunshot wounds, to the heart and lungs. Ballistic evidence indicated that the gun was fired within two to four feet of the victim. The evidence also indicated that one shot had been fired while the victim was on the floor.

The defense offered evidence from friends and coworkers who noticed a deterioration in Schnopps's physical and emotional health after the victim had left Schnopps. Schnopps wept at work and at home; he did not eat or sleep well; he was distracted and agitated. On two occasions, he was taken home early by supervisors because of emotional upset and agitation. He was drinking.

Schnopps was diagnosed at a local hospital as suffering from a "severe anxiety state." He was given Valium. Schnopps claimed he was receiving threatening telephone calls.

Schnopps and the Commonwealth each offered expert testimony on the issue of criminal responsibility.

Schnopps's expert claimed Schnopps was suffering from a "major affective disorder, a major depression," a "psychotic condition," at the time of the slaying. The expert was of the opinion Schnopps was not criminally responsible.

The Commonwealth's expert claimed that Schnopps's depression was a grief reaction, a reaction generally associated with death. The expert was of the opinion Schnopps was grieving over the breakup of his marriage, but that he was criminally responsible.

The judge instructed the jurors on every possible verdict available on the evidence. The jurors were told they could return a verdict of murder in the first degree on the ground of deliberately premeditated malice aforethought; murder in the second degree; manslaughter; not guilty by reason of insanity; or not guilty.

OPINION

On appeal, Schnopps does not now quarrel with that range of possible verdicts nor with the instruction which the trial court gave to the jury. . . . Nor does . . . Schnopps now dispute that there may be some view of . . . some of the evidence which might support the verdict returned in this matter.

Rather, Schnopps claims that his case is "not of the nature that judges and juries, in weighing evidence, ordinarily equate with murder in the first degree." Schnopps therefore concludes that this is an appropriate case in which to exercise our power under G.L. c. 278, § 33E. We do not agree.

Pursuant to G.L. c. 278, § 33E, we consider whether the verdict of murder in the first degree was against the weight of the evidence, considered in a large or nontechnical sense. Our power under § 33E is to be used with restraint.

Moreover, "we do not sit as a second jury to pass anew on the question of Schnopps's guilt." Schnopps argues that the evidence as a whole demonstrates that his wife was the emotional aggressor, and that her conduct shattered him and destroyed him as a husband and a father. Schnopps points to the fact that he was not a hoodlum or gangster, that he had no prior criminal record, and that he had a "good relationship" with his wife prior to the last six months of their marriage. Schnopps concludes these factors should be sufficient to entitle him to a new trial or the entry of a verdict of a lesser degree of guilt.

The Commonwealth argues that the evidence is more than ample to sustain the verdict. The Commonwealth points out that at the time of the killing there was not a good relationship between the parties; that Schnopps had threatened to harm his wife physically on several occasions; and that he had threatened to kill his wife. Schnopps obtained a gun and ammunition the day before the killing.

Schnopps arranged to have his younger child cared for by a neighbor when his wife came to see him. The jury could have found that Schnopps lured his wife to the apartment by suggesting that he might leave and let her live in it with the children. The evidence permits a finding that the killing occurred within a few minutes of the victim's arrival at Schnopps's apartment and before she had time to take off her jacket.

From the facts, the jury could infer that Schnopps had planned to kill his wife on October 13, and that the killing was not the spontaneous result of the quarrel but was the result of a deliberately premeditated plan to murder his wife almost as soon as she arrived.

Ballistic evidence indicated that as the victim was lying on the floor, a third bullet was fired into her. From the number of wounds, the type of weapon used, as well as the effort made to procure the weapon, the jurors could find that Schnopps had "a conscious and fixed purpose to kill continuing for a length of time." If conflicting inferences are possible, "it is for the jury to determine where the truth lies." There was ample evidence which suggested the jurors' conclusion that Schnopps acted with deliberately premeditated malice aforethought.

On appeal, Schnopps complains that the prosecutor's summation, which stressed that premeditated murder requires "a thought and an act," could have confused the jurors by suggesting that if "at any time earlier Schnopps merely thought about killing that person," that was sufficient to constitute deliberately "premeditated malice aforethought."

We do not read the prosecutor's argument as suggesting that conclusion. The prosecutor focused on the Commonwealth's evidence of deliberately premeditated malice aforethought throughout his argument. There was no error.

In any event, the argument, read as a whole, does not create a "substantial likelihood of a miscarriage of justice." Schnopps's domestic difficulties were fully explored before the jury. The jurors rejected Schnopps's claim that his domestic difficulties were an adequate ground to return a verdict of a lesser degree of guilt. The degree of guilt, of course, is a jury determination. The evidence supports a conclusion that Schnopps, angered by his wife's conduct, shot her with deliberately premeditated malice aforethought.

The jurors were in the best position to determine whether the domestic difficulties were so egregious as to require a verdict of a lesser degree of guilt. We conclude, on review of the record as a whole, that there is no reason for us to order a new trial or direct the entry of a lesser verdict.

Judgment AFFIRMED.

Questions

1. If you were a juror, could you in good conscience say that Schnopps was adequately provoked? Explain your answer, relying on the facts in the case, the court's opinion, and the text prior to the excerpt.

2. If so, was it the adultery that provoked him or the provocative words his wife used to describe her adulterous relationship?

3. Do you think the prohibition against provocative words makes sense?

4. If you were writing a voluntary manslaughter law, state the elements of the offense as you believe they should be.

EXPLORING FURTHER

Provocation

Who's a "Reasonable Person"?

People v. Washington (1976)

FACTS Merle Francis Washington shot his gay partner following a lover's quarrel brought on by the victim's unfaithfulness. The jury was instructed that to reduce the homicide from murder to manslaughter upon the ground of sudden quarrel or heat of passion, the conduct must be tested by the ordinarily reasonable man test.

Washington argued that the instruction was in error because

> Homosexuals are not at present a curiosity or a rare commodity. They are a distinct third sexual class between that of male and female, are present in almost every field of endeavor, and are fast achieving a guarded recognition not formerly accorded them. The heat of their passions in dealing with one another should not be tested by standards applicable to the average man or the average woman, since they are aberrant hybrids, with an obvious diminished capacity.

Washington argued that since the evidence showed that

> he was acting as a servient homosexual during the period of his relationship with the victim, that his heat of passion should have been tested, either by a standard applicable to a female, or a standard applicable to the average homosexual, and that it was prejudicial error to instruct the jury to determine his heat of passion defense by standards applicable to the average male.

DECISION The court disagreed:

> In the present condition of our law it is left to the jurors to say whether or not the facts and circumstances in evidence are sufficient to lead them to believe that the defendant did, or to create a reasonable doubt in their minds as to whether or not he did, commit his offense under a heat of passion.

> The jury is further to be admonished and advised by the court that this heat of passion must be such a passion as would naturally be aroused in the mind of an ordinarily reasonable person under the given facts and circumstances, and that, consequently, no defendant may set up his own standard of conduct and justify or excuse himself because in fact his passions were aroused, unless further the jury believe that the facts and circumstances were sufficient to arouse the passions of the ordinarily reasonable man.

> Thus no man of extremely violent passion could so justify or excuse himself if the exciting cause be not adequate, nor could an excessively cowardly man justify himself unless the circumstances were such as to arouse the fears of the ordinarily courageous man. Still further, while the conduct of the defendant is to be measured by that of the ordinarily reasonable man placed in identical circumstances, the jury is properly to be told that the exciting cause must be such as would naturally tend to arouse the passion of the ordinarily reasonable man.

 Go to the Criminal Law 9e website for the full text of the Exploring Further excerpt (see excerpt on provocation) and to find Exercise 9.3 to learn more about voluntary manslaughter: www.thomsonedu.com/criminaljustice/samaha.

Involuntary Manslaughter

The central elements in **involuntary manslaughter** are its *actus reus* (voluntary act or omission) and its *mens rea* (unintentional killing). Of course, as in all crimes of criminal conduct causing criminal harm, involuntary manslaughter also includes the elements of causation and resulting harm (death). We won't repeat our discussion of causation from Chapter 4 here.

We'll examine two kinds of involuntary manslaughter:

1. *Criminal negligence manslaughter* Despite its name, it includes the mental elements of both recklessness and negligence.

2. **Unlawful act manslaughter** (also called misdemeanor manslaughter) This is for deaths that occur during the commission of unlawful acts.

Criminal Negligence/Vehicular/Firearms Manslaughter   Although it goes by the name of criminal negligence manslaughter in some statutes and cases, in reality, criminal negligence manslaughter consists of two elements:

1. *Actus reus* The defendant's acts create a high (substantial and unjustifiable) risk of death or serious bodily injury.

2. *Mens rea* The defendant is aware the risk of death or serious bodily injury is high but commits the acts anyway.

Recall that when you're acting recklessly, you *know* you're creating a high risk of harm; when you're acting negligently, you *should*, but don't, know you're creating the risk. There may be confusion in the labels, and in the minds of legislators and judges, but the reality is that most of the time, the mental element is recklessness. So if you find it difficult to keep the difference clear in your mind, you have company in high places. When there's a doubt about the meaning, criminal negligence *probably* means criminal recklessness in involuntary manslaughter.

Criminal negligence statutes cover a wide field. Most of the cases involve unintentional deaths caused by operating vehicles and firearms. But they also include practicing medicine, handling explosives, delivering dangerous drugs, allowing vicious animals to run free, failing to care for a sick child, and not providing fire exits in

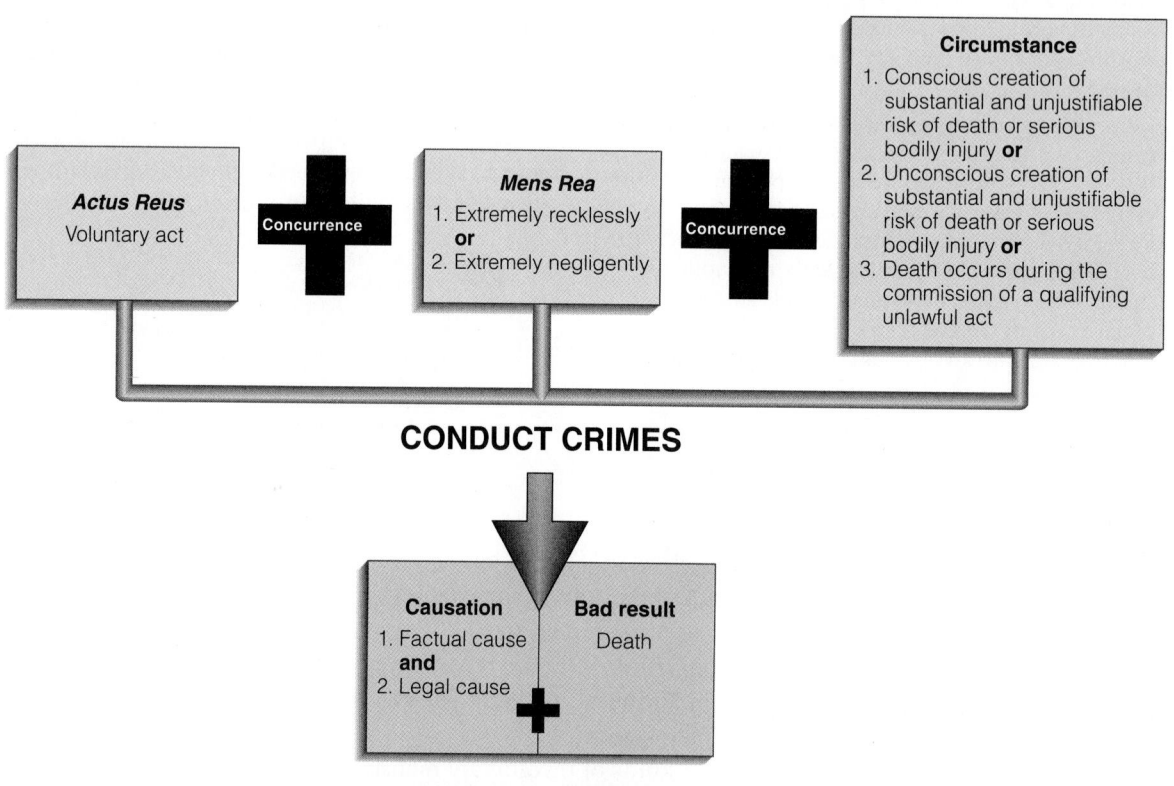

Elements of Involuntary Manslaughter

businesses. In *State v. Mays* (2000), the Ohio Court of Appeals applied its vehicular homicide statute to 19-year-old Nicholas Mays, who killed his victim when he "messed with" him by "nudging" him with his car.

Did He Commit Aggravated Vehicular Homicide?

State v. Mays
743 N.E.2d 447 (OhioApp. 2000)

HISTORY

Upon convictions entered pursuant to guilty pleas, Nicholas Mays, defendant, was sentenced by the Hamilton County Court of Common Pleas to five years' incarceration for aggravated vehicular homicide. He appealed. The Ohio Court of Appeals affirmed in part, and reversed and remanded in part.

DOAN, J.

FACTS

On August 19, 1999, nineteen-year-old Mays was operating an automobile in which his cousin was a passenger. At approximately 1:45 A.M., they saw a pedestrian, later identified as Michael Boumer, in a grocery store parking lot. According to Mays, Boumer appeared to be intoxicated. (Investigating officers confirmed that Boumer had consumed some alcohol. However, the record also indicates that Boumer was mentally handicapped.) The two young men decided that they would "mess with" Boumer by appearing to offer him a ride. Mays intended to nudge Boumer with the vehicle and then drive away.

Mays did drive the vehicle in the direction of Boumer, but instead of merely nudging him, he inadvertently ran over him, causing him fatal injuries. Upon seeing that Boumer was injured, Mays drove to another location and called for emergency aid. He then went to a car wash, where he cleaned the vehicle to remove evidence of the fatal collision.

On the day after the incident, Mays took a planned trip to Florida, during which his mother convinced him that he should report his involvement in the crime. Mays did so, returning to Cincinnati and giving a full confession to the police.

OPINION

[The Ohio Revised Code vehicular homicide statute (Section 2903.06) reads in part:

(A) No person, while operating or participating in the operation of a motor vehicle, motorcycle, snowmobile, locomotive, watercraft, or aircraft, shall cause the death of another or the unlawful termination of another's pregnancy in any of the following ways:

(2) Recklessly;

(3) Negligently;

(1) Whoever violates division (A) . . . (2) of this section is guilty of aggravated vehicular homicide and shall be punished as provided in divisions (B)(1) (b) of this section. . . .

(b) Except as otherwise provided in this division, aggravated vehicular homicide committed in violation of division (A)(2) of this section is a felony of the third degree. . . . In addition to any other sanctions imposed, the court shall suspend the offender's driver's license, commercial driver's license, temporary instruction permit, probationary license, or nonresident operating privilege for a definite period of three years to life. . . .

(2) Whoever violates division (A)(3) of this section is guilty of vehicular homicide. Except as otherwise provided in this division, vehicular homicide is a misdemeanor of the first degree. . . .]

. . . Mays first argues that the court erred in imposing terms of incarceration greater than the minimum. To impose a prison term more than the minimum for the offender's first prison term, the court must find that the minimum sentence would demean the seriousness of the offense or not adequately protect the public from future crime. Here, the trial court found both to be applicable.

We hold that the trial court's finding with respect to the seriousness of the offenses is supported by the record. Mays conceded that his intention was to "mess with" a person whom he perceived to be impaired in some way, and in doing so, he deprived the thirty-nine-year-old victim of his life. Mays did not immediately seek help for Boumer, but instead thought first of his own interest in evading detection for the crime. His concealment of the crime was compounded when he washed the car and left the jurisdiction. Under these circumstances, the trial court reasonably concluded that the minimum term would demean the seriousness of the offenses. Because the trial court's finding with respect to the seriousness of the offenses was proper, we need not address Mays's argument concerning the adequate protection of the public.

In his second argument, Mays claims that the trial court erred in imposing the maximum sentence for aggravated vehicular homicide. Before imposing the maximum term of incarceration for an offense, the court must find that the offender has committed the worst form of the offense, poses the greatest likelihood of recidivism, or is of a certain class of repeat offenders. In the case at bar, the court found that Mays had committed the worst form of aggravated vehicular homicide. We disagree.

In past cases, this court has grappled with the somewhat vague concept of what constitutes the "worst form" of an offense. And while the concept is difficult to define in concrete terms, we hold that Mays's conduct in the case at bar did not constitute the worst form of aggravated vehicular homicide. Though the evidence certainly indicates that Mays exercised extremely poor judgment in carrying out his wish to "mess with" Boumer, there is no indication that he harbored any malice toward the victim.

Instead, the record indicates that Mays's conduct started as a reckless, poorly conceived prank and ended in tragedy. And while we in no way wish to minimize the loss of a human life or to condone Mays's actions, this is not the type of conduct for which the legislature has reserved the maximum sentence.

Furthermore, although he admittedly thought of his own interests before seeking help for Boumer, Mays did take steps to ensure that emergency personnel were notified promptly. His actions therefore did not reflect an utter lack of concern for Boumer or otherwise demonstrate a perversity of character that would justify the imposition of the maximum sentence.

Further, there is no indication that the victim suffered for a prolonged period of time before he died or suffered to a greater degree than any other victim of a vehicular homicide.

Finally, Mays surrendered to authorities and confessed to the crimes. Under these circumstances, we cannot say that Mays committed the worst form of the offense within the meaning of R.C. 2929.14(C). We therefore hold that the trial court erred in imposing the maximum term for that offense.

Mays next argues that the trial court erred in imposing consecutive sentences. To impose consecutive terms of imprisonment, the court must find that consecutive sentences are necessary to protect the public from future crime and that consecutive sentences are not disproportionate to the offender's conduct and to the danger the offender poses to the public.

The trial court must also find one of the following:

(1) that the offenses occurred while the offender was under community control;

(2) that the harm caused was great or unusual or

(3) that the offender's criminal history requires consecutive sentences.

Of the latter factors, the court in the instant case found that the harm caused was unusual or great.

We agree with Mays that the trial court's findings with respect to consecutive sentences are not supported by the record. Concerning the protection of the public from future crime, Mays's criminal record included no adult convictions and only one juvenile delinquency adjudication. Thus, there is little indication that Mays is likely to recidivate.

Also, the trial court revoked Mays's operator's license, thereby reducing the likelihood that future vehicular offenses would occur.

Further, as to the finding that consecutive terms were not disproportionate to Mays's conduct and to the danger that he posed to the public, we have already noted that Mays's conduct, while reckless and ill-conceived, was not the product of malice.

Given the revocation of Mays's license, his confession, and his demonstrated remorse, the conduct also appears not likely to be repeated. The investigating officers and the author of the presentence-investigation report indicated that Mays was genuinely remorseful.

Finally, the harm caused by the offense, while senseless and tragic, was not greater than the harm caused in every other aggravated-vehicular-homicide case. Under these circumstances, we hold that the trial court erred in imposing consecutive sentences.

Having held that the trial court erred in imposing the maximum sentence for the aggravated vehicular homicide and in otherwise imposing consecutive sentences, we hereby reverse those parts of the trial court's judgment and remand the cause for resentencing in accordance with law.

Judgment affirmed in part, reversed in part and cause remanded.

DISSENT

HILDEBRANDT, P.J.

. . . Mays senselessly took the life of the victim because he wished to "mess with" him. The wantonness of that conduct alone could have justified the trial court in imposing the maximum sentence. However, Mays compounded his misconduct by leaving the scene of the collision, thereby making it clear that he valued his own interest in evading detection above the life of Boumer. The majority concedes as much, yet persists in holding that Mays did not commit the worst form of the offense. His eventual call for emergency aid and his subsequent remorse for his actions did not erase the fact that his conduct was egregious and deserving of the greatest punishment.

For many of the same reasons, I believe that the imposition of consecutive sentences was proper. The utter lack of regard for human life that Mays exhibited by using his automobile to "mess with" a person whom he believed to be impaired provided ample support for the trial court's conclusion that consecutive sentences were necessary to prevent future crimes and to protect the public. Moreover, the fact that death is caused in all aggravated-vehicular-homicide cases should not prevent a finding that the harm caused in the instant case was great or unusual. Mays's

CHAPTER 9/CRIMES AGAINST PERSONS I: CRIMINAL HOMICIDE

taking of a life in such a wanton manner justified the court in finding that the harm done was great or unusual. . . . In my view, nine years of incarceration is not excessive when weighed against the taking of a human life under these circumstances. I therefore respectfully dissent in part.

Questions

1. How does the Ohio statute define *vehicular homicide*?

2. Relying on the evidence in the case and referring to the Ohio provision, explain why Nicholas Mays was guilty of aggravated vehicular homicide.

3. How would you define *vehicular homicide*? Defend your definition.

4. Do you agree with the majority opinion's reasons for reversing the sentence? Or do the dissent and the trial court have the better arguments? Back up your answer.

 Go to the Criminal Law 9e website to find Exercise 9.4 and learn more about involuntary manslaughter: www.thomsonedu.com/criminaljustice/samaha.

Unlawful Act Manslaughter   In 1260, long before the division between murder and manslaughter was created by the common-law judges, the great jurist Bracton wrote that unintended deaths during unlawful acts are criminal homicides. Some time after the judges created the offense of manslaughter, unlawful act homicides became a form of involuntary manslaughter. In modern times, statutes have restricted unlawful act manslaughter because it's considered too harsh. In fact, there's a trend to abolish unlawful act manslaughter, leaving criminal negligent manslaughter as the only kind of involuntary manslaughter.

Unlawful acts taken literally could include everything from committing felonies, misdemeanors, and even traffic violations, city ordinances, administrative crimes, and noncriminal wrongs, such as civil trespass and other torts (Chapter 1). Misdemeanors are certainly included among these possibly unlawful acts; that's why unlawful act manslaughter is often called "misdemeanor manslaughter."

The most common misdemeanors that come up in the cases are speeding and drunk driving. Another is ordinary battery, mostly hitting someone who dies from the blow. This is what happened in *People v. Datema* (1995). Greg and Pamela Datema were sitting around in their living room with friends talking, smoking pot, and drinking.

The conversation turned to their previous romances. Pam and Greg started arguing about the people they'd slept with. Pam claimed she'd had sex with some of her paramours in front of their sons. Greg slapped her in the face—once. Pam slumped back; the other three thought she'd passed out. After 10 minutes, they got worried. When they shook her and she didn't wake up, they called for an ambulance. Pam never regained consciousness.

The medical examiner found that Pam Datema had a blood-alcohol level between 0.03 and 0.05 percent. He stated that death was caused by a tear in an artery in the head that occurred as a result of Greg's slap:

> Most people, when slapped, reflexively stiffen their necks and avoid serious injury. Occasionally, however, when a person is intoxicated, the reflexes do not react quickly enough, and a blow could result in a tearing. Generally, a higher blood-alcohol level is necessary, but the ingested marijuana, which was not able to be tested, was undoubtedly a contributing factor. (274)

There's a trend toward abolishing unlawful act manslaughter; about half of the states have already done so (LaFave 2003a, 801). Where it still exists, the states have placed limits on it. Most states limit the underlying offense to *mala in se* offenses. Recall *mala in se* offenses are ones that are inherently evil—for example, the battery in *People v. Datema* and the "nudge" in *State v. Mays*. To count an offense as a *malum prohibitum* crime, death has to be a foreseeable consequence of the unlawful act. In *Todd v. State* (1992), Todd ran off with the church collection plate. A congregation member jumped in his car and pursued the thief. He suffered a heart attack, hit a tree, and died of cardiac arrest. The court held this wasn't a case of unlawful act manslaughter because death is not a foreseeable risk in petty theft.

SUMMARY

I. Killing is different.
  A. It's the most serious of all crimes.
  B. Criminal homicides are very rare events.

II. The meaning of "person" or "human being" is integral to homicide law.
  A. Killing another person is central to criminal homicide liability, because it defines who is a victim.
  B. Throughout most of history, homicide law followed the born alive rule, meaning that a baby had to be "born alive" and capable of breathing and maintaining a heartbeat on its own to be a victim of homicide.
  C. Defining when life ends has become more and more complex with advances in organ transplants and artificial life support.
  D. The Uniform Brain Death Act provides that an individual who has suffered irreversible cessation of all brain functions, including those of the brain stem, is dead.

III. *Murder* Common law and modern criminal codes recognized two kinds of homicide:
  A. Murder
  B. Manslaughter

IV. The history of murder
  A. English common-law judges first divided homicide into two broad categories, criminal and noncriminal.
  B. By the 1550s, common-law judges further divided criminal homicide into murder and manslaughter and noncriminal homicide into justifiable and excusable homicide.
  C. In the 1550s, the definition of killing with "malice aforethought" separated murder as intentional or unintentional.
  D. By 1700, the English law of homicide recognized three kinds of homicide:
    1. Justifiable homicide
    2. Excusable homicide
    3. Criminal homicide
  E. Eventually, criminal homicide was divided into murder and manslaughter.
  F. Judges soon added several other murder scenarios, including:
    1. Manslaughter
    2. Deaths occurring during the commission of a felony
    3. Depraved heart murder
    4. Intent-to-cause-serious-bodily-injury murder
  G. "Express" vs. "implied" malice aforethought

1. "Express" malice aforethought was reserved for killings that fit the original meaning of murder—intentional killings planned in advance.
2. "Implied" malice aforethought referred to four additional kinds of murder:
   a. Intentional killings without premeditation or reasonable provocation
   b. Unintentional killings during the commission of felonies
   c. Depraved heart killings
   d. Intent to inflict grievous bodily harm killings

V. *Elements of murder* **Murder is a result crime; therefore, proving murder requires proof beyond a reasonable doubt of these elements:**
   A. *Actus reus* The act of killing is the heart of murder.
   B. *Mens rea* Purpose, knowledge, or extreme recklessness can qualify as the mental element in murder.
   C. *Causation* The act caused death.
   D. *Attendant circumstance* If any exists, it has to be proved.

VI. *Degrees of murder* **Dividing murder into degrees was a continuation of the idea that not all murderers should be executed.**

VII. **First-degree murder**
   A. There are two types of first-degree murder:
      1. Premeditated, deliberate, intent-to-kill murders
      2. Felony murders
   B. First-degree murder is the only crime today in which the death penalty can be imposed.
   C. The death penalty is discretionary in all states where the penalty is authorized.
   D. Since the 1970s, several limits have been placed on the death penalty:
      1. Mandatory death sentences are banned.
      2. Unguided discretionary death penalty decisions are banned.
      3. Mitigating factors are required.
      4. Additional aggravating factors are allowed.
   E. Bifurcation mandates that the death penalty decision be made in two phases:
      1. A trial to determine guilt
      2. A second separate proceeding, after a finding of guilt, to consider the aggravating for, and mitigating factors against, capital punishment
   F. First-degree murder *mens rea* All murder that is perpetrated by willful, deliberate, and premeditated killing is murder in the first degree.
   G. First-degree murder *actus reus* can be critical when it comes to deciding whether to sentence a convicted person to death or to prison for life without parole.

VIII. **Second-degree murder**
   A. The creation of second-degree murder was to limit capital punishment without eliminating it.
   B. Depraved heart murders, unintentional but extremely reckless murders, fall under second-degree murder.
   C. Second-degree murder is sometimes treated as the catchall for all murders that aren't first-degree murders.
   D. Unintentional deaths that occur during the commission of some felonies are called "felony murders" in most states; these felonies include:
      1. Criminal sexual conduct
      2. Kidnapping
      3. Robbery

    4. Arson

    5. Burglary

E. Felony murder *mens rea* does not require the intent to kill or to inflict serious bodily injury; the intent to commit the designated felonies substitutes for the intent to kill or inflict serious bodily injury.

F. Felony murder laws have three rationales:

    1. Deter offenders

    2. Reduce violence

    3. Punish wrongdoers

G. Dangerous felonies

    1. Many states limit felony murder to deaths that occur during the commission of other "dangerous felonies."

    2. The determination of whether felonies are dangerous arises in at least two situations:

       a. Where statutes use the term *inherently dangerous* without defining it

       b. Where statutes have a first-degree felony murder statute and a catchall second-degree murder statute that provides that "all murders not first degree are second-degree murders"

H. Courts use two ways to determine if the felony being committed when the killing occurred was "dangerous" to life:

    1. The inherently dangerous felony approach, in which courts look at the elements of the felony without looking at how it was carried out in the specific case before them to see if the elements amount to a dangerous felony

    2. The case-by-case approach, which weighs the facts and circumstances surrounding the way the felony was committed in the particular case to consider whether it was dangerous to human life

IX. Corporation murder

A. Most criminal codes apply to corporate criminal homicide in the same way that they apply to other crimes committed for the corporation's benefit.

B. Federal prosecutors are reluctant to prosecute corporations for murder because the public hesitates to view corporations as persons.

C. It's extremely rare to prosecute a corporation for murder.

X. Manslaughter

A. Manslaughter is the unlawful killing of another, which may be either

    1. Voluntary upon a sudden heat

    2. Involuntary where one had no intent to do another any personal harm

XI. Voluntary manslaughter

A. Voluntary manslaughter consists of the elements of *actus reus, mens rea,* causation, and death. But it has one element not present in murder, adequate provocation, which is the trigger that sets off the sudden killing of another person.

B. Adequate provocation has to be both subjective and objective:

    1. *Subjective* The defendant herself must be provoked.

    2. *Objective* Provocation has to be reasonable.

C. The common law and many states today recognize four reasonable provocations:

    1. Mutual combat (fighting that goes too far)

    2. Assault and battery

    3. Trespass

    4. Adultery

D. Because voluntary manslaughter is a "heat of passion" killing, courts apply an objective test of cooling-off time: Would a reasonable person under the same circumstances have had time to cool off? If yes, the law views the killings as murders.

E. To prove voluntary manslaughter, the prosecution has to prove that the provocation *caused* the passion *and* the killing.

F. Provocation by words in some states is adequate provocation to kill in the heat of passion, whereas other states have adopted the "last straw" rule or extreme mental or emotional disturbance manslaughter provision.

G. According to the common-law paramour rule, a husband who caught his wife in the act of adultery had adequate provocation to kill.

XII. Involuntary manslaughter

A. There are two kinds of involuntary manslaughter:
1. Criminal negligence manslaughter, consists of two elements:
   a. *Actus reus* The defendant's actions create a high (substantial and unjustifiable) risk of death or serious bodily injury.
   b. *Mens rea* Despite its name, the *mens rea* of involuntary manslaughter is recklessness; namely, the defendant is aware of the risk of death or serious bodily injury is high but commits the acts anyway.
2. Unlawful act manslaughter, which occurs during the commission of unlawful acts (mostly connected with vehicles, such as speeding and drunk driving)

REVIEW QUESTIONS

1. Identify when life begins and ends in order for one to be charged with the killing of a "person."

2. Identify and describe the difference between the two kinds of homicide that modern criminal codes and the MPC recognize.

3. Briefly describe the history of murder law from the time of common-law judges to the four present divisions.

4. Describe the difference between "express" and "implied" malice aforethought.

5. Identify and state the five elements the prosecution has to prove beyond a reasonable doubt.

6. Pennsylvania was the first state to have two degrees of murder. Explain the reasons for the division.

7. Identify and describe two kinds of first-degree murder.

8. According to the U.S. Supreme Court, what four requirements have to be met before the death penalty can be administered?

9. Identify the two parts of a bifurcated trial in capital murder cases. Explain what happens at each of the two stages. When and why is it required?

10. Identify seven aggravating circumstances that can qualify a murder for the death penalty.

11. Identify eight mitigating factors that can disqualify a murder for the death penalty.

12. Explain both specific-intent-plus-real-premeditation-deliberation and the equivalent-of-specific-intent mental attitudes and how they relate to first-degree murder.

13. Explain the difference between depraved heart murders and reckless manslaughter.

14. State the *mens rea* element of felony murder.

15. Identify and explain three rationales for felony murder laws.

16. Why are prosecutors reluctant to charge corporations with murder?

17. Identify the elements of voluntary manslaughter, and explain the difference between murder and voluntary manslaughter.

18. Explain how adequate provocation is both objective and subjective.

19. Identify and give an example of four reasonable provocations that can reduce murder to voluntary manslaughter.

20. Explain the objective test of cooling-off time.

21. Identify, explain, and give an example of the two types of involuntary manslaughter.

KEY TERMS

born-alive rule, p. 275
feticide, p. 277
murder, p. 277
manslaughter, p. 277
justifiable homicide, p. 278
excusable homicide, p. 278
criminal homicide, p. 278
malice aforethought, p. 279
depraved heart murder, p. 279
intent-to-cause-serious-bodily-injury murder, p. 280
"express" malice aforethought, p. 280
"implied" malice aforethought, p. 280
murder *actus reus*, p. 281

murder *mens rea*, p. 282
capital cases, p. 283
bifurcation, p. 283
criteria for decision, p. 283
specific-intent-plus-real-premeditation-deliberation definition, p. 286
equivalent-of-specific-intent definition, p. 287
first-degree murder, p. 292
second-degree murder, p. 295
felony murder, p. 300
third-party exception, p. 302
resisting-victim exception, p. 302
inherently dangerous felony approach, p. 302

case-by-case approach, p. 303
voluntary manslaughter, p. 311
adequate provocation, p. 311
objective test of cooling-off time, p. 312
last-straw rule, p. 313
extreme mental or emotional disturbance, p. 313
paramour rule, p. 314
involuntary manslaughter, p. 317
criminal negligence manslaughter, p. 317
unlawful act manslaughter, p. 318
unlawful act, p. 321

Crimes Against Persons II: Criminal Sexual Conduct, Bodily Injury, and Personal Restraint

MAIN POINTS

- Crimes against persons boil down to four types: taking a life, unwanted sexual invasions, bodily injury, and personal restraint.
- Rape is regarded by the law and society as second only to murder as the most serious crime.
- Under consensual circumstances, behaviors connected with sexual assault are legal, healthy, and desired.
- Criminal law originally recognized two types of sex offenses: rape and sodomy.
- The vast majority of rape victims are raped by men they know.
- Aggravated rape and unarmed acquaintance rape are two classes of rape used in prosecuting defendants accused of rape.
- Until the 1970s, rape was a capital offense.
- The 1970s and 1980s gave way to reform in modern criminal sexual conduct and assault statutes; gender-neutral sex offenses were incorporated, including unwanted sexual penetrations and contacts.
- Most states recognize four degrees of criminal sexual assault or conduct.
- Force and resistance are necessary elements to convict a defendant accused of rape. Actual force isn't required to satisfy the force requirement; the threat of force is enough.
- No resistance is required if victims were incapacitated at the time of the assault by intoxication, mental deficiency, or insanity.
- Rape is a general-intent crime; defendants intended to commit the act defined in the crime.
- Courts vary on whether consent is a defense to sexual assault of adult victims; some recognize negligent mistake, others require reckless mistake, and some adopt a strict liability approach.
- Critics argue that rape is too serious a charge and the penalties are too severe to allow convictions based on negligent, reckless, or no-fault mistakes.
- Statutory rape consists of having sex with minors; force isn't a necessary element because of the immaturity of the victim. Most states define statutory rape as a strict liability crime with regard to the element of the victim's age.
- Assault and battery, although combined in many modern statutes, are two separate crimes. Battery is an unwanted and unjustified offensive touching in which body contact is the central element; assault is either an attempted or a threatened battery and requires no physical contact.
- Stalking, however ancient in practice, is a relatively new *crime*.
- Stalking leads to depression, substance abuse, phobias, anxiety, obsessive-compulsive behaviors, and dissociative disorders in the victim.
- The right of locomotion allows people to come and go as they please; kidnapping and false imprisonment violate that right.

10

ELLER

STATUTORY RAPE

Sex with a minor is a major crime.

A Minor Is Under 18

Sponsored by the California Department of Health Services,
Partnership for Responsible Parenting

0933

© Michael Newman/PhotoEdit

Statutory rape consists of having sex with minors. Statutory rapists don't have to use force; the victim's immaturity takes the place of force. Furthermore, non-consent isn't an element, nor is consent a defense because minors can't legally consent to sex. In other words, statutory rape is a strict liability crime in most states.

Did He Rape Her?

A college student left her class, went to her dormitory room where she drank a martini, and then went to a lounge to wait for her boyfriend. When her boyfriend didn't show up, she went to another dormitory to find a friend, Earl Hassel. She knocked on the door, but no one answered. She tried the doorknob and, finding it unlocked, went in and found a man sleeping on the bed. At first, she thought the man was Hassel, but he turned out to be Hassel's room-mate, Robert Berkowitz. Berkowitz asked her to stay for a while and she agreed. He asked for a backrub and she turned him down. He suggested that she sit on the bed, but she said no and sat on the floor instead.

Berkowitz moved to the floor beside her, lifted up her shirt and bra and massaged her breasts. He then unfastened his pants and unsuccessfully attempted to put his penis in her mouth. They both stood up, and he locked the door. He came back, pushed her onto the bed, and removed her undergarments from one leg. He then penetrated her vagina with his penis.

(continued)

After withdrawing and ejaculating on her stomach, he stated, "Wow, I guess we just got carried away," to which she responded, "No, we didn't get carried away, you got carried away." ⊚

(COMMONWEALTH V. BERKOWITZ 1994)

Rape is second only to murder in being regarded by law and society as the most serious crime. This isn't just true today. From colonial times until 1977, when the U.S. Supreme Court declared it was cruel and unusual punishment (Chapter 2; *Coker v. Georgia* 1977), rape was punishable by death in several states. Rape is a serious crime even if victims suffer no physical injury, not even minor cuts and bruises. That's because rape violates intimacy and autonomy in a way that physical injuries can't. Even less-invasive sexually generated touching, such as pinching buttocks or fondling breasts, is treated as a serious felony.

Rape and other sexual assaults are different from all other felonies in one very important respect. Under other circumstances, the behaviors connected with them aren't just legal, they're healthy and desired. One of the most critical problems in sex offenses is to distinguish flirting and seduction from sexual assault. In prosecuting the grave crimes against individual autonomy and violence involved in these offenses, we don't want to inhibit the healthy pursuit of consensual, desirable, healthy, legal sexual activity.

We devote most of this chapter to the elements of rape and other sexual assaults. But you'll also learn a little bit about the elements of two other kinds of crimes against persons—nonsexual assaults and bodily injury (battery, its close relative assault, and stalking)—and criminal restraints on liberty (kidnapping and false imprisonment). Most of these crimes can be result crimes, in which case, they include elements of causing a result as well as act, state of mind, and attendant circumstance elements. As we did in homicide, we'll leave discussion of the elements of causation and result to what you've already learned in the "Principle of Causation" section of Chapter 4. Here, we'll concentrate on the act or omission, the state of mind, and frequently the attendant circumstance elements.

SEX OFFENSES

Originally, the criminal law recognized only two sex offenses—rape and sodomy. **Common-law rape** was strictly limited to intentional, forced, nonconsensual, heterosexual vaginal penetration. It was aimed at the traditional view of rape: a male stranger leaps from the shadows at night and sexually attacks a defenseless woman. Legally, men couldn't rape their wives. **Common-law sodomy** meant anal intercourse between two males.

Modern court opinions have relaxed the strict definitions of rape, and **sexual assault,** or **criminal sexual conduct, statutes** enacted in the 1970s and the 1980s (discussed below) have expanded the definition of sex offenses to embrace a wide range of nonconsensual penetrations and contacts, even if they fall far short of violent. Statutes and cases refer to sex offenses as either "sexual assault" or "criminal sexual conduct." In the text, we'll use the terms interchangeably.

These reforms in sex offense law were brought about because of a dirty secret finally made public: The vast majority of rape victims are raped by men they know. In this chapter, we'll distinguish between two kinds of rape: (1) **aggravated rape**—rape by strangers or men with weapons who physically injure their victims—and **unarmed acquaintance rape**—nonconsensual sex between "dates, lovers, neighbors, co-workers, employers, and so on" (Bryden 2000, 318).

The criminal justice system deals fairly well with aggravated rapes, but it has failed miserably when it comes to unarmed acquaintance rapes. Why? Several reasons.

- Victims aren't likely to report them, or they don't recognize them as rapes.
- When victims do report them, the police are less likely to believe them than the victims of aggravated rape.
- Prosecutors are less likely to charge unarmed acquaintance rapists.
- Juries are less likely to convict them.
- Unarmed acquaintance rapists are likely to escape punishment if their victims don't follow the rules of middle-class morality.

According to Professor David P. Bryden's excellent article "Redefining Rape" (2000):

> An acquaintance rapist is most likely to escape justice if his victim violated traditional norms of female morality and prudence: for example, by engaging in casual sex, drinking heavily, or hitchhiking. When the victim is a norm-violating woman, people often blame her rather than the rapist. (318)

The criminal justice system's poor performance in dealing with unarmed acquaintance rapes would be a serious problem in any case, but it's made worse by the social reality that the overwhelming number of rapes are acquaintance rapes. In one survey of women who didn't report rapes to the police, more than 80 percent of the women said they were raped by men they knew (Williams 1984). In three separate surveys of college women, one in five reported being "physically forced" to have sexual intercourse by her date (Foreman 1986, 27).

Another aspect of the social reality of rape is the substantial number of rapes committed against men (McMullen 1990). It's almost impossible to get details about male rape victims. The FBI's Uniform Crime Reports, the most widely cited statistics of crimes reported to the police, doesn't break down the numbers of rape victims by gender. The National Crime Victim Survey, the most thorough government victimization survey, reports that about 8 percent of sexual assault victims are males, but it includes no further details. A few scattered numbers from rape counseling and rape crisis centers report between 8 and 10 percent of their clients are men (Rochman n.d.).

To learn more about how the law treats rape, in this section we'll study the history of rape law; statutes defining criminal sexual conduct; the elements of modern rape law; statutory rape; and how the law grades the seriousness of sex offenses and the penalties it prescribes for them.

The History of Rape Law

As early as the year 800, rape was a capital offense in Anglo-Saxon England. In 1769, William Blackstone, the leading 18th-century authority on the common law in both England and the colonies, defined *common-law rape* as the "carnal knowledge of a woman [sexual intercourse] forcibly and against her will" (210). This definition boiled down to four elements:

1. Sexual intercourse by force or a threat of severe bodily harm (*actus reus*)

2. Intentional vaginal intercourse (*mens rea*)

3. Intercourse between a man and a woman who wasn't his wife (attendant circumstance)

4. Intercourse without the woman's consent (attendant circumstance)

The common law required proof beyond a reasonable doubt of all four elements because, as Lord Hale, the highly regarded 17th-century lawyer and legal scholar of the criminal law, noted:

> It is true that rape is a most detestable crime, and therefore ought severely and impartially to be punished; but it must be remembered, that it is an accusation easy to be made, hard to be proved, and harder to be defended by the party accused, though innocent. . . .
>
> The heinousness of the offence many times transporting the judge and jury with so much indignation, that they are overhastily carried to the conviction of the person accused thereof, by the confident testimony of sometimes false and malicious witnesses. (Blackstone 1769, 215)

In common-law trials, rape victims were allowed to testify against accused rapists; it was up to the jury to decide whether to believe them. But the victim's credibility depended on three conditions, always difficult (and often impossible) to satisfy:

1. Her chastity

2. Whether she promptly reported the rape

3. Whether other witnesses corroborated the rape

Blackstone (1769) talked tough enough when he asserted that even prostitutes could be of good fame, but he undermined his own words when he added this warning about victim witnesses:

> If the ravished be of evil fame, and stand unsupported by others; if she concealed the injury for any considerable time after she had opportunity to complain; if the place where the fact was alleged to be committed, was where it was possible she might have been heard, and she made no outcry; these and the like circumstances carry a strong, but not conclusive, presumption that her testimony is false or feigned. (213–14)

Criminal Sexual Conduct Statutes

The 1970s and 1980s were a time of major reform in the law of sex offenses. First, states made changes to rape prosecution procedures that had been in effect since the 1600s. Many states abolished the **corroboration rule** that required the prosecution to back up rape victims' testimony with that of other witnesses (rarely possible to obtain). Also, most states passed **rape shield statutes,** which banned introducing evidence of victims' past sexual conduct. Many states also relaxed the **prompt-reporting rule** that banned prosecution unless women promptly reported rapes.

States also made changes in the definition of rape. For example, all but a few states abolished the **marital rape exception,** the old common-law rule that husbands couldn't rape their wives.

Sexual assault statutes have also shifted the emphasis away from whether there was consent by the victim to unwanted advances by the perpetrator. For example, the Pennsylvania Superior Court, in *Commonwealth v. Mlinarich* (1985), ruled that the common-law emphasis on lack of consent had "worked to the unfair disadvantage of the woman who, when threatened with violence, chose quite rationally to submit to her assailant's advances rather than risk death or serious bodily injury."

The MPC (ALI 1985 2:279–81) eliminated consent as an element in rape because of its "disproportionate emphasis upon objective manifestations by the woman." But the drafters of the code also recognized that a complex relationship exists between force and consent. Unlike the acts in all other criminal assaults, under ordinary, consensual circumstances victims may desire the physical act in rape—sexual intercourse:

> This unique feature of the offense requires drawing a line between forcible rape on the one hand and reluctant submission on the other, between true aggression and desired intimacy. The difficulty in drawing this line is compounded by the fact that there will often be no witness to the event other than the participants and that their perceptions may change over time. The trial may turn as much on an assessment of the motives of the victim as of the actor. (281)

The most far-reaching reforms in the definition of rape are included in the sexual assault statutes of the 1970s and the 1980s, which consolidated the sex offenses into one statute. They expanded the definition of rape and other sex offenses to include all sexual *penetrations*: vaginal, anal, and oral. Then, they created less serious crimes of sexual *contacts*—such as offensive touching of breasts and buttocks. Finally, they made sex offenses gender-neutral; men can sexually assault men or women, and women can sexually assault women or men (Minnesota Criminal Code 2005, § 341).

The seriousness of sex offenses under the new codes is graded according to several criteria:

1. Penetrations are more serious than contacts.

2. Forcible penetrations and contacts are more serious than simple nonconsensual penetrations and contacts.

3. Physical injury to the victim aggravates the offense.

4. Rapes involving more than one rapist, "gang rapes," are more serious than those involving a single rapist.

One of the earliest and best known of the new sexual assault laws is Michigan's statute, which incorporated language defining unwanted sexual conduct in 1974 (Michigan Criminal Code 2005, § 750.520). It provides:

- *First degree:* This consists of "sexual penetration," defined as sexual intercourse, cunnilingus, fellatio, anal intercourse, "or any other intrusion, however slight, of any part of a person's body or of any object into the genital or anal openings of another person's body." In addition one of the following must have occurred:

  1. The defendant must have been armed with a weapon.

  2. Force or coercion was used, and the defendant was aided by another person.

  3. Force or coercion was used, and personal injury to the victim was caused.

- *Second degree:* This consists of "sexual contact," defined as the intentional touching of the victim's or actor's personal parts or the intentional touching of the clothing covering the immediate area of the victim's intimate parts for purposes of sexual arousal or gratification.

"Intimate parts" is defined as including the primary genital area, groin, inner thigh, buttock, or breast. In addition, one of the circumstances required for first-degree criminal sexual conduct must have existed.

- *Third degree:* This consists of sexual penetration accomplished by force or coercion.
- *Fourth degree:* This consists of sexual contact accomplished by force or coercion.

Despite these advances in rape law, keep in mind Professor David Bryden's (2000) assessment of the reality of current sexual assault law:

> Most legislatures and courts still define rape narrowly. In acquaintance rape cases, in most states, nonconsensual sex is not rape unless the perpetrator employs force or a threat of force, or the victim is unconscious, badly drunk, underage, or otherwise incapacitated. Even if the victim verbally declines sex, the encounter is not rape in most states unless the man employs "force." Sex obtained by nonviolent threats ("you'll lose your job," etc.), or by deception, usually is not a crime. (321)

 Go to the Criminal Law 9e website to learn more about David Bryden's research: www.thomsonedu.com/criminaljustice/samaha.

The Elements of Modern Rape Law

Most traditional rape statutes, and the newer criminal sexual assault laws, define **rape** as intentional sexual penetration by force without consent. There are many variations in the statutes, but in *most* jurisdictions, rape today boils down to three elements:

1. Actus reus Sexual penetration by force or threat of force
2. Mens rea Intentional sexual penetration
3. *Circumstance* Nonconsent by the victim

Let's look at each of these elements.

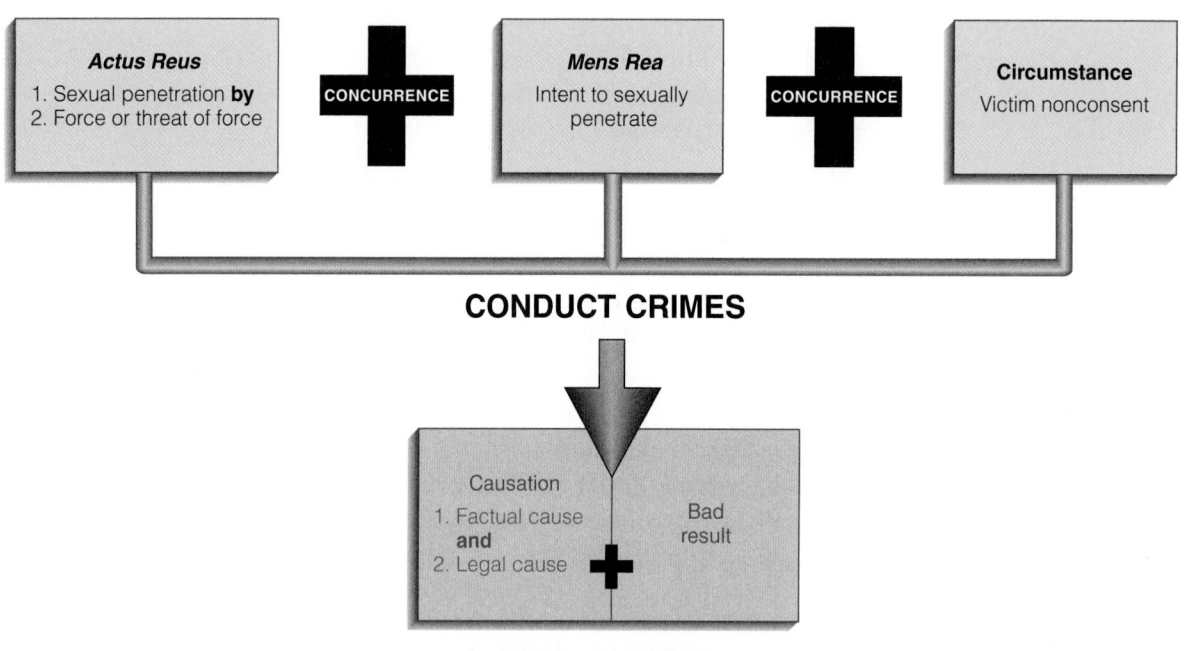

Elements of Rape

Rape Actus Reus: The Force and Resistance Rule Rape is a crime of violence; its *actus reus* is sexual intercourse by force. For most of its history, **rape *actus reus*** was governed by the **force and resistance rule.** The "force" part of the rule wasn't satisfied if victims consented to sexual intercourse. In practice, the prosecution didn't have to prove that victims consented; victims had to prove they didn't consent. This is where the "resistance" part of the rule comes in. Victims had to prove they didn't consent by proving they resisted the force of the accused rapist.

According to an early frequently cited case, *Reynolds v. State* (1889):

> Voluntary submission by the woman, while she has power to resist, no matter how reluctantly yielded, removes from the act an essential element of the crime of rape . . . if the carnal knowledge was with the consent of the woman, no matter how tardily given, or how much force had theretofore been employed, it is not rape. (904)

Proof of nonconsent by resistance is peculiar to the law of rape. In no other crime where lack of consent is an element of the crime does the law treat passive acceptance as consent. Robbery requires taking someone's property by force or threat of force, but it's outrageous even to think that the element of force puts the burden on victims to prove they resisted. Entering an unlocked apartment house without consent to commit a crime is burglary, but it would be absurd to demand that residents prove they didn't consent to the entry. The same is true of theft. According to Lani Anne Remick (1993):

> A common defense to a charge of auto theft . . . is that the car's owner consented to the defendant's use of the vehicle. A mere showing that the owner never gave the defendant permission to take the car is enough to defeat this defense; no showing that the owner actually told the defendant not to take the car is necessary.
>
> In rape law, however, the "default" position is consent. Proof of the absence of affirmative indications by the victim is not enough to defeat a consent defense; instead, the prosecution must show that the alleged victim indicated to the defendant through her overt actions and/or words that she did not wish to participate in sexual activity with him.
>
> Thus, "the law presumes that one will not give away that which is his to a robber, but makes no similar presumption as to the conduct of women and rapists." In fact, quite the opposite is true: in the context of sexual activity the law presumes consent. For example, proving both that a woman did not verbally consent and that her actions consist of lying still and not moving does not raise a presumption of nonconsent but of consent. Only through evidence of some sort of overt behavior such as a verbal "no" or an attempt to push away the defendant can the prosecution meet its burden of proving nonconsent. (1111)

Factors that have influenced the courts' view of nonconsent include the amount of resistance the victim offered, the threat of force, and the danger to the victim if she resisted. We'll look at each of these and exceptions to the force and resistance rule.

The amount of resistance: The amount of resistance required to prove lack of consent has changed over time. From the 1800s until the 1950s, the **utmost resistance standard** prevailed. According to the standard, to show they didn't consent, victims had to resist with all the physical power they possessed. In *Brown v. State* (1906), a 16-year-old virgin testified that her neighbor grabbed her, tripped her to the ground, and forced himself on her.

> I tried as hard as I could to get away. I was trying all the time to get away just as hard as I could. I was trying to get up; I pulled at the grass; I screamed as hard as I could, and he told me to shut up, and I didn't, and then he held his hand on my mouth until I was almost strangled. (538)

The jury convicted the neighbor of rape, but, on appeal, the Wisconsin Supreme Court reversed, deciding the victim hadn't resisted enough:

> Not only must there be entire absence of mental consent or assent, but there must be the most vehement exercise of every physical means or faculty within the woman's power to

resist the penetration of her person, and this must be shown to persist until the offense is consummated. (538)

In *Casico v. State* (1947), the Nebraska Supreme Court described resistance in even tougher terms:

The general rule is that a mentally competent woman must in good faith resist to the utmost with the most vehement exercise of every physical means or faculty naturally within her power to prevent carnal knowledge, and she must persist in such resistance as long as she has the power to do so until the offense is consummated. (900)

In the 1950s, most courts softened the utmost resistance definition to the **reasonable resistance rule,** the rule followed in almost all states today. According to the rule, the amount of resistance depends on the totality of circumstances in each case. For example, in *Jones v. State* (1984), Marvin Jones ran N. M. off the road while she was on the way to a fast-food store with her daughters. Jones opened the door, grabbed her arm, choked her, and forced her toward his car.

Fearing for her life, M. S. got into the car with her daughters. Jones drove to a secluded spot, threatened her, and forced her to commit oral sodomy. Then, he took her out on the road and raped her. At his first-degree rape and oral sodomy trial, Jones argued that N. M. consented. He was convicted and sentenced to 50 years in prison. He appealed, arguing there wasn't enough evidence that N. M. submitted because of "the threat of immediate and great bodily harm." The Oklahoma Court of Criminal Appeals affirmed his conviction and sentence:

In Oklahoma, a woman threatened with rape is not required to resist to the uttermost; instead, she is not required to do more than her age, strength, and the surrounding circumstances make reasonable. In light of the facts of this case, as recited above, we find that there was more than ample evidence to establish that the prosecutrix submitted due to the threats of great bodily harm. (757)

Many new rape or sexual assault statutes have dropped the resistance requirement. This has little or no effect in practice in stranger rape cases, because it's pretty clear that these rapists use force against victims they don't know.

Unarmed acquaintance rapes are a different matter; evidence of reasonable resistance is often critical. In practical terms, force means resistance. This is because acquaintance rapists don't use force unless victims resist their advances. In other words, force and resistance are two sides of the same coin; if force is an element, then so is resistance (Bryden 2000, 356).

Jones v. State (1992) illustrates this close, often inseparable connection between force and reasonable resistance in acquaintance rape. The victim, 26-year-old C. L., lived in the same home with Jones, Jones's wife and child, and C. L's foster mother. One night, when Jones had been drinking, he came into C. L's bedroom and asked her to have sex with him. She said "no" and asked him why he didn't have intercourse with his wife.

He asked her again to have intercourse; she refused again "because it wouldn't be fair to his wife and child." He asked her a third time and C. L. testified that she "just let him have it, you know." She was lying on her side, and he turned her over and had sexual intercourse with her. She testified he told her not to tell anyone, particularly not to tell his wife.

She said she didn't give him permission to have sexual intercourse with her. She didn't yell out or cry for help because she was afraid. She testified on cross-examination that she was afraid of Jones, his wife, and her own foster mother; that it was difficult to tell her foster mother; that Jones didn't have a weapon; and that she didn't think to hit him (242).

In the trial court, Jones was convicted of rape under Indiana's rape statute, which defined a rapist as someone who "knowingly or intentionally has sexual intercourse with a member of the opposite sex when the other person is compelled by force or imminent threat of force. . . ." The Indiana Supreme Court reversed the conviction:

> There was no evidence that Jones used any force or threats to encourage C. L. to engage in sexual intercourse. He asked her three times, and on the third time she "just let him have it." There was no evidence of any previous threats or force against C. L. from which the trier of fact could infer a fear of force or threats on this occasion. The circumstances do not lead to an inference of constructive or implied force. C. L. stated she was afraid to yell for help, but there was no evidence she was afraid because Jones had forced her to do anything or threatened her. There are reasons a person might be afraid to attract attention other than fear of forced activity. (243)

The court didn't mention the word "resistance," but the implication is clear that resistance was an implied requirement. Otherwise, how could the court have concluded this was a consensual case? You might think of it this way: If Jones had been a stranger, is there any doubt that this would be rape?

Courts today have adopted either of two definitions of "force":

1. *Extrinsic force* Requires some act of force in addition to the muscular movements needed to accomplish penetration. The amount of force required varies according to the circumstances of particular cases.

2. *Intrinsic force* Requires only the amount of physical effort necessary to accomplish penetration.

We'll use the next two case excerpts to show you how important the facts in each case are in applying the extrinsic and intrinsic force requirements to acquaintance rape. We look first at the Pennsylvania Supreme Court's application of the extrinsic force standard to the facts of *Commonwealth v. Berkowitz* (1994).

C A S E — *Did He Have Sexual Intercourse by Force?*

Commonwealth v. Berkowitz
609 A.2d 1338 (Pa.Sup. 1992)
641 A.2d 1161 (Pa. 1994)

HISTORY

Robert Berkowitz, the defendant, was convicted in the Court of Common Pleas, Monroe County, of rape and indecent assault and he appealed. The Superior Court, Philadelphia, reversed the rape conviction. The Pennsylvania Supreme Court affirmed the Superior Court's reversal of the conviction.

FACTS
609 A.2d 1338 (Pa.Sup. 1992)

PER CURIAM

In the spring of 1988, Robert Berkowitz and the victim were both college sophomores at East Stroudsburg State University, ages twenty and nineteen years old, respectively. They had mutual friends and acquaintances. On April nineteenth of that year, the victim went to appellant's dormitory room. What transpired in that dorm room between appellant and the victim thereafter is the subject of the instant appeal.

During a one-day jury trial held on September 14, 1988, the victim gave the following account during direct examination by the Commonwealth. At roughly 2:00 on the afternoon of April 19, 1988, after attending two morning classes, the victim returned to her dormitory room. There, she drank a martini to "loosen up a little bit" before going to meet her boyfriend, with whom she had argued the night before. Roughly ten minutes later she walked to her boyfriend's dormitory lounge to meet him. He had not yet arrived.

Having nothing else to do while she waited for her boyfriend, the victim walked up to Berkowitz's room to look for Earl Hassel, Berkowitz's roommate. She knocked on the door several times but received no answer. She therefore wrote a note to Mr. Hassel, which read, "Hi Earl, I'm drunk. That's not why I came to see you. I haven't seen you in a while. I'll talk to you later, [Victim's name]." She did so, although she had not felt any intoxicating effects from the martini, "for a laugh."

After the victim had knocked again, she tried the knob on Berkowitz's door. Finding it open, she walked in. She saw someone lying on the bed with a pillow over his head, whom she thought to be Earl Hassel. After lifting the pillow from his head, she realized it was Berkowitz. She asked him which dresser was his roommate's. He told her, and the victim left the note.

Before the victim could leave Berkowitz's room, however, he asked her to stay and "hang out for a while." She complied because she "had time to kill" and because she didn't really know Berkowitz and wanted to give him "a fair chance." Berkowitz asked her to give him a back rub but she declined, explaining that she did not "trust" him. He then asked her to have a seat on his bed. Instead, she found a seat on the floor, and conversed for a while about a mutual friend. On cross-examination, the victim testified that during this conversation she had explained she was having problems with her boyfriend. No physical contact between the two had, to this point, taken place.

Thereafter, however, appellant moved off the bed and down on the floor, and "kind of pushed [the victim] back with his body. It wasn't a shove, it was just kind of a leaning-type of thing." Next Berkowitz "straddled" and started kissing the victim. The victim responded by saying, "Look, I gotta go. I'm going to meet [my boyfriend]." Then Berkowitz lifted up her shirt and bra and began fondling her. The victim then said "no."

After roughly thirty seconds of kissing and fondling, Berkowitz "undid his pants and he kind of moved his body up a little bit." The victim was still saying "no" but "really couldn't move because Berkowitz was shifting her body so he was over me." Berkowitz then tried to put his penis in her mouth. The victim did not physically resist, but rather continued to verbally protest, saying "No, I gotta go, let me go," in a "scolding" manner.

Ten or fifteen more seconds passed before the two rose to their feet. Berkowitz disregarded the victim's continual complaints that she "had to go," and instead walked two feet away to the door and locked it so that no one from the outside could enter. The victim testified that she realized at the time that the lock was not of a type that could lock people inside the room.

Then, in the victim's words, "He put me down on the bed. It was kind of like—he didn't throw me on the bed. It's hard to explain. It was kind of like a push but no. . . ." She did not bounce off the bed. "It wasn't slow like a romantic kind of thing, but it wasn't a fast shove either. It was kind of in the middle."

Once the victim was on the bed, Berkowitz began "straddling" her again while he undid the knot in her sweatpants. He then removed her sweatpants and underwear from one of her legs. The victim did not physically resist in any way while on the bed because Berkowitz was on top of her, and she "couldn't like go anywhere." She did not scream out at anytime because, "it was like a dream was happening or something."

Berkowitz then used one of his hands to "guide" his penis into her vagina. At that point, after Berkowitz was inside her, the victim began saying "no, no to him softly in a moaning kind of way . . . because it was just so scary." After about thirty seconds, Berkowitz pulled out his penis and ejaculated onto the victim's stomach.

Immediately thereafter, Berkowitz got off the victim and said, "Wow, I guess we just got carried away." To this the victim retorted, "No, we didn't get carried away, you got carried away." The victim then quickly dressed, grabbed her school books and raced downstairs to her boyfriend who was by then waiting for her in the lounge.

Once there, the victim began crying. Her boyfriend and she went up to his dorm room where, after watching the victim clean off Berkowitz's semen from her stomach, he called the police.

Defense counsel's cross-examination elicited more details regarding the contact between Berkowitz and the victim before the incident in question. The victim testified that roughly two weeks prior to the incident, she had attended a school seminar entitled, "Does 'no' sometimes means 'yes'?" Among other things, the lecturer at this seminar had discussed the average length and circumference of human penises. After the seminar, the victim and several of her friends had discussed the subject matter of the seminar over a speaker-telephone with Berkowitz and his roommate Earl Hassel. The victim testified that during that telephone conversation, she had asked Berkowitz the size of his penis. According to the victim, Berkowitz responded by suggesting that the victim "come over and find out." She declined.

When questioned further regarding her communications with Berkowitz prior to the April 19, 1988 incident, the victim testified that on two other occasions, she had stopped by Berkowitz's room while intoxicated. During one of those times, she had laid down on his bed. When asked whether she had asked Berkowitz again at that time what his penis size was, the victim testified that she did not remember.

Berkowitz took the stand in his own defense and offered an account of the incident and the events leading up to it which differed only as to the consent involved. According to Berkowitz, the victim had begun communication with him after the school seminar by asking him of the size of his penis and of whether he would show it to her. Berkowitz had suspected that the victim wanted to pursue a sexual relationship with him because she had stopped by his room twice after the phone call while intoxicated, laying down on his bed with her legs spread and again asking to see his penis. He believed that his suspicions were confirmed when she initiated the April 19, 1988 encounter by stopping by his room (again after drinking), and waking him up.

Berkowitz testified that, on the day in question, he did initiate the first physical contact, but added that the victim warmly responded to his advances by passionately returning his kisses. He conceded that she was continually "whispering . . . no's," but claimed that she did so while "amorously . . . passionately" moaning. In effect, he took such protests to be thinly veiled acts of encouragement. When asked why he locked the door, he explained that "that's not something you want somebody to just walk in on you doing."

According to Berkowitz, the two then laid down on the bed, the victim helped him take her clothing off, and he entered her. He agreed that the victim continued to say "no" while on the bed, but carefully qualified his agreement, explaining that the statements were "moaned passionately." According to Berkowitz, when he saw a "blank look on her face," he immediately withdrew and asked "is anything wrong, is something the matter, is anything wrong." He ejaculated on her stomach thereafter because he could no longer "control" himself. Berkowitz testified that after this, the victim "saw that it was over and then she made her move. She gets right off the bed . . . she just swings her legs over and then she puts her clothes back on." Then, in wholly corroborating an aspect of the victim's account, he testified that he remarked, "Well, I guess we got carried away," to which she rebuked, "No, we didn't get carried, you got carried away."

OPINION

641 A.2d 1161 (Pa. 1994)

CAPPY, J.

The crime of rape is defined as follows:

§ 3121. RAPE

A person commits a felony of the first degree when he engages in sexual intercourse with another person not one's spouse:

(1) by forcible compulsion;

(2) by threat of forcible compulsion that would prevent resistance by a person of reasonable resolution;

(3) who is unconscious; or

(4) who is so mentally deranged or deficient that such person is incapable of consent.

The victim of a rape need not resist.

The force necessary to support a conviction of rape . . . need only be such as to establish lack of consent and to induce the [Victim] to submit without additional resistance. . . . The degree of force required to constitute rape is relative and depends on the facts and particular circumstance of the case.

In regard to the critical issue of forcible compulsion, the complainant's testimony is devoid of any statement which clearly or adequately describes the use of force or the threat of force against her. In response to defense counsel's question, "Is it possible that [when Appellee lifted your bra and shirt] you took no physical action to discourage him," the complainant replied, "It's possible." When asked, "Is it possible that [Berkowitz] was not making any physical contact with you . . . aside from attempting to untie the knot [In the drawstrings of complainant's sweatpants]," she answered, "It's possible." She testified that "He put me

down on the bed. It was kind of like—He didn't throw me on the bed. It's hard to explain. It was kind of like a push but not—I can't explain what I'm trying to say."

She concluded that "it wasn't much" in reference to whether she bounced on the bed, and further detailed that their movement to the bed "wasn't slow like a romantic kind of thing, but it wasn't a fast shove either. It was kind of in the middle." She agreed that Appellee's hands were not restraining her in any manner during the actual penetration, and that the weight of his body on top of her was the only force applied.

She testified that at no time did Berkowitz verbally threaten her. The complainant did testify that she sought to leave the room, and said "no" throughout the encounter. As to the complainant's desire to leave the room, the record clearly demonstrates that the door could be unlocked easily from the inside, that she was aware of this fact, but that she never attempted to go to the door or unlock it. As to the complainant's testimony that she stated "no" throughout the encounter with Berkowitz, we point out that, while such an allegation of fact would be relevant to the issue of consent, it is not relevant to the issue of force. . . . Where there is a lack of consent, but no showing of either physical force, a threat of physical force, or psychological coercion, the "forcible compulsion" requirement under 18 Pa.C.S. § 3121 is not met. . . . The degree of physical force, threat of physical force, or psychological coercion required under 18 Pa.C.S. § 3121 . . . must be sufficient to "prevent resistance by a person of reasonable resolution," but . . . the "peculiar situation" of the victim and other subjective factors should be considered by the court in determining "resistance," "assent," and "consent." . . .

Reviewed in light of the above described standard, the complainant's testimony simply fails to establish that the Appellee forcibly compelled her to engage in sexual intercourse as required under 18 Pa.C.S. § 3121. Thus, even if all of the complainant's testimony was believed, the jury, as a matter of law, could not have found Appellee guilty of rape. Accordingly, we hold that the Superior Court did not err in reversing Appellee's conviction of rape. . . .

Accordingly, the order of the Superior Court reversing the rape conviction is AFFIRMED.

Questions

1. Explain how the court came to the conclusion that the Pennsylvania rape statute required extrinsic force.

2. List all the facts relevant to deciding whether Robert Berkowitz's actions satisfy the extrinsic force requirement.

3. Assume you're the prosecutor, and argue that Robert Berkowitz did use extrinsic force to achieve sexual penetration.

4. Now, assume you're the prosecutor, and argue that Robert Berkowitz did *not* use extrinsic force to achieve sexual penetration.

Now, let's look at how the New Jersey Supreme Court applied the intrinsic force standard in *State in the Interest of M. T. S.* (1992).

C A S E   *Did He Use Force to Rape?*

State in the Interest of M. T. S.
609 A.2d 1266 (N.J. 1992)

HISTORY

The trial court determined that M. T. S., a juvenile, was delinquent for committing a sexual assault. The Appellate Division reversed. The New Jersey Supreme Court granted the State's petition for certification to review the law regarding the element of force in rape, and reversed.

HANDLER, J.

FACTS

On Monday, May 21, 1990, fifteen-year-old C. G. was living with her mother, her three siblings, and several other people, including M. T. S. and his girlfriend. A total of ten people resided in the three-bedroom town home at the time of the incident. M. T. S., then age seventeen, was temporarily residing at the home with the permission of C. G.'s mother; he slept downstairs on a couch. C. G. had her own room on the second floor.

At approximately 11:30 P.M. on May 21, C. G. went upstairs to sleep after having watched television with her mother, M. T. S., and his girlfriend. When C. G. went to bed, she was wearing underpants, a bra, shorts, and a shirt. At trial, C. G. and M. T. S. offered very different accounts concerning the nature of their relationship and the events that occurred after C. G. had gone upstairs. The trial court did not credit fully either teenager's testimony.

C. G. stated that earlier in the day, M. T. S. had told her three or four times that he "was going to make a surprise visit up in her bedroom." She said that she had not taken M. T. S. seriously and considered his comments a joke because he frequently teased her. She testified that M. T. S. had attempted to kiss her on numerous other occasions and at least once had attempted to put his hands inside of her pants, but that she had rejected all of his previous advances.

C. G. testified that on May 22, at approximately 1:30 A.M., she awoke to use the bathroom. As she was getting out of bed, she said, she saw M. T. S., fully clothed, standing in her doorway. According to C. G., M. T. S. then said that "he was going to tease [her] a little bit." C. G. testified that she "didn't think anything of it"; she walked past him, used the bathroom, and then returned to bed, falling into a "heavy" sleep within fifteen minutes.

The next event C. G. claimed to recall of that morning was waking up with M. T. S. on top of her, her underpants and shorts removed. She said "his penis was into [her] vagina." As soon as C. G. realized what had happened, she said, she immediately slapped M. T. S. once in the face, then "told him to get off [her], and get out." She did not scream or cry out. She testified that M. T. S. complied in less than one minute after being struck; according to C. G., "he jumped right off of [her]." She said she did not know how long M. T. S. had been inside of her before she awoke.

C. G. said that after M. T. S. left the room, she "fell asleep crying" because "she couldn't believe that he did what he did to her." She explained that she did not immediately tell her mother or anyone else in the house of the events of that morning because she was "scared and in shock." According to C. G., M. T. S. engaged in intercourse with her "without [her] wanting it or telling him to come up [To her bedroom]." By her own account, C. G. was not otherwise harmed by M. T. S.

At about 7:00 A.M., C. G. went downstairs and told her mother about her encounter with M. T. S. earlier in the morning and said that they would have to "get [him] out of the house." While M. T. S. was out on an errand, C. G.'s mother gathered his clothes and put them outside in his car; when he returned, he was told that "[he] better not even get near the house." C. G. and her mother then filed a complaint with the police.

According to M. T. S., he and C. G. had been good friends for a long time, and their relationship "kept leading on to more and more." He had been living at C. G.'s home for about five days before the incident occurred; he testified that during the three days preceding the incident they had been "kissing and necking" and had discussed having sexual intercourse. The first time M. T. S. kissed C. G., he said, she "didn't want him to, but she did after that." He said C. G. repeatedly had encouraged him to "make a surprise visit up in her room." M. T. S. testified that at exactly 1:15 A.M. on May 22, he entered C. G.'s bedroom as she was walking to the bathroom.

He said C. G. soon returned from the bathroom, and the two began "kissing and all," eventually moving to the bed. Once they were in bed, he said, they undressed each other and continued to kiss and touch for about five minutes. M. T. S. and C. G. proceeded to engage in sexual intercourse.

According to M. T. S., who was on top of C. G., he "stuck it in" and "did it [Thrust] three times, and then the fourth time [he] stuck it in, that's when [she] pulled [him] off of her." M. T. S. said that as C. G. pushed him off, she said "stop, get off," and he "hopped off right away." According to M. T. S., after about one minute, he asked

C. G. what was wrong; she replied with a backhand to his face. He recalled asking C. G. what was wrong a second time, and her replying, "how can you take advantage of me or something like that."

M. T. S. said that he proceeded to get dressed and told C. G. to calm down, but that she then told him to get away from her and began to cry. Before leaving the room, he told C. G., "I'm leaving . . . I'm going with my real girlfriend, don't talk to me . . . I don't want nothing to do with you or anything, stay out of my life . . . don't tell anybody about this . . . it would just screw everything up." He then walked downstairs and went to sleep.

On May 23, 1990, M. T. S. was charged with conduct that if engaged in by an adult would constitute second-degree sexual assault of the victim, contrary to N.J.S.A. 2C:142c(1). . . .

Following a two-day trial on the sexual assault charge, M. T. S. was adjudicated delinquent. After reviewing the testimony, the court concluded that the victim had consented to a session of kissing and heavy petting with M. T. S. The trial court did not find that C. G. had been sleeping at the time of penetration, but nevertheless found that she had not consented to the actual sexual act. Accordingly, the court concluded that the State had proven second-degree sexual assault beyond a reasonable doubt.

On appeal, following the imposition of suspended sentences on the sexual assault and the other remaining charges, the Appellate Division determined that the absence of force beyond that involved in the act of sexual penetration precluded a finding of second-degree sexual assault. It therefore reversed the juvenile's adjudication of delinquency for that offense.

OPINION

Under New Jersey law a person who commits an act of sexual penetration using physical force or coercion is guilty of second-degree sexual assault. The sexual assault statute does not define the words "physical force." The question posed by this appeal is whether the element of "physical force" is met simply by an act of nonconsensual penetration involving no more force than necessary to accomplish that result.

That issue is presented in the context of what is often referred to as "acquaintance rape." The record in the case discloses that the juvenile, a seventeen-year-old boy, engaged in consensual kissing and heavy petting with a fifteen-year-old girl and thereafter engaged in actual sexual penetration of the girl to which she had not consented. . . .

. . . Pre-reform rape law in New Jersey, with its insistence on resistance by the victim, greatly minimized the importance of the forcible and assaultive aspect of the defendant's conduct. Rape prosecutions turned then not so much on the forcible or assaultive character of the defendant's actions as on the nature of the victim's response. . . . That the law put the rape victim on trial was clear. . . .

The New Jersey Code of Criminal Justice [reformed the law of rape in 1978]. . . . The Code does not refer to force

in relation to "overcoming the will" of the victim, or to the "physical overpowering" of the victim, or the "submission" of the victim. It does not require the demonstrated nonconsent of the victim. . . .

In reforming the rape laws, the Legislature placed primary emphasis on the assaultive nature of the crime, altering its constituent elements so that they focus exclusively on the forceful or assaultive conduct of the defendant. . . .

. . . We conclude, therefore, that any act of sexual penetration engaged in by the defendant without the affirmative and freely given permission of the victim to the specific act of penetration constitutes the offense of sexual assault. . . .

Today the law of sexual assault is indispensable to the system of legal rules that assures each of us the right to decide who may touch our bodies, when, and under what circumstances. The decision to engage in sexual relations with another person is one of the most private and intimate decisions a person can make. Each person has the right not only to decide whether to engage in sexual contact with another, but also to control the circumstances and character of that contact. . . .

Notwithstanding the stereotype of rape as a violent attack by a stranger, the vast majority of sexual assaults are perpetrated by someone known to the victim. . . . Contrary to common myths, perpetrators generally do not use guns or knives and victims generally do not suffer external bruises or cuts. Although this more realistic and accurate view of rape only recently has achieved widespread public circulation, it was a central concern of the proponents of reform in the 1970s. . . .

We acknowledge that cases such as this are inherently fact sensitive and depend on the reasoned judgment and common sense of judges and juries. The trial court concluded that the victim had not expressed consent to the act of intercourse, either through her words or actions. We conclude that the record provides reasonable support for the trial court's disposition.

Accordingly, we REVERSE the judgment of the Appellate Division and reinstate the disposition of juvenile delinquency for the commission of second-degree sexual assault.

Questions

1. List all of the evidence relevant to determining whether M. T. S.'s actions satisfied the intrinsic force element of the New Jersey sexual assault statute.

2. Summarize the reasons the court gives for adopting the intrinsic force standard.

3. Taking into account the evidence, decision, and reasoning of *Commonwealth v. Berkowitz*, which do you think is the better approach to the force requirement—intrinsic or extrinsic force? Defend your answer.

4. Should legislatures or courts decide whether to adopt the intrinsic or extrinsic force standard? Defend your answer.

TABLE 10.1   The Antioch College Sexual Offense Policy

All sexual contact and conduct on the Antioch College campus and/or occurring with an Antioch community member must be consensual. . . .

Consent

1. For the purpose of this policy, "consent" shall be defined as follows: the act of willingly and verbally agreeing to engage in specific sexual contact or conduct.
2. If sexual contact and/or conduct is not mutually and simultaneously initiated, then the person who initiates sexual contact/conduct is responsible for getting the verbal consent of the other individual(s) involved.
3. Obtaining consent is an on-going process in any sexual interaction. Verbal consent should be obtained with each new level of physical and/or sexual contact/conduct in any given interaction, regardless of who initiates it. Asking "Do you want to have sex with me?" is not enough. The request for consent must be specific to each act.
4. The person with whom sexual contact/conduct is initiated is responsible to express verbally and/or physically her/his willingness or lack of willingness when reasonably possible.
5. If someone has initially consented but then stops consenting during a sexual interaction, she/he should communicate withdrawal verbally and/or through physical resistance. The other individual(s) must stop immediately.
6. To knowingly take advantage of someone who is under the influence of alcohol, drugs and/or prescribed medication is not acceptable behavior in the Antioch community.
7. If someone verbally agrees to engage in specific contact or conduct, but it is not of her/his own free will due to any of the circumstances stated in (a) through (d) below, then the person initiating shall be considered in violation of this policy if:
   a. the person submitting is under the influence of alcohol or other substances supplied to her/him by the person initiating;
   b. the person submitting is incapacitated by alcohol, drugs, and/or prescribed medication;
   c. the person submitting is asleep or unconscious;
   d. the person initiating has forced, threatened, coerced, or intimidated the other individual(s) into engaging in sexual contact and/or sexual conduct.

Source: David S. Hall 1998.

5. Study Table 10.1, "Antioch College, Sexual Offense Policy." Do you agree with this critic (Crichton and others 1993) of the policy?

> Deep among the cornfields and pig farms of central Ohio in the town of Yellow Springs, Antioch prides itself on being "A Laboratory for Democracy." The dress code is grunge and black; multiple nose rings are de rigueur, and green and blue hair are preferred (if you have hair). Seventy percent of the student body are womyn (for the uninitiated, that's women—without the dreaded m-e-n). And the purpose of the Sexual Offense Policy is to empower these students to become equal partners when it comes time to mate with males.
>
> The goal is 100 percent consensual sex, and it works like this: it isn't enough to ask someone if she'd like to have sex, as an Antioch women's center advocate told a group of incoming freshmen this fall. You must obtain consent every step of the way. "If you want to take her blouse off, you have to ask. If you want to touch her breast, you have to ask. If you want to move your hand down to her genitals, you have to ask. If you want to put your finger inside her, you have to ask" (52).
>
> How silly this all seems; how sad. It criminalizes the delicious unexpectedness of sex—a hand suddenly moves to here, a mouth to there. What is the purpose of sex if not to lose control? (To be unconscious, no.) The advocates of sexual correctness are trying to take the danger out of sex, but sex is inherently dangerous. It leaves one exposed to everything from euphoria to crashing disappointment. That's its great unpredictability. But of course, that's sort of what we said when we were all made to use seat belts.
>
> What is implicit in the new sex guidelines is that it's the male who does the initiating and the woman who at any moment may bolt. Some young women rankle at that. "I think it encourages wimpy behavior by women and [The idea] that women need to be handled with kid gloves," says Hope Segal, 22, a fourth-year Antioch student. Beware those boys with their swords, made deaf by testosterone and, usually, blinded by drink. (54)

Threat of force: The *actual* use of force isn't required to satisfy the force requirement. The threat of force is enough. To satisfy the **threat-of-force requirement,** the prosecution has to prove the victim experienced two kinds of fear:

1. *Subjective fear* The victim honestly feared imminent and serious bodily harm.

2. *Objective fear* The fear was reasonable under the circumstances.

Brandishing a weapon satisfies the requirement. So do verbal threats—such as threats to kill, seriously injure, or kidnap. But the threat doesn't have to include showing weapons or using specifically threatening words. Courts can consider all of the following in deciding whether the victim's fear was reasonable (Edwards 1996, 260–61):

- The respective ages of the perpetrator and the victim

- The physical sizes of the perpetrator and the victim

- The mental condition of the perpetrator and the victim

- The physical setting of the assault

- Whether the perpetrator had a position of authority, domination, or custodial control over the victim

Resistance and danger to the victim: Some empirical research from the late 1970s and early 1980s reported that resistance "may threaten rape victims' lives" (Schwartz 1983, 577). Fifty-five percent of rapists in one widely publicized study reported "getting more violent, sometimes losing control" when their victims resisted (579). Another study, funded by the U.S. Department of Justice, found that 66 percent of victims who resisted were injured compared to 34 percent who didn't (580).

More recent studies from the 1990s have uncovered shortcomings in these earlier findings. For one thing, stranger rapes were overrepresented because it's easier to study convicted rapists, who are overwhelmingly violent stranger rapists. As you've already learned, acquaintance rapists far outnumber stranger rapists.

Let's add some details about acquaintance rape that are helpful in understanding the effect of victim resistance. First, victims usually resist unwanted advances, because they're not afraid men they know will hurt them. Second, and important, they're right: Resistance usually succeeds. According to Patricia Dooze and her colleagues, "Most rapes are attempted but not completed and the woman succeeds in escaping with little or no injury" (Bryden 2000, 366, n. 196). As to injuries, the National Victim Center's report, *Rape in America,* reported that 4 percent of acquaintance rape victims reported serious injuries, 24 percent reported minor injuries, and 70 percent reported no injuries (Bryden 2000, 367, n. 198).

Finally, the most sophisticated empirical studies of the 1990s found that it's not initial victim resistance that provokes rapists to injure their victims. It's the other way around; initial rapist violence provokes victim resistance (Bryden 2000, 367).

Exceptions to the force and resistance rule: The law has never required physical resistance in all cases. No resistance is required if victims were incapacitated at the time of the assault by intoxication, mental deficiency, or insanity.

Also, deception (fraud) can substitute for force. These cases involve doctors who trick their patients into having sexual intercourse. These cases fall into two categories, fraud in the fact and fraud in the inducement. **Fraud in the fact** consists of tricking the victim into believing the act she consented to wasn't sexual intercourse. This type of intercourse is rape. In a famous old case still cited, *Moran v. People* (1872), Dr. Moran told a patient he needed to insert an instrument into her vagina for treatment. She consented. In fact, the doctor was engaging in intercourse. The court rejected the argument that his victim consented, and the appeals court upheld the doctor's rape conviction.

Intercourse obtained by **"fraud in the inducement"** is *not* rape. For example, "Dr. Feelgood" in the 1980s had sexual assault charges against him dropped, but he didn't benefit from his victims' consent, because his fraud was in the benefits he promised his victims, not in the act of intercourse. Daniel Boro, posing as "Dr. Feelgood," tricked several women into believing he could cure their fatal blood disease by having sexual intercourse with him. He convinced them that they had two choices: they could undergo an extremely painful and expensive surgery or have intercourse with a donor (Boro, of course) who'd been injected with a special serum. The court ruled the women consented even though Bono used fraud to induce them to have intercourse with them (*Boro v. Superior Court* 1985).

Finally, sexual intercourse with a minor who consented is rape, because the law doesn't recognize the consent of minors. You'll learn more about statutory rape later in the chapter.

Rape Mens Rea   Rape is a general-intent crime. Recall from Chapter 4 that one common meaning of *general intent* is that defendants intended to commit the act defined in the crime—in the case of rape, the act is forcible sexual penetration. This, of course, doesn't mean there can't be a different state of mind regarding circumstance elements, specifically nonconsent. These circumstance elements center around mistakes—mistakes about age in the cases involving underage victims or mistakes about the consent to sexual penetration by competent adult victims.

It's impossible to purposely, or even knowingly, make a mistake. That leaves three possibilities: reckless mistakes, negligent mistakes, or no-fault mistakes (strict liability). The states are divided as to which mental element to require.

At one extreme are states that adopt strict liability. An example of strict liability regarding consent is *Commonwealth v. Fischer* (1998). Kurt Fischer and another Lafayette College freshman gave "grossly divergent" stories regarding their encounter in Fischer's dorm room. The victim testified that when they went to his room, Fischer locked the door, pushed her onto the bed, straddled her, held her wrists above her head, and forced his penis into her mouth. She struggled through the whole encounter, warned him that "someone would find out," told him she had to be at a class, and didn't want to have sex with him. Fischer ignored all this, forced his hands inside a hole in her jeans, pushed his penis through the hole, removed it, and ejaculated on her face, hair, and sweater (1112–13).

Fischer testified that when they got to his room, the victim told him it would have to be a "quick one." Fischer admitted he held the victim's arms above her head, straddled her, and put his penis in her mouth, and said, "I know you want my dick in your mouth." When she replied, "no," Fischer said, "no means yes." After Fischer insisted again that she "wanted it," and she replied, "No, I honestly don't," he stopped trying. Then they just lay on the bed fondling and kissing each other (1113).

The jury found Fischer guilty of involuntary deviate sexual intercourse and aggravated indecent assault; he was sentenced to 5 years in prison. On appeal, Fischer argued that he honestly, but mistakenly, believed the victim consented. The Pennsylvania Superior Court expressed approval of an **honest and reasonable mistake rule**—that is, a negligence mental element—because of changing sexual habits, particularly on college campuses (1114).

Nevertheless, the court ruled, it didn't have the authority to replace the state's strict liability rule with a negligence rule on its own. Quoting from a rape case involving two

Temple University students, the court said the reasonable and honest mistake of fact rule regarding consent

> is not now and has never been the law of Pennsylvania. When one individual uses force or the threat of force to have sexual relations with a person not his spouse and without the person's consent he has committed the crime of rape. *If the element of the defendant's belief as to the victim's state of mind is to be established as a defense to the crime of rape then it should be done by the legislature which has the power to define crimes and defenses. We refuse to create such a defense.* (1114)

Several states have adopted the negligence standard that the court in *Commonwealth v. Fischer* referred to favorably. A frequently cited example is *People v. Mayberry* (1975). Booker T. Mayberry and "Miss B." gave conflicting stories of what happened. Miss B. testified that Mayberry repeatedly hit her and threatened to hurt her if she didn't come to his apartment for sex. Mayberry testified that she came voluntarily to his apartment where she willingly engaged in sexual intercourse with him.

The trial court refused Mayberry's request that the judge instruct the jury as to mistake of fact regarding Mayberry's belief that Miss B. consented to the intercourse. The California Supreme Court reversed the conviction. Although the statute said nothing about the mental attitude required for consent, the court read into the statute the requirement that Mayberry's mistake as to Miss B.'s consent had to be negligent:

> The severe penalty imposed for . . . [rape] and the serious loss of reputation following conviction make it extremely unlikely that the legislature intended to exclude . . . the element of wrongful intent. If a defendant entertains a reasonable and bona fide belief that a prosecutrix voluntarily consented to accompany him and to engage in sexual intercourse, it is apparent he does not possess the wrongful intent that is a prerequisite . . . to a conviction of . . . rape by means of force or threat. (1345)

A few courts have adopted a **recklessness requirement,** requiring that the defendant has to be aware that there's a risk the victim hasn't consented to sexual intercourse. The most famous example of requiring recklessness is the controversial English case, *Regina v. Morgan* (1975), which the court with great understatement, called "somewhat bizarre." The case generated enormous attention and great criticism, not just in the United Kingdom but in the United States.

William Morgan, an officer in the RAF was out drinking with Robert McDonald, Robert McClarty, and Michael Parker, three other RAF men, much younger and junior in rank to Morgan. The four men weren't just drinking, they were looking for women. When they couldn't find any women to have sex with, Officer Morgan suggested that they go back to his house and have sex with his wife Daphne. The younger men were complete strangers to Mrs. Morgan and at first didn't take their superior's suggestion seriously. But they realized Morgan was serious when he told them stories about Mrs. Morgan's "sexual aberrations" and then gave them condoms to wear.

Morgan told the men to expect his wife to resist but not to take her resistance seriously, "since it was a mere pretense whereby she stimulated her own sexual excitement." The men went to Morgan's house; Mrs. Morgan did resist. All four men overcame her resistance, and each had sexual intercourse with Mrs. Morgan while the others watched.

Daphne Morgan's account of what happened was that

> she was awakened from sleep in a single bed in a room which she shared with one of her children. Her husband and the other men in part dragged and in part carried her out on to a landing and thence into another room which contained a double bed. She struggled and screamed and shouted to her son to call the police, but one of the men put a hand over her mouth. Once on the double bed the defendants had intercourse with her in turn, finishing with her husband. During intercourse with the other three she was continuously being

held, and this, coupled with her fear of further violence, restricted the scope of her struggles, but she repeatedly called out to her husband to tell the men to stop.

McDonald, McClarty, and Parker were charged with and convicted of rape. Officer Morgan was charged with and convicted of aiding and abetting the rapes by the younger men. (The marital rape exception prevented charging Morgan with rape.) They appealed. Their case eventually reached England's highest court, the House of Lords, where they argued that their convictions should be overturned because they believed Mrs. Morgan consented to the rape.

There was long and detailed argument about mistake and consent. It centered on whether a negligent mistake regarding Daphne Morgan's consent was enough to satisfy the *mens rea* requirement or whether recklessness was required. After more than fifty pages of analysis, the Lords decided on recklessness and reversed the convictions. Lord Hailsham put it succinctly:

> In rape the prohibited act is intercourse without the consent of the victim and the mental element lies in the intention to commit the act willy-nilly or not caring whether the victim consents or not. A failure to prove this element involves an acquittal, because an essential ingredient is lacking and it matters not that it is lacking because of a belief not based on reasonable ground.

Critics argue that rape is too serious a charge and the penalties are too severe to allow convictions based on a negligent or even a reckless mistake. They demand that defendants have to *know* their victims didn't consent before they can be subjected to the stigma of such a heinous crime and such severe punishment.

Law professor Susan Estrich (1987), a rape law scholar and herself a rape victim, disagrees:

> If inaccuracy or indifference to consent is "the best that this man can do" because he lacks the capacity to act reasonably, then it might well be unjust and ineffective to punish him for it. . . . More common is the case of the man who could have done better but did not; heard her refusal or saw her tears, but decided to ignore them.
>
> The man who has the inherent capacity to act reasonably but fails to has, through that failure, made a blameworthy choice for which he can justly be punished. The law has long punished unreasonable action which leads to the loss of human life as manslaughter—a lesser crime than murder, but a crime nonetheless. . . . The injury of sexual violation is sufficiently great, the need to provide that additional incentive pressing enough, to justify negligence liability for rape as for killing. (97–98)

Statutory Rape

Statutory rape consists of having sex with minors. Statutory rapists don't have to use force; the victim's immaturity takes the place of force. Furthermore, nonconsent isn't an element, nor is consent a defense because minors can't legally consent to sex. In other words, statutory rape is a strict liability crime in most states.

A few states, such as California and Alaska, however, do permit the defense of **reasonable mistake of age.** In those states, the defense applies if a man reasonably believes his victim is over the age of consent. In other words, negligence is the required *mens rea* regarding the circumstance element of age.

Grading the Degrees of Rape

Most statutes divide rape into two degrees: simple (second-degree) rape and aggravated (first-degree) rape. *Aggravated rape* involves at least one of the following circumstances:

- The victim suffers serious bodily injury.

- A stranger commits the rape.

- The rape occurs in connection with another crime.
- The rapist is armed.
- The rapist has accomplices.
- The victim is a minor and the rapist is several years older.

All other rapes are **"simple" rapes,** for which the penalties are less severe. The criminal sexual conduct statutes comprise a broad range of criminal sexual penetrations and contacts that grades penetrations more seriously than contacts but also takes into account the aggravating circumstances just listed.

BODILY INJURY CRIMES

Assault and battery, although combined in many modern statutes, are two separate crimes. A **battery** is an unwanted and unjustified offensive touching. Body contact is central to the crime of battery. An **assault** is either an attempted or a threatened battery, depending on how the statute defines it. The essential difference between assault and battery is that assault requires no physical contact; an assault is complete before the offender touches the victim. **Stalking** involves intentionally scaring another person by following, tormenting, or harassing him or her.

In this section, we'll look at bodily injury crimes involving battery, assault, and stalking.

Battery

The *actus reus* of battery is unlawful touching, but not every offensive physical contact is unlawful. Spanking children is offensive, at least to the children, but it's not battery. Why? Because the law recognizes it as the *lawful* act of disciplining children. Unlawful

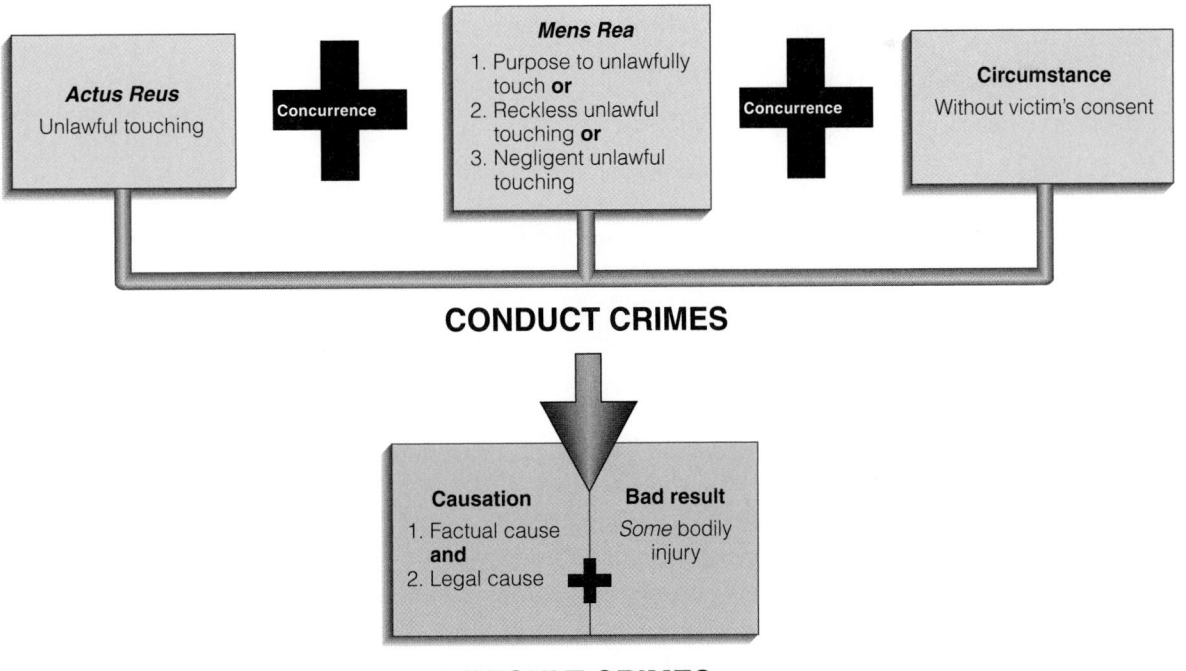

Elements of Battery

touching includes a broad spectrum of acts but usually means any unjustified touching without consent. Some courts have even included spitting in the face of someone you want to insult (*State v. Humphries* 1978).

Statutes don't always spell out the battery *mens rea*. At common law, battery was an intentionally inflicted injury. Modern courts and statutes extend battery *mens rea* to include reckless and negligent contacts. The MPC (ALI 1953, no. 11) defines battery *mens rea* as "purposely, recklessly, or negligently causing bodily injury," or "negligently causing bodily injury . . . with a deadly weapon."

Some state statutes call this expanded offense by a different name. Louisiana (Louisiana Statutes Annotated 1974, 17-A, 14.39), for example, provides that "inflicting any injury upon the person of another by criminal negligence" is "negligent injuring."

Battery requires *some* injury. Batteries that cause minor physical injury or emotional injury are misdemeanors in most states. Batteries that cause serious bodily injury are felonies. Some code provisions are directed at injuries caused by special circumstances. For example, injuries caused by pit bulls prompted the Minnesota legislature (Minnesota Statutes Annotated 1989, § 609.26) to enact the following provision:

> Section 609.26. A person who causes great or substantial bodily harm to another by negligently or intentionally permitting any dog to run uncontrolled off the owner's premises, or negligently failing to keep it properly confined is guilty of a petty misdemeanor. . . .
>
> Subd. 3. If proven by a preponderance of the evidence, it shall be an affirmative defense to liability under this section that the victim provoked the dog to cause the victim's bodily harm.

Injuries and deaths resulting from drug abuse led the same legislature to enact this provision:

> 609.228 Whoever proximately causes great bodily harm by, directly or indirectly, unlawfully selling, giving away, bartering, delivering, exchanging, distributing, or administering a controlled substance . . . may be sentenced to imprisonment for not more than ten years or to payment of a fine of not more than $20,000, or both.

The MPC grades bodily harm offenses as follows:

§ 211.1 2.

Bodily injury is a felony when

a. such injury is inflicted purposely or knowingly with a deadly weapon; or

b. serious bodily injury is inflicted purposely, or knowingly or recklessly under circumstances manifesting extreme indifference to the value of human life.

c. except as provided in paragraph (2), bodily injury is a misdemeanor, unless it was caused in a fight or scuffle entered into by mutual consent, in which case it is a petty misdemeanor.

Assault

Assaults are either attempted batteries or threatened batteries, depending on the state. (Notice both kinds are complete crimes without touching the victim.) **Attempted battery assault** consists of having the specific intent to commit a battery and taking substantial steps toward carrying it out without actually completing the attempt. **Threatened battery assault,** sometimes called the crime of "intentional scaring," requires only that actors intend to frighten their victims, thus expanding assault beyond attempted battery. Threatened battery doesn't require actually having the intent to injure their victims physically; the intent to frighten victims into believing the actor will hurt them is enough.

Victims' awareness is critical to proving threatened battery assault. Specifically, victims' fear of an immediate battery has to be reasonable. Words alone aren't assaults; threatening gestures have to accompany them. But this requirement isn't always fair. For example, what if an assailant approaches from behind a victim, saying, "Don't move, or I'll shoot!" These words obviously are reasonable grounds to fear imminent injury, but they aren't assault because they are, after all, only words.

Conditional threats aren't enough either, because they're not immediate. The conditional threat, "I'd punch you out if you weren't a kid," isn't immediate because it depends on the victim's age. In a few jurisdictions, a present ability to carry out the threat has to exist. But in most, even a person who approaches a victim with a gun she knows is unloaded, points the gun at the victim, and pulls the trigger (intending only to frighten her victim) has committed threatened battery (*Encyclopedia of Crime and Justice* 1983, 1:89).

Attempted and threatened battery assaults address separate harms. Attempted battery assault deals with an incomplete physical injury. Threatened battery assault is directed at a present psychological or emotional harm—namely, putting a victim in fear.

So in attempted battery assault, a victim's awareness doesn't matter; in threatened battery assault, it's indispensable.

The MPC deals with threatened and attempted battery assaults as follows:

§ 211.1 SIMPLE ASSAULT

A person is guilty of assault if he:

a. attempts to cause . . . bodily injury to another; or

b. attempts by physical menace to put another in fear of imminent serious bodily harm.

Simple assault is a misdemeanor unless committed in a fight or scuffle entered into by mutual consent, in which case the assault is a petty misdemeanor. (ALI 1985)

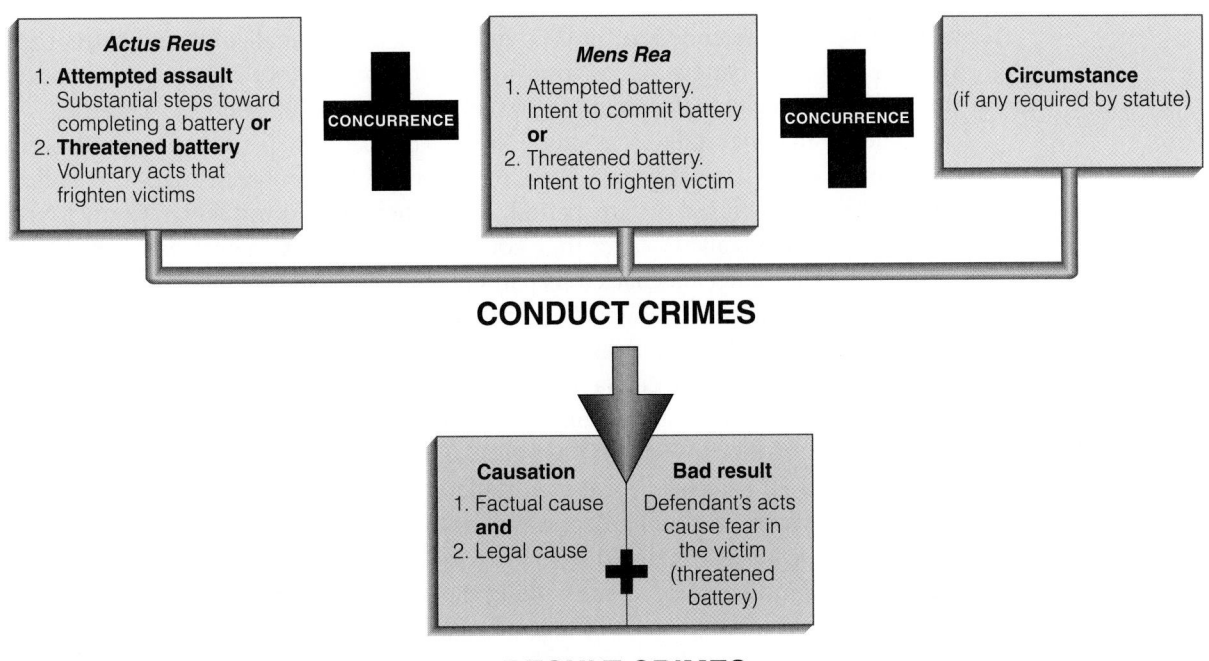

Elements of Assault

Historically, all assaults were misdemeanors. However, modern statutes have created several aggravated or felonious assaults. Most common are assaults with the intent to commit violent felonies (murder, rape, and robbery, for example), assaults with deadly weapons (such as guns and knives), and assaults on police officers.

The MPC includes a comprehensive assault and battery statute that integrates, rationalizes, and grades assault and battery. It takes into account *actus reus*, *mens rea*, circumstance elements, and intended harm. Note the careful attention paid to these elements:

§ 211.2

A person is guilty of aggravated assault if he:

a. attempts to cause serious bodily injury to another, or causes such injury purposely, knowingly or recklessly under circumstances manifesting extreme indifference to the value of human life; or

b. attempts to cause or purposely or knowingly causes bodily injury to another with a deadly weapon.

Aggravated assault under paragraph (a) is a felony of the second degree; aggravated assault under paragraph (b) is a felony of the third degree.

§ 211.3

A person commits a misdemeanor if he recklessly engages in conduct which places or may place another person in danger of death or serious bodily injury. Recklessness and danger shall be presumed where a person knowingly points a firearm at or in the direction of another, whether or not the actor believed the firearm to be loaded. (ALI 1985)

Stalking

Stalking is an ancient practice but only a modern crime; it involves intentionally scaring another person by following, tormenting, or harassing him or her. Statutes criminalizing stalking "intended to fill gaps in the law by criminalizing conduct that fell short of assault or battery . . . by insuring that victims did not have to be injured or threatened with death before stopping a stalker's harassment" (*Curry v. State* 2002).

Statutes making stalking a crime began in California, after actress Rebecca Schaeffer was murdered at her Los Angeles apartment by an obsessed fan who stalked her for 2 years. Within a 5-week period, four other women in Orange County were murdered by their stalkers—*after* they got restraining orders against them (Bradfield 1998, 243–44). California enacted its pathbreaking antistalking statute in 1990.

Other states quickly followed California's example; today every state and the U.S. government have stalking statutes. The laws reflect widespread concern over the "stalking phenomenon" (LaFave 2003a, 828–29). Although many victims are celebrities like Rebecca Schaeffer and other prominent individuals, the vast majority are "ordinary" people, most of them women. Nearly 1.5 million people are stalked every year. Seventy-five to 80 percent involve men stalking women. Stalking has major negative effects on its victim, including depression, substance abuse, phobias, anxiety, obsessive-compulsive behaviors, and dissociative disorders (829).

We'll look more closely at antistalking statutes, the *actus reus* and the *mens rea* of stalking, the bad result in stalking, and cyberstalking.

Antistalking Statutes   The antistalking statutes vary enormously from state to state and the U.S. statute. Let's begin with the National Criminal Justice Association's model stalking law. It was commissioned by the U.S. Department of Justice's National Institute of Justice, resulting from considerable effort. Many states have adopted parts of it:

SECTION 1

For purposes of this code:

(a) "Course of conduct" means repeatedly maintaining a visual or physical proximity to a person or repeatedly conveying verbal or written threats or threats implied by conduct or a combination thereof directed at or toward a person;

(b) "Repeatedly" means on two or more occasions; and

(c) "Immediate family" means a spouse, parent, child, sibling, or any other person who regularly resides in the household or who within the past six months regularly resided in the household.

SECTION 2

Any person who

(a) Purposely engages in a course of conduct directed at a specific person that would cause a reasonable person to fear bodily injury to himself or herself or a member of his or her immediate family or to fear the death of himself or herself or a member of his or her immediate family; and

(b) Has knowledge or should have knowledge that the specific person will be placed in reasonable fear of bodily injury to himself or herself or a member of his or her immediate family or to fear the death of himself or herself or his or her immediate family; and

(c) Whose acts induce fear in the specific person of bodily injury to himself or herself or a member of his or her immediate family or induce fear in the specific individual of the death of himself or herself or a member of his or her immediate family; is guilty of stalking.

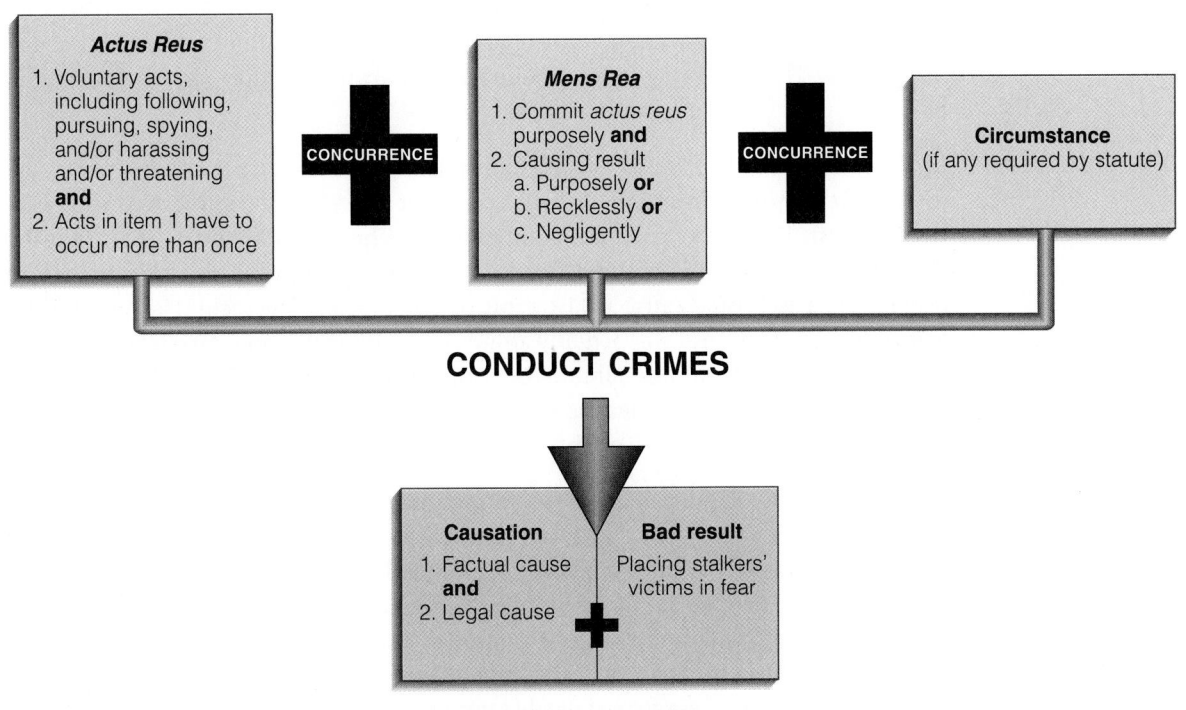

Elements of Stalking

Stalking Actus Reus   Despite great diversity from state to state, the stalking statutes all share some common requirements when it comes to the criminal act. First, as in the model code, all 50 states require that the act happen more than once (LaFave 2003a, 831). Some codes use the word "repeatedly"; others, as in the model code, say there has to be a "course of conduct."

As to the *kind* of conduct that has to be repeated, all states require some variation of the model code's "maintaining a visual or physical proximity." These acts include following, pursuing, spying, and/or harassing. About half the states require some kind of threat, including the model code's "verbal or written threats or threats implied by conduct," "threat," "terroristic threat," or "credible threat" (LaFave 2003a, 832).

Other statutes list very specific acts, including one or more of the following: interfering with the victim; approaching or confronting the victim; appearing at the victim's job or home; placing objects on the victim's property; causing damage to the victim's pet; calling the victim on the phone, or sending letters or e-mail to the victim (832).

Stalking Mens Rea   Stalking is a result crime. All statutes require a specific intent to commit the acts discussed in the *actus reus* section. They also require some mental attitude causing the bad result, but the exact mental attitude varies considerably among the states (836).

Slightly more than half the states require some level of *subjective fault;* recall that subjective fault refers to purpose, knowledge, or recklessness. Most of these states require that the actor's purpose was to cause the bad result. A few of these subject fault states require either that stalkers know their acts will cause the bad result or that they act recklessly; that is, they know their acts create a substantial and unjustifiable risk of causing the bad result (837).

About one-third of the states require only *objective fault*—namely, negligence. In other words, the requirement is objective reasonableness: actors don't *know* their acts are creating a substantial and unjustifiable risk of causing the bad result, but they *should* know. The remaining states require no mental attitude; they provide for strict liability. The only requirement is a voluntary act (837).

Bad Result   The bad result in stalking is placing stalkers' victims in fear. States take four different approaches to the fear caused. Most states adopt a **subjective and objective fear test.** The model code is a good example. The defendant's acts "induce fear in the specific person"; this is subjective fear. It also requires objective fear; that is, the defendant's acts "would cause a reasonable person to fear." The second is the **subjective fear only test:** the victim was actually afraid. The third is the **objective fear only test;** a reasonable person would be afraid. The fourth is the **intent-to-instill-fear test.** Here, the actor's intent to instill fear is enough, whether the acts actually caused fear or would've caused fear in a reasonable person (LaFave 2003a, 835–36).

Cyberstalking   The Internet is a "fertile ground for stalking" (Merschman 2001, 275). This "dark side of the Web" provides cyberstalkers with cheap and powerful tools for instilling fear in their victims—mostly e-mail but also chat rooms and bulletin boards. **Cyberstalking** is defined as "the use of the Internet, e-mail or other electronic communications devices to stalk another person through threatening behavior" (Mishler 2000, 117). In 1999, the Los Angeles and Manhattan District Attorneys reported that 20 percent of its stalking victims were cyberstalked (Attorney General 1999).

Cyberstalking reaches victims in their homes, where they feel safest; what's worse, stalkers can stalk from the comfort of *their* homes. "Make no mistake: this kind of stalking can be as frightening and as real as being followed and watched in your neighborhood or in your home" (Mishler 2000, 117).

Ted Hoying, in our next case excerpt, *State v. Hoying* (2005), insisted his endless e-mails didn't cause his co-worker Kelly Criswell either physical or mental harm. He also argued that he wasn't aware that Criswell believed he'd caused her any harm. Hoying also objected to the severity of his sentence. This excerpt gives you a chance to see how the court applies the elements of stalking in a cyberstalking setting and to consider the degree and purposes of the sentence.

CASE   *Did He Cyberstalk Her?*

State v. Hoying
WL 678989 (OhioApp. 2005)

HISTORY

Theodore Hoying, Defendant, was convicted by a jury in the Court of Common Pleas, of menacing by stalking and intimidation of a victim. He was sentenced to a total of $6^{1}/_{2}$ years in prison. Defendant appealed. The Ohio Court of Appeals affirmed.

BROGAN, J.

FACTS

Ted Hoying met the victim, Kelly Criswell, when they both worked at a local restaurant. In June 2002, Hoying asked Criswell for a date, and became quite angry when she declined. When Hoying persisted in contacting Ms. Criswell after she left her employment with the restaurant, Ms. Criswell obtained a civil protection order against Hoying in February 2003. Subsequently, between August 15, 2003, and September 7, 2003, Hoying sent 105 e-mails to Ms. Criswell in violation of the protection order.

In the first e-mail, which is dated August 15, 2003, Hoying acknowledged that he could get in trouble for writing. He then asked Ms. Criswell to remove the civil protection order. Ms. Criswell did not reply to any of Hoying's e-mails, which became increasingly agitated.

The first threatening e-mail is dated August 16. This e-mail states, "Maybe I still have your picture and I will post it on the Net. Fair is fair. Ted." Subsequently, Hoying wrote, "Why don't you tell the authorities I shot three boxes of shells at clay birds yesterday. I'm going to do that the rest of my life at least once a week. I don't give a rat's ass what number eight says on that civil protection order. Ted." That e-mail is also dated August 16, 2003.

In another e-mail dated August 16, 2003, Hoying threatened to come to Ms. Criswell's place of employment unless she met with him. The same day, in another e-mail message, Hoying indicated that he would persist in sending e-mails until Ms. Criswell agreed to talk to him.

In an e-mail dated August 17, 2003, Hoying made a significant threat to Ms. Criswell. Specifically, he said:

> "Kelly, set me free. I'm no longer a man. I'm shackled like a beast. What is a man if he is not free. Let me take away your freedom and you feel the sting. Also, it's not pleasant. Set me free. Ted H."

In another e-mail written on the same day, Hoying again threatened to come to Ms. Criswell's place of employment. He reiterated that threat in another e-mail, which was also written on August 17, 2003.

As a result of receiving these e-mails, Ms. Criswell filed charges in Xenia Municipal Court, alleging that Hoying had violated the Civil Protection Order. Hoying acknowledged receiving the charge in an e-mail dated August 28, 2003. In that e-mail, Hoying said: "Kelly, why did you do that at Xenia? All I wanted was for things to be normal. I thought you could be nice." The same day, Hoying threatened to file criminal charges against Ms. Criswell's boyfriend, whom Hoying thought was named "Grinstead."

Subsequently, on August 30, 2003, Hoying sent Ms. Criswell another message. In that e-mail, Hoying threatened that "If the stuff in Xenia is not handled then some things are going to happen." The next day, Hoying sent a message, which says:

> "Ms. Criswell, tell your old man to get rid of the Xenia stuff or the hammer is going to fall heavy on him. It will take three years to get all of this stuff straightened out. If not, remember you are going to be subpoenaed for the thefts since you supplied some of the info, so you might as well say good bye to your job. I've been nice to you. I don't deserve to be paid back like this. I don't want to hurt you, but if you choose their side then that is that. This is such high school shit. I'm not coming to court anyway. I have an important doctor's appointment. My life is just as important as yours. If it is not handled and they come for me, they better bring an army. Ted."

As a result of the e-mails, Ms. Criswell changed her address, changed her license plate, changed employment, and eventually moved away. (Ms. Criswell's current living arrangement was not revealed in court, for her protection). Ms. Criswell also testified that she could possibly need psychiatric or psychological assistance in the future because of everything Hoying had done.

OPINION

. . . Hoying claims that his conviction for menacing by stalking was based on insufficient evidence. As support for this contention, Hoying notes that he did not cause physical harm to Ms. Criswell and she did not seek professional help for mental distress. He also notes a lack of evidence that he was aware that Ms. Criswell believed he would cause her physical harm or mental distress. . . .

The essential elements of menacing by stalking are found in R.C. 2903.211, which provides, in pertinent part, that:

(A) No person by engaging in a pattern of conduct shall knowingly cause another person to believe that the offender will cause physical harm to the other person or cause mental distress to the other person. . . .

(B) Whoever violates this section is guilty of menacing by stalking.

. . . (2) Menacing by stalking is a felony of the fourth degree if any of the following applies:

(g) At the time of the commission of the offense, the offender was the subject of a protection order issued under section 2903.213 or 2903.214 of the Revised Code, regardless of whether the person to be protected under the order is the victim of the offense or another person.

After reviewing the evidence, we agree with the State that a reasonable jury could have inferred from the content of the e-mails that Hoying knew Ms. Criswell would consider the messages to be a threat to her physical safety or to that of her father. A reasonable jury could also have found that the messages would cause Ms. Criswell mental distress. The fact that Ms. Criswell previously sought a civil protection order was some evidence that she was afraid of the defendant, and the e-mails were sent after the protection order was issued to the defendant. Ms. Criswell also testified that she was "scared to death" of Hoying and that he had caused her much mental distress.

As an additional matter, Hoying's conduct in court did not help his case, as he interrupted Ms. Criswell's testimony several times with inappropriate comments, including calling her a liar. In one outburst, Hoying made what could be interpreted as a threat, stating, "She'd better start telling the truth and quit lying, that's for sure."

Hoying did not present any evidence to counteract the victim's testimony, or to prove that she was lying. Accordingly, any rational trier of fact had more than an ample basis for finding Hoying guilty of menacing by stalking. . . .

[Hoyer also] challenges the trial court's action in sentencing Hoying to the maximum term for the conviction of menacing by stalking, which is a fourth-degree felony, at least under the circumstances of this case. See R.C. 2903.211(B)(2)(g). Although community control sanctions are available for fourth-degree felonies, Hoying admits that they are not guaranteed. Hoying further concedes that he probably forfeited the ability to obtain community control by his conduct during trial and the sentencing hearing, and by his refusal to participate in the presentence investigation process. Having reviewed the record, we fully agree with that statement.

Nonetheless, Hoying contends that he should not have received the maximum sentence for menacing by stalking because the record does not support a finding that he poses the greatest likelihood of recidivism. We disagree.

Under R.C. 2929.14(A)(4), the potential term for a fourth degree felony is six to eighteen months. R.C. 2929.14(C) additionally states that:

except as provided in division (G) of this section or in Chapter 2925. of the Revised Code, the court imposing a sentence upon an offender for a felony may impose the longest prison term authorized for the offense pursuant to division (A) of this section only upon offenders who committed the worst forms of the offense, upon offenders who pose the greatest likelihood of committing future crimes, upon certain major drug offenders under division (D)(3) of this section, and upon certain repeat violent offenders in accordance with division (D)(2) of this section.

When a trial court imposes maximum sentences, it must state its findings and reasoning at the sentencing hearing. . . . Also, . . . when a trial court states its reasons for imposing a maximum sentence, it must connect those reasons to the finding which the reason supports. The court cannot merely pronounce causes that objectively may be its reasons. The court must also identify which of those causes are the particular reasons for each of the statutory findings that the court made.

In the present case, the trial court complied with the requirement of making findings at the sentencing hearing. The court also adequately connected its reasons for imposing a maximum sentence to the finding that the reason supported. At the sentencing hearing, the court stated that it found that Hoying had the greatest likelihood to re-offend, and that Hoying had committed the worst form of the offense.

Before reciting the court's specific reasons for these findings, we should note that the very night the jury verdict was issued, Hoying attempted to contact the victim. According to the State, Hoying attempted to contact Ms. Criswell five times. Hoying denied making five attempts, but did admit that he tried to contact the victim after the verdict to ask for help with his appeal. In view of the nature of the crime (menacing by stalking) and the jury verdict of "guilty," an attempt to contact the victim of the crime shows either a disconnection from reality or an obstinate refusal to submit to the authority of the law.

Hoying also refused to cooperate in any way with the presentence investigation. In addition, Hoying disrupted the sentencing process, showering foul language and abuse on the victim, her family, and even the court, to the point that Hoying eventually had to be removed from the courtroom. Ultimately, in discussing the length of the sentence, the trial court specifically connected the following reasons to its findings, by stating that:

> when the victim in this case testified, the Defendant's conduct as to her testimony was absolutely parallel to the conduct of the crime in which he was charged, beginning with his sense of enjoyment of the presence of the victim as she testified, and as her testimony became less beneficial to the Defendant, he proceeded to become more aggravated and agitated, writing notes, ultimately basically yelling at the victim during the course of that testimony, clearly, giving an indication as to his attitude and conduct toward the victim in this matter which brought this case forward in the first place.

> For that reason, the Court finds that the shortest prison term would not protect the public from future crimes, and the court has the greatest fear for Kelly Criswell, which the record will reflect, has moved from the immediate area and has taken extraordinary steps to prevent her location from being identified by this Defendant.

> The Court notes for the record that testimony in this case and the information subsequently received indicates that the particular victim in this case had no relationship whatsoever with the Defendant, can't even suggest there ever was a scintilla of a relationship, yet the Defendant's attitude toward her is just a classic stalking attitude, and the harm caused to her is so significant that it is necessary to take extreme measures so the Court can protect her, as well as others from future crime.

> The Court clearly feels the Defendant's conduct as demonstrated at his arrest, at his arraignment, during the conduct of this matter, the trial, and the sentencing here demonstrates an attitude on his part of failure to comply with authority, the failure to respect the integrity of other individuals, and quite candidly, makes this Defendant a very dangerous individual.

> The shortest prison term will demean the seriousness of the Defendant's conduct.

> The Court further finds based upon the facts stated herein and the information provided, which will be made a part of the record in this matter, that the Defendant's conduct has, to a great degree, established the worst form of the offense. I do not discount Counsel's statement that a first time offender is one in which there is an indication from the legislature that the least restrictive setting should apply; however, this Court can say unequivocally, in all the time that I've been on the Bench, I've never seen a Defendant that I'm more sure of is a serious threat to society and to the public.

The Court also finds the Defendant clearly poses the greatest likelihood to commit future crimes in this matter, and as such, the Court makes reference particularly to the competency report prepared earlier this year where the Defendant indicated in his evaluation, quote, I know I'm not crazy. I knew what I was doing when I contacted her knowing I was violating the order, end quote.

We find that the above discussion by the trial court fully complies with requirements for imposing maximum sentences. We also agree with the trial court that a maximum sentence was warranted. The record in this case is quite troubling, since it portrays an individual who either has no remorse for his actions, or refuses to admit he needs mental health treatment. Even though Hoying was found competent to stand trial, that does not mean that he is free of mental health problems that should be addressed, hopefully while he is in the prison system.

[Hoyer was also convicted of the separate crime of intimidation, not discussed here. The trial court sentenced him to consecutive sentences, amounting to a total of $6^1/_2$ years in prison. He objected]

to imposition of consecutive sentences. Consecutive sentences may be imposed for convictions of multiple offenses,

> if the court finds that the consecutive service is necessary to protect the public from future crime or to punish the offender and that consecutive sentences are not disproportionate to the seriousness of the offender's conduct and to the danger the offender poses to the public, and if the court also finds any of the following:

> (a) The offender committed one or more of the multiple offenses while the offender was awaiting trial or sentencing, was under a sanction imposed pursuant to section 2929.16, 2929.17, or 2929.18 of the Revised Code, or was under post-release control for a prior offense.

> (b) At least two of the multiple offenses were committed as part of one or more courses of conduct, and the harm caused by two or more of the multiple offenses so committed was so great or unusual that no single prison term for any of the offenses committed as part of any of the courses of conduct adequately reflects the seriousness of the offender's conduct.

> (c) The offender's history of criminal conduct demonstrates that consecutive sentences are necessary to protect the public from future crime by the offender. R.C. 2929.14(E)(4).

In imposing consecutive sentences, the trial court relied on R.C. 2929.14(E)(4)(b) and(c). Specifically, the court commented that:

> a consecutive term would be appropriate in this case because it's necessary to protect the public from future

crime by this Defendant, and I believe that the evidence presented in the trial in this matter, the Defendant's behavior during the trial, his failure to comply with the simplest matters of completing the presentence investigation clearly indicates that the Defendant's desire to not follow authority is quite clear. In fact, the Court would go so far as to make that finding beyond a reasonable doubt.

The Court further finds that consecutive sentences would be appropriate to punish the offender for the conduct he committed, and consecutive sentences in this case are not disproportionate to the seriousness of the Defendant's conduct and to the danger the Defendant clearly and unequivocally poses to the victim in this case and to the public generally.

The Court further finds that the harm caused in this case is so great that no single sentence would adequately reflect the seriousness of the Defendant's conduct, and the information received by the Prosecuting Attorney, which was made a part of the record in this case, indicating that the Defendant, even after his arrest, attempted to make continued contact with the victim, likewise dictates the Court's finding in this particular regard.

[Hoyer objected that the court used the same reasons to support the maximum sentence for both crimes.]

. . . One factor in imposing maximum sentences is whether an offender has committed the worst form of an offense. Similarly, a factor in deciding if consecutive sentences are warranted is whether the harm caused by two or more of the multiple offenses is "so great or unusual that no single prison term for any of the offenses . . . adequately reflects the seriousness of the offender's conduct." R.C. 2929.14(E)(4)(b). As merely one way in which these factors can overlap, we note that the harm caused by a particular offense will certainly bear on the determination of whether an offender has committed the worst form of the offense. . . . We see nothing wrong with a court using the same or similar reasons for more than one finding. . . .

. . . The judgment of the trial court is affirmed.

Questions

1. State the elements of stalking according to the Texas stalking statute.

2. List all the facts relevant to deciding whether the prosecution proved each of the elements.

3. Assume you're the prosecutor. Relying on the facts of the case and the reasoning of the trial and appellate court, argue that Hoying was guilty of stalking.

4. Assume you're Hoying's attorney. Relying on the facts of the case and Hoying's arguments, argue that Hoying wasn't guilty of stalking.

5. In *your* opinion, do the facts support a guilty verdict? Was the $6^1/_2$-year sentence too harsh? Explain your answers.

PERSONAL RESTRAINT CRIMES

One of the greatest things about living in a free society is the right to control our freedom of movement, even though we may not appreciate it until it's taken away from us. The 18th century called it the **right of locomotion,** meaning the right to come and go as we please, to stay if we don't want to move, and to move if we don't want to stay. I'm reminded of how precious this right is every time we get several inches of snow (which can be pretty often here in Minnesota). My house has a long driveway that needs plowing before I can get out. As much as I love my house, I start feeling confined if the snowplow doesn't get there within an hour. This is a silly example, but it underscores the issues of the two crimes against personal liberty we'll look at in this section: kidnapping and false imprisonment.

Kidnapping

Kidnapping is an ancient result crime that originally involved holding the king's relatives for ransom. Of course, it was considered a serious offense because it interfered with the personal liberty of members of royal families. Kidnapping is taking and carrying away another person with the intent to deprive that person of personal liberty.

At common law, kidnapping consisted of six elements:

1. Seizing,

2. Carrying away (**asportation** of) and

3. Confining

4. By force, threat of force, fraud, or deception

5. Another person

6. With the intent to deprive the other person of his or her liberty.

In the 1900s, kidnapping came to be considered a very serious felony in the United States—even a capital offense in some states. The seriousness had nothing to do with royalty but a lot to do with events during the first half of the 20th century.

During Prohibition (1919 to 1933), kidnapping was prevalent in the organized crime world. One gang member might abduct a rival, "take him for a ride," and kill him. Much more frequently, rivals were captured and held hostage for ransom. Before long, kidnapping spread to include the spouses and children of law-abiding wealthy and prominent citizens. The most famous case was *State v. Hauptmann* (1935), involving the prosecution of the man charged and convicted of the ransom kidnap and murder of Charles Lindbergh's son. The famous and beloved aviator captured Americans' hearts and imaginations when he flew solo across the Atlantic Ocean.

Kidnapping was a misdemeanor in New Jersey in 1932 when the crime occurred, but the tremendous sympathy that Lindbergh's popular hero status generated, and the public outrage toward what was perceived as a rampant increase in random kidnappings of America's "pillars of wealth and virtue," led legislatures to enact harsh new kidnapping statutes. These statutes remain largely in force today, even though they were passed in an emotional overreaction to a few notorious cases.

In 1974, another widely publicized case breathed new life into these harsh statutes when Patricia Hearst, heiress to newspaper tycoon William Randolph Hearst, was kidnapped. The case met with public outrage, not only because of sympathy for the prominent Hearst family but also because of shock at the psychological and physical dimensions of the crime. The kidnappers were self-styled revolutionaries calling themselves the Symbionese Liberation Army (SLA). One of the SLA's first demands was that Hearst's father, Randolph, distribute $1 million in food to the poor of California. Later on, much to her parents' and the public's horror, Patricia Hearst was accused of converting to the SLA and was later convicted of participating in bank robberies to raise money for the "revolution."

All this took place during a time when radicalism and violence were very much feared and when the Vietnam War protest and airline hijackings for terrorist political purposes were very much on the public's mind. The public saw Patty Hearst's capture and her family's deep trauma not just as one family's suffering but a threat to destroy American society.

The Hearst case focused attention on how monstrous kidnapping can be. It drew together in one story, capture, detention, terror, violence, and political radicalism. The details were trumpeted every day in newspapers and on radio and television. Hope that existing harsh and sweeping kidnapping legislation would be reassessed calmly vanished in this inflamed, emotional atmosphere.

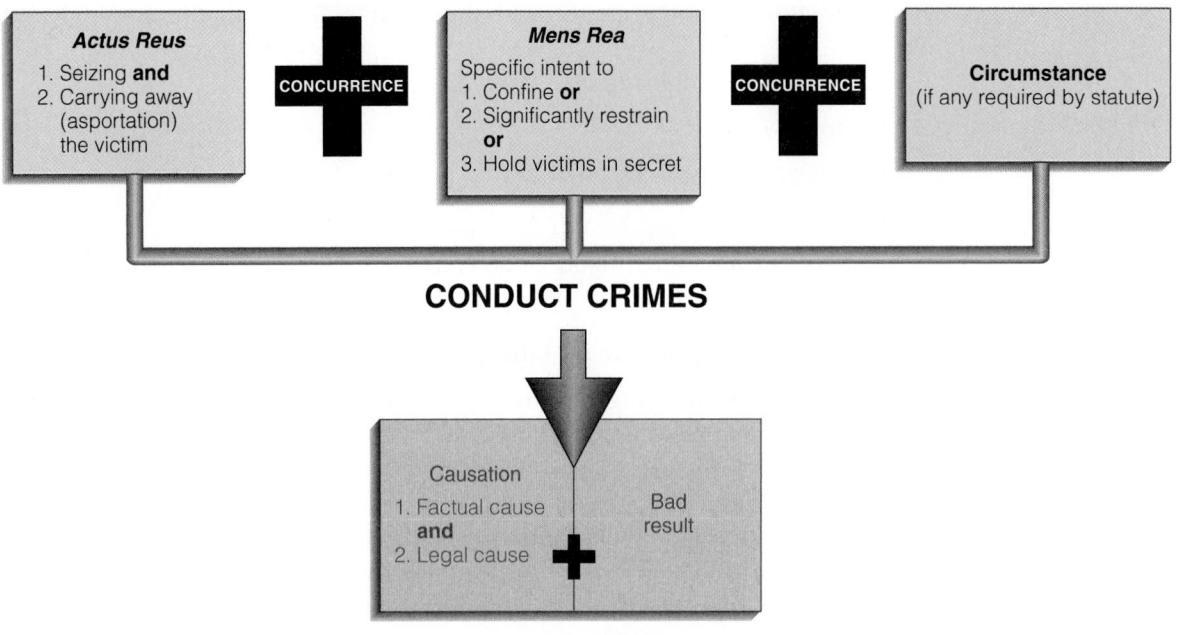

Elements of Kidnapping

President Nixon expressed his hope—a hope that many others shared—that the Supreme Court wouldn't declare capital punishment for kidnapping to be unconstitutional. California Governor Ronald Reagan reflected the deep public outrage against kidnapping when he wished aloud that the kidnappers' demand for a free food program would set off a botulism epidemic among the poor.

Let's look at the *actus reus* and *mens rea* elements of kidnapping and at how the law grades the seriousness of acts of kidnapping.

Kidnapping Actus Reus   The heart of kidnapping *actus reus* consists of seizing and carrying away (asportation) the victim. Since at least the 18th century, carrying a victim into a foreign country where no friends or family could give her aid and comfort, and the law couldn't offer protection, added a terrifying dimension to kidnapping.

In the early days, the victim had to be carried at least as far as another county and usually across its border. Modern interpretations have made the asportation requirement meaningless. The notorious case of *People v. Chessman* (1951) is the best example. Caryl Chessman was a serial rapist who, in one instance, forced a young woman to leave her car and get into his, which was only 22 feet away. The court held that the mere fact of moving the victim, not how far she was moved, satisfied the asportation requirement. So moving his victim 22 feet was enough to convict and sentence Chessman to the gas chamber.

In our next case excerpt, a carjacking, *People v. Allen* (1997), the California Supreme Court ruled that it's not the number of feet the carjacker moved the victims but the "quality and character" of his movement that matters in asportation.

Did He Move Her a "Substantial" Distance?

People v. Allen
64 Cal.Rptr.2d 497 (1997)

HISTORY

Tyrone Allen was convicted in the Superior Court, City and County of San Francisco, of kidnapping of a person under the age of 14. He appealed. The Court of Appeal affirmed.

RUVOLO, J.

FACTS

On August 7, 1995, May SunYoung and her family lived at 2951 Treat Street in San Francisco. That morning, Ms. SunYoung was on her way to take her 7-year-old daughter, Kirstie, to summer camp and stopped her automobile briefly in the driveway to close her garage door manually as she was backing out onto the street.

As Ms. SunYoung closed her garage door, a man approached her from behind and said, "Excuse me, can you do me a favor?" While turning around she saw Tyrone Allen getting into her vehicle, whose engine was still running. He then locked the car doors. Kirstie was still in the vehicle with her seatbelt on and began crying. Because the driver's side window was rolled down about seven inches, Ms. SunYoung put her arms through the window and struggled with appellant in an attempt to reach the ignition key and turn off the engine.

Allen then released the parking brake, put the vehicle in reverse, and backed out of the driveway with Kirstie inside and Ms. SunYoung running alongside the vehicle still attempting to reach the ignition key. The vehicle backed across Treat Street, which was a two-lane road with two parking lanes, until it hit the opposite curb and came to a stop. Allen estimated the vehicle movement was 30–40 feet. While Allen now claims this estimate to be "speculation," both sides at different times suggested that the distance moved was approximately 5 car lengths, or 50 feet.

Allen exited the vehicle, threw the car keys onto the ground, shoved Ms. SunYoung against a fence, and ran down the street carrying her purse which had been left in the vehicle. Shortly thereafter, a neighbor on Treat Street several blocks away saw a man run by. In response to the neighbor's attempts to stop the man, the fleeing suspect stated, "Stay back, I got a gun." After a brief struggle, the man ran off but was later apprehended by San Francisco police officers and identified as appellant.

The jury instruction given regarding the simple kidnapping count was CALJIC No. 9.52, which sets forth the elements of kidnapping of a person under 14 years of age as follows:

Every person who unlawfully and with physical force or by any other means of instilling fear moves any other person under 14 years of age without her consent for a substantial distance, that is, a distance more than slight or trivial, is guilty of the crime of kidnapping. . . . (Pen. Code, § 208, subd. (b); all further statutory references are to the Penal Code unless otherwise indicated.)

OPINION

The only element of the crime for which appellant asserts there was insufficient evidence and inadequate jury instructions is asportation. For "simple" kidnapping, that is, a kidnapping not elevated to a statutory form of "aggravated" kidnapping, the movement needed must be "substantial," or a distance that is more than "trivial, slight, or insignificant."

Allen . . . argues that his conviction for simple kidnapping must be reversed because the minimum distance requirement for asportation is not met. He asserts the movement of Ms. SunYoung's vehicle 30–50 feet down her driveway and across Treat Street with Kirstie inside as a matter of law cannot be "substantial," or a distance that is more than "trivial, slight or insignificant."

Allen is correct that under most cases decided pre-1981 which have examined only the actual distance involved, the movement here would not meet the legal test of substantiality. . . . Those cases which have considered the quality and character of the movement in addition to its absolute distance have weighed the purpose for the movement, whether it posed an increased risk of harm to the victim, and the context of the environment in which the movement occurred.

Purposes for movement found to be relevant have been those undertaken to facilitate the commission of a further crime, to aid in flight, or to prevent detection. We believe these factors are appropriate considerations.

"Substantiality" implies something more than only measured distance. While "slight" is consistent with a quantitative analysis, the term "trivial" is a qualitative term suggestive of the conclusion that more is envisioned in determining whether a kidnapping occurs than simply how far the victim is moved. The legal requirement for asportation is satisfied by a finding of either.

In so holding, we conclude that while in absolute footage the distance moved here may have been empirically short, it was of a character sufficient to justify a finding of "substantiality" by the jury. The movement, in part, was plainly made to prevent Ms. SunYoung from regaining possession of her vehicle and to facilitate appellant's flight from the area with Kirstie. In addition to evasion of capture, the vehicle was moved from a position of relative safety onto a thoroughfare. The boundary crossed was significant because it placed Kirstie at greater risk of injury.

We confirm these factors, coupled with the distance traveled, are sufficient to satisfy the "substantial movement" requirement for the crime of simple kidnapping. . . .

AFFIRMED.

DISSENT

KLINE, J.

. . . Movement as short a distance as that shown here—30 to 40 feet—has never been held to satisfy the asportation requirement of kidnapping. Indeed, considerably greater distances have often been held insufficient. As the majority opinion points out, movement of 90 feet, nearly three times the distance the victim in this case was moved, was held insufficient. . . . The shortest distance this court has ever held to be "substantial" for this purpose was a full city block.

People v. Brown (1974) 523 P.2d 226 also dramatically demonstrates that the movement in the present case must be deemed trivial as a matter of law. The defendant in Brown had gone to the victim's residence in search of her husband, whose name he had discovered in the home of his estranged wife. He forced the victim to accompany him in a search of the house for her husband.

When a neighbor who heard the victim scream telephoned and asked if she needed help, the defendant dragged her out of the house and along a narrow passageway between her house and the house next door. A neighbor then ordered the defendant to release the victim and told him the police were on their way. Defendant released her and fled.

All in all he had taken her approximately 40 to 75 feet from the back door of her house. A unanimous Supreme Court had little difficulty concluding that "the asportation of the victim within her house and for a brief distance outside the house must be regarded as trivial." . . .

I agree that by moving the child in the vehicle across the street Allen committed a crime other than carjacking and the various other offenses of which he was properly convicted; that crime was not kidnapping, however, but false imprisonment (Pen.Code, § 236), which does not require any movement. . . .

Because the asportation in this case was trivial within the meaning of the applicable case law, I would reverse the judgment of conviction of simple kidnapping for lack of evidentiary support. I agree that in all other respects the judgment should be affirmed.

Questions

1. What test did the court establish to determine how far defendants have to move victims to satisfy the asportation element of kidnapping *actus reus*?

2. What reasons does the majority give to support its definition of asportation?

3. How does the dissent's definition of asportation differ from that of the majority's?

4. What reasons does the dissent give for its definition?

5. Do you agree with the majority or the dissent's definition of asportation? Defend your answer.

Kidnapping Mens Rea   Kidnapping *mens rea* is stated usually as the specific intent to confine, significantly restrain, or hold victims in secret. The Wisconsin statute, for example, defines a kidnapper as one who "seizes or confines another without his consent and with intent to cause him to be secretly confined." Whatever the exact wording of the statutes, the heart of the kidnapping mental attitude remains to "isolate the victim from the prospect of release or friendly intervention" (Wisconsin Criminal Code 2006, ß 940.31).

Grading Kidnapping Seriousness   Kidnapping is usually divided into two degrees: simple and aggravated. The most common aggravating circumstances include kidnapping for the purpose of:

- Sexual invasions

- Obtaining a hostage

- Obtaining ransom

- Robbing the victim

- Murdering the victim
- Blackmailing
- Terrorizing the victim
- Achieving political aims

The penalty for aggravated kidnapping is usually life imprisonment and, until recently, occasionally even death.

False Imprisonment

False imprisonment is a lesser form of personal restraint than kidnapping, but the heart of the crime remains depriving others of their personal liberty. It's a lesser offense because there's no asportation requirement; the deprivation of liberty is brief; and the detention is less stressful. *False imprisonment* was succinctly defined as compelling a person "to remain where he does not wish to remain" (*McKendree v. Christy* 1961, 381).

Most forcible detentions or confinements, however brief, satisfy the *actus reus* of false imprisonment. This doesn't include restraints authorized by law—for example, when parents restrict their children's activities or victims detain their victimizers.

The Model Penal Code (MPC) requires the restraint to "interfere substantially with the victim's liberty," but, in most state statutes, *any* interference with another person's liberty is enough. For example, here's the way the Florida statute defines the *actus reus* of false imprisonment:

> False imprisonment means forcibly, by threat, or secretly confining, abducting, imprisoning, or restraining another person without lawful authority and against her or his will. (Florida Criminal Code 2006)

Although physical force often accomplishes the detention, it doesn't have to; threatened force is enough. So the threat, "If you don't come with me, I'll drag you along," is enough. Even nonthreatening words can qualify, such as when a police officer who has no right to do so orders someone on the street into a squad car, asserting, "You're under arrest."

False imprisonment is a specific-intent crime. According to a typical statute: False imprisonment consists of intentionally confining or restraining another person without his consent. . . . (New Mexico Criminal Code 2006) The motive for the detention doesn't matter. For example, if police officers make unlawful arrests, they can be prosecuted for false imprisonment even if they believed the arrests were lawful.

SUMMARY

I. Rape
    A. Rape is regarded by the law and society as second only to murder as the most serious crime.
    B. Rape is a crime even if victims suffer no physical injury, not even minor cuts and bruises.
    C. Rape and other sexual assaults are different from all other felonies in that under other circumstances, the behaviors connected with them are not just legal but desired.

II. Sex offenses
 A. Common-law origins only recognized two sex offenses: common-law rape and common-law sodomy.
  1. Common-law rape was strictly limited to intentional forced heterosexual vaginal penetration.
  2. Common-law sodomy meant anal intercourse between two males.
 B. Since the 1970s and 1980s, court opinions have relaxed the definition of rape and criminal sexual conduct and assault statutes.
 C. The vast majority of rape victims are raped by men they know.
 D. There are two types of rape: aggravated and unarmed acquaintance rape.
  1. In aggravated rape, a victim is raped by strangers or men with weapons who physically injure their victims.
  2. Unarmed acquaintance rape is nonconsensual sex between "dates, lovers, neighbors, co-workers, employers, and so on."
 E. Acquaintance rapes make up an overwhelming number of rapes, some 80 percent of all rapes.
 F. There are a substantial number of rapes committed against men; 8 percent of all sexual assault victims are male.

III. The history of rape law
 A. As early as 800, rape was a capital offense in Anglo-Saxon England.
 B. The 1769 definition of rape by Blackstone consisted of four elements:
  1. Sexual intercourse by force or a threat of severe bodily harm (*actus reus*)
  2. Intentional vaginal intercourse (*mens rea*)
  3. Intercourse between a man and a woman who wasn't his wife (attendant circumstance)
  4. Intercourse without the woman's consent (attendant circumstance)
 C. A victim's credibility was considered on three elements:
  1. Her chastity
  2. Whether she promptly reported the rape
  3. Whether other witnesses corroborated the rape

IV. Criminal sexual conduct statutes
 A. The 1970s and 1980s gave way to great change in the formal law of sex offenses.
  1. Many states abolished the corroboration rule, which required the prosecution to back up rape victims' testimony with that of other witnesses.
  2. Most states passed rape shield statutes, which banned introducing evidence of victims' past sexual conduct.
  3. Many states relaxed the prompt-reporting rule, which banned prosecution unless women promptly reported rapes.
  4. States also changed the marital rape exception, the old common-law rule that husbands couldn't rape their wives.
  5. Sexual assault statutes shifted the emphasis away from consent by the victim to unwanted advances by the perpetrator and also consolidated the sex offenses into one statute.
 B. The seriousness of sex offenses under the new codes is graded according to several criteria:
  1. Penetrations are more serious than contacts.

2. Forcible penetrations and contacts are more serious than simple nonconsensual penetrations and contacts.
3. Physical injury to the victim aggravates the offense.
C. Michigan's statute, instituted in 1974, is the best known; it divides sexual assault into four degrees.

V. The elements of modern rape law

A. Most traditional rape statutes define *rape* as intentional sexual penetration by force without the victim's consent.
B. Rape boils down to three elements:
1. The *actus reus* is sexual penetration by force or threat of force.
2. The *mens rea* is intentional sexual penetration.
3. The circumstance is nonconsent by the victim.
C. Rape *actus reus* is governed by the force and resistance rule.
1. Originally, this meant that victims had to prove they didn't consent and, therefore, resisted the unwanted sexual act to the utmost of their power.
2. Today, courts recognize two types of force: extrinsic and intrinsic force.
   a. Extrinsic force requires some act of force in addition to the muscular movements needed to accomplish penetration. The amount of force required varies according to the circumstances of particular cases.
   b. Intrinsic force requires only the amount of physical effort necessary to accomplish penetration.
3. Actual use of force isn't required to satisfy the force requirement; the threat of force is enough.
4. To satisfy the threat-of-force requirement, the prosecution has to prove two things: subjective fear and objective fear.
   a. Subjective fear means the victim honestly feared imminent and serious bodily harm.
   b. Objective fear means the fear was reasonable under the circumstances.
D. Rape *mens rea*
1. Rape is a *general-intent* crime, meaning defendants intend to commit the act defined in the crime.
2. Exceptions to the *mens rea* element include reckless mistakes, negligent mistakes, or no-fault mistakes (strict liability).
   a. A negligent mistake occurs when the defendant falsely believes the victim's state of mind is one of consenting to sex.
   b. Courts have also adopted a reckless requirement, requiring that the defendant has to be aware that there's a risk the victim hasn't consented to sexual intercourse.
   c. Strict liability occurs when the defendant engages in the sexual act without consent.
E. Statutory rape consists of having sex with minors.
1. In most states, rape is a strict liability offense with respect to the circumstance of the age of the victim, meaning that the perpetrator's belief that the victim was above the age consent, even if reasonable, doesn't affect liability.
2. In some states, reasonable mistake regarding age is a defense.
F. Most statutes divide rape into two degrees: simple rape and aggravated rape.
1. Aggravated rape usually requires one of the following circumstances:
   a. The victim suffers serious bodily injury.

     b. A stranger commits the rape.

     c. The rape occurs in connection with another crime.

     d. The rapist is armed.

     e. The rapist has accomplices.

     f. The victim is a minor and the rapist is several years older.

  2. All other rapes are simple rapes.

VI. Bodily injury crimes

A. Assault and battery are two separate crimes, although they are often combined in many modern statutes.

  1. Battery is an unwanted and unjustified offensive touching; body contact is central to battery.

  2. Assault is either an attempted or a threatened battery, depending on how the statute defines it.

  3. Assault requires no physical contact; an assault is complete before the offender touches the victim.

B. Battery

  1. The *actus reus* of battery is unlawful touching without consent.

  2. Battery requires some injury. Minor physical injury and emotional injury are misdemeanors in most states, whereas batteries that cause serious bodily injury are felonies.

C. Assaults are either attempted batteries or threatened batteries, depending on the state's statute.

  1. Attempted battery assault consists of having the specific intent to commit a battery and taking substantial steps toward carrying it out without actually completing the attempt.

  2. Threatened battery assault requires only that actors intend to frighten their victims.

D. Stalking

  1. Stalking laws ensure that victims don't have to be injured or threatened with death before stopping a stalker's harassment.

  2. *Actus reus* requires that the stalking take place more than once.

  3. The *mens rea* of stalking, which is a result crime, requires that stalkers' actions cause their victims to be put in fear.

  4. States use four different tests to determine whether the stalker's acts caused the bad result of fear in the victim:

     a. Subjective and objective fear

     b. Subjective fear only

     c. Objective fear only

     d. Intent to instill

  5. *Cyberstalking* is defined as the use of the Internet, e-mail, or other electronic communications devices to stalk another person through threatening behavior.

VII. Personal restraint crimes

A. Kidnapping is an ancient crime that interferes with the right of locomotion.

  1. The heart of kidnapping *actus reus* consists of seizing and carrying away the victim.

  2. Kidnapping *mens rea* is usually stated as the specific intent to confine, significantly restrain, or hold victims in secret.

3. Kidnapping has two degrees: aggravated and simple.
   B. False imprisonment is a specific-intent crime—namely, intent to detain without consent.
      1. It's a lesser offense than kidnapping because of three differences:
         a. The victim isn't moved from the place of detention.
         b. The detention is brief.
         c. The detention is less stressful.
      2. Most forcible detentions or confinements satisfy the *actus reus* of false imprisonment.
      3. The motive for detention is irrelevant.

REVIEW QUESTIONS

1. How are rape and other sexual assaults different from all other felonies?

2. Define *common-law rape* and *common-law sodomy*.

3. Describe the differences between aggravated and unarmed acquaintance rape.

4. Identify four reasons why the criminal justice system has failed when it comes to unarmed acquaintance rape.

5. Identify and describe the four elements in Blackstone's definition of rape.

6. List and summarize the main reforms in the law of rape adopted in the statutes enacted in the 1970s and the 1980s.

7. Identify three criteria used to grade the seriousness of sex offenses in the criminal conduct statutes of the 1970s and the 1980s.

8. Identify and define the four degrees of criminal sexual conduct in Michigan's 1974 criminal sexual conduct statute.

9. Trace the history of the force and resistance rule.

10. What's the difference between extrinsic force and intrinsic force in rape law?

11. Identify the two prongs of the subjective and objective test to satisfy the threat-of-force requirement.

12. Identify four elements that meet the threat-of-force requirement in rape.

13. List and describe the *mens rea* element of reckless mistakes, negligent mistakes, and no-fault, or strict liability, mistakes.

14. Describe why statutory rapists don't have to use force to be held accountable for rape.

15. Identify five of the six circumstances that qualify rape as aggravated rape.

16. Describe the difference between battery and assault.

17. Identify the difference between attempted battery assault and threatened battery assault.

18. Describe the history behind modern antistalking statutes.

19. Identify three elements fault states use to define the *mens rea* element of stalking.

20. Describe four different approaches states use to test for the bad result of fear caused by acts of stalking.

21. In what way is cyberstalking different from "normal" stalking?

22. Describe the history behind kidnapping laws.

23. Identify six of the eight aggravating circumstances involving kidnapping.

24. Define the right of locomotion.

25. Why is false imprisonment a lesser offense than kidnapping?

KEY TERMS

common-law rape, p. 330
common-law sodomy, p. 331
sexual assault statutes, p. 331
criminal sexual conduct statutes, p. 331
aggravated rape, p. 331
unarmed acquaintance rape, p. 331
corroboration rule, p. 332
rape shield statute, p. 332
prompt-reporting rule, p. 332
marital rape exception, p. 333
rape, p. 334
rape *actus reus*, p. 335
force and resistance rule, p. 335
utmost resistance standard, p. 335

reasonable resistance rule, p. 336
extrinsic force, p. 337
intrinsic force, p. 337
threat-of-force requirement, p. 343
fraud in the fact, p. 343
fraud in the inducement, p. 344
honest and reasonable mistake rule (regarding consent in rape), p. 344
recklessness requirement (regarding consent in rape), p. 345
statutory rape, p. 346
reasonable mistake of age, p. 346
simple rape, p. 347
battery, p. 347

assault, p. 347
stalking, p. 347
attempted battery assault, p. 348
threatened battery assault, p. 348
conditional threats (in assault), p. 349
subjective and objective fear test, p. 352
subjective fear only test, p. 352
objective fear only test, p. 352
intent-to-instill-fear test, p. 352
cyberstalking, p. 352
right of locomotion, p. 356
kidnapping, p. 356
asportation, p. 357
false imprisonment, p. 361

Crimes Against Property

MAIN POINTS

- Crimes against other people's property are of three types: taking property, damaging or destroying property, and invading property.
- The crime of theft grew out of the general social concern with violent crimes against persons.
- It's illegal to receive stolen property only if you intend to keep it permanently.
- The heart of robbery is the use of actual or threatened force to obtain someone else's property right now.
- Extortion differs from robbery in that the threat is to use force some time in the future.
- Arson is a felony; criminal mischief is a misdemeanor.
- The heart of both burglary and criminal trespass is *invading* other people's property, not taking, destroying, or damaging it.
- Criminal trespass used to be limited to unauthorized invasions of physical property, but now it includes unauthorized access to electronic information systems.
- Identity theft is the most prevalent crime in the United States.
- Intellectual property theft results in billions of dollars in losses each year.

Tim and Helen Remsburg pose in their home in Hudson, NH, with a photo of Helen's daughter, Amy Boyer. Liam Yovens, who murdered Boyer, had chronicled his obsession with her and his plot to kill her on a website, and he paid Docusearch Inc. the Internet information broker, about $150 to get her Social Security number and other information, including her work address.

What's the Right Response to These Victims?

A well-known Nashville-based songwriter wrote a track on Jessica Simpson's best-selling album "Sweet Kisses." By the time Simpson's album was released in 1999, this songwriter had used his talent and hard work to build a major song-writing firm in Nashville that employed eight additional songwriters and an office assistant. As with many songwriting businesses in New York and Los Angeles, the Nashville firm depended on royalties to pay salaries and cover expenses. "Sweet Kisses" was a commercial success for them and sold more than three million copies. But, during a three-week period after its release, the album was illegally downloaded more than 1.2 million times, according to a Nashville-based firm that tracked the online theft of the album. As more and more of the firm's songs were illegally downloaded, the firm saw less and less income from royalties. The Nashville songwriter was forced to downsize, ultimately laying off all nine of his employees. Today, he is a one-man songwriting operation.

(U.S. DEPARTMENT OF JUSTICE 2004, III)

There are three kinds of crimes against other people's property:

1. Taking it
2. Damaging or destroying it
3. Invading it

Our discussion will focus on the elements of a few specific crimes of each kind. First, we'll look at three ways of taking someone else's property: by theft (sneaking away with an iPod left unattended in the library; robbery (sticking a gun in someone's side and demanding the $100 she just withdrew from an ATM machine); and receiving stolen property (buying a new notebook computer for $75 that you know is stolen). Then, we'll look at destroying someone else's property through arson (setting a house on fire) and damaging someone else's property through criminal mischief (driving your car up on an obnoxious neighbor's new sod and spinning the wheels). Finally, we'll look at invasions of someone else's property through burglary (unlawfully entering someone else's house with the intent to steal a TV inside) and criminal trespass (entering your neighbor's yard where a "no trespassing" sign is posted).

The examples given in the last paragraph represent the traditional ways you can take, destroy, damage, and invade other people's property. **Cybercrime,** crimes committed through the Internet or some other computer network, is a serious and rapidly growing new problem. There are four types of cybercrimes (Yang and Hoffstadt 2006, 203–4):

1. *Crimes against information brokers* Data collectors (credit reporting agencies) and data aggregators (LexisNexis)
2. *Crimes against manufacturers and distributors of digital media* Movie, recording, and software companies
3. *Crimes against online product and service sales* Businesses that offer their products and services for sale on the Internet
4. *Crimes against business computer systems* Internal computer systems connected to the Internet, used to conduct daily business affairs, house companies' asset data, including their trade secrets

We often call cybercrimes "new crimes." But they're really only new *ways* (admittedly sometimes very complex and sophisticated ways) to commit the three ancient kinds of crimes against property: taking it, damaging or destroying it, and invading it. According to *The Electronic Frontier* (2000):

> Advances in technology—the advent of the automobile and the telephone for instance—have always given wrongdoers new means for engaging in unlawful conduct. The internet is no different: it is simply a new medium through which traditional crimes can now be committed.

TAKING OTHER PEOPLE'S PROPERTY

The long history of taking other people's property resulted in the expansion of the criminal law into protecting property. It began as part of the general social concern with violent crimes against the person (such as those you learned about in Chapters 9 and 10). That concern led to the creation of the common-law felony of **robbery**—taking property by force or the threat of force—which is a violent crime against persons *and* their property.

Criminal law next expanded to taking property without consent even if the thief used no force. The first nonconsensual taking felony was **larceny,** the ancient crime of sneaking away with (stealing) someone else's property without their consent and, most of the time, without their knowledge. Larceny was born as the common-law instrument to protect the Anglo-Saxons' most valuable possession—livestock—from dishonest or untrustworthy thieves (LaFave and Scott 1986, chap. 8; Perkins and Boyce 1982, chap. 4)

Larceny didn't protect the property of those who voluntarily handed it over to a caretaker—for example, a carrier who delivered property to someone else or a bank that held depositors' money. Larceny required that thieves "take and carry away" the property. Caretakers did neither; what they did was "convert" property that was lawfully in their possession to their own use.

As society advanced, this gap in the law of larceny failed increasingly to protect the exploding quantities and kinds of valuable possessions from clever, trusted people who wanted to get their hands on other people's property entrusted to them. These included **tangible property** (for example, jewelry) and **intangible property** (stock options, bonds, and promissory notes—paper worth nothing by itself but which was proof of something of value).

As society became more complex, caretakers converting property that had been voluntarily handed over to them to their own use grew into an enormous problem. Legislatures responded to this problem of unlawful conversion of property by creating the felony of **embezzlement.** The earliest embezzlement statutes were directed at occupations like bank clerks. Eventually, statutes reached broadly to include all kinds of breaches of trust. According to the MPC reporter (ALI 1985, 2:223.1):

> A few American legislatures enacted fraudulent-conversion statutes penalizing misappropriation by anyone who received or had in his possession or control the property of another, or property which someone else "is entitled to receive and have." Indeed, some modern embezzlement statutes go so far as to penalize breach of faith without regard to whether anything is misappropriated. Thus, the fiduciary who makes forbidden investments, the official who deposits public funds in an unauthorized depository, the financial advisor who betrays his client into paying more for a property than fair market value, may be designated an embezzler. (129)

These **abuse-of-trust crimes** are the first examples of what eventually became **white-collar crimes**—crimes growing out of opportunities to get someone else's property because of the perpetrator's occupation. Although the term was first used to refer only to business executives, it's now used to include property crimes that grow out of opportunities created by any lawful occupation. Statutes and courts are still creating new crimes to combat the same old evil of satisfying the excessive desire to get other people's property by the new methods of stealing their identities using computers and the Internet.

Larceny applied to those who sneaked away with someone else's property. Embezzlement covered those who kept permanently someone else's property they had only a temporary right to possess. But what about owners who were tricked into giving up possession or ownership? The deceivers hadn't "taken" the property, because the owners willingly gave it to them. They hadn't converted it either, because they didn't even have a temporary right to possess it.

The crime of obtaining property by **false pretenses** (also called **theft by deceit or trick**) filled the gap left by larceny and embezzlement when it came to criminally getting other people's property. In false pretenses *actus reus*, "deceiving" replaces "taking" in larceny and "converting" in embezzlement. Deception requires a lie, like making a promise to deliver something when you can't, or don't intend to, keep the promise. False pretenses *mens rea* requires the purpose or specific intent to obtain property by deceit and lies.

False pretenses includes three circumstance elements. Victims have to had parted with property; they have to had parted with it because they believed the lie; and the property they parted with has to be worth an amount named in the false pretenses statute.

Theft

There's a lot more history than reason behind dividing these three ways to get other people's property into separate crimes. As we saw earlier, when society changed, embezzlement supplemented larceny, and then theft by deceit (false pretenses) supplemented both larceny and embezzlement to fight the new ways of unlawfully taking other people's money. Most states have turned away from divisions of theft based on history and moved toward logic by consolidating larceny, embezzlement, and false pretenses into one offense called **theft.** They accept the social reality that all these ancient crimes were aimed at the same evil—intentionally getting control of someone else's property.

Consolidated theft statutes eliminate the artificial need to separate theft into distinct offenses according to their *actus reus*. Theft includes the *actus reus* of either "taking and carrying away" or "converting" or "swindling" someone else's property. The *mens*

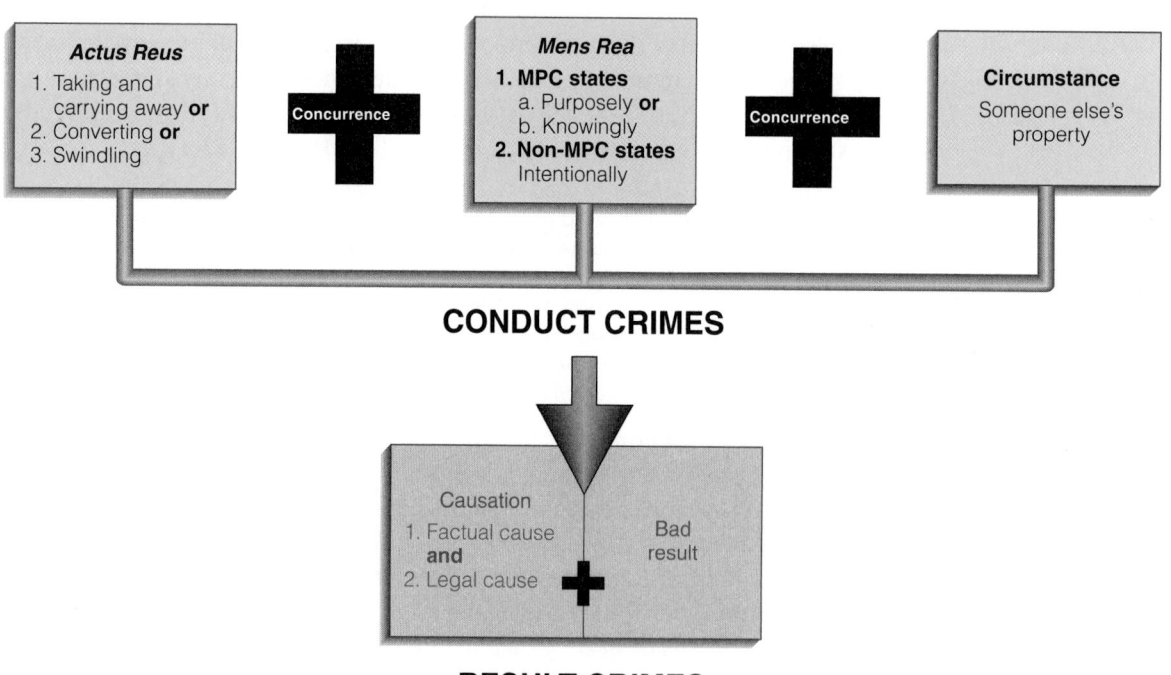

Elements of Theft

rea is acquiring someone else's property "purposely" or "knowingly" in MPC language or "intentionally" in non-MPC states.

Let's look at one other nonviolent misappropriation of property crime that most consolidated theft statutes don't include: receiving stolen property.

Receiving Stolen Property

It's not only a crime to steal someone else's property, it's also a crime to "receive" (accept) property someone else has already stolen. Called **receiving stolen property**, the purpose of making this a crime is to prevent and to punish individuals who benefit from someone else's theft, even though they didn't have anything to do with the original theft. Although the crime is primarily directed at *fences* (professionals who sell stolen property for profit), it also targets people whose mental attitude is that they know, or should know, they're buying stolen stuff because the prices are too low.

Receiving Stolen Property Actus Reus   The *actus reus* of receiving stolen property is the act of receiving the property. Receiving requires that the receiver control the property, at least briefly. But the receiver doesn't have to possess the property physically. So if I buy a stolen TiVo from a fence for a friend, and the fence hands it over directly to my friend, I've received the stolen TiVo, even though I've never seen or touched it. If my friend gives the TiVo to her friend, her friend also has received the stolen TiVo. Also, anyone who temporarily hides stolen goods for someone else has received the stolen goods.

Receiving Stolen Property Mens Rea   The receiving stolen property *mens rea* varies. In some states, receivers have to *know* the goods are stolen. In others, *believing* the goods are stolen is enough. In all jurisdictions, knowledge may be inferred from

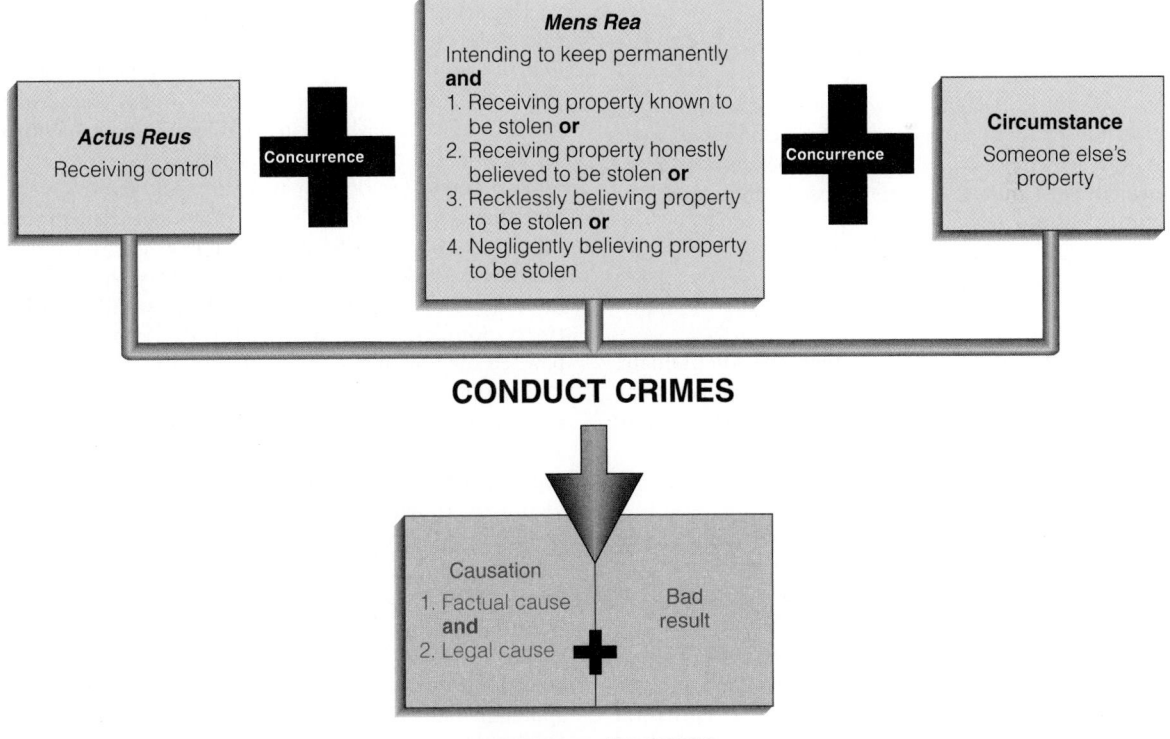

Elements of Receiving Stolen Property

surrounding circumstances, such as receiving goods from a known thief or buying goods at a fraction of their real value (for example, buying a new top-of-the-line HDTV for $275). Some jurisdictions require only that receivers were reckless or negligent about whether the property was stolen. Recklessness and negligence as to whether the property was stolen are often directed at likely fences, usually junk dealers and pawn shop operators.

Another aspect of the *mens rea* of receiving stolen property is that receivers have to intend to keep the property permanently. This excludes police officers who knowingly accept stolen property and secretly place it in the hands of suspected fences to catch them. They haven't received stolen property because they don't intend to keep it, only to use it as bait.

Texas is one state that requires that receivers *know* the property they control is stolen. The state has to prove actual knowledge beyond a reasonable doubt, but the prosecution can use circumstantial evidence to meet its burden of proof. In our next case excerpt, *Sonnier v. State*, a Texas trial court convicted Olga Sonnier of receiving stolen property and sentenced her to 15 years in prison for knowingly pawning four stolen P. V. amplifier speakers for $275; they were worth $1400. The Texas Court of Criminal Appeals reversed the trial court's conviction.

CASE   *Did She Know the Speakers Were Stolen?*

Sonnier v. State

849 S.W.2d 828 (Tex.App. 1992)

HISTORY

Olga Lee Sonnier, Defendant, was convicted after a bench trial in the 230th District Court, Harris County, of theft. She was sentenced to 15 years confinement, and she appealed. The Court of Appeals reversed and judgment of acquittal was ordered.

MIRABAL, J.

FACTS

On November 2, 1989, John L. Clough, the complainant, discovered several items missing from his establishment, the Houstonian Club. Among the items missing were four amplifier speakers, known as "P. V." or "Peavey" speakers. The speakers are the type that are connected to an amplifier system when bands play at the club. When the four speakers are stacked and connected, they stand about four feet tall and three feet wide. The speakers were valued at $1400 when purchased, and could not be replaced for less than $2000.

The complainant last saw the speakers on the night of November 1, 1989. He did not know appellant, she was not his employee, and he did not give anyone permission to take the speakers from his club. An employee, Gaylord or "Ricky" Burton, worked for him a couple of months, but vanished at the same time the speakers did. Burton was supposed to be at the club on the morning the speakers disappeared.

The complainant reported the theft to the police. He told them he believed Burton had stolen the speakers. One of complainant's employees had seen Burton take the speakers the morning of November 2, 1989. The speakers were found in a pawn shop. The complainant identified the speakers by their serial numbers.

Two employees of the pawn shop said two men came into the shop on November 2, 1989, and tried to pawn the speakers. The men had no identification, and the employees could not accept the speakers without some identification. The men came back later with appellant (Olga Sonnier), who had a driver's license, and she pawned the four speakers for $225.

The police, after an investigation, were unable to locate Burton, but did locate appellant because her name, address, and signature were on the pawn tickets. Appellant was charged with theft. A pawn shop employee positively identified appellant as the woman who pawned the speakers. Appellant called two witnesses, an employee of the pawn shop, Anthony Smith, and Sergeant Graves of the Houston Police Department. Appellant did not testify.

Smith testified two men tried to pawn the speakers. When he would not accept the speakers without some identification, the men left, but came back later with appellant. She presented a driver's license and pawned the speakers. Sergeant Graves testified appellant phoned him and said she pawned the speakers for some friends who did not have a driver's license.

OPINION

In her first point of error, appellant asserts that the evidence is insufficient to show she had actual knowledge that the speakers were stolen. The essential elements of theft by receiving are:

(1) that a theft occurred by another person;

(2) the defendant received the stolen property; and

(3) when the defendant received the stolen property she knew it was stolen.

Note:

TEXAS CRIMINAL CODE SEC. 31.03. THEFT

(1) A person commits an offense if he unlawfully appropriates property with intent to deprive the owner of property.

(2) Appropriation of property is unlawful if:
 (1) it is without the owner's effective consent;
 (2) the property is stolen and the actor appropriates the property knowing it was stolen by another. . . .

Under the statute and the indictment, the State had the burden to prove beyond a reasonable doubt, that appellant had *actual subjective* knowledge that the speakers were stolen. The evidence, viewed in the light most favorable to the prosecution, shows:

- On the same day the speakers were stolen, two men brought them to a pawn shop to hock them.

- When the pawn shop refused to accept the speakers because neither man would offer identification, the two men left, and then returned with appellant.

- Appellant pawned the four speakers for the two men. She used her driver's license, giving her correct name and address. She received $225 for the four speakers, about $56 for each, while they were worth at least $350 each.

The State emphasized in the trial court, and on appeal, that the sheer value of the speakers is enough for the trial court to find appellant knew they were stolen. The State argues that selling stolen property for less than market value is some evidence that the seller knew the property was stolen.

However, here the speakers were pawned, not sold, and the evidence does not indicate that the pawn shop paid an unusually low amount to pawn the speakers. Further, the evidence does not show that appellant, or any reasonable person of common experience, would likely even know the market value of the speakers.

We cannot say that the circumstances in this case exclude every other reasonable hypothesis except the hypothesis that appellant knew the speakers were stolen when she pawned them. We find, under the circumstances, appellant just as reasonably could have been doing a favor for her friends or acquaintances when she accompanied them to the pawn shop and used her own ID so the speakers could be pawned. We sustain appellant's point of error one.

In point of error three, appellant asserts the evidence was also insufficient to support her conviction under the "straight theft" paragraph of the indictment which alleged appellant

(1) unlawfully appropriated the speakers by acquiring them and otherwise exercising control over them,

(2) with the intent to deprive the owner of the property,

(3) without the effective consent of the owner. Tex.Penal Code Ann. ß 31.03(a), (b)(1). . . .

The evidence before the trial court placed appellant in possession of the speakers on the day they were stolen. The unexplained possession of stolen property may be sufficient to sustain a conviction for theft. To warrant such an inference of guilt from the circumstances of possession alone, the possession must be personal, recent, unexplained, and must involve a distinct and conscious assertion of a right to the property by the defendant.

When the party in possession gives a *reasonable* explanation for having the recently stolen property, the State must prove the explanation is false. Whether the explanation is reasonable and true is a question of fact. The fact finder is not bound to accept a defendant's explanation for possession of recently stolen property. A trial judge, sitting without a jury, is authorized to accept or reject any or all of the evidence.

Appellant was in possession of the speakers when she pledged them at the pawn shop. This was a distinct and conscious assertion of a right to the property. She pawned the speakers on the day they were stolen, a "recent" possession. The explanation for appellant's possession of the speakers came from the State's witnesses, as well as appellant's. The evidence is uncontradicted that two men possessed the speakers and tried to pawn them. It was only when the two men were not allowed to pawn the speakers that they left, and then returned to the same pawn shop accompanied by appellant.

The explanation for appellant's possession or control over the speakers is clear and uncontested—the two men requested her help in getting the speakers pawned. There is no evidence of what the two men told appellant in order to get her help. We find nothing in the record to contradict the hypothesis that appellant may have believed the speakers belonged to one of the two men. There is not one shred of evidence placing appellant at the complainant's club at the time the speakers were removed; the evidence, instead, points only to complainant's prior employee, Burton, as the likely thief.

In addition to the inference of guilt raised by possession of recently stolen property, the evidence when viewed as a whole must still be sufficient under normal standards of appellate review, and if the evidence supports a reasonable hypothesis other than the guilt of appellant, a finding of guilt beyond a reasonable doubt is not a rational finding.

When viewed in its totality, we find the evidence in this case does not support a guilty verdict. . . .

We reverse the judgment and order a judgment of acquittal.

Questions

1. State the elements of theft without consent of the owner and the elements of receiving stolen property in the Texas theft statute.

2. List all the facts relevant to deciding each of the elements of theft without consent and receiving stolen property.

3. Assume you're the prosecutor. Argue that Olga Sonnier is guilty of theft without consent and receiving stolen property. Back up your answer with the facts you listed in (2).

4. Assume you're the defense counsel. Argue that Olga Sonnier should be acquitted of theft without consent and receiving stolen property. Back up your answer with the facts you listed in (2).

EXPLORING FURTHER

Receiving Stolen Property

Did He "Receive" the Stolen Astro by Sitting in It?

In the Interest of C. W. 485 S.E.2d 561, (Ga.App. 1997)

FACTS A 1992 Chevrolet Astro van was stolen from a mobile home park in Spalding County. The van was subsequently utilized in a drive-by shooting on August 28, 1996. Later on the same day, Corporal Bradshaw of the Spalding County Sheriff's Department observed the van and recognized it as being similar to one that was reported stolen, as well as one that was reported as being involved in a drive-by shooting a few hours earlier. Corporal Bradshaw followed the van and could see four to five black males inside; he couldn't determine who was driving.

While Corporal Bradshaw was following the van, it abruptly turned into a driveway, where two or three men jumped out and ran from the scene. Without the driver, the van, which was left in the "drive" mode, rolled backward into the patrol car. Then, two young men, one of whom was the appellant, attempted to exit the van through the passenger door but were caught by Corporal Bradshaw before they could flee and were arrested at the scene.

The arresting officer was never able to determine who the driver had been or who had been in control of the stolen vehicle. The car keys were never found. When questioned by an investigator after receiving *Miranda* warnings, C. W. stated that he had only been along for a ride and didn't know that the van was stolen. At the hearing, the appellant's co-defendant, D. L. S., testified that C. W. had

only gone for a ride in the van and didn't have control of the vehicle at any time.

The juveniles were charged with theft by receiving stolen property because they had been in the stolen vehicle. They were tried in Spalding County Juvenile Court on October 23, 1996. The juvenile court judge determined that C. W. was delinquent and sentenced him to 90 days in custody. The appellant appealed, asserting that the adjudication of delinquency was contrary to the law and to the evidence. Did C. W. receive the stolen van?

DECISION No, according to the Georgia Court of Appeals:

Mere proximity to stolen property is insufficient to establish possession or control. In a similar vein, riding in a stolen van or automobile as a passenger does not support a conviction for theft by receiving unless the accused also, at some point, acquires possession of or controls the vehicle, i.e., has the right to exercise power over a corporeal thing. Therefore, one cannot be convicted of the crime of receiving stolen property absent exercise of control over the stolen goods, or if one is a passenger, intentionally aiding and abetting the commission of the crime.

. . . No evidence was presented by the state that the appellant ever retained, disposed of, acquired possession of, or controlled the stolen van, nor was any evidence presented of any affirmative act by the appellant that rose to the level of aiding and abetting the crime. The undisputed evidence indicates that the appellant got into the van while it was driven by an acquaintance, known as "Rat," and that Rat previously had acquired the van from a "Geek Monster," i.e., a crack addict, who apparently traded the van for cocaine.

Appellant denied ever driving the van, an assertion supported by his co-defendant, D. L. S. In addition, there was no evidence that appellant ever exercised control over the van, i.e., determined where it would go, who it would transport, etc., or that the appellant otherwise actively aided and abetted the crime. All evidence indicates that appellant was simply along for the ride.

While appellant admitted being in the van while another passenger shot at an acquaintance in a drive-by shooting, appellant was not charged with being an accessory to that offense. Therefore, lacking evidence that the appellant ever possessed or controlled the van under OCGA § 1687(A) or affirmatively acted as a party to the crime under OCGA § 16220(B), his adjudication of delinquency for the offense of theft by receiving stolen property must be reversed.

 Go to the Criminal Law 9e website to find the full text of the Exploring Further excerpt: www.thomsonedu .com/criminaljustice/samaha. (Excerpt on receiving stolen property.)

Let's turn now to two violent misappropriation-of-property crimes, robbery and extortion.

Robbery

The core of robbery is theft accomplished under circumstances calculated to terrorize the victim. The circumstances are actual injury or the threat of *immediate* injury (ALI 1985, 2:222.1, 98). Robbery is really two crimes, theft and assault (Chapter 10). But the criminal law has never treated it that way, because robbery is considered more serious than the sum of these two parts. The MPC reporter explains why:

> The violent petty thief operating in the streets and alleys of big cities—the "mugger"—is one of the main sources of insecurity and concern in the population at large. There is a special element of terror in this kind of depredation. The ordinary citizen does not feel particularly threatened by the surreptitious larceny, embezzlement, or fraud. But there is understandable abhorrence of the robber who accosts on the streets and who menaces his victims with actual or threatened violence against which there is a general sense of helplessness. In proportion as the ordinary person fears and detests such behavior, the offender exhibits himself as seriously deviated from community norms, thus justifying more serious sanctions. In addition, the robber may be distinguished from the stealthy thief by the hardihood that enables him to carry out his purpose in the presence of his victim and over his opposition—obstacles that might deter ordinary sneak thieves and that justify the feeling of special danger evoked by the robber. (98)

As a victim of more than one mugging on city streets, I can vouch for the fear, anger, and sense of violation that goes along with losing something valuable, like the watch my mother gave me as a graduation present. But it's more than the value of what I lost that signifies. It's the personal violation that goes along with fear and humiliation, even when there's no *real* threat. During the second mugging, I gave up my money because the mugger showed me his "weapon" bulging in his coat pocket. After I handed over the money, he pulled the "weapon" out of his pocket—a comb—and ran

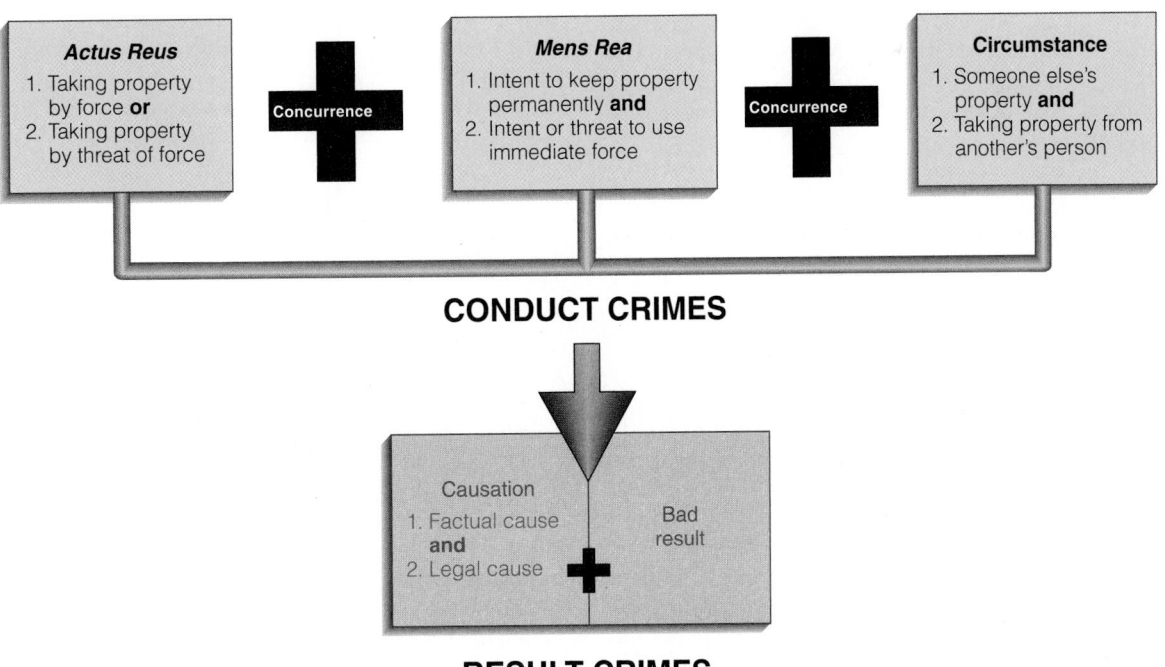

Elements of Robbery

his thumb down the spokes, sneering, "Hey man, you should be more careful in the future," as he swaggered away snickering.

Let's look at the elements of robbery: its *actus reus*, *mens rea*, and required attendant circumstances.

Robbery Actus Reus The use of force, or the threat of force, is the essence of robbery *actus reus*. Any amount of force beyond the amount needed to take and carry away someone else's property is enough. Picking a pocket isn't robbery because picking pockets is defined as requiring only enough force to remove the contents of the pocket. But even slightly mishandling the victim, like a push, turns the pickpocket into a robber. Robbery doesn't even require the use of actual force; threatened force (a drawn gun or knife) is enough.

In our next case excerpt, *State v. Curley* (1997), the New Mexico Court of Appeals decided that under the state's robbery statute, the jury should've had the opportunity to decide whether Erwin Curley's "shove" was enough force to rob or only enough physical strength to steal the money in his victim's purse by snatching it.

CASE *Did He Take Her Purse by Force?*

State v. Curley
939 P.2d 1103 (N.M.App., 1997)

HISTORY

Erwin Curley, Defendant, was convicted of robbery in the District Court, McKinley County. Defendant appealed. The Court of Appeals, Pickard, J., held that defendant was entitled to requested instruction on the lesser included offense of larceny. The Court reversed and remanded for a new trial.

PICKARD, J.

This case requires us to determine: (1) what force suffices to turn a larceny into a robbery and (2) whether there is any view of the evidence pursuant to which that force was not shown. . . .

FACTS

The prosecution arose out of a purse snatching. The evidence was that the victim was walking out of a mall with her daughter when Erwin Curley (Defendant) grabbed her purse and ran away. The victim described the incident as follow: "I had my purse on my left side . . . and I felt kind of a shove of my left shoulder where I had my purse strap with my thumb through it and I kind of leaned—was pushed—toward my daughter, and this person came and just grabbed the strap of my purse and continued to run."

The victim used the words "grab" or "pull" to describe the actual taking of the purse and "shove" or "push" to describe what Defendant did as he grabbed or "pulled [the purse] from her arm and hand." However, there was also evidence that the victim's thumb was not through the strap of the purse, but was rather on the bottom of the purse. The purse strap was not broken, and the victim did not testify that she struggled with Defendant for the purse in any way or that any part of her body offered any resistance or even moved when the purse was pulled from her arm and hand.

Defendant presented evidence that he was drunk and did not remember the incident at all.

OPINION

Robbery is theft by the use or threatened use of force or violence. NMSA 1978, ß 30-16-2 (Repl.Pamp.1994). Because the words "or violence" refer to the unwarranted exercise of force and do not substantively state an alternative means of committing the offense, we refer simply to "force" in this opinion. The force must be the lever by which the property is taken.

Although we have cases saying . . . that even a slight amount of force, such as jostling the victim or snatching away the property, is sufficient, we also have cases in which a taking of property from the person of a victim has been held not to be robbery, (wallet taken from victim's pocket while victim was aware that the defendant was taking the wallet).

A defendant is entitled to a lesser-included-offense instruction when there is some evidence to support it. There must be some view of the evidence pursuant to which the lesser offense is the highest degree of crime committed, and that view must be reasonable. Thus, in this case, to justify giving Defendant's larceny instruction, there must be some view of the evidence pursuant to which force sufficient to constitute a robbery was not the lever by which Defendant removed the victim's purse.

Defendant contends that such evidence exists in that the jury could have found that Defendant's shoving of the victim was part of his drunkenness, and then the purse was taken without force sufficient to constitute robbery. We agree. . . . The applicable rule in this case is as follows: when property is attached to the person or clothing of a victim so as to cause resistance, any taking is a robbery, and not larceny, because the lever that causes the victim to part with the property is the force that is applied to break that resistance; however, when no more force is used than would be necessary to remove property from a person who does not resist, then the offense is larceny, and not robbery. . . .

[According to] the minority rule adopted by Massachusetts . . . any purse snatching not accomplished by stealth would be robbery. We are not inclined to overrule cases such as *Sanchez*, in which we held that the taking of a wallet accompanied by just so much force as is necessary to accomplish the taking from a person who was not resisting was not robbery. Rather, we adhere to what we perceive to be the majority rule.

According to the majority rule, robbery is committed when attached property is snatched or grabbed by sufficient force so as to overcome the resistance of attachment. In cases such as this one, where one view of the facts appears to put the case on the border between robbery and larceny, it is necessary to further explore what is meant by the concept of "the resistance of attachment." Our exploration is informed by the interests protected by the two crimes.

. . . [Robbery] may be classified not only as an offense against property but also as an offense against the person. It is the aspect of the offense that is directed against the person which distinguishes the crime of robbery from larceny and also justifies an increased punishment. Thus, the resistance of attachment should be construed in light of the idea that robbery is an offense against the person, and something about that offense should reflect the increased danger to the person that robbery involves over the offense of larceny.

The great weight of authority . . . supports the view that there is not sufficient force to constitute robbery when the thief snatches property from the owner's grasp so suddenly that the owner cannot offer any resistance to the taking. On the other hand, when the owner, aware of an impending snatching, resists it, or when the thief's first attempt being ineffective to separate the owner from his property, a struggle for the property is necessary before the thief can get possession thereof, there is enough force to make the taking robbery. Taking the owner's property by stealthily picking his pocket is not taking by force and so

is not robbery; but if the pickpocket or his confederate jostles the owner, or if the owner, catching the pickpocket in the act, struggles unsuccessfully to keep possession, the pickpocket's crime becomes robbery. To remove an article of value, attached to the owner's person or clothing, by a sudden snatching or by stealth is not robbery unless the article in question (e.g., an earring, pin or watch) is so attached to the person or his clothes as to require some force to effect its removal.

Thus, it would be robbery, not larceny, if the resistance afforded is the wearing of a necklace around one's neck that is broken by the force used to remove it and the person to whom the necklace is attached is aware that it is being ripped from her neck. On the other hand, it would be larceny, not robbery, if the resistance afforded is the wearing of a bracelet, attached by a thread, and the person to whom the bracelet is attached is not aware that it is being taken until she realizes that it is gone.

. . . Subtle differences in the amount of force used, alone, is neither a clear nor reasonable basis to distinguish the crime of robbery from that of larceny. However, if we remember that the reason for the distinction in crimes is the increased danger to the person, then an increase in force that makes the victim aware that her body is resisting could lead to the dangers that the crime of robbery was designed to alleviate. A person who did not know that a bracelet was being taken from her wrist by the breaking of a string would have no occasion to confront the thief, thereby possibly leading to an altercation. A person who knows that a necklace is being ripped from her neck might well confront the thief.

We now apply these rules to the facts of this case. Although the facts in this case are simply stated, they are rich with conflicting inferences. Either robbery or larceny may be shown, depending on the jury's view of the facts and which inferences it chooses to draw.

In the light most favorable to the State, Defendant shoved the victim to help himself relieve her of the purse, and the shove and Defendant's other force in grabbing the purse had that effect. This view of the facts establishes robbery, and if the jury believed it, the jury would be bound to find Defendant guilty of robbery.

However, there is another view of the facts. Defendant contends that the evidence that he was drunk allows the jury to infer that the shove was unintentional and that the remaining facts show the mere snatching of the purse, thereby establishing larceny. Two issues are raised by this contention that we must address:

(1) is there a reasonable view of the evidence pursuant to which the shove was not part of the robbery? and

(2) even disregarding the shove, does the remaining evidence show only robbery?

We agree with Defendant that the jury could have inferred that the shove was an incidental touching due to Defendant's drunkenness. Defendant's testimony of his drunkenness and the lack of any testimony by the victim or any witness that the shove was necessarily a part of the robbery permitted the jury to draw this inference. Once the jury drew the inference that the shove was independent of the robbery, the jury could have found that Defendant formed the intent to take the victim's purse after incidentally colliding with her.

Alternatively, the jury could have found that Defendant intended to snatch the purse without contacting the victim and that the contact (the shove) was not necessary to, or even a part of, the force that separated the victim from her purse. The victim's testimony (that she felt "kind of a shove" and then Defendant grabbed her purse) would allow this inference. Thus, the jury could have found that the shove did not necessarily create a robbery.

The question would then remain, however, whether the grabbing of the purse was still robbery because more force was used than would have been necessary to remove the purse if the victim had not resisted. Under the facts of this case, in which the victim did not testify that she held the strap tightly enough to resist and in which there was some evidence that she was not even holding the strap, we think that there was a legitimate, reasonable view of the evidence that, once the shove is eliminated from consideration, Defendant used only such force as was necessary to remove the purse from a person who was not resisting. Under this view of the facts, Defendant took the purse by surprise from a person who was not resisting, and not by force necessary to overcome any resistance. Therefore, the trial court should have given Defendant's tendered larceny instructions. . . .

Defendant's conviction is reversed and remanded for a new trial.

Questions

1. List all of the evidence relevant to determining whether the purse snatching was a robbery.

2. State both the majority and the minority rule regarding the element of force in purse snatching.

3. Summarize the evidence in favor of and against each rule.

4. In your opinion, which is the better rule? Defend your answer. See the Exploring Further case that follows.

Robbery Mens Rea   Robbery *mens rea* is the same as theft *mens rea* (the intent to take another person's property and keep it permanently) but with the additional intent to use immediate force, or the threat of immediate force, to get it. So it's not robbery to take an iPod away from someone if you honestly, but mistakenly, believe it's yours. Of course, it's still a crime (battery if you use force or assault if you threaten to use it); it's just not robbery (LaFave and Scott 1986, 778–79).

The Degrees of Robbery   Most states have divided robbery into degrees according to whether robbers are armed and the injury they cause to their victims. New York's Penal

Code (2003, § 160.00) is typical. First-degree robbers (§ 160.15) carry deadly weapons (or "play weapons" that look real) and seriously injure their victims. Second-degree robbers (§ 160.10) have accomplices or display play weapons and inflict some injury on their victims. Third-degree robbers (§ 160.05) are unarmed, and they inflict no injury on their victims.

Extortion

Theft by **extortion** (also called **blackmail**) is taking someone else's property by threats of *future* harm. The circumstance of time separates extortion from robbery: robbery is hurting, or threatening to hurt, someone right now if they don't give up their property; extortion is a threat to hurt someone later if they don't hand over the property.

The elements of extortion consist of:

1. Mens rea The specific intent to take someone else's property by means of a variety of threats.

2. Actus reus A wide range of specific threats by which the taking of property is accomplished.

The MPC's "Theft by Extortion" (ALI 1985 2:223.4) provision is an excellent example of a comprehensive statute based on existing state law:

> § 223.4. THEFT BY EXTORTION
>
> A person is guilty of theft if he purposely obtains property of another by threatening to:
>
> > (1) inflict bodily injury on anyone or commit any other criminal offense; or
> >
> > (2) accuse anyone of a criminal offense; or
> >
> > (3) expose any secret tending to subject any person to hatred, contempt or ridicule, or to impair his credit or business repute; or
> >
> > (4) take or withhold action as an official, or cause an official to take or withhold action; or
> >
> > (5) bring about or continue a strike, boycott or other collective unofficial action, if the property is not demanded or received for the benefit of the group in whose interest the actor purports to act; or
> >
> > (6) testify or provide information or withhold testimony or information with respect to another's legal claim or defense; or
> >
> > (7) inflict any other harm which would not benefit the actor.
>
> It is an affirmative defense to prosecution based on paragraphs (2), (3) or (4) that the property obtained by threat of accusation, exposure, lawsuit or other invocation of official action was honestly claimed as restitution or indemnification for harm done in the circumstances to which such accusation, exposure, lawsuit or other official action relates, or as compensation for property or lawful services.

Notice that threats don't have to be spelled out in detail; they can be indirect. The MPC's reporter puts it this way:

> It is sufficient, for example, that the actor ask for money in exchange for "protection" from harms where the actor intends to convey the impression that he will in some fashion instigate the harm from which he proposes to "protect" the victims. (ALI 1985, 2:205–6)

Also, threats don't have to be directed at hurting the victim; threats to hurt anyone are good enough, according to the code.

DAMAGING AND DESTROYING OTHER PEOPLE'S PROPERTY

In this section, we'll discuss two crimes of destroying property: **arson** (damaging or destroying buildings by burning) and **criminal mischief** (damaging or destroying personal property).

Arson

In the 1700s, *arson* was defined as "the malicious and willful burning of the house or outhouses of another." Blackstone (1769) called it an "offense of very great malignity, and much more serious than simple theft." According to Blackstone, here's why:

> Because, first, it is an offence against that right, of habitation, which is acquired by the law of nature as well as the laws of society. Next, because of the terror and confusion that necessarily attends it. And, lastly, because in simple theft the thing stolen only changes its master, but still remains in essence for the benefit of the public, whereas by burning the very substance is absolutely destroyed. (220)

Arson has grown far beyond its origins in burning houses to include burning almost any kind of building, vessel, or vehicle. Also, the property burned doesn't have to be someone else's. Today, arson is a crime against possession and occupancy, not just against ownership. So even where owners aren't in possession of or don't occupy their own property, arson can still be committed against it. For example, if I lease my house and become its landlord, and I set fire to it to collect insurance on it, I've committed arson because I transferred occupancy to my tenant.

One thing hasn't changed; arson is still a very serious crime against property *and* persons. Arson kills hundreds and injures thousands of people every year. It damages and destroys more than a billion dollars worth of property and costs millions in lost taxes and jobs. It has also significantly increased insurance rates. Most states prescribe harsh penalties for arson. For example, in Texas and Alabama, arson is punishable by life imprisonment.

Let's look further at the *actus reus*, *mens rea*, and degrees of arson.

Actus Reus: *Burning*   At common law, **burning** had its obvious meaning— setting a building on fire. However, just setting the fire wasn't enough; the fire had to

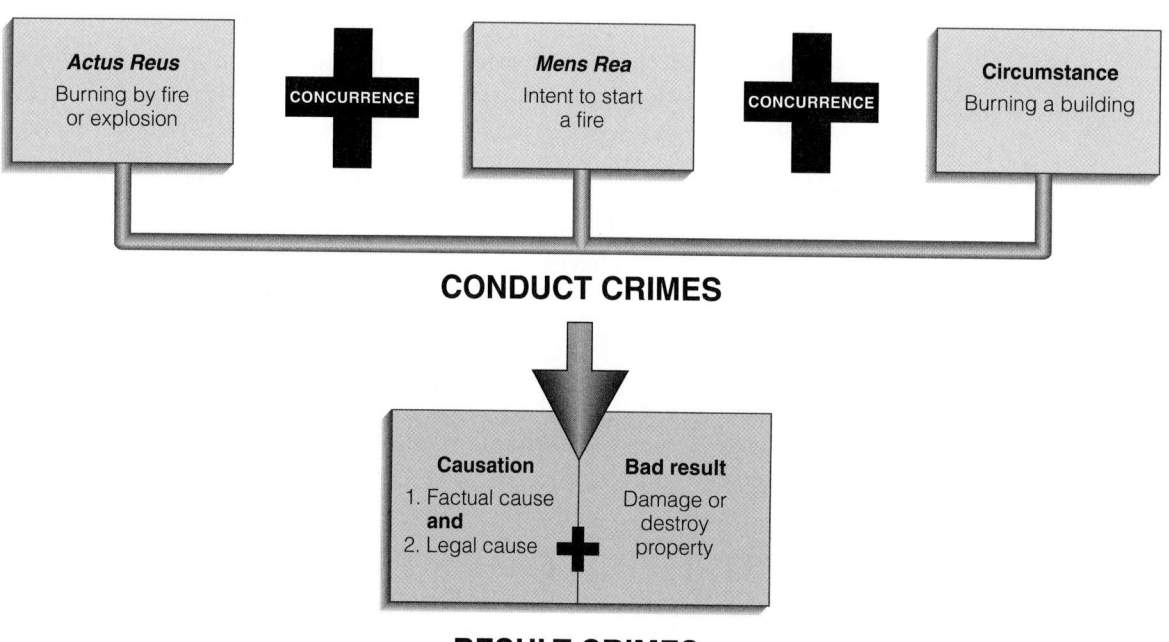

Elements of Arson

reach the structure and burn it. But burning didn't mean burning to the ground. Once the building caught on fire, the arson was complete, however slight the actual burning was.

Modern statutes have adopted the common-law rule, and the cases pour great effort into deciding whether the smoke from the fire only blackened or discolored buildings, whether the fire scorched them, or whether the fire burned only the outside wall or the wood under it. The MPC (ALI 1985, 2:2, 3) tries to clear up many of the technical questions in common-law arson by providing that *burning* means "starting a fire," even if the fire never touches the structure it was meant to burn. The drafters justify this expansion of common-law burning on the ground that there's no meaningful difference between a fire that has already started but hasn't reached the structure and a fire that's reached the structure but hasn't done any real damage to it.

Burning also includes explosions, even though the phrase "set on fire" doesn't usually mean "to explode." In *Williams v. State* (1992), when Tonyia Williams, one of the guests at a New Year's Eve party, started a fire, "the only physical damage caused by fire was smoke throughout the house and soot and smoke damage to one of the walls in the basement" (963).

Indiana's arson statute defined *arson* as: "A person who, by means of fire or explosive, knowingly or intentionally damages: (1) a dwelling of another person without his consent" (964). Williams argued that the "soot and smoke damage to the wall of the basement do not constitute 'damages' within the meaning of the arson statute." She argued that arson "requires proof of burning or charring as was the case at common law" (964). The state argued that

> damages in our present statute is not tied to the common law definition of the word "burning" and should therefore be construed in its plain and ordinary sense. Any damage, even smoke damage, would therefore be enough to satisfy the requirements of the statute. (964)

Williams was convicted, and she appealed. According to the Indiana Appeals Court:

> Traditionally the common law rigidly required an actual burning. The fire must have been actually communicated to the object to such an extent as to have taken effect upon it. In general, any charring of the wood of a building, so that the fiber of the wood was destroyed, was enough to constitute a sufficient burning to complete the crime of arson.

However, merely singeing, smoking, scorching, or discoloring by heat weren't considered enough to support a conviction (964). The Appeals court agreed with the state: "We find . . . that the smoke damage and the soot on the basement wall were enough to support a conviction for arson" (965).

Arson Mens Rea   Most arson statutes follow the common-law *mens rea* requirement that arsonists have to "maliciously and willfully" burn or set fire to buildings. Some courts call arson *mens rea* general intent. According to the general-intent definition, purpose refers to the act in arson (burning or setting fire to buildings), not to the resulting harm (damaging or destroying them). So a prisoner who burned a hole in his cell to escape was guilty of arson because he purposely started the fire. So was a sailor who lit a match to find his way into a dark hold in a ship to steal rum. The criminal intent in arson is general—an intent to start a fire, even if there is no intent to burn a specific structure.

The Degrees of Arson   Typically, there are two degrees of arson. Most serious, first-degree arson, is burning homes or other occupied structures (such as schools, offices, and churches) where there's danger to human life. Second-degree arson includes burning unoccupied structures, vehicles, and boats.

The MPC divides arson into two degrees, based on defendants' blameworthiness. The most blameworthy are defendants who intend to destroy buildings, not merely set fire to or burn them; these are first-degree arsonists. Second-degree arsonists set buildings on fire for other purposes. For example, if I burn a wall with an acetylene torch because I want to steal valuable fixtures attached to the wall, I'm guilty of second-degree arson for "recklessly" exposing the building to destruction even though I meant only to steal fixtures.

Statutes don't grade arson according to motive, but it probably ought to play some part, if not in formal degrees, then in sentencing. Why? Because arsonists act for a variety of motives. Some are so consumed by rage they burn down their enemies' homes. Then there are the pyromaniacs, whose psychotic compulsion drives them to set buildings on fire for thrills. And there are the rational, but equally deadly, arsonists who burn down their own buildings or destroy their own property to collect insurance. Finally, and most deadly and difficult to catch, the professional torch commits arson for hire.

 Go to the Criminal Law 9e website to find Exercise 11.2 and learn more about arson statutes: www.thomsonedu.com/criminaljustice/samaha.

Criminal Mischief

Arson under the common law was, and still is, the serious felony of intentionally burning occupied buildings. *Criminal mischief* descends from another common-law crime, the misdemeanor called "malicious mischief." Malicious mischief consisted of destroying or damaging tangible property ("anything of value" that you can see, weigh, measure, or feel).

The modern counterpart of malicious mischief (the MPC calls it "criminal" mischief) includes three types of harm to tangible property:

1. Destruction or damage by fire, explosives, or other "dangerous acts" (the original malicious mischief)

2. Tampering with tangible property so as to endanger property

3. Deception or threat that causes someone to suffer money loss

All three forms of damage and destruction usually are defined as felonies but less serious felonies than the more serious felony arson.

Criminal Mischief Actus Reus   The *actus reus* of criminal mischief mirrors the three types of criminal mischief. In *destruction or damage* criminal mischief, the *actus reus* is burning, exploding, flooding, or committing some other dangerous act. *Tampering* is any act that creates a danger to property, even if it doesn't actually cause any damage to the property. So a cross burning on the lawn of an interracial couple's house wasn't "tampering" with the property, because the burning cross by itself created no damage and it didn't pose a threat of damage to the property (*Commonwealth v. Kozak* 1993).

Deception or *threat actus reus* usually consists of "expensive practical jokes," like "sending a false telegram notifying the victim that his mother is dying so that he spends several hundred dollars on a vain trip," or "misinforming a neighboring farmer that local tests of a particular seed variety have been highly successful, so that he wastes money and a year's work planting that seed" (ALI 1985, 2:2, 49).

Criminal Mischief Mens Rea   Generalizations about criminal mischief *mens rea* are impossible because statutes are all over the place, including whether they

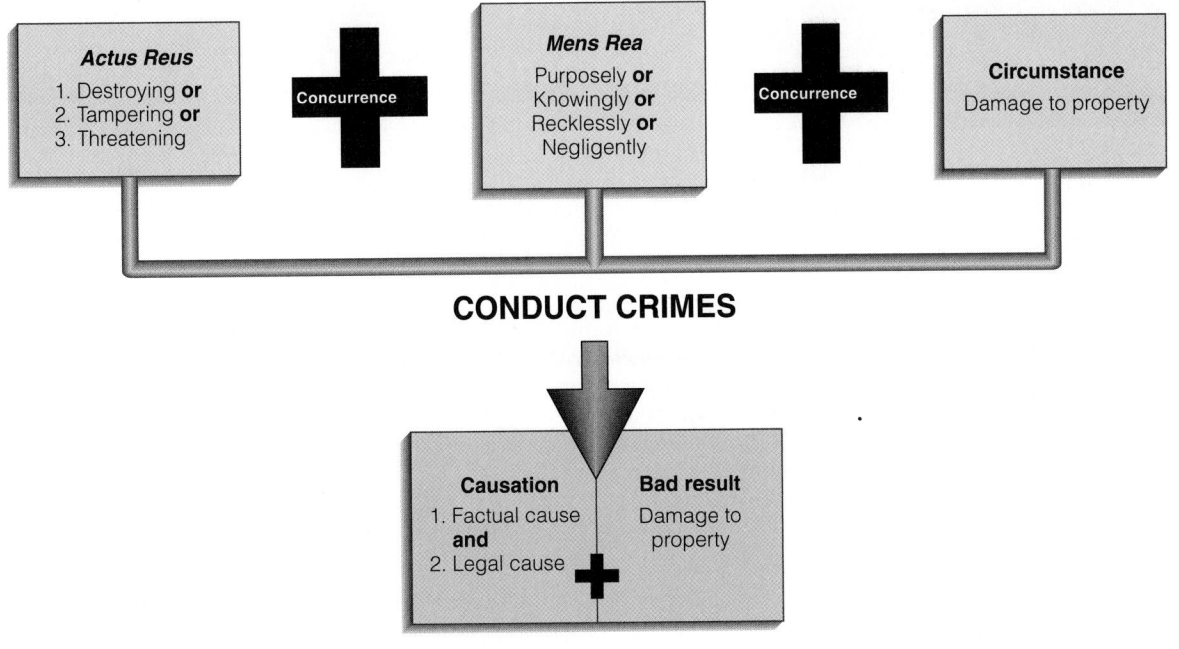

CONDUCT CRIMES

RESULT CRIMES

Elements of Criminal Mischief

contain all the mental states we've encountered throughout the book (purposely, knowingly, recklessly, and negligently). So you need to check the malicious (or criminal) mischief statute of an individual state to find out how it defines the element of criminal intent.

We'll quote the MPC's provision because its *actus reus* and *mens rea* requirements make sense, and they're comprehensive.

§ 220.3. CRIMINAL MISCHIEF

(1) Offense Defined. A person is guilty of criminal mischief if he:
   (a) damages tangible property of another purposely, recklessly, or by negligence in the employment of fire, explosives, or other dangerous means; or
   (b) purposely or recklessly tampers with tangible property of another so as to endanger person or property; or
   (c) purposely or recklessly causes another to suffer pecuniary loss by deception or threat.
(2) Grading. Criminal mischief is a felony of the third degree if the actor purposely causes pecuniary loss in excess of $5,000, or a substantial interruption or impairment of public communication, transportation, supply of water, gas or power, or other public service. It is a misdemeanor if the actor purposely causes pecuniary loss in excess of $100, or a petty misdemeanor if he purposely or recklessly causes pecuniary loss in excess of $25. Otherwise criminal mischief is a violation.

Pennsylvania's criminal mischief statute closely tracks the MPC provision. In our next case excerpt, *Commonwealth v. Mitchell* (1993), the Pennsylvania Superior Court affirmed Duane Mitchell's conviction for criminal mischief by painting "nigger," "KKK," and other racial slurs on Betty Jo and James Johnson's house.

Commonwealth v. Mitchell

WL 773785 (Pa.Com.Pl. 1993)

HISTORY

Following a non-jury trial, held on December 22, 1992, Duane Mitchell (defendant) was convicted of the criminal mischief . . . graded as a misdemeanor of the third degree. Defendant filed timely post-trial motions, which were denied, and the defendant was sentenced to pay a fine of $150. The defendant filed post trial motions which were denied. The Superior Court affirmed the trial court's denial of the motions.

CRONIN, JR., J.

FACTS

Following a report to the Upper Darby Police Department on Sunday, June 21, 1992 at 9:49 P.M., Lieutenant Michael Kenney and Officer Mark Manley of the Upper Darby Police Department, proceeded to 7142 Stockley Road, Upper Darby, Pennsylvania. Upon arriving at the above location, both officers observed the following: painted on the front walk the word "nigger," the letters "KKK"; and a cross painted under three dark marks; on each of the steps leading to the house was spray painted the word "nigger"; the front screen door had a painted cross with three marks above it; the patio was painted with the word "nigger" and a cross with three dark marks; the front walk had the word "nigger" and a cross with three dark marks; the front walk had the words "nigger get out" painted on it; the rear wall had painted the words "nigger get out or else" and a cross with the letters "KKK"; and, the rear door had the words "KKK Jungle Fever Death" and a cross painted on it.

The owners of 7142 Stockley Road, Upper Darby, Pennsylvania are James and Betty Jo Johnson, who had made settlement on the property on June 15, 1992, but had not occupied the home with their 7-year-old daughter, Zena. The Johnsons are an interracial couple, James Johnson being Afro-American and Betty Jo Johnson being Caucasian. The Johnsons had not given the defendant or any other person permission to spray paint on their property.

On June 25, 1992, defendant, Duane Mitchell, was taken into custody by the Upper Darby Police. The defendant voluntarily waived, in writing, his right to counsel and his right to remain silent and freely gave a statement to the police. The defendant told the Upper Darby Police that he, the defendant, alone spray painted the above-mentioned words and symbols on the Johnson property located at 7142 Stockley Road, Upper Darby, Pennsylvania; at the time that he did the spray painting, he had been drinking.

Following a non-jury trial, held on December 22, 1992, defendant was convicted of the summary offense of criminal mischief and the offense of ethnic intimidation, graded as a misdemeanor of the third degree in accordance with 18 Pa.C.S. § 2710(B). Defendant filed timely post-trial motions, which were denied by the order of trial court dated May 17, 1993.

OPINION

Criminal mischief is defined at 18 Pa.C.S. § 3304 as follows:

§ 3304. CRIMINAL MISCHIEF

(A) Offense Defined—A person is guilty of criminal mischief if he:

(1) damages the tangible property of another intentionally, recklessly, or by negligence in the employment of fire, explosives, or other dangerous means listed in section 3302(A) of this title (relating to causing or risking catastrophe);

(2) intentionally or recklessly tampers with tangible property of another so as to endanger person or property; or

(3) intentionally or recklessly causes another to suffer pecuniary loss by deception or threat. 18 Pa.C.S. § 3304(A)

The defendant argues that the evidence was insufficient to prove that tangible property was damaged in the employment of fire, explosion, or other dangerous means. 1 Pa.C.S. § 1903 states that "(A) Words and phrases shall be construed according to rules of grammar and according to their common usage; . . ." Section 1 of 18 Pa.C.S. § 3304 makes a person guilty of the crime of criminal mischief if that person either intentionally damages the tangible property of another; recklessly damages the tangible property of another; or negligently damages the tangible personal property of another in the employment of fire, explosives or other dangerous means listed in section 3302(A) of title 18.

In this case it is abundantly clear that the defendant spray painted the phrases and words mentioned herein on the Johnsons' home located at 7142 Stockley Road, Upper Darby, Pennsylvania and that the defendant did so without the permission of the Johnsons. Sufficient evidence exists to support a verdict if the evidence, when viewed in a light most favorable to the verdict winner along with all reasonable inferences drawn therefrom, allows a fact finder to find that all elements of a crime have been established beyond a reasonable doubt.

The evidence was sufficient to prove beyond a reasonable doubt that the defendant intentionally damaged the tangible property of the Johnsons.

A court must interpret a statute to ascertain the intent of the legislature. It is clear from the use of the conjunctive "or" in section 1 of 18 Pa.C.S. § 3304, that the legislature intended to punish either the intentional or the reckless or the negligent damaging of the tangible property of another person. The intentional spray painting of graffiti on the walls of a building is factually sufficient to support a conviction for criminal mischief.

It is equally clear that the commission of any of the other acts specified in either section 1 or section 2 or section 3 of 18 Pa.C.S. § 3304 is sufficient to support a conviction for criminal mischief since the conjunctive "or" is used between sections 2 and 3 of 18 Pa.C.S. § 3304 and the conjunctive "or" is to be given the same meaning and legislative intent as "or" is given with the states of mind (intent, reckless or negligent) in section 1 of 18 Pa.C.S. § 3304. See 1 Pa.C.S. § 1903(A), 1 Pa.C.S. § 1921(A)(B).

For the foregoing reasons the defendant's post-trial motions were denied.

Questions

1. State the elements of *actus reus* and *mens rea* as the Pennsylvania criminal mischief statute defines them.

2. List the facts relevant to each of the elements.

3. Assume you're Duane Mitchell's lawyer, and argue that the facts don't prove the elements beyond a reasonable doubt.

4. Assume you're the state's prosecutor, and argue that the facts prove the elements beyond a reasonable doubt.

INVADING OTHER PEOPLE'S PROPERTY

The heart of burglary and criminal trespass is *invading* others' property, not taking, destroying, or damaging it. Invasion itself is the harm. So the two main crimes of invading someone else's property, homes, and other occupied structures **(burglary)** or invading other property **(criminal trespass)** are crimes of criminal conduct; they don't require causing a bad result. So they're crimes even if no property is taken, damaged, or destroyed during the invasion.

Burglary

> Burglary, or nighttime housebreaking . . . has always been looked upon as a very heinous offense, not only because of the abundant terror that it naturally carries with it, but also as it is a forcible invasion and disturbance of that right of habitation, which every individual might acquire in a state of nature. . . . And the law of England has so particular and tender regard to the immunity of a man's house, that it styles it a castle and will never suffer it to be violated. (Blackstone 1769, 223)

Blackstone's definition of burglary just before the American Revolution emphasizes the special nature of homes. Why are they special? For many people, their homes are their most valuable if not their only material asset. But homes are more than property that's worth money. The novelist Sinclair Lewis (1922) described this difference between homes as things with money value and homes as special places ("castles") that can't be measured by money alone:

> The Babbitts' house was five years old. . . . It had the best of taste, the best of inexpensive rugs, a simple and laudable architecture, and the latest conveniences. Throughout, electricity took the place of candles and slatternly hearth-fires. Along the bedroom baseboard were three plugs for electric lamps, concealed by little brass doors. In the halls were plugs for the vacuum cleaner, and in the living-room plugs for the piano lamp, for the electric fan. The trim dining-room (with its admirable oak buffet, its leaded-glass cupboard, its

creamy plaster walls, its modest scene of a salmon expiring upon a pile of oysters) had plugs which supplied the electric percolator and the electric toaster.

In fact there was but one thing wrong with the Babbitt house: *It was not a home.* (chap. 2) (emphasis added)

Lewis means that a house is the material thing worth money, but a home is the haven of refuge where security and privacy from the outside world are possible.

The elements of common-law burglary from which our modern law of burglary descends included:

1. Breaking and entering (*actus reus*)

2. The dwelling of another (circumstance element)

3. In the nighttime (circumstance element)

4. With the intent to commit a felony inside (*mens rea*)

Modern burglary has outgrown its common-law origin of just protecting homes. Now, you can "burglarize" all kinds of structures, even vehicles, at any time of the day or night. Definitions such as "any structure" or "any building" are common in many statutes. One writer (Note 1951, 411) who surveyed the subject concluded that any structure with "four walls and a roof" was included.

Here's California's list of "structures" you can burglarize:

Every person who enters any house, room, apartment, tenement, shop, warehouse, store, mill, barn, stable, outhouse or other building, tent, vessel, . . . floating home . . . , locked or sealed cargo container, whether or not mounted on a vehicle, trailer coach . . . , any house car, inhabited camper . . . , vehicle . . . , when the doors are locked, aircraft . . . , or mine or any underground portion thereof. . . . (California Penal Code 2003, § 459)

Let's look at the elements needed to prove burglary, and then the degrees of burglary.

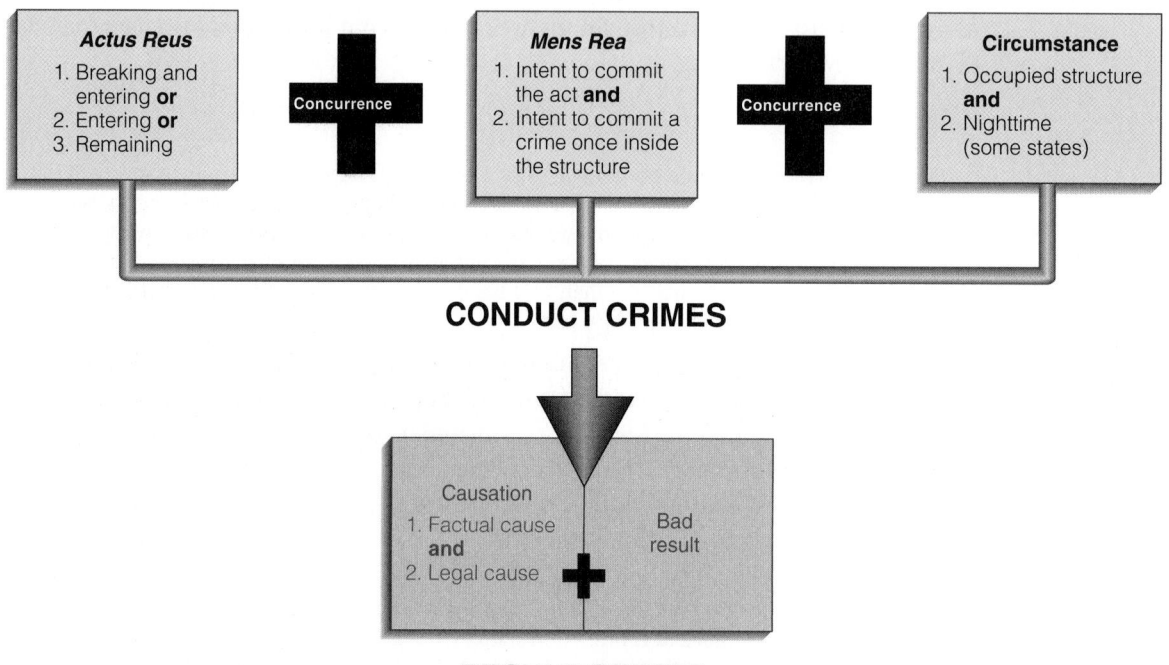

Elements of Burglary

Burglary Actus Reus   Until the 1900s, burglary *actus reus* consisted of two actions—breaking and entering. In the early days of the common law, *breaking* meant making a violent entry, usually knocking down doors and smashing windows. By 1900, the common-law element of breaking had become a mere technicality, and most modern statutes have eliminated it entirely, leaving entering as the only element. A few states—for example, Massachusetts—have retained the ancient definition, "Whoever, in the night time, breaks and enters . . ." (Massachusetts Criminal Code 2003, chap. 266 § 16).

Entering, like breaking, has a broad meaning in burglary law. From about 1650, partial entry was enough to satisfy burglary. One court (*Rex v. Bailey* 1818) ruled that a burglar "entered" a house because his finger was inside the windowsill when he was caught. Today, some statutes have completely removed the entering element by providing that "remaining" in a structure lawfully entered is enough. So it's burglary to go into a store during business hours and wait in a rest room until the store closes with the intent to steal.

Some states don't even require burglars to get inside; it's enough if they try to get in. In *State v. Myrick* (1982), a man who got a door ajar but never set foot inside was convicted because the state's burglary statute didn't require entering or remaining. To some criminal law reformers, substituting remaining for breaking and entering badly distorts burglary's core idea—nighttime invasions into homes.

The MPC and several states take a middle ground between the old common-law requirement of actual entry and eliminating entering completely. They've adopted a **surreptitious remaining element,** which means the burglar entered lawfully (for example, going into a bank during business hours) and waited inside to commit a crime.

Circumstances   The MPC's (ALI 1985, 2:2, 60) definition limits burglary to occupied structures, because they're the "intrusions that are typically the most alarming and dangerous." According to the code, *occupied structure* means "any structure, vehicle, or place adapted for overnight accommodations of persons, or for carrying on business therein, whether or not a person is actually present" (72). Most states take occupancy into account either as an element or as part of grading burglary as "aggravated burglary."

Another circumstance element of common-law burglary was that burglars had to break and enter the dwelling "of another." Modern law has expanded the common-law definition to include your own property; now, for example, landlords can burglarize their tenants' apartments. In *Jewell v. State* (1996), the Indiana Court of Appeals affirmed Barry Jewell's conviction for burglarizing his own house.

C A S E   *Did He Burglarize His Own Home?*

Jewell v. State
672 N.E.2d 417 (Ind.App. 1996)

HISTORY

Barry L. Jewell, after a jury trial, was convicted of burglary with a deadly weapon resulting in serious bodily injury, a class A felony, and battery resulting in serious bodily injury, a class C felony. Jewell was sentenced to an aggregate term of 48 years imprisonment. After a re-trial Jewell appealed. The Indiana Court of Appeals affirmed.

ROBERTSON, J.

FACTS

In 1989, Bridget Fisher, who later married Jewell and changed her name to Bridget Jewell, purchased a home on contract in her maiden name from her relatives. Bridget and Jewell lived in the house together on and off before and after they married in 1990. Jewell helped fix the house up, and therefore, had some "sweat equity" in the house.

Jewell and Bridget experienced marital difficulties and dissolution proceedings were initiated. Jewell moved out of the house and Bridget changed the locks so that Jewell could not reenter. At a preliminary hearing in the dissolution proceedings, Bridget's attorney informed Jewell that Bridget wanted a divorce and wanted Jewell to stop coming by the house. Jewell moved into a friend's house, agreeing to pay him $100.00 per month in rent and to split the utility expenses.

Bridget resumed a romantic relationship with her former boyfriend, Chris Jones. Jewell told a friend that he wanted to get Jones in a dark place, hit him over the head with a 2 × 4 (a board), and cut his "dick" off. Jewell confronted Jones at his place of employment and threatened to kill him if he were to continue to see Bridget.

Jewell was observed on numerous occasions watching Bridget's house. Jewell used a shortwave radio to intercept and listen to the phone conversations on Bridget's cordless phone.

At approximately 4:00 A.M. on the morning of June 13, 1991, Jewell gained entry to Bridget's house through the kitchen window after having removed a window screen.

Bridget and Jones were inside sleeping. Jewell struck Jones over the head with a 2 × 4 until he was unconscious, amputated Jones' penis with a knife, and fed the severed penis to the dog. Bridget awoke and witnessed the attack, but she thought she was having a bad dream and went back to sleep. Bridget described the intruder as the same size and build as Jewell and as wearing a dark ski mask similar to one she had given Jewell. She observed the assailant hit Jones on the head with a board, and stab him in the lower part of his body.

A bloody 2 × 4 was found at the scene. The sheets on the bed where Bridget and Jones had been sleeping were covered in blood. Bridget discovered that one of her kitchen knives was missing. However, the police did not preserve the sheets or take blood samples and permitted Bridget to dispose of the sheets. A police officer involved explained that the possibility that any of the blood at the

crime scene could have come from anyone other than Jones had not been considered.

Jones' severed penis was never found and he underwent reconstructive surgery. His physicians fashioned him a new penis made from tissue and bone taken from his leg. Jones experienced complications and the result was not entirely satisfactory.

OPINION

. . . Jewell attacks the sufficiency of evidence supporting his conviction of Burglary, which is defined as: A person who breaks and enters the building or structure of another person, with intent to commit a felony in it, commits burglary. Ind. Code 354321 Jewell argues he was improperly convicted of breaking into his own house. . . .

The Burglary statute's requirement that the dwelling be that "of another person" is satisfied if the evidence demonstrates that the entry was unauthorized. . . . In the present case, Bridget had purchased the house in her own name before the marriage. When she and Jewell experienced marital difficulties, Jewell moved out and Bridget changed the locks to prevent Jewell from reentering the house. Bridget alone controlled access to the house. Jewell entered the house at 4:00 A.M. through the kitchen window after having removed the screen.

The evidence supports the conclusion that the entry was unauthorized; and, therefore, we find no error. . . .

Judgment AFFIRMED.

Questions

1. List all of the facts relevant to determining whether Barry Jewell burglarized his own home.
2. How does the state of Indiana define the "dwelling of another" element?
3. How did the court arrive at the conclusion that Barry Jewell burglarized his own home?
4. What's the reason for the "unauthorized entry" requirement?
5. Do you agree with it? Defend your answer.

At common law, another circumstance element was "in the nighttime." There were three reasons for the nighttime element. First, it's easier to commit crimes at night. Second, it's harder to identify suspects you've seen at night. Third, and probably most important, nighttime intrusions frighten victims more than daytime intrusions. At least eighteen states retain the nighttime requirement. Some do so by making nighttime an element of the crime. Others treat nighttime invasions as an aggravating circumstance. Some have eliminated the nighttime requirement entirely.

Burglary Mens Rea   Burglary is a specific-intent crime. The prosecution has to prove two *mens rea* elements:

1. The intent to commit the *actus reus* (breaking, entering, or remaining)

2. The intent to commit a crime once inside the structure broken into, entered, or remained in

The intended crime doesn't have to be serious. Intent to steal is usually good enough, but some states go further to include "any crime," "any misdemeanor," or even "any public offense" (Note 1951, 420).

Keep in mind another important point: It isn't necessary to complete or even attempt to commit the intended crime. Suppose I sneak into my rich former student Patrick's luxurious condo in Kona, Hawaii, while he's out making more money, intending to steal one of his three wireless notebook computers he doesn't need or use. Right after I get inside the front door, and not even close to where the notebooks are, my conscience gets the better of me. I say to myself, "I can't do this, even if Pat does have three notebook computers," and I slink back out the front door. I still committed burglary, because the burglary was complete the moment I was inside with the intent to steal one of the notebooks.

The Degrees of Burglary   Because burglary is defined so broadly, many states divide it into several degrees. Alabama's burglary statute is typical:

§ 13A-7-5. BURGLARY IN THE FIRST DEGREE

(a) A person commits the crime of burglary in the first degree if he knowingly and unlawfully enters or remains unlawfully in a dwelling with intent to commit a crime therein, and, if, in effecting entry or while in dwelling or in immediate flight therefrom, he or another participant in the crime:
(1) Is armed with explosives or a deadly weapon; or
(2) Causes physical injury to any person who is not a participant in the crime; or
(3) Uses or threatens the immediate use of a dangerous instrument.

Sentence: 10 years to life

§ 13A-7-6. BURGLARY IN THE SECOND DEGREE

(a) A person commits the crime of burglary in the second degree if he knowingly enters or remains unlawfully in a building with intent to commit theft or a felony therein and, if in effecting entry or while in the building or in immediate flight therefrom, he or another participant in the crime:
(1) Is armed with explosives or a deadly weapon; or
(2) Causes physical injury to any person who is not a participant in the crime; or
(3) Uses or threatens the immediate use of a dangerous instrument.

(b) In the alternative to subsection (a) of this section, a person commits the crime of burglary in the second degree if he unlawfully enters a lawfully occupied dwelling-house with intent to commit a theft or a felony therein.

Sentence: 2–20 years

§ 13A-7-7. BURGLARY IN THE THIRD DEGREE

(a) A person commits the crime of burglary in the third degree if he knowingly enters or remains unlawfully in a building with intent to commit a crime therein.

Sentence: 1–10 years

Despite efforts to grade burglary according to seriousness, the broad scope of the offense invites injustices in most statutes. This is true in large part because burglary punishes the invasion and not the underlying crime—namely, the crime the burglar entered to commit. In many cases, the penalty for burglary is a lot harsher than the penalty for the intended crime. The difference between a 5-year sentence and a 20-year sentence sometimes depends upon the largely philosophical question of whether a thief forms the intent to steal before or after entering a building.

Criminal Trespass

Criminal trespass is a broader but less serious crime than burglary. It's broader because it's not limited to invasions of occupied buildings, and the trespasser doesn't have to intend to commit a crime in addition to the trespass. The heart of criminal trespass is unwanted presence. The ancient misdemeanor called "trespass" referred to unwanted presence on (invasion of) another person's land. Not all unwanted presence was (or is) criminal trespass; only unauthorized presence qualifies. So, of course, law enforcement officers investigating a crime or gas company employees reading the meter, no matter how unwanted they are, aren't trespassers because they're authorized to be there.

Trespass used to be limited to unauthorized invasions of physical property. At first, only entry onto land was included; then entering and remaining on land and buildings were added; and since the explosion of computers and the Internet, unauthorized access to electronic information systems has been included.

Let's look at the elements and degrees of criminal trespass and at the special trespassing offense of computer trespass.

The Elements of Criminal Trespass The *actus reus* of criminal trespass is the unauthorized entering of or remaining on the premises of another person (ALI 1985, 2:2, 87). The *mens rea* varies, including:

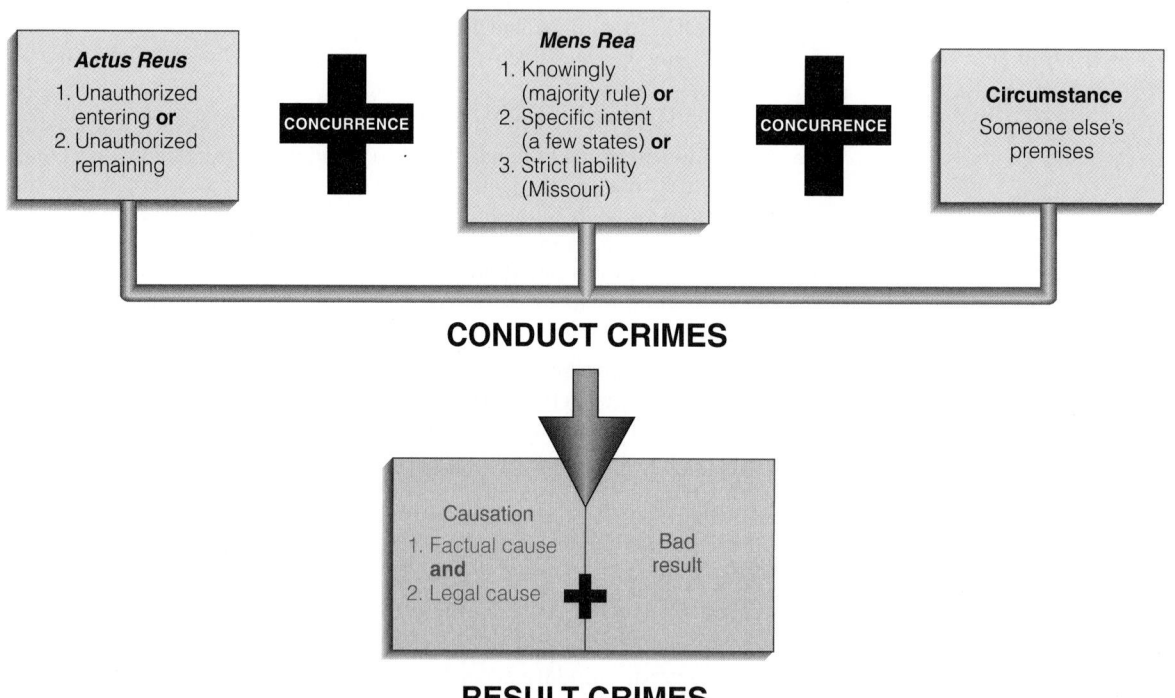

Elements of Criminal Trespass

1. The defendant knowingly enters or remains without authority or by invitation, license, privilege, or legality (most states).

2. The defendant has the specific intent to enter or remain without authority for some unlawful purpose (a few states).

3. The defendant bears strict liability for entering or remaining (Missouri, enters "unlawfully"). (88)

The Degrees of Criminal Trespass   The MPC created three degrees of criminal trespass:

1. *Misdemeanor* Entering or remaining in an occupied dwelling at night

2. *Petty misdemeanor* Entering or remaining in any occupied building or structure

3. *Violation* Entering or remaining in any place where a "no trespass" notice is given (warning to person, "no trespassing" sign, or fence)

CYBERCRIMES

We live in the Information Age. Computers and the Internet have greatly enhanced the capacity to exploit information about individuals and about ideas. "Life is built upon computerized data bases" (V. Johnson 2005, 255) that can be used for good and for ill.

Personal information about our health, our finances, and our likes and dislikes helps doctors, banks, and merchants help us. But it also helps identity thieves take our money and wreck our lives (V. Johnson 2005, 256–57) and, in extreme cases, even kill us and the people we love (see the *Remsburg v. Docusearch, Inc.* case excerpt later in this section).

Ideas and their practical application, **intellectual property,** can be the most valuable of all property any individual, business, or society can have. Whether this intellectual property is the copyright of a popular song; the patent on a breakthrough drug; a trade secret to an innovative product; or a trademark to a valuable brand, it's a source of wealth, jobs, and social and economic strength and stability (U.S. Department of Justice 2006, 13). But with these strengths, enhanced by computers and the Internet, come enhanced vulnerabilities to *cybercrime*, crimes aimed at the valuable information contained in computers, especially computer databases accessible through the Internet (Yang and Hoffstadt 2006, 201; also *U.S. v. Ancheta*, case excerpt later in this section).

Let's look at two cybercrimes that can be enhanced by computers and the Internet: identity theft and intellectual property theft.

Identity Theft

Identity theft is the crime committed most often in the United States (see Figure 11.1). This isn't surprising given the enormous range of personal information contained in business, nonprofit organization, and government electronic databases. These organizations collect, update, and use "masses of computerized information" about anyone who "voluntarily or involuntarily" deals with their institutions (Table 11.1).

The consequences of wrongful access to personal information can be devastating, and they go beyond the money victims lose to identify thieves. The more than nine million annual identity theft "victims spend an average of 600 hours over 2 to 4 years and $1400 to clear their names (V. Johnson 2005, 257, n. 7). Victims may also lose job opportunities; be refused loans, education, housing, or cars; and be arrested for crimes they didn't commit (FDA 2005). In extreme cases, victims are blackmailed (a former chemistry graduate student found a security flaw in a commercial website and

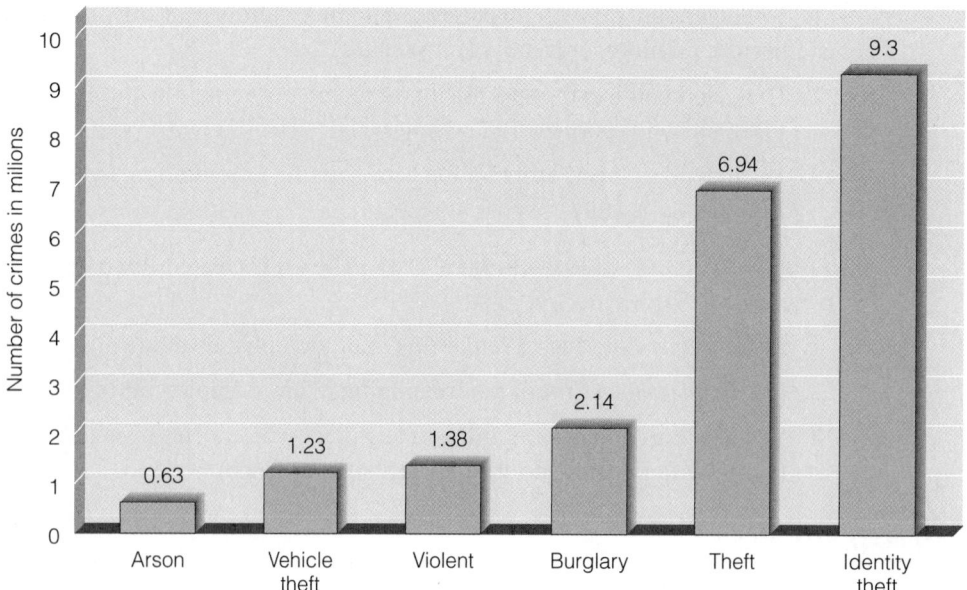

FIGURE 11.1 Number of Crimes 2005

demanded ransom from the company to keep his mouth shut (Rustad 2001, 63); or stalked (Chapter 10, case excerpt, *State v. Hoying*); or even murdered (later in this section, case excerpt *Remsburg v. Docusearch, Inc.*).

The motivations for stealing other people's identity vary. They may be jilted lovers (*Remsburg v. Docusearch, Inc.*); or "bored juveniles, disgruntled employees, corporate spies, or organized crime networks" (Rustad 2001, 65); or just your "run-of-the-mill" thieves (V. Johnson 2005, 257).

Whatever their reasons for stealing identities, they're hard to catch. When they are caught, they're hard to convict (McMahon 2004). That has led some victims to turn to suing the providers of victims' identity. That's the route Helen Remsburg took. Liam Youens got Remsburg's 20-year-old daughter Amy's Social Security number, home address, and her job location from Docusearch, Inc. It cost him $204. A week later, Youens went to Amy's workplace. As she was leaving work, he shot her and then himself to death. This is the subject of our next case excerpt, *Remsburg v. Docusearch, Inc.*

TABLE 11.1	Types of Information Collected by Government, Business, and Nonprofit Organizations
Types	**Examples of the Information Collected**
Names	First, middle, and last names
Relationships	Family members and employers
Contact information	Phone, physical addresses, e-mail addresses, websites
Personal information	Birthday, medical information, physical description, educational records
Official identifiers	Social security, driver's license, passport numbers
Financial records	Bank, credit card, frequent fliers, and investment accounts

Source: V. Johnson (2005, 256).

Is She Entitled to Damages from the Identity Information Providers?

Remsburg v. Docusearch, Inc.

816 A.2d 1001 (N.H. 2003)

HISTORY

After her daughter was fatally shot at her workplace, Helen Remsburg, administrator of the estate of her daughter, Amy Lynn Boyer, sued in the U.S. District Court for the District of New Hampshire, defendants Docusearch, Inc., Wing and a Prayer, Inc., Daniel Cohn, Kenneth Zeiss and Michele Gambino for wrongful death; invasion of privacy through intrusion upon seclusion; invasion of privacy through commercial appropriation of private information; violation of the federal Fair Credit Reporting Act, 15 U.S.C. §§ 1681a et seq.; and violation of the New Hampshire Consumer Protection Act, N.H.Rev.Stat. Ann. 358-A:1 et seq.

Defendants Docusearch, Inc., Wing and a Prayer, Inc., Daniel Cohn and Kenneth Zeiss filed motions for summary judgment.

[Summary judgment means the facts don't amount to a case against the defendant and should be dismissed without further proceedings.]

The material facts supporting the motions are undisputed.

Because the "motions raised important questions of New Hampshire law that should be resolved by the New Hampshire Supreme Court rather than a federal court," the U.S. District Court judge sent the following questions to the N.H. Supreme Court.

(1) investigation service had duty to exercise reasonable care in disclosing personal information about daughter to client;

(2) daughter's work address was not something secret, secluded or private, and thus disclosure of that address could not support claim for invasion of privacy by intrusion upon seclusion;

(3) New Hampshire recognizes cause of action for invasion of privacy by appropriation of individual's name or likeness;

(4) mother did not have a cause of action for appropriation; and

(5) investigation service, which obtained daughter's work address through a pretextual phone call, was subject to liability for damages under Consumer Protection Act.

DALIANIS, J.

FACTS

We adopt the district court's recitation of the facts. Docusearch, Inc. and Wing and a Prayer, Inc. (WAAP) jointly own and operate an Internet-based investigation and information service known as Docusearch.com. Daniel Cohn and Kenneth Zeiss each own 50% of each company's stock. Cohn serves as president of both companies and Zeiss serves as a director of WAAP. Cohn is licensed as a private investigator by both the State of Florida and Palm Beach County, Florida.

On July 29, 1999, New Hampshire resident Liam Youens contacted Docusearch through its Internet website and requested the date of birth for Amy Lynn Boyer, another New Hampshire resident. Youens provided Docusearch his name, New Hampshire address, and a contact telephone number. He paid the $20 fee by credit card. Zeiss placed a telephone call to Youens in New Hampshire on the same day. Zeiss cannot recall the reason for the phone call, but speculates that it was to verify the order. The next day, July 30, 1999, Docusearch provided Youens with the birth dates for several Amy Boyers, but none was for the Amy Boyer sought by Youens.

In response, Youens e-mailed Docusearch inquiring whether it would be possible to get better results using Boyer's home address, which he provided. Youens gave Docusearch a different contact phone number.

Later that same day, Youens again contacted Docusearch and placed an order for Boyer's Social Security number (SSN), paying the $45 fee by credit card. On August 2, 1999, Docusearch obtained Boyer's Social Security number from a credit reporting agency as a part of a "credit header" and provided it to Youens. A "credit header" is typically provided at the top of a credit report and includes a person's name, address and Social Security number.

The next day, Youens placed an order with Docusearch for Boyer's employment information, paying the $109 fee by credit card, and giving Docusearch the same phone number he had provided originally. Docusearch phone records indicate that Zeiss placed a phone call to Youens on August 6, 1999. The phone number used was the one Youens had provided with his follow-up inquiry regarding Boyer's birth date. The phone call lasted for less than one minute, and no record exists concerning its topic or whether Zeiss was able to speak with Youens.

On August 20, 1999, having received no response to his latest request, Youens placed a second request for Boyer's employment information, again paying the $109 fee by credit card. On September 1, 1999, Docusearch refunded Youens' first payment of $109 because its efforts to fulfill his first request for Boyer's employment information had failed.

With his second request for Boyer's employment information pending, Youens placed yet another order for information with Docusearch on September 6, 1999. This time, he requested a "locate by social security number" search for Boyer. Youens paid the $30 fee by credit card, and received the results of the search—Boyer's home address—on September 7, 1999.

On September 8, 1999, Docusearch informed Youens of Boyer's employment address. Docusearch acquired this address through a subcontractor, Michele Gambino, who had obtained the information by placing a "pretext" telephone call to Boyer in New Hampshire. Gambino lied about who she was and the purpose of her call in order to convince Boyer to reveal her employment information. Gambino had no contact with Youens, nor did she know why Youens was requesting the information.

On October 15, 1999, Youens drove to Boyer's workplace and fatally shot her as she left work. Youens then shot and killed himself. A subsequent police investigation revealed that Youens kept firearms and ammunition in his bedroom, and maintained a website containing references to stalking and killing Boyer as well as other information and statements related to violence and killing.

OPINION

Question 1

All persons have a duty to exercise reasonable care not to subject others to an unreasonable risk of harm. Whether a defendant's conduct creates a risk of harm to others sufficiently foreseeable to charge the defendant with a duty to avoid such conduct is a question of law because the existence of a duty does not arise solely from the relationship between the parties, but also from the need for protection against reasonably foreseeable harm. Thus, in some cases, a party's actions give rise to a duty. Parties owe a duty to those third parties foreseeably endangered by their conduct with respect to those risks whose likelihood and magnitude make the conduct unreasonably dangerous.

In situations in which the harm is caused by criminal misconduct, however, determining whether a duty exists is complicated by the competing rule that a private citizen has no general duty to protect others from the criminal attacks of third parties. This rule is grounded in the fundamental unfairness of holding private citizens responsible for the unanticipated criminal acts of third parties, because under all ordinary and normal circumstances, in the absence of any reason to expect the contrary, the actor may reasonably proceed upon the assumption that others will obey the law.

In certain limited circumstances, however, we have recognized that there are exceptions to the general rule where a duty to exercise reasonable care will arise. We have held that such a duty may arise because:

(1) a special relationship exists;

(2) special circumstances exist; or

(3) the duty has been voluntarily assumed.

The special circumstances exception includes situations where there is an especial temptation and opportunity for criminal misconduct brought about by the defendant. This exception follows from the rule that a party who realizes or should realize that his conduct has created a condition which involves an unreasonable risk of harm to another has a duty to exercise reasonable care to prevent the risk from occurring. The exact occurrence or precise injuries need not have been foreseeable. Rather, where the defendant's conduct has created an unreasonable risk of criminal misconduct, a duty is owed to those foreseeably endangered.

Thus, if a private investigator or information broker's (hereinafter "investigator" collectively) disclosure of information to a client creates a foreseeable risk of criminal misconduct against the third person whose information was disclosed, the investigator owes a duty to exercise reasonable care not to subject the third person to an unreasonable risk of harm. In determining whether the risk of criminal misconduct is foreseeable to an investigator, we examine two risks of information disclosure implicated by this case: stalking and identity theft. . . .

[The court's discussion of stalking is omitted.]

Identity theft, *i.e.*, the use of one person's identity by another, is an increasingly common risk associated with the disclosure of personal information, such as a SSN. A person's SSN has attained the status of a quasi-universal personal identification number. At the same time, however, a person's privacy interest in his or her SSN is recognized by state and federal statutes, including RSA 260:14, IV-a (Supp.2002) which prohibits the release of SSNs contained within drivers' license records. Armed with one's SSN, an unscrupulous individual could obtain a person's welfare benefits or Social Security benefits, order new checks at a new address on that person's checking account, obtain credit cards, or even obtain the person's paycheck.

Like the consequences of stalking, the consequences of identity theft can be severe. The best estimates place the number of victims in excess of 100,000 per year and the dollar loss in excess of $2 billion per year. LoPucki, *Human Identification Theory and the Identity Theft Problem*, 80 Tex. L.Rev. 89, 89 (2001).

[See the "Number of Crimes, 2005" graph in your text for much higher numbers in 2005.]

Victims of identity theft risk the destruction of their good credit histories. This often destroys a victim's ability to obtain credit from any source and may, in some cases, render the victim unemployable or even cause the victim to be incarcerated.

The threats posed by stalking and identity theft lead us to conclude that the risk of criminal misconduct is sufficiently foreseeable so that an investigator has a duty to exercise reasonable care in disclosing a third person's personal information to a client. And we so hold. This is especially true when, as in this case, the investigator does not know the client or the client's purpose in seeking the information.

Questions 2 and 3

A tort action based upon an intrusion upon seclusion must relate to something secret, secluded or private pertaining to the plaintiff. Moreover, liability exists only if the defendant's conduct was such that the defendant should have realized that it would be offensive to persons of ordinary sensibilities. It is only where the intrusion has gone beyond the limits of decency that liability accrues.

In addressing whether a person's SSN is something secret, secluded or private, we must determine whether a person has a reasonable expectation of privacy in the number. SSNs are used to identify people to track social security benefits, as well as when taxes and credit applications are filed. In fact, "the widespread use of SSNs as universal identifiers in the public and private sectors is one of the most serious manifestations of privacy concerns in the Nation. As noted above, a person's interest in maintaining the privacy of his or her SSN has been recognized by numerous federal and state statutes. As a result, the entities to which this information is disclosed and their employees are bound by legal, and, perhaps, contractual constraints to hold SSNs in confidence to ensure that they remain private. Thus, while a SSN must be disclosed in certain circumstances, a person may reasonably expect that the number will remain private.

Whether the intrusion would be offensive to persons of ordinary sensibilities is ordinarily a question for the fact-finder and only becomes a question of law if reasonable persons can draw only one conclusion from the evidence. The evidence underlying the certified question is insufficient to draw any such conclusion here, and we therefore must leave this question to the fact-finder. In making this determination, the fact-finder should consider "the degree of intrusion, the context, conduct and circumstances surrounding the intrusion as well as the intruder's motives and objectives, the setting into which he intrudes, and the expectations of those whose privacy is invaded." Accordingly, a person whose SSN is obtained by an investigator from a credit reporting agency without the person's knowledge or permission may have a cause of action for intrusion upon seclusion for damages caused by the sale of the SSN, but must prove that the intrusion was such that it would have been offensive to a person of ordinary sensibilities.

We next address whether a person has a cause of action for intrusion upon seclusion where an investigator obtains the person's work address by using a pretextual phone call. We must first establish whether a work address is something secret, secluded or private about the plaintiff.

In most cases, a person works in a public place. On the public street, or in any other public place, [a person] has no legal right to be alone. A person's employment, where he lives, and where he works are exposures which we all must suffer. We have no reasonable expectation of privacy as to our identity or as to where we live or work. Our commuting to and from where we live and work is not done clandestinely and each place provides a facet of our total identity.

Question 4

One who appropriates to his own use or benefit the name or likeness of another is subject to liability to the other for invasion of his privacy. . . . New Hampshire recognizes the tort of invasion of privacy by appropriation of an individual's name or likeness. . . . The interest protected by the rule is the interest of the individual in the exclusive use of his own identity, in so far as it is represented by his name or likeness, and in so far as the use may be of benefit to him or to others.

Tortious liability for appropriation of a name or likeness is intended to protect the value of an individual's notoriety or skill. Thus, . . . in order that there may be liability under the rule . . . the defendant must have appropriated to his own use or benefit the reputation, prestige, social or commercial standing, public interest or other values of the plaintiff's name or likeness. The misappropriation tort does not protect one's name *per se*; rather it protects the value associated with that name.

Appropriation is not actionable if the person's name or likeness is published for purposes other than taking advantage of [the person's] reputation, prestige or other value" associated with the person. Thus, appropriation occurs most often when the person's name or likeness is used to advertise the defendant's product or when the defendant impersonates the person for gain.

An investigator who sells personal information sells the information for the value of the information itself, not to take advantage of the person's reputation or prestige. The investigator does not capitalize upon the goodwill value associated with the information but rather upon the client's willingness to pay for the information. In other words, the benefit derived from the sale in no way relates to the social or commercial standing of the person whose information is sold. Thus, a person whose personal information is sold does not have a cause of action for appropriation against the investigator who sold the information.

Question 5

The last issue relates to the construction of the Consumer Protection Act, RSA chapter 358-A. On questions of statutory interpretation, this court is the final arbiter of the intent of the legislature as expressed in the words of a statute considered as a whole. We begin by considering the plain meaning of the words of the statute. In conducting our analysis we will focus on the statute as a whole, not on isolated words or phrases. We will not consider what the legislature might have said or add words that the legislature did not include.

RSA 358-A:2 (1995) states, in pertinent part:

It shall be unlawful for any person to use . . . any unfair or deceptive act or practice in the conduct of any trade or commerce within this state. Such . . . unfair or deceptive act or practice shall include, but is not limited to, the following:

. . .

III. Causing likelihood of confusion or of misunderstanding as to affiliation, connection or association with . . . another.

Pretext phone calling has been described as the use of deception and trickery to obtain a person's private information for resale to others. The target of the phone call is deceived into believing that the caller is affiliated with a reliable entity who has a legitimate purpose in requesting the information. RSA 358-A:2, III explicitly prohibits this conduct. The pretext clearly creates a misunderstanding as to the investigator's affiliation.

The defendant argues that . . . an investigator who makes a pretextual phone call to obtain information for sale does not conduct any "trade" or "commerce" with the person deceived by the phone call. The Consumer Protection Act defines "trade" and "commerce" as including "the advertising, offering for sale, sale, or distribution of any services and any property. . . ."

There is no language in the Act that would restrict the definition of "trade" and "commerce" to that affecting the party deceived by the prohibited conduct. In fact, the Act explicitly includes "trade or commerce directly or *indirectly* affecting the people of this state." (emphasis added). . . . Here, the investigator used the pretext phone call to complete the sale of information to a client. Thus, the investigator's pretextual phone call occurred in the conduct of trade or commerce within the State. . . .

We conclude that an investigator who obtains a person's work address by means of pretextual phone calling, and then sells the information, may be liable for damages under RSA chapter 358-A to the person deceived.

Remanded.

Questions

1. State the five questions the U.S. District Court asked the New Hampshire Supreme Court to answer.

2. Summarize the court's answers and the reasons for its answers.

3. If you were a juror, would you vote to award Helen Remsburg damages? How much? Back up your answer with the rich facts supplied by the court.

4. Consider the final outcome in the case and the Remburgs' reaction to the case. About a year after the New Hampshire Supreme Court decided the case, the Remsburgs settled for $85,000.

> Tim Remsburg, Amy Boyer's stepfather, said he and his wife wanted their day in court but grew frustrated with the court system. "This has never been about money," he said Wednesday. "There's just so many things that are still wrong, but we had to make a decision. We needed to get our lives back and focus on putting this behind us a little bit."
>
> Remsburg said the couple will continue to honor Amy's memory by spreading her story to the public and policy makers. And he believes the lawsuit, though it never went to trial, received enough publicity that information brokers such as Docusearch now think twice about selling private information. (Ramer 2004)

Describe your reaction to the case after reading the excerpt and the final outcome.

Intellectual Property Theft

> The Congress shall have power . . . to promote the progress of science and useful arts, by securing for limited times to authors and inventors the exclusive right to their respective writings and discoveries. (U.S. Constitution, Article I, Section 8)

The importance of intellectual property wasn't lost on our nation's founders. They wrote it into the Constitution. We recognize it today in the copyright laws that protect unauthorized copying and distribution of books, films, music compositions, sound recordings, software programs. Other laws protect intellectual property from infringement on trademarks, trade secrets, and patents and thefts, damage, and destruction of intellectual property.

Intellectual property definitely needs protection, even more today than before the widespread use of computers and the Internet. First, intellectual property theft costs at least $250 billion every year (Department of Justice 2006, 13). The cost may be a lot higher because businesses don't report these thefts, fearing it'll hurt business. Second, intellectual property thefts go undetected because of the difficulty of catching cyber-criminals (Rustad 2001, 65).

Third, cybercriminals are smart, skilled, and highly motivated, not just by money but by the darker and dangerous side of our nature—revenge, hate, ideology, and the powerful, seductive, addictive thrill of hacking.

> Hackers on the borderless Internet have obtained unauthorized access into computer systems to rob banks, infringe copyrights, commit fraud, distribute child pornography, and plan terrorist attacks. (Rustad 2001, 63–64)

A whole new vocabulary has grown up to describe the ways hackers commit cybercrimes. In addition to viruses and wiretapping, methods known even to functional computer illiterates like me, here's a list of some others compiled by Professor Michael Rustad (2001, 64):

- *Spoofing* When an attacker compromises routing packets to direct a file or transmission to a different location.

- *Piggybacking* Programs that hackers use to piggyback on other programs to enter computer systems.

- *Data diddling* The practice by employees and other knowledgeable insiders of altering or manipulating data, credit limits, or other financial information.

- *Salami attack* A series of minor computer crimes—slices of a larger crime—that are difficult to detect. (For example, a hacker finds a way to get into a bank's computers. He quietly skims off a penny or so from each account. Once he has $200,000, he quits.)

- *E-mail flood attacks* When so much e-mail is sent to a target that the transfer agent is overwhelmed, causing other communication programs to destabilize and crash the system.

- *Password sniffing* Using password sniffing programs to monitor and record the name and password of network users as they log in and impersonating the authorized users to access restricted documents.

- *Worm* Uses a network to send copies of itself to other systems and it does so without any intervention. In general, worms harm the network and consume bandwidth, whereas viruses infect or corrupt files on a targeted computer. Viruses generally do not affect network performance, as their malicious activities are mostly confined within the target computer itself.

Our last case excerpt in this chapter, *U.S. v. Ancheta* (2006), involves one cyberthief who got caught and pleaded guilty to multiple counts of computer fraud. Twenty-year-old Jeanson Acheta worked in an Internet café in Downey, California. According to his aunt, he had modest ambitions—to join the military reserves, but he lived a luxurious lifestyle as an Internet café employee. He was often seen driving his BMW and spending more than $600 a week on new clothes and car parts. The explanation was the profits he made from the results of a worm he authored. The worm allowed him to infect as many computers on the Internet as he could with off-the-shelf remote access Trojans (RATs) (Vamosi 2006).

Ancheta pleaded guilty to multiple counts of cybercrime fraud; he received 57 months in prison—the longest prison cybercrime theft sentence to date—and had to forfeit his BMW. Before you read the case excerpt, study the provisions in the federal "Fraud and Related Activity in Connection with Computers" (U.S. Code 2006, Title 18, Part I, Chapter 47 ß1030(a)(5)(A)(i); 1030(a)(5)(B)(i), and 1030(b)) that Ancheta pleaded guilty to. Make sure you can state the *actus reus*, *mens rea*, circumstance, and bad result elements:

"FRAUD AND RELATED ACTIVITY IN CONNECTION WITH COMPUTERS"

(a) Whoever— . . .

    (5)(A)

        (i) knowingly causes the transmission of a program, information, code, or command, and as a result of such conduct, intentionally causes damage without authorization, to a protected computer. . . .

    (5) (B) by conduct described in clause (i), (ii), or (iii) of subparagraph (A), caused (or, in the case of an attempted offense, would, if completed, have caused)—

        (i) loss to 1 or more persons during any 1-year period (and, for purposes of an investigation, prosecution, or other proceeding brought by the United States only, loss resulting from a related course of conduct affecting 1 or more other protected computers) aggregating at least $5,000 in value. . . .

(b) Whoever attempts to commit an offense under subsection (a) of this section shall be punished as provided in subsection (c) of this section.

(c) The punishment for an offense under subsection (a) or (b) of this section is—

    (1)(A) a fine under this title or imprisonment for not more than ten years, or both, in the case of an offense under subsection (a)(1) of this section which does not occur after a conviction for another offense under this section, or an attempt to commit an offense punishable under this subparagraph; and

    (B) a fine under this title or imprisonment for not more than twenty years, or both, in the case of an offense under subsection (a)(1) of this section which occurs after a conviction for another offense under this section, or an attempt to commit an offense punishable under this subparagraph. . . .

CASE — *Fraud and Related Activity in Connection with Computers*

U.S v. Ancheta
(C.D. Cal. 2006)

HISTORY

Concluding the first prosecution of its kind in the United States, a well known member of the "botmaster underground" was sentenced this afternoon to nearly five years in prison for profiting from his use of "botnets"—armies of compromised computers—that he used to launch destructive attacks, to send huge quantities of spam across the Internet, and to receive surreptitious installations of adware.

FACTS

Jeanson James Ancheta, 21, of Downey, California, was sentenced to 57 months in federal prison by United States District Judge R. Gary Klausner in Los Angeles. During the sentencing hearing, Judge Klausner characterized Ancheta's crimes as "extensive, serious and sophisticated." The prison term is the longest known sentence for a defendant who spread computer viruses.

Ancheta pleaded guilty in January to conspiring to violate the Computer Fraud Abuse Act, conspiring to violate the CAN-SPAM Act, causing damage to computers used by the federal government in national defense, and accessing protected computers without authorization to commit fraud. When he pleaded guilty, Ancheta admitted using computer servers he controlled to transmit malicious code over the Internet to scan for and exploit vulnerable computers. Ancheta caused thousands of compromised computers to be directed to an Internet Relay Chat channel, where they were instructed to scan for other computers vulnerable to similar infection, and to remain "zombies" vulnerable to further unauthorized accesses.

Ancheta further admitted that, in more than 30 separate transactions, he earned approximately $3,000 by selling access to his botnets. The botnets were sold to other computer users, who used the machines to launch distributed denial of service (DDOS) attacks and to send unsolicited commercial email, or spam. Ancheta acknowledged specifically discussing with the purchasers the nature and extent of the DDOS attacks or proxy spamming they were interested in conducting. Ancheta suggested the number of bots or proxies they would need to accomplish the specified acts, tested the botnets with them to ensure that the DDOS attacks or proxy spamming were successfully carried out, and advised them on how to properly maintain, update and strengthen their purchased armies.

In relation to the computer fraud scheme, Ancheta admitted generating for himself and an unindicted co-conspirator more than $107,000 in advertising affiliate proceeds by downloading adware to more than 400,000 infected computers that he controlled. By varying the download times and rates of the adware installations, as well as by redirecting the compromised computers between various servers equipped to install different types of modified adware, Ancheta avoided detection by the advertising affiliate companies who paid him for every install. Ancheta further admitted using the advertising affiliate proceeds he earned to pay for, among other things, the multiple servers he used to conduct his illegal activity.

Following the prison term, Ancheta will serve three years on supervised release. During that time, his access to computers and the Internet will be limited, and he will be required to pay approximately $15,000 in restitution to the Weapons Division of the United States Naval Air Warfare Center in China Lake and the Defense Information Systems Agency, whose national defense networks were intentionally damaged by Ancheta's malicious code. The proceeds of Ancheta's illegal activity—including more than $60,000 in cash, a BMW automobile and computer equipment—have been forfeited to the government.

Addressing the defendant at the conclusion of the sentencing hearing, Judge Klausner said: "Your worst enemy is your own intellectual arrogance that somehow the world cannot touch you on this." This case was investigated by the Los Angeles Field Office of the Federal Bureau of Investigation, which received assistance from the Southwest Field Office of the Naval Criminal Investigative Service and the Western Field Office of the Defense Criminal Investigative Service.

Questions

1. State the *actus reus*, *mens rea*, attendance circumstance(s), and "bad result" elements of the federal "Fraud and Related Activity in Connection with Computers" statute.

2. List the relevant facts Ancheta admitted, and match them up with the elements you stated in (1).

3. What purposes of punishment do the forfeiture and sentence reflect? Recall the purposes of punishment laid out in Chapter 1: punishment requires (a) condemnation *and* hard treatment; (b) retribution; (c) a means of prevention (general and special deterrence, incapacitation, and rehabilitation); and (d) restitution. Back up your answer using the purposes of punishment.

4. Was the sentence fair? Too harsh? Too lenient? Explain your answer.

SUMMARY

I. Crimes against other people's property

  A. There are three kinds of crimes people can commit against other people's property:

    1. They can take it.

      a. Theft

      b. Robbery

      c. Receive stolen property

    2. They can damage or destroy it.

      a. Arson

      b. Criminal mischief

    3. They can invade it.

      a. Burglary

      b. Criminal trespass

  B. Cybercrime is a rapidly growing problem with the advent of modern computers.

II. Taking other people's property

A. Theft

1. In most states, theft is a combined definition of larceny, embezzlement, and false pretenses.
2. Consolidated theft statutes eliminate the artificial need to separate theft into distinct offenses according to their *actus reus*.
3. The *mens rea* is acquiring someone else's property purposely, knowingly, or intentionally.

B. Receiving stolen property

1. The purpose of making it a crime to receive stolen property is to punish individuals who benefit from someone else's theft.
2. The *actus reus* of receiving stolen property is the very act of receiving the property, no matter how briefly.
3. The *mens rea* requirement varies in most states:
   a. In some states receivers have to know the goods are stolen.
   b. In others, if receivers believe the goods are stolen, that's enough to prove the *mens rea*.
   c. Receivers can also obtain property recklessly or negligently.
   d. Receivers also have to intend to keep the property permanently.

C. Robbery

1. The core of robbery is theft accomplished under circumstances calculated to terrorize the victim through actual injury or threat of immediate injury.
2. The use of force, or the threat of force, is the essence of robbery *actus reus*.
3. Robbery *mens rea* is the intent to take another person's property and keep it permanently but with the additional intent or threat to use immediate force.
4. Robbery is divided into degrees according to whether the robbers were armed and the injury they caused to their victims.

D. Extortion

1. Theft by extortion, often called "blackmail," is taking someone else's property by threats of future harm.
2. The elements of extortion include:
   a. Mens rea The specific intent to take someone else's property by means of a variety of threats
   b. Actus reus A wide range of specific threats by which the taking of property is accomplished

III. Damaging and destroying other people's property

A. Arson

1. Arson has grown far beyond its origins in burning houses to include burning almost any kind of building, vessel, or vehicle.
2. Arson is a crime against possession and occupancy, not just against ownership.
3. In the MPC, *actus reus* burning is starting a fire, even if the fire never touches the structure it was meant to burn; explosions are also included in "burning."
4. Most arson statutes follow the common-law *mens rea* requirement that arsonists have to "maliciously and willfully" burn or set fire to buildings.

5. There are two degrees of arson:
   a. First-degree arson includes burning homes and other occupied structures.
   b. Second-degree arson includes burning unoccupied structures, vehicles, and boats.
B. Criminal mischief
   1. Criminal mischief includes three types of harm to tangible property:
      a. Destruction or damage by fire, explosives, or other "dangerous acts"
      b. Tampering with tangible property so as to endanger property
      c. Deception or threat that causes someone to suffer money loss
   2. The *actus reus* of criminal mischief mirrors the three types of criminal mischief:
      a. In destruction or damage, the *actus reus* is burning, exploding, flooding, or committing some other dangerous act.
      b. Tampering is any act that creates a danger to property, even if it doesn't actually cause any damage to the property.
      c. Deception or threat usually consists of "expensive practical jokes."
   3. The *mens rea* element of criminal mischief varies according to state statutes.

IV. Invading other people's property
A. Burglary
   1. The heart of burglary is invading others' property, not taking, destroying, or damaging it; it doesn't require causing a bad result.
   2. Until the 1900s, burglary *actus reus* consisted of two actions—breaking and entering; today many states define burglary as an attempt to break in.
   3. The MPC's definition limits burglary to occupied structures.
   4. Some statutes still require that burglary has to occur in the nighttime.
   5. Burglary is a specific-intent crime; the prosecution has to prove two *mens rea* elements:
      a. The intent to commit the *actus reus.*
      b. The intent to commit a crime once inside the structure broken into, entered, or remained in. Completion of the crime isn't necessary.
B. Criminal trespass
   1. The heart of criminal trespass is unwanted presence.
   2. In addition to unauthorized invasions of physical property, unauthorized access to electronic information systems has been included in the definition of criminal trespass.
   3. The *actus reus* of criminal trespass is the unauthorized entering of or remaining on the premises of another person.
   4. The *mens rea* varies:
      a. The defendant knowingly enters or remains without authority (most states).
      b. The defendant had the specific intent to enter or remain without authority (a few states).
      c. The defendant has strict liability for entering or remaining unlawfully— (Missouri).

V. Cybercrimes
A. *Identity theft* It's the crime committed most often in the United States with more than 9 million victims annually.

B. Intellectual property theft
   1. Intellectual property theft costs at least $250 billion every year.
   2. Intellectual property thefts go undetected because of the difficulty of catching cybercriminals.
   3. Cybercriminals are smart, skilled, and highly motivated.

REVIEW QUESTIONS

1. Identify three kinds of crimes one can commit against other people's property. Give a specific example of each.

2. Identify and describe four types of cybercrimes.

3. Describe the history behind common-law statutes involving taking other people's property.

4. Explain the differences among the *actus reus* of larceny, embezzlement, and false pretenses.

5. What's the difference between tangible and intangible property?

6. What's the purpose of making receiving stolen property a crime?

7. Identify both the *actus reus* and the *mens rea* elements in receiving stolen property, and give an example of each.

8. How do robbery and extortion differ from other crimes of taking other people's property?

9. Define the amount of force necessary to satisfy the *actus reus* requirement in robbery.

10. What special circumstance makes the *mens rea* of robbery different from ordinary theft?

11. Explain the difference between robbery and extortion.

12. Describe the history behind modern arson statutes.

13. State and give examples of arson *actus reus* and *mens rea*.

14. Identify the heart of burglary and criminal trespass.

15. Summarize the significance of the quote from Sinclair Lewis's novel *Babbitt* (page 387).

16. Identify the four elements of common-law burglary from which our modern law of burglary descends, and give an example of each.

17. Identify three reasons for the "nighttime element" in common-law burglary.

18. How has the definition of criminal trespass broadened in light of computers?

19. Identify four vocabulary words hackers use to describe the crimes they commit.

20. What's the key to taking other people's property by means of identity theft?

21. Identify and describe two ways states have responded to the effects of computers and the Internet on the law of theft.

KEY TERMS

Crimes Against Public Order and Morals

MAIN POINTS

- Some disorderly conduct crimes are now called "quality of life" crimes, but they're still aimed at the same conduct—"bad manners" in public.
- Efforts to control bad manners in public underscore the tension between order and liberty in constitutional democracies.
- Quality-of-life crimes are minor offenses, but the "broken windows" theory claims (based on mixed empirical results) they're linked to serious crime.
- There's widespread public support among all classes, races, and communities for controlling the bad behaviors of "street people" and "street gangs."
- Most people are more worried about bad public manners than they are about serious crimes.
- "Victimless" crimes against public decency (the ancient "crimes against public morals") are a hot-button issue between those who believe the criminal law should enforce morality and those who believe the nonviolent behavior of competent adults is none of the law's business.

© Clayton Sharrard/PhotoEdit

12

The broken-windows theory suggests that physical disorder in a neighborhood leads to further neglect, which can lead to small crimes and eventually become a setting for major crimes. Do you assume anything about the quality of life in this neighborhood by the state of this building?

What's the Best Way to Control Street Gangs?

Rocksprings is an urban war zone. The four-square-block neighborhood, claimed as the turf of a gang variously known as Varrio Sureno Town, Varrio Sureno Treces (VST), or Varrio Sureno Locos (VSL), is an occupied territory. Gang members, all of whom live elsewhere, congregate on lawns, on sidewalks, and in front of apartment complexes at all hours of the day and night. They display a casual contempt for notions of law, order, and decency—openly drinking, smoking dope, sniffing toluene, and even snorting cocaine laid out in neat lines on the hoods of residents' cars. The people who live in Rocksprings are subjected to loud talk, loud music, vulgarity, profanity, brutality, fistfights, and the sound of gunfire echoing in the streets. Gang members take over sidewalks, driveways, carports, and apartment parking areas, and impede traffic on the public thoroughfares to conduct their drive-up drug bazaar. Murder, attempted murder, drive-by shootings, assault and battery, vandalism, arson, and theft are commonplace.

(PEOPLE EX REL. GALLO V. ACUNA 1997)

The last species of offenses which especially affect the commonwealth are . . . the due regulation and domestic order of the kingdom. The individuals of the state, like members of a well-governed family, are bound to conform their general behavior to the rules of propriety, good neighborhood, and good manners; and to be decent, industrious, and inoffensive. . . . This head of offenses must therefore be very miscellaneous, as it comprises all such crimes as especially affect public society. (Blackstone 1769, 162)

Blackstone's 18th-century introduction to his chapter on crimes related to the "regulation and domestic order of the kingdom" is a good way to introduce you to the subject of this chapter, crimes against public order and morals. These crimes cover two vast areas of criminal law that involve mostly very minor crimes but, nonetheless, affect many more people than the crimes against persons and their property we've already discussed (Chapters 9–11) and the crimes against the state we'll discuss in Chapter 13.

We'll first look at disorderly conduct crimes—the misdemeanor of individual disorderly conduct and the group disorderly conduct felony of riot. Next, we'll examine in depth the application of disorderly conduct laws to what are now called **"quality of life" crimes.** These are crimes of "bad manners" in public.

Significant numbers of people across the spectrums of age, sex, race, ethnicity, and class believe strongly that "bad manners" in public places create disorder and threaten the quality of life of ordinary people (Skogan 1990). Others believe just as strongly that making bad manners a crime denies individuals their liberty without due process of law (5th and 14th Amendments to the U.S. Constitution; Chapter 2).

Constitutional democracy can't survive without order and liberty, but there's a natural tension between them because they're fundamental values in conflict. The U.S. Supreme Court has recognized the need to balance order and liberty by holding repeatedly that "ordered liberty" is a fundamental requirement of our constitutional system (Chapter 2). In this chapter, **order** refers to acting according to ordinary people's standard of "good manners." **Liberty** refers to the right of individuals to come and go as they please without government interference.

Throughout most of our history, "bad manners" crimes have been called **crimes against public order.** Today, we call them "quality of life" crimes. The list of quality-of-life offenses is long, including public drinking and drunkenness; begging and aggressive panhandling; threatening behavior and harassment; blocking streets and public places; graffiti and vandalism; street prostitution; public urination and defecation; unlicensed vending; and even "squeegeeing"—washing the windshields of stopped cars and demanding money for the "service."

Finally, we'll examine **"victimless" crimes,** crimes involving willing participants, or participants who don't see themselves as victims.

DISORDERLY CONDUCT

Disorderly conduct crimes are offenses against public order and morals. Except for riot, they are minor crimes that legislators, judges, and scholars didn't pay much attention to until the 1950s when the Model Penal Code (MPC) was adopted by the American Law Institute (ALI). Why the lack of attention? The punishment was minor (small fines or a few days in jail); most defendants were poor; and convictions were rarely appealed. But disorderly conduct offenses are an important part of the criminal justice system for three reasons: They "affect large numbers of defendants, involve a great proportion of public activity, and powerfully influence the view of public justice held by millions of people" (ALI 1985, Part II, Vol. 3, Art. 250, 251, 309).

We'll divide our discussion of these crimes into two sections: the minor offenses included in individual disorderly conduct statutes (fighting in public) and the felony of riot (group disorderly conduct).

Individual Disorderly Conduct

Disorderly conduct statutes grew out of the ancient common-law crime known as "breach of the peace" (Chapter 1, "Common-Law Origins" section). It included both the misdemeanors of **actual disorderly conduct** (fighting in public, making unreasonable noise) and **constructive disorderly conduct,** which was conduct that "tends to provoke or excite others to break it [the peace]" (Blackstone 1769, 148).

Some statutes define disorderly conduct in general terms. Wisconsin's is a good example:

> Whoever, in a public or private place, engages in violent, abusive, indecent, profane, boisterous, unreasonably loud or otherwise disorderly conduct under circumstances in which the conduct tends to cause or provoke a disturbance is guilty of a Class B misdemeanor. (Wisconsin Criminal Code 2003, § 947.01)

Here's the other extreme, the frequently quoted Chicago disorderly conduct ordinance, which one court (*Landry v. Daley* 1968, 969) called "one of the most charming grab bags of criminal prohibitions ever assembled":

> All persons who shall make, aid, countenance or assist in making any improper noise, riot, disturbance, breach of the peace or diversion tending to a breach of the peace, within the limits of the city; all persons who shall collect in bodies or crowds for unlawful purposes, or for any purpose, to the annoyance or disturbance of other persons; all persons who are idle or dissolute and go about begging; all persons who use or exercise any juggling or other unlawful games, all persons who are found in houses of ill-fame or gaming houses; all persons lodging in or found at any time in sheds, barns, stables, or unoccupied buildings, or lodging in the open air and not giving a good account of themselves; all persons who shall wilfully assault another in the city, or be engaged in, aid, abet in any fight, quarrel, or other disturbance in the city; all persons who stand, loiter, or stroll about in any place in the city, waiting or seeking to obtain money or other valuable things from others by trick or fraud, or to aid or assist therein; all persons that shall engage in any fraudulent scheme, device or trick to obtain money or other valuable thing in any place in the city, or who shall aid, abet, or in any manner be concerned therein; all touts, rapers, steerers, or cappers, so called, for any gambling room or house who shall ply or attempt to ply their calling on any public way in the city; all persons found loitering about any hotel, block barroom, dramshop, gambling house, or disorderly house, or wandering about the streets either by night or day without any known lawful means of support, or without being able to give a satisfactory account of themselves; all persons who shall have or carry any pistol, knife, dirk, knuckles,

slingshot, or other dangerous weapon concealed on or about their persons; and all persons who are known to be narcotic addicts, thieves, burglars, pickpockets, robbers or confidence men, either by their own confession or otherwise, or by having been convicted of larceny, burglary, or other crime against the laws of the state, who are found lounging in, prowling, or loitering around any steamboat landing, railroad depot, banking institution, place of public amusement, auction room, hotel, store, shop, public way, public conveyance, public gathering, public assembly, court room, public building, private dwelling house, house of ill-fame, gambling house, or any public place, and who are unable to give a reasonable excuse for being so found, shall be deemed guilty of disorderly conduct, and upon conviction thereof, shall be severally fined not less than one dollar nor more than two hundred dollars for each offense. (Quoted in ALI 1985, Part II, Vol. 3, 326–27)

Both types of statutes create two problems. First, they're too vague to give individuals and law enforcement officers notice of what the law prohibits (Chapter 2, "Void-for-Vagueness Doctrine" section). Second, neither requires *mens rea* (Chapter 4). The MPC (ALI 1985, Part II, Vol. 3, 324–25) addresses both of these problems in Section 250.2:

§ 250.2. DISORDERLY CONDUCT

(1) Offense Defined. A person is guilty of disorderly conduct if, with purpose to cause public inconvenience, annoyance or alarm, or recklessly creating a risk thereof, he:
  (a) engages in fighting or threatening, or in violent or tumultuous behavior; or
  (b) makes unreasonable noise or offensively coarse utterance, gesture or display, or addresses abusive language to any person present; or
  (c) creates a hazardous or physically offensive condition by any act which serves no legitimate purpose of the actor.

"Public" means affecting or likely to affect persons in a place to which the public or a substantial group has access; among the places included are highways, transport facilities, schools, prisons, apartment houses, places of business or amusement, or any neighborhood.

(2) Grading. An offense under this section is a petty misdemeanor if the actor's purpose is to cause substantial harm or serious inconvenience, or if he persists in disorderly conduct after reasonable warning or request to desist. Otherwise disorderly conduct is a violation.

Notice that Section 250.2(1) requires a mental attitude of subjective fault (Chapter 4)—namely, either knowledge or recklessness. So conscious risk creation is the minimum level of culpability; negligence isn't good enough (Chapter 4, "The MPC's Mental Attitudes" section). Next, notice that the MPC limits conduct that qualifies as disorderly conduct *actus reus* to three actions:

1. Fighting in public

2. Making "unreasonable noise" or using "abusive language" (Chapter 2, "Free Speech" section)

3. Creating a "hazardous or physically offensive condition," such as strewing garbage, setting off "stink bombs," or turning off lights in crowded public places

In practice, the most common use of disorderly conduct statutes is the ban on fighting in public. Fighting can cause two harms: disturbing community peace and quiet and disturbing or endangering innocent bystanders.

The MPC also includes several "special" sections devoted to other specifically defined acts of disorderly conduct (Table 12.1). The majority of states have adopted the *actus reus* and the *mens rea* provisions of the MPC.

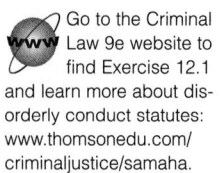 Go to the Criminal Law 9e website to find Exercise 12.1 and learn more about disorderly conduct statutes: www.thomsonedu.com/criminaljustice/samaha.

TABLE 12.1	Model Penal Code Special Disorderly Conduct Sections	
Offense	**Element**	**Description**
False public alarms (250.3)	*Mens rea*	Knowingly
	Actus reus	Initiating or circulating a report or warning of a bombing or a catastrophe
	Harm	Likely to cause evacuation or public inconvenience or alarm
Public drunkenness (250.5)	*Actus reus*	Appearing in a public place "manifestly under the influence of alcohol, narcotics, or other drug, not therapeutically administered"
	Harm	To the degree it may "endanger himself or other persons or property, or annoy persons in his vicinity"
Loitering or prowling (250.6)	*Actus reus*	Loitering or prowling
	Circumstances	"In a place, at a time, or in a manner not usual for law-abiding individuals" Warrant "alarm for the safety of persons or property in the vicinity"
Obstructing highways or other public passages (250.7)	*Mens rea*	Purposely or recklessly
	Actus reus	Obstructs highway or public passage (except if exercising lawful First Amendment rights) (Chapter 2)
Disrupting meetings and processions (250.8)	*Mens rea*	Purposely
	Actus reus	Prevent or disrupt a lawful meeting, procession, or gathering either physically or by words, gestures, or displays designed to "outrage the sensibilities of the group"

Group Disorderly Conduct (Riot)

Group disorderly conduct consisted of three misdemeanors at the common law: unlawful assembly, rout, and riot. All three were aimed at preventing "the ultimate evil of open disorder and breach of the public peace" (ALI 1985, 3:313).

Unlawful assembly was committed when a group of at least three persons joined for the purpose of committing an unlawful act. If the three or more took action toward achieving their purpose, they committed **rout**. If the group actually committed an unlawful violent act, or performed a lawful act in a "violent or tumultuous manner," they committed **riot**.

Committing riot didn't require the group to plan their unlawful violent act before they got together; it was enough that once together they came up with the riotous plan of violence. The Riot Act of 1714 turned the common-law misdemeanor of riot into a felony. The felony consisted of 12 or more persons who "being unlawfully, riotously, and tumultuously assembled together" stayed together for one hour after being warned to disperse by the reading of a proclamation. (Now you know the original meaning of "reading the riot act.") Here's Queen Victoria's version:

> Our sovereign lady the Queen chargeth and commandeth all persons being assembled immediately to disperse themselves and peaceably to depart to their habitations or to their lawful business, upon the pains contained in the Act made in the first year of King George for preventing tumults and riotous assemblies. God Save the Queen. (ALI 1985, 3:314, n. 8)

Riot is still a felony under modern law for two reasons. First, it lets the law provide harsher penalties for disorderly conduct when group behavior gets "especially alarming or dangerous." Second, it allows the law to punish persons in a disorderly crowd who disobey police orders to disperse (ALI 1985, 3:316–17). Every state has some form of riot act; many have adopted the MPC provision:

> RIOT §250.1(1) (1) RIOT
>
> A person is guilty of riot, a felony of the third degree, if he participates with [two] or more others in a course of disorderly conduct:
>
> (a) with purpose to commit or facilitate the commission of a felony or misdemeanor;
>
> (b) with purpose to prevent or coerce official action; or
>
> (c) when the actor or any other participant to the knowledge of the actor uses or plans to use a firearm or other deadly weapon.

"QUALITY OF LIFE" CRIMES

In the 1980s, two prominent scholars sensed a deep public yearning for recovering what they called a lost sense of public "good manners," especially in our largest cities. Professors James Q. Wilson and George L. Kelling (1982) suggested that what were labeled "petty crimes" weren't just "bothering" law-abiding people and creating a yearning for a more polite past; they were connected to serious crime. They called this connection between disorderly conduct and serious crime the **broken-windows theory.** According to Kelling, research conducted since the article was written in 1982 has demonstrated "a direct link between disorder and crime. . . ."

Wilson described the broken-windows theory in 1996 more cautiously. In the foreword to a book written by Kelling and Catherine M. Coles, *Fixing Broken Windows* (1996), Wilson wrote:

> We used the image of broken windows to explain how neighborhoods might decay into disorder and even crime if no one attends faithfully to their maintenance. If a factory or office window is broken, passersby observing it will conclude that no one cares or no one is in charge. In time, a few will begin throwing rocks to break more windows. Soon all the windows will be broken, and now passersby will think that, not only is no one in charge of the building no one is in charge of the street on which it faces. Only the young, the criminal, or the foolhardy have any business on an unprotected avenue, and so more and more citizens will abandon the street to those they assume prowl it. Small disorders lead to larger and larger ones, and perhaps even to crime. (xiv)

Professor Wesley G. Skogan (1990), the author of some of the research on which Kelling relies, has also characterized his and others' research more cautiously than Kelling:

> Our concern with common crime is limited to whether disorder is a *cause* of it. . . . Neighborhood levels of disorder are closely related to crime rates, to fear of crime, and the belief that serious crime is a neighborhood problem. This relationship could reflect the fact that the link between crime and disorder is a *causal* one, or that both are dependent on

some third set of factors (such as poverty or neighborhood instability). (10) [emphasis added]

Despite the caution, Skogan still concluded that the data "support the proposition that disorder needs to be taken seriously in research on neighborhood crime and that, both directly and through crime, it plays an important role in neighborhood decline" (75).

Professor Bernard Harcourt (2001) at the University of Chicago Law School replicated Skogan's research and found a weak-to-no-causal link between disorder and serious crime (8–9). The best and most recent research strongly suggests that disorder and serious crime have common causes, but they don't cause each other, at least not directly (Sampson and Raudenbush 1999, 637–38).

Most of the national debate over crime, criminal law books (this one included), and criminal justice courses concentrate on the serious crimes we've analyzed in Chapters 9–11. But there's a disconnect between this national focus on one side and local concern on the other. Mayors and local residents do worry about murder, rape, burglary, and theft, but they also care a lot about order on their streets, in their parks, and in other public places. In a careful and extensive survey of a representative sample of high- and low-crime neighborhoods in major cities, public drinking, followed closely by loitering youths, topped the list of worries among all classes, races, and ethnic groups, among both men and women.

Survey participants also listed begging, street harassment, noisy neighbors, vandalism, street prostitution, and illegal vending (Skogan 1990, 2). Prosecutor Karen Hayter found this out when she created Kalamazoo, Michigan's Neighborhood Prosecutor Program. When Hayter "asked residents what crimes worried them the most, she thought it would be the big ones: murder, assault, breaking and entering," but that's not what she was told. Instead, said Hayter, "Loud noise, littering, loitering, curfew violations, junk autos, rundown houses—those are considered quality-of-life crimes, and they're very important to residents in an area" (National Public Radio 2003).

Any examination of criminal law has to recognize quality-of-life crimes as part of early 21st-century life. Since the 1980s, state statutes and city ordinances have reinvigorated and molded the old crimes against public order and morals to fit the public's demand that criminal justice preserve, protect, and even restore the quality of life in their communities. The courts have assumed the burden of balancing the social interest in public order against the social interest in individual liberty and privacy (Skogan 1990, 21).

Let's examine how states and localities have shaped traditional public order and morals laws to control the public behavior of two groups—"street people" and street gangs—and the quality-of-life crimes commonly associated with them: vagrancy, loitering, panhandling, and gang activity.

Vagrancy and Loitering

For at least six hundred years, it's been a crime for poor people to roam around without visible means of support **(vagrancy)** or to stand around with no apparent purpose **(loitering)**. The Articles of Confederation specifically denied to paupers the freedom to travel from state to state. In 1837, in *Mayor of New York v. Miln*, the U.S. Supreme Court approved the efforts by the state of New York to exclude paupers arriving by ship. According to the Court, it's as necessary for a state to provide precautionary measures against the moral pestilence of paupers, vagabonds, and possibly convicts as it is to guard against physical pestilence, which may arise from unsound and infectious articles. Every state in the union had and enforced vagrancy and loitering statutes that wrote the Court's view into law (Simon 1992, 631).

Vagrancy Laws targeting poor people's behavior, and the attitudes behind them, began to change during the Great Depression of the 1930s. In 1941, the U.S. Supreme Court struck down a vagrancy statute that prohibited the importation of paupers into California.

In response to the argument that the regulation of paupers enjoyed a long history, the Court dismissed the earlier decisions as out of date. According to the Court, "We do not think that it will now be seriously contended that because a person is without employment and without funds he constitutes a 'moral pestilence.'" In a concurring opinion, Justice Robert Jackson encouraged the Court to "say now, in no uncertain terms, that a mere property status, without more, cannot be used by a state to test, qualify, or limit his rights as a citizen of the United States" (*Edwards v. California* 1941, 184).

During the 1960s and 1970s, courts began to strike down vagrancy laws because they unfairly discriminated against the poor. The following excerpt from an opinion written by Chief Justice Thompson of the Nevada Supreme Court in *Parker v. Municipal Judge* (1967) reflects this trend:

> It is simply not a crime to be unemployed, without funds, and in a public place. To punish the unfortunate for this circumstance debases society. The comment of [U.S. Associate Supreme Court] Justice Douglas is relevant: "How can we hold our heads high and still confuse with crime the need for welfare or the need for work?"

In *Papichristou v. City of Jacksonville* (1972), the U.S. Court struck down the Jacksonville, Florida, vagrancy ordinance, which was nearly identical to virtually every other vagrancy law in the country. Writing for a unanimous Court, Justice Douglas declared the ordinance void for vagueness, because it both failed to give adequate notice to individuals and it encouraged arbitrary law enforcement (Chapter 2). The Court warned that criminal statutes aimed at the poor

> teach that the scales of justice are so tipped that even-handed administration of the law is not possible. The rule of law, evenly applied to minorities as well as majorities, to the poor as well as the rich, is the great mucilage that holds society together. (169)

Loitering In *Kolender v. Lawson* (1983), the U.S. Supreme Court tightened the constitutional restrictions on loitering statutes. The counterpart to *vagrancy*, which means to roam about with no visible means of support, *loitering* means to "remain in one place with no apparent purpose." In *Kolender,* the Court struck down a California statute that combined ancient vagrancy and loitering into a new crime defined as "wandering the streets and failing to produce credible identification" when a police officer asked for it. As it did with the vagrancy statute in *Papichristou,* the Court ruled that the statute was void for vagueness.

According to Harry Simon (1992), staff attorney for the Legal Aid Society in Santa Ana, California:

> With the Supreme Court's decisions in *Papichristou* and *Kolender,* loitering and vagrancy laws ceased to be effective tools to punish and control the displaced poor. While judicial attitudes on vagrancy and loitering laws had changed, local officials perceived the invalidation of these laws as a dangerous assault on their authority to enforce social order. (645)

According to Robert C. Ellickson (1996), professor of Property and Urban Law at the Yale Law School:

Many judges at the time seemed blind to the fact that their constitutional rulings might adversely affect the quality of urban life and the viability of city centers. It is one thing to protect unpopular persons from wrongful confinement; it is another to imply that these persons have no duty to behave themselves in public places. In addition, federal constitutional rulings are one of the most centralized and inflexible forms of lawmaking. In a diverse and dynamic nation committed to separation of powers and federalism, there is much to be said for giving state and local legislative bodies substantial leeway to tailor street codes to city conditions, and for giving state judges ample scope to interpret the relevant provisions of state constitutions. (1213–14)

At the same time these decisions were easing up on control over the behavior of poor people in public, other events were creating a rapidly—and to many a frightening—growth of an underclass. Mental institutions were in the midst of major deinstitutionalization of the mentally ill; family breakdowns and breakups were increasing steeply; crack cocaine was becoming more available on the streets; hard economic times were upon us; and budgets for social programs were tightening.

By the late 1980s, this rising underclass and its public presence and behavior led many city dwellers to conclude that things had gone too far. The liberal columnist Ellen Goodman, in "Swarms of Beggars Cause 'Compassion Fatigue,'" captured this attitude when she wrote, "Today at least, this tourist, walking from one block to another, one cup to another, one city to another, wants to join in a citizens' chorus: 'Enough's enough'" (Simon 1992, 1218).

Municipal codes reflected this growing intolerance of street people's behavior. By the late 1990s, Juliette Smith (1996) found that "at least thirty-nine American cities had initiated or continued policies that criminalize activities associated with homelessness" (29).

Enforcing the laws regulating the behavior of homeless and other street people generates controversy because these laws seem to target the poorest and weakest members of the community to provide for the comfort and convenience of better-off residents. But James Q. Wilson defends these laws, noting that the special competence of courts lies in defining and applying rights; courts typically hear the cases of "an individual beggar, sleeper, or solicitor." Such an individual rarely poses a threat to anyone, "and so the claims of communal order often seem, in the particular case, to be suspect or overdrawn."

> But the effects on a community of many such individuals taking advantage of the rights granted to an individual (or often, as the court sees it, an abstract depersonalized individual) are qualitatively different from the effects of a single person. A public space—a bus stop, a market square, a subway entrance—is more than the sum of its parts; it is a complex pattern of interactions that can become dramatically more threatening as the scale and frequency of those interactions increase. As the number of unconventional individuals increases arithmetically, the number of worrisome behaviors increases geometrically. (Kelling and Coles 1996, xiv)

San Francisco is one of many cities whose officials enforced the "quality of life" laws against the "bad public manners" of street people, but it's also a city where a few individuals turned to the courts to fight for the constitutional rights of homeless people. In *Joyce v. City and County of San Francisco* (1994), U.S. District Judge Lowell Jensen heard a motion to grant a **preliminary injunction** (a temporary court order to do or to stop doing something) to stop the city of San Francisco from continuing its Matrix Program. The program was designed to preserve the quality of life on San Francisco streets and other public places. Be aware that granting a preliminary injunction *isn't* a decision that the plaintiff is right; it only means the plaintiff has presented enough evidence to justify a temporary freeze to give the court time to decide whether to rule in the plaintiff's favor.

Did the Program Violate the Rights of Homeless People?

Joyce v. City and County of San Francisco
846 F. Supp. 843 (N.D.Cal. 1994)

HISTORY

Bobby Joe Joyce, Timothy E. Smith, Thomas O'Halloran, and Jim Tullah, homeless persons, brought an action against the city seeking a preliminary injunction against the Matrix Program which targeted violation of certain ordinances ("quality of life offenses") and thus allegedly penalized homeless persons for engaging in life sustaining activities. U.S. District Judge Lowell Jensen denied the plaintiffs' motion for a preliminary injunction.

JENSEN, J.

FACTS

Plaintiffs to this action seek preliminary injunctive relief, an order to stop enforcing the ordinances, on behalf of themselves and a class of homeless individuals alleged to be adversely affected by the City and County of San Francisco's (the "City's") "Matrix Program." Institution of the Matrix Program followed the issuance of a report in April of 1992 by the San Francisco Mayor's Office of Economic Planning and Development, which attributed to homelessness a $173 million drain on sales in the City.

In August of 1993, the City announced commencement of the Matrix Program, and the San Francisco Police Department began stringently enforcing a number of criminal laws. The City describes the Program as "initiated to address citizen complaints about a broad range of offenses occurring on the streets and in parks and neighborhoods. . . . [The Matrix Program is] a directed effort to end street crimes of all kinds."

The program addresses "quality of life" offenses including public drinking and inebriation, obstruction of sidewalks, lodging, camping or sleeping in public parks, littering, public urination and defecation, aggressive panhandling, dumping of refuse, graffiti, vandalism, street prostitution, and street sales of narcotics, among others.

A four-page intradepartmental memorandum addressed to the Police Department's Southern Station Personnel condemned "Quality of Life" violations, "type of behavior [which] tends to make San Francisco a less desirable place in which to live, work or visit," and directed the vigorous enforcement of eighteen specified code sections, including prohibitions against trespassing, public inebriation, urinating or defecating in public, removal and possession of shopping carts, solicitation on or near a highway, erection of tents or structures in parks, obstruction and aggressive panhandling.

The memorandum directed all station personnel, "when not otherwise engaged, pay special attention and enforce observed 'Quality of Life' violations. . . .

In a Police Department Bulletin entitled "Update on Matrix Quality of Life Program," Deputy Chief Thomas Petrini referred to the intended nondiscriminatory policy of the Program's enforcement measures:

All persons have the right to use the public streets and places so long as they are not engaged in specific criminal activity. Factors such as race, sex, sexual preference, age, dress, unusual or disheveled or impoverished appearance do not alone justify enforcement action. Nor can generalized complaints by residents or merchants or others justify detention of any person absent such individualized suspicion.

The memorandum stated that the "rights of the homeless must be preserved," and included as an attachment a Department Bulletin on "Rights of the Homeless," which stated that:

[All members of the Department] are obligated to treat all persons equally, regardless of their economic or living conditions. The homeless enjoy the same legal and individual rights afforded to others. Members shall at all times respect these rights. . . .

The Police Department has, during the pendency of the Matrix Program, conducted continuing education for officers regarding nondiscriminatory enforcement of the Program. . . .

Plaintiffs, pointing to the discretion inherent in policing the law enforcement measures of the Matrix Program, allege certain actions taken by police to be "calculated to punish the homeless." As a general practice, the Program is depicted by plaintiffs as "targeting hundreds of homeless persons who are guilty of nothing more than sitting on a park bench or on the ground with their possessions, or lying or sleeping on the ground covered by or on top of a blanket or cardboard carton."

The City contests the depiction of Matrix as a singularly focused, punitive effort designed to move "an untidy problem out of sight and out of mind." The City emphasizes its history as one of the largest public providers of assistance to the homeless in the State, asserting that "individuals on general assistance in San Francisco are eligible for larger monthly grants than are available almost anywhere else in California." . . . By its own estimate, the City will spend $46.4 million for services to the homeless for 1993–94. Of that amount, over $8 million is specifically earmarked to provide housing, and is spent primarily on emergency shelter beds for adults, families, battered women and youths. An additional $12 million in general assistance grants is provided to those describing themselves as homeless, and free health care is provided by the City to the homeless at a cost of approximately $3 million.

. . . Since its implementation, the Matrix Program has resulted in the issuance of over 3,000 citations to homeless persons. . . .

OPINION

. . . The Court is called upon to decide whether to grant a preliminary injunction. . . . Such relief constitutes an extraordinary use of the Court's powers, and is to be granted sparingly and with the ultimate aim of preserving the status quo pending trial on the merits. . . . The decision whether to grant preliminary injunctive relief is largely left to its discretion. However, this discretion has been circumscribed by the presence or not of various factors, notably, the likelihood that the moving party will prevail on the merits and the likelihood of harm to the parties from granting or denying the injunctive relief. . . .

The injunction sought by plaintiffs at this juncture of the litigation must be denied for each of two independent reasons. First, the proposed injunction lacks the necessary specificity to be enforceable, and would give rise to enforcement problems sufficiently inherent as to be incurable by modification of the proposal. Second, those legal theories upon which plaintiffs rely are not plainly applicable to the grievances sought to be vindicated, with the effect that the Court cannot find at this time that, upon conducting the required balance of harm and merit, plaintiffs have established a sufficient probability of success on the merits to warrant injunctive relief. . . .

Equal Protection Clause

[Denial of equal protection requires proof that] governmental action [was] undertaken with an intent to discriminate against a particular individual or class of individuals. Such intent may be evinced by statutory language, or in instances where an impact which cannot be explained on a neutral ground unmasks an invidious discrimination. Under the latter approach, a neutral law found to have a disproportionately adverse effect upon a minority classification will be deemed unconstitutional only if that impact can be traced to a discriminatory purpose.

In the present case, plaintiffs have not at this time demonstrated a likelihood of success on the merits of the equal protection claim, since the City's action has not been taken with an evinced intent to discriminate against an identifiable group. . . . Various directives issued within the Police Department mandate the nondiscriminatory enforcement of Matrix. Further, the Police Department has, during the pendency of the Matrix Program, conducted continuing education for officers regarding nondiscriminatory enforcement of the Program. It has not been proven at this time that Matrix was implemented with the aim of discriminating against the homeless. That enforcement of Matrix will, de facto, fall predominantly on the homeless does not in itself effect an equal protection clause violation. . . .

Even were plaintiffs able at this time to prove an intent to discriminate against the homeless, the challenged sections of the Program might nonetheless survive constitutional scrutiny. Only in cases where the challenged action is aimed at a suspect classification, such as race or gender, or premised upon the exercise of a fundamental right, will the governmental action be subjected to a heightened scrutiny.

Counsel for plaintiff proposed at the hearing that this Court should be the first to recognize as a fundamental right the "right to sleep." This is an invitation the Court, in its exercise of judicial restraint, must decline. . . . The discovery of a right to sleep concomitantly requires prohibition of the government's interference with that right. This endeavor, aside from creating a jurisprudential morass, would involve this unelected branch of government in a legislative role for which it is neither fit, nor easily divested once established. . . .

Due Process of Law

Plaintiffs contend the Matrix Program has been enforced in violation of the due process clause . . . of the United States . . . Constitution. . . . Plaintiffs specifically argue that due process has been violated by employing punitive policing measures against the homeless for sleeping in public parks. . . .

Plaintiffs claim that San Francisco Park Code section 3.12 has been applied by police in an unconstitutional manner. That section provides,

> No person shall construct or maintain any building, structure, tent or any other thing in any park that may be used for housing accommodations or camping, except by permission from the Recreation and Park Commission.

Plaintiffs contend the Police Department has impermissibly construed this provision to justify citing, arresting, threatening and "moving along" those "persons guilty of nothing more than sitting on park benches with their personal possessions or lying on or under blankets on the ground." Plaintiffs have submitted declarations of various homeless persons supporting the asserted application of the San Francisco Park Code section. It appears, if plaintiffs have accurately depicted the manner in which the section is enforced, that the section may have been applied to conduct not covered by the section and may have been enforced unconstitutionally. . . .

Conclusion

In common with many communities across the country, the City is faced with a homeless population of tragic dimension. Today, plaintiffs have brought that societal problem before the Court, seeking a legal judgment on the efforts adopted by the City in response to this problem. The role of the Court is limited structurally by the fact that it may exercise only judicial power, and technically by the fact that plaintiffs seek extraordinary pretrial relief.

The Court does not find that plaintiffs have made a showing at this time that constitutional barriers exist which preclude that effort. Accordingly, the Court's judgment at this stage of the litigation is to permit the City to continue enforcing those aspects of the Matrix Program now challenged by plaintiffs.

. . . Accordingly, plaintiffs' motion for a preliminary injunction is DENIED. IT IS SO ORDERED.

Questions

1. Describe the main elements of the Matrix Program.
2. Why did San Francisco adopt the Matrix Program?
3. What are the plaintiffs' objections to the Matrix Program?
4. Assume you're the attorney for San Francisco, and argue that the court should deny the injunction.
5. Assume you're the attorney for the homeless people, and argue that the court should issue the injunction.
6. If you could, what terms would you include in an injunction in this case?

Panhandling

> On the concrete plaza outside [San Francisco] City Hall here, day or night, dozens of homeless men and women shuffle from bench to grate dragging blankets or pushing shopping carts stuffed with all they own. They beg, they bicker, they sleep. It is a ragged, aimless procession that never ends. It is also a sight that this ever-tolerant city is tired of seeing. Frustrated by how difficult it is to end homelessness even in robust economic times, and facing pressure to make neighborhoods and business centers safe and clean, San Francisco has become the latest in a growing number of cities deciding that it is time to get tougher. (Sanchez 1998, A3)

This quote comes from *Washington Post* reporter Renee Sanchez's article about the continuing backlash against the so-called rights revolution of the 1960s and 1970s.

According to Robert Tier (1993), general counsel for the American Alliance for Rights and Responsibilities:

> Many City Councils have been convinced to adopt new and innovative controls on antisocial behavior to maintain minimal standards of public conduct and to keep public spaces safe and attractive. . . . One of the most common examples of these efforts are ordinances aimed at aggressive begging. (286)

These "new and innovative controls" rely on ancient laws against begging, or *panhandling*. **Panhandling** is stopping people on the street to ask them for food or money. At the outset, keep in mind that these new antibegging ordinances don't apply to organized charities. So although it's a crime for a private beggar to panhandle for money, it's legal for the Salvation Army to ring their bells to get contributions.

Why the distinction? Supporters of the distinction say the rights revolution has simply gone too far. It's reached the point, they say, where the rights of a minority of offensive individuals trump the quality of life of the whole community. Associate Supreme Court Justice Clarence Thomas (1996) commenting on "how judicial interpretations of the First Amendment and of 'unenumerated' constitutional rights have affected the ability of urban communities to deal with crime, disorder, and incivility on their public streets," told the Federalist Society:

> Vagrancy, loitering, and panhandling laws were challenged [during the rights revolution] because the poor and minorities could be victims of discrimination under the guise of broad discretion to ensure public safety. Moreover, as a consequence of the modern tendency to challenge society's authority to dictate social norms, the legal system began to prefer the ideal of self-expression without much attention to self-discipline or self-control.

What resulted was a culture that declined to curb the excesses of self-indulgence—vagrants and others who regularly roamed the streets had rights that could not be circumscribed by the community's sense of decency or decorum. (269)

"Hey, buddy, can you spare some change?" is clearly speech. And, of course, the First Amendment guarantees individuals freedom of speech. But free speech doesn't mean you can say anything you want anywhere at anytime (Chapter 2). The U.S. Supreme Court has "rejected the notion that a city is powerless to protect its citizens from unwanted exposure to certain methods of expression which may legitimately be deemed a public nuisance" (Scheidegger 1993, 7).

The Court has established a number of tests to determine whether ordinances violate the First Amendment guarantee of free speech. One is to look at the place where the speech takes place. In traditional public forums—streets, sidewalks, and parks—where people have since ancient times expressed their views, the freedom to solicit is virtually unrestricted. In designated public forums—places the government chooses to make available to the public—the government has more leeway to regulate solicitation.

In nonpublic forums—airports, bus stations, railroad stations, subways, and shopping malls—the government has broad power to restrict and even prohibit solicitation (Scheidegger 1993, 7–9).

The First Amendment free speech clause also permits time, place, and manner regulations. According to the U.S. Supreme Court (*R. A. V. v. City of St. Paul* 1992; Chapter 2), to be constitutional, restrictions have to satisfy three elements of a **time, place, and manner test:**

1. They're not based on the content of the speech.
2. They serve a significant government interest—for example, maintaining the free flow of pedestrian traffic.
3. They leave open other channels of expression.

The first element in the test bars the use of the regulation to suppress any message about social conditions that panhandlers are trying to convey. The second element is often hotly debated. Advocates for panhandlers argue that the regulation of panhandling is really a government policy of removing "unsightly" poor people from public view. Others maintain that the "purpose is to permit people to use the streets, sidewalks, and public transportation free from the borderline robbery and pervasive fraud which characterizes so much of today's panhandling" (Scheidegger 1993, 10–11).

The third element requires the regulation to allow panhandlers to beg in other ways. So a panhandling ordinance that prohibits "aggressive panhandling" leaves panhandlers free to beg peaceably. So do bans on fraudulent panhandling or panhandling in subways. Panhandlers can beg honestly or on streets and in parks (10–11).

In addition to forum and time, place, and manner restrictions, the First Amendment gives the government considerable leeway to regulate nonverbal expression (expressive conduct; Chapter 2). This would allow direct efforts to stop panhandlers from approaching people or blocking the sidewalk to beg or receiving the money they solicited.

Finally, the First Amendment grants commercial speech (advertising and other means of "asking for" money) less protection than other types of speech. Because begging relies on talking listeners into handing over their money, panhandling is commercial speech. Jimmy Gresham, a homeless person, challenged the constitutionality of Indianapolis's aggressive panhandling ordinance in U.S. District Court and asked for an injunction against the enforcement of the ordinance. The District Court rejected his challenge and denied his request for the injunction. The U.S. Court of Appeals for the Seventh Circuit affirmed the District Court's decision in *Gresham v. Peterson* (2000).

CASE · *Was the Panhandling Ordinance Vague, and Did It Violate Free Speech?*

Gresham v. Peterson
225 F.3d 899 (7th Cir. 2000)

HISTORY

Jimmy Gresham challenged an Indianapolis ordinance that limits street begging in public places and prohibits entirely activities defined as "aggressive panhandling." The U.S. District Court granted the city summary judgment on Gresham's request for a permanent injunction. Gresham appealed. The U.S. Circuit Court affirmed the District Court's decision.

KANNE, J.

FACTS

Jimmy Gresham is a homeless person who lives in Indianapolis on Social Security disability benefits of $417 per month. He supplements this income by begging, using the money to buy food. He begs during both the daytime and nighttime in downtown Indianapolis. Because different people visit downtown at night than during the day, it is important to him that he be able to beg at night.

Gresham approaches people on the street, tells them he is homeless and asks for money to buy food. Gresham has not been cited for panhandling under the new ordinance, but he fears being cited for panhandling at night or if an officer interprets his requests for money to be "aggressive" as defined by the law.

Gresham filed this class action shortly after the ordinance took effect, requesting injunctive and declaratory relief. Gresham moved for a preliminary injunction barring enforcement of the ordinance on the grounds that it was unconstitutionally vague and violated his right to free speech. The district court, after hearing oral argument . . ., entered a final order denying the motion for preliminary injunction and dismissing the case.

OPINION

Gresham raises two principal arguments. First, he contends that the provisions defining aggressive panhandling are vague because they fail to provide clear criteria to alert panhandlers and authorities of what constitutes a violation and because they fail to include an intent element.

Second, he argues that the statute fails the test for content-neutral time, place and manner restrictions on protected speech.

A. The First Amendment

Laws targeting street begging have been around for many years, but in the last twenty years, local communities have breathed new life into old laws or passed new ones. Cities, such as Indianapolis, have tried to narrowly draw the ordinances to target the most bothersome types of street solicitations and give police another tool in the effort to make public areas, particularly downtown areas, safe and inviting.

While the plaintiff here has focused the inquiry on the effects of the ordinance on the poor and homeless, the ordinance itself is not so limited. It applies with equal force to anyone who would solicit a charitable contribution, whether for a recognized charity, a religious group, a political candidate or organization, or for an individual. It would punish street people as well as Salvation Army bell ringers outside stores at Christmas, so long as the appeal involved a vocal request for an immediate donation.

The ordinance bans panhandling by beggars or charities citywide on any "street, public place or park" in three circumstances.

First, it would prohibit any nighttime panhandling. § 407-102(b).

Second, it would prohibit at all times—day or night—panhandling in specified areas. § 407-102(c).

Third, it would prohibit "aggressive panhandling" at all times. § 407-102(d)(1)-(6).

The defendants emphatically point out that the ordinance allows a great deal of solicitation, including "passive" panhandling, which does not include a vocal appeal, street performances, legitimate sales transactions and requests for donations over the telephone or any other means that is not "in person" or does not involve an "immediate donation." Under the ordinance, one could lawfully hold up a sign that says "give me money" and sing "I am cold and starving," so long as one does not voice words to the effect of "give me money." . . .

[The U.S. Supreme Court has held that] government may enact "reasonable regulations" so long as they reflect "due regard" for the constitutional interests at stake. . . . Governments may "enforce regulations of the time, place and manner of expression which are content neutral, are narrowly tailored to serve a significant government interest, and leave open ample alternative channels of communication." . . .

Because the parties here agree that the regulations are content neutral . . . , the Indianapolis ordinance should be upheld if it is narrowly tailored to achieve a significant governmental purpose and leaves open alternate channels of communication.

The city has a legitimate interest in promoting the safety and convenience of its citizens on public streets. The plaintiff concedes this much, but argues that a total night-time ban on verbal requests for alms is substantially broader than necessary and therefore cannot be considered narrowly tailored. However, a government regulation can be considered narrowly tailored "so long as the . . . regulation promotes a substantial government interest that would be achieved less effectively absent the regulation." This means the regulation need not be a perfect fit for the government's needs, but cannot burden substantially more speech than necessary. Furthermore, a time, place or manner restriction need not be the least restrictive means of achieving the government purpose, so long as it can be considered narrowly tailored to that purpose.

The city determined that vocal requests for money create a threatening environment or at least a nuisance for some citizens. Rather than ban all panhandling, however, the city chose to restrict it only in those circumstances where it is considered especially unwanted or bothersome—at night, around banks and sidewalk cafes, and so forth. These represent situations in which people most likely would feel a heightened sense of fear or alarm, or might wish especially to be left alone. By limiting the ordinance's restrictions to only those certain times and places where citizens naturally would feel most insecure in their surroundings, the city has effectively narrowed the application of the law to what is necessary to promote its legitimate interest.

Finally, the plaintiff contends that the statute fails to provide ample alternative channels of communication. We disagree.

An adequate alternative does not have to be the speaker's first or best choice, or one that provides the same audience or impact for the speech. However, the Court has "shown special solicitude for forms of expression that are much less expensive than feasible alternatives," and so an alternative must be more than merely theoretically available. It must be realistic as well.

Furthermore, an adequate alternative cannot totally foreclose a speaker's ability to reach one audience even if it allows the speaker to reach other groups. The Indianapolis ordinance allows many feasible alternatives to reach both the daytime and nighttime downtown Indianapolis crowds. Under the ordinance, panhandlers may ply their craft vocally or in any manner they deem fit (except for those involving conduct defined as aggressive) during all the daylight hours on all of the city's public streets.

Gresham contends that soliciting at night is vital to his survival, a fact we do not dispute, but the ordinance leaves open many reasonable ways for him to reach the night-time downtown crowd. He may solicit at night, so long as he does not vocally request money. He may hold up signs requesting money or engage in street performances, such as playing music, with an implicit appeal for support.

Although perhaps not relevant to street beggars, the ordinance also permits telephone and door-to-door solicitation at night. Thus to the extent that "give me money" conveys an idea the expression of which is protected by the First Amendment, solicitors may express themselves vocally all day, and in writing, by telephone or by other non-vocal means all night.

Furthermore, they may solicit in public places on all 396.4 square miles of the city, except those parts occupied by sidewalk cafes, banks, ATMs and bus stops. . . .

B. Vagueness

Gresham next challenges certain provisions of the ordinance as unconstitutionally vague. Specifically, he contends that the definition[s] of aggressive panhandling in sections (d)(4) and (d)(5) are not sufficiently clear to direct authorities on the enforcement of the law, nor to allow panhandlers such as Gresham to avoid violating the law.

Section (d)(4) prohibits "following behind, ahead or alongside a person who walks away from the panhandler after being solicited." [Chapter 2, Void-for-Vagueness section] Gresham argues hypothetically that police could cite a person for inadvertently violating this section merely by walking in the same direction as the solicited person, without intending to engage in "aggressive panhandling." Also, section (d)(5) refers to making a person "fearful or feel compelled" without defining what the terms mean in relation to panhandling. A generalized guilt at economic inequality might make one "feel compelled" even by the meekest request for money.

The void-for-vagueness doctrine forbids the enforcement of a law that contains "terms so vague that [persons] of common intelligence must necessarily guess at its meaning and differ as to its application." Legislative enactments must articulate terms "with a reasonable degree of clarity" to reduce the risk of arbitrary enforcement and allow individuals to conform their behavior to the requirements of the law. A statute that "vests virtually complete discretion in the hands of the police" fails to provide the minimal guidelines required for due process. . . .

Paragraph (d)(5) could be construed to prohibit "any statement, gesture, or other communication" that makes a reasonable person feel they face danger if they refuse to donate, that they are being compelled out of physical fear. The possibility that a polite request for a donation might be heard as a threatening demand by an unusually sensitive or timid person is eliminated by the "reasonable person" standard included in the ordinance.

A statement that makes a reasonable person feel compelled to donate out of physical fear amounts to a prohibition on robbery or extortion, which of course would be constitutional. While it is not a certainty that the state courts would adopt constitutional interpretations of the panhandling provisions, they are entitled to the opportunity to do so, and we will not interfere with that right. The district court did not err in refusing to enjoin the ordinance based on the vagueness concerns.

Conclusion

For the foregoing reasons, we AFFIRM the district court's denial of a permanent injunction and dismissal of Gresham's complaint.

Questions

1. State the main elements in Indianapolis's panhandling ordinance.

2. Summarize the positions of the city of Indianapolis and Jimmy Gresham regarding the ordinance.

3. Should there be a distinction between organized charities and individual beggars when it comes to asking for money in this ordinance? Explain your answer.

4. According to the court, what's the difference between solicitation and commercial speech? What's the significance of distinguishing between them?

5. According to the court, why doesn't the ordinance violate the free speech clause of the First Amendment?

6. Should panhandling be considered speech? Defend your answer.

7. Assuming that panhandling is speech, is this ordinance a reasonable "time, place, and manner" regulation of free speech?

8. Summarize the arguments the court gives for ruling that the ordinance isn't unconstitutionally vague. Do you agree? Defend your answer.

Gang Activity

"Bands of loitering youth" seriously threaten their quality of life, say many city residents (Skogan 1990, 23). Gangs can include everything from casual groups of kids who are just hanging out drinking a little bit all the way to "organized fighting squads" who terrorize neighborhoods. The casual groups do little more than "bother" residents. According to one observer, "They are neighborhood kids, and they sometimes make a nuisance of themselves. Actually they stand there because they have no place to go" (23). Gangs composed of older, rowdier members are more threatening.

According to a resident in a neighborhood with one of these gangs:

> Sometimes I walk out of my house and start to try to walk down the street, and a gang will cross the street and try to scare me and my mother. A gang used to sit and drink beer and smoke pot in front of our stairs. My mom used to come out and tell them to get off; they would, and then when she would go into the house they'd come back, sit down, and look at us. Actually we're afraid to walk around in the neighborhood after it gets dark. I stay right in front of the house where my mom can see me. (24)

A number of state and city governments have passed criminal laws to regulate gang behavior. In some places, it's a crime to participate in a gang. Some statutes and ordinances have stiffened the penalties for crimes committed by gang members. Others make it a crime to encourage minors to participate in gangs. Some have applied organized crime statutes to gangs. A few have punished parents for their children's gang activities. Cities have also passed ordinances banning gang members from certain public places, particularly city parks.

In addition to criminal penalties, cities have also turned to civil remedies to control gang activity. For example, in the ancient civil remedy **injunction to abate public nuisances,** which is still used, city attorneys ask courts to declare gang activities and gang members public nuisances and to issue injunctions (court orders) to abate (eliminate) the public nuisance.

According to the California Supreme Court, in *People ex rel. Gallo v. Acuna* (1997), a public nuisance may be any act

> which alternatively is injurious to health or is indecent, or offensive to the senses; the result of the act must interfere with the comfortable enjoyment of life or property; and those affected by the act may be an entire neighborhood or a considerable number of people.

The city attorney of Santa Clara in *Acuna* asked for an injunction ordering gang members to stop doing all of the following:

(a) Standing, sitting, walking, driving, gathering or appearing anywhere in public view with any other defendant herein, or with any other known "VST" (Varrio Sureno Town or Varrio Sureno Locos) member;

(b) Drinking alcoholic beverages in public excepting consumption on properly licensed premises or using drugs;

(c) Possessing any weapons including but not limited to knives, dirks, daggers, clubs, nunchukas, BB guns, concealed or loaded firearms, and any other illegal weapons as defined in the California Penal Code, and any object capable of inflicting serious bodily injury including but not limited to the following: metal pipes or rods, glass bottles, rocks, bricks, chains, tire irons, screwdrivers, hammers, crowbars, bumper jacks, spikes, razor blades, razors, sling shots, marbles, ball bearings;

(d) Engaging in fighting in the public streets, alleys, and/or public and private property;

(e) Using or possessing marker pens, spray paint cans, nails, razor blades, screwdrivers, or other sharp objects capable of defacing private or public property;

(f) Spray painting or otherwise applying graffiti on any public or private property, including but not limited to the street, alley, residences, block walls, vehicles and/or any other real or personal property;

(g) Trespassing on or encouraging others to trespass on any private property;

(h) Blocking free ingress and egress to the public sidewalks or street, or any driveways leading or appurtenant thereto in "Rocksprings";

(i) Approaching vehicles, engaging in conversation, or otherwise communicating with the occupants of any vehicle or doing anything to obstruct or delay the free flow of vehicular or pedestrian traffic;

(j) Discharging any firearms;

(k) In any manner confronting, intimidating, annoying, harassing, threatening, challenging, provoking, assaulting and/or battering any residents or patrons, or visitors to "Rocksprings," or any other persons who are known to have complained about gang activities, including any persons who have provided information in support of this Complaint and requests for Temporary Restraining Order, Preliminary Injunction and Permanent Injunction;

(l) Causing, encouraging, or participating in the use, possession and/or sale of narcotics;

(m) Owning, possessing or driving a vehicle found to have any contraband, narcotics, or illegal or deadly weapons;

(n) Using or possessing pagers or beepers in any public space;

(o) Possessing channel lock pliers, picks, wire cutters, dent pullers, sling shots, marbles, steel shot, spark plugs, rocks, screwdrivers, "slim jims" and other devices capable of being used to break into locked vehicles;

(p) Demanding entry into another person's residence at any time of the day or night;

(q) Sheltering, concealing or permitting another person to enter into a residence not their own when said person appears to be running, hiding, or otherwise evading a law enforcement officer;

(r) Signaling to or acting as a lookout for other persons to warn of the approach of police officers and soliciting, encouraging, employing or offering payment to others to do the same;

(s) Climbing any tree, wall, or fence, or passing through any wall or fence by using tunnels or other holes in such structures; .

(t) Littering in any public place or place open to public view;

(u) Urinating or defecating in any public place or place open to public view;

(v) Using words, phrases, physical gestures, or symbols commonly known as hand signs or engaging in other forms of communication which describe or refer to the gang known as "VST" or "VSL" as described in this Complaint or any of the accompanying pleadings or declarations;

(w) Wearing clothing which bears the name or letters of the gang known as "VST" or "VSL";

(x) Making, causing, or encouraging others to make loud noise of any kind, including but not limited to yelling and loud music at any time of the day or night.

The California trial court issued the injunction, and the California Supreme Court upheld the injunction against challenges that it both violated freedom of association and was void for vagueness. Injunctions, like crimes that outlaw gang activities, call for balancing community and individual rights. The community interest in the quality of life requires peace, quiet, order, and a sense of security. At the same time, even members of street gangs have the right to associate, express themselves, travel freely, and be free from vague laws (see Chapter 2, "Void-for-Vagueness Doctrine" section).

In 1992, Chicago was facing a skyrocketing increase in crime rates that many outspoken people blamed on street gangs. But unlike the sweeping injunction approved in California, the Chicago City Council passed a modern version of the ancient loitering ordinances (discussed in the "Loitering" section). Chicago's ordinance gave its police the power to order groups of loiterers (people who "remain in one place with no apparent purpose") to disperse or face arrest if officers reasonably believed that one of the loiterers was a gang member (Poulos 1995, 379–81).

No one was surprised when the ordinance set off an angry debate. Mayor Richard Daley, Jr., expressed one view, "In some areas of the city, street gangs are terrorizing residents and laying claim to whole communities." Bobbie Crawford, a waitress, expressed another view, "When kids reach a certain age they hang around on street corners. I sure wouldn't like my children taken to a police station for hanging around." And Joan Suglich, mother of six, asked, "What if somebody asks his boys to walk him home so gang members don't jump him. Are police going to arrest them?"

Nor was anyone surprised when the debate ended up in the U.S. Supreme Court. In *City of Chicago v. Morales* (1999), a divided Court decided that the ordinance was void for vagueness. Several justices, but not a majority, also argued that the ordinance also violated the right to come and go as you please without unreasonable government interference.

CASE   *Was the Loitering Ordinance Void for Vagueness?*

City of Chicago v. Morales
527 U.S. 41 (1999)

HISTORY

Jesus Morales and other defendants in several separate cases were charged in the Circuit Court of Cook County, with violating the Chicago Anti-Gang ordinance. Morales and defendants in one case, moved to dismiss the actions against them. The Circuit Court, Cook County, granted the motion. The City appealed. The Illinois Appellate Court affirmed.

Defendants in a second case were charged with violating the ordinance. The Circuit Court dismissed the charges. The Appellate Court affirmed. The City petitioned for leave to appeal, which the Appellate Court granted.

In a third case, defendants were charged, in the Circuit Court, with violating the ordinance, were convicted, and sentenced to jail terms. Defendants appealed. The Appellate Court reversed. The City petitioned for leave to appeal.

After granting the petitions to appeal in all three cases, and consolidating the cases for one hearing, the Supreme Court of Illinois affirmed.

The U.S. United States Supreme Court granted certiorari and affirmed the judgment of the Illinois Supreme Court.

STEVENS, J.

Announced the judgment of the Court and delivered the following opinion.

FACTS

In 1992, the Chicago City Council enacted the Gang Congregation Ordinance, which prohibits "criminal street gang members" from "loitering" with one another or with other persons in any public place.

The ordinance creates a criminal offense punishable by a fine of up to $500, imprisonment for not more than six months, and a requirement to perform up to 120 hours of community service. Commission of the offense involves four elements.

First, the police officer must reasonably believe that at least one of the two or more persons present in a "public place" is a "criminal street gang member."

Second, the persons must be "loitering," which the ordinance defines as "remain[ing] in any one place with no apparent purpose."

Third, the officer must then order "all" of the persons to disperse and remove themselves "from the area."

Fourth, a person must disobey the officer's order. If any person, whether a gang member or not, disobeys the officer's order, that person is guilty of violating the ordinance.

Two months after the ordinance was adopted, the Chicago Police Department promulgated General Order 92-4 to provide guidelines to govern its enforcement. That order purported to establish limitations on the enforcement discretion of police officers "to ensure that the anti-gang loitering ordinance is not enforced in an arbitrary or discriminatory way."

The limitations confine the authority to arrest gang members who violate the ordinance to sworn "members of the Gang Crime Section" and certain other designated officers, and establish detailed criteria for defining street gangs and membership in such gangs.

In addition, the order directs district commanders to "designate areas in which the presence of gang members has a demonstrable effect on the activities of law abiding persons in the surrounding community," and provides that the ordinance "will be enforced only within the designated areas." The city, however, does not release the locations of these "designated areas" to the public. . . .

During the three years of its enforcement, the police issued over 89,000 dispersal orders and arrested over 42,000 people for violating the ordinance. In the ensuing enforcement proceedings, two trial judges upheld the constitutionality of the ordinance, but eleven others ruled that it was invalid.

The city believes that the ordinance resulted in a significant decline in gang-related homicides. It notes that in 1995, the last year the ordinance was enforced, the gang-related homicide rate fell by 26%. In 1996, after the ordinance had been held invalid, the gang-related homicide rate rose 11%. However, gang-related homicides fell by 19% in 1997, over a year after the suspension of the ordinance.

Given the myriad factors that influence levels of violence, it is difficult to evaluate the probative value of this statistical evidence, or to reach any firm conclusion about the ordinance's efficacy.

OPINION

The basic factual predicate for the city's ordinance is not in dispute. The very presence of a large collection of obviously brazen, insistent, and lawless gang members and hangers-on on the public ways intimidates residents, who become afraid even to leave their homes and go about their business. That, in turn, imperils community residents' sense of safety and security, detracts from property values, and can ultimately destabilize entire neighborhoods.

We have no doubt that a law that directly prohibited such intimidating conduct . . . [as described in the facts] would be constitutional, but this ordinance broadly covers a significant amount of additional activity. Uncertainty about the scope of that additional coverage provides the basis for respondents' claim that the ordinance is too vague. . . .

The freedom to loiter for innocent purposes is part of the "liberty" protected by the Due Process Clause of the Fourteenth Amendment. We have expressly identified this "right to remove from one place to another according to inclination" as "an attribute of personal liberty" protected by the Constitution. Indeed, it is apparent that an individual's decision to remain in a public place of his choice is as much a part of his liberty as the freedom of movement inside frontiers that is "a part of our heritage" or the right to move "to whatsoever place one's own inclination may direct" identified in Blackstone's *Commentaries*. . . .

Vagueness may invalidate a criminal law for either of two independent reasons. First, it may fail to provide the kind of notice that will enable ordinary people to understand what conduct it prohibits; second, it may authorize and even encourage arbitrary and discriminatory enforcement. . . .

. . . A law fails to meet the requirements of the Due Process Clause if it is so vague and standardless that it leaves the public uncertain as to the conduct it prohibits." . . . It is difficult to imagine how any citizen of the city of Chicago standing in a public place with a group of people would know if he or she had an "apparent purpose." If she were talking to another person, would she have an apparent purpose? If she were frequently checking her watch and looking expectantly down the street, would she have an apparent purpose?

Since the city cannot conceivably have meant to criminalize each instance a citizen stands in public with a gang member, the vagueness that dooms this ordinance is not the product of uncertainty about the normal meaning of "loitering," but rather about what loitering is covered by the ordinance and what is not.

The Illinois Supreme Court emphasized the law's failure to distinguish between innocent conduct and conduct threatening harm. . . . Its decision followed the precedent set by a number of state courts that have upheld ordinances that criminalize loitering combined with some other overt act or evidence of criminal intent (ordinance criminalizing loitering with purpose to engage in drug-related activities; ordinance criminalizing loitering for the purpose of engaging in or soliciting lewd act). . . .

The city's principal response to this concern about adequate notice is that loiterers are not subject to sanction until after they have failed to comply with an officer's order to disperse. "Whatever problem is created by a law that criminalizes conduct people normally believe to be innocent is solved when persons receive actual notice from a police order of what they are expected to do."

We find this response unpersuasive for at least two reasons. First, the purpose of the fair notice requirement is to enable the ordinary citizen to conform his or her conduct to the law. No one may be required at peril of life, liberty or property to speculate as to the meaning of penal statutes. . . . Such an order cannot retroactively give adequate warning of the boundary between the permissible and the impermissible applications of the law.

Second, the terms of the dispersal order compound the inadequacy of the notice afforded by the ordinance. It provides that the officer "shall order all such persons to disperse and remove themselves from the area." This vague phrasing raises a host of questions. After such an order issues, how long must the loiterers remain apart? How far must they move? If each loiterer walks around the block and they meet again at the same location, are they subject to arrest or merely to being ordered to disperse again? As we do here, we have found vagueness in a criminal statute exacerbated by the use of the standards of "neighborhood" and "locality." . . . Both terms are elastic and, dependent upon circumstances, may be equally satisfied by areas measured by rods or by miles.

The Constitution does not permit a legislature to set a net large enough to catch all possible offenders, and leave it to the courts to step inside and say who could be rightfully detained, and who should be set at large. This ordinance is therefore vague "not in the sense that it requires a person to conform his conduct to an imprecise but comprehensible normative standard, but rather in the sense that no standard of conduct is specified at all."

The broad sweep of the ordinance also violates the requirement that a legislature establish minimal guidelines to govern law enforcement. There are no such guidelines in the ordinance. In any public place in the city of Chicago, persons who stand or sit in the company of a gang member may be ordered to disperse unless their purpose is apparent.

The mandatory language in the enactment directs the police to issue an order without first making any inquiry about their possible purposes. It matters not whether the reason that a gang member and his father, for example, might loiter near Wrigley Field is to rob an unsuspecting fan or just to get a glimpse of Sammy Sosa leaving the ballpark; in either event, if their purpose is not apparent to a nearby police officer, she may—indeed, she "shall"—order them to disperse.

Recognizing that the ordinance does reach a substantial amount of innocent conduct, we turn, then, to its language to determine if it "necessarily entrusts lawmaking to the moment-to-moment judgment of the policeman on his beat."

. . . The principal source of the vast discretion conferred on the police in this case is the definition of loitering as "to remain in any one place with no apparent purpose." . . . [That definition] provides absolute discretion to police officers to determine what activities constitute loitering. . . .

It is true . . . that the requirement that the officer reasonably believe that a group of loiterers contains a gang member does place a limit on the authority to order dispersal. That limitation would no doubt be sufficient if the ordinance only applied to loitering that had an apparently harmful purpose or effect, or possibly if it only applied to loitering by persons reasonably believed to be criminal gang members. Not all of the respondents in this case, for example, are gang members.

The city admits that it was unable to prove that Morales is a gang member but justifies his arrest and conviction by the fact that Morales admitted "that he knew he was with criminal street gang members." But this ordinance . . . requires no harmful purpose and applies to non-gang members as well as suspected gang members. It applies to everyone in the city who may remain in one place with one suspected gang member as long as their purpose is not apparent to an officer observing them. Friends, relatives, teachers, counselors, or even total strangers might unwittingly engage in forbidden loitering if they happen to engage in idle conversation with a gang member. . . .

In our judgment, the Illinois Supreme Court correctly concluded that the ordinance does not provide sufficiently specific limits on the enforcement discretion of the police "to meet constitutional standards for definiteness and clarity."

We recognize the serious and difficult problems testified to by the citizens of Chicago that led to the enactment of this ordinance. We are mindful that the preservation of liberty depends in part on the maintenance of social order.

However, in this instance the city has enacted an ordinance that affords too much discretion to the police and too little notice to citizens who wish to use the public streets.

Accordingly, the judgment of the Supreme Court of Illinois is AFFIRMED.

DISSENT

SCALIA, J.

. . . Until the ordinance that is before us today was adopted, the citizens of Chicago were free to stand about in public places with no apparent purpose—to engage, that is, in conduct that appeared to be loitering. In recent years, however, the city has been afflicted with criminal street gangs. . . . These gangs congregated in public places to deal in drugs, and to terrorize the neighborhoods by demonstrating control over their "turf." Many residents of the inner city felt that they were prisoners in their own homes. . . . Chicagoans decided that to eliminate the problem it was worth restricting some of the freedom that they once enjoyed. . . .

The minor limitation upon the free state of nature that this prophylactic arrangement imposed upon all Chicagoans seemed to them (and it seems to me) a small price to pay for liberation of their streets.

The majority today invalidates this perfectly reasonable measure by . . . elevating loitering to a constitutionally guaranteed right, and by discerning vagueness where, according to our usual standards, none exists. . . . The fact is that the present ordinance is entirely clear in its application, cannot be violated except with full knowledge and intent, and vests no more discretion in the police than innumerable other measures authorizing police orders to preserve the public peace and safety. . . .

DISSENT

THOMAS, J. JOINED BY REHNQUIST, J. AND SCALIA, J.

The duly elected members of the Chicago City Council enacted the ordinance at issue as part of a larger effort to prevent gangs from establishing dominion over the public streets. By invalidating Chicago's ordinance, I fear that the Court has unnecessarily sentenced law-abiding citizens to lives of terror and misery. The ordinance is not vague. Any fool would know that a particular category of conduct would be within its reach. Nor does it violate the Due Process Clause. The asserted "freedom to loiter for innocent purposes," is in no way "deeply rooted in this Nation's history and tradition." . . .

The human costs exacted by criminal street gangs are inestimable. In many of our Nation's cities, gangs have "virtually overtaken certain neighborhoods, contributing to the economic and social decline of these areas and causing fear and lifestyle changes among law-abiding residents." . . .

Ordinary citizens like Ms. D'Ivory Gordon explained that she struggled just to walk to work:

When I walk out my door, these guys are out there. . . . They watch you. . . . They know where you live. They know what time you leave, what time you come home. I am afraid of them. I have even come to the point now that I carry a meat cleaver to work with me. . . . I don't want to hurt anyone, and I don't want to be hurt. We need to clean these corners up. Clean these communities up and take it back from them.

Eighty-eight-year-old Susan Mary Jackson echoed her sentiments, testifying,

We used to have a nice neighborhood. We don't have it anymore. . . . I am scared to go out in the daytime . . . you can't pass because they are standing. I am afraid to go to the store. I don't go to the store because I am afraid. At my age if they look at me real hard, I be ready to holler.

Another long-time resident testified:

I have never had the terror that I feel everyday when I walk down the streets of Chicago. . . . I have had my windows broken out. I have had guns pulled on me. I have been threatened. I get intimidated on a daily basis, and it's come to the point where I say, well, do I go out today? Do I put my ax in my briefcase? Do I walk around dressed like a bum so I am not looking rich or got any money or anything like that? . . .

Today, the Court focuses extensively on the "rights" of gang members and their companions. It can safely do so—the people who will have to live with the consequences of today's opinion do not live in our neighborhoods. Rather, the people who will suffer from our lofty pronouncements are people like Ms. Susan Mary Jackson; people who have seen their neighborhoods literally destroyed by gangs and violence and drugs.

They are good, decent people who must struggle to overcome their desperate situation, against all odds, in order to raise their families, earn a living, and remain good citizens. As one resident described, "There is only about maybe one or two percent of the people in the city causing these problems maybe, but it's keeping 98 percent of us in our houses and off the streets and afraid to shop."

By focusing exclusively on the imagined "rights" of the two percent, the Court today has denied our most vulnerable citizens the very thing that Justice STEVENS, elevates above all else—the "freedom of movement." And that is a shame.

Questions

1. List the four elements in the Chicago gang loitering ordinance.
2. List the specific arguments the majority gave to support its conclusion that the ordinance was vague.

3. Explain specifically all of the reasons why the dissenting judges disagreed.

4. Would "any fool know" what conduct this ordinance prohibited? Defend your answer.

5. Did the majority properly balance the interest in community order with the individual liberty? Explain your answer.

6. If the majority didn't properly strike the balance, how would you do it differently? Explain your answer.

 Go to the Criminal Law 9e website to find Exercise 12.2 and learn more about gangs, *Chicago v. Morales*, and the Constitution: www.thomsonedu.com/criminaljustice/samaha.

"VICTIMLESS" CRIMES

Let me be clear about how we're going to use the term "victimless" crime in this section. First, it applies only to consenting adults, not minors. Second, it refers to crimes committed by adults who don't see themselves as victims of their behavior. Let's look at the controversy surrounding the issue and then at two crimes that are generally considered victimless—prostitution and solicitation.

The Victimless Crime Controversy

Referring to many crimes in which the perpetrators don't see themselves as victimized as "victimless" crimes is controversial; Table 12.2 lists some of these crimes. We've already examined the question of adult drug use in a constitutional democracy (Chapters 2 and 3, *Robinson v. California* and *Powell v. Texas*). And we've discussed the application of the principles of *actus reus* and *mens rea* to drug crimes (Chapters 3 and 4).

Let's look a little closer at a few offenses that involve consensual adult sexual conduct. First, a little history: In medieval days, when the Church was more powerful than kings and queens, ecclesiastical courts had total power to try and punish crimes against "family and morals," including all nonviolent sexual behavior and marital relations breaches. As monarchs grew stronger, royal courts eventually gained control over most of these offenses. Once the monarch's courts took them over, they became the crimes against public morals, most of which would be on the list of anyone who subscribes to the idea of victimless crimes (Morris and Hawkins 1970, chap. 1).

TABLE 12.2	"Victimless" Crimes
Substance abuse (Chapters 2 and 3)	
Internet censorship	
Loitering	
Prostitution	
Sodomy (*Lawrence v. Texas*, Chapter 2)	
Seat-belt law violations	
Helmet law violations	
Violating bans on bungee jumping	
Assisted suicide	

Controversy makes it tough to balance public good and individual privacy in these cases. There's broad agreement that the crimes against persons and property you read about in Chapters 9–11 deserve punishment. However, no such agreement exists when it comes to whether those listed in Table 12.2 should be crimes. In fact, there's a deep rift between those who believe criminal law should enforce morals to "purify" society and those who just as deeply believe that consenting adults' nonviolent sexual conduct is none of the criminal law's business (Morris and Hawkins 1970).

Perhaps no issue in criminal policy has caused more acrimonious debate over a longer time than that of the role law should play in enforcing public morals. Two English Victorian scholars, the philosopher John Stuart Mill and the historian Sir James F. Stephen, started the debate. Their two major positions were summed up in the widely known and debated Wolfendon Report, an English document recommending the decriminalization of private sexual conduct of two types: between adult consenting male homosexuals and between adult sex workers and their customers."

Here's the summary of the majority of the commission's position:

> There remains one additional argument which we believe to be decisive, namely, the importance which society and the law ought to give to individual freedom of choice and action in matters of private morality. Unless a deliberate attempt is to be made by society, acting through the agency of the law, to equate the sphere of crime with that of sin, there must remain a realm of private morality and immorality which is, in brief and crude terms, not the law's business. To say this is not to condone or encourage private immorality. On the contrary, to emphasize the personal private nature of moral or immoral conduct is to emphasize the personal and private responsibility of the individual for his own actions, and that is a responsibility which a mature agent can properly be expected to carry for himself without the threat of punishment from the law. (Wolfendon Report 1957, 20–21)

And here's English jurist Sir Patrick Devlin's rebuttal to the majority position:

> I think, therefore, that it is not possible to set theoretical limits to the power of the State to legislate against immorality. It is not possible to settle in advance exceptions to the general rule or to define inflexibly areas of morality into which the law is in no circumstances to be allowed to enter. Society is entitled by means of its laws to protect itself from dangers, whether from within or without. Here again I think that the political parallel is legitimate.
>
> The law of treason is directed against aiding the king's enemies and against sedition from within. The justification for this is that established government is necessary for the existence of society and therefore its safety against violent overthrow must be secured. But an established morality is as necessary as good government to the welfare of society. Societies disintegrate from within more frequently than they are broken up by external pressures.
>
> There is disintegration when no common morality is observed and history shows that the loosening of moral bonds is often the first state of disintegration, so that society is justified in taking the same steps to preserve its moral code as it does to preserve its government and other essential institutions. The suppression of vice is as much the law's business as the suppression of subversive activities; it is no more possible to define a sphere of private morality than it is to define one of private subversive activity. (Wolfendon Report 1957, 48)

Prostitution and Solicitation

Nonviolent sex offenses cover a broad spectrum (Table 12.3). Let's look at a few of these crimes related to prostitution. Prostitution is an ancient business, prospering in all cultures at all times no matter the condemnation of religion and morals.

TABLE 12.3	**Prostitution and Related Offenses**

Fornication

Prostitution

Solicitation of prostitution ("pimping")

Adult consensual sex outside marriage

Adultery

It's also a crime nearly everywhere in the United States, persisting no matter how severe the laws or how tough the efforts of police to enforce them. Prostitution used to be reserved for describing the act of selling sexual intercourse for money—and only selling, not buying, sex was included.

Now it means all contacts and penetrations (Chapter 10 defines these terms) as long as they're done with the intent to gratify sexual appetite. And both patrons (buyers) and prostitutes (sellers) can commit prostitution. In the past, the law recognized only women as prostitutes. Now both men and women who sell sex are prostitutes.

It's a crime not only to buy and sell sex but also to solicit prostitution (sometimes called "promoting prostitution," "pimping," or "pandering"). Soliciting prostitution means getting customers for prostitutes and/or providing a place for prostitutes and customers to engage in sex for money.

Prostitution and promoting prostitution are misdemeanors in most states, but it's a serious felony when circumstances such as minors, violence, and weapons are involved.

Here's an edited version of Minnesota's elaborate and detailed statute on prostitution, promotion, and aggravating circumstances:

ß 609.324. PROSTITUTION

Subdivision 1. Engaging in, hiring, or agreeing to hire a minor to engage in prostitution; penalties.

(a) Whoever intentionally does any of the following may be sentenced to imprisonment for not more than 20 years or to payment of a fine of not more than $40,000, or both:
  (1) engages in prostitution with an individual under the age of 13 years; or
  (2) hires or offers or agrees to hire an individual under the age of 13 years to engage in sexual penetration or sexual contact.

(b) Whoever intentionally does any of the following may be sentenced to imprisonment for not more than ten years or to payment of a fine of not more than $20,000, or both:
  (1) engages in prostitution with an individual under the age of 16 years but at least 13 years; or
  (2) hires or offers or agrees to hire an individual under the age of 16 years but at least 13 years to engage in sexual penetration or sexual contact.

(c) Whoever intentionally does any of the following may be sentenced to imprisonment for not more than five years or to payment of a fine of not more than $10,000, or both:
  (1) engages in prostitution with an individual under the age of 18 years but at least 16 years; or
  (2) hires or offers or agrees to hire an individual under the age of 18 years but at least 16 years to engage in sexual penetration or sexual contact.

Subd. 2. Solicitation or acceptance of solicitation to engage in prostitution; penalty.

Whoever solicits or accepts a solicitation to engage for hire in sexual penetration or sexual contact while in a public place may be sentenced to imprisonment for not more than one year or to payment of a fine of not more than $3,000 or both. Except as otherwise provided in subdivision 4, a person who is convicted of violating this subdivision while acting as a patron must, at a minimum, be sentenced to pay a fine of at least $1,500.

Subd. 3. Engaging in, hiring, or agreeing to hire an adult to engage in prostitution; penalties.

Whoever intentionally does any of the following may be sentenced to imprisonment for not more than 90 days or to payment of a fine of not more than $700, or both:

> (1) engages in prostitution with an individual 18 years of age or above; or
> (2) hires or offers or agrees to hire an individual 18 years of age or above to engage in sexual penetration or sexual contact.

Except as otherwise provided in subdivision 4, a person who is convicted of violating clause (1) or (2) while acting as a patron must, at a minimum, be sentenced to pay a fine of at least $500.

Whoever violates the provisions of this subdivision within two years of a previous conviction may be sentenced to imprisonment for not more than one year or to payment of a fine of not more than $3,000, or both.

Except as otherwise provided in subdivision 4, a person who is convicted of a gross misdemeanor violation of this subdivision while acting as a patron, must, at a minimum, be sentenced as follows: (1) to pay a fine of at least $1,500; and (2) to serve 20 hours of community work service.

The court may waive the mandatory community work service if it makes specific, written findings that the community work service is not feasible or appropriate under the circumstances of the case.

Subd. 4. Community service in lieu of minimum fine.

The court may order a person convicted of violating subdivision 2 or 3 to perform community work service in lieu of all or a portion of the minimum fine required under those subdivisions if the court makes specific, written findings that the convicted person is indigent or that payment of the fine would create undue hardship for the convicted person or that person's immediate family. Community work service ordered under this subdivision is in addition to any mandatory community work service ordered under subdivision 3.

Subd. 5. Use of motor vehicle to patronize prostitutes; driving record notation.

When a court sentences a person convicted of violating this section while acting as a patron, the court shall determine whether the person used a motor vehicle during the commission of the offense. If the court finds that the person used a motor vehicle during the commission of the offense, it shall forward its finding to the commissioner of public safety who shall record the finding on the person's driving record. . . .

SUMMARY

I. Issues of public order include
- A. Disorderly conduct crimes
- B. Quality-of-life crimes
- C. Victimless crimes

II. Disorderly conduct crimes
- A. Historically, these were largely ignored misdemeanors.
- B. The Model Penal Code provision has two main purposes:
  - 1. It defines *actus reus* more precisely than "disorderly conduct."
  - 2. It adds a *mens rea* element to what used to be strict liability offenses.
- C. Individual disorderly conduct in the Model Penal Code
  - 1. There are three kinds of *actus reus:*
    - a. Fighting
    - b. Making unreasonable noise, using offensive language
    - c. Creating hazardous or offensive conditions

2. The *mens rea* of disorderly conduct is acting purposely, knowingly, or recklessly.
3. There are several special individual disorderly conduct sections in the Model Penal Code:
   a. Knowingly spreading false alarms
   b. Appearing drunk in public (no *mens rea* requirement)
   c. Loitering or prowling (no *mens rea* requirement)
   d. Purposely or recklessly obstructing highways or other public passages
   e. Purposely disrupting lawful meetings, processions, or gatherings
D. Group disorderly conduct ("riot")
   1. Background
      a. There were three ancient misdemeanor group disorderly conduct crimes: unlawful assembly, rout, and riot.
      b. The Riot Act of 1714 made riot a felony.
      c. "Reading the riot act" comes from the 1714 act.
   2. Elements
      a. The *actus reus* is participating in disorderly conduct.
      b. The *mens rea* requires that:
         (1) The defendant had a specific intent or purpose to commit or facilitate the commission of a felony.
         (2) The defendant had the purpose to prevent or coerce an official action.
         (3) The defendant had knowledge that any participant used or planned to use a deadly weapon.

III. "Quality-of-life" crimes
A. These crimes are meant to control "bad manners" in public places (sidewalks, streets, parks).
B. These are ancient offenses (crimes against public order) applied to new situations ("street people" and "gangs") and called by a new name (quality-of-life crimes).
C. They underscore the tension between liberty and order in a constitutional democracy.
D. They apply due process of liberty (Chapter 2) to maintaining order in public.
E. "Broken windows" theory
   1. Theory—There's a link between "minor" quality-of-life offenses (public drunkenness, panhandling, graffiti, vandalism, prostitution, loitering) and serious crimes (rape, robbery, burglary).
   2. Reality
      a. The national debate concentrates on serious crime, whereas local officials and the public are more worried about quality-of-life offenses.
      b. Empirical findings as to whether there's a link between serious crime and disorder are mixed.
         (1) Some find a causal relationship. (Kelling, Skogan)
         (2) Others find common origins but not a causal link. (Sampson and Raudenbush)
F. Wide public agreement on what "bad public manners" consists of exists.
G. Vagrancy and loitering
   1. Two ancient offenses aimed at roaming around (vagrancy) with no visible means of support and at standing around (loitering).
   2. Vagrancy and loitering have been tailored to meet the modern problems of "bad public manners" of street people and gangs.

3. Due process (void for vagueness) restricts the power to criminalize vagrancy (*Papichristou v. City of Jacksonville* 1972) and loitering (*Kolender v. Lawson* 1983).
4. Vagrancy and loitering can overcome the vagueness objection if they're defined to include more than just roaming around or standing around.

H. Panhandling
1. Panhandling statutes call the ancient crime of public begging into service to control "aggressive" begging by "street people."
2. Bans on panhandling don't apply to "organized charities" (Salvation Army).
3. Panhandling is "speech" protected by the First Amendment.
   a. The right to panhandle is "commercial speech," and so it's less protected than other types of speech.
   b. States can control the time, place (subways), and manner ("aggressive") of panhandling.
   c. States can't control the content of panhandling (the right to ask for money).

I. Street gangs
1. "Bands of loitering youth" scare ordinary people.
2. Antigang ordinances raise due process questions (liberty and void for vagueness).
3. Antigang ordinances meet due process and liberty requirements if they define loitering more specifically than "hanging out with no apparent purpose" (OK to ban loitering "for the purpose of committing a crime").

IV. "Victimless" crimes
A. The term applies only to adults.
B. It refers to crimes committed by adults who don't see themselves as victims.
C. Referring to these crimes as "victimless" is controversial.
D. The Wolfendon Report in 1950s England recommended decriminalizing private sexual conduct between consenting adults with regard to homosexuality and prostitution.
E. Today, both patrons and prostitutes (male or female) commit prostitution.

REVIEW QUESTIONS

1. Why is there a natural tension between order and liberty in a constitutional democracy?

2. Explain the difference between individual and group disorderly conduct, and give an example of each.

3. Summarize public opinion regarding quality-of-life crimes.

4. Describe the disconnect between the national crime debate and the attitude of local officials and the public.

5. Describe the "broken windows" theory.

6. Summarize the empirical findings regarding the validity of the broken-windows theory.

7. What's the difference between loitering and vagrancy?

8. Trace the constitutional history of vagrancy statutes.

9. What's the significance of the *Papichristou v. City of Jacksonville* case?

10. What's the significance of the *Kolender v. Lawson* case?

11. What was the columnist Ellen Goodman referring to with her comment "Enough's enough"?

12. Summarize James Q. Wilson's defense of laws targeting "street people."

13. Describe and explain the distinction between panhandling and organized charities in panhandling ordinances.

14. What's the difference between "commercial" and other speech, and why is the distinction constitutionally important?

15. Describe the spectrum of groups included within the meaning of "gang."

16. Describe the behavior included in criminal laws regulating gangs.

17. Describe the gang activities that fall within the definition of "public nuisance" in the injunction asked for by the Santa Clara, California, city attorney.

18. Summarize the California Supreme Court decision in *People ex rel. Gallo v. Acuna*.

19. Summarize the Chicago ordinance and the debate over it that finally reached the U.S. Supreme Court in *Chicago v. Morales*.

20. Summarize the controversy over victimless crimes.

KEY TERMS

"quality of life" crimes, p. 408
order, p. 408
liberty, p. 408
crimes against public order, p. 408
"victimless" crimes, p. 408
disorderly conduct, p. 409
actual disorderly conduct, p. 409

constructive disorderly conduct, p. 409
unlawful assembly, p. 411
rout, p. 411
riot, p. 411
broken-windows theory, p. 412
vagrancy, p. 413

loitering, p. 413
preliminary injunction, p. 415
panhandling, p. 418
time, place, and manner test, p. 419
injunction to abate public nuisance, p. 422

Crimes Against the State

MAIN POINTS

- This chapter is about applying the enduring idea of balancing security and freedom during wartime emergencies.
- Treason is a fundamental weapon against *present* allegiance and support to foreign enemies.
- Crimes against *potential* terrorist attacks are subject to the limits placed on traditional criminal law.
- The most commonly prosecuted crime against the state since September 11, 2001, is "providing material support or resources" to terrorists or terrorist organizations.

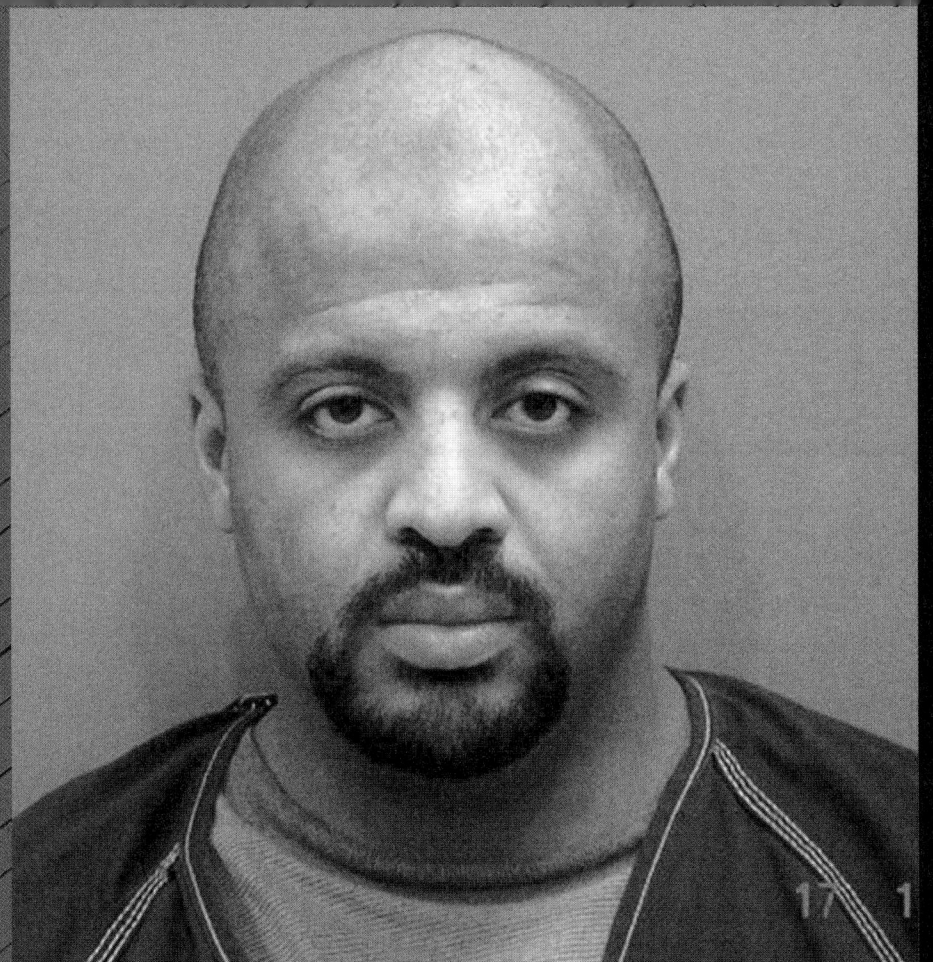

© Associated Press

13

Zacarias Moussaoui has often been referred to as "the 20th hijacker" in the September 11th attacks, bu whether the self-confessed al-Qaeda operative was a serious plotter or just a fringe figure has been unclear. Jurors at his trial concluded that his silence in the run-up to 9/11 made him responsible for at least one death on that day, and that made him eligible for the death penalty. They ultimately rejected the deatf penalty, however, and he was sentenced to six life terms in prison without the possibility of parole.

Balance in Times of Emergency

Whoever, within the United States or subject to the jurisdiction of the United States, knowingly provides material support or resources to a foreign terrorist organization, or attempts or conspires to do so, shall be fined under this title or imprisoned not more than 10 years, or both.

USA PATRIOT ACT (2001)

You don't have to wait until the fuse is being lit. If that were the standard, a lot of bombs would go off and a lot of people would lose their lives.

MICHAEL CHERTOFF,

U.S. DEPARTMENT OF HOMELAND

SECURITY (ANDERSON 2003)

If you cast too wide a net and you don't use appropriate discretion to limit these prosecutions, you risk ensnaring innocent people and you demean the entire process of prosecuting terror.

NEAL SONNETT,
NATIONAL ASSOCIATION OF
CRIMINAL DEFENSE LAWYERS
(ANDERSON 2003)

In the different views of the Patriot Act quoted in the opener, you can see the tension between two core values in our constitutional democracy—the need for safety and security and the desire for privacy and liberty.

The **USA Patriot Act** (2001) is an acronym for "Uniting and Strengthening America by Providing Appropriate Tools Required to Intercept and Obstruct Terrorism." Aimed at fighting and preventing international terrorism, it was passed and signed into law on October 16, 2001, after the September 11 attacks on the World Trade Center and the Pentagon.

This chapter is about how we apply the enduring principles of criminal law (Chapters 1–4) to protect the core values of security and freedom in a time of great testing by threats from terrorist groups who are prepared to kill innocent Americans both in the United States and around the world. Grave as the threat may be today, we should remember our Constitution was adopted during a time of similar major threats to our nation's security.

We'll examine the history and modern law of treason, the other ancient crimes of disloyalty (sedition, sabotage, and espionage), and the specific crimes against domestic and international terrorism enacted after the Oklahoma City bombing in 1993 and the attacks on the World Trade Center and the Pentagon on September 11, 2001.

 TREASON

Treason is the only crime defined in the U.S. Constitution. This is how Article III, Section 3 defines this most heinous of all crimes against the state:

> Treason against the United States, shall consist only in levying War against them, or, in adhering to their Enemies, giving them Aid and Comfort. No Person shall be convicted of Treason unless on the Testimony of two Witnesses to the same overt Act, or on Confession in open Court.

There's also a U.S. Code (2006) treason statute that includes the constitutional definition and adds this penalty provision:

> Whoever, owing allegiance to the United States, levies war against them or adheres to their enemies, giving them aid and comfort within the United States or elsewhere, is guilty of treason and shall suffer death, or shall be imprisoned not less than five years and fined under this title but not less than $10,000; and shall be incapable of holding any office under the United States. (Title 18, Part I, Chapter 115, § 2381)

Let's look at how treason laws were viewed both before and after the Revolution.

DISTRUST OF TREASON LAWS AND THE AMERICAN REVOLUTION

The revolutionaries who wrote the U.S. Constitution knew very well the new government they were about to create couldn't survive without the active support (or at least the passive submission) of most of the people. They also realized it was going to be some time before this new republican form of government took hold among the people.

The people's allegiance would be especially important to the newborn nation's survival in the early years following the Revolution, a time of gigantic threats from enemies inside and outside the new country. From within, Benedict Arnold's betrayal of General Washington was fresh in their minds, and English royalists among them remained deeply loyal to King George III.

From without, unfriendly countries had designs on the new country's territory. To the north in Canada, England was hovering, smarting from the loss of the American colonies and looking for payback. Spain to the south had just taken back Florida and claimed the whole Mississippi Valley. And France had only recently been thrown out of the Ohio Valley. These unfriendly nations formed alliances with Native American nations by taking advantage of deep injustices the Americans continued to inflict on the tribes.

These threats led the authors of the Constitution to take a tough stand against individuals who broke their allegiance in the face of these dangers. But there was a flip side to their tough stand. Many of the drafters' ancestors had fled to the colonies to escape persecution for heresy and prosecution for treason. More to the point, almost all of them were traitors themselves under British law. English treason consisted either of levying war against the king or giving aid and comfort to the king's enemies. They'd done both. They'd levied war against the King of England by fighting the Revolutionary War, and they'd given aid and comfort to England's bitterest enemy, France.

Everything they did to further the interests of the colonies was done under threat of prosecution for treason. English prosecutions for treason weren't pretty. Thomas Jefferson referred to the English law of treason as a "deadly weapon" in the hands of "tyrannical kings" and "weak and wicked Ministers which had drawn the blood of the best and honestest men in the kingdom" (Jefferson 1853, 1:215). Treason prosecutions were probably on Benjamin Franklin's mind when he quipped at the signing of the Declaration of Independence, "We must all hang together, or most assuredly we shall all hang separately" (Lederer 1988, 27).

What were they worried about? The existing law of treason in England defined treason as **"adherence to the enemy."** *Adherence* here means breaking allegiance to your own country by forming an "attachment to the enemy. " Criminalizing attachment—joining the enemy's military forces—wasn't an issue; everybody agreed that was treason. But what about "giving aid and comfort to the enemy"? With this loose phrase, "attachment" could lead to attacks on thoughts and feelings. Suppose "disloyalty" took the forms of sympathy for our enemies or even apathy toward our own cause. Were they treason, too? (They were in England.) And would zealous patriotism, so needed in troubled times, tempt the government to bend the rules in its attempt to protect the country? (It did in England.)

The worries that treason law would be abused boiled down to two concerns:

1. That peaceful opposition to the government, not just rebellion, would be repressed.

2. That innocent people might be convicted of treason because of perjury, passion, and/or insufficient evidence. The authors of the Constitution were determined that disloyal feelings or opinions and the passions of the time wouldn't be a part of the law of treason.

So as much as they recognized the need for allegiance to the new government, their fear of abusive prosecutions for treason led them to adopt "every limitation that the practice of governments had evolved or that politico-legal philosophy to that time had advanced" (*Cramer v. U.S.* 1945, 23–24). By the time the Constitution was adopted, government and philosophy had come to limit treason to two disloyal behaviors: (1) levying war against your own country and (2) giving aid and comfort to the enemy.

The authors of the Constitution adopted these two acts and then, for more protection, added three more limits to the reach of treason:

1. They banned legislatures and courts from creating new treasons.

2. They required two witnesses to at least one overt (unconcealed) act of treason or a confession in open court.

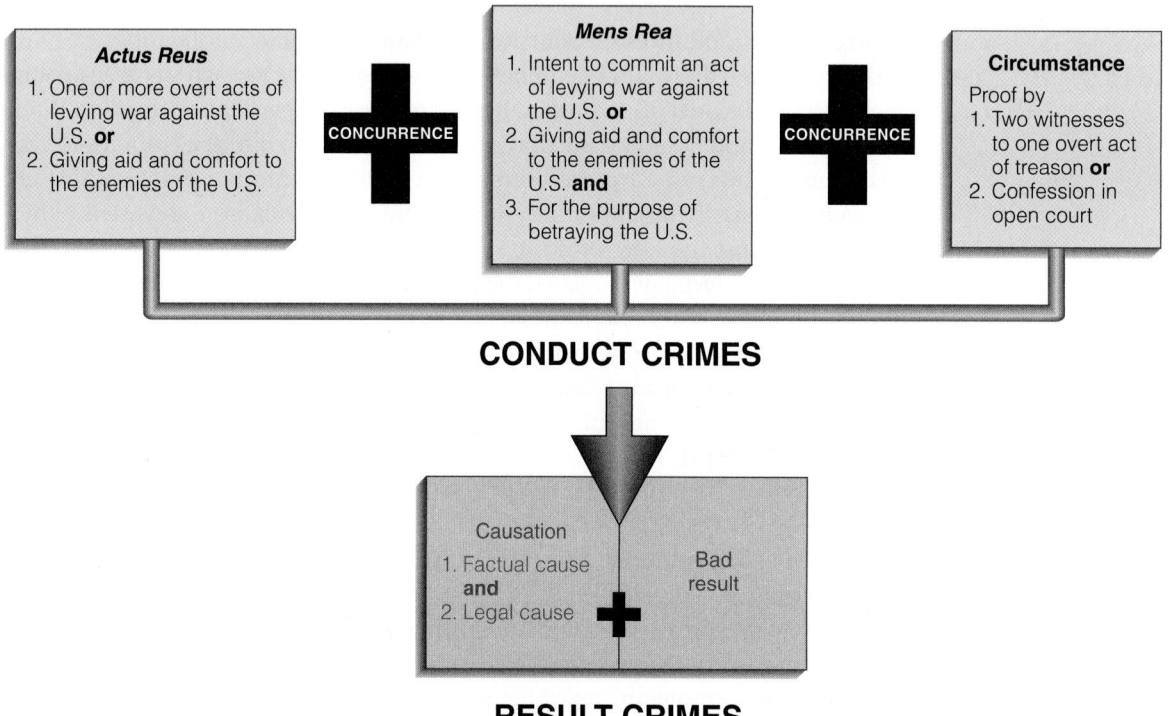

Elements of Treason

3. They wrote these limits into the body of the U.S. Constitution, where it would be very tough to tamper with them because of the intentionally cumbersome constitutional amendment process.

Treason consists of three elements. First, treason *actus reus* consists of either levying war against the United States or giving aid and comfort to the enemies of the United States. Second, treason *mens rea* consists of intentionally giving aid and comfort for the very purpose of betraying the United States. Third, proof of treason requires either two witnesses to the *actus reus* or confession in open court.

Associate U.S. Supreme Court Robert Jackson stated the elements of treason in this straightforward language in one of the very few treason cases in U.S. history, *Cramer v. U.S.* (1945):

> The crime of treason consists of two elements: adherence to the enemy; and rendering him aid and comfort. A citizen intellectually or emotionally may favor the enemy and harbor sympathies or convictions disloyal to this country's policy or interest, but so long as he commits no act of aid and comfort to the enemy, there is no treason. On the other hand, a citizen may take actions, which do aid and comfort the enemy—making a speech critical of the government or opposing its measures, profiteering, striking in defense plants or essential work, and the hundred other things which impair our cohesion and diminish our strength—but if there is no adherence to the enemy in this, if there is no intent to betray, there is no treason. (29)

Treason Law Since the Adoption of the U.S. Constitution

Distrust of treason prosecutions didn't end with the adoption of the Constitution. Throughout U.S. history, the government has prosecuted only a handful of people for treason, and presidents have pardoned or at least mitigated death sentences of most of those few who've been found guilty. The only exception was President Eisenhower's refusal to stop the execution of Ethel Rosenberg, convicted of conspiring to give atomic bomb secrets to the Soviet Union. She and her husband Julius were executed in 1951. There's still plenty of controversy surrounding the Rosenbergs' executions (Meerpol 2003).

In 1945, six years before the Rosenbergs' executions, the U.S. Supreme Court dealt with *disloyalty*—giving aid and comfort to Nazi Germany for the purpose of betraying the United States—and proving it, in *Cramer v. U.S.* (1945). This case was part of the fallout from the darkest days of World War II.

Early in June 1942, when the war was going badly for the Allies, German submarines were able to get close enough to the East Coast of the United States to allow eight Germans to get ashore, four on Long Island and four in Florida. They managed to bring along several crates of dynamite and lots of cash. The plan was to blow up bridges, factories, and maybe a department store owned by Jews. The object of the plot was, first, to sabotage the war effort by destroying strategic places. Second, they planned to demoralize the American public by terror—namely, by the brazen act of coming right onto U.S. soil and blowing up our places of defense and business.

The saboteurs never committed sabotage. Within days of their landing, they turned themselves in to the FBI. The reason they went to the FBI isn't clear. They may have had a change of heart, or feared getting caught, or perhaps they never were really saboteurs at all but Germans disillusioned with Hitler, hoping to escape to the United States (Nazi Saboteur Case 1942, "Transcript of Military Commission"). Whatever the reason, the eight saboteurs were immediately tried by a secret military commission and convicted. Six were quickly executed; two were sentenced to life in prison.

Shortly before the saboteurs were caught, Anthony Cramer got together with two of them, Werner Thiel and Edward Kerling, at the Lexington Inn in New York City. Later that day, Cramer had dinner with Werner Thiel at Thompson's Cafeteria in New York City.

In 1943, Cramer was arrested and charged with treason based on his meetings with the by-then executed Thiel and Kerling. At Cramer's treason trial, two FBI agents testified they had witnessed his meetings with Thiel and Kerling and that the three ate, drank, and "engaged long and earnestly in conversation."

The government claimed these acts amounted to "giving aid and comfort to the enemy" and that the FBI agents' testimony satisfied the constitutional requirement of two witnesses. The trial judge and jury agreed; Cramer was convicted (*Cramer v. U.S.*, 1945). However, the U.S. Supreme Court, by a vote of 5–4, disagreed and reversed Cramer's conviction. According to Justice Jackson, writing for the majority, two witnesses to the dinner wasn't good enough to prove treason:

> The whole purpose of the constitutional [two witness] provision is to make sure that a treason conviction shall rest on direct proof of two witnesses and not even a little on imagination.
>
> And without the use of some imagination it is difficult to perceive any advantage which this meeting afforded to Thiel and Kerling as enemies or how it strengthened Germany or weakened the United States in any way whatever. It may be true that the saboteurs were cultivating Cramer as a potential "source of information and an avenue for contact." But there is no proof either by two witnesses or by even one witness or by any circumstance that Cramer gave them information. . . .
>
> Meeting with Cramer in public drinking places to tipple and trifle was no part of the saboteurs' mission and did not advance it. It may well have been a digression which jeopardized its success. (38)

Go to the Criminal Law 9e website to find Exercise 13.1 for a full report of *Cramer v. U.S:* www.thomsonedu .com/criminaljustice/samaha.

SEDITION, SABOTAGE, AND ESPIONAGE

The lesson of *Cramer v. U.S.* is clear: It's very hard to convict someone of treason—and as you've already learned, that's just what the authors intended. But treason isn't the only crime aimed at combating disloyalty and keeping the allegiance of our citizens. Let's look at three of these crimes, which are very much like ancient crimes with the same names—sedition, sabotage, and espionage. Then, we'll examine some specific antiterrorism laws that borrowed from these three ancient crimes.

Sedition

For centuries, it's been a crime against the state not just to commit treason but to "stir up" others to overthrow the government by violence. Advocating the violent overthrow of the government was called **sedition**. The "stirring up" could be done by speeches **(seditious speech)**, writings **(seditious libel)**, or agreement **(seditious conspiracy)**.

In 1798, during the French Revolution and impending war with France, the U.S. Congress enacted the country's first sedition act. Banning a lot more than stirring up the violent overthrow of the government, it made it a crime to

> unlawfully combine or conspire together with intent to oppose any measure or measures of the government of the United States . . . , or to impede the operation of any law of the United States, or to intimidate or prevent any [official] . . . from undertaking, performing, or executing his . . . duty. (Urofsky and Finkelman 2002a, I:141)

The Sedition Act also made it a crime to

write, print, utter, or publish any . . . false, scandalous and malicious writing or writings . . ." with intent to "defame" the U.S. Government . . . or excite the hatred of the good people [against the U.S. Government]. (142)

The U.S. Criminal Code (2006) definition of seditious conspiracy sticks to conspiracies that advocate violence. It provides:

If two or more persons in any State or Territory, or in any place subject to the jurisdiction of the United States, conspire to overthrow, put down, or to destroy by force the Government of the United States, or to levy war against them, or to oppose by force the authority thereof, or by force to prevent, hinder, or delay the execution of any law of the United States, or by force to seize, take, or possess any property of the United States contrary to the authority thereof, they shall each be fined under this title or imprisoned not more than twenty years, or both. (Title 18, Part I, Chapter 115, § 2384)

In the **Smith Act of 1940,** Congress made it a crime to conspire to teach or advocate overthrowing the government by force or to be a member of a group that advocated the violent overthrow of the government. In 1948, a federal grand jury indicted 12 national leaders of the U.S. Communist Party. After an often-explosive trial that lasted 9 months, the leaders were convicted in 1949 (Urofsky and Finkelman 2002b, II: 758–59). In *Dennis v. U.S.* (1951), the U.S. Supreme Court upheld the convictions of the Communist Party leaders against a challenge that the Smith Act violated the First Amendment's ban on laws that "abridge" free speech and association.

 Go to the Criminal Law 9e website to find Exercise 13.2 and read the full version of *Dennis v. U.S:* www.thomsonedu.com/criminaljustice/samaha.

Sabotage

Sabotage is the crime of damaging or destroying property for the purpose of interfering with and hindering preparations for war and defense during national emergencies. Here's how the U.S. Criminal Code (2006, Title 18, Part I, Chapter 105, § 2153) defines the sabotage of war and defense materials, buildings, and utilities:

Whoever, when the United States is at war, or in times of national emergency . . . with intent to injure, interfere with, or obstruct the United States or any associate nation in preparing for or carrying on the war or defense activities, or, with reason to believe that his act may injure, interfere with, or obstruct the United States or any associate nation in preparing for or carrying on the war or defense activities, willfully injures, destroys, contaminates or infects, or attempts to so injure, destroy, contaminate or infect any war material, war premises, or war utilities, shall be fined under this title or imprisoned not more than thirty years, or both.

Other sections of Chapter 105 apply to similar acts against forts, harbors, and sea areas (§ 2152); production of defective war (§ 2154) or national defense (§ 2155) material, premises, and utilities; and destruction of national defense materials, premises, and utilities. Utilities include

railroads, railways, electric lines, roads of whatever description, any railroad or railway fixture, canal, lock, dam, wharf, pier, dock, bridge, building, structure, engine, machine, mechanical contrivance, car, vehicle, boat, aircraft, airfields, air lanes, and fixtures or appurtenances thereof, or any other means of transportation whatsoever, whereon or whereby such war material or any troops of the United States, or of any associate nation, are being or may be transported either within the limits of the United States or upon the high seas or elsewhere; and all air-conditioning systems, dams, reservoirs, aqueducts, water and gas mains and pipes, structures and buildings, whereby or in connection with which air, water or gas is being furnished, or may be furnished, to any war premises or to the Armed Forces of the United States, or any associate nation, and all electric light and power, steam or pneumatic power, telephone and telegraph plants, poles, wires, and fixtures, and wireless stations, and the buildings connected with the maintenance and operation thereof used to supply air, water, light, heat, power, or facilities of communication to any war premises or to the Armed Forces of the United States, or any associate nation. (§ 2151)

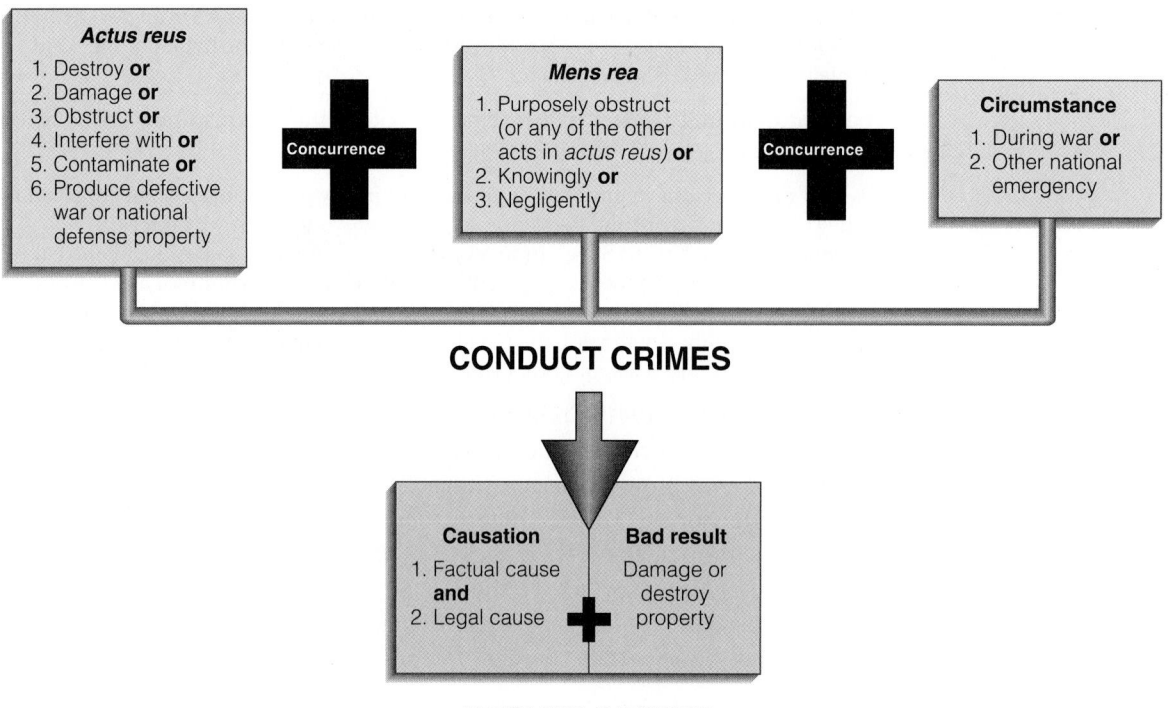

Actus reus
1. Destroy **or**
2. Damage **or**
3. Obstruct **or**
4. Interfere with **or**
5. Contaminate **or**
6. Produce defective war or national defense property

Concurrence

Mens rea
1. Purposely obstruct (or any of the other acts in *actus reus)* **or**
2. Knowingly **or**
3. Negligently

Concurrence

Circumstance
1. During war **or**
2. Other national emergency

CONDUCT CRIMES

Causation
1. Factual cause **and**
2. Legal cause

Bad result
Damage or destroy property

RESULT CRIMES

Elements of Sabotage

The code isn't completely clear about the required mental attitude. Most of the time, it's expressed as "willfully," sometimes "with intent to," and at least once "with reason to believe." Whatever the exact words, it's probably closest to the highest level of culpability—purpose (Chapter 4).

Espionage

You probably know **espionage** by its more common name "spying." Merriam-Webster (2003) defines *espionage* as

> the systematic secret observation of words and conduct . . . by special agents upon people of a foreign country or upon their activities or enterprises (for example, war production or scientific advancement in military fields) and the accumulation of information (intelligence gathering) about such people, activities, and enterprises for political or military uses.

The U.S. Code (2006, Title 18, Chapter 37, § 794) separates spying into two crimes: espionage during peace and espionage during war. The code defines espionage during peace as turning or attempting to turn over information about national defense to any foreign country with "intent or with reason to believe" the information is "to be used" to either hurt the United States or help any foreign country. The penalty is any term of imprisonment up to life or, if someone died as a result of the espionage, death (§ 794[a]).

The crime of espionage during war consists of collecting, recording, publishing, or communicating (or attempting to do any of these) "any information" about troop movements, ships, aircraft, or war materials and any other information "which might be useful to the enemy." The penalty is death or any term of imprisonment up to life (§794[b]).

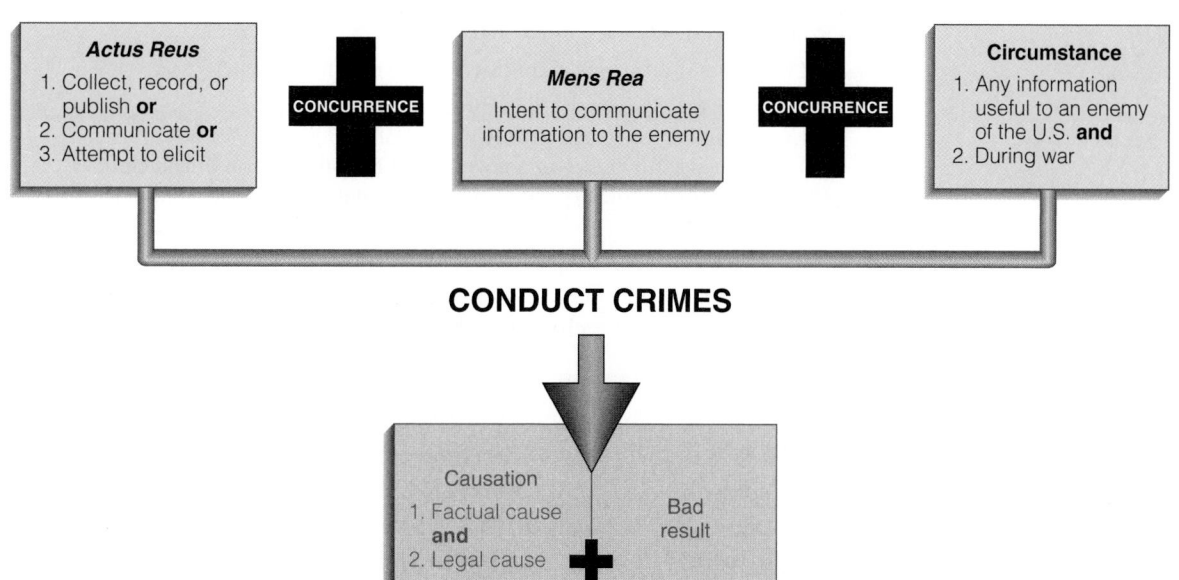

CONDUCT CRIMES

Causation
1. Factual cause **and**
2. Legal cause

Bad result

RESULT CRIMES

Elements of Espionage

ANTITERRORISM CRIMES

Go to the Criminal Law 9e website to find Exercise 13.3 and read the full text of the terrorism sections in the U.S. Code: www.thomsonedu.com/criminaljustice/samaha.

A number of sections of the U.S. Code are available for prosecuting crimes related to terrorists and terrorist organizations. (**Terrorism,** in the nonlegal sense, means the use of violence and intimidation in the pursuit of political aims.) These include the crimes we've already discussed—treason, sedition, sabotage, and espionage. Naturally, prosecutors can also use the murder, attempted murder, and conspiracy to murder provisions in the code. Then, there are some specific antiterrorism crimes—mainly, U.S. Code Chapter 113B, "Terrorism" (Title 18, Part I), the **Anti-Terrorism and Effective Death Penalty Act (AEDPA)** (1996), and the USA Patriot Act (2001). These acts include the following crimes:

1. Use of certain weapons of mass destruction (§ 2332a)

2. Acts of terrorism transcending national boundaries (§ 2332b)

3. Harboring or concealing terrorists (§ 2339)

4. Providing material support to terrorists (§ 2339A)

5. Providing material support or resources to designated foreign terrorist organizations (§ 2339B)

Before we examine these crimes, it's important that you know the elements of terrorism as they're defined in the U.S. Code (§ 2331). The code divides terrorism into two kinds: international terrorism and domestic terrorism. According to the code:

International terrorism (§ 2331[1]) consists of violent acts or acts dangerous to human life that

1. Are committed outside the United States

2. Would be crimes if they were committed inside the United States

3. Are committed, or appear to be committed, with the intent
    (a) To intimidate or coerce a civilian population;
    (b) To influence the policy of a government by intimidation or coercion; or
    (c) To affect the conduct of a government by mass destruction, assassination, or kidnapping

Domestic terrorism (§ 2331[5]) consists of the same elements, but the acts are committed inside the United States. Now that you know the definitions, let's look at some specific terrorist crimes included in the U.S. Code.

The Use of Weapons of Mass Destruction

According to the U.S. Code (2006), it's a felony punishable by up to life imprisonment, or execution if someone dies, to use, to threaten to use, or attempt or conspire to use, a weapon of mass destruction against a U.S. citizen outside the United States (Title 18, Part I, Chapter 113B, § 2332a); any person or property inside the United States (§ 2332a); any property owned, leased, or used by the U.S. government inside or outside the United States (§ 2332a[3]); or any property owned, leased, or used by a foreign government inside the United States (§ 2332a[4]). **"Weapons of mass destruction"** means "any **destructive device,**" including any:

1. Explosive, incendiary, or poison gas

2. Bomb

3. Grenade

4. Rocket that has a propellant charge over 4 ounces

5. Missile that has an explosive or incendiary charge over 1.4 ounce

6. Mine

7. Device similar to the devices listed in (1)–(6) (U.S. Code, Title 18, Part I, Chapter 44, § 921)

   The following are also defined as weapons of mass destruction:

- Any weapon intended to cause death or serious bodily injury by poisonous chemicals, or their precursors

- Any weapon involving a disease mechanism

- Any weapon designed to release radiation or radioactivity at a level dangerous to human life (§ 2332[c][2])

Acts of Terrorism Transcending National Boundaries

According to U.S. Code, § 2332b, it's a felony for anyone whose **"conduct transcends national boundaries"**—that is, acts that take place partly outside and partly inside the United States—to

1. Kill, kidnap, maim, assault resulting in serious bodily injury, or assault with a deadly weapon any person within the United States; or

2. "Create a substantial risk of serious bodily injury to any other person" by destroying or damaging any structure, conveyance, or other property within the United States; or

3. Threaten, or attempt, or conspire to commit (1) or (2) if the following circumstance elements are present:
   a. The victim, or intended victim is the U.S. government, a member of the uniformed services, or any official, officer, employee, or agent of the legislative, executive, or judicial branches, or of any department or agency, of the United States.
   b. The structure, conveyance, or other property is owned by or leased by the United States

The penalties are:

1. Death or up to life imprisonment for killing or for death resulting from the conduct

2. Up to life imprisonment for kidnapping

3. Up to 35 years for maiming

4. Up to 30 years for assault with a deadly weapon or assault resulting in serious bodily injury

5. Up to 25 years for damaging or destroying property

Harboring or Concealing Terrorists

Section 2339 of the U.S. Code provides:

> Whoever harbors or conceals any person who he knows, or has reasonable grounds to believe, has committed, or is about to commit, an offense under section 32 (relating to destruction of aircraft or aircraft facilities), section 175 (relating to biological weapons), section 229 (relating to chemical weapons), section 831 (relating to nuclear materials), paragraph (2) or (3) of section 844(f) (relating to arson and bombing of government property risking or causing injury or death), section 1366(a) (relating to the destruction of an energy facility), section 2280 (relating to violence against maritime navigation), section 2332a (relating to weapons of mass destruction), or section 2332b (relating to acts of terrorism transcending national boundaries) of this title, section 236(a) (relating to sabotage of nuclear facilities or fuel) of the Atomic Energy Act of 1954 (42 U.S.C. 2284(a)), or section 46502 (relating to aircraft piracy) of title 49, shall be fined under this title or imprisoned not more than ten years, or both.

The *actus reus* consists of harboring or concealing persons who have committed or are about to commit a list of terrorist-related crimes. The *mens rea* requires knowing (or that a reasonable person should have known) the *actus reus* was about to be committed. The penalty is a fine or up to 10 years of imprisonment.

All of the crimes we've covered so far in this chapter are *available* to the U.S. government for prosecuting suspected terrorists and convicting guilty ones. But, as of August, 2006, the only person convicted of any of those crimes has been Zacarias Moussaoui, the so-called 20th hijacker. After a trial lasting more than four years, Moussaoui eventually pleaded guilty to all six crimes he was charged with, all of them conspiracies (U.S. Department of Justice 2001):

1. Conspiracy to commit acts of terrorism

2. Conspiracy to commit aircraft piracy

3. Conspiracy to destroy aircraft

4. Conspiracy to use airplanes as weapons of mass destruction

5. Conspiracy to murder government employees

6. Conspiracy to destroy property

TABLE 13.1	Types of "Material Support"

Currency or monetary instruments or financial securities

Financial services

Lodging

Training

Expert advice or assistance

Safe houses

False documentation or identification

Communications equipment

Facilities

Weapons

Lethal substances, explosives

Personnel

Transportation

Other physical assets, except medicine or religious materials

In the penalty phase of the trial, the jury declined to recommend his execution, recommending life imprisonment instead. Most of the 9/11 families seemed satisfied with the jury's decision; most professionals didn't.

There are a few other cases not yet decided, but the government's clear charges of choice are "providing material support or resources to individual terrorists" (U.S. Code 2003, Title 18, Part I, Chapter 113B, § 2339A), and/or to "terrorist organizations" (§ 2339B) (Roth 2003; Table 13.1). Let's turn to those most important crimes now.

Providing "Material Support" to Terrorists and/or Terrorist Organizations

The felony of providing **material support** was first created in the 1996 Anti-Terrorism and Effective Death Penalty Act (AEDPA) (§ 323), which was aimed at *domestic* terrorist acts. It was passed after Timothy McVeigh bombed the federal building in Oklahoma City, Oklahoma.

The AEDPA felony, with harsher penalties, became Sections 2339A and B of the 2001 USA Patriot Act. The Patriot Act is a huge law (300+ pages long) passed with lightning speed only 6 weeks after the September 11 attacks. Most of the act deals with criminal procedure, surveillance and intelligence, law enforcement information sharing, search and seizure, interrogation, and detention. Of course, these are extremely important, but we won't discuss them here because they're subjects for criminal procedure, not criminal law.

Section 2339A makes it a federal felony to provide, attempt, or conspire to "provide material support or resources" to commit any of a long list of federal crimes. It aims at providing support to *individual* terrorists. Section 2339B bans providing, attempting to provide, or conspiring to provide "material support or resources to a designated foreign terrorist *organization*."

The crimes of providing material support to individuals or organizations are proximity crimes. **Proximity crimes** ban conduct because of its closeness to other crimes—in this case, 44 other federal crimes individual terrorists or terrorist organizations

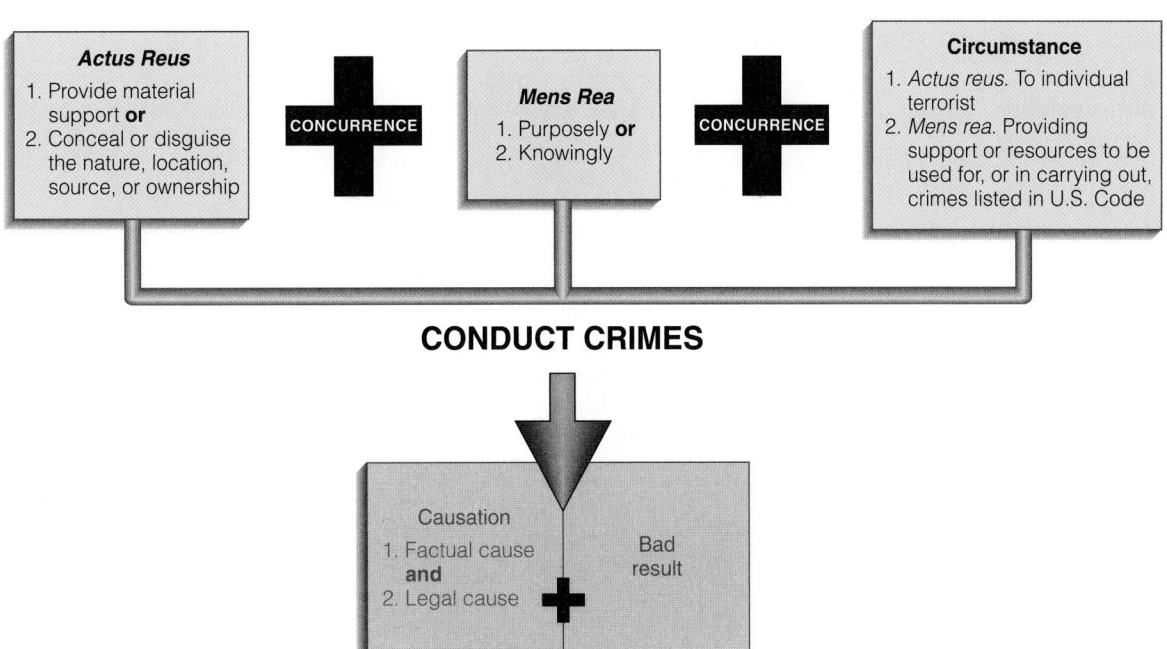

Elements of Material Support to Terrorists

might commit (Doyle 2005, 1–2, 7–8). They aim at "nipping terrorism in the bud." They try to prevent what we most want to prevent—killing and destruction by terrorist acts.

A few decisions in the U.S. District Courts and U.S. Courts of Appeals have ruled that parts of the material support provisions violate the U.S. Constitution (Table 13.2). These same decisions have also applied a demanding interpretation of "knowingly," the *mens rea* element in the material support provisions.

TABLE 13.2   Material Support Provisions

SEC. 2339A.—PROVIDING MATERIAL SUPPORT TO TERRORISTS

Offense.—Whoever provides material support or resources or conceals or disguises the nature, location, source, or ownership of material support or resources, knowing or intending that they are to be used in preparation for, or in carrying out, a violation of [a list of provisions related to terrorist acts in the U.S. Code] or in preparation for, or in carrying out, the concealment or an escape from the commission of any such violation, or attempts or conspires to do such an act, shall be fined under this title, imprisoned not more than 15 years, or both, and, if the death of any person results, shall be imprisoned for any term of years or for life. . . .

Definition.—In this section, the term "material support or resources" means . . . [the list of items in Table 13.1].

SEC. 2339B.—PROVIDING MATERIAL SUPPORT OR RESOURCES TO DESIGNATED FOREIGN TERRORIST ORGANIZATIONS

(a) *Prohibited Activities.*—
 (1) Unlawful conduct.—
 Whoever, within the United States or subject to the jurisdiction of the United States, knowingly provides material support or resources to a foreign terrorist organization, or attempts or conspires to do so, shall be fined under this title or imprisoned not more than 15 years, or both, and, if the death of any person results, shall be imprisoned for any term of years or for life.

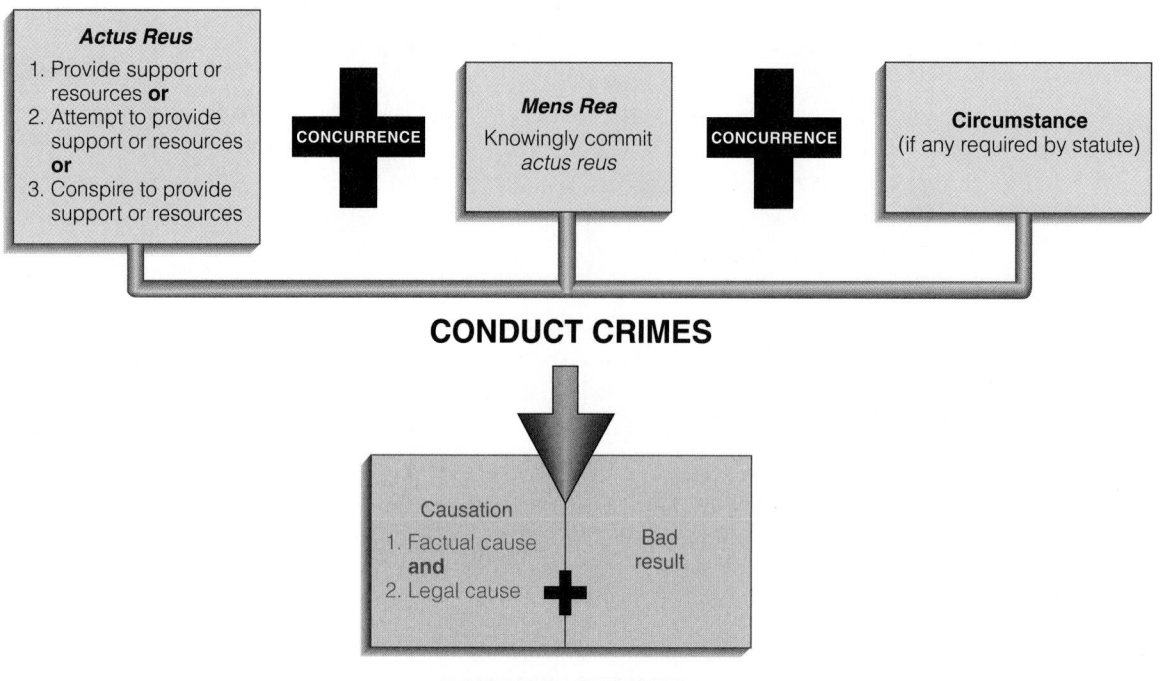

CONDUCT CRIMES

Causation
1. Factual cause
and
2. Legal cause

Bad result

RESULT CRIMES

Elements of Material Support to Terrorist Organizations

None of the cases has reached the U.S. Supreme Court, but a few have reached and been decided in the U.S. District Courts and the U.S. Courts of Appeals. One of the cases that challenged the material support sections' constitutionality was the prosecution of John Walker Lindh, the "American Taliban." Lindh attended a military training camp in Pakistan run by Harakut ul-Mujahideen, whose followers had been designated by the U.S. Secretary of State as a "terrorist group dedicated to an extremist view of Islam"; traveled to Afghanistan; and joined the Taliban. There, he informed Taliban personnel "that he was an American and that he wanted to go to the front lines to fight." Lindh was captured by the Northern Alliance, an ally of the United States in the war in Afghanistan. Later, he was indicted for providing and conspiring to provide material support to Harakut ul-Mujahideen.

In *U.S. v. Lindh*, Lindh tried and failed to get the indictment dismissed on the ground that the material support provisions are void for vagueness and violate the First Amendment because of overbreadth (Chapter 2). His case, heard in the U.S. District Court, Eastern District of Virginia, never went to trial because Lindh reached a guilty plea agreement with the United States. According to the terms of the agreement, Lindh pleaded guilty to two crimes ("supplying services to the Taliban" and "carrying an explosive during the commission of a felony") in exchange for receiving less than a life sentence. He was sentenced to 10 years for each offense, to be served consecutively (one after the other), and 3 years of supervised release following his 20 years in prison and fined $250,000 for each offense (*U.S. v. Lindh* 2002).

Lindh's acts were clearly within the *actus reus* of "providing material support" to al Qaeda and the Taliban—he trained, carried a weapon and a grenade, and fought on their side. And the First Amendment clearly didn't protect his association with them. Other cases aren't so clear. Several federal court decisions have ruled that parts of ßß 2339 A and B violate the First Amendment rights of free speech and assembly and that they're void for vagueness (Chapter 2).

In addition to the constitutional challenges, some cases have also read a very high standard of *mens rea* into the sections. Particularly troubling to some courts were the uncertain meaning of "training," "personnel," "expert advice or assistance," and "service." In *Humanitarian Law Project v. Reno* (2000), the Ninth Circuit U.S. Court of Appeals declared "personnel" vague because it might include "the efforts of a simple advocate" (1137–38); "training" because it might include innocent academic instruction (1138); and "expert advice or assistance" because it might, like "training" and "personnel," include constitutionally protected First Amendment speech (1185).

To cure these constitutional and interpretation problems, Congress amended the "material support" provisions in ß 6603 of the Intelligence Reform and Prevention of Terrorism Act of 2004 (Doyle 2005, 2). Section 6603 enacted new definitions of the uncertain terms (Doyle 2006, 2–3):

> *Training.* The term "training" means instruction or teaching designed to impart a specific skill, as opposed to general knowledge.
>
> *Expert advice or assistance.* The term "expert advice or assistance" means advice or assistance from scientific, technical, or other specialized knowledge.
>
> *Personnel.* No person may be prosecuted under this section in connection with the term "personnel" unless that person has knowingly provided, attempted to provide, or conspired to provide a foreign terrorist organization with 1 or more individuals (who may include himself) to work under that terrorist organization's direction or control, or otherwise direct the operation of that organization. Individuals who act entirely independently of the foreign terrorist organization shall not be considered to be working under the organization's direction and control.

The case excerpt, *Humanitarian Law Project v. Gonzales* (2005), is the first case decided since Congress tried to stave off constitutional challenges to the material support sections. The case gave Congress's efforts "mixed grades." Section 6603 cured the vagueness problem in "personnel" but not in "training" or in "expert advice or assistance." It added that "service" was also vague.

CASE — *Are the "Material Support" Provisions Vague or Not?*

Humanitarian Law Project v. Gonzales
205 F.Supp. 2d 1130 (C.D. Cal. 2005)

HISTORY

The Humanitarian Law Project, Ralph Fertig, Ilankai Thamil Sangam, Dr. Nagalingam Jeyalingam, World Tamil Coordinating Committee, Federation of Tamil Sangams of North America, and Tamil Welfare and Human Rights Committee (collectively, "Plaintiffs") desire to provide support for the lawful activities of two organizations that have been designated as foreign terrorist organizations.

Plaintiffs seek summary judgment and an injunction to prohibit the enforcement of the criminal ban on providing material support to such organizations. Alberto Gonzales (in his official capacity as United States Attorney General), the United States Department of Justice, Condoleeza Rice (in her official capacity as Secretary of the Department of State), and the United States Department of State (collectively, "Defendants") bring a motion to dismiss and cross-motion for summary judgment.

After considering the parties' submissions, the arguments of counsel, and the case file, the Court hereby denies Defendants' motion to dismiss and GRANTS IN PART and DENIES IN PART the parties' cross-motions for summary judgment.

COLLINS, J.

This action involves a challenge to portions of the Antiterrorism and Effective Death Penalty Act and the

Intelligence Reform and Terrorism Prevention Act. Specifically, the parties seek summary judgment regarding the constitutionality of the prohibition on providing material support or resources, including "training," "expert advice or assistance," "personnel," and "service," to designated foreign terrorist organizations.

FACTS

Plaintiffs are five organizations and two United States citizens seeking to provide support to the lawful, nonviolent activities of the Partiya Karkeran Kurdistan (Kurdistan Workers' Party) ("PKK") and the Liberation Tigers of Tamil Eelam ("LTTE"). The PKK and the LTTE have been designated as foreign terrorist organizations.

The PKK is a political organization representing the interests of the Kurds in Turkey, with the goal of achieving self-determination for the Kurds in Southeastern Turkey. Plaintiffs allege that the Turkish government has subjected the Kurds to human rights abuses and discrimination for decades. The PKK's efforts on behalf of the Kurds include political organizing and advocacy, providing social services and humanitarian aid to Kurdish refugees, and engaging in military combat with Turkish armed forces.

Plaintiffs wish to support the PKK's lawful and nonviolent activities towards achieving self-determination. Specifically, Plaintiffs seek to provide training in the use of humanitarian and international law for the peaceful resolution of disputes, engage in political advocacy on behalf of the Kurds living in Turkey, and teach the PKK how to petition for relief before representative bodies like the United Nations.

The LTTE represents the interests of Tamils in Sri Lanka, with the goal of achieving self-determination for the Tamil residents of Tamil Eelam in the Northern and Eastern provinces of Sri Lanka. Plaintiffs allege that the Tamils constitute an ethnic group that has for decades been subjected to human rights abuses and discriminatory treatment by the Sinhalese, who have governed Sri Lanka since the nation gained its independence in 1948. The LTTE's activities include political organizing and advocacy, providing social services and humanitarian aid, defending the Tamil people from human rights abuses, and using military force against the government of Sri Lanka.

Plaintiffs wish to support the LTTE's lawful and nonviolent activities towards furthering the human rights and well-being of Tamils in Sri Lanka. In particular, Plaintiffs emphasize the desperately increased need for aid following the tsunamis that devastated the Sri Lanka region in December 2004, especially in Tamil areas along the Northeast Coast. Plaintiffs seek to provide training in the presentation of claims to mediators and international bodies for tsunami-related aid, offer legal expertise in negotiating peace agreements between the LTTE and the Sri Lankan government, and engage in political advocacy on behalf of Tamils living in Sri Lanka.

In 1996, Congress enacted the Antiterrorism and Effective Death Penalty Act (the "AEDPA") proscribing all material support and resources to designated foreign terrorist organizations in the interests of law enforcement and national security. Specifically, the AEDPA sought to prevent the United States from becoming a base for terrorist fundraising. Congress recognized that terrorist groups are often structured to include political or humanitarian components in addition to terrorist components. Such an organizational structure allows terrorist groups to raise funds under the guise of political or humanitarian causes. Those funds can then be diverted to terrorist activities.

Following the September 11, 2001, terrorist attacks on the World Trade Center Twin Towers in New York, Congress enacted the Uniting and Strengthening America by Providing Appropriate Tools Required to Intercept and Obstruct Terrorism Act (the "USA PATRIOT Act") and the Intelligence Reform and Terrorism Prevention Act (the "IRTPA") in 2001 and 2004, respectively, to further its goal of eliminating material support or resources to foreign terrorist organizations. The USA PATRIOT Act and the IRTPA amended the AEDPA.

While Plaintiffs are committed to providing the above-mentioned support, they fear doing so would expose them to criminal prosecution under the AEDPA for providing material support and resources to foreign terrorist organizations. Accordingly, Plaintiffs challenge the portion of the AEDPA, as amended by the IRTPA, providing as follows:

> Whoever knowingly provides material support or resources to a foreign terrorist organization, or attempts or conspires to do so, shall be fined under this title or imprisoned not more than 15 years, or both, and, if the death of any person results, shall be imprisoned for any term of years or for life. 18 U.S.C. ß 2339B(a).

The AEDPA, as amended by the USA PATRIOT Act and the IRTPA, defines "material support or resources" as:

> any property, tangible or intangible, or service, including currency or monetary instruments or financial securities, financial services, lodging, *training, expert advice or assistance,* safe houses, false documentation or identification, communications equipment, facilities, weapons, lethal substances, explosives, *personnel* (1 or more individuals who may be or include oneself), and transportation, except medicine or religious materials. 18 U.S.C. ß 2339A(b)(1) (emphasis added). . . .

The Prohibition on Providing Material Support or Resources Does Not Violate the Fifth Amendment

. . . Plaintiffs argue that the AEDPA's prohibition on providing material support or resources to foreign terrorist organizations violates due process under the Fifth Amendment. Specifically, Plaintiffs contend that the prohibition imposes vicarious criminal liability without requiring proof of specific intent to further the terrorist activities of foreign terrorist organizations. Plaintiffs, therefore, urge the Court to read a specific intent *mens rea* requirement into 18 U.S.C. ß 2339B in order to avoid Fifth Amendment due process concerns.

Defendants, in contrast, assert that the AEDPA does not impose vicarious criminal liability, but instead prohibits only the conduct of giving material support or resources to foreign terrorist organizations. Moreover, Defendants point to Congressional intent regarding the *mens rea* required and Congress's wide latitude to legislate in the foreign affairs arena. Defendants also contend that the Ninth Circuit previously rejected the specific intent argument in [a previous case involving Humanitarian Law Project]. . . . Finally, Defendants note that the IRTPA amendment requiring that a donor know that the recipient of the material support is a foreign terrorist organization adequately addresses Plaintiffs' concerns regarding specific intent.

. . . The Court finds that the AEDPA does not violate due process under the Fifth Amendment and, therefore, declines to read a specific intent requirement into the statute. . . . The clear and unambiguous Congressional intent to exclude a specific intent requirement precludes a judicial interpretation of a specific intent element. Finally, the statute's current requirement that a donor know that the recipient of material support is a foreign terrorist organization eliminates any Fifth Amendment due process concerns. . . .

The *Mens Rea* Requirement in ß 2339B Satisfies Any Due Process Concerns

. . . Congress's recent clarification of the *mens rea* required under ß 2339B satisfies any due process issues under the Fifth Amendment. Significantly, the Ninth Circuit in [the previous HLP case] . . . held that it was sufficient to "avoid due process concerns" to require that the government "prove beyond a reasonable doubt that the accused knew that the organization was designated as a foreign terrorist organization or that the accused knew of the organization's unlawful activities that caused it to be so designated." The AEDPA, as amended by the IRTPA, incorporates this reading of *mens rea* and prohibits the provision of material support to a recipient that the donor knows is a foreign terrorist organization. Accordingly, Congress's clarification of the *mens rea* requirement satisfies the notion of personal guilt under the Due Process Clause because an offender must know that he or she was materially supporting a foreign terrorist organization.

The Prohibitions on "Training," "Expert Advice or Assistance," and "Service" Are Impermissibly Vague, but "Personnel" Is Permissible

. . . A challenge to a statute based on vagueness grounds requires the court to consider whether the statute is "sufficiently clear so as not to cause persons 'of common intelligence . . . necessarily [to] guess at its meaning and [to] differ as to its application.'" Vague statutes are void for three reasons: "(1) to avoid punishing people for behavior that they could not have known was illegal; (2) to avoid subjective enforcement of the laws based on 'arbitrary and discriminatory enforcement' by government officers; and (3) to avoid any chilling effect on the exercise of First Amendment freedoms."

Perhaps the most important factor affecting the clarity that the Constitution demands of a law is whether it threatens to inhibit the exercise of constitutionally protected rights. If, for example, the law interferes with the right of free speech or of association, a more stringent vagueness test should apply. The requirement of clarity is enhanced when criminal sanctions are at issue or when the statute abuts upon sensitive areas of basic First Amendment freedoms. Thus, under the Due Process Clause, a criminal statute is void for vagueness if it "fails to give a person of ordinary intelligence fair notice that his contemplated conduct is forbidden by the statute." A criminal statute must therefore "define the criminal offense with sufficient definiteness that ordinary people can understand what conduct is prohibited. . . .

After considering the arguments, the Court finds that the terms "training," "expert advice or assistance," and "service" are impermissibly vague under the Fifth Amendment. With respect to the term "personnel," the Court finds that the IRTPA amendment to "personnel" sufficiently cures the previous vagueness concerns. The Court addresses each of these terms separately below.

"Training" Is Impermissibly Vague

This Court previously concluded that "training," an undefined term, was impermissibly vague because it easily reached protected activities, such as teaching how to seek redress for human rights violations before the United Nations. The IRTPA amendment now defines "training" as "instruction or teaching designed to impart a specific skill, as opposed to general knowledge." 18 U.S.C. ß 2339A(b)(2).

Plaintiffs contend that the amendment to "training" exacerbates the vagueness problem because Plaintiffs must now guess whether teaching international law, peacemaking, or lobbying constitutes a "specific skill" or "general knowledge." Defendants respond that training encompasses a broad range of conduct, ranging from flying lessons to training in the use of weapons.

The Court agrees with Plaintiffs that the IRTPA amendment to "training" (distinguishing between "specific skill" and "general knowledge") fails to cure the vagueness concerns that the Court previously identified. Even as amended, the term "training" is not sufficiently clear so that persons of ordinary intelligence can reasonably understand what conduct the statute prohibits. Moreover, the IRTPA amendment leaves the term "training" impermissibly vague because it easily encompasses protected speech and advocacy, such as teaching international law for peacemaking resolutions or how to petition the United Nations to seek redress for human rights violations.

Defendants contend that the AEDPA prohibits Plaintiffs from providing "advice or training 'on how to engage in human rights advocacy on their own behalf and on how to use international law to seek redress for human rights violations.'"

This position is in direct contrast to the Ninth Circuit and this Court's holdings, which recognized that such activities are protected under the First Amendment rights to free speech and association. In fact, the Ninth Circuit indicated in HLP I that limiting "training" to the "imparting of skills" would be insufficient because such a definition would encompass protected speech and advocacy activities. The Ninth Circuit explained:

> Again, it is easy to imagine protected expression that falls within the bounds of this term. For example, a plaintiff who wishes to instruct members of a designated group on how to petition the United Nations to give aid to their group could plausibly decide that such protected expression falls within the scope of the term "training." The government insists that the term is best understood to forbid the imparting of skills to foreign terrorist organizations through training. Yet, presumably, this definition would encompass teaching international law to members of designated organizations. The result would be different if the term "training" were qualified to include only military training or training in terrorist activities. *HLP I*, 205 F.3d at 1138.

"Training" implicates, and potentially chills, Plaintiffs' protected expressive activities and imposes criminal sanctions of up to fifteen years imprisonment without sufficiently defining the prohibited conduct for ordinary people to understand. Therefore, the Court finds that "training" fails to satisfy the enhanced requirement of clarity for statutes touching upon protected activities under the First Amendment or imposing criminal sanctions.

"Expert Advice or Assistance" Is Impermissibly Vague

The Court previously found "expert advice or assistance," an undefined term, to be impermissibly vague under the same analysis it applied to "training" and "personnel" because "expert advice or assistance" could be construed to include First Amendment protected activities. Plaintiffs seek to offer includes advocacy and associational activities protected by the First Amendment, which Defendants concede are not prohibited under the USA PATRIOT Act.").

The IRTPA amendments define "expert advice or assistance" as "scientific, technical, *or other specialized knowledge*." 18 U.S.C. ß 2339A(b)(3) [emphasis added]. Plaintiffs contend that the "specialized knowledge" portion of this definition is vague because it merely repeats what an expert is and provides no additional clarity. Similar to their attack on the term "training," Plaintiffs assert that they must now guess whether their expert advice constitutes "specialized knowledge." Defendants argue that "expert advice or assistance" is not vague because the definition is derived from the established Federal Rules of Evidence regarding expert testimony.

The Court agrees with Plaintiffs that the IRTPA amendment to "expert advice or assistance" (adding "specialized knowledge") does not cure the vagueness issues. Even as amended, the statute fails to identify the prohibited conduct in a manner that persons of ordinary intelligence can reasonably understand. Similar to the Court's discussion of "training" above, "expert advice or assistance" remains impermissibly vague because "specialized knowledge" includes the same protected activities that "training" covers, such as teaching international law for peacemaking resolutions or how to petition the United Nations to seek redress for human rights violations. Moreover, the Federal Rules of Evidence's inclusion of the phrase "scientific, technical, or other specialized knowledge" does not clarify the term "expert advice or assistance" for the average person with no background in law. Accordingly, the Court finds that the "expert advice or assistance" fails to provide fair notice of the prohibited conduct and is impermissibly vague. . . .

"Service" Is Impermissibly Vague

Plaintiffs attack the IRTPA's insertion of the undefined term "service" to the definition of "material support or resources" on vagueness grounds. According to Plaintiffs, the prohibition on "service" is at least as sweeping as the prohibitions on "training," "expert advice or assistance," and "personnel," as each of these could be construed as services. Defendants concede that the term "service" is broad, but argue that it is a common term that the dictionary defines (among other definitions) as "an act done for the benefit or at the command of another" or "useful labor that does not produce a tangible commodity." Defendants' Opposition at 21. Plaintiffs reply that Defendants' own definition is vague and would infringe on all sorts of speech and advocacy done for the benefit of another that is clearly protected by the First Amendment.

In addition, Plaintiffs note that Defendants' argument that any activity done *"for the benefit of another"* would violate the ban on "services" contradicts Defendants' concession that Plaintiffs could freely engage in "human rights and political advocacy on *behalf of* the PKK and the Kurds before any forum of their choosing." Plaintiffs argue that this supposed distinction proves their point. In other words, "service" is impermissibly vague because it forces Plaintiffs to guess whether their human rights and political advocacy constitutes action taken "on behalf of another," which Defendants concede is protected action, or "for the benefit of another," which Defendants argue is prohibited.

The Court finds that the undefined term "service" in the IRTPA is impermissibly vague, as the statute defines "service" to include "training" or "expert advice or assistance," terms the Court has already ruled are vague. Like "training" and "expert advice or assistance," "it is easy to imagine protected expression that falls within the bounds of" the term "service." Moreover, there is no readily apparent distinction between taking action "on behalf of another" and "for the benefit of another." Defendants' contradictory arguments on the scope of the prohibition only underscore the vagueness. As with "training" and "expert advice or assistance," the term "service" fails to meet the enhanced requirement of clarity for statutes affecting protected expressive activities and imposing criminal sanctions.

"Personnel" Is Not Impermissibly Vague

The Court previously found personnel to be impermissibly vague because it "broadly encompasses the type of human resources which Plaintiffs seek to provide, including the distribution of LTTE literature and informational materials and working directly with PKK members at peace conferences and other meetings." The Ninth Circuit affirmed, finding that the ban on personnel "blurs the line between protected expression and unprotected conduct," as an individual "who advocates the cause of the PKK could be seen as supplying them with personnel."

The IRTPA amendment now limits prosecution for providing "personnel" to the provision of "one or more individuals" to a foreign terrorist organization "to work under that terrorist organization's direction or control or to organize, manage, supervise, or otherwise direct the operation of that organization." 18 U.S.C. ß 2339B(h). Further, the statute states that "[i]ndividuals who act entirely independently of the foreign terrorist organization to advance its goals or objectives shall not be considered to be working under the foreign terrorist organization's direction and control." Plaintiffs argue that the new language distinguishing between acting under an organization's "direction and control" and acting "independently" still impinges on protected activities. Defendants respond that the IRTPA amendments use clear terms that are readily understandable to persons of ordinary intelligence.

The Court finds that the IRTPA amendment sufficiently narrows the term "personnel" to provide fair notice of the prohibited conduct. Limiting the provision of personnel to those working under the "direction or control" of a foreign terrorist organization or actually managing or supervising a foreign terrorist organization operation sufficiently identifies the prohibited conduct such that persons of ordinary intelligence can reasonably understand and avoid such conduct.

The Prohibitions on "Training," "Expert Advice or Assistance," "Personnel," and "Service" Are Not Substantially Overbroad

Plaintiffs also contend that the prohibitions on "training," "expert advice or assistance," "personnel," and "service" are sweepingly overbroad because they proscribe a substantial amount of speech activity that is protected by the First Amendment.

. . . Under the overbreadth doctrine, a "showing that a law punishes a substantial amount of protected free speech, judged in relation to the statute's plainly legitimate sweep, suffices to invalidate *all* enforcement of that law, until and unless a limiting construction or partial invalidation so narrows it as to remove the seeming threat or deterrence to constitutionally protected expression.

However, the Supreme Court has recognized that "there comes a point at which the chilling effect of an overbroad law, significant though it may be, cannot justify prohibiting all enforcement of that law—particularly a law that reflects 'legitimate state interests in maintaining comprehensive controls over harmful, constitutionally unprotected conduct.'" Accordingly, the Supreme Court requires that the "law's application to protected speech be 'substantial,' not only in an absolute sense, but also relative to the scope of the law's plainly legitimate applications before applying the 'strong medicine' of the overbreadth invalidation."

. . . Plaintiffs have failed to establish that the prohibitions on "training," "personnel," "expert advice or assistance," and "service" are substantially overbroad, as the prohibitions are content-neutral and their purpose of deterring and punishing the provision of material support to foreign terrorist organizations is legitimate. Further, the statute's application to protected speech is not "substantial" both in an absolute sense and relative to the scope of the law's plainly legitimate applications. The Court, therefore, declines to apply the "strong medicine" of the overbreadth doctrine, finding instead that as-applied litigation will provide a sufficient safeguard for any potential First Amendment violation. . . .

CONCLUSION

. . .

1. The Court finds that the lack of a specific intent requirement to further the terrorist activities of foreign terrorist organizations in the AEDPA's prohibition on providing material support or resources to foreign terrorist organizations does not violate due process under the Fifth Amendment. The Court therefore GRANTS Defendants' motion and DENIES Plaintiffs' motion on this ground.

2. The Court finds that the AEDPA's prohibitions on material support or resources in the form of "training," "expert advice or assistance," "personnel," and "service" are not overbroad under the First Amendment. The Court therefore GRANTS Defendants' motion and DENIES Plaintiffs' motion on this ground.

3. The Court finds that the term "personnel" is not impermissibly vague under the Fifth Amendment. The Court therefore GRANTS Defendants' motion and DENIES Plaintiffs' motion on this ground.

4. The Court finds that the terms "training"; "expert advice or assistance" in the form of "specialized knowledge"; and "service" are impermissibly vague under the Fifth Amendment. The Court therefore

GRANTS Plaintiffs' motion and DENIES Defendants' motion on this ground. . . .

Accordingly, Defendants, their officers, agents, employees, and successors are ENJOINED from enforcing 18 U.S.C. ß 2339B's prohibition on providing "training"; "expert advice or assistance" in the form of "specialized knowledge"; or "service" to the PKK or the LTTE against any of the named Plaintiffs or their members. The Court declines to grant a nationwide injunction.

IT IS SO ORDERED.

Questions

1. Identify the terms in the material assistance provisions that the defendants challenged as violating the Constitution.

2. Summarize the court's arguments for its decision about the constitutionality of each of the challenged terms.

3. Are the terms clear to an ordinary reasonable person? Are they clear to you? What's the difference between the two? Explain your answers.

SUMMARY

I. The criminal law during national emergencies

A. The USA Patriot Act reflects conflicting values in our constitutional democracy.
1. On the one hand, there's a need for public safety and security.
2. But there's also a strong desire for privacy and freedom.
B. Problem: How can the government apply enduring principles of criminal law when terrorists and terrorist groups have killed and are still trying to kill Americans at home and around the world?
C. Allegiance and loyalty were especially critical during national emergencies.
D. The Constitution was written during a time of emergency.

II. Treason

A. Treason is the only crime defined in the Constitution.
B. After the Revolution, the fragile, new government needed time for loyalty and allegiance to take hold.
1. England, Spain, France, and Native American nations threatened from all directions.
2. Traitors, spies, and other disloyal individuals and groups threatened from within.
C. The authors of the Constitution had mixed feelings about treason.
1. They were tough on traitors who broke allegiance and were disloyal.
2. Their own ancestors had fled from religious persecution and prosecution for treason.
3. Treason was broadly defined in England to include thoughts and feelings that led to prosecution of innocent people.
4. The authors of the Constitution had two worries:
   a. They feared repression of peaceful opposition to government.
   b. They wanted to avoid conviction of the innocent because of perjury, passion, and/or insufficient evidence.
D. Treason is defined in the body of the Constitution, where it's tough to change.
E. Elements
1. *Actus reus*
   a. Treason requires levying war against the United States.
   b. It also requires giving aid and comfort to enemies of the United States.

2. *Mens rea*
   a. Defendants must have had the intent to give aid and comfort.
   b. And it must have been for the very purpose of betraying the United States by means of that aid and comfort.
3. Proof
   a. Two witnesses to the *actus reus* are required.
   b. Confession in open court is also proof.

III. More crimes against disloyalty
   A. Sedition
   1. *Sedition* is the ancient crime of "stirring up" treason (advocate violent overthrow of government) by
      a. Speech
      b. Writing (libel)
      c. Conspiracy
   2. In the U.S. Code, sedition includes only advocating the violent overthrow of the government.
   B. Sabotage
   1. *Sabotage* is damaging and/or destroying property related to war and defense material, buildings, and utilities (which includes transportation and harbors).
   2. It's also producing defective property related to war and defense.
   3. Elements
      a. *Actus reus*
         (1) Destroy
         (2) Damage
         (3) Obstruct
         (4) Interfere
         (5) Contaminate
         (6) Produce defective war or national defense materials
      b. *Mens rea*
         (1) The defendant has to purposely obstruct (or commit any other acts in *actus reus*).
         (2) The defendant has to knowingly obstruct (or commit any other acts in *actus reus*).
         (3) The defendant has to negligently obstruct (or commit any other acts in *actus reus*).
      c. Circumstance
         (1) The sabotage has to take place when the United States is at war.
         (2) It can also take place during a national emergency.
   C. Espionage (spying)
   1. *Espionage* is secret intelligence gathering by spies about foreign people, activities, and enterprises for political and military uses.
   2. U.S. Code espionage elements (at any time)
      a. *Actus reus*
         (1) Communicate
         (2) Deliver
         (3) Transmit
         (4) Attempt to (1), (2), or (3) intelligence (information harmful to the U.S.)

b. *Mens rea*
    (1) The defendant has to injure purposely.
    (2) The defendant has to have reason to believe use of the intelligence will cause injury.
c. Circumstances
    (1) Intelligence was provided to a foreign government.
    (2) Intelligence was provided to a foreign faction or party.
    (3) Intelligence was provided to a foreign military or naval force.
    (4) Intelligence was provided to a foreign representative, officer, agent, employee, subject, or citizen.

3. U.S. Code espionage elements (during war)
  a. *Actus reus*
    (1) Collect any intelligence useful to the enemy.
    (2) Publish it.
    (3) Communicate it.
    (4) Attempt to do so.
  b. The *mens rea* is the intent to communicate information to the enemy.
  c. The circumstance is that it's a time of war.

IV. Antiterrorism crimes
  A. The general crimes applicable to terrorist acts are treason, sedition, sabotage, and espionage.
  B. Murder, attempted murder, and conspiracy to murder also apply.
  C. Use of weapons of mass destruction
    1. Elements
      a. *Actus reus*
        (1) Use
        (2) Threaten to use
        (3) Attempt or conspire to use
      b. The *mens rea* is without lawful authority (voluntarily).
      c. Circumstance(s)
        (1) Use against a U.S. "national" outside the United States.
        (2) Use against any "person" inside the United States.
        (3) Use against any U.S. government property inside or outside the United States.
        (4) Use against any foreign government's property inside the United States.
    2. The definition of *weapon of mass destruction* is
      a. "Any destructive device"—explosive, incendiary, poison gas; bomb; grenade; rocket; missile; mine; or similar device
      b. Any weapon intended to cause death or serious bodily injury by poisonous chemicals or precursor
      c. Any weapon involving a disease mechanism
      d. Any weapon designed to release radiation or radioactivity at levels dangerous to human life
  D. Acts of terrorism transcending national boundaries
    1. The definition is conduct occurring partly inside and partly outside the United States.
    2. It includes three types of conduct (*actus reus*):
      a. Committing violent crimes against any person inside the United States

    b. Creating a substantial risk of serious bodily injury by destroying or damaging property within the United States

    c. Threatening, or attempting, or conspiring to commit (a) or (b)

3. Circumstances

    a. The victims are the U.S. government; members of uniformed services; or officials, employees, and agents of the United States.

    b. The acts target property owned or leased by the United States.

4. Penalties

    a. Death for killing or death resulting from the act

    b. Up to life for kidnapping

    c. Up to 35 years for maiming

    d. Up to 30 years for assault

    e. Up to 25 years for damaging or destroying property

E. Harboring or concealing terrorists

1. The *actus reus* is harboring or concealing persons who have committed or are about to commit a list of terrorist-related crimes.

2. The *mens rea* is knowing (or a reasonable person should have known) the crimes in (1) were going to be committed.

3. The penalty is a fine or up to 10 years of imprisonment.

F. Providing material support to terrorists (§ 2339A) and terrorist organizations (§ 2339B)

1. Prosecutions for violating Section 2339B are the most frequent in practice.

2. Material support crimes were created after the Oklahoma City bombing in the Anti-Terrorism and Effective Death Penalty Act (AEDPA) of 1996.

3. An amendment increased the AEDPA penalty in the USA Patriot Act (Uniting and Strengthening America by Providing Appropriate Tools to Intercept and Obstruct Terrorism) of 2001.

4. The 300+-page Patriot Act is devoted mainly to criminal procedure— surveillance and intelligence, law enforcement information sharing, search and seizure, detention, and interrogation.

5. *Material support* includes

    a. Currency or monetary instruments or financial securities

    b. Financial services

    c. Lodging

    d. Training

    e. Expert advice or assistance

    f. Safe houses

    g. False documentation or identification

    h. Communications equipment

    i. Facilities

    j. Weapons, lethal substances, explosives

    k. Personnel

    l. Transportation

    m. Other physical assets, except medicine or religious materials

6. Material support to individual terrorists

    a. *Actus reus*

      (1) Provide material support to individual terrorists.

      (2) Conceal or disguise the nature, location, source, or ownership of material support or resources.

b. The *mens rea* is intending or knowing that support or resources are to be used in preparing or committing a list of crimes helpful to terrorists.
7. Material support to terrorist organizations
   a. The *actus reus* is providing material support or resources to terrorist organizations.
   b. The *mens rea* is knowingly providing material support.
8. The most-argued issues in material support cases are constitutional.
   a. Due process—Is the term *material support* void for vagueness?
   b. First Amendment—Does providing material support violate the right to free speech and association?

REVIEW QUESTIONS

1. Why did the authors of the U.S. Constitution define *treason* in the body of the U.S. Constitution?

2. State the elements of the constitutional crime of treason.

3. State the two worries the authors of the Constitution had about abuse of the treason law.

4. According to the authors of the Constitution, what place do feelings, opinions, and passions have in the law of treason, and why?

5. By the time the authors defined treason in the Constitution, what were the two limits government and philosophy had come to accept? What two limits of their own did the authors add?

6. Identify and explain the three elements of treason as it's defined in Article III, § 3 of the U.S. Constitution.

7. Why is it so hard to convict individuals for treason in the United States?

8. What did Justice Jackson point out with respect to combating disloyalty and the law of treason?

9. Identify and distinguish among the three forms of sedition.

10. How does the U.S. Code define seditious conspiracy, and how does the crime contrast with the first sedition law?

11. State the elements of sabotage as it's defined in the U.S. Code.

12. State the elements of espionage during war and at other times as it's defined in the U.S. Code.

13. How does the U.S. Code define domestic and international terrorism?

14. How does the U.S. Code define the crime of "use of weapons of mass destruction"?

15. List the kinds of "destructive devices" included within the meaning of "weapons of mass destruction."

16. List the kinds of weapons of mass destruction that aren't included within the meaning of "destructive devices."

17. How does the U.S. Code define "harboring or concealing terrorists"?

18. What's the most frequently prosecuted antiterrorism crime?

19. Identify and state the elements of the crime of providing material support to individual terrorists, and compare them with providing material support to terrorist organizations.

20. Identify the two most common issues raised in prosecutions for providing material assistance to terrorists and terrorist organizations.

KEY TERMS

USA Patriot Act, p. 438
treason, p. 438
adherence to the enemy, p. 439
sedition, p. 442
seditious speech, p. 442
seditious libel, p. 442
seditious conspiracy, p. 442

Smith Act of 1940, p. 443
sabotage, p. 443
espionage, p. 444
terrorism, p. 445
Anti-Terrorism and Effective Death Penalty Act (AEDPA), p. 445
international terrorism, p. 445

domestic terrorism, p. 446
weapons of mass destruction, p. 446
destructive device, p. 446
conduct transcending national boundaries, p. 446
material support, p. 448
proximity crimes, p. 448

APPENDIX
Selected Amendments of the Constitution of the United States

Amendment I [1791]

Congress shall make no law respecting an establishment of religion, or prohibiting the free exercise thereof; or abridging the freedom of speech, or of the press; or the right of the people peaceably to assemble, and to petition the Government for a redress of grievances.

Amendment VIII [1791]

Excessive bail shall not be required, nor excessive fines imposed, nor cruel and unusual punishments inflicted.

Amendment XIV [1868]

Section 1 All persons born or naturalized in the United States, and subject to the jurisdiction thereof, are citizens of the United States and of the State wherein they reside. No State shall make or enforce any law which shall abridge the privileges or immunities of citizens of the United States; nor shall any State deprive any person of life, liberty, or property, without due process of law; nor deny to any person within its jurisdiction the equal protection of the laws.

Section 2 Representatives shall be apportioned among the several States according to their respective numbers, counting the whole number of persons in each State, excluding Indians not taxed. But when the right to vote at any election for the choice of electors for President and Vice President of the United States, Representatives in Congress, the Executive and Judicial officers of a State, or the members of the Legislature thereof, is denied to any of the male inhabitants of such State, being twenty-one years of age, and citizens of the United States, or in any way abridged, except for participation in rebellion, or other crime, the basis of representation therein shall be reduced in the proportion which the number of such male citizens shall bear to the whole number of male citizens twenty-one years of age in such State.

Section 3 No person shall be a Senator or Representative in Congress, or elector of President and Vice-President, or hold any office, civil or military, under the United States, or under any State, who having previously taken an oath, as a member of Congress, or as an officer of the United States, or as a member of any State legislature, or as an executive or judicial officer of any State, to support the Constitution of the United States, shall have engaged in insurrection or rebellion against the same, or given aid or comfort to the enemies thereof. But Congress may by a vote of two thirds of each House, remove such disability.

Section 4 The validity of the public debt of the United States, authorized by law, including debts incurred for payment of pensions and bounties for services in suppressing insurrection or rebellion, shall not be questioned. But neither the United States nor any State shall assume or pay any debt or obligation incurred in aid of insurrection or rebellion against the United States, or any claim for the loss or emancipation of any slave; but all such debts, obligations and claims shall be held illegal and void.

Section 5 The Congress shall have power to enforce, by appropriate legislation, the provisions of this article.

 Go to the Criminal Law 9e website for the full text of the Constitution of the United States.

Glossary

abuse-of-trust crimes (in property crime) crimes committed by caretakers.

accessories the parties liable for separate, lesser offenses following a crime.

accomplices the parties liable as principals before and during a crime.

actual disorderly conduct completed disorderly conduct (fighting).

actual possession physical possession; on the possessor's person.

actus reus the criminal act or the physical element in criminal liability.

adequate provocation the circumstance element in voluntary manslaughter that is the trigger that sets off the sudden killing of another person; acts that qualify as reducing murder to manslaughter.

adherence to the enemy (in treason) breaking allegiance to your own country.

administrative crimes violations of federal and state agency rules.

affirmative defense defense in which the defendant bears the burden of production.

aggravated rape (first degree) rape committed with a weapon, by more than one person, or causing serious physical injury to the victim.

American bystander rule there's no legal duty to rescue or call for help to aid someone who's in danger even if helping poses no risk whatsoever to the potential rescuer.

Anti-Terrorism and Effective Death Penalty Act (AEDPA) law defining new crimes of domestic terrorism and increasing the penalties for domestic terrorism crimes.

arson intentionally burning a house or other structure.

asportation the carrying away of another's property.

assault an attempt to commit a battery or intentionally putting another in fear.

attempt *actus reus* steps taken to complete a crime that's never completed.

attempt *mens rea* specific intent to commit a crime that's never completed.

attempted battery assault consists of having the specific intent to commit a battery and taking substantial steps toward carrying it out without actually completing the attempt.

attendant circumstances a "circumstance" connected to an act, an intent, and/or a result required to make an act criminal.

barbaric punishments punishment considered no longer acceptable.

battery unwanted and unjustified offensive touching.

bifurcation a mandate that the death penalty decision be made in two phases: a trial to determine guilt and a second separate proceeding, after a finding of guilt, to consider the aggravating factors for, and mitigating factors against, capital punishment.

blameworthiness (also called "culpability") the idea that we can only punish people that we can blame, and we can only blame people that are responsible for what they do.

born-alive rule homicide law once said that to be a person, and therefore a homicide victim, a baby had to be "born alive" and capable of breathing and maintaining a heartbeat on its own.

broken-windows theory theory that minor offenses or disorderly conduct can lead to a rise in serious crime.

burden of persuasion the responsibility to convince the fact finder of the truth of the defense.

burden of production the responsibility to introduce initial evidence to support a defense.

burglary breaking and entering a building with intent to commit a crime inside the building.

burning (*actus reus* in arson) setting a building on fire, and the fire actually reaches the structure.

"but for" cause cause in fact (also called *sine qua non* cause); the actor's conduct sets in motion a chain of events that, sooner or later, leads to a result; see **factual ("but for") cause.**

capital case death penalty cases in death penalty states and "mandatory life sentence without parole" cases in non–death penalty states.

case-by-case approach the facts and circumstances surrounding the way the felony was committed in the particular case, not the elements of the crime in the abstract, may be considered to determine whether it was dangerous to human life.

cause in fact the objective determination that the defendant's act triggered a chain of events that ended as the bad result, such as death in homicide.

chain conspiracies participants at one end of the chain may know nothing of those at the other end, but every participant handles the same commodity at different points, such as manufacture, distribution, and sale.

chilling effect when people hesitate to express themselves because they fear criminal prosecution even though the Constitution protects their speech.

choice-of-evils defense defense of making the right choice—namely, choosing the lesser of two evils.

civil commitment involuntary confinement not based on criminal conviction.

code states states that have abolished the common law.

common-law crimes crimes originating in the English common law.

common-law rape intentional forced heterosexual vaginal penetration by a man with a woman not his wife.

common-law sodomy anal intercourse between two males.

complicity the principle regarding parties to crime that establishes the conditions under which more than one person incurs liability before, during, and after committing crimes; when one person is liable for another person's crime.

concurrence the requirement that *actus reus* must join with *mens rea* to produce criminal conduct or that conduct must cause a harmful result.

conditional threats not enough to satisfy the *mens rea* of assault because they're not immediate.

conduct crimes crimes requiring a criminal act triggered by criminal intent.

conduct transcending national boundaries (in terrorist crimes) element in new antiterrorism crime statute that cites acts of terrorism that take place partly outside and partly inside the United States.

consolidated theft statutes eliminate the artificial need to separate theft into distinct offenses according to their *actus reus*.

conspiracy agreeing to commit a crime.

conspiracy *actus reus* consists of two parts: (1) an agreement to commit a crime (in all states) and (2) an overt act in furtherance of the agreement (in about half the states).

conspiracy *mens rea* specific intent to commit a crime, or specific intent to commit a legal act by illegal means.

constructive disorderly conduct acts that tend toward causing others to breach the peace.

constructive possession legal possession or custody of an item or substance.

corroboration rule element in rape that the prosecution had to prove rape by the testimony of witnesses other than the victim.

crimes against public order crimes that harm the public peace generally (for example, disorderly conduct).

criminal attempt intending to commit a crime and taking steps to complete it but something interrupts the completion of the crime's commission.

criminal codes definitions of crimes and punishments by elected legislatures.

criminal conspiracy agreement between two or more persons to commit a crime.

criminal homicide a homicide that's neither justified nor excused.

criminal mischief (in property crimes) misdemeanor of damaging or destroying other people's property.

criminal negligence manslaughter includes the mental elements of both recklessness and negligence.

criminal objective the criminal goal of an agreement to commit a crime.

criminal omission two forms: (1) mere failure to act or (2) failure to intervene in order to prevent a serious harm.

criminal punishment punishments prescribed by legislatures.

criminal sexual conduct statutes expanded the definition of sex offenses to embrace a wide range of nonconsensual penetrations and contact.

criminal solicitation urging another person to commit a crime, even though the person doesn't respond to the urging.

criminal trespass (in property crimes) the crime of invading another person's property.

criteria for decision (in death penalty cases) must be limited by the criteria established and announced *before* the decision to sentence the defendant to death but includes aggravating factors for and mitigating factors against imposing death.

culpability blameworthiness based on *mens rea;* deserving of punishment because of individual responsibility for actions.

curtilage the area immediately surrounding a dwelling.

cybercrime crimes committed through the Internet or some other computer network.

cyberstalking the use of the Internet, e-mail, or other electronic communications devices to stalk another person through threatening behavior.

damages money plaintiffs get for the injuries they suffer.

dangerous act rationale (in attempt law) looking at how closely a defendant came to completing a crime.

dangerous person rationale (in attempt law) looking at how fully a defendant developed a criminal purpose to commit a crime.

dangerous proximity test to success test/physical proximity test looking at the seriousness of the offense intended; the closeness to completion of the crime; and the probability the conduct would actually have resulted in completion of the crime.

defense of consent a justification defense that says if mentally competent adults want to be crime victims, no paternalistic government should get in their way.

defense of duress excuse of being forced to commit a crime.

defense of voluntary abandonment the actor voluntarily and completely gives up his criminal purpose before completing the offense.

depraved heart murder extremely reckless killing.

destructive device (in terrorist crimes) device used to commit terrorist acts (for example, bombs, poison gas).

diminished capacity mental capacity less than "normal" but more than "insane"; an attempt to prove that the defendant incapable of the requisite intent of the crime charged is innocent of that crime but may well be guilty of a lesser one.

diminished responsibility a defense of excuse in which the defendant argues, "What I did was wrong, but under the circumstances I'm *less* responsible."

discretionary decision making judicial criminal lawmaking power that leaves judges lots of leeway for making decisions based on their professional training and experience.

disorderly conduct crimes against public order and morals.

domestic terrorism terrorist crimes committed inside the United States.

elements of a crime the parts of a crime that the prosecution must prove beyond a reasonable doubt, such as *actus reus, mens rea,* concurrence, causation, and bad result.

embezzlement the crime of lawfully gaining possession of someone else's property and later converting it to one's own use.

entrapment government actions that induce individuals to commit crimes that they otherwise wouldn't commit.

equivalent-of-specific-intent definition some courts define a willful, premeditated, deliberate killing as the same as specific intent, which may render the difference between first- and second-degree murder meaningless.

espionage the crime of spying for the enemy.

excusable homicide accidental killings done by someone "not of sound memory and discretion" (insane and immature).

excuses defenses defendants admit what they did was *wrong* but claim that under the circumstances, they weren't *responsible* for what they did.

ex post facto laws laws passed after the occurrence of the conduct constituting the crime.

express malice aforethought intentional killings planned in advance.

extortion (blackmail) misappropriation of another's property by means of threats to inflict bodily harm in the future.

extraneous factor a condition beyond the attempter's control.

extreme mental or emotional disturbance a defense that reduces criminal homicide to manslaughter if emotional disturbance provides a reasonable explanation for the defendant's actions.

extrinsic force requires some force in addition to the amount needed to accomplish the penetration.

factual ("but for") cause conduct that, in fact, leads to a harmful result.

factual impossibility the defense that some extraneous factor made it impossible to complete a crime.

failure-of-proof theory defendant disproves the prosecution's case by showing he or she couldn't have formed the state of mind required to prove the mental element of the crime.

failure to intervene (criminal omission) one type of omission *actus reus*.

failure to report (criminal omission) one type of omission *actus reus*.

false imprisonment the heart of the crime is depriving others of their personal liberty.

false pretenses in modern law it's often called "theft by deceit," and it means having the specific intent to obtain property by deceit and lies.

felonies serious crimes that are generally punishable by one year or more in prison.

felony murder unintentional deaths that occur during the commission of felonies.

feticide law defining when life begins for purposes of applying the law of criminal homicide.

first-degree murder premeditated, deliberate killings and other particularly heinous capital murders.

force and resistance rule victims had to prove to the courts they didn't consent to rape by demonstrating that they resisted the force of the rapist.

fraud in the fact (in rape) when a rapist fraudulently convinces his victim that the act she consented to was something other than sexual intercourse.

fraud in the inducement the fraud is in the benefits promised, not in the act.

general deterrence (also called general prevention) aims by threat of punishment to deter criminal behavior in the general population.

general intent intent to commit the *actus reus*—the act required in the definition of the crime.

general intent plus "general intent" refers to the intent to commit the *actus reus* of the crime and "plus" refers to some "special mental element" in addition to the intent to commit the criminal act.

general part of criminal law principles that apply to all crimes.

general principle of necessity (defense to crime) the justification of committing a lesser crime to avoid the imminent danger of a greater crime.

"Good Samaritan" doctrine doctrine that imposes a legal duty to render or summon aid for imperiled strangers.

honest and reasonable mistake rule a negligence mental element in rape cases in which the defendant argues that he honestly, but mistakenly, believed the victim consented to sex.

identity theft stealing another person's identity for the purpose of getting something of value.

ignorance of the law a defense that the defendant didn't know the rules, so he couldn't know he was breaking the law.

imminent danger element in self-defense that injury or death is going to happen right now.

imperfect defenses defenses reducing, but not eliminating, criminal liability.

implied malice aforethought killings that weren't intentional or planned but still resulted from the intention to do harm.

incapacitation punishment by imprisonment, mutilation, and even death.

inchoate offenses offenses based on crimes not yet completed.

indispensable element test (attempt law) asks whether defendants have gotten control of everything they need to complete the crime.

inherently dangerous felony approach courts look at the felony in the abstract—if a felony *can* be committed in a way that's *not* dangerous to life, even if it was committed in a dangerous way in the case before the court, then it's not inherently dangerous.

initial aggressor a person who begins a fight can't claim the right to self-defense.

injunction to abate public nuisances an action in which city attorneys ask the courts to declare gang activities and gang members public nuisances and to issue injunctions to abate their activities.

insanity legal term for a person who is excused from criminal liability because a mental disease or defect impairs his *mens rea*.

intangible property property that lacks a physical existence (examples include stock options, trademarks, licenses, and patents).

intellectual property nformation and services stored in and transmitted to and from electronic data banks; a rapidly developing area of property crimes.

intent-to-cause-serious-bodily injury murder when death results following acts triggered by the intent to inflict serious bodily injury short of death.

intent-to-instill-fear test did the actor intend to instill fear?

international terrorism terrorist acts dangerous to U.S. citizens committed outside the United States.

intervening cause the cause that either interrupts a chain of events or substantially contributes to a result.

intrinsic force requires only the amount of force necessary to accomplish the penetration.

involuntary manslaughter criminal homicides caused either by recklessness or gross criminal negligence.

irresistible impulse test tests whether the will is so impaired that it makes it impossible for the person to control the impulse to do wrong.

judicial waiver when a juvenile court judge uses her discretion to transfer a juvenile to adult criminal court.

justifiable homicide killing in self-defense, capital punishment, and police use of deadly force.

justification defenses defendants admit they were responsible for their acts but claim what they did was right (justified) under the circumstances.

kidnapping taking and carrying away another person with intent to deprive the other person of personal liberty.

knowing possession awareness of physical possession.

knowledge (in *mens rea*) consciously acting or causing a result.

larceny taking and carrying away another person's property without the use of force with the intent to permanently deprive its owner of possession.

last proximate act rule your acts brought you as close as possible to completing the crime.

last-straw rule a smoldering resentment or pent-up rage resulting from earlier insults or humiliating events, culminating in a triggering event that, by itself, might be insufficient to provoke the deadly act.

legal cause a subjective judgment as to whether it's fair and just to blame the defendant for the result; cause recognized by law to impose criminal liability.

legal duty (in criminal omission) liability only for duties imposed by contract, statute, or "special relationships."

legal fiction (in *actus reus*) treating as a fact something that's not a fact if there's a good reason for doing so.

legal impossibility the defense that what the actor attempted was not a "crime."

liability the technical legal term for responsibility.

liberty the right of individuals to go about in public free of undue interference.

loitering remaining in one place with no apparent purpose.

malice aforethought killing on purpose after planning it.

malum in se a crime inherently bad or evil.

malum prohibitum a crime not inherently bad or evil but merely prohibited.

manifest criminality the requirement in law that intentions have to turn into criminal deeds to be punishable.

manslaughter unlawful killing of another person without malice aforethought.

marital rape exception legally, husbands can't rape their wives.

material support (in terrorist crimes) element in terrorist crimes that consists of helping terrorists or terrorist organizations.

mens rea the "state of mind" the prosecution has to prove beyond a reasonable doubt; criminal intent from an evil mind; the mental element in crime, including purpose, knowledge, recklessness, and negligence.

mere possession physical possession.

mere presence rule a person's presence at the scene of a crime doesn't by itself satisfy the *actus reus* requirement of accomplice liability.

misdemeanors minor crimes for which the penalty is usually less than one year in jail or a fine.

mistake of fact to be mistaken about the law or fact; to believe the facts are one thing when they're really another; a defense whenever the mistake prevents the formation of any fault-based mental attitude.

M'Naghten rule see **right-wrong test.**

Model Penal Code the code developed by the American Law Institute to guide reform in criminal law.

motive the reason why a defendant commits a crime.

murder intentionally causing the death of another person with "malice aforethought.

murder *actus reus* causing a death of a person.

murder *mens rea* the purposeful, knowing, reckless, or negligent killing of a person.

necessity (choice-of-evils defense) general principle of an honest and reasonable belief that it's necessary to commit a lesser crime (evil) to prevent the imminent danger of a greater crime (evil).

negligence the unconscious creation of substantial and unjustifiable risks.

no fault liability that requires neither subjective nor objective fault.

objective fault requires no purposeful or conscious bad mind in the actor; it sets a standard of what the "average person should have known."

objective fear only test would a reasonable person be afraid?

objective test of cooling-off-time in voluntary manslaughter, the element of whether in similar circumstances a reasonable person would've had time to cool off.

objective test of entrapment focuses on the actions that government agents take to induce individuals to commit crimes.

offenses of general application describes the inchoate crimes, which are partly general and partly specific.

order behavior in public that comports with minimum community standards of civility.

overt act (in conspiracy) requirement of conspiracy *actus reus* of some act toward completing the crime in addition to the agreement.

panhandling stopping people on the street to ask them for food or money.

paramour rule a husband who caught his wife in the act of adultery had adequate provocation to kill and could reduce criminal homicide to voluntary manslaughter.

perfect defenses defenses that lead to outright acquittal.

Pinkerton rule the rule that conspiracy and the underlying crime are separate offenses.

plaintiffs those who sue for wrongs in tort cases.

precedent prior court decision that guides judges in deciding future cases.

preliminary injunction a temporary order issued by a court after giving notice and holding a hearing.

preponderance of the evidence more than 50 percent of the evidence proves justification or excuse.

present danger danger that's probably going to happen some time in the future but not right now (self-defense).

prevention punishing offenders to prevent crimes in the future.

principle of causation requirement that criminal conduct cause a harm defined in the criminal code.

principle of concurrence some mental fault has to trigger the *actus reus* in criminal conduct crimes and the cause in bad-result crimes; see **concurrence.**

principle of legality a principle stating that there can be no crime or punishment if there are no specific laws forewarning citizens that certain specific conduct will result in a particular punishment.

principle of *mens rea* see *mens rea.*

principle of proportionality a principle of law stating that the punishment must be proportional to the crime committed.

principle of utility permitting only the minimum amount of pain necessary to prevent the crime as punishment.

probable desistance test a dangerous person test that focuses on how far defendants have gone, not on what's left for them to do to complete the crime.

product-of-mental-illness test a test to determine whether a crime was a product of mental disease or defect.

prompt-reporting rule rape victims have to report the rape soon after it occurs.

proximate cause the main cause of the result of criminal conduct; legal cause.

proximity crimes ban conduct because of its closeness to other crimes.

proximity tests tests of dangerous conduct: physical proximity, dangerous proximity, and indispensable element.

punitive damages damages that make an example of defendants and punish them for their behavior.

purpose (in *mens rea***)** the specific intent to act and/or cause a criminal harm.

quality-of-life crimes breaches of minimum standards of decent behavior in public.

rape intentional sexual penetration by force without consent.

rape *actus reus* the act of sexual penetration.

rape shield statutes statutes that prohibit introducing evidence of victims' past sexual conduct.

reasonable mistake of age a defense to statutory rape in California and Alaska if the defendant reasonably believed his victim was over the age of consent.

reasonable resistance rule (in rape) the amount of force required to repel rapists to show nonconsent in rape prosecutions.

receiving stolen property benefiting from someone else's property without having participated in the wrongful acquisition in the first place.

recklessness the conscious creation of substantial and unjustifiable risk.

recklessness requirement (regarding consent in rape) adopted by some states in rape cases, it requires that the defendant has to be aware that there's a risk the victim hasn't consented to sexual intercourse.

rehabilitation prevention of crime by treatment.

resisting-victim exception exception to the third-party exception to felony murder, in which the defendant can be charged with the killing of his accomplice committed by the resisting victim.

result crimes serious crimes that include causing a criminal harm in addition to the conduct itself, for example, criminal homicide.

retreat rule you have to retreat but only if you reasonably believe that backing off won't unreasonably put you in danger of death or serious bodily harm.

retribution punishment based on just deserts.

retroactive criminal lawmaking a person can't be convicted of, or punished for, a crime unless the law defined the crime and prescribed the punishment *before* she acted; *"the* first principle of criminal law."

right of locomotion the right to come and go without restraint.

right to privacy a right that bans "all governmental invasions of the sanctity of a man's home and the privacies of life."

right-wrong test (*M'Naghten* **rule)** test used in insanity defense to determine the defendant's capacity to either know right from wrong or to know the act is against the law.

riot disorderly conduct committed by more than three persons.

robbery taking and carrying away another's property by force or threat of force with the intent to permanently deprive the owner of possession.

rout three or more people moving toward the commission of a riot.

rule of lenity when judges apply a criminal statute to the defendant in the case before them, they have to stick "clearly within the letter of the statute," resolving all ambiguities in favor of defendants and against the application of the statute.

sabotage damaging or destroying property for the purpose of hindering preparations for war and national defense during national emergencies.

scienter the Latin name for "awareness."

second-degree murder a catchall offense including killings that are neither manslaughter nor first-degree murder; unintentional killings.

sedition the crime of "stirring up" treason by words.

seditious conspiracy agreement to "stir up" treason.

seditious libel writings aimed at "stirring up" treason.

seditious speech "stirring up" treason by means of the spoken word.

sexual assault statutes expanded the definition of sex offenses to embrace a wide range of nonconsensual penetrations and contacts.

simple rape (second degree) rape without aggravated circumstances.

Smith Act of 1940 U.S. statute aimed at Communists who advocated the violent overthrow of the government.

solicitation trying to get someone to commit a crime.

solicitation *actus reus* urging another person to commit a crime.

solicitation *mens rea* intent to get another person to commit a crime.

special deterrence the threat of punishment aimed at individual offenders in the hope of deterring future criminal conduct.

special part of criminal law defines the elements of specific crimes.

specific intent the attitude represented by subjective fault, where there's a "bad" mind or will that triggers the act; the intent to do something beyond the *actus reus*.

specific-intent-plus-real-premeditation-deliberation definition the law looks at three areas to determine whether a killing was premeditated and deliberate: signs of planning, motive, and deliberate method in the killing.

stalking intentionally scaring another person by following, tormenting, or harassing.

stand-your-ground rule if you didn't start the fight, you can stand your ground and kill.

stare decisis the principle that binds courts to stand by prior decisions and to leave undisturbed settled points of law.

status (as *actus reus*) who we are as opposed to what we do; a condition that's not an action can't substitute for action as an element in crime.

statutory rape to have carnal knowledge of a person under the age of consent whether or not accomplished by force.

strict liability liability without fault, or in the absence of *mens rea*; it's based on voluntary action alone.

subjective and objective fear test did the defendant's acts "induce fear in the victim, and would the acts cause a reasonable person to fear?

subjective fault fault that requires a "bad mind" in the actor.

subjective fear only test was the victim actually afraid?

subjective test of entrapment focuses on the predisposition of defendants to commit crimes.

substantial capacity test insanity due to mental disease or defect impairing the substantial capacity either to appreciate the wrongfulness of conduct or to conform behavior to the law.

"substantial steps" test (in attempt *actus reus*) in the Model Penal Code, substantial acts toward completion of a crime and that strongly corroborate the actor's intent to commit the crime.

surreptitious remaining element entering a structure lawfully with the intent to commit a crime inside.

syndrome novel defenses of excuse based on symptoms of conditions such as being a Vietnam vet suffering from post–traumatic stress disorder or having premenstrual symptoms.

tangible property personal property (not real estate).

terrorism in the nonlegal sense, it means the use of violence and intimidation in the pursuit of political aims.

theft the consolidated crimes of larceny, embezzlement, and false pretenses.

theft by deceit or trick obtaining someone else's property by deceit and lies.

third-party exception defense to felony murder that someone other than the felon caused the death during the commission of a felony.

threatened battery assault sometimes called the crime of "intentional scaring," it requires only that actors intend to frighten their victims, thus expanding assault beyond attempted battery.

threat-of-force requirement prosecution must prove a sexual assault victim feared imminent bodily harm and that the fear was reasonable.

time, place, and manner test three-part test to determine whether a statute places legitimate limits on the First Amendment right of free speech.

torts private wrongs for which you can sue the party who wronged you and recover money.

treason crime of levying war against the United States or of giving aid and comfort to its enemies.

unarmed acquaintance rape nonconsensual sex between people who know each other; rape involving dates, lovers, neighbors, co-workers, employers, and so on.

unequivocality test/*res ipsa loquiter* test ("act speaks for itself") examines the likelihood the defendant won't complete the crime (attempt law).

unilateral approach (in conspiracy) not all the conspirators need to agree to commit a crime to impose criminal liability (conspiracy *actus reus*).

unlawful act include everything from committing felonies, misdemeanors, and even traffic violations, city ordinances, administrative crimes, and noncriminal wrongs, such as civil trespass and other torts.

unlawful act manslaughter sometimes called "misdemeanor manslaughter," it's involuntary manslaughter based on deaths that take place during the commission of another crime.

unlawful assembly ancient crime of three or more persons gathering together to commit an unlawful act.

USA Patriot Act act passed by Congress following September 11, 2001, creating some new (and enhancing the penalties for existing) crimes of domestic and international terrorism.

utmost resistance rule the requirement that rape victims must use all the physical strength they have to prevent penetration.

vagrancy ancient crime of poor people wandering around with no visible means of support.

vicarious liability the principle of liability for another based on relationship.

"victimless" crimes crimes without complaining victims (for example, recreational illegal drug users).

void-for-overbreadth doctrine the principle that a statute is unconstitutional if it includes in its definition of undesirable behavior conduct protected under the U.S. Constitution.

void-for-vagueness doctrine the principle that statutes violate due process if they don't clearly define crime and punishment in advance.

voluntary manslaughter intentional killings committed in the sudden heat of passion upon adequate provocation.

weapons of mass destruction any destructive device used to commit acts of terror.

wheel conspiracies one or more defendants participate in every transaction.

white-collar crimes crimes growing out of opportunities to get someone else's property provided by the perpetrator's occupation.

withdrawal exception if initial aggressors completely withdraw from fights they provoke, they can claim the defense of self-defense.

Bibliography

Ainsworth, Bill. 2004. "Poll Finds Broad Support for Limits on 3-Strikes Laws." *San Diego Union,* 10 June.

Alabama Criminal Code. 1975. http://www.legislature.state.al.us/CodeofAlabama/1975/coatoc.htm (visited April 29, 2006).

Allen, Francis A. 1993. *The Habits of Legality: Criminal Justice and the Rule of Law.* New York: Oxford University Press.

American Law Institute (ALI). 1953. *Model Penal Code Tentative Draft No. 1.* Philadelphia: ALI.

———. 1985. *Model Penal Code and Commentaries.* Philadelphia: ALI.

American Psychiatric Association. 2003. "Questions and Answers on Using 'Insanity' as a Legal Defense." http://healthyminds.org/insanitydefense.cfm (visited October 20, 2006).

Andenæs, Johannes. 1983. "Deterrence." *Encyclopedia of Crime and Justice.* Edited by Sanford H. Kadish. New York: Free Press.

Anderson, Curt. 2003. "'Material Support' Charge under Legal Eye." *Associated Press,* 13 August.

Arizona Criminal Code. 2003. Effect of Alcohol or Drug Use. http://www.azleg.state.az.us/ars/13/00503.htm.

Atkins v. Virginia. 2002. 536 U.S. 304.

Attorney General. 1999. *1999 Report on Cyberstalking: A New Challenge for Law Enforcement and Industry.* Washington D.C.: U.S. Department of Justice. http:// www.usdoj .gov/criminal/cybercrime/cyberstalking.htm.

Bachun v. U.S. 1940. 112 F.2d 635 (4th Cir.).

Bailey v. U.S. 1969. 416 F.2d 1110 (D.C. Cir.).

Barnes v. Glen Theatre, Inc., et al. 1991. 501 U.S. 560.

Barstow, David. 2003. "When Workers Die: A Trench Caves In; a Young Worker Is Dead. Is It a Crime?" *New York Times,* 21 December.

Batey, Robert. 1997. "Vagueness and the Construction of Criminal Statutes—Balancing Act." *Virginia Journal of Social Policy and Law* 5:1.

Beasley v. State. 1886. 8 So. 234. (Miss.).

Beazell v. Ohio. 1925. 269 U.S. 167.

Benekos, Peter, and Alido Merlo. 1995 (March). "Three Strikes and You're Out!: The Political Sentencing Game." *Federal Probation.*

Black, Henry Campbell. 1983. *Black's Law Dictionary.* St. Paul Minn.: West.

Blackstone, Sir William. 1769. *Commentaries on the Laws of England, IV.* Oxford: Clarendon Press.

Blakely, Richard, and Mark Gettings. 1980. "Racketeer Influenced and Corrupt Organizations (RICO): Basic Concepts—Criminal and Civil Remedies." *Temple Law Quarterly* 53.

Board of Commissioners v. Backus. 1864. 29 How. Pr. 33.

Bond, Julian P., ed. 1950. *Papers of Thomas Jefferson.* Vol. 2. Princeton, N.J.: Princeton University Press.

Boro v. Superior Court. 1985. 210 Cal.Rptr.122 (Cal.App.).

Bowers v. Hardwick. 1986. 478 U.S. 186.

Bracton, Henry of. 1968. *On the Laws and Customs of England.* Translated by Samuel E. Thorne. Cambridge: Harvard University Press.

———. 1968–77. *On the Laws and Customs of England.* Translated by Samuel E. Thorne. Cambridge: Harvard University Press.

Bradfield, Jennifer L. 1998. "Anti-Stalking Laws: Do They Adequately Protect Stalking Victims?" *Harvard Women's Law Journal* 21:229, 249.

Bradley v. Ward. 1955. N.Z.L.R. 471.

Branson, Serene. 2006 (April 13). "Racist Video Game Targets Immigrants." CBS Channel 13. Sacramento. http://cbs13.com/topstories/local_story_104000846 .html (visited April 27, 2006).

Brodie, Kyle S. 1995. "The Obviously Impossible Attempt: A Proposed Revision to the Model Penal Code." *Northern Illinois University Law Review* 15:237.

Brown v. State. 1906. 106 N.W. 536 (Wis.).

———. 1997. 955 S.W.2d 276 (Tex.).

Bryden, David P. 2000. "Redefining Rape." *Buffalo Criminal Law Review* 3:318.

Buck v. Bell. 1927. 274 U.S. 200.

Burnet v. Coronado Oil and Gas Co. 1932. 285 U.S. 393.

Burnett v. State. 1999. 807 So.2d 573 (Ala.App.).

Burrows v. State. 1931. 297 P. 1029.

Byford v. State. 2000. 994 P.2d 700 (Nev.).

California Penal Code. 2003. http://www.leginfo.ca.gov/ .html/pen_table_of_contents.html.

———. 2006. http://caselaw.lp.findlaw.com/cacodes/ pen.html (visited July 16, 2006).

———. 2006. Section 187–199. http://www.leginfo.ca.gov/ cgi-bin/displaycode?section=pen&group=00001- 01000&file=187-199.

Campbell v. State. 1982. 444 A.2d 1034.

Cardozo, Benjamin. 1921. *The Nature of the Judicial Process.* New Haven, Conn.: Yale University Press.

Carlson, Jonathan C. 1987. "The Act Requirement and the Foundations of the Entrapment Defense." *Virginia Law Review* 73:1011.

Carney, Robert Mark, and Brian D. Williams. 1983. "Premenstrual Syndrome: A Criminal Defense." *Notre Dame Law Review* 59:263–69.

Casico v. State. 1947. 25 N.W.2d 897 (Neb.).

Chambers v. Florida. 1940. 309 U.S. 227.

Chaney v. State. 1970. 477 P.2d 441 (Alaska).

Chaplinsky v. New Hampshire. 1942. 315 U.S. 568.

Chicago v. Roman. 1998. 705 N.E.2d 81 (Ill.).

City of Chicago v. Morales. 1999. 527 U.S. 41.

Clark v. Arizona. 2006. 548 U.S. _____ (Slip Opinion).

Coffee, John C., Jr. 1992. "Paradigms Lost: The Blurring of the Criminal and Civil Law Models—and What Can Be Done about It." *Yale Law Journal* 101:1875.

Cohen, Fred. 1985. "Old Age Defense." *Criminal Law Bulletin* 21.

Coker v. Georgia. 1977. 433 U.S. 584.

Commonwealth v. Barnette. 1998. 699 N.E.2d 1230 (Mass.App.).

Commonwealth v. Berkowitz. 1992. 609 A.2d 1338 (Pa.Super.).

———. 1994. 641 A.2d 1161 (Pa.).

Commonwealth v. Drum. 1868. WL 7210 (Pa.).

Commonwealth v. Fischer. 1998. 721 A.2d 1111 (Pa.Super.).

Commonwealth v. Gagne. 2000. 735 N.E.2d 1277.

Commonwealth v. Gilliam. 1980. 417 A.2d 1203 (Pa.Super.).

Commonwealth v. Golston. 1977. 249, 366 N.E.2d 744 (Mass.).

Commonwealth v. Kozak. 1993. WL 768932 (Pa.Com.Pl.).

Commonwealth v. McCloskey. 2003. 835 A.2d 801 (Pa.Super.).

Commonwealth v. Mitchell. 1993. WL 773785 (Pa.Com.Pl.).

Commonwealth v. Mlinarich. 1985. 542 A.2d 1335 (Pa.).

Commonwealth v. Peaslee. 1901. 59 N.E. 55 (Mass.).

Commonwealth v. Pestinakas. 1992. 617 A.2d 1339.

Commonwealth v. Rhodes. 1996. 920 S.W.2d 531 (Ky.App.).

Commonwealth v. Rozanski. 1965. 213 A.2d 155 (Pa.Super.)

Commonwealth v. Schnopps. 1983. 459 N.E.2d 98 (Mass.).

Commonwealth v. Zangari. 1997. 677 N.E.2d 702 (Mass.App.).

Corrado, Michael. 1994. "Is There an Act Requirement in the Criminal Law?" *University of Pennsylvania Law Review* 142:1529.

Costello, George. 2005 (November 29). "The Supreme Court's Overruling of Constitutional Precedent: An Overview." Washington, D.C.: Congressional Research Service.

Cramer v. U.S. 1945. 325 U.S. 1.

Crichton, Sarah, Debra Rosenberg, Stanley Holmes, Martha Brant, Donna Foote, and Nina Biddle. 1993. "Sexual Correctness: Has It Gone Too Far?" *Newsweek,* 25 October, pp. 52–54.

Cullen, Francis T., William J. Maakestad, and Gray Cavender. 1987. *Corporate Crime under Attack: The Ford Pinto Case and Beyond.* Cincinnati: Anderson.

Curry v. State. 2002. 811 So.2d 736 (Fla.App.).

Darby, Joe. 2003. "Penalty for Rape May Not Stand: Louisiana Law May Be Unconstitutional." *New Orleans Times-Picayune,* 28 August.

Dennis v. State. 1995. 105 Md.App. 687.

Dennis v. U.S. 1951. 341 U.S. 494.

DePasquale v. State. 1988. 757 P.2d 367.

Dershowitz, Alan. 1994. *The Abuse Excuse and Other Cop-Outs, Sob Stories, and Evasions of Responsibility.* Boston: Little, Brown.

Diamond, John L. 1996. "The Myth of Morality and Fault in Criminal Law." *American Criminal Law* 34.

DiFonzo, James. 2001. "Parental Responsibility for Juvenile Crime." *Oregon Law Review* 80:1.

Direct Sales Co. v. U.S. 1943. 319 U.S. 703.

Doyle, Charles. 2005. "Material Support of Terrorists and Foreign Terrorist Organizations: Sunset Amendments." Washington, D.C.: Congressional Research Service.

Dressler, Joshua. 2001. *Understanding Criminal Law.* 3rd ed. Danvers, Mass.: LexisNexis.

Dubber, Markus D. 2001. "Policing Possession: The War on Crime and the End of Criminal Law." *Journal of Criminal Law and Criminology* 91:829.

———. 2002. *Criminal Law: Model Penal Code.* New York: Foundation Press.

———, and Mark G. Kelman. 2005. *American Criminal Law.* New York: Foundation Press.

Duest v. State. 1985. 462 So.2d 446 (Fla.).

Durham v. U.S. 1954. 214 F.2d 862 (D.C. Cir.).

Dutile, Ferdinand, and Harold F. Moore. 1979. "Mistake and Impossibility: Arranging a Marriage between Two Difficult Partners." *Northwestern University Law Review* 74.

Edwards, Daphne. 1996. "Acquaintance Rape and the 'Force' Element: When 'No' Is Not Enough." *Golden Gate Law Review* 26:241.

Edwards v. California. 1941. 314 U.S. 162.

Ehrlich, Isaac. 1975. "The Deterrent Effect of Capital Punishment: A Question of Life and Death." *American Economic Review* LXV(3):414.

Eisenstadt v. Baird. 1972. 405 U.S. 438.

Electronic Frontier. 2000. Executive Summary. http://www.usdoj.gov/criminal/cybercrime/unlawful.htm.

Ellickson, Robert C. 1996. "Controlling Chronic Misconduct in City Spaces: Of Panhandlers, Skid Rows, and Public-Space Zoning." *Yale Law Journal* 105.

Elton, Geoffrey R. 1972. *The Tudor Constitution.* Cambridge, UK: Cambridge University Press.

Encyclopedia of Crime and Justice. 1983. Vol. 1. New York: Free Press.

Enker, Arnold. 1977. "*Mens Rea* in Criminal Attempt." *American Bar Foundation Research Journal.*

Enmund v. Florida. 1982. 458 U.S. 782.

Eskridge, William N., Jr. 1991. "Overriding Supreme Court Statutory Interpretation Decisions." *Yale Law Journal* 101:331.

Estrich, Susan. 1987. *Real Rape*. Cambridge, Mass.: Harvard University Press.

Ewing v. California. 2003. 538 U.S. 11.

Falco v. State. 1981. 407 So.2d 203 (Fla.).

Farnsworth, Clyde. 1994. "Mercy Killing in Canada Stirs Calls for Changes in Law." *New York Times*, 21 November.

Farrand, Max, ed. 1929. Introduction. *The Laws and Liberties of Massachusetts*. Cambridge, Mass.: Harvard University Press.

FBI. 2005. *Crime in the U.S.* Washington, D.C.: Department of Justice. http://www.fbi.gov/ucr/cius_04/offenses_reported/property_crime/index.html (visited July 18, 2006).

FDA. 2005. "Be Aware and Beware of Identity Theft." *FDA Consumer Magazine*. http://www.fda.gov/fdac/departs/2005/405_fda.html (visited August 12, 2006).

Federal Criminal Code and Rules. 1988. St. Paul, Minn.: West.

Feeley, Malcolm M. 1983. *Court Reform on Trial*. New York: Basic Books.

Fisse, Brian. 1986. "Sanctions against Corporations: Economic Efficiency?" In *Punishment and Privilege*. Edited by W. Byron Groves and Graeme Newman. Albany, N.Y.: Harrow and Heston.

Fletcher, George. 1978. *Rethinking Criminal Law*. Boston: Little, Brown.

———. 1988. *A Crime of Self-Defense: Bernhard Goetz and the Law on Trial*. New York: Free Press.

———. 1996. "Justice for All, Twice." *New York Times*, 24 April.

Florida Constitution. 1998. http://www.flsenate.gov/Statutes/index.cfm?Mode=Constitution&Submenu=3&Tab=statutes#A01S23.

Florida Criminal Code. 2006. § 787.02. http://www.flsenate.gov/statutes/index.cfm?App_mode=Display_Statute&Search_String=&URL=Ch0787/SEC02.HTM&Title=->2002->Ch0787->Section%2002.

Foreman, Judy. 1986. "Most Rape Victims Know Assailant, Don't Report to Police, Police Report Says." *Boston Globe*, 16 April.

Fox, Everett. 1995. *The Five Books of Moses*. New York: Schocken Books.

Franck, Matthew J. 2006 (January 9). "Staring Down the Constitution: *Roe* and *Stare Decisis*." *National Review*. http://article.nationalreview.com/?q=MWZkNDQzOTJjYzAwZmRiZjRlOTRhN2Q3MWZlMmU2MTE=.

Fried, Joshua Mark. 1996. "Forcing the Issue: An Analysis of the Various Standards of Forcible Compulsion in Rape." *Pepperdine Law Review* 23:120.

Fries, Jacob H. 2001. "4,000 Cars Seized in Effort to Halt Drunk Driving." *New York Times*, 3 July.

Furman v. Georgia. 1972. 408 U.S. 238.

Gainer, Ronald L. 1988 (Spring). "The Culpability Provisions of the Model Penal Code." *Rutgers Law Journal* 19:575–91.

Ganeson v. State. 2001. 45 S.W.3d 197 (Tex.).

Gansberg, M. 1964. "37 Who Saw Murder Didn't Call. . . ." *New York Times*, 17 March.

Garner v. Jones. 2000. 529 U.S. 244.

Gaylin, Willard. 1982. *The Killing of Bonnie Garland*. New York: Simon and Schuster.

General v. State. 2002. 789 A.2d 102 (Md.).

Georgia Criminal Code. 2006. http://www.legis.ga.gov/legis/GaCode/?title=16&chapter=3&section=3 (visited June 30, 2006).

Gibeaut, John. 1997. "Sobering Thoughts." *American Bar Association Journal* 83.

Gitlow v. New York. 1925. 268 U.S. 652.

Gordon, Brenda. 1999. "A Criminal's Justice or a Child's Justice? Trends in the Waiver of Juvenile Court Jurisdiction and the Flaws in the Arizona Response." *Arizona Law Review* 41:193.

Grayned v. City of Rockford. 1972. 408 U.S. 104.

Gray v. State. 1979. 403 A.2d 853.

Greenhouse, Linda. 2003. "Justices Deny Appeal in Execution of Juveniles." *New York Times*, 27 January.

Greenhouse, Steven. 1985. "Three Executives Convicted of Murder for Unsafe Workplace Conditions." *New York Times*, 15 June.

Gregg v. Georgia. 1976. 428 U.S. 153.

Gresham v. Peterson. 2000. 225 F.3d 899 (7th Cir.).

Grindstaff v. State. 1964. 377 S.W.2d 921 (Tenn.).

Griswold v. Connecticut. 1965. 381 U.S. 479.

Gross, Hyman. 1978. *A Theory of Criminal Justice*. New York: Oxford University Press.

Hall, David S. 1998 (August 10). "Consent for Sexual Behavior in a College Student Population." *Electronic Journal of Human Sexuality* 1. http://www.ejhs.org/volume1/conseapa.htm (visited August 1, 2006).

Hall, Jerome. 1960. *The General Principles of Criminal Law*. 2nd ed. Indianapolis: Bobbs-Merrill.

Hall, John Wesley, Jr. 1991. *Search and Seizure*. 2nd ed. Deerfield, Ill.: Clark Boardman Callaghan.

Harcourt, Bernard E. 2001. *Illusions of Order*. Cambridge, Mass.: Harvard University Press.

———. 2005. "Carceral Imaginations." *Carceral Notebooks* 1:3–19.

Harmelin v. Michigan. 1991. 501 U.S. 957.

Hart, Henry M., Jr. 1958. "The Aims of the Criminal Law." *Law and Contemporary Problems* 23:401.

———, and Albert M. Sacks. 1994. *The Legal Process: Basic Problems in the Making and Application of Law*. Edited by William N. Eskridge, Jr., and Philip P. Frickey. New York: Foundation Press.

Haupt v. U.S. 1947. 330 U.S. 631.

Hawkins, Beth. 2003 (May 7). "The Sad, Strange Case of Darren Odell and the Sorry State of Our Insanity Laws." *City Pages*. www.citypages.com/databank/24/1170/article11221.asp (visited June 30, 2006).

Healy, Thomas. 2001. "Stare Decisis as a Constitutional Requirement." *West Virginia Law Review* 104:43.

Henyard v. State. 1996. 689 So.2d 239 (Fla.).

Holmes, Oliver Wendell. 1963. *The Common Law*. Boston: Little, Brown.

Holy Bible: King James Version. 2000. http://www.bartleby.com/108/03/24.html.

Iorton v. City of Oakland. 2000. 98 Cal.Rptr.2d 371.

Howe, Mark DeWolfe, ed. 1953. *Holmes-Laski Letters.* Cambridge, Mass: Harvard University Press.

Hughes v. State. 1994. 888 P.2d 730 (Okla.).

Humanitarian Law Project v. Gonzales. 2005. 205 F.Supp. 2d 1130 (C.D. Cal.).

Humanitarian Law Project v. Reno. 2000. 205 F.3d. 1130.

Human Rights Watch. 2002. "World Report. U.S. Death Penalty." http://www.hrw.org/wr2k2/us.html# Death%20Penalty (visited October 2, 2006).

Hutto v. Davis. 1982. 454 U.S. 370.

Hyde v. U.S. 1912. 225 U.S. 347.

Illinois Criminal Law and Procedure. 1988. St. Paul, Minn.: West.

In re Kemmler. 1890. 136 U.S. 436.

In re Medley. 1890. 134 U.S. 160.

In the Interest of C. W. 1997. 485 S.E.2d 561 (Ga.App.).

Iowa Criminal Code. 1999. http://www.legis.state.ia.us/ IACODE/1999/707/2.html.

Jefferson, Thomas. 1853. *The Writings of Thomas Jefferson.* Edited by Albert Ellery Bergh. Washington, D.C.: U.S. Government.

Jewell v. State. 1996. 672 N.E.2d 417 (Ind.App.).

Johnson, Bryan. 2005 (March 3). "Burlington Man Arrested, Jailed for Overdue Library Books." KOMO News. Burlington, Washington. http://www.komotv .com/news/story.asp?ID=35531 (visited June 14, 2006).

Johnson, Vincent R. 2005. "Cybersecurity, Identity Theft, and the Limits of Tort Liability." *South Carolina Law Review* 57:255.

Jones v. State. 1984. 682 P.2d 757 (Okla.Crim.App.).

———. 1992. 589 N.E.2d 241 (Ind.).

Joyce v. City and County of San Francisco. 1994. 846 F.Supp. 843 (N.D.Cal.).

Kadish, Sanford. 1987. *Blame and Punishment.* New York: Macmillan.

Kahan, Dan M. 1994. "Lenity and Federal Common Law Crimes." *Supreme Court Review* 345.

———. 1996. "What Do Alternative Sanctions Mean?" *University of Chicago Law Review* 63:591.

———. 1997. "Some Realism about Retroactive Criminal Lawmaking." *Roger Williams University Law Review* 3:95–117.

Kansas Criminal Code. 2005-6. http://www.kslegislature .org/legsrvstatutes/getStatuteInfo.do (visited November 8, 2006).

Keeler v. Superior Court. 1970. 470 P.2d 617 (Cal.).

Kelling, George L., and Catherine M. Coles. 1996. *Fixing Broken Windows.* New York: Free Press.

Kolender v. Lawson. 1983. 461 U.S. 352.

Koppersmith v. State. 1999. 742 So.2d 206 (Ala.App.).

Kotila v. Commonwealth. 2003. 114 S.W.3d 226. (Ky.).

Kring v. Missouri. 1883. 107 U.S. 221.

Krulewitch v. U.S. 1949. 336 U.S. 440.

LaFave, Wayne R. 2003a. *Criminal Law.* 4th ed. St. Paul, Minn.: Thompson West.

———. 2003b. *Substantive Criminal Law.* 2nd ed. Vol. 1. St Paul, Minn.: Thompson West.

———, and Austen Scott. 1986. *Criminal Law.* 2nd ed. St. Paul, Minn.: West.

Landry v. Daley. 1968. 280 F.Supp. (N.D.Ill.).

Lanzetta v. New Jersey. 1939. 306 U.S. 451.

Lawrence v. Texas. 2003. 123 S.Ct. 2472.

Law v. State. 1974. 318 A.2d 859 (Md.App.).

———. 1975. 349 A.2d 295 (Md.App.).

Le Barron v. State. 1966. 145 N.W.2d 79 (Wis.).

Lederer, Richard. 1988. *Get Thee to a Punnery.* New York: Bantam Doubleday.

Levett's Case. 1638. 79 Eng. Rep. 1034.

Lewin, Tamar. 1985. "Criminal Onus on Executives." *New York Times,* 5 March.

Lewis, C. S. 1953. "The Humanitarian Theory of Punishment." *Res Judicata* 6:224.

Lewis, Sinclair. 1922. *Babbitt.* New York: Harcourt Brace.

Lewis et al. v. State. 1952. 251 S.W.2d 490 (Ark.).

Liptak, Adam. 2003. "Louisiana Sentence Renews Debate on the Death Penalty." *New York Times,* 28 August.

Livermore, Joseph, and Paul Meehl. 1967. "The Virtues of M'Naghten." *Minnesota Law Review* 51:800.

Loewy, Arnold. 1987. *Criminal Law.* St. Paul, Minn.: West.

Logan, Wayne A. 2001. "The Shadow Criminal Law of Municipal Governance." *Ohio State Law Journal* 62:1409.

Louisiana Statutes Annotated. 1974. Rev. Stat. tit. 17-A.

Low, Peter. 1990. *Criminal Law.* St. Paul, Minn.: West.

Macias v. State. 1929. 283 P. 711.

Madison, James. 1961. "The Federalist No. 51." In *The Federalist.* Edited by Jacob E. Cooke. Middletown, Conn.: Wesleyan University Press.

Marcus, Paul. 1986. "The Development of Entrapment Law." *Wayne Law Review* 33:5.

Martinson, Robert. 1974. "What Works? Questions and Answers about Prison Reform." *Public Interest* 35:22–54.

Maryland Criminal Code. 2006. Criminal Law. § 2-201 (Murder). http://mlis.state.md.us/cgi-win/web_ statutes.exe (visited November 8, 2006).

Massachusetts Criminal Code. 2003. http://www.mass.gov/ legis/laws/mgl/266-16.htm.

Matheney v. Commonwealth. 2006. WL 733985 (Ky.).

Mayer, Andre, and Michael Wheeler. 1982. *The Crocodile Man: A Case of Brain Chemistry and Criminal Violence.* Boston: Houghton-Mifflin.

Mayor of New York v. Miln. 1837. 36 U.S. (11 Pet.) 102.

McKendree v. Christy. 1961. 172 N.E.2d 380.

McMahon, R. Bradley. 2004. "After Billions Spent to Comply with HIPPA and GBA Provisions, Why Is Identity Theft the Most Prevalent Crime in America?" *Villanova Law Review* 49:625.

McMullen, Richie. 1990. *Male Rape: Breaking the Silence on the Last Taboo.* London: Gay Men Press.

McNally v. U.S. 1987. 483 U.S. 350.

Meerpol, Robert. 2003. *An Execution in the Family: One Son's Journey.* New York: St. Martin's Press.

Merriam-Webster. 2003. *The Unabridged Dictionary.* http://unabridged.merriam-webster.com/.

Merschman, Joseph. 2001. "The Dark Side of the Web: Cyberstalking and the Need for Contemporary Legislation." *Harvard Women's Law Journal* 24:255.

Michael, Jerome, and Herbert Wechsler. 1937. "A Rationale of the Law of Homicide." *Columbia Law Review* 701, 1261.

Michael M. v. Superior Court of Sonoma County. 1981. 450 U.S. 464.

Michigan Criminal Code. 2005. http://www.legislature .mi.gov/(S(gp0glz552tmoxh45i5emeu45))/mileg.asp x?page=getObject&objectName=mcl-328-1931-LXXVI.

———. 2006. http://www.legislature.mi.gov/ (S(chfhmr55ac4mdwzsscw41s55))/mileg.aspx?page= getobject&objectname=mcl-750-17&queryid= 15730297&highlight=317.

Miller v. State. 1999. 6 S.W.3d 812 (Ark.App.).

Minnesota Criminal Code. 2005. http://www.revisor.leg .state.mn.us/stats/609/341.html.

Minnesota Statutes Annotated. 1989. Cumulative Supplement.

Mishler, Joanna Lee. 2000 (December). "Cyberstalking: Can Communication via the Internet Constitute a Credible Threat, and Should an Internet Service Provider Be Liable If It Does?" *Santa Clara Computer and High Technology Law Journal* 17:115.

Mitford, Jessica. 1969. *The Trial of Dr. Spock.* New York: Knopf.

M'Naghten's Case. 1843. 8 Eng.Rep. 718.

Moore, Michael S. 1999. "The Principle of Legality." In *Foundations of Criminal Law.* Edited by Leo Katz, Michael S. Moore, and Stephen J. Morse. New York: Foundation Press.

Moran v. People. 1872. 25 Mich. 356.

Moriarty, Daniel G. 1989. "Extending the Defense of Renunciation." *Temple Law Review* 62.

Morris, Herbert. 1976. *On Guilt and Innocence.* Los Angeles: University of California Press.

Morris Norval. 1951. "Somnambulistic Homicide: Ghosts, Spiders, and North Koreans." *Res Judicata* 5.

———. 1974. *The Future of Imprisonment.* Chicago: University of Chicago Press.

———, and Gordon Hawkins. 1970. *An Honest Politician's Guide to Crime Control.* Chicago: University of Chicago Press.

National Public Radio. 2003. Morning Edition. 18 September.

Nazi Saboteur Case. 1942. Transcript of Military Commission (copy owned by author). Washington, D.C.: National Archives.

Nesson, Charles. 1982. Letter to the Editor. *New York Times,* 1 July.

New Mexico Criminal Code. 2006. § 30-4-3. http://nxt .ella.net/NXT/gateway.dll?f=templates$fn=default .htm$vid=nm:all.

New York Penal Code. 2003. http://public.leginfo.state .ny.us/menugetf.cgi?COMMONQUERY=LAWS.

Note. 1951. "Statutory Burglary: The Magic of Four Walls and a Roof." *University of Pennsylvania Law Review* 100:411.

Nourse, Victoria. 1997. "Passion's Progress: Modern Law Reform and the Provocation Defense." *Yale Law Journal* 106:1331.

Novak, William J. 1996. *The People's Welfare: Law and Regulation in Nineteenth-Century America.* Chapel Hill: University of North Carolina Press.

Oliver v. State. 1985. 703 P.2d 869.

Olmstead v. U.S. 1928. 277 U.S. 438.

Packer, Herbert L. 1968. *The Limits of the Criminal Sanction.* Stanford, Calif.: Stanford University Press.

Papichristou v. City of Jacksonville. 1972. 405 U.S. 156.

Parker v. Municipal Judge. 1967. 427 P.2d 642 (Nev.).

Parsons v. State. 1877. 2 So. 854 (Ala.).

Pennsylvania Laws. 1794. Ch. 257, §§ 1–2.

Penry v. Lynaugh. 1989. 492 U.S. 302.

People ex rel. Gallo v. Acuna. 1997. 929 P.2d 596.

People v. Allen. 1997. 64 Cal.Rptr.2d 497.

People v. Anderson. 1968. 447 P.2d 942.

People v. Armitage. 1987. 239 Cal.Rptr.515 (Cal.App.).

People v. Chavez. 1947. 176 P.2d 92 (Cal.App.).

People v. Chessman. 1951. 238 P.2d 1001 (Cal.).

People v. Datema. 1995. 533 N.W.2d 272 (Mich.).

People v. Decima. 1956. 138 N.E.2d 799 (N.Y.).

People v. Disimone. 2002. 650 N.W.2d 436 (Mich.App.).

People v. Dover. 1990. 790 P.2d 834 (Colo.).

People v. Drew. 1978. 583 P.2d 1318 (Cal.).

People v. Goetz. 1986. 497 N.E.2d 41 (N.Y.).

People v. Guenther. 1987. 740 P.2d 971 (Colo.).

People v. Johnson. 1987. 750 P.2d 72 (Colo.App.)

People v. Kemp. 1961. 359 P.2d 913 (Cal.).

People v. Kibbe. 1974. 362 N.Y.S.2d 848.

People v. Kimball. 1981. 311 N.W.2d 343 (Mich.App.).

People v. Mayberry. 1975. 542 P.2d 1337 (Cal.).

People v. Mills. 1904. 70 N.E. 786.

People v. Moreland. 2002. WL 459026 (Cal.App. 2 Dist.).

People v. Muñoz. 1960. 200 N.Y.S.2d 957.

People v. Oliver. 1989. 258 Cal.Rptr.138.

People v. O'Neil. 1990. 550 N.E.2d 1090 (Ill.App.).

People v. Penman. 1915. 110 N.E. 894.

People v. Phillips. 1966. 414 P.2d 353 (Cal.).

People v. Poplar. 1970. 173 N.W.2d 732.

People v. Protopappas. 1988. 201 Cal.App.3d 152 (Cal.App.).

People v. Rizzo. 1927. 158 N.E. 888 (N.Y.App.).

People v. Rokicki. 1999. 718 N.E.2d 333 (Ill.App.).

People v. Schmidt. 1915. 216 N.Y. 324.

People v. Shabtay. 2006. 42 Cal.Rptr.3d 227.

People v. Steele. 2002. 47 P.3d 225. (Cal.).

People v. Thomas. 1978. 272 N.W.2d 157 (Mich.App.).

People v. Washington. 1976. 130 Cal.Rptr.96.

People v. Williams. 1965. 205 N.E.2d 749 (Ill.App.).

Perkins, Rollin M., and Ronald N. Boyce. 1982. *Criminal Law.* 3rd ed. Mineola, N.Y.: Foundation Press.

Perlin, Michael. 1989–90. "Unpacking the Myths: The Symbolism Mythology and Insanity Defense Jurisprudence." *Case Western Reserve Law Review* 40:599.

Pinkerton v. U.S. 1946. 328 U.S. 640.

Plato. 1975. *Laws,* trans., Trevor J. Saunders. Middlesex, England: Penguin Books.

Porter v. State. 2003. WL 1919477 (Ark.App.).

Poulos, Peter W. 1995. "Chicago's Ban on Gang Loitering: Making Sense Out of Vagueness and Overbreadth in Loitering Laws." *California Law Review* 83:379.

Powell v. Texas. 1967. Brief for Appellant. WL 113841 (visited June 9, 2006).

———. 1968. 392 U.S. 514.

———. 1968. Brief for Appellee. WL 129298 (visited June 9, 2006).

Press, Ann, and Peggy Clausen. 1982. "Not Guilty Because of PMS?" *Newsweek*, November 8.

Preyer, Kathryn. 1983. "Crime, the Criminal Law and Reform in Post-Revolutionary Virginia." *Law and History Review* 1.

Queen v. Dudley and Stephens. 1884. 14 Q. B. 273.

Ramer, Holly. 2004. "Mother of Slain Woman Settles Lawsuit Against Info-Broker." *Associated Press*, 10 March.

R. A. V. v. City of St. Paul. 1992. 505 U.S. 377, 112 S.Ct. 2538.

Regina v. Morgan. 1975. 2. W.L.R. 923 (H.L.).

Reinhold, Robert. 1985. "Trial Opens in Death at Texas Nursing Home." *New York Times*, 1 October.

Remick, Lani Anne. 1993. "Read Her Lips: An Argument for a Verbal Consent Standard in Rape." *University of Pennsylvania Law Review* 141:1103.

Remsburg v. Docusearch, Inc. 2003. 816 A.2d 1001 (N.H.).

Rex v. Bailey. 1818. *Crown Cases Reserved.*

Rex v. Scofield. 1784. Cald. 397.

Reynolds v. State. 1889. 42 N.W. 903.

Rimer, Sara, and Raymond Bonner. 2000. "Whether to Kill Those Who Killed as Youths." *New York Times*, 22 August.

Roberts, Sam. 1989. "Metro Matters; Exploring Laws and the Legacy of the *Goetz* Case." *New York Times*, 23 January.

Robinson, Paul, and Markus Dubber. 2004. "An Introduction to the Model Penal Code of the American Law Institute." http://papers.ssrn.com/sol3/papers.cfm?abstract_id=661165 (visited May 7, 2006).

Robinson v. California. 1962. 370 U.S. 660.

Rochman, Sue. n.d. "Silent Victims: Bring Male Rape Out of the Closet." http://www.interactivetheatre.org/resc/silent.html.

Roper v. Simmons. 2005. 543 U.S. 551.

Rosenberg, Ben. 2002. "The Growth of Federal Criminal Common Law." *American Journal of Criminal Law* 29:193.

Roth, Siobahn. 2003. "Material Support Law: Weapon in the War on Terror." *Legal Times*, 9 May.

Rothman, David J. 1980. *Conscience and Convenience.* Boston: Little, Brown.

Rustad, Michael L. 2001. "Private Enforcement of Cybercrime on the Electronic Frontier." *Southern California Interdisciplinary Law Journal* 11:63.

Safire, William. 1989. "The End of RICO." *New York Times*, 30 January.

Samaha, Joel. 1974. *Law and Order in Historical Perspective.* New York: Academic Press.

———. 1978. "Hanging for Felony." *Historical Journal* 21.

———. 1981. "The Recognizance in Elizabethan Law Enforcement." *American Journal of Legal History* 25.

Sampson, Robert J., and Stephen W. Raudenbush. 1999. "Deterrent Effect of the Police on Crime." *American Journal of Sociology* 105:163–89.

Sanchez, Renee. 1998. "City of Tolerance Tires of Homeless: San Francisco Aims to Roust Street Dwellers." *Washington Post*, 28 November.

Sayre, Francis Bowes. 1921–22. "Criminal Conspiracy." *Harvard Law Review* 35:399.

———. 1932. "*Mens Rea.*" *Harvard Law Review* 45:974.

Scheidegger, Kent S. 1993. *A Guide to Regulating Panhandling.* Sacramento, Calif.: Criminal Justice Legal Foundation.

Schenck v. U.S. 1919. 249 U.S. 47.

Schopp, Robert F. 1988. "Returning to *M'Naghten* to Avoid Moral Mistakes: One Step Forward, or Two Steps Backward for the Insanity Defense?" *Arizona Law Review* 30:135.

Schwartz, Richard. 1983. "Rehabilitation." *Encyclopedia of Crime and Justice.* New York: Free Press.

Shenon, Philip. 1985. "Dispute over Intent in Drug Cases Divided F.D.A. and Justice Department." *New York Times*, 19 September.

Shepherd, Joanna. 2002 (January). "Fear of the First Strike: The Full Deterrent Effect of California's Two- and Three-Strikes Legislation." *Journal of Legal Studies* XXXI:159.

Sherman, Rorie. 1994 (March 28). "Insanity Defense: A New Challenge." *National Law Journal.*

Sherman v. U.S. 1958. 356 U.S. 369.

Siegel, Barry. 1996. "Held Accountable for Son's Burglaries." *Los Angeles Times*, 10 May.

Simon, Harry. 1992. "Towns without Pity: A Constitutional and Historical Analysis of Official Efforts to Drive Homeless Persons from American Cities." *Tulane Law Review* 66.

Simons, Kenneth W. 1997. "When Is Strict Liability Just?" *Journal of Criminal Law and Criminology* 87:1075.

Skilton, Robert H. 1937. "The Requisite Act in a Criminal Attempt." *University of Pennsylvania Law Review* 3:308.

Skogan, Wesley G. 1990. *Disorder and Decline.* New York: Free Press.

Smith, Juliette. 1996. "Arresting the Homeless for Sleeping in Public: A Paradigm for Expanding the *Robinson* Doctrine." *Columbia Journal of Law and Social Problems* 29.

Solem v. Helm. 1983. 463 U.S. 277.

Sonnier v. State. 1992. 849 S.W.2d 828 (Tex.App.).

Stanford v. Kentucky. 1989. 492 U.S. 361.

Stanley v. Georgia. 1969. 394 U.S. 557.

State in the Interest of M.T.S. 1992. 609 A.2d 1335 (Pa.).

State v. Aguillard. 1990. 567 So.2d 674 (La.).

State v. Akers. 1979. 400 A.2d 38 (N.H.).

State v. Anderson. 1991. 566 N.E. 2d 1224 (Ohio).

State v. Brown. 1976. 364 A.2d 27 (N.J.).

State v. Celli. 1978. 263 N.W.2d 145 (S.D.).
State v. Chism. 1983. 436 So.2d 464 (La.).
State v. Cotton. 1990. 790 P.2d 1050 (N.M.App.).
State v. Cotton. 2000. 5 P.3d. 918 (Ariz.App.).
State v. Crawford. 1996. 472 S.E.2d 920 (N.C.).
State v. Curley. 1997. WL 242286 (N.Mex.App.).
State v. Damms. 1960. 100 N.W.2d 592 (Wis.).
State v. Fiero. 1979. 603 P.2d 74.
State v. Flory. 1929. 276 P. 458 (Wyo.).
State v. Foster. 1987. 522 A.2d 277 (Conn.).
State v. Fransua. 1973. 510 P.2d 106 (N.Mex.App.).
State v. Good. 1917. 195 S.W. 1006.
State v. Hall. 1974. 214 N.W.2d 205.
State v. Hamlet. 1984. 321 S.E.2d 837 (N.C.).
State v. Harrell. 2002. 811 So.2d 1015 (La.App.).
State v. Harrison. 1977. 564 P.2d 1321 (N.M.).
State v. Hauptmann. 1935. 180 A.2d 809 (N.J.).
State v. Hiott. 1999. 987 P.2d 135 (Wash.App.).
State v. Hobbs. 1961. 107 N.W.2d 238.
State v. Hoying. 2005. WL 678989 (OhioApp.).
State v. Hudson. 1999. 745 So. 2d. 997 (Fla.App.)
State v. Humphries. 1978. 586 P.2d. 130 (Wash.App.).
State v. Hundley. 1985. 693 P.2d 475 (Kans.).
State v. Jantzi. 1982. 56, 57, 641 P.2d 62 (Ore.App.).
State v. Jerrett. 1983. 307 S.E.2d 339.
State v. Kennamore. 1980. 604 S.W.2d 856 (Tenn.).
State v. Kimberley. 2003. 103 S.W.2d (Mo.App.).
State v. Kordas. 1995. 528 N.W.2d 483 (Wis.).
State v. K. R. L. 1992. 840 P.2d 210 (Wash.App.).
State v. Kuntz. 2000. 995 P.2d 951 (Mont.).
State v. Loge. 2000. 608 N.W.2d 152 (Minn.).
State v. Mays. 2000. WL 1033098 (OhioApp. Dist. 1).
State v. Metzger. 1982. 319 N.W.2d 459 (Neb.).
State v. Miranda. 1998. 715 A.2d 680.
State v. Mitcheson. 1977. 560 P.2d 1120 (Utah).
State v. Myrick. 1982. 291 S.E.2d 577.
State v. Noren. 1985. 371 N.W.2d 381 (Wis.).
State v. O'Dell. 1984. 684 S.W.2d 453.
State v. Ownbey. 2000. 996 P.2d 510 (Ore.App.).
State v. Phipps. 1994. 883 S.W.2d 138 (Tenn.App.).
State v. Quarles. 1986. 504 A.2d 473 (R.I.).
State v. Robins. 2002. 646 N.W.2d 287 (Wis.).
State v. Schleifer. 1923. 432 121 A. 805.
State v. Shelley. 1997. 929 P.2d 489 (Wash.App.).
State v. Snowden. 1957. 313 P.2d 706 (Idaho).
State v. Stark. 1992. 832 P.2d 109 (Wash.App.).
State v. Stewart. 1988. 763 P.2d 572 (Kans.).
———. 1995. 663 A.2d 912 (R.I.).
State v. Taylor. 2002. 650 N.W.2d 190 (Minn.).
State v. Thomas. 1999. 590 N.W.2d 755 (Minn.).
State v. Thompson. 1990. 792 P.2d. 1103 (Mont.).
——— . 2003. 65 P.3d 420 (Ariz.).
State v. Tomaino. 1999. 733 N.E.2d 1191 (OhioApp.).
State. v. Ulvinen. 1981. 313 N.W.2d 425 (Minn.).
State v. Vargas. 2003. 812 A.2d. 205.
State v. Walden. 1982. 293 S.E.2d 780.
State v. Wilson. 1996. 685 So.2d 1063.
State v. Zeta Chi Fraternity. 1997. 686 A.2d. 530 (N.H.).

Stephen, Sir James F. 1883. *A History of the Criminal Law of England.* London: Macmillan.
Swann v. U.S. 1994. 648 A.2d 928.
"Symposium: Wrongful Convictions and Systemic Reform." 2005. *American Criminal Law Reform* 42:4.
Tennessee Criminal Code. 2005. http://198.187.128.12/tennessee/lpext.dll?f=templates&fn=fs-main.htm&2.0 (visited July 20, 2006).
Texas v. Johnson. 1989. 491 U.S. 397.
Thomas, Clarence. 1996. "Federalist Society Symposium: The Rights Revolution." *Michigan Law and Policy Review* 1:269.
Thompson v. Oklahoma. 1988. 487 U.S. 815.
Tier, Robert. 1993. "Maintaining Safety and Civility in Public Spaces: A Constitutional Approach to Aggressive Begging." *Louisiana Law Review* 54:285.
Todd v. State. 1992. 594 So.2d 802 (Fla.App.).
Trop v. Dulles. 1958. 356 U.S. 86.
Turner, J. W. Cecil. 1934. *Cambridge Law Journal* 5:230–47.
Turner, Michael, Jody Sundt, Brandon Applegate, and Francis Cullen. 1995 (September). "'Three Strikes and You're Out' Legislation: A National Assessment." *Federal Probation.*
Urofsky, Melvin, and Paul Finkelman. 2002a. *Documents of American Constitutional and Legal History.* New York: Oxford University Press.
———. 2002b. *A March of Liberty.* New York: Oxford University Press.
USA Patriot Act. 2001. http://frwebgate.access.gpo.gov/cgi-bin/getdoc.cgi?dbname=107_cong_bills&docid=f:h3162enr.txt.pdf.
U.S. Code. 2003. 18 U.S.C.A. § 17.
———. 2006. Destructive Device. Title 18, Part I, Chapter 44, Section 921. http://www4.law.cornell.edu/uscode/html/uscode18/usc_sec_18_00000921----000-.html.
———. 2006. Fraud and Related Activity in Connection with Computers. Title 18, Part I, Chapter 47, Section 1030. http://www4.law.cornell.edu/uscode/html/uscode18/usc_sec_18_00001030----000-.html (visited August 5, 2006).
———. 2006. Gathering or Delivering Defense Information to Aid Foreign Government. Title 18, Part I, Chapter 37, Section 794. http://www4.law.cornell.edu/uscode/html/uscode18/usc_sec_18_00000794----000-.html.
———. 2006. Sabotage. Title 18, Part I, Chapter 105. http://www4.law.cornell.edu/uscode/html/uscode18/usc_sup_01_18_10_I_20_105.html.
———. 2006. Sedition. Title 18, Part I, Chapter 115, Section 2384. http://www4.law.cornell.edu/uscode/html/uscode18/usc_sec_18_00002384----000-.html.
———. 2006. Terrorism. Title 18, Part I, Chapter 113B. http://www4.law.cornell.edu/uscode/html/uscode18/usc_sup_01_18_10_I_20_113B.html.
———. 2006. Treason. Title 18, Part I, Chapter 115, Section 2381. http://www4.law.cornell.edu/uscode/html/uscode18/usc_sec_18_00002381----000-.html.

U.S. Department of Justice. 2001. "Moussaoui Indictment." http://www.usdoj.gov/ag/moussaouiindictment.htm (visited August 20, 2006).

———. 2004. Report of the Department of Justice's Task Force on Intellectual Property. iii–iv. http://www.eff.org/IP/20041013_DOJ_IPTaskForceReport.pdf.

———. 2006. Progress Report of the Department of Justice's Task Force on Intellectual Property. Washington D.C.: Department of Justice.

U.S. v. Aguilar et al. 1989. 883 F.2d 662 (CA9).

U.S. v. Ancheta. 2006. (C.D. Cal.). http://www.usdoj.gov/criminal/cybercrime/anchetaSent.htm (visited, August 13, 2006).

U.S. v. Bass. 1971. 404 U.S. 336.

U.S. v. Blue Thunder. 1979. 604 F.2d 550 (8th Cir.).

U.S. v. Bruno. 1939. 105 F.2d 921.

U.S. v. Cordoba-Hincapie. 2001. 825 F.Supp. 485.

U.S. v. Downs. 1995. 56 F.3d 973 (8th Cir.).

U.S. v. Feola. 1975. 420 U.S. 671.

U.S. v. Garcia. 1998. 151 F.3d 1243 (CA9).

U.S. v. Grimaud. 1911. 220 U.S. 506.

U.S. v. Hudson and Goodwin. 1812. 11 U.S. 32.

U.S. v. Lanier. 1997. 520 U.S. 259.

U.S. v. Lindh. 2002. "Plea Agreement." U.S. District Court, E.D. Virginia, Crim. No. 02-37A.

U.S. v. Nofziger. 1989. 878 F.2d 442 (2nd Cir.).

U.S. v. Peoni. 1938. 100 F.2d 401 (2nd Cir.).

U.S. v. Peterson. 1973. 483 F.2d 1222 (2nd Cir.).

U.S. v. Reese. 1875. 92 U.S. 214.

U.S. v. Simpson. 1987. 813. F.2d 1462 (CA9).

U.S. v. Treas-Wilson. 1993. 3 F.3d 1406 (10th Cir.).

Vamosi, Robert. 2006. "An American Cybervillain." CNET Reviews http://reviews.cnet.com/4520-3513_7-6427016-1.html (visited August 13, 2006).

Velazquez v. State. 1990. 561 So.2d 347 (Fla.App.).

Von Hirsh, Andrew, and Andrew Ashworth. 2004. *Proportionate Sentencing.* Oxford University Press.

Weems v. U.S. 1910. 217 U.S. 349.

Weiss, Baruch. 2002. "What Were They Thinking? The Mental States of Aider and Abettor, and the Causer under Federal Law." *Fordham Law Review* 70:1341.

West's California Penal Code. 1988. St. Paul, Minn.: West.

West's Florida Statutes Annotated. 2005. Title XLVI, § 775.01. http://www.flsenate.gov/Statutes/index.cfm?App_mode=Display_Index&Title_Request=XLVI#TitleXLVI (visited May 5, 2006).

Williams, Glanville. 1961. *Criminal Law.* 2nd ed. London: Stevens and Sons.

Williams, Linda. 1984. "The Classic Rape: When Do Victims Report?" *Social Problems* 31:464.

Williams v. State. 1992. 600 N.E.2d 962 (Ind.App.).

Wilson, James Q. 1975. *Thinking about Crime.* New York: Basic Books.

———, and Richard Herrnstein. 1985. *Crime and Human Nature.* New York: Simon and Schuster.

———, and George L. Kelling. 1982 (March). "Broken Windows." *Atlantic Monthly.*

Wisconsin Criminal Code. 2003. http://folio.legis.state.wi.us/cgi-bin/om_isapi.dll?clientID=547736967&infobase=stats.nfo&jump=ch.%20947.

———. 2006. § 940.31. http://nxt.legis.state.wi.us/nxt/gateway.dll?f=templates&fn=default.htm&vid=WI:Default&d=stats&jd=ch.%20940.

Wolfendon Report. 1957. Report of Committee on Homosexual Offenses and Prostitution. London: Stationer's Office.

Yang, Debra Wong, and Brian M. Hoffstadt. 2006. "Countering the Cyber-Crime Threat." *American Criminal Law Review* 43:201.

Young v. State. 1985. 493 A.2d 352 (Md.).

Case Index

Index

Attempt *actus reus*, 240–247, **465**
Attempted battery assault, 348, **465**
Attempted murder, 233
Attempt liability, 235–256
    elements, 237–247
    historical perspectives, 235–236
    rationales, 236
Attempt *mens rea*, 237–240, **465**
Attendant circumstance, 81, 332, **465**
Attribution. *See* Causation, principle of
Authorized consent, 164
Autonomy, retribution and, 15
Awareness (scienter), 116, **472**

B

"Bad manners," in public places, 408
Bad-results crimes
    causation and, 124–129
    definition of, 80, 82
Barbaric punishments, 64–65, **465**
Battery
    definition of, 347, **465**
    elements of, 347–348
    injury as requirement for, 348
Battery *actus reus*, 347–348
Battery *mens rea*, 348
BB gun shooting, consent defense, 167
"Benefit of clergy," 282
Bentham, Jeremy, 16
Bifurcation, 283, **465**
Bill of Rights
    free speech, 55–60
    privacy, 60–64
Blackmail (extortion), 381, **468**
Blameworthiness (culpability)
    definition of, 15, 106, **465, 467**
    intoxication defense and, 193
    Model Penal Code provisions, 113
Bodily injury crimes
    assault, 348–350
    battery, 347–348
    personal restraint crimes, 356–361
    stalking, 350–356
Bodily movements
    involuntary, 84
    voluntary, 84
"Booby trap," as justifiable deadly
    force, 157
Born-alive rule, 275–276, **465**
Bracton, 20, 107, 158
Brain death, 277
Breach of the peace, 55
Breaking, common-law, 389
"Briefing" cases, 39–40
Broken windows theory, 412–413, **465**
Burden of persuasion, 139, **465**
Burden of production, 139, **465**
Burden of proof, for insanity defense,
    186–187
Burglary, 387–392
    capacity to commit, age and, 173,
      189–191
    choice-of-evils defense, 163

circumstances, 389
common-law, 388
definition of, 387, **466**
degrees of, 391–392
elements of, 11, 388
home, 389–390
number of cases, 394
Burglary *actus reus*, 389
Burglary *mens rea*, 391
Burning (*actus reus* in arson),
    382–383, **465**
Business, information collection by, 394
Business crimes, vicarious liability,
    221–223
"But for" cause (*sine qua non* cause),
    124, **466**
Bystanders, legal duty of, 94–95

C

California, antistalking statute, 350
Capacity, diminished, 187–188, **467**
Capacity to commit crimes, age and, 173,
    188–191
Capital cases, 283, **466**
Capital offenses, 282
Capital punishment, 17, 283–284
Case-by-case approach, 303, **466**
Cases. *See also specific cases*
"briefing," 39–40
    excerpts
      briefing, 39–40
      parts of, 37–39
    finding, 40
    strange, 3–6
    text-case method and, 36–40
"Casing a joint," 244
Causation
    principle of, 124–129, **470**
    proving, 124–129
    voluntary manslaughter and, 313
Cause in fact, 106, **466**
Chain conspiracies, 262, **466**
Child enticement, 252
Child rape, death penalty for, 47, 66–68
Chilling effect, 56, 58–59, **466**
Choice-of-evils defense, **466**. *See also*
    Necessity defense
Choices, "right," in Moral Penal
    Code, 159
Circumstances
    aggravating, 284, 360–361
    attendant, 81, 332, **465**
    in loitering, 411
    rape and, 334
Citation, 38
Civil commitment, 175, **466**
Classification of crimes, 10–12
Clear and present danger doctrine, 55–56
Clemency, 19
Code states, 29, **466**
Collection, of materials used to commit
    crime, 244
Colonial America, codified offenses in, 31

Commission of crime
    participation after, 216–220
    participation before and during,
      209–216
Common-law burglary, 388
Common-law crimes
    definition of, 28, **466**
    federal, 30
    state, 29–30
Common-law murder. *See* Murder,
    common-law
Common-law rape, 330–332, **466**
Common-law sodomy, 331, **466**
Complicity, 12, 208, **466**. *See also*
    Accomplices
Comprehensive Crime Control Act, 187
Concealing terrorists, 447–448
Concurrence (in criminal conduct
    crimes), 81, **466**
Concurrence, principle of, 123–124,
    470–471
Conditional threats, 349, **466**
Conduct
    criminal, proof of, 138
    expressive, 55, 59–60
Conduct, unjustifiably inflicting harm, 7
Conduct crimes, 81–82, **466**
Conduct transcending national
    boundaries, in terrorist crimes,
    446–447, **466**
Confessions, 109
Confinement, 14
Consensual crimes, 195
Consent
    authorized, 164
    knowing, 164
Consent defense
    case, 165–168
    definition of, 163–164
    exceptions, 164
Consolidated theft statutes, 372–373, **466**
Conspiracy, 256–263
    criminal objective, 262–263
    definition of, 209, 256–257, **466**
    justifications for criminal liability, 257
    large-scale, 261–262
    overt act requirement, 262
    parties to, 261
Conspiracy *actus reus*, 257–260, **466**
Conspiracy *mens rea*, 260–262, **466**
Constitution. *See* United States
    Constitution
Constitutional democracy, 48
Constructive disorderly conduct, 409, **466**
Constructive possession, 97, **466**
Contact, in rape and sexual offenses, 333
Contraceptive use, privacy rights and,
    61–63
Conviction, 8–9
Cooper, Kentucky Supreme Court Justice
    William, 26
Corporate criminal liability, 221
Corporation murder, 307–310

Fraud in the inducement, 344, **468**
Free speech rights, 55–60
  hate crimes and, 55–59
  infringement on, 58
  time, place and manner regulations, 419
Free will, retribution and, 15, 16
Fundamental rights, 60

G

Gang activity, 422–427
General deterrence (general prevention), 16, **468**
General intent, 108, 110, **468**
General intent "plus," 111, **468**
General part of criminal law, 12–13, **468**
General principle of necessity (defense to crime), 158, **468**
Gestures, insulting, 312
Ginsburg, Justice, 70
"Good Samaritan" doctrine, 91, **468**
Government
  compelling interest of, 55
  information collection by, 394
Grand larceny, accessory after the fact, 219–220
Grand theft, punishment for, 72–74
Guilt, legal *vs.* factual, 37
Guilty but mentally ill verdict, 175
Guilty verdict, 37
Gun, unloaded, as factual impossibility, 248–351

H

"Hanging judge," 49
Harboring or concealing terrorists, 447–448
Harm, unjustifiable infliction of, 7
Hate crimes, violation of free speech and, 55–59
Highways, obstruction of, 411
HIV exposure, 114–115
Holmes, Oliver Wendell
  on attempt *mens rea*, 237
  on blameworthiness, 106
  on criminal punishment, 17–18
  definition of objective fair warning, 51
  on freedom of speech, 56
  on voluntary acts, 83
Home
  burglary, 389–390
  defense of, 153–157
  as special place, 387–388
Home confinement sentence, 10
Homeless people, rights of, 416–418
Homicide. *See also* Criminal homicide
  justifiable, 278, **469**
  negligent, 216
  unintentional, 16
Honest and reasonable mistake rule, 344–345, **468**
Hospitalization, for mental patient, 14
Human being, meaning of, 275–277

I

Identity theft, 393–398
  case excerpt, 395–398
  definition of, **468**
  motivations for, 394
  number of cases, 393, 394
Ignorance of the law, 129, 130–131, **468**
Illegal drug possession, 97–99, 100
Illegal immigrants, transporting/harboring, choice-of-evils defense, 160–162
Immediacy of threats, duress and, 192
Imminent danger
  definition of, **468**
  determination of, 149–150
  self-defense and, 140, 141–145
  vs. present danger, 145–149
Imperfect defenses, 139, **468**
Implied malice aforethought, 280, **468**
Impossibility, 248–253
Imprisonment, principle of proportionality and, 70–74
Imputation (causation, principle of), 124–129
Incapacitation, 16, 18, **469**
Inchoate crimes, 232–271
  abandonment, 253–256
  attempt liability, 235–256
  conspiracy, 256–263
  definition of, **469**
  dilemma of, 234
  impossibility, 248–253
  solicitation, 263–266
Inchoate offenses, 234
Incomplete criminal conduct, 234
Indeterminant sentencing laws, 19
Indispensable element test (attempt law), 242, **469**
Information collection, by government, business and nonprofit organizations, 394
Inherently dangerous felony approach, 302–307, **469**
Inhumane, rehabilitation as, 19
Initial aggressor, 140, **469**
Injunction to abate public nuisances, 422, **469**
Injury
  accidental, strict liability and, 120–123
  attempted, 239
  as requirement for battery, 348
  as robbery requirement, 377
Insanity
  definition of, **469**
  faking, 176
  as legal concept, 175
Insanity defense, 175–187
  burden of proof, 186–187
  diminished capacity, 187–188
  irresistible impulse test, 181–182
  myths about, 176
  product-of-mental-illness test, 186

right-wrong test or M'Naghten rule, 175, 177–180
  risks from, 176
  substantial capacity test, 182–185
  use of, 175, 176
Intangible property, 371, **469**
Intellectual property
  definition of, 393, **469**
  theft of, 398–401
Intelligence Reform and Prevention of Terrorism Act of 2004, 451
Intent, premeditated and deliberate, proving, 286–287
Intentional killing, 279
"Intentional scaring," 348
Intent-to-cause-serious-bodily-injury, 280, **469**
Intent-to-instill-fear test, 352, **469**
Intent to kill, 239–230
Interference with prosecution. *See* Accessories after the fact
International terrorism, 445–446, **469**
Intervening cause, 125, **469**
Intoxication
  involuntary, 193–194
  voluntary, 193
Intoxication defense, 193–194
Intrinsic force, 337, **469**
Invasion, of others' property
  burglary, 387–392
  criminal trespass, 392–393
  cybercrimes, 393–401
Involuntary bodily movements, 84
Involuntary manslaughter, 317–322
  case excerpts, 125–127, 319–321
  by criminal negligence, 317–321
  definition of, **469**
  elements of, 317
  by unlawful act, 318, 321–322
Irresistible impulse test, 181–182, **469**

J

Jail sentence. *See* Sentencing
Jefferson, Thomas, 439
Judges
  application of rule of lenity and, 25
  in case excerpt, 38
  criminal lawmaking power, 23
  "hanging," 49
Judgment (decision), 38
Judicial policies, stare decisis and, 25–27
Judicial retroactive criminal lawmaking, 22–28
  limits on, 23
  precedent, 25–28
  rule of lenity, 23–25
  stare decisis, 26–28
Judicial waiver, 189, **469**
"Just deserts," 20
Justice, retribution and, 15
Justifiable homicide, 278, **469**
Justification, principle of, 12

mental attitudes, 112–113
mental element in murder, 282
MPC test. *See* Substantial steps test
offenses of general application, 234
overt act requirement, 262
rehabilitation and, 20
"right" choices, 159
riot, 412
states of mind, 106
structure of, 32
theft by extortion, 381
unlawful entry provision, 244
Moral duties, failure to perform, 91
Morality, free speech and, 55
Motive, 108–109, **470**
MPC. *See* Model Penal Code
MPC test. *See* Substantial steps test
Municipal codes, 415
Municipal ordinances, 33–34
Murder, 277–310
    accomplices to, 12, 211–213
    attempted, 233, 239
    attempted, voluntary abandonment of, 256
    Biblical view of, 274
    common-law
        elements of, 278–279
        history of, 282
    concurrence in, 124
    corporation, 307–310
    definition of, 36, 277, **470**
    deliberate, 284–288
    elements of, 280–282
    felony. *See* Felony murder
    first-degree. *See* First-degree murder
    insanity defense for, 176
    intent and, 131
    justification, defense of home, 154–156
    kinds or degrees of, 282–283
    law, history of, 278–280
    M'Naghten defense, 178–179
    premeditated, 284–288
    reckless or negligent, 119–120
    second-degree. *See* Second-degree murder
    as voluntary act, 86–87
    vs. manslaughter, 321
Murder *actus reus*, 281–282, **470**
Murder *mens rea*, 282, **470**
Music, illegal downloads of, 369

N

National Crime Victim Survey, 331
Nature and quality of the act, 177
Necessity defense (choice-of-evils defense), 158–163
    case excerpt, 160–163
    definition of, **470**
    history of, 158–159
    justification defense and, 140
    Model Penal Code, 159
    self-defense and, 140, 141–145

Negligence
    as culpability requirement, 113, 118–120
    definition of, **470**
    rape and, 345–346
    stalking *mens rea*, 352
Negligent injuring, 348
Negligent mistake, regarding consent for sexual intercourse, 346
New York Penal Code
    of 1881, 31
    of 1976, 31–32
    duress, 192
NGRI (Not Guilty By Reason of Insanity), 176
Ninth Amendment, privacy rights and, 61
No fault liability, **470**. *See also* Strict liability
"Nonclergyable" offenses, 282
Noncriminal wrongs, 7. *See also* Torts
Nonprofit organizations, information collection by, 394
Not Guilty By Reason of Insanity (NGRI), 176
Not guilty verdict, 37
Nude dancing, as expressive conduct, 59

O

Objective fault, 109–110, 352, **470**
Objective fear, 343
Objective fear test only, 352, **470**
Objective morality, criminal law as, 131
Objective test of cooling-off time, 312–313, **470**
Objective test of entrapment, 198, **470**
Obscenity, 55
Obstruction of justice. *See* Accessories after the fact
Offenses of general application, 12–13, 234, **470**
Old Testament, retribution and, 14, 15
Omissions, 90–95
Opinion of court, 38–39
Order, 408, **470**
Organized criminal behavior, 263
Overt act, in conspiracy, 258, **470**

P

Palgrave, Sir Francis, 18
"Panacea phenomenon," 71
Panhandling, 418–422, **470**
Paramour rule, 314, **470**
Pardons, 19
Parent-child relationship, vicarious liability and, 226–228
Parties to crime, 208–220
    accessories after the fact, 208, 216–220
    accessories before the fact, 208
    accomplices. *See* Accomplices
    principals in the first degree, 208
    principals in the second degree, 208
Password sniffing, 399
Peel, Sir Robert, 177

Penetrations, in rape and sexual offenses, 333
Pennsylvania, murder statute, 282
The People's Welfare (Novak), 33
Perception of the facts, 131
Per curiam, 293
Perfect defenses, 139, **470**
Person, meaning of, 275–277
Personal restraint crimes
    false imprisonment, 361
    kidnapping, 356–361
Persuasion, burden of, 139, **465**
Petitioners, 38
Physical proximity test, 241–242
Piggybacking, 399
Pinkerton rule, 209, **470**
Plaintiffs, 8, **470**
Plurality opinion, 39
PMS (premenstrual syndrome), as excuse defense, 199
Police methods, unsavory, 198
Poor, criminal statutes and, 414
Pornography, privacy rights and, 63
Possession, 96–100
    actual, 97, **465**
    constructive, 97, **466**
    of illegal drugs, 97–100
    knowing, 97, **469**
    of materials used to commit crime, 244
    mere, 97
    of weapons, 99–100
Post-traumatic stress syndrome, as excuse defense, 199–201
Precedent, 25–26, **470**
Preemptive strikes, 140
Preferred status, 55
Preliminary injunction, 415, **470**
Premeditated murder, 284–288
Premenstrual syndrome (PMS), as excuse defense, 199
Prenatal injuries, fetal death from, 276
Preparation for crime
    substantial steps test, 247
    vs. criminal attempt, 244
Preponderance of the evidence, 139, **470**
Present danger, 145–149, **470**
Prevention, 16–19, **470**
Principals in the first degree, 208
Principals in the second degree, 208
Principle of causation, 124–129, **470**
Principle of concurrence, 123–124, **470–471**
Principle of justification, 12
Principle of legality, 20–21, **471**
Principle of legality ("rule of law"), 20–21
Principle of *mens rea*. *See Mens rea*
Principle of proportionality, 65–74
    death penalty and, 65–70
    definition of, **471**
    history of, 65
    imprisonment and, 70–74
Principle of utility, 16–17, **471**
Prison release, dependent on rehabilitation, 19

Photo Credits

P. 3, ©Jean Coughlin

P. 47, ©Larry Downing/Reuters/Landov

P. 79, ©Time & Life Pictures/Getty Images (for the street), The New York Times Photo Archives/Redux (for the inset)

P. 105, ©Ted Soqui/Corbis (for the accident scene), ©AP Images/Nick Ut (for the inset)

P .137, ©AP Images/Contra Costa Times/Dan Rosenstrauch

P. 173, ©Associated Press

P. 207, *The Scream* 1893 by Edvard Munch (1863–1944 Norwegian). Tempera and pastel on board, National Gallery, Oslo, Norway. ©2007. The Munch Museum/The Munch-Ellingsen Group/Artists Rights Society (ARS) New York.

P. 233, ©Dennis Van Tine/Landov

P. 273, ©Lee Celano/Reuters/Landov

P. 329, ©Michael Newman/PhotoEdit

P. 369, ©AP Images/Jim Cole

P. 407, ©Clayton Sharrard/PhotoEdit

P. 437, ©Associated Press

TO THE OWNER OF THIS BOOK:

I hope that you have found *Criminal Law,* Ninth Edition useful. So that this book can be improved in a future edition, would you take the time to complete this sheet and return it? Thank you.

School and address:_____

Department:_____

Instructor's name:_____

1. What I like most about this book is:_____

_____

_____

2. What I like least about this book is:_____

_____

_____

3. My general reaction to this book is:_____

_____

_____

4. The name of the course in which I used this book is:_____

_____

5. Were all of the chapters of the book assigned for you to read?_____

   If not, which ones weren't?_____

6. In the space below, or on a separate sheet of paper, please write specific suggestions for improving this book and anything else you'd care to share about your experience in using this book.

_____

_____

_____

_____

THOMSON

WADSWORTH ™

BUSINESS REPLY MAIL
FIRST-CLASS MAIL   PERMIT NO. 34   BELMONT CA

POSTAGE WILL BE PAID BY ADDRESSEE

Attn: Carolyn Henderson Meier, Criminal
Justice Editor

Wadsworth/Thomson Learning
10 Davis Dr
Belmont CA 94002-9801

FOLD HERE

OPTIONAL:

Your name:_____ Date: _____

May we quote you, either in promotion for *Criminal Law,* Ninth Edition or in future
publishing ventures?

Yes: _____ No: _____

Sincerely yours,

Joel Samaha